COMPANY LAW AND C

LAW IN CONTEXT

Editors: Robert Stevens (Haverford College, Pennsylvania), William Twining (University of Warwick) and Christopher McCrudden (Balliol College, Oxford)

ALREADY PUBLISHED

Accidents, Compensation and the Law (*Third Edition*), P.S. Atiyah
Karl Llewellyn and the Realist Movement, William Twining
Cases and Materials on the English Legal System (*Third Edition*), Michael Zander
Computers and the Law, Colin Tapper
Tribunals and Government, J.A. Farmer
Government and Law, T.C. Hartley and J.A.G. Griffith
Land, Law and Planning, Patrick McAuslan
Landlord and Tenant (*Second Edition*), Martin Partington
How to do things with Rules, William Twining and David Miers
Evidence, Proof and Probability, Richard Eggleston
Family Law and Social Policy, John Eekelaar
Consumers and the Law, Ross Cranston
Law and Politics, Robert Stevens
Obscenity, Geoffrey Robertson
Labour Law, Paul Davies and Mark Freedland
Charities, Trusts and Social Welfare, Michael Chesterman
The Law-making Process, Michael Zander
An Introduction to Law, Phil Harris

Company Law and Capitalism

SECOND EDITION

TOM HADDEN

Lecturer in Law in the Queen's University of Belfast

WEIDENFELD AND NICOLSON
London

Weidenfeld and Nicolson
91 Clapham High Street London SW4

ISBN 0 297 77334 8 Cased
ISBN 0 297 77335 6 Paperback

Printed in Great Britain by
Redwood Burn Limited
Trowbridge & Esher

CONTENTS

	Preface	viii
	Table of cases	xi
	Table of statutes	xvii
	PART ONE: CAPITALISM	
Chapter 1	The development of capitalism	3
	1 The growth of industrial capitalism	4
	2 The development of the joint stock enterprise	9
	3 Capitalism in economic and socialist theory	25
Chapter 2	The realities of modern capitalism	37
	1 The range of registered companies	38
	2 The economic analysis of commercial organization	47
	3 Patterns of company finance	58
	4 The stock market mechanism	69
	5 Patterns of ownership and control	75
	6 The managerial revolution	81
	7 National and multi-national capitalism	87
	8 Conclusions	90
	PART TWO: COMPANY LAW	
Chapter 3	Introductory concepts: sole traders, partnerships, companies and business accounting	95
	1 The sole trader	95
	2 The partnership	97
	3 The limited company	103
	4 Business accounts	124
Chapter 4	The small private business	141
	1 The legal effects of incorporation	142
	2 The basis of association in small businesses	152
	3 Financing small businesses	168
	4 The rights of creditors	181
	5 Bankruptcy	186

	6 Company liquidation	194
	7 Disclosure by small businesses	205
	8 The taxation of small businesses	212
	9 A new small business statute	222
Chapter 5	The unquoted company	231
	1 The status and duties of directors	233
	2 Directors and shareholders	239
	3 Problems of transition	286
Chapter 6	The quoted company: legal controls and the disclosure system	296
	1 Public issues and the disclosure system	298
	2 Legal sanctions and remedies	306
	3 Quoted companies and their directors	316
	4 Shareholders and investors	324
Chapter 7	The quoted company and public dealing: administrative controls	336
	1 Control of non-market dealings	338
	2 Control over quotations	340
	3 Control of market dealings	342
	4 Official intervention	352
Chapter 8	Take-overs and mergers	364
	1 The cases and types of take-overs	364
	2 Legal controls	369
	3 The City Code	374
Chapter 9	Groups	389
Chapter 10	Investment institutions	401
Chapter 11	Co-operatives and communes	414
	PART THREE: THE MIXED ECONOMY	
Chapter 12	Perspective for the future	425
Chapter 13	Industrial democracy	439
	1 Levels of industrial democracy	440
	2 Board-level participation	447
	3 Shop-floor democracy	471
	4 Financial participation and workers' control	477
	5 Conclusion	483

Chapter 14 The modern corporation and government 486

1 Monopolies, restrictive practices and prices and incomes policies 487

2 Government intervention: aid and rationalization 496

3 Nationalization 501

4 Multi-national companies 505

Index 512

PREFACE

British company law is not unworkable. But it is tied to a conception of capitalism which has been discarded by all but the most ardent free-market economists. It has also ceased to reflect the realities of the commercial and industrial world.

The intention of this book is to explain and analyse the existing law as it is applied in practice to the three main types of business enterprise which operate as limited companies under the Companies Acts : small private businesses, larger unquoted or family companies and quoted companies. This restructuring on functional lines has in itself suggested a number of ways in which the law might be restated or reformed in order to provide a more realistic framework for the regulation of each class of enterprise. It has also highlighted the triviality of some of the topics traditionally dealt with at some length in company law texts. These have accordingly been excluded or drastically pruned. In dealing with changes in substantive law since the first edition of this book appeared in 1972 I have adopted the same approach. The main statutory reforms and developments in the case-law have been incorporated. But I have paid equal attention to developments in the practical operation of the law and to the likely impact of current proposals for industrial democracy and of current practice in governmental intervention on the future of the capitalist system in a mixed economy.

I have also tried to meet some of the criticisms with which the generally favourable response to the first edition was tempered. In the first chapter I have attempted to live better up to my title by including a good deal more material on the origins of capitalism and by dealing more fully with the alternative theoretical explanations of free market and Marxist economists. In the second I have added some material on multi-nationals and the mixed economy to bring up to date the analysis of trends in modern capitalism. These two chapters now form Part I which is intended as a general non-legal introduction to the development and organization of the capitalist system.

As a result of this rearrangement I have been able to gather together in Part II all the chapters which deal with the basic rules of company law and practice, dealing in turn with small participatory companies, unquoted or family companies, quoted (listed) companies, and the administrative regulation of stock market dealings, of take-overs and mergers and of investment institutions. By abolishing the chapter on the concepts of company law and reallocating some of the material in it on a more functional basis I hope to meet the criticism that the material on certain topics was too scattered for teaching, or indeed any other, purposes. I have also attempted to remedy some of the errors and omissions which my more attentive readers have pointed out. In this Part the principal new material will be found in the section on inflation accounting in Chapter 3, in the discussion of oppression and its remedies, including the important new case of *Wallersteiner v. Moir*, in Chapter 5, and in the reorganized section on groups in Chapter 9. The main provisions of the Companies Act 1976 and the revised version of the City Code of April 1976 have been incorporated.

Finally I have attempted in Part III to analyse the practical choices facing the capitalist system. What is now Chapter 13 on Industrial Democracy has been completely rewritten, excising the material on individual and collective rights of employees and bringing in a much more detailed discussion of the experience of co-determination in Germany and of the proposals of the Bullock Committee in Britain. The final section on governmental intervention in Chapter 14 has been expanded to cover the provisions of the Industry Act 1975 and the operations of the National Enterprise Board.

I should like to thank a number of people who have read and commented on drafts of various sections of this new edition or otherwise assisted in its preparation: they are Phyllis Bateson (Queen's University), Ben Buchan (Weidenfeld and Nicolson), Rosemary Chesney (Queen's University), Mike Chesterman (University of Warwick), Paul Davies (University of Oxford), Ian Grigg-Spall (University of Kent), Geoffrey Hornsey (Queen's University), Rosemary Jack (who drew another drawing), Peter Lee (City Panel), Marie McAlister (Queen's University), David McLellan (University of Kent), Chris Moffat (Lloyd-Baker Institute), Carol Robinson (Queen's University), William Twining (University of Warwick), Jack Winkler (Cranfield Institute) and Malcolm Wood (Queen's University). I have not accepted all their criticisms, but I am grateful to them all, and particularly to Mike Chesterman, for trying so hard to straighten out my legal, theoretical and political deviations.

February 1977

Derrybroughas
Portadown
Co. Armagh

TABLE OF CASES

Aaron's Reefs Ltd. v. Twiss [1896] A.C. 273 **310–11**
Allen v. Hyatt (1914) 30 T.L.R. 444 **256**
In re Allied Produce Co. Ltd. [1967] 1 W.L.R. 1469 358
Ammonia Soda Co. v. Chamberlain [1918] 1 Ch. 266 **132**
Ashbury Railway Carriage and Iron Co. v. Riche (1875) L.R. 7 H.L. 653 **113**
Automatic Self-Cleansing Filter Syndicate Co. Ltd. v. Cunninghame [1906] 2 Ch. 34 **156**

Bamford v. Bamford [1970] Ch. 212 273
Bank voor Handel en Sheepvart v. Slatford [1953] 1 Q.B. 248 **112**
In re Jon Beauforte (London) Ltd. [1953] Ch. 131 **114**
Bell Houses Ltd. v. City Wall Properties Ltd. [1966] 2 Q.B. 656 **115**, 148
In re Bellador Silk Ltd. [1965] 1 All E.R. 667 267
Re Black Bolt and Nut Association's Agreement (1960) L.R. 2 R.P. 50; (1961) L.R. 3 R.P. 43 492
Blue Chip Stamps v. Manor Drug Stores (1975) 421 U.S. 723 351
Brace v. Calder [1895] 2 Q.B. 253 **99**
Henry Brown & Sons v. Smith [1964] 2 Lloyds List 476 **144**
In re Bugle Press Ltd. [1961] 1 Ch. 270 **372–3**
Bushell v. Faith [1970] A.C. 1099 **106**, 246

In re Carlton Holdings Ltd. [1971] 1 W.L.R. 918 372
Charterbridge Corporation Ltd. v. Lloyds Bank Ltd. [1970] Ch. 62 395
Clemens v. Clemens Bros Ltd. [1976] 2 All E.R. 179 **269**, 290
In re City Equitable Fire Insurance Co. [1925] 1 Ch. 407 238

Consten and Grundig v. EEC Commission (1966) C.M.L.R. 418 495
Conway v. Petronius Clothing Co. Ltd. (1977) The Times 28 April 464
Cook v. Deeks [1916] 1 A.C. 554 **235**, 253, 259
Cox v. Hickman (1860) 8 H.L.C. 268 **98**, 167, 169
Cunliffe-Owen v. Teather & Greenwood [1967] 1 W.L.R. 1421 **343**
In re Cutts [1956] 1 W.L.R. 728 **190–1**

D.H.N. Food Distributors Ltd. v. Tower Hamlets L.B.C. [1976] 1 W.L.R. 852 **394**
Dafen Tinplate Co. v. Llanelly Steel Co. [1907] 2 Ch. 124 **260**
In re Davis & Collett Ltd. [1935] 1 Ch. 693 **157**
De Beers Consolidated Mines Ltd. v. Howe [1906] A.C. 455 145
Derry v. Peek (1889) 14 App. Cas. 337 **311**
Diamond v. Oreamuno (1969) 24 N.Y. 2d. 494 **351**
Dimbula Valley (Ceylon) Tea Co. Ltd. v. Laurie [1961] 1 Ch. 353 **132**
In re Duomatic Ltd. [1969] 2 Ch. 365 242, **258–9**

Edwards v. Halliwell [1950] 2 All E.R. 1064 **272**
Eisenberg v. Central Zone Property Corp. (1957) 335 U.S. 884 278
Elder v. Elder & Watson Ltd. [1952] S.C. 49 263
Ernst & Ernst v. Hochfelder (1976) 96 S.Ct. 1375 351
Europemballage Corp. and Continental Can Co. v. EEC Commission (1973) C.M.L.R. 199 495

In re F G Films Ltd. [1953] 1 W.L.R. 483 **146**
In re F L E Holdings Ltd. [1967] 1 W.L.R. 1397 **200**
Featherstonhaugh v. Fenwick (1810) 17 Ves. Jun. 298 **101**
In re Five Minute Car Wash Service Ltd. [1966] 1 W.L.R. 745 **264**
Foss v. Harbottle (1843) 2 Hare 641 240, **271**, 272–80
Freeman & Lockyer v. Buckhurst Park Properties (Mangal) Ltd. [1964] 2 Q.B. 480 **119–20**, 166

In re Galvanized Tank Manufacturers' Association's Agreement (1965) L.R. 5 R.P. 315 492
In re Thomas Gerrard & Son Ltd. [1968] Ch. 455 **139**
Gething v. Kilner [1972] 1 W.L.R. 337 **370**
In re Glamorganshire Banking Co. (1884) 28 Ch. D. 620 **281**

Governments Stock & Other Securities Investment Co. Ltd. v. Christopher [1956] 1 All E.R. 490 301
Greenhalgh v. Arderne Cinemas Ltd. [1951] 1 Ch. 286 **261**
In re Grierson, Oldham & Adams Ltd. [1967] 1 W.L.R. 385 372
In re The Grosvenor and West-end Railway Terminus Hotel Co. (1897) 76 L.T. 337 352
Guthrie v. Harkness (1905) 199 U.S. 1149 **282**

In re H R Harmer Ltd. [1959] 1 W.L.R. 62 **266**
Harrison v. Tennant (1856) 21 Beav. 482 **102**
Hedley Byrne & Co. v. Heller & Partners [1964] A.C. 465 **251**, 312
In re Hellenic & General Trust Ltd. [1976] 1 W.L.R. 123 **394**
Hely-Hutchinson v. Brayhead Ltd. [1968] 1 Q.B. 549 **243**
Hogg v. Cramphorn Ltd. [1967] Ch. 254 **245–6**, 274, 280
In re Holders Investment Trust Ltd. [1971] 1 W.L.R. 583 **262**
In re Eric Holmes (Property) Ltd. [1965] Ch. 1052 **200**
Holroyd v. Marshall (1862) 10 H.L.C. 191 172
Houldsworth v. City of Glasgow Bank (1880) 5 App. Cas. 317 311
Hughes v. Trapnell [1963] 1 Q.B. 737 339
Hutton v. West Cork Railway Co. (1883) 23 Ch. D. 654 **317–8**

ICI and Commercial Solvents Corp. v. EEC Commission (1974) C.M.L.R. 309 495
Independent Automatic Sales Ltd. v. Knowles & Foster [1962] 1 W.L.R. 974 **173–4**
Industrial Development Consultants Ltd. v. Cooley [1972] 1 W.L.R. 443 **253**, 254
IRC v. Crossman [1937] A.C. 26 69
IRC v. Phillips [1951] 1 Ch. 225 189
Introductions Ltd. v. National Provincial Bank Ltd. [1970] Ch. 199 114, **115–16**, 148

In re Jermyn Street Turkish Baths Ltd. [1970] 1 W.L.R. 1194; reversed [1971] 1 W.L.R. 1071 **265–6**, 268–9
Jones v. Lipman [1962] 1 W.L.R. 832 **146**

Kendal v. Wood (1871) L.R. 6 Exch. 243 **164**
In re Kingston Cotton Mill Co. (No. 2) [1896] 2 Ch. 279 **138**
Knapp v. Bankers Securities Corp. (1956) 230 F. 2d. 717 **270**
Re Kodak (1970) C.M.L.R. D19 495

Lagunas Nitrate Co. v. Lagunas Syndicate [1899] 2 Ch. 392 **237**, 314
Lee v. Neuchatel Asphalte Co. (1889) 41 Ch. D. 1 **131**, 132
In re William C Leitch Bros. Ltd. [1932] 2 Ch. 71 204
Lindgren v. L & P Estates Ltd. [1968] Ch. 572 **236**, 395
In re Lundie Bros. Ltd. [1965] 1 W.L.R. 1051 158, **160**, 266–7
Lyle & Scott Ltd. v. Scotts Trustees [1959] A.C. 763 **369**

Macaura v. Northern Assurance Co. [1925] A.C. 619 **144**
McEntire & Maconchy v. Crossley Bros. Ltd. [1895] A.C. 457 **177**
Mann v. Goldstein [1968] 1 W.L.R. 1091 **197**
Maxwell v. Department of Trade and Industry [1974] Q.B. 523 **357**
Morgan v. Tate & Lyle [1955] A.C. 21 **319**
Mutual Life and Citizens' Assurance Co. Ltd. v. Evatt [1971] A.C. 793 **251**

In re Net Book Agreement (1962) L.R. 3 R.P. 246 493
In re New York Taxicab Co. Ltd. [1913] 1 Ch. 1 **183–4**
Northern Counties Securities Ltd. v. Jackson & Steeple Ltd. [1974] 1 W.L.R. 1133 **247**

In re Othery Construction Ltd. [1966] 1 W.L.R. 69 **196**
Otter Tail Power Co. v. US (1973) 410 U.S. 366 490

In re Panama, New Zealand and Australian Royal Mail Co. (1870) L.R. 5 Ch. App. 318 172
Parke v. Daily News Ltd. [1962] Ch. 927 **318**, 463
In re Patrick & Lyon Ltd. [1933] Ch. 786 201, 204
Pavlides v. Jensen [1956] Ch. 565 **274**
Percival v. Wright [1902] 2 Ch. 421 236, 252, **255**, 257, 347
In re Pergamon Press Ltd. [1971] Ch. 388 **356–7**
Phipps v. Boardman [1967] 2 A.C. 46 **234**
Polsky v. S & A Services Ltd. [1951] 1 All E.R. 185 & 1062 **177–8**

R. v. Arthur (1967) The Times 14 March **112**
R. v. de Berenger (1814) 3 M. & S. 67 **344**
R. v. Grunwald [1963] 1 Q.B. 935 309, 370
R. v. Gurney (1868) 11 Cox C.C. 414 308
R. v. ICR Haulage Ltd. [1944] 1 K.B. 551 **111**
R. v. Lord Kylsant [1932] 1 K.B. 442 **307–8**
R. v. McDonnell [1966] 1 Q.B. 233 **145**

R. v. Mackinnon [1959] 1 Q.B. 150 308
R. v. Salter [1968] 2 Q.B. 793 189
R. v. Schildkamp [1971] A.C. 1 204
In re Rampgill Mill Ltd. [1967] Ch. 1138 **199**
Regal (Hastings) Ltd. v. Gulliver [1942] 1 All E.R. 378 **235**, 254
Rights and Issues Investment Trust Ltd. v. Stylo Shoes Ltd. [1965] Ch. 250 **247**
In re W & M Roith Ltd. [1967] 1 W.L.R. 432 244–5
Royal British Bank v. Turquand (1856) 6 E. & B. 327 **119**, 165
Salaman v. Warner (1891) 65 L.T. 132 345
Salmon v. Hamborough Co. (1671) 1 Ch. Cas. 204 **12**, 20
Salomon v. Salomon & Co. [1897] A.C. 22 **143**, 200, 202
Schein v. Chasen (1975) 313 So. 2d 739 351
Scott v. Brown, Doering & McNab [1892] 2 Q.B. 724 **345**
Scottish Co-operative Wholesale Society Ltd. v. Meyer [1959] A.C. 324 **263–4**, 396
SEC v. Texas Gulf Sulphur Co. (1968) 401 F. 2d 833 **350**
Seddon v. North Eastern Salt Co. [1905] 1 Ch. 326 314
Selangor United Rubber Estates Ltd. v. Cradock (No. 3) [1968] 1 W.L.R. 1555 374
John Shaw & Sons (Salford) Ltd. v. Shaw [1935] 2 K.B. 113 **106–7**, 275–6
Sidebottom v. Kershaw, Leese & Co. [1920] 1 Ch. 154 260
Smith v. Anderson (1880) 15 Ch. D. 247 411
Re Smith & Fawcett [1942] Ch. 304 **154–5**, 290
A P Smith Mfg. Co. v. Barlow (1953) 346 U.S. 861 **319**
Howard Smith Ltd. v. Ampol Petroleum Ltd. (1974) A.C. 821 **246**, 290
In re South of England Natural Gas and Petroleum Co. Ltd. [1911] 1 Ch. 573 **249–50**
In re Standard Manufacturing Co. [1891] 1 Ch. 627 174
Stekel v. Ellice [1973] 1 W.L.R. 191 **99**, 161
Stoneleigh Finance Ltd. v. Phillips [1965] 2 Q.B. 537 **178**
Strong v. Repide (1909) 213 U.S. 419 **256**
Sykes v. Beadon (1879) 11 Ch. D. 170 411

Taylor v. Wright (1945) 69 Cal. App. 2d 371 256
Thomas v. Kelly (1888) 13 App. Cas. 506 174
Trevor v. Whitworth (1887) 12 App. Cas. 409 129, **130**
Tunstall v. Steigman [1962] 2 Q.B. 593 **111**, 144

In re Victoria Steamboats Ltd. [1897] 1 Ch. 158 183

Wallersteiner v. Moir (No. 2) [1975] Q.B. 373 **279**, 280
In re Westbourne Galleries Ltd. [1970] 1 W.L.R. 1378; reversed (1971) Ch. 799; reaffirmed (1973) A.C. 360 **158–9**, 267–8
White v. Bristol Aeroplane Co. [1953] Ch. 65 **261**
In re W. R. Willcocks & Co. Ltd. [1974] 1 Ch. 163 **159**

In re Yenidje Tobacco Co. Ltd. [1916] 2 Ch. 426 145, **157**
In re Yeovil Glove Co. Ltd. [1965] Ch. 148 **201**

TABLE OF STATUTES

Aircraft and Shipbuilding Industries Act 1977 505

Bankruptcy Act 1914
s.1 187–8
s.14 188
s.15 189
s.16 185
s.19 189
s.20 189
s.33 189
s.38 175, 192, 194
ss.42–3 190
s.44 190
s.45 190
s.54 190
s.154 192
s.155 192
s.158 192
Bankruptcy Act 1924, s.33 193
Bills of Sale Act 1854 173
Bills of Sale Act 1878 173, 177
Bills of Sale (Amendment) Act 1882 173, 174, 177

Coal Industry Nationalization Act 1946 502–3
Companies Act 1862 20, 22, 173
Companies Act 1929, s.356 338
Companies Act 1948
s.1 103, 110, 123, 149, 165
s.2 104, 110
s.5 107
s.8 104
s.10 108, 261
s.11 104
s.12 208
ss.17–19 104, 105
s.20 105
s.23 107, 108
s.27 390, 397
s.28 122
s.31 166
s.38 301
s.39 301
s.40 303
s.41 303
s.43 312
s.44 306
s.45 300

s.47 302
s.48 302
ss.49–53 302
s.52 208
s.54 129, 130, 370, 393–4, 478
s.55 301
s.56 129
s.61 107
ss.66–8 108, 129, 169, 262
ss.69–71 169
s.72 108, 261
s.94 199
s.95 173, 208
s.109 116
s.110–11 117, 208
s.124 208
s.130 116
s.131 116, 324
s.132 116, 324
s.136 324
s.140 324
s.149 250
s.150 391–2
s.153 392
s.154 390, 466
ss.156–8 117
s.159 138, 212
s.160 138
s.162 138–9
s.164 283, 354
s.165 283, 354, 355
s.167 355
s.172 354
ss.176–7 117
s.183 326
s.184 106, 324, 326
s.187 192
s.190 241
s.200 208
ss.206–8 197, 212, 262, 370–1, 389
s.209 370, 371, 389
s.210 160, 228, 262–70, 400
s.212 165
s.222 157, 195, 262
s.223 196
s.225 262
s.236 198, 358
s.270 198, 358
s.283 195, 358
ss.284–91 195
ss.292–300 195, 198
s.306 185
ss.311–5 195
s.319 198, 199
s.320 199
s.322 201
s.328 203, 204
s.332 166, 204
s.334 198, 358
s.353 121, 198
s.434 102
s.441 282
s.448 243, 249, 252, 258, 315
s.455 109, 300

Table A, Part I:

art.76 323
art.80 117, 156
art.81 117, 321, 461
art.84 248
arts.89–92 326
art.95 326
arts.107–9 117, 321, 461
art.116 130

ss.191–3 242, 243
s.195 117
s.197 242
s.199 242, 323
art.125 281
Table A, Part II:
art.3 122, 154
Table B 104
Schedule 4 302

Companies Act (Northern Ireland) 1960, s.201 268
Companies Act 1967
s.2 241
ss.4–5 392
ss.6–8 208, 323, 392
s.13 139, 212
s.14 138–9, 212
s.16 208, 323
s.17 208, 392
s.18 208, 392
s.19 208, 320
s.20 208, 320
ss.25–6 208, 241, 242, 258, 323, 347
ss.27–9 117, 208, 242, 258, 304, 347
s.30 241
s.31 304
s.32 354
ss.33–4 304
s.35 358
s.37 284, 358
s.40 283
s.43 149
s.50 358
s.109 283, 355
s.120 102
Schedule 2 128, 382

Companies Act 1976
ss.4–6 152, 208
s.8 391
s.12 117, 208
s.13 139
s.15 139, 212
s.16 139
s.18 393
ss.24–5 304
s.26 304
s.27 304

Companies Clauses Consolidation Act 1845 20
Companies (Winding-Up) Act 1890 194
Consumer Credit Act 1974 180–1
Cotton Industry Act 1959 497
County Courts Act 1959 185
Counter-Inflation Act 1973 496

Deeds of Arrangement Act 1914 185
Development of Inventions Acts 1948–54 497
Directors' Liability Act 1890 312

Employment Protection Act 1975 199, 445, 465
European Communities Act 1972, s.9 114, 148, 166

Fair Trading Act 1973 489
Finance Act 1960 219
Finance Act 1965 292
Finance Act 1971 292
Finance Act 1972 215, 217
Finance Act 1975 134, 292
Finance (No. 2) Act 1975 134
Finance Act 1976 215, 323, 506
Friendly Societies Act 1974 418
Friendly and Industrial and Provident Societies Act 1968 418

Health and Safety Act 1974 476

Income and Corporation Taxes Act 1970
s.233 170 s.460 219
ss.282–3 217 ss.485–8 393, 506
Industrial Common Ownership Act 1976 419
Industrial Expansion Act 1968 497
Industrial and Provident Societies Act 1965 417
Industrial Relations Act 1971 428, 464, 476
Industry Act 1972 498
Industry Act 1975 498–501, 506–7
Insolvency Act 1976 96, 188, 189, 192, 193, 195, 198
Insurance Companies Act 1974 406

Joint Stock Companies Act 1844 19
Joint Stock Companies Act 1856 21

Leeman's Act: Banking Companies' (Shares) Act 1867 343
Limited Partnership Act 1907 167, 224

Mercantile Law (Amendment) Act 1865 98, 167
Misrepresentation Act 1967 250, 312

Monopolies and Restrictive Practices (Inquiry and Control) Act 1948 488
Monopolies and Mergers Act 1965 489

Partnership Act 1890
s.1 98
s.5 100, 148, 164
ss.20–4 100, 101
ss.26–7 154
ss.29–30 101
s.35 102, 157
s.40 154
Policy Holders Protection Act 406
Prevention of Fraud (Investments) Act 1958 306, 308, 338–40, 411
s.1 338
s.2 338
s.3 338
s.5 339
s.13 306, 308
s.14 339, 340
s.15 340
s.16 340
Protection of Depositors Act 1963 405
s.21 307, 308, 339

Registration of Business Names Act 1916 96–7, 100, 207
Resale Prices Act 1976 493
Restrictive Trade Practices Act 1976 491–2

Shipbuilding Industry Acts 1967–71 497
Stock Exchange (Completion of Bargains) Act 1976 343

Theft Act 1968
s.18 241
s.19 241, 306
Trade Union and Labour Relations Act 1974 476

City Code on Take-overs and Mergers 1976
Introduction 366, 378
General Principle 1 377
General Principle 3 378, 386
General Principle 4 367, 378, 385
General Principle 6 379
General Principle 8 366, 379
General Principle 9 366, 379
General Principle 10 379
General Principle 11 378
Rule 16 380
Rule 17 347
Rule 21 384
Rule 23 383
Rule 27 383
Rule 30 348
Rule 31 379, 382, 384, 385

Rule 32 384
Rule 33 385
Rule 34 368,386
Rule 37 385
Rule 38 367, 385
Practice Note 1 367
Practice Note 3 381
Practice Note 4 381
Practice Note 7 382
Practice Note 9 385

PART ONE: CAPITALISM

I

The development of capitalism

Company law is about capitalism. It provides the formal legal structure necessary to the operation of the capitalist system. The capitalist invests in shares in a company set up and managed by an entrepreneur, who employs on his behalf as many workers, or machines, as are necessary to the profitable operation of the business. The shareholders supply the finance, the managers provide the drive and the organization, and the employees do the work. The managers and the other employees are paid a salary or wage out of the takings of the business. The remaining profit goes exclusively to the shareholders who own and control the business, and who also bear the risk of any loss which may be incurred. In Marxist terms all the surplus value created in the business is appropriated by the capitalists.

In addition in public companies, through the mechanism of the stock market, the capitalist is able to withdraw his money from any particular enterprise by selling his shares to another at the market price. He is then free to spend his money, or to reinvest it more profitably elsewhere if he can. This should result in the flow of capital being directed to the most profitable enterprises, which in its turn should lead to the optimum allocation of resources throughout the economy. The ideal capitalist economy is one in which the greatest possible number of shareholders makes the greatest possible profit.

All this is grossly simplified. The relationship between the capitalist and the entrepreneur has typically been much more complex and variable than such a skeletal model suggests. There have probably not been very many pure entrepreneurs with no capital of their own, and even if a few did start without any, most have soon been able to use their initial profit to finance at least some of their expansion. The captains of industry in the heyday of capitalism have been both capitalists and entrepreneurs. In addition the structure of ownership and management in any enterprise alters as the business grows and prospers. The sharp separation between capitalist owners and professional managers which the model prescribes seems only to occur at a relatively late stage in development. Only the worker fills the precise and limited role allotted to him.

Even if there is very little historical truth in such a pure model of capitalism, it none the less provides the theoretical justification for the basic organization of industry and commerce throughout most of the western world. There is nothing necessary or natural about this. The ownership and control of business enterprises, and the distribution of profits arising in them, can be structured in any number of ways. Some of the possible alternatives will be considered below. For the moment the important question is how we came to accept as so fundamental the structure which we now have.

I THE GROWTH OF INDUSTRIAL CAPITALISM

The origins of a social or economic institution like capitalism can be traced as far back as historical sources permit. There are no neat discontinuities between the ancient world of Egypt, China, Greece and Rome, the feudal structure of the middle ages and the modern capitalist age. Many of the elements of capitalism as we know it – international trade, the division of labour, mass production, and the accumulation of wealth to finance it – can be found in virtually every large scale society.[1] Trade, whether by barter or monetary payment, in which one or other party may be said to have made a profit is a more or less universal human activity: well-organized and regular distribution networks have been discovered for neolithic axes, arrowheads and pottery, for oriental goods in the middle ages, and for agricultural and craft products in the so-called primitive communities of New Guinea and elsewhere. The social division of

[1] See generally, on the development of capitalism, M. Dobb, *Studies in the Development of Capitalism* (1946), and on pre-urban communities, M. Sahlins, *Stone Age Economics* (1974); comparative material on ancient urban economies is not readily available, but see for instance J. Crook, *Law and Life of Rome* (1967).

labour in the production of consumer goods is equally widespread: specialized full-time craftsmen in pottery and metal-work were recognized as separate social classes in ancient India and China and in Celtic Ireland. Most urban communities have developed and depended on the mass production of consumer goods for sale: pottery factories and workshops for other household goods and building materials were commonplace in ancient Greece and Rome and in many oriental cultures. Not all were based on slave labour. Moneylending and banking in one form or another are found in all but the smallest tribal communities.

Capitalism in the more precise sense introduced at the start of this chapter is a modern western European phenomenon, though it has been exported to the rest of the world by political colonialism and economic empire-building. Various explanations have been put forward for this fact. Weber and others have tied the development of capitalism to certain aspects of Protestantism, notably an ethic which favoured hard work and the accumulation of wealth.[2] Some Marxists have argued that technological developments were the determining force. A search for causes in matters of this kind, however, is probably fruitless, given the complex interrelationship of social, economic, political and ideological factors. It is better to attempt a brief description of what appears to have happened in countries like Britain, France and Germany where the capitalist system developed out of broadly similar feudal structures. Since the developments in different countries and regions and in different industries within them were far from uniform this can only be given in a highly generalized form.

The basis of feudalism in western Europe was the superimposition of Germanic and later Norman lords on a relatively well-developed Roman colonial economy. The incoming conquerors dismantled the dominant urban living patterns and replaced them with a much smaller scale pattern of rural settlement in which military leaders offered protection and certain essential services like milling to their subjects in return for certain services in kind, notably regular work on the lords' lands and military service when the occasion demanded. The ramifications and regional variations in the medieval feudal system from its beginnings in the fifth and sixth centuries to its

[2] M. Weber, *The Protestant Ethic and the Spirit of Capitalism* (English edn., 1930); see also R. H. Tawney, *Religion and the Rise of Capitalism* (1926).

apogee in Norman England and France in the eleventh and twelfth centuries cannot be discussed here. But it is clear that by the thirteenth century the personal non-monetary relationships of pure feudalism were already proving inconvenient. The more settled conditions after the Germanic migrations and Nordic invasions led to the regeneration of urban living and to a rapid growth in trade and craftwork. This was centred on the wool trade, but extended to the provision of the wide range of materials required for the construction and furnishing of the massive castles and cathedrals which dominated economic life in the period. All this, together with the growth in the size and financial requirements of royal and princely courts in the process of state centralization, led to the replacement of feudal exchange relationships by monetary payment.

The centre of this new economic activity was in the towns in which the growing numbers of merchants and craftsmen established themselves. The merchants organized regular markets and developed their own structures for internal and long-distance moneylending and banking. The craftsmen formed themselves into local associations or guilds to organize the training of new recruits and to protect themselves from competition. Some master craftsmen also employed fully trained apprentices as 'journeymen' for a money wage, but each craftsman could look forward to becoming a master and a guild member in his own right. The merchants and guilds in the main centres eventually won legal recognition for their restrictive and monopolistic practices from the royal or feudal authorities, often in return for direct money payments or continuing taxes or levies.

Thus far there was little to distinguish the urban economies of Italy, Holland and England from their counterparts in the ancient world or the orient. Two important differences soon began to appear. The first was the growth of wage labour in place of the household retinue of the merchant and the relative independence of each guild craftsman. The second was the growth of legal institutions which facilitated the accumulation of monetary resources, or capital, for trading purposes. Though the second of these – the commercial as opposed to the industrial revolution – is the more important in the context of this book, a brief generalized account must be given of the first.

A system of wage labour appears to have developed in response to a similar combination of forces both in the countryside and in the towns. The progression may have been started by a simple growth in population and the resulting pressure on land. It may also have been linked to the desire of the royal authorities and the subordinate lords for money payments in place of feudal dues in kind, and the consequent impoverishment of the less prosperous peasants. Many of these were forced by the usual pressures of debt and interest to mortgage their land and eventually to cede it to their creditors. Whatever the explanation, it is certain that there was an increasing number of landless peasants. Some of them became entirely dependent on their lord or on other wealthy farmers who could employ them on their own holdings in the production of surplus food for sale in the towns. Others drifted to the towns in search of an alternative livelihood. These self-generating processes were later supplemented in England by the forced enclosure of the common land upon which the remaining feudal tenants relied for grazing and other purposes.

These displaced persons could not readily be absorbed in the established structures in the towns. Entry to the trade and craft guilds was strictly limited by the apprenticeship system. The merchants were essentially middlemen with little need for more than their household retinue of servants. Some of the migrants found employment as household servants for the merchants or for the more prosperous craftsmen. Others took refuge in military or naval service. Many had to be supported at public expense through the elaborate local structures for relief, as for instance the Tudor and Elizabethan Poor Laws. But the most significant development was the rapid extension in paid productive labour. Small workshops, owned and managed by the more prosperous master craftsmen, began to displace the old guild organizations, particularly in those spheres where a measure of mass production for sale was possible. Some merchants and landowners also began to organize increased production of woollen goods and other fabrics through what is termed the outwork system. Under this the materials of production, and sometimes the necessary looms and tools, were supplied by the merchant to labourers in the towns and villages and to poorer cottagers in the countryside, who were then paid on a piecework basis for what they produced.

In these various ways the mass of the population in both town and country became increasingly dependent on selling their labour to the more prosperous members of the community, either for agricultural or industrial production or as household servants. The final stage in the industrial revolution as we now know it was factory production. At first this was merely a matter of gathering together the scattered outworkers and their individual looms in a single 'manufactory' where the flow of production could be more effectively and cheaply supervised and controlled. As science and technology progressed, particularly in the development of motive power and of larger scale machinery, factory production and the division of labour within each manufacturing process developed rapidly in all spheres. The result was a rapid increase in the drift of workers from the country to the new industrial towns, where the mill-owners were beginning to provide cheap terrace housing for them. The pressure to increase production and keep down costs meant that in many cases the new class of workers were kept at their machines from dawn to dusk, and sometimes even at night. The women and children were employed as well, not least because their labour was less costly. The market for the greatly increased production which all this made possible was provided both by the rapid increase in population which accompanied the industrial revolution and by the opening up of colonial territories overseas. Where necessary the mill- and factory-owners were ready to seek legal protection from competition from potential competitors, as for instance in the penal taxation of industrial production in Ireland in the eighteenth century.

The most obvious social result of this new economic structure was an increasing separation between the two main classes of Marxist analysis, the bourgeoisie and the urban proletariat. The bourgeoisie organized and financed the new methods of production and took the profit from them. The proletariat did the work when work was required and was paid a bare living wage in return; in the recurring slumps they were paid off and suffered even greater hardship. But the pattern of development from the mid-nineteenth century, when there was general anxiety among the bourgeoisie about the growing militancy and organization among the workers and the unemployed, notably in the Chartist movement, has been rather different from that which Marx inferred from his analysis of the internal momentum of capitalist production methods. Capitalist entrepreneurs were not left to pursue the maximization of profit without regard to the interests of their workers. The state intervened to prevent the worst excesses of the factory system. Those employers who were not already turning their attention to the welfare of their workers out of self-interest or from humanitarian motives were required to restrict their working hours, to stop employing children, to improve the health and safety of their mines and factories, and to observe minimum standards in the provision of housing for the working classes. The increasing strength of the trade unions, despite the attempts of employers, the courts and the legislature to outlaw their activities, helped to win a larger share for ordinary workers in the prosperity which they were creating. Furthermore, as production methods and the division of labour became more complex, there was an increasing differentiation between different groups of workers. Skilled and prosperous employees in the various branches of productive industry and ancillary trades and services organized themselves in separate trade unions and pursued their own sectional interests rather than the interests of the proletariat as a whole. There also developed a growing class of technical and administrative 'white-collar' workers whose interests and attitudes overlapped with those of both the managers and the workers. As a result the simple opposition between the bourgeoisie and the workers became less rather than more prominent as the twentieth century progressed. These developments do not alter the fundamental critique of the capitalist system mounted by its opponents. But the cumulative if occasionally erratic improvement in the working conditions and living standards of ordinary workers in advanced capitalist countries is a fact which cannot be ignored in any realistic analysis of the capitalist system.

This account of the development of capitalism is not complete. There have been equally significant changes in industrial and commercial organization since the introduction of factory production methods in the nineteenth century. But many of these are directly linked to parallel developments in the legal and financial structures which form the second limb of the capitalist system. To understand these fully it is necessary to return to the beginnings of commercial development in the middle ages.

2 THE DEVELOPMENT OF THE JOINT STOCK ENTERPRISE

The idea of a commercial enterprise in which risk and profit are shared between financiers and traders as joint participants is as old as western civilization itself. Wealthy nobles and merchants in Greece and Rome and later in the Italian city states habitually contributed to the initial outlay and expenses of trading expeditions and ventures undertaken by shipowners and other traders in return for a share of the eventual profit. The legal rules for the *commenda*, perhaps the earliest formalized system of commercial joint enterprise, facilitated this type of transaction by allowing the liability of the investor, who had no direct control over the conduct of the venture, to be limited to the amount he had contributed. Apart from this the ancient world did not produce any lasting form of permanent trading association. But Roman lawyers did develop the conception of an association of persons, the *societas*, with legal rights and duties independent of its individual members, which laid the foundation of the modern idea of the company as a separate legal entity.

The structure of the modern trading company in Europe has been derived more or less directly from the concepts of the *commenda* and the *societas*. Its origins in England, as might be expected, were more closely related to historical institutions than legal theory.[3] On a formal basis the trading company was a direct development from the medieval guilds and companies formed by charter for the regulation first of general trading activities in the towns, and later of specific trades and skills. These charters normally provided for the appointment of masters or governors and councillors with powers to make rules for the conduct of the trade concerned usually in return for some form of monopoly, either locally or nationally. They also granted the right to hold property and to conduct litigation in the corporate name. But only those who were genuine masters of the trade or profession would be permitted to join : hence the complex apprenticeship system. And the actual trading was carried out by the individual members on their own account. The finances of the corporation as such, raised from entry subscriptions and levies and fines on members, would be spent only on maintaining some form of headquarters and on suitable business entertainment. The objective of these early charters was to regulate and control a particular branch of trade rather than to create any form of corporate trading association.

As international trade grew in importance, however, charters were increasingly granted to groups of traders who directed their activities to particular regions. As in the case of the guilds the principal object of the exercise was to provide for the regulation of the trade. In the grant of a charter to the merchants of Andalusia in 1530, for

[3] See generally W. R. Scott, *Joint Stock Companies to 1720*, 3 vols. (1912), from which the account which follows is largely drawn, and C. A. Cooke, *Corporation, Trust and Company* (1950).

instance, provision was made for the appointment of councillors with full power and authority to levy impositions both on traders in the region and on goods imported or exported, and to make statutes and ordinances for their general wealth. Little else by way of formal legal provision was necessary.

The joint stock system

Foreign trade was particularly suitable for joint ventures in which several members of the company would pool their resources in a single expedition, and in time it came to be accepted practice for the company itself to organize the various ventures, for which members would be entitled or even expected to contribute money or goods. At the end of each voyage the profits would then be shared out pro rata with the amount invested. This type of venture came to be known as a joint stock, since each, instead of trading with his own stock, agreed to pool it in a common enterprise. 'In long and dangerous voyages', as it was said of the trade to Russia for example, 'a joint stock was held necessary, for in that voyage one alone will not venture.'

Hence grew up a distinction between the 'regulated', or rather regulating companies in which each member was free to trade as he pleased, subject to the company's rules, and the joint stock company in which individual trading might even be forbidden. During the sixteenth century, for example, the directors of the Muscovy Company appear to have managed the whole trade for their members, numbering some 150, 'limiting to every man the proportion of stock which he should trade for . . .', a practice vigorously attacked in the debates on monopolies in 1604. Not that this distinction between regulation and joint trading was at all clearly marked in the formal constitutions of the various companies. The object of the grant of a charter was the mercantilist one of restricting and regulating trade. Whether the trade was carried out by means of a joint stock or by individual traders was not a matter of crucial concern to the government and seems to have been left to the discretion of the individual companies.

The joint stock system, however, soon became popular in other spheres for the operation of any new trading venture in which a large initial capital was required. The Company of the Mines Royal, for instance, which was founded in 1564, seems to have been organized from the start on a joint stock basis, twenty-four shares being issued at an average price of £1,200. And the closely related Company of Mineral and Battery Works, founded in 1565, raised its initial capital by making a series of calls on the thirty-six shares which had been created. The charters granted to these companies did not include any express power to raise capital in this way. It was not until some time later that established commercial practice in this respect was formally reflected in newly granted charters: as, for example, in that granted to the Mineral and Battery Works Company in 1603, stated expressly to be 'for the better execution of [its] ... privileges, benefits and immunities, and for the raising of a convenient stock to be employed in the building of waterworks ... etc'. And it was not until much later still, in 1671, that the power to raise calls on shares to meet ordinary trade obligations was finally established in the House of Lords, sitting in its judicial capacity.

The company, the Merchant Adventurers of England, incorporated by letters patent, had been raising large loans by contract under its common seal. The plaintiff lent the company £2,000. But when he sought to recover in 1656 it was objected that the company had no common stock and those in control refused to levy actions on its members to meet the obligation. The Lords finally agreed to order the company 'to make such a leviation upon every member as shall be sufficient to satisfy the said sum'. *Salmon v. Hamborough Company* (1671) 1 Ch. Cas. 204

The same slow process in the legal recognition of trading practice seems to have taken place in respect of the transferability of shares. There is little doubt that a share in a joint stock was regarded as a saleable asset as soon as the joint stock system became established. According to Scott, 'as early as the sixteenth century shares were sold outside personal acquaintances, and without limiting conditions.' But it was not until the seventeenth century that provision for the assignment of shares began to appear in company charters as a matter of course: as for example in that granted to the Royal Africa Company in 1660 giving power to grant or assign any share or shares to any other person whatsoever. By the middle of the seventeenth century the ownership of a share had clearly come to be regarded as a matter of financial rather than personal participation. And by the end of the century there was a flourishing public market in London for the shares of all the major companies.

The formal problems relating to the raising of capital and the transfer of shares, though both were essential to the joint stock system, were of concern primarily to lawyers. The importance of the system in economic terms was the encouragement it gave to overseas trade, and other new projects. In the words of Scott, during the first 130 years from 1553 the progress of the joint stock company was 'inseparably connected with British naval and maritime progress'. A large proportion of the earliest trading companies was directly concerned either with the exploitation of new foreign markets or with the development of new industries dependent on the navy for their prosperity, as, for example, the copper mining operations of the Mines Royal; some others were in the nature of public utilities, as, for example, the New River Company formed in 1606 to bring fresh water to London. The colonizations of the later seventeenth century were also largely carried out under the lead of joint stock companies. But in a sense the development of the system through which these activities were carried out was of even greater importance. Through the joint stock company it was now possible to raise large sums of capital for any profit-making enterprise from persons who could not in any way be regarded as having any direct connection with the enterprise. Capitalism of this kind was the base upon which our modern commercial society has been founded.

The beginnings of public dealing

The growth of a public market in shares was also of real practical importance. It was clearly necessary to protect the company's enterprise from the withdrawal of capital by those who had invested in it. It is not easy to conduct a business if provision must always be made for the repayment of individual shares. In the early companies in which participation was an essentially personal matter the irrevocable commitment of capital was a natural deduction from the nature of the enterprise. When capital was raised on a much wider basis, however, and participation became more financial than personal, it was necessary to provide a means by which individual contributors could withdraw their money without injuring or interrupting the affairs of the company. A public market, in which individual shareholders could recoup their initial contribution when they wished, together with any undistributed profits due, by disposing of their shares to someone else who was prepared to tie up his surplus capital, was the simplest and most practical solution. The much wider base for the raising of capital which it permitted was soon reflected in the proliferation of new joint stock enterprises of all kinds in the 1690s and early 1700s.

Public share dealing also produced its own special problems. The rapid succession of booms and slumps in the period resulted in a number of over-optimistic flotations, and a high failure rate: of ninety-three joint stock companies known to have been trading between 1690 and 1695 only twenty could be traced in 1698. According to the report of the Commissioners of Trade in 1696:

> The pernicious art of stock jobbing so wholly perverted the end and design of companies and corporations erected for the introducing or carrying on of manufactures to the private profit of the first projectors, that the privileges granted to them have commonly been made no other use of by the first procurers and subscribers but to sell again with advantage to ignorant men, drawn in by the reputation, falsely raised and artfully spread, concerning the thriving state of their stock.

The additional allegation that brokers had 'confederated themselves together to raise or fall from time to time the value [of stock] as might be most convenient for their own private interest' does not seem to be justified by the available evidence. But the Commissioners' report did lead to the passing of an Act in 1697 to regulate and control the buying and selling of stock: all brokers were to be licensed up to a maximum number of a hundred and were not to engage in personal dealings; brokerage charges were to be limited and forward dealings were to be unenforceable. The immediate impact of these measures is not clear. But it is certainly not without significance that the first appearance of investment on a large scale by ordinary persons interested exclusively in financial profit, whether by way of speculative capital appreciation or by the accumulation of dividends, was so quickly followed by direct governmental intervention in an attempt to prevent the exploitation and manipulation of the market. The capitalist system had enormous economic potential, but it was clearly open to abuse.

Whatever the effect of the 1697 Act on the practice of the brokers, it seems to have caused little slackening in the rapid development of the joint stock system. In the early decades of the eighteenth century there was a continuing series of booms and slumps, marked by bursts of company flotation and failure respectively. A number of companies turned their attention to banking on a joint stock basis, following the foundation of the Bank of England in 1694, despite the fact that their charters made no provision for operations of this type, and there was a sudden insurance boom in 1710. The failures in both these fields also led to statutory intervention: a virtual monopoly of joint stock banking was given to the Bank of England in 1708, and the formation of insurance societies was restricted in 1710 and 1711. Legislation of this kind was all the more necessary in this early period when there was no readily available and effective court action by which companies could be prevented from exceeding the powers granted to them in their charters. The only effective means of control was through a parliamentary petition and investigation, which could only be resorted to in extreme circumstances.

It was also becoming increasingly common for 'companies' to be formed on a joint stock basis without formal legal incorporation of any kind, by charter or otherwise. This practice seems to have dated back to the mid-seventeenth century, when for various reasons the government was reluctant to grant formal charters to new enterprises. From the lawyer's point of view there seems in fact to have been no strict need for a charter, except for the grant of special monopolistic rights or privileges, since all the necessary provisions for the raising of a joint stock could be made by means of a deed of association which individual parties might join simply by signature. In consequence the distinction between incorporated and unincorporated companies was of little practical significance.

It was thus in the context of a well-established though scarcely sophisticated market for shares in both official and unofficial companies that the story of the notorious South Sea Company must be judged. The company was founded by statute in 1710 with the joint objectives of exploiting the opportunities for trade with South America and serving as a means of relieving the government of the burden of the national debt. In essence the capital of the company was to be formed by the conversion of government annuities into stock, which would then in some sense serve as a 'fund of credit' for commercial trading operations which in their turn would provide for the interest due on the converted stock. The scheme was not a success. The company's trading ventures were not particularly profitable, and the operation came to depend more and more on the buoyancy of the stock market, which had at all costs to be maintained. The directors of the South Sea Company resorted to spreading encouraging rumours, and eventually to supporting the price of its shares by lending the company's money on the security of its own shares. Not unnaturally others took advantage of the speculative fever on which the South Sea Company was dependent and a large number of new trading companies were formed, most of them without formal incorporation, and many of them patently unsound or even fraudulent. Eventually in 1720 the 'bubble' burst. The directors of the South Sea Company were summoned before Parliament and fined for their 'notorious fraud and breach of trust', the only effective way in which a breach of the terms of a statutory charter could be dealt with.

The unincorporated company: 1720–1844

The impact of the South Sea Bubble on the major established joint stock companies has often been exaggerated.[4] Most of them continued their operations more or less regardless of the state of the stock market, and new chartered joint stock companies continued to be formed by governmental or legislative grant throughout the eighteenth century. But the episode did have a considerable influence on the development of the law of commercial organization. The so-called 'Bubble Act', rushed through in 1720 as part of a final effort to shore up the market for South Sea shares by suppressing some of its competitors, made it a criminal offence to form any company 'presuming to be a corporate body' or to raise 'transferable stocks without legal authority'. As a result, apart from some few larger enterprises of a semi-public nature which were able to secure charters, such as the new canal companies, the commercial community was forced to operate within the limits of the unincorporated partnership, in which the participation of the various parties was an essentially personal matter, and which were expressly exempted from the operation of the Act. The crucial issue was the transferability of shares. A number of the more respectable unincorporated concerns consulted a certain Serjeant Pengelly immediately on the passing of the Act as to the risk of prosecution, and were advised that they might safely continue if special attention were given to the method of transferring shares. But the net effect of the statute was naturally to reduce the numbers of persons who might safely pool their

[4] On this period see generally A. Dubois, *The English Business Company after the Bubble Act 1720–1800* (1938), B. C. Hunt, *The Development of the Business Corporation in England 1800–1867* (1936) and R. R. Formoy, *The Historical Foundation of Modern Company Law* (1923).

resources in a joint enterprise, and so to discourage the aggregation of capital on a large scale.

There were other more technical problems in the use of the simple partnership for joint stock trading. As an unincorporated association the partnership was not entitled to own property nor to conduct legal proceedings in the name of the partnership as such. All formal transactions had in law to be carried on in the name of all the partners together, since the liability of each partner could be assessed only in respect of the period during which he was a member. There was no simple means by which disputes among the partners could be resolved. And finally the death or withdrawal of any partner in theory determined the partnership, which would then in strict law have to be reconstituted.

Means were eventually developed by the legal profession to avoid some of the most inconvenient of these technicalities. The property of the concern could be put into the hands of a small number of trustees to hold on behalf of all the partners, and provision could be made for the transfer of shares without either dissolving the partnership or too obviously contravening the Bubble Act. The unincorporated partnership was thus developed throughout the eighteenth century as a standard form of commercial organization by way of substitute for the joint stock company. In fact many of the standard form clauses developed by the lawyers for these associations were later to be crystallized in the early Companies Acts in the mid-nineteenth century. In the words of Du Bois, the permanent effect of the Bubble Act was to help ensure the continued importance in England of the unincorporated joint stock company free from the restrictive policy of the government in the grant of official charters.

As the century progressed, however, and commercial concerns grew larger and more numerous, the prohibitions on claims to corporate status and on the free transferability of shares became more and more inconvenient. The Bubble Act was in consequence increasingly ignored, and full scale companies began to spring up again in the main commercial centres. In 1796, for instance, the Birmingham Flour and Bread Company was established with a capital of 20,000 £1 shares, and by 1808 there were some 8,000 shareholders; and in London in 1807 prospectuses were circulated for a London Paper Manufacturing Company, and a London Distillery Company, in which there were to be respectively 2,500 and 2,000 transferable shares of £50. These new companies were similar in all but their legal status to chartered companies created by the Crown or by Act of Parliament, but they were subject to none of the official controls on formation which formal incorporation involved. Nor would their affairs be subject to official investigation in the event of fraud or scandal as was the case with any chartered company.

It is not surprising, therefore, that proceedings were eventually brought against companies of this type on the grounds of their blatant breach of the provisions of the Bubble Act. The gist of the charges in a number of test cases brought between 1808 and 1810 was the assumption of corporate status and the quite unjustified claim that the liability of subscribers would be limited to the sum subscribed for. The promoters' defence was simply that the companies were genuine commercial enterprises and that no grievance, prejudice or injury to the public, as required under the Act, could be proved. The attempt to resurrect the Bubble Act achieved little. The judges were clearly reluctant to hold that all large unincorporated associations were illegal. The whole operation in fact did little more than highlight the absurdity of the old law. And eventually in 1825, probably as a result of the official embarrassment caused by a sudden spate of new unincorporated flotations, the Act was repealed. More important, Parliament was induced to provide additional powers for the Crown to facilitate the creation of chartered companies on increasingly standardized terms.

It was now increasingly clear that what was required was a form of corporate organization through which capital could be freely raised for new commercial projects and which would be readily available without prior government sanction. Official authorization of some kind was perhaps necessary for projects such as railway and canal companies, if only to grant the necessary powers of compulsory acquisition and to avoid totally uneconomic competition. But the same arguments could not be applied to ordinary commercial concerns. Even with the new streamlined statutory procedures and the adoption of standard form charters, the expense of obtaining the privileges of incorporation was too great. And the drawbacks of unincorporated association, despite the efforts of the lawyers to mitigate them, could not always be completely avoided. The fact that all partners were legally liable for all the debts of the partnership, for example, regardless of the extent of their interest, caused serious difficulties. Even a cursory glance at the history of the proceedings in *Von Sandau v. Moore*,[5] an action against the directors of an unincorporated company in which some 300 parties were involved, and which dragged on for several decades, will show how difficult it might be to bring any legal proceedings to a successful conclusion. Eventually in 1837 an eminent barrister, Bellenden Ker, was appointed to make a comprehensive review of 'the present state of the law of partnership' with special reference to the difficulty of suing and being sued and the question of limited liability. His report recommended further standardization of the system for granting charters, and a complete rationalization of the law relating to large trading partnerships.[6]

The first Companies Acts: 1844–62

The immediate motive for legislative action, as so often in this field, was the desire to control flagrant abuses of the existing system. Both in 1824–5 and in 1834–6 the commercial world was disrupted by periods of intense activity in company flotation, duly followed by a large number of failures and consequential loss on the part of the less sophisticated investors. Most of the projects were probably genuine, but there was also undoubtedly a good deal of fraud and manipulation of the market. It was in fact a new outbreak of insurance and annuity frauds in the early 1840s which led directly to the appointment of the first comprehensive company law reform committee, under the chairmanship of William Gladstone. The legislation which the committee recommended was directed primarily at providing a system in which frauds and malpractices would be less likely to occur and more easily dealt with when they did. The solution adopted was to provide a simple method of incorporation for all joint stock companies, without any form of prior authorization, but on terms which would minimize the incidence of malpractice and fraud. Provision was accordingly made in the Companies Acts of 1844 for the registration and publication of the details of the organization and membership of all newly incorporated companies, 'so that the public would have the means of knowing with whom they were dealing.' Provision was also made for the holding of periodic meetings and the auditing of accounts in order to discourage mismanagement or abuse of trust in the conduct of companies' affairs. It was in this way that the basic principle of English company law,

[5] (1825) 1 *Russ.* 441.
[6] Parl. Papers, 1837, XLIV, 399.

freedom of incorporation on standard terms with compulsory registration and disclosure, was adopted.

The details of the provisions for internal organization and control were then adapted from the existing standard forms for charters and deeds of association for the larger unincorporated companies, and were crystallized in the early Companies Clauses Acts and later in the 'Table A' model clauses addended to the 1862 Companies Act. The current terminology – boards of directors, annual general meetings, auditors and the like – was given statutory force, and has become a permanent feature of British company law.

The introduction of limited liability

The one remaining issue to be settled was that of limited liability. It seems to have been assumed without formal provision that the liability of shareholders in the earliest chartered companies was limited to the amount of their subscribed contributions, though additional calls could be made in certain circumstances. Then in the Hamborough Company case of 1671 it was finally established that creditors of the company could look to the shareholders for the settlement of company debts (see above p. 12). As a result it became relatively common in eighteenth-century charters for special provision to be made for the liability of shareholders to be limited to the amount subscribed, and the larger unincorporated companies in the early nineteenth century often petitioned for special rights in this respect along with the right to sue and be sued in the name of their trustees. In wholly unincorporated companies on the other hand all shareholders, or partners, were fully liable without limitation for all the debts of the partnership. The making of unauthorized claims that liability would be limited, it will be remembered, was one of the main grounds on which the provisions of the Bubble Act were resurrected.

The advantages and disadvantages of limited liability were in fact the principal subject of dispute in the mid-nineteenth-century discussions on company law. Bellenden Ker in his report on partnership law in 1837 had considered the existing French system of *sociétés en commandite*, a development of the old civil law concept of the *commenda*, under which only those in direct control of the concern were fully liable for its debts and obligations while those who merely put up capital were not liable to lose more than they had contributed. But he did not make any clear recommendations for its adoption.

The system for liquidation with full liability for all shareholders which was adopted in 1844, however, was soon shown to be virtually unworkable in the aftermath of a number of important failures in the later 1840s. Quite apart from the fact that it was often impossible to ascertain which shareholders should be personally responsible in the event of a failure, since many of them were likely to have sold or bought their shares after the main losses had been incurred, the effect of maintaining full personal responsibility for shareholders was thought to discourage men of substance from buying shares in enterprises in which there was any degree of risk. Such persons risked their entire personal fortunes in return for a relatively small gain, since in the event of failure it was clear that they would be the first to be sued by unpaid creditors. The smaller and less wealthy shareholder, on the other hand, though he might be more hard hit by the loss of the capital invested, was unlikely in practice to be sued for any further liabilities.[7]

This essentially economic argument for limited liability, that it would encourage much wider investment in joint stock enterprises, eventually prevailed over the dire warnings of the more conservative commentators, who gloomily forecast that any change in the law would merely serve to encourage recklessness and fraud on the part of company promoters and directors. After a heated battle the principle of limited liability was finally adopted in 1855, though a number of safeguards were provided, for example a provision that seventy-five per cent of the nominal capital must have been subscribed and that the company would not carry on business if more than seventy-five per cent of its capital had been lost. These restrictive provisions, however, were soon dropped. From 1856 any company which complied with the terms of the Companies Act in adding the word 'limited' to its formal title by way of warning to all those dealing with it was entitled to limit its liability, and that of its members, to the amount of its subscribed capital. As Robert Lowe put it in introducing the Companies Act of 1856:

> The principle we should adopt is this, not to throw the slightest obstacle in the way of limited companies being formed . . . and when difficulties arise to arm the courts of justice with sufficient powers to check extravagance or roguery . . . That is the only way the legislature should interfere, with the

[7] See, for instance, *Report of the Select Committee on Investments for the Savings of the Middle and Working Classes*, Parl. Papers 1850, XIX, 169.

single exception of giving the greatest publicity to the affairs of such companies that everyone may know on what grounds he is dealing.[8]

The consolidation of company law

With the passing of the consolidating Companies Act of 1862 the broad structure of company law as we now know it was firmly established. Within this framework the courts and textwriters have built up an increasingly complex conceptual account of the respective rights and duties of shareholders and directors inside the company and their relations with the company's creditors. The legislature has also intervened from time to time, primarily to deal with the particular abuses which have manifested themselves at various periods and to increase the ambit and accuracy of statutory disclosure provisions. The most significant of these statutory interventions were the introduction of a new and more effective system of liquidation in the 1880s, and of more stringent rules governing prospectuses issued by companies seeking to raise money from the public in 1901, the formal separation of public and private companies in 1907 and the prohibition of door-to-door or postal share-pushing in the 1930s. The principal additions to the disclosure rules were in 1907 when all public companies were required to disclose their annual balance sheets, in 1927 when this was extended to include annual trading accounts and in 1967 when the disclosure of accounts was extended to all companies and larger companies were required to give additional information on directors' fees, employment, turnover and exports. There has also been a progressive tightening of the informal controls exercised by the Stock Exchange over publicly quoted companies, notably the administrative vetting of new applications for quotation in the early 1930s and the development of the City Code on Take-overs and Mergers in the late 1960s. The details of these various reforms are dealt with in their legal and administrative context in Part II.

Corporate capitalism

This legal consolidation was not immediately reflected in the real industrial world. The bulk of new company flotations in the mid-nineteenth century were in the field of railways, shipping and mining, both in Britain and abroad. All these needed substantial

[8] Parl. Deb., 1856, Vol. 140, col. 131.

initial capital of the kind which could be accumulated through the stock market in London and the main provincial centres. But the firms which were engaged in the production of cotton, iron and steel and other manufactured goods did not for the most part begin in that way. Most of them were set up and operated as unincorporated partnerships through which individual factory masters and financiers could make what arrangements they and their lawyers pleased. It has been estimated that by 1885 at most between five and ten per cent of the total number of important business organizations in Britain were limited companies, and that only in shipping, iron and steel and cotton could their influence be said to be considerable.[9] As time passed more and more of the established businesses converted themselves to the new corporate form. But so too did a myriad of small private businesses and retail shops, employing no more than a handful of paid assistants in addition to the working proprietors. By 1911, when accurate figures for the division into public and private companies introduced in 1907 were published, almost two-thirds of the total of 50,000 registered companies were private companies (see Table 2.1, p. 39).

The practical effect of the new corporate structures was thus limited in its initial stages to the narrow range of operations like the railway and shipping companies which could probably not have been financed in any other way than through the public market for capital, at least on the scale which was actually attained. And it must not be forgotten that many of the early flotations were anything but successful, and that not a few were unsound or fraudulent from the start. At a later stage however the corporate form did play a part in the increasing concentration of large firms in the leading commercial and industrial spheres, in what may be regarded as the second stage of industrial capitalism. In the 1890s there was a spate of mergers and amalgamations undertaken on a voluntary basis by the owners of large existing mills and factories, with a view to increasing their joint market power. In some cases the resulting giant combines were unwieldy associations of relatively independent productive units. Thus, for example, in the 'relatively efficient and integrated Associated Portland Cement Manufacturers Ltd. there were in addition to the managing directors, not less than forty ordinary

[9] P. L. Payne, *British Entrepreneurship in the Nineteenth Century* (1974) p. 19, quoting J. B. Jeffreys, *Trends in Business Organisation in Great Britain since 1856* (unpublished thesis 1938).

directors . . . because there were so many interests to be considered'; there were similar problems in the Calico Printers Association formed in 1889 by the amalgamation of fifty-nine firms controlling about eighty-five per cent of the industry and controlled initially by eight managing and seventy-six other directors.[10] In others the take-overs were promoted by unscrupulous financiers more interested in making a quick profit on the stock market than in industrial efficiency. But there can be little doubt that such massive accumulations of capital could not have been achieved without the legal and financial framework which had been developed over the preceding centuries.

During the twentieth century the trend towards this kind of accumulation or concentration has greatly increased. Established and profitable companies have been able to use the revenue which they have generated internally or capital which they have been able to raise on the open market by the issue of new shares to buy their smaller competitors. In some cases the companies taken over have simply been absorbed by their purchasers, but more often they have been left in existence as wholly owned subsidiaries. A further sophistication which has arisen in the post-war period has been the acquisition of new subsidiaries merely by an increase in the share capital of the purchasing company which is then issued in exchange for the shares of the company being purchased, without any hard cash changing hands at all. The potential for this kind of operation within the framework of the law and the stock market is virtually unlimited. In theory one might predict the eventual absorption of all existing companies under the umbrella of one massive conglomerate giant by cumulative merger and take-overs. The combination of further industrial and commercial concentration and of individual profit which the techniques of stock market management and manipulation have made possible has been described as finance capitalism by some commentators.

A second development has been an increasing separation between those who own the shares in large publicly quoted companies and those who control their operations and the allocation of the profit which is generated. Though this separation is inherent in the formal structures of company law with its clearly distinct roles for shareholders as owners and directors as managers, it has developed much

[10] Ibid., pp. 21–2.

further than the entrepreneurial factory masters and company promoters of the nineteenth century would have thought possible. Few of the directors and managers of the largest modern corporations in industry or commerce own more than a tiny proportion of the shares in the companies which they control. Yet management in these companies is a self-perpetuating and increasingly autonomous group. This overall process is generally described as the managerial revolution.

The financial and managerial revolutions, like the industrial revolution, have been prevented from fulfilling their own inherent potential. The government has intervened to discourage and prevent some forms of concentration by legislation on monopolies and mergers. It has also sought to exercise some control over financial manipulation and managerial power. In some instances it has itself completed the process of concentration by nationalization and thus imposed direct political control over the affairs of the resulting national corporations. The combined effect of these conflicting forces of internal concentration and external intervention among large companies is a matter of some complexity which will be investigated in the next chapter.

3 CAPITALISM IN ECONOMIC AND SOCIALIST THEORY

One further element which is essential to an understanding of the development of capitalism is the theoretical analysis of the story which has just been outlined. Though the history of capitalism is in one sense a factual matter, the analysis of what the word means and what the system implies is hotly disputed. This is not just a matter of words. The different interpretations of capitalism adopted by traditional market economists and by socialist and Marxist economists differ substantially in their implications for practical action. The more general aspects of this difference in approach cannot be dealt with here, but the centrality of corporate organization in free market and socialist economies alike calls for some discussion of the respective accounts of corporate capitalism in its various stages of development.

The company in free market economics

The main focus of traditional economic theory has been the operation of the market as a pricing mechanism and as a method of resource allocation. Starting from the simple laws of supply and demand economists from Adam Smith onwards have sought to demonstrate how free market competition in the various factors of production – labour, capital and raw materials – can operate to produce the most democratic and beneficial distribution of goods and services in a given economy. In recent years there has been rather more concentration on the effect of various forms of interference and intervention in the market, both at the micro-economic level of the firm as a result of monopoly or oligopoly and at the macro-economic level in terms of governmental action on the supply of money, interest rates and levels of public expenditure. But the underlying commitment to the principles of free competition and consumer sovereignty has remained. This is stated in forthright terms by Samuelson in a leading modern textbook on basic economics:

> The price mechanism, working through supply and demand in competitive markets, operates to answer the three fundamental problems of economic organization in our mixed private enterprise system; the system is far from perfect but it is one way to solve the What, How and For Whom.[11]

This approach obviously requires some consideration of the costs of production, including those of the necessary wage labour in relation to that of plant, machinery and raw materials, and their effect on prices and competition. But relatively little attention has been paid to the internal structure of the firms which produce the goods and services or to the allocation of profit within them. This is perhaps because the nature of the firm or company as an organization is theoretically superfluous. The economic theory of free market competition can be stated most directly in terms of the pure entrepreneur who supplies his own capital and manages his own enterprise. The model of capitalism which has been developed within this framework is attractively simple. Capital or stock – the terms were originally fully interchangeable – is merely the physical means of production (fixed capital) and the material and products necessary to maintain it (circulating capital). The entrepreneur must provide this capital in order to set up and operate his factory. In return he is entitled to any balance between the costs of production, including labour and raw materials at the market rate, and the proceeds of his sales. This profit or return from the investment of capital may

[11] P. Samuelson, *Economics* (10th edn., 1976), p. 53.

then be variously explained either as a payment to the entrepreneur for his skill and enterprise in organizing production at a competitive price, or less directly as a reward for postponing expenditure or consumption. The simpler of these two alternatives may be illustrated from a current elementary textbook:

> Profit is the reward (the entrepreneur) receives for taking the risk of producing in advance for an uncertain demand. . . .[12]

The more sophisticated view, which emphasizes the need for a market price for capital as for any other factor of production, is adopted by Samuelson:

> Thrift in the sense of abstaining from consuming past capital accumulation and waiting for future consumption goods rather than consuming now interacts with the technical net productiviy of capital goods to determine the developing pattern of interest rates and capital formation.'[13]

Neither of these views, it may be thought, provides a very compelling justification for the massive differentials in the rewards for labour and entrepreneurial activity which free market capitalism has often produced. The theory of market economics is equally unsatisfactory in its account of the corporate form of organization, and consequently of the role of the shareholder as a disinterested capitalist. Adam Smith certainly had little time for the joint stock company.[14] He objected to the limitation of risk to the amount of the capital subscribed, and to the management of the company's affairs by its directors, since, though they were subject to the general control of the proprietors, 'the greater part of those proprietors seldom pretended to understand anything of the business of the company.' The formation of a company, he admitted, could allow greater sums of capital to be raised, but this had to be set off against the fact that the directors, 'being the managers rather of other people's money than of their own' could not well be expected to 'watch over it with the same anxious vigilance with which the partners in a private copartnery frequently watch over their own. . . . Negligence and profusion, therefore, must always prevail, more or less, in the management of such companies.' The only trades which a joint stock company could in consequence carry on successfully

[12] J. Harvey, *Elementary Economics* (3rd edn., 1971), p. 274.
[13] Ibid., p. 611.
[14] *The Wealth of Nations* (1776); see generally Book V, Ch. I, Pt. III.

were those 'in which all the operations were capable of being reduced to what is called a routine or to such uniformity of method as permits of little or no variation', such as banking, insurance and such public utilities as canals or water companies. In sum, in Smith's view, no joint stock company should be established 'except for some purpose of remarkable utility requiring a larger capital than can be provided by a private partnership'.

The economist's image of the company had scarcely altered by the time of Alfred Marshall a century later.[15] The entrepreneur or businessman was still the key figure: it was he who 'adventured or undertook the risks of directing production, brought together the capital and the labour required for the work, . . . arranged or engineered its general plan and superintended its minor details.' Marshall did admit that joint stock companies were taking an increasing share in the management of business and commerce, but this he attributed mainly to the needs of those with good business ability but with little capital of their own, who could make use of the corporate form in order to facilitate investment in their concerns. He could only marvel at the 'growth in recent times of a spirit of honesty and uprightness in commercial matters', and the fact that 'the leading officers of great public companies yielded as little as they did to the vast temptations which lay in their way.' The impression is still of a reluctant acceptance of trading companies as a slightly improper form of economic organization which managed to succeed in spite of rather than because of the laws of economics.

As companies came to dominate the economic scene from the mid-nineteenth century, it was no longer possible to regard them as peripheral to economic theory. The gradual replacement of the solitary entrepreneur by larger and larger joint stock companies had to be accounted for in theory as well as recorded in practice. The most direct attempt is perhaps Schumpeter's.[16] Economic development, for Schumpeter, was dependent on new combinations of labour, materials and methods, and these could normally be financed only by capital supplied by other than the entrepreneurs or innovators themselves:

> The possessor of wealth, even if it is the greatest combine, must resort to credit if he wishes to carry out a new combination which cannot like an

[15] *The Principles of Economics* (1890); see generally Book IV, Ch. 12.

[16] J. A. Schumpeter, *The Theory of Economic Development* (1934).

established business be financed by returns from previous production. To provide this credit is clearly the function of that class of individuals which we call capitalists.

The payment of profit to these capitalists was not then a reward for initiative or innovation as in the case of an entrepreneur, but simply a payment for the risk which they ran of losing their security. Such was the typical position of shareholders, who 'were never entrepreneurs but merely capitalists who in consideration of their submitting to certain risks participate in profit'.

The stock market in economic theory

There is one further element in what may be termed the classical economic account of the capitalist system: the role of the open market in capital. In a free market the individual investor will ideally choose to make his money available to those new or existing enterprises which offer the best prospect of immediate or continuing profit. And since he is entitled to withdraw his money from a less profitable enterprise by selling his shares, as long as he can find a buyer, and to reinvest it, he will continually be looking for new and more profitable outlets for his money. The ordinary laws of supply and demand, however, apply to capital just as to any other commodity, so that a market price for capital will be fixed in relation to the amount of capital available, the outlets open to it and the nature of the risk run by the investor in relation to the expected return. The net effect of the system should be an approximation of an optimum allocation of capital throughout the economy. To revert to Schumpeter: 'the money market is as it were the headquarters of the capitalist system ... and that which is debated and decided there is always in essence the settlement of plans for further development.'

For the economist, therefore, the stock market is in theory 'the allocator of resources par excellence'; and though there is 'some uneasiness about the untoward effects of speculation', it is generally regarded as 'an allocative mechanism of remarkable efficiency'.[17] The proper achievement of its function, however, is dependent on the nature of the market itself. It must be a free market, not only in the sense that all those in search of capital have the right to apply to it for funds, but in that individual investors must be free to allocate

[17] W. Baumol, *The Stock Market and Economic Efficiency* (1965), p. 4.

their capital within the market as they please. It must also be so organized that those who deal on it are fully informed of all the relevant details of the enterprises in which they are being asked to invest. Translated into the terminology of company law this means simply that the facilities of the market shall be available to all public companies and that each shareholder or potential shareholder must be free to withdraw his money from a particular company and reinvest it in another. All those concerned must also be provided with the information necessary to permit them to make investment decisions on a fully rational basis.

Protecting the market

The practical implications of this approach to companies and the stock market may be seen in governmental policies throughout the western world. There has been a progressive increase in the disclosure requirements of the Companies Acts in Britain, both in relation to the past performance and future prospects of all those companies seeking to raise capital on the stock market, and also in respect of the current performance of all quoted companies. The thinking behind these requirements was aptly summarized by the Davey Committee in 1895 in relation to disclosure in prospectuses:

> It is, therefore, of the utmost importance that the prospectus upon which the public are invited to subscribe shall not only not contain any misrepresentation but shall satisfy a high standard of good faith. . . . That a prospectus shall disclose everything which could reasonably influence the mind of an investor of average prudence . . . is the ideal to be aimed at.[18]

These legal requirements have been further reinforced by even more stringent regulations imposed as a condition of quotation by the Stock Exchange regulations on all quoted companies, and by the rule that there shall be a sufficient number of shares in every quoted company on the open market to ensure a reasonable level of supply and demand.

As the size and economic power of major companies and groups of companies has increased, there have also been repeated attempts to protect the free market in goods and services from distortion as a result of restrictive pricing agreement or cartels or of monopoly or oligopoly power. The anti-trust laws in the United States date back to the 1890s, when corporate concentration first became an

[18] C.7179 (1895), p. vi.

issue of general political concern. In Britain formal legislation against monopolies and restrictive practices was not developed in any systematic way until the 1940s, as described in Chapter 14. But the general objective in both cases has clearly been to preserve a state of affairs which approximates as closely as circumstances permit to the unfettered competitive market of traditional economic theory.

More recently there has been some recognition of the impracticality of this strategy in the face of the growing power of the largest corporations to control and on occasions even to create public demand for their products through advertising. Some modern economists, like Galbraith and Marris, have sought to build up an alternative theory of corporate capitalism which takes account of the dominating influence on the market exercised by these corporations.[19] But most leading economists in the western tradition, led by the so-called monetary theorists of the Chicago school, still adhere to the principles of market competition. Samuelson, for instance, adopts the objective of 'workable competition':

> By public regulation of utilities and by various formal and informal anti-trust activities of the state, some of the checks and balances that are not automatically enforceable by perfect competition can be achieved by governmental action.[20]

Even when individual governments have felt obliged in the interests of maintaining employment to protect or support their ailing industries from foreign competition, as has happened with increasing frequency in recent years, lip service continues to be paid to the concept of free international competition.

The socialist theory of capitalism

Socialist economists are not bound by any commitment to a free market. The basis of their alternative to free market capitalism is an economy in which all aspects of economic activity are controlled by the state for the common good. The ultimate goal is a system of production under which the communist ideal – 'from each according to his ability, to each according to his need' – can be attained. The socialist analysis of capitalism is accordingly focused on the social relations of production, and in particular on the claim that

[19] J. K. Galbraith, *The New Industrial State* (1969) and *Economics and Public Purpose* (1974); R. Marris, *The Economic Theory of Managerial Capitalism* (1964).

[20] Op. cit., p. 532.

under capitalism ownership of the means of production has been appropriated by a single class, the bourgeoisie, with the result that the mass of the working class is denied a just share in the goods and services which it produces.

Marx developed this simple conclusion from an elaborate analysis of the nature of capital.[21] He distinguished three forms: usurer's capital, merchant's capital and industrial capital. These three forms developed cumulatively in the succeeding stages of capitalist growth from feudalism to industrial production which have already been outlined, but in each case the element of exploitation which is inherent in the nature of capital was clearly stressed. From the feudal period onwards both the poor and the idle rich were the victims of usurer's interest on the money which they were forced into borrowing to meet their basic needs and social obligations. In the early period of capitalist development the population at large were the victims of the profits which merchants could make by using their capital to buy cheap and sell dear, taking advantage of temporary fluctuations in supply and demand in different areas, though Marx also argued that much of the initial trade was in luxury goods and that much of the initial capital was derived from piracy. In the final stages of industrial capitalism the whole working class was the victim of the continuing exploitation of wage labour, through which the employer was able to appropriate the whole of the surplus value created by his workers.

The concept of surplus value lies at the foundation of Marx's analysis. In simple terms what he meant by it was that part of each worker's production over and above that which was necessary to feed and clothe his family and himself. In an agricultural society that meant any surplus food or produce. In an urban society it meant anything over and above the wage which was required to buy the necessaries of life. In either case, on Marx's view, the surplus product or value properly belonged to the person who produced it. This view was directly related to what is termed the labour theory of value, originally developed by Adam Smith and Ricardo, under which the true value of any product is no more and no less than the labour which is socially necessary to produce it.

Marx then argued that the social effect of these three forms of

[21] For a modern account see E. Mandel, *Marxist Economic Theory* (English edn., 1962).

capitalist exploitation – interest, trading profit and surplus value – was bound to be cumulative. As the capitalist class accumulated more and more capital, so their exploitation of the proletariat was bound to grow. This was principally a matter of a larger and larger proportion of the population losing control over the means of their production and thus being reduced to the status of wage labourers, while more and more capital would be accumulated in the hands of a diminishing number of capitalists. Marx showed remarkable foresight in predicting that the expropriation of the means of production would extend gradually from the individual producers affected at the start of the industrial revolution to the smaller and medium sized capitalists who would themselves be absorbed at a later stage; he also accurately predicted the 'transformation of the actual functioning capitalist into a mere manager' who would be paid the wage for a specific type of skilled labour, and 'of the owner of capital into a ... mere money capitalist' whose profit would eventually be received as compensation for owning capital that was entirely divorced from the actual process of production.[22]

More important, however, was the social disruption caused by these general processes. Though in certain periods it would be in the interests of the capitalist class to pay higher wages in order to sustain a market for their products, the inherent imbalance between the productive capacity of the capitalist system and the capacity of society, including the proletariat, to pay for it would contribute to a series of ever more exaggerated booms and slumps and an ever increasing mass of unemployed workers. The final culmination of these forces might be delayed by colonial expansion in search of extended markets and cheaper labour. But Marx was never in any doubt about the ultimate end, which he described in a number of well-known passages of which the following is a typical example:

> Along with the constantly diminishing number of the magnates of capital, who usurp and monopolize all advantages of this process of transformation, grows the mass of misery, oppression, slavery, degradation, exploitation; but with this too grows the revolt of the working class, a class always increasing in numbers, and disciplined, united, organized by the very mechanism of the process of capitalist production itself.... The knell of capitalist private property sounds. The expropriators are expropriated.[23]

[22] See, generally, *Capital*, Vol. III, Ch. 27.

[23] *Capital*, Vol. I, Ch. 32.

This account of the self-destroying force of capitalism was linked by Marx to another phenomenological claim. He argued in his early writings that the only natural and satisfying relationship between a worker and his work was one in which he or she was in full control of the means of production. This requirement was fulfilled in primitive communal societies, and to a lesser extent in agricultural production and craft work under the feudal system. Under capitalist production methods, however, the means of production were owned exclusively by the capitalist and the worker was thus increasingly alienated from his or her work. When the full extent of this alienation was recognized and a state of revolutionary consciousness attained, there would then be a proletarian uprising against the capitalist expropriators. The workers would collectively seize control of the means of production and so remedy their alienation through the development of a new form of social or collective ownership :

> ... the ultimate development of capitalist production is a necessary transitional phase towards a reconversion of capital into the property of producers, although no longer as the private property of the individual producers but rather as the property of the associated producers, as outright social property.[24]

This analysis cannot be refuted simply by pointing out that the promised proletarian revolution has not materialized in the most advanced industrial countries. The force of the Marxist position lies in the flexibility of its predictions and of its programmes for revolutionary action. The theory of alienation is immune from any empirical refutation, since by its very nature it requires the mass acceptance of an ideological position as a condition of its own validity. But there is a price to be paid for this immunity. There are serious difficulties in deriving any detailed prescriptions for economic organization on the basis of Marxist economic theory. The labour theory of value, for instance, breaks down very quickly when an attempt is made to use it to derive differential rates of pay for different kinds of work without any reference to market forces. It provides no measure for assessing the contribution of 'non-productive' labour carried out by managerial and administrative staff, and even for production workers there is an obvious difficulty in settling any hard figure for a 'socially necessary' standard of living. There are equally large technical difficulties in working out the precise implica-

[24] *Capital*, Vol. III, Ch. 27.

tions of Marx's law of diminishing profit and other consequences of the fact that surplus value was calculated on the cost of labour alone.

It is hardly surprising in this light that Marx failed to provide any satisfactory model for economic organization in an advanced industrial society. His economic theory was eminently forceful and persuasive, but essentially simplistic. He recognized the injustice of the industrial structures of the mid-nineteenth century, and saw clearly that capitalism by its own momentum would 'establish a monopoly in certain spheres and thereby require state intervention'.[25] But his prescription for an alternative to the capitalist system he described so well was vague and ill-defined.

The role of company law

It will be clear from this brief account of the conflicting theories of market and socialist economics that there is much common ground in factual if not in evaluative terms between them. It is also clear that neither provides a very satisfactory basis for the allocation of rewards to workers, managers and investors in large modern companies, or for solving the problems of corporate organization whether in a mixed or a socialist economy. The Marxist account provides the better foundation for the analysis of the development of capitalism and its impact on society. But many of the problems of private monopoly capitalism, notably those of controlling the power of the managerial class and meeting the legitimate wishes of the working population, are equally real under state monopoly capitalism.[26]

The contribution of a book on company law to the better understanding of the interrelationship of socialist ideals and market forces in the real world is necessarily limited. But some attempt can be made to analyse the social and economic relations of those who contribute in various ways to the production of goods and services within the business enterprise. This will involve a detailed analysis of the rights and duties of the three main groups involved, in capitalist, mixed and socialist economies alike: the workers, the managers and the suppliers of capital. For obvious practical reasons the main emphasis will be on the formal rights and obligations of

[25] *Capital*, Vol. III, Ch. 27.

[26] See generally M. Djilas, *The New Class* (English edn., 1957).

investors and managers as they are currently defined in law and in practice. But in the final part of the book some of the possible developments in industrial democracy and governmental involvement in a non-revolutionary framework will also be explored.

2

The realities of modern capitalism

If the law is to provide the commercial community with a more effective framework for business operations, lawyers clearly require a better appreciation of commercial and economic realities than is usually expected of them. So too do those politicians and political economists who are concerned with the reform or reconstruction of the capitalist structures which we have inherited from the past. The object of this chapter is to describe in simple terms the nature and range of the business enterprises which must be taken into account, and to document more precisely some of the major trends and developments in the capitalist system over the past few decades.[1] One of the major problems with much current political and economic analysis is the tendency to focus exclusively on the largest companies on the assumption that trends and developments in the dominant sector are bound to be followed in the rest of the economy. The reality, as will be seen, is much more diverse. Smaller companies have proved remarkably resilient in the past and are likely to remain so.

The analysis which follows is based largely on statistics relating to companies and other business enterprises in England and Wales or in Britain as a whole. But there is little doubt that a broadly similar pattern would emerge from a corresponding analysis of other common law jurisdictions such as those in the United States, Canada or Australia, and in substantive if not in legal terms in most west European countries. The relative size and distribution of the various

[1] Readers who are not already acquainted with the basic terminology of company law and commercial practice may find it helpful to read the introductory legal account in Chapter 3 before beginning on this chapter.

forms of enterprise will naturally reflect the stage of development which has been reached in the particular country or industry. But the essentials of the analysis will not be affected.

I THE RANGE OF REGISTERED COMPANIES

An obvious starting point for analysis is the total number of companies actually in existence. The figures in Table 2.1 (see p. 39) show clearly that there has been a startling increase in the number of incorporations in Britain since 1945. The current total is more than half a million, or more than four times that of the mid-1930s. This massive increase has been almost exclusively due to the formation of new private companies. The number of public companies has remained more or less static at a figure of some 15,000 since early in the century. The relative stability in the number of large companies is also shown by the figures for the number of securities and companies quoted on the London Stock Exchange.

Company formation practice

These crude figures are not particularly revealing in themselves, except perhaps as a reflection of the changing patterns in the practice of company formation. As already indicated, there were relatively few incorporations in the years following the enactment of the first modern Companies Acts in 1844, most of them involving new enterprises in search of public capital on a fairly large scale. The number of companies newly registered each year during the 1860s, for instance, varied only between four and nine hundred. As the century progressed, however, it became more and more of a standard practice for established manufacturing and commercial concerns to convert themselves into limited companies, both for administrative convenience and to take advantage of the provision of limited liability. In most cases the value of individual share units was rather higher than at present, at £10 or even £100 per share, though in the case of new issues the subscribers would not normally be expected to contribute the full amount all at once, or even at all. A balance of uncalled capital to meet emergencies, or for future development, was regarded as a normal form of financial reserve.

By the 1890s it was becoming common practice for much smaller concerns, whether owned and controlled by individual traders or by partnerships, to seek the protection of limited liability. Concern was

TABLE 2.1

Public and private companies in England and Wales and securities and companies quoted on the London Stock Exchange for selected years, 1911–75

Year	Public companies No.	Public companies %	Private companies No.	Private companies %	Total	London Stock Exchange Companies	London Stock Exchange Securities
1911	18,600	37	31,400	62	50,000	n.a.	n.a.
1921	12,700	17	62,300	83	75,000	n.a.	n.a.
1931	16,831	15	92,499	85	109,330	n.a.	n.a.
1938	15,872	11	134,882	89	150,754	n.a.	10,297 (1939)
1946	15,428	8	189,575	92	205,003	n.a.	9,615
1951	14,504	6	230,721	94	245,225	n.a.	9,706
1956	14,195	5	276,068	95	290,263	n.a.	9,988
1961	14,491	4	368,702	96	383,193	n.a.	9,355
1966	14,027	3	489,588	97	503,615	4,269	9,431
1970	14,151	3	480,945	97	495,096	3,805	9,180
1975	14,273	3	547,825	97	562,098	3,524	8,743 (1976)

Sources: *Annual Reports on Companies* (HMSO), *Stock Exchange Factbooks*

expressed at the time both in the Board of Trade's annual reports and in the courts, culminating in the Salomon case (see p. 143), at this 'misuse' or 'abuse' of the provisions of the Companies Acts. But the practice was eventually given statutory blessing in 1907 by the introduction of the status of private company to distinguish between these small closely owned concerns and the larger 'public' companies in which shareholding was relatively widespread.

The bulk of new registrations since that date has been of small private companies, whether on the formation of new enterprises or through the incorporation of existing businesses or partnerships. It is difficult to be precise about the reasons for this trend. Many businessmen and their professional advisers have undoubtedly been attracted by the legal and administrative advantages of incorporation, principally the limitation of personal liability and formal separation of personal and business property. A major factor at least until 1965 was probably the belief that there were tax advantages to be obtained from incorporation. Surtax could often be avoided by the retention of profits in a company, and if they were distributed they could be paid out in the form of directors' fees and thus rank as earned rather than unearned income more or less regardless of the degree of active participation in the business. The impact of death duties on small family businesses could also be cushioned more readily by the redistribution of company shares within the family than by the transfer of personal or partnership assets. Many accountants also advised their clients on similar grounds to form what may be called 'tax companies' to own and manage their existing assets, whether in the form of real property or stocks and shares, though the operation would not normally be regarded as a business enterprise.

The massive proliferation of small private companies has been accompanied by a considerable increase in the number of companies which exist in law but do not represent any real business operations. One explanation for this is the practice adopted by some company registration agents of registering large numbers of 'off-the-peg' companies for sale to anyone in search of instant incorporation. There is no legal requirement that a company shall be formed only for the purposes of a genuine and existing or prospective business. They may be formed with a minimal paid up capital of as little as £2 and with a memorandum and articles of association drawn widely enough to suit virtually any prospective business. The number of non-operative companies on the register is swollen by what may be termed 'defunct companies'. The mass of new company registrations of all types is naturally offset by the decline and disappearance of others. Many small companies, and some larger ones, simply go out of business on the failure of the enterprise or on the death or retirement of the individuals principally concerned. Others are swallowed up by their more successful competitors, whether by the direct purchase of the business or by a formal take-over of the company by the purchase of its shares.

It would naturally be assumed that in all these cases the company would be wound up in due course, and thus cease to exist in law as well as in practice. But frequently this does not happen. In the case of take-overs the buying company, having purchased all the shares in the business required, often leaves the old company formally in being, though the actual businesses will often be inextricably merged even for internal accounting purposes. Even when an independent company really does cease to exist for practical purposes, there is often no practical pressure to wind it up in a formal sense. If its outstanding debts are negligible or if for some other reason its creditors do not wish to press for their money, or can see that there is no money to be had, there is no reason why anyone should take the trouble of initiating formal liquidation proceedings. The defunct company simply disappears from the commercial scene, and it is only when the Registrar of Companies finally notices that the statutory returns have ceased to flow that official action is taken to have it struck off the register.

The net result of these various practices is that there is a considerable number of what are for all practical purposes dormant companies on the register at any given time. The total will be made up from various sources: 'off-the-peg' companies registered in advance of requirements, wholly owned subsidiaries with no independent existence, and defunct companies which no one has taken the trouble to liquidate formally. No precise estimate of their numbers can be given, but they probably represent at least one-fifth, and perhaps even a quarter of the total number of registered companies.

The flow of incorporations

The range of figures involved in this general process of registration and deregistration may be illustrated by the statistics for the flow of incorporations in 1970, as set out in Figure 2.1. This shows clearly

Figure 2.1 The flow of company formation, liquidation and deregistration in 1970 showing the net increase in companies on the register during the year

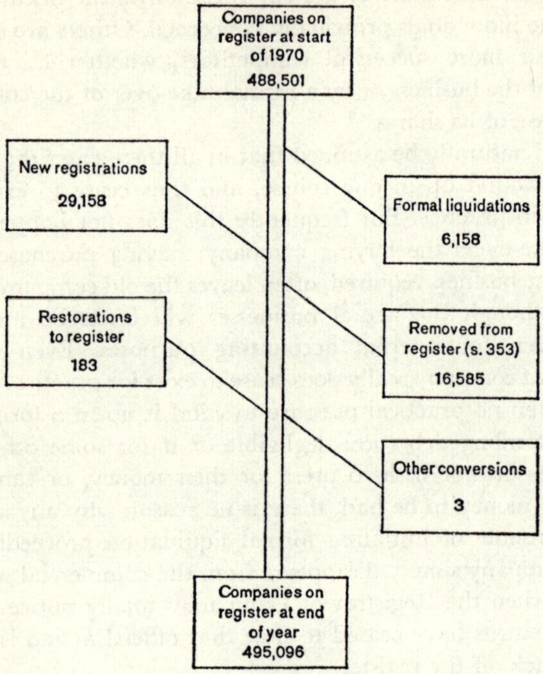

Source: *Companies in 1970* (HMSO)

how the official liquidation procedures are overshadowed by the ad hoc striking off procedures employed in the case of those companies which have died a natural rather than a formal death. Furthermore the fact that the number of new registrations in any one year far exceeds the number of companies liquidated and struck off the register is not in itself any guarantee that there has been any real increase in the number of genuinely operative concerns. The statistics for company registrations and deregistrations from year to year are a highly unreliable index of anything other than the work of the administrative departments involved.

The development of individual companies

In tracing the development of company formation practice the emphasis has naturally been on the gradual shift from the flotation of large and heavily capitalized public and family concerns in the mid-nineteenth century to the modern concentration on vast numbers of very small individualized companies frequently floated with minimal capital and sometimes with no genuine trading operations in view. Within the individual company, however, the tendency is clearly in the opposite direction. Typically, the small business is started without corporate status and is then transformed into a small private company with two or three shareholders only. As time passes the initial shareholdings become dispersed among the sons and other relatives of the original founders, until the company can readily be classed as an extended family company with anything from twenty or thirty to a hundred shareholders, though any increase over the figure of fifty will require its formal conversion into a public company. Then, at any given point, the need for further finance, or simply the growing size of the enterprise may induce the company to 'go public' by seeking a quotation on a stock market, as a result of which the range of shareholding will be rapidly increased. From that point, the company may continue to grow, either by its own internal expansion or through the assimilation of other smaller companies, into one of the massive industrial or commercial complexes which dominate the scene in any particular sphere. Or it may itself be absorbed by a more successful competitor.

This pattern of development is not of course universal. Many enterprises, particularly in the nineteenth century, were founded from the start as quoted companies making use of public investment capital as the prime source of finance. Others have continued from generation to generation at essentially the same level of operation, whether as small private companies, extended family companies or as quoted public companies, though in any one of these there may be occasional changes in internal control by sale or otherwise. But these static concerns are the exception. The normal rule is growth or decline.[2] The average life of a small private company as such is probably only a few decades, or the working life of those involved; that of a larger family company perhaps twice as long. A survey carried out for the Bolton Committee on Small Firms found that

[2] See generally J. Boswell, *The Rise and Decline of Small Firms* (1973).

the median age of small firms in 1963 varied from nineteen years for retail and motor trades to twenty-two for manufacturing, twenty-nine for wholesale and sixty-nine for construction.[3] Death comes swiftly, whether in the form of failure and liquidation or more frequently in the form of assimilation into a larger enterprise. Yet even the most rapid expansion is no protection for the public company. The laws of corporate survival in an age of frequent take-over and merger are a good deal more complex. None the less the account which has been given of the typical progression of a successful concern does emphasize the fact that the nature of any company is likely to alter appreciably through the passage of time.

The classification and distribution of companies in Britain

These patterns of company formation practice and of individual corporate development may appropriately be used as the basis for an overall classification of companies both for statistical and legal purposes. The rough classification and estimate of distribution which follows is little more than an attempt to lend precision to the discursive account which has already been given, but it should help to clarify the task which faces the legislature in embarking on any major reform of company law.[4]

i *The participant or partnership company*. The base of the corporate pyramid is formed of small incorporated businesses, in which the shares are held exclusively by those directly concerned in the management of the business, or by their close relatives. For some purposes it may be useful to draw a distinction between the one-man company and the partnership company in this context, but the formal nature of the company as a business enterprise is not normally affected by the number of persons involved in running it. The Bolton Committee reported that ninety-nine per cent of small firms in their sample, whether companies or not, had five or fewer participators: roughly forty per cent had a single controlling owner, forty-five per cent two controlling shareholder/partners and the remainder more than two.[5] If an upper limit is set at five participants it is probable that about six in ten of all existing companies, or some 300,000 in

[3] Cmnd. 4811 (1971), p. 7.

[4] The figures for each group are an informed guess based on a small random survey of companies on the register for England and Wales in 1969.

[5] Cmnd. 4811, p. 6.

all, fall into this group, of which about one-third might be one-man companies and the rest partnership companies. Within the group, however, there is a large number of non-operative concerns, either formed in advance of requirements or not formally wound up on failure. These dormant companies may amount to as many as 100,000 or one-third of the total. Of the remainder an appreciable number are formed and operated to hold and manage individual property assets in the most advantageous and convenient way.

ii *The extended partnership company.* When all shareholders cease to be active participants in the operation of the company's business an important new factor is introduced, the interest of the 'external' shareholder. Such companies develop naturally from participant or partnership companies as shares are made over to the wives and children of the principal participants, whether for tax purposes or on the retirement or death of the original participants. Many tax companies will be floated in this form from the start. If these are considered along with the first group, the combined total probably accounts for four-fifths of all companies.

iii *The large unquoted company.* At a certain stage of size or development it becomes natural to think of the company as a continuing entity rather than merely a mechanism through which the participants conduct their business. There is no precise dividing line in this context: the age of the company, the size of its business and the number of participants and external shareholders are all relevant. In some cases the company remains almost exclusively in the hands of one or two families, and may appropriately be termed a private family company. In others companies with fairly widespread shareholding are floated as a means of investment or property management. If all private companies with more than ten independent shareholdings are included it is probable that there are some 50,000 unquoted companies of this type.

iv *Quoted public companies.* Where there is a genuine public market in the shares of a company, through the mechanism of the stock market or otherwise, there is an important additional element of public interest which distinguishes it from the large private company. This must not be confused with the purely legal distinction between public and private companies. There are in Britain some 10,000 public companies with share capital, but of these only some 4,000 are quoted on stock exchanges.

v *Subsidiary companies.* Finally, there is a residual group of subsidiary companies, wholly owned and controlled by other companies. This group cuts across the distinction between public and large private companies as just explained, in the sense that subsidiaries of both types are included, and there is also an appreciable number of subsidiaries which would otherwise fall within the first two groups. Many subsidiaries retain an independent existence, as operational or accounting divisions. Others are completely swallowed up by the parent organization. But if all types are covered the category probably accounts for about one-tenth of the total or a further 50,000 companies.

vi *Non-commercial concerns.* In addition there is an entirely separate group of companies incorporated for non-commercial reasons, for instance to hold the property of clubs and societies, or to carry on charitable activities. It is usual in such cases for the company to be formed without share capital since there is no question of dividend payments, though if limited liability is required provision must be made for a guaranteed fund in lieu of share capital. In recent years these non-commercial companies have been formed at the rate of three or four hundred a year. Though precise figures are not available, they may amount in total to some 20,000.

The general picture of the range and distribution of companies in England and Wales at the close of the 1960s in accordance with this classification is summarized in Table 2.2.

TABLE 2.2

Estimated distribution of companies in Britain, 1970

1 Participant/partnership companies:	active	200,000
	dormant	100,000
2 Extended partnership companies:	active	75,000
	dormant	25,000
3 Larger private and family companies		50,000
4 Quoted public companies		5,000
5 Subsidiaries		50,000
6 Non-commercial companies		20,000

2 THE ECONOMIC ANALYSIS OF COMMERCIAL ORGANIZATION

No description of companies in terms of internal structure and membership, or of the legal nature of the undertaking, will satisfy the economist. In the first place, the list of registered companies, less those which can be shown to be economically dormant, does not exhaust the range of economically relevant concerns. There is no obligation on businessmen to operate as limited companies, and though most large concerns are companies, many smaller ones of considerable economic importance in the aggregate if not individually are not. Secondly, the economist will wish to know a good deal more about the various concerns than can be obtained from the type of analysis undertaken above. How many firms are there in each size group? What are their profit margins? Are they growing, and if so how is the expansion financed? What is the rate of concentration towards larger units of organization? None of these questions is strictly legal. But the answers in some cases at least are relevant to the more general question of the most appropriate legal structure for commercial concerns of various types and sizes.

The analysis which follows is again based largely on the current British situation. There is some evidence, however, of similar patterns in other countries.[6] In any case what is relevant is the broad pattern and structure and development rather than precise statistical detail. Much of the analysis is therefore of general application to advanced industrial economies, though the non-British reader may wish to modify some of the general conclusions on the basis of the statistics available on his own economy.

An economic classification of concerns

The most comprehensive figures for the number and size of trading concerns in Britain are compiled by the Inland Revenue. All profit-making trading concerns are included, regardless of whether they are involved in manufacturing, distribution or service trades and regardless of their legal status as companies, partnerships or individual traders. Non-operating or dormant concerns will normally be excluded. There are some drawbacks to this form of analysis : the

[6] Sargant Florence, *The Logic of British and American Industry* (1961); Bolton Committee on Small Firms, Cmnd. 4811, Ch. 6.

TABLE 2.3

The number and relative size of commercial enterprises in the UK in terms of annual taxable income

Range of annual income		1951–2 000s No.	%	1960–1 000s No.	%	1971 000s No.	%
£0–£1,000	Individuals	1,423	87	1,326	82	1,170	75
	Partnerships	112	7	130	8	91	6
	Companies	107	6	165	10	290	19
	Total	1,642		1,622		1,551	
£1,000–£10,000	Individuals	128	50	188	52	706	71
	Partnerships	70	27	119	33	227	23
	Companies	58	23	52	14	68	7
	Total	257		359		1,001	
£10,000–£100,000	Individuals	1	5	1	3	60	53
	Partnerships	3	15	5	21	22	20
	Companies	19	81	19	76	31	27
	Total	23		25		113	
£100,000–£1m.	Partnerships	–		0·1	3	0·3	5
	Companies	3	100	3·4	97	6·1	95
	Total	3		3·5		6·4	
Over £1m.	Companies	0·3	100	0·3	100	0·7	100
All sizes	Individuals	1,551	81	1,515	75	1,882	72
	Partnerships	185	10	255	13	340	13
	Companies	185	10	240	12	396	15
	Grand total	1,922		2,010		2,618	

Source: *Inland Revenue Statistics*

part-time earnings of individuals taxed under Schedule D are included, though they might not be considered to represent independent trading concerns; and the effective trading profit of companies as opposed to partnerships and individuals is underestimated in that salaries and fees paid to directors and managers are excluded, while the remuneration of partners and individual traders is included. But the returns do give the best overall picture of the range of commercial concerns in any given period. Figures for three selected years, 1951–2, 1960–1 and 1971, are set out in Table 2.3.

The figures show clearly the overwhelming numbers of small

compared with large trading concerns. The vast majority of tax-paying trading concerns are small or very small. Some two-thirds of the total had taxable earnings of less than £1,000; fewer than one in twenty earned more than £10,000 even on the latest 1971 returns. Up to that level roughly three-quarters were individual traders, though allowance must be made for the large number of individuals who trade only on a part-time basis in addition to regular employment. Even if individuals are ignored roughly half the concerns up to the £10,000 level traded as partnerships rather than as companies. Only among concerns earning more than £10,000 were companies clearly dominant; among concerns earning more than £100,000 the corporate form was almost universal.

This picture of widespread variation among smaller concerns is borne out by the more detailed analysis carried out for the Bolton Committee on Small Firms, summarized in Table 2.4. Though more than four-fifths of manufacturing concerns with fewer than two hundred employees were limited companies, only one-third of non-manufacturing concerns below the size limits defined by the Committee were companies, and almost half were sole traders. The figures also show that the level of incorporation was much higher in construction and wholesaling than in retailing and catering. The predominance of sole traders over partnerships both in the manufacturing and non-manufacturing sectors indicated by the Inland Revenue returns is also confirmed.

Even at the top end of the scale there is a good deal of variation in the precise form of organization. It has already been seen that there are some 4,000 quoted public companies in Britain. The Inland Revenue returns in Table 2.3 show that until the mid-1960s fewer than 4,000 concerns earned more than £100,000. But it cannot be assumed that the two groups were co-extensive. All but a handful of the very largest concerns are quoted companies, but there is a good deal of overlap in the middle ranges of income. A Board of Trade survey of tax returns for 1960–1 showed that even then there were well over 2,000 unquoted companies with incomes of more than £50,000; a parallel survey of more than 2,000 of the largest quoted companies showed that eighteen per cent had average earnings in the three-year period from 1961 to 1963 of less than £100,000.[7] At a rough estimate perhaps only half of all companies

[7] *Economic Trends*, No. 136 (1965), No. 169 (1967).

TABLE 2.4

The legal status of small firms in manufacturing and non-manufacturing sectors in Britain, 1969

Type of firm	Legal status Quoted company %	Unquoted company %	Unlimited company %	Partner-ships %	Sole owner %
A Manufacturing					
1–25 employees	–	77	3	7	13
25–99 employees	1	95	1	2	1
100–199 employees	5	92	2	1	1
Total manufacturing	0	81	2	6	10
B Non-manufacturing					
Catering	–	7	–	25	69
Retail distribution	0	35	1	23	42
Road transport	1	35	–	20	45
Motor trades	–	47	0	21	32
Construction	–	72	0	9	18
Wholesale distribution	1	83	2	5	10
Total non-manufacturing	0	33	0	20	46

Source: *Bolton Committee on Small Firms*, Research Report No. 17

with earnings of more than £50,000 have a Stock Exchange quotation.

The dominance of larger firms

The predominance of small concerns in numerical terms must be set against the concentration of earning power in large companies. The Inland Revenue returns of the taxable income of all concerns within various size ranges when reduced to percentages of the total taxable income of all concerns, as shown in Table 2.5, show that the ninety-five per cent of all concerns with taxable income of less than £10,000

TABLE 2.5

The distribution of the annual taxable income of trading concerns of various sizes as a percentage of total income of all concerns

Range of incomes		1951–2 %	1960–1 %	1971 %
£0–£10,000	Individuals	22·3	20·9	18·8
	Partnerships	7·2	8·3	7·3
	Companies	6·4	4·8	2·7
£10,000–£1m.	Individuals	0·6	0·3	1·0
	Partnerships	1·8	2·6	5·0
	Companies	39·9	35·6	25·9
Over £1m.	Individuals	—	—	—
	Partnerships	—	—	—
	Companies	21·6	27·3	39·1
All sizes	Individuals	22·9	21·2	19·8
	Partnerships	9·0	10·9	12·3
	Companies	67·9	67·7	67·7

Source: *Inland Revenue Statistics*

produced less than one-third of the total income in each of the three selected years; conversely in 1971 the 700 companies earning more than £1m produced almost four-tenths of the total. It is easy to deduce from figures like these that the economy as a whole is dominated by a relatively small number of very large firms.

This pattern is not limited to the analysis of income. The returns for the number of persons employed in *manufacturing* concerns from the periodic Census of Production, summarized in Table 2.6, reveal a similar pattern. Though the returns for concerns with fewer than ten employees are highly unreliable and have thus been excluded from the percentage calculations, the figures show that while three-quarters of the concerns employed between ten and one hundred persons, more than three-quarters of the total work force were employed by concerns with more than one hundred employees. Similarly it has been estimated by the Board of Trade that during the 1960s eighty-two per cent of the totals for income, for assets and for exports of an estimated 250,000 industrial and commercial concerns were attributable to the 5,000 largest firms. A more recent

TABLE 2.6

The size of manufacturing concerns in Britain in terms of the number of persons employed

		1935		1961		1973	
		No.	%	No.	%	No.	%
Under 10	Concerns	132,338		140,000		50,000	
	Employees	536		560		250	
10–100	Concerns	37,614	77	40,049	73	45,888	77
	Employees (000s)	1,318	26	1,642	20	1,487	20
100–1,000	Concerns	10,797	22	13,906	25	12,740	21
	Employees (000s)	2,733	53	3,715	45	3,487	47
Over 1000	Concerns	533	1	1,206	2	1,131	2
	Employees (000s)	1,106	21	2,821	34	2,402	33
Total concerns with 10 or more employees		48,944	100	55,161	100	59,741	100
Total employees (000s)		5,158	100	8,178	100	7,376	100

Source: *Census of Production*; figures for concerns with fewer than ten employees are official estimates and those for 1961 are probably incorrect

analysis of the importance of the 'top hundred' manufacturing companies reached the following conclusion:

The broad picture emerging from the ranking by UK sales is that in the early 1970s the top one hundred manufacturing companies in the private sector accounted for about two-fifths of manufacturing industry's net assets, employment and inward direct investment from overseas; they exported between two-fifths and one half of merchandise exports, carried out seventy per cent of industrial expenditure on research and development, and accounted for about three-quarters of direct investment in manufacturing industry by UK companies (excluding oil).[8]

Ever increasing concentration?

Figures of this kind are frequently produced to demonstrate the extent of capitalist concentration in developed industrial economies

[8] *Economic Trends*, No. 274 (1976).

like those of Britain and America. It is important to distinguish their factual content from their latent implications. Any of the figures may be statistically and psychologically reversed to give an entirely different flavour. They show, for example, that even in 1971 one-third of the total taxable income was produced by concerns with earnings of less than £10,000, or that in 1973 almost one-quarter of the manufacturing work force was employed in firms with fewer than one hundred employees. There is none the less a widespread belief that the days of the small firm and of the small shop are limited. The argument may be put in two ways. It may be claimed that only those firms which are geared to modern technology and mass production methods can survive and prosper, given the organizational and economic economies of scale. Alternatively it may be argued that the financial and economic power of the largest companies permits them to absorb or eliminate their smaller competitors regardless of their relative efficiency. In either case it follows that the number of economically significant firms is bound to decrease at an ever increasing rate, whether by direct competition or through take-overs and mergers.

This general theme is a significant element in the Marxist analysis of capitalism. It has also been taken up by some explicitly non-Marxist writers. In their classic analysis of corporate development in the United States in the 1930s Berle and Means calculated that the two hundred largest non-banking corporations controlled almost exactly half the assets of non-banking wealth.[9] In addition they estimated that if the trend continued at the then current rate it would take only thirty or forty years for *all* corporate activity and practically all industrial activity to be absorbed by two hundred giant corporations.[10] Forty years have now passed and it is clear that these alarming conclusions have not been borne out in practice. But there has undoubtedly been a continuing trend towards greater concentration, as Berle and Means themselves have shown : their latest analysis shows that the proportion of net assets of all manufacturing corporations held by the hundred largest manufacturing corporations rose from forty-four per cent in 1933 to fifty-eight per cent in 1962.[11]

Similar trends can be established in Britain. The figures on the

[9] A. Berle and G. Means, *The Modern Corporation and Private Property* (1932); revised edn. (1968), p. 33.

[10] Ibid., p. 41.

[11] Ibid., pp. 343 ff.

numbers employed in manufacturing industries for 1935 and 1973, set out in Table 2.6, show that the proportion employed in the largest firms with over a hundred employees rose from sixty-eight per cent in 1935 to seventy-seven per cent in 1973, and that the proportion of such firms itself doubled from six per cent to thirteen per cent. Similarly the Inland Revenue returns for the shorter period between 1951 and 1971, as set out in Table 2.5 (see p. 51), show that the proportion of the total assessable income from all concerns attributable to the largest companies earning more than £1m rose from twenty-two per cent in 1951–2 to thirty-nine per cent in 1971. The Bolton Committee on Small Firms confirmed this relative decline. The extent of concentration found by the Committee's research team varied considerably from sector to sector: the figures for the proportion of total employment and net output in the manufacturing sector contributed by establishments employing 200 persons or less, as set out in Table 2.7 (below), have fallen from forty-four per cent and forty-two per cent respectively in 1924 to twenty-nine

TABLE 2.7

Figures for the numbers, employment and output of small establishments, employing 200 or fewer persons, as a proportion of the total manufacturing sector, UK 1924–68

Year	No. of establishments		% of total employment in small establishments	% of net output (1963 prices) in small establishments
	Small (000s)	Larger (000s)		
1924	160,000	3,000	44	42
1930	164,000	4,000	43	40
1935	144,000	4,000	44	41
1948	103,000	5,000	37	37
1951	96,000	6,000	35	32
1954	91,000	6,000	33	29
1958	85,000	8,000	32	28
1963	82,000	8,000	31	27
1968	n.a.	n.a.	29*	25*

Source: *Bolton Committee on Small Firms, Tables* 5.I, 5.II *and* 5.III; figures are for establishments rather than enterprises; *those for 1968 are provisional estimates

TABLE 2.8

Take-over and merger activity by large companies in Britain, 1964–75

Year	Companies acquired Quoted	Unquoted	Total consideration Quoted	Unquoted	Type of consideration Cash %	Ordinary shares %	Loan capital %
1964	71	868	£262m.	£240m.	60	33	7
1965	75	920	£347m.	£160m.	48	41	11
1966	78	727	£330m.	£117m.	41	45	14
1967	84	577	£630m.	£151m.	33	43	24
1968	140	458	£1,515m.	£137m.	16	70	14
1969	846		£1,069m.		28	52	20
1970	793		£1,123m.		22	53	25
1971	884		£911m.		31	48	21
1972	1,210		£2,532m.		20	58	23
1973	1,205		£1,304m.		53	36	11
1974	504		£508m.		68	22	9
1975	315		£291m.		59	32	9

Source: *Monopolies Commission: Survey of Mergers and Take-overs* (1964–68); *Board of Trade Journal* (1969–75)

per cent and twenty-five per cent in 1968. A substantial decline in the number and importance of small firms was also found in the retail, distributive and construction trades; only in road haulage and to a lesser extent in motor distributive trades did the small firm, as defined by the Committee, appear to have held its own.[12]

Equally striking evidence of concentration among the larger firms themselves as well as of the elimination of their smaller competitors is provided by a Monopolies Commission survey of take-over and merger activity between 1964 and 1968. The total number of firms absorbed, as shown in Table 2.8, amounted to more than 3,500 non-quoted and almost 450 quoted companies, and the number of companies covered in the survey was reduced as a result by almost one-third, from 1,312 to 908. Subsequent figures show that the level of take-over and merger activity, as revealed by reports in the financial press, reached a peak in the boom of 1972 and 1973, though since then it has decreased considerably. It is also noticeable that the

[12] Cmnd. 4811 (1971), Ch. 5.

vast majority of these take-overs and mergers, especially in boom periods, have been carried out by the issue of shares rather than cash payment to the shareholders of the company acquired. The implications of this trend and its relationship to the City Code on Take-overs and Mergers will be discussed in greater detail in Chapter 8.

These findings on the extent of commercial and industrial concentration in terms of assets, earnings, employment and output have prompted far-reaching conclusions on the inevitable accumulation of economic power in the hands of the directors of a diminishing number of national and multi-national corporations within advanced industrial economies.[13] The trend has apparently gone further in Britain than elsewhere,[14] and has been assisted by governmental policies on rationalization and nationalization, as discussed below. But it is now generally accepted that quite apart from the effects of legislative intervention to encourage or discourage concentration there are some natural limits to the process. In particular the continual development and decline of individual firms in response to market opportunities and technical discoveries helps to counteract the prevailing trend. This factor is sometimes ignored in the picture presented by the more alarmist commentators, as too is the distorting effect of inflation on some forms of analysis. It is significant, for instance, that the proportion of total taxable income earned by the corporate sector in Britain remained virtually static at sixty-seven per cent in the two decades from 1952 to 1971, as shown in Table 2.5 (see p. 51), though allowance must be made for the differences in taxation rules already referred to. There is also some evidence that new developments in technology in the service as opposed to the manufacturing sector favour the development of smaller units of operation. The latest American and Canadian statistics have revealed a levelling off in the past decade in the decline of small firms, and in some cases a slight upturn in the proportion of the total work force employed in them.[15] Though there is clear evidence of a shift in the balance of power from predominance by small firms to predominance by large firms in particular sectors, there is none to suggest any serious decline in the number of small firms which fulfil what the Bolton Committee called the 'seed-bed' function, or of any decline

[13] J. K. Galbraith, *The New Industrial State* (1969).
[14] Bolton Committee on Small Firms, Cmnd. 4811 (1971), Ch. 6.
[15] Ibid., Table 6.III.

in the total number of new business enterprises. There is accordingly no reason to predict the disappearance of small and medium sized concerns.

The role of the smaller firm

Though the threat of extinction for the smaller firm may thus be safely discounted, it has focused attention on the important part played by smaller firms within the economy, a part which has all too frequently been ignored both by economists and by government.[16] Emphasis is laid on different aspects of their role in different industries: the flexibility in management which independence from the bureaucratic tendencies of large organization allows; the greater possibilities for experimentation in new methods of production or other technological innovations; the provision of specialized products or services which cannot readily be integrated in a mass production organization; the freedom to concentrate on individual requirements.

These advantages must of course be set off against those which follow from increased size and concentration: the economies of mass production, or of vertical or horizontal integration; greater resources for research and development; greater control over the market and the consequent freedom to influence if not to dictate the patterns of demand in such a way as to ease the problems of meeting that demand. It is of course just such economies of scale that have shifted the balance of advantage in favour of the larger firm. It follows that in many cases the products and services of the smaller firm will be more costly than those of its largest rivals. But cost and economic utility are not at all the same thing, either in theoretical or practical terms. Economic utility lies in the provision of goods and services to meet a genuine demand, and there are many goods and services to which the economies of scale are not applicable. To take a simple example, the fact that goods can be sold at a lower cost in a large supermarket with a high turnover does not make all corner shops economically redundant. Corner shops supply the same goods at slightly higher prices but more conveniently and often more quickly and so provide a different service from that offered by the supermarket. It is not through economic inefficiency or inertia that Berle and Means' predictions have not been fully borne out. As long as

[16] These issues are discussed at length by the Bolton Committee on Small Firms: see especially Chapters 3 and 7.

there is a demand for specialized or individualized services, in whatever sphere, there will be a function for the small firm to perform, and perform more effectively than its larger competitors.

The difficulty as far as the small firm is concerned, as the Bolton Committee argued, is that the natural tendency of governmental agencies to think primarily of the larger firms in developing their economic policies has often resulted in the adoption of measures which have tilted the balance of advantage in favour of the larger firm. It is arguable that the current British system of company taxation, the latest disclosure provisions in the Companies Act 1967 and even the methods adopted by government for the collection of economic statistics, have made the life of small firms relatively harder than their larger competitors. These particular issues will be dealt with in greater detail in Chapters 4 and 5 in so far as they affect company law. The important general point which emerges from the economic analysis of large and small firms is that the problems which face them are sufficiently different to raise the question whether a single range of legal and administrative controls under the Companies Acts and other statutes can adequately reflect the wide variation in size and structure of the firms subjected to them. The idea that the absence of legislative interference provides an economically neutral climate in which the relative efficiency and profitability of large and small firms can be ascertained by market processes is highly questionable. The apparent absence of such interference merely indicates that the balance which has been built up piecemeal in the past has come to be accepted as 'normal'.

3 PATTERNS OF COMPANY FINANCE

The principal contribution of the law to the modern system of commercial organization in economic terms has been the provision of a formal mechanism for the financing of enterprises. The machinery of joint stock trading is open to all. But it is put to different uses by companies of different sizes and types. The smallest companies will normally be financed initially by the personal capital of those who run the business, supplemented by short-term bank loans under personal guarantee, or by debentures secured on the company's assets. As the company expands into a medium sized private family company more and more reliance will be placed on these external loans and debentures in place of increases in subscribed share capital. It is only the largest companies which have effective access to the excess capital of ordinary investors through the public stock market.

This account of company financing, based on the classification of companies introduced above, is less than adequate for economic purposes, in that it ignores the crucial question of self-financing. The principal source of funds for expansion in almost every enterprise, whatever its size and nature, is its profit on past or current trading. This profit may be immediately reinvested in new stock or plant, or accumulated over a period of years by making transfers to the company's liquid reserves and then used to acquire new subsidiaries. In either case the theoretical source of the funds is the shareholders who would have been entitled to the profit had it been distributed. In addition the impact of ordinary trade credit must be taken into account. Clearly to the extent that increases in the level of production can be financed by obtaining the necessary supplies on extended or short term credit, or by obtaining new plant on hire purchase terms, there will be all the less need for direct loans or capital issues. The realities of company finance can only be understood when all these different sources of funds are considered together.

The flow of funds

The most revealing way to achieve an overall view of this kind is to tabulate for a given period both the sources of company finance and the uses to which the money or credit was put. The figures set out in Tables 2.9 and 2.10 show the results of this type of analysis as applied to the accounts of companies of varying sizes and types: the details of the various groups are as follows:

i *Large quoted companies:* for 1950–2 and 1960–2 the figures are for some 2,000 companies quoted on stock exchanges with annual profits of more than £50,000 or assets of more than £250,000; for 1970–2 they are for some 1,200 such companies with gross incomes of more than £200,000 or net assets of £2m or more in 1968;

ii *Medium sized unquoted companies:* figures for a sample of 331 (then) exempt private companies with an annual profit in 1956 of between £20,000 and £50,000;

iii *Small private companies:* figures for a sample of 334 (then)

TABLE 2.9

The financing of quoted companies: sources and uses of funds

	1950–2 £m	1950–2 %	1960–2 £m	1960–2 %	1970–2 £m	1970–2 %
Sources of funds						
A Internal						
Trading profit	£1,357	75	£2,369	69	£4,760	65
Other revenue	£52	3	£125	4	£260	3
B External						
Ordinary and preference shares (cash) }					£112	2
Ordinary and preference shares (exchanged for subsidiaries) }	£88	5	£416	11	£562	8
Loan capital (cash) }					£294	4
Loan capital (exchanged for subsidiaries) }	£67	4	£144	4	£222	3
New bank loans and trade credit	£253	14	£403	12	£1,092	15
Total funds	£1,817	100	£3,457	100	£7,302	100
Uses of funds						
Taxation	£677	36	£882	24	£1,027	15
Loan interest	£22	1	£78	2	£352	5
Investment (fixed assets)	£426	23	£1,277	35	£2,079	30
(including allowance for depreciation)	**(£189)**		**(£572)**		**(£1,297)**	
Investment (subsidiaries)	£34	2	£336	9	£1,115	16
Other investment					£203	3
Increase in stock and current debtors	£525	28	£605	17	£1,218	17
Dividends	£170	9	£462	13	£918	14
Donations	£12	1	£19	1	£6	—
Total uses	£1,866	100	£3,659	100	£6,918	100

Source: *Annual Abstract of Statistics*; each column is an average of a three-year period; the figures for 1950–2 and 1960–2 are for a sample of more than 2,000 quoted companies, those for 1970–2 for a sample of some 1,200 quoted companies.

TABLE 2.10

The financing of unquoted companies: sources and uses of funds in medium sized and small companies in 1961–2

	Medium sized companies (£000s)	%	Small companies (£000s)	%
Sources of funds				
A Internal				
Trading profit	£11,255	82	£3,432	70
Other revenue	£523	4	£155	3
B External				
Ordinary shares issued	£223	2	£83	2
Preference shares issues	£88	1	£17	—
New long-term loans	£220	2	£80	2
New bank loans trade credit	£1,350	10	£1,107	23
Total sources	£13,659	100	£4,874	100
Uses of funds				
Taxation	£4,832	37	£1,328	25
Loan interest	£97	1	£38	1
Investment (fixed assets)	£4,754	37	£1,854	37
(**including allowance for depreciation**)	(**£2,368**)		(**£859**)	
Investment (subsidiaries)	£450	3	£221	4
Other investment	£85	1	£37	1
Increase in stock/debtors	£1,237	9	£1,210	24
Dividends	£1,549	12	£372	7
Total uses	£13,004	100	£5,060	100

Source: *Economic Trends Nos. 169 & 136*; details of the samples of companies covered are given in the text.

exempt private companies with an annual profit in 1956 of between £4,000 and £20,000.

It should be noted that these groups are defined solely in terms of the profitability or value of the company in a single year, rather than its underlying size in terms of capital employed or the number of employees. Nor is there any necessary correlation between these groups and the classification proposed earlier in the chapter. The resulting table does, however, provide a simple comparative picture of the flow of funds in various sizes of concern.

It is clear from these figures that the principal source of finance in firms of all sizes is internal. Most new expenditure is financed out of profits retained and ploughed back into the business. If depreciation is ignored, the proportion of all new funds provided in this way was consistently more than two-thirds in larger quoted companies, and a good deal more in medium sized (eighty-two per cent) and smaller private companies (seventy per cent). Though there are important differences of degree, companies of all sizes are self-financing to a considerable extent.

The difference between the various groups is more marked in respect of other sources. Large quoted companies do rely on the public market to supply some of their requirements through new issues of share or loan capital. In recent years this has amounted in the aggregate to some ten to twenty per cent of their total funds, though the picture is complicated by the fact that many of the shares are issued for the purpose of a take-over without any cash payment. It must be remembered that in any one year only a small proportion of firms will make a new issue so that for those that do the proportion provided in this way is very much larger. The figures also indicate that substantial sums are now raised through longer term loans or debentures whether publicly quoted or not.

Smaller unquoted companies are not in a position to rely on the open market, unless they have the prospective net market value of £500,000 required for a Stock Exchange quotation. The figures indicate that medium sized and small companies raised a good deal less proportionally through the issue of ordinary or preference shares (two or three per cent) than their larger competitors (ten to twenty per cent). The principal external source of funds for these companies was through short-term loans from banks or other financial institutions or through increases in trade credit. It is also worth noting that on these figures the medium sized companies tended to rely more on internal sources than small companies. It may be that banks and other financial houses are less ready or able to provide sums of the size required by the larger unquoted companies, so that they are thrown back on their own internal funds to an even greater extent than both their larger and smaller rivals.

Whatever the ultimate explanation, these figures provide hard evidence of the continuing existence of what is termed the 'Macmillan gap', following the report of the Macmillan Committee on Finance and Industry[17] in 1931. The Committee pointed out the difficulty experienced by medium sized and smaller firms in obtaining that portion of the funds necessary for expansion which in the case of quoted public companies would be sought from a public issue. Various expedients have been tried in an attempt to redress this imbalance in the availability of capital. In 1945 the government sponsored the formation of the Industrial and Commercial Finance Corporation. This is an independent company whose main function is to raise capital from its major shareholders, the clearing banks, and since 1959 from public issues, with a view to making funds available to those companies which for one reason or another are not able to make a public issue themselves. Since that date the Corporation has been lending more than £30m. per year to small and medium sized companies. Though studies in the late 1950s indicated that it was failing to concentrate its lending in the ranges from £10,000 to £20,000 and from £150,000 to £300,000 which were critical to the growth of small and medium sized firms, figures for 1969 showed that more than forty per cent of its loans were less than £20,000.[18] The Radcliffe Committee on the Working of the Monetary System in 1959[19] drew attention to the additional problem that small companies may not always be able to persuade such institutions that the risk of investment is a good one and that such institutions may not in any case be psychologically accessible to smaller companies. There is no evidence that this problem has yet been satisfactorily solved.[20]

The uses of capital

The second part of Tables 2.9 and 2.10 showing the use to which the available funds were put, reveals some equally significant trends. In all companies the first call on profit is taxation, which in the mid-1960s accounted for between one-third and one-quarter of total funds in all sizes of company. But the figures from quoted companies show a clear downward trend from the 1950s to the 1970s, by which

[17] Cmd. 3897.

[18] J. Bates, *The Financing of Small Business* (2nd edn., 1971).

[19] Cmnd. 827.

[20] Bolton Committee on Small Firms, Cmnd. 4811 (1971), Ch. XII.

time the proportion of company profits taken in direct taxation had fallen to less than one-sixth. These figures are not an accurate representation of the total contribution of the corporate sector to public funds, since they ignore the increasing sums levied in payroll taxes of one form or another. But they help to counteract the impression given in some quarters of an increasing rather than diminishing reliance by government on the corporate sector.

A second figure of contemporary relevance is the proportion of available funds ploughed back into company operations by way of investment in fixed assets, that is in plant and machinery. Standard company accounts allow a specific amount for the replacement of wasting assets by way of depreciation. Though in a period of inflation it is difficult to place much reliance on such provisions as an indication of the real cost of maintaining the company's business, the true amount of new investment is expenditure in excess of simple replacement. The figures on this show that for all sizes of company in the years covered the amount ploughed back represented roughly one-third of total funds and roughly double the amount provided by way of depreciation. They also show an increasing trend among larger public companies to invest their surplus funds in the acquisition of subsidiaries : the proportion of resources used in this way increased from two per cent in the early 1950s to sixteen per cent in the early 1970s, though allowance must again be made for the increased use of capital exchange rather than cash for this purpose which has already been illustrated in Table 2.8 (see p. 55). Whether the figures for real investment have been adequate in economic and competitive terms in relation to that in other capitalist and socialist economies cannot be assessed in this context, but the trend does perhaps indicate a greater focus among leading British companies on increasing their size and market share than on productive capacity and efficiency, a theme which will be taken up again in the next section.

A final figure of relevance to any discussion of the operation of the capitalist system is the level of dividend distribution. The amount actually paid to shareholders in this way is one measure of the actual benefit to shareholders from their investment. The figures for quoted companies in Table 2.9 show that in recent years there has been a small increase in the proportion of funds distributed as dividends. If a measure more closely approximating to the Marxist concept of surplus value extracted from the corporate sector is sought, however, account must also be taken of loan interest and of the money recirculated into the system by reinvestment in new share or loan capital. On this basis the proportion of funds extracted amounted in 1970–2 to some nineteen per cent as against some six per cent reinvested in real terms, making a net extraction rate of some thirteen per cent. The difficulty with any calculation of this kind is that shareholders can also be said to benefit in terms of capital appreciation of their shares from any funds reinvested by the company itself, particularly since many wealthier shareholders may prefer a capital gain to current income for tax purposes. A further difficulty is that employees also benefit from reinvestment in the longer term. This kind of dispute is perhaps best taken as an indication of the inadequacy of the conception of surplus value for all but simple propaganda purposes. A more relevant issue is the extent to which employees participate in decision-making on investment and on the allocation of any eventual benefit, as discussed in Part III.

The balance sheet and capital structure

The drawback with any form of flow analysis is its limited time span. The figures apply only to the period covered and can give no indication of the underlying financial position. For that purpose we require an account of the origin and use of all the funds or capital employed by the company and of the current balance between its assets and liabilities. This is obviously the function of the company balance sheet. But the traditional way of presenting the balance sheet, with the company's assets on one side balanced by capital and reserves on the other, is not readily intelligible to the uninitiated. The figures in Table 2.11 have therefore been presented in a somewhat different form, now increasingly adopted to explain a company's finances to ordinary shareholders: at the top of a single column the book value of the company's property, less accumulated depreciation, is set down and to this is added, or subtracted, the balance of sums currently owed by and owing to the company; the resulting figure for the net book value of the company's business is then stated to be represented by the share and loan capital of the company plus any reserves of accumulated and undistributed profits. By this means the relationship between the value of the company's business and its capital structure is clearly shown.

Several aspects of this analysis merit some comment. First it is clear from the figures in the table that in every size of company the

TABLE 2.11 *The assets and capital structure of large quoted, medium sized and small companies in Britain*

	Quoted companies (£ms)						Medium-sized companies (£000s)		Small companies (£000s)	
	1950–2		1960–2		1970–2		1961–2		1961–2	
Fixed assets, goodwill and investments	3,560		9,047		16,911		27,804		11,426	
Less accumulated depreciation	1,400		3,860		9,076		17,341		5,927	
	2,160		5,187		7,835		10,463		5,499	
Current assets	5,835		10,122		22,225		64,171		24,145	
Less current liabilities	2,660		4,975		14,253		33,419		15,841	
	3,175		5,147		7,972		30,752		8,304	
Total assets (book value)	5,335		10,337		15,807		41,215		13,803	
Represented by										
Ordinary shares	1,615	30%	5,369	42%	6,478	41%	14,926	36%	4,629	34%
Preference shares	860	16%	985	10%	513	3%	3,160	8%	933	7%
Total shareholders' contribution	2,475	46%	5,354	52%	6,991	44%	18,086	44%	5,662	41%
Minority interests	240	5%	434	4%	977	6%	96	—	2	—
Long-term loans	630	12%	1,599	15%	5,310	34%	1,469	4%	871	6%
Taxation reserves	436	8%	623	6%	809	5%	3,605	9%	1,058	8%
Balancing reserves	1,554	29%	2,327	23%	1,721	11%	18,151	44%	6,314	45%
	5,335	100%	10,337	100%	15,807	100%	41,215	100%	13,803	100%

net book valuation of the business is far in excess of the amount of capital actually subscribed. This is of course simply a reflection of the profitability of the enterprises linked to the tendency which has already been noted for companies to plough back a good deal of that profit instead of paying it out to shareholders in the form of dividends. The result of this in accounting terms is that large 'reserves' must be entered in the lower section of the balance sheet, so that the total book value of the assets is exactly balanced. These 'balancing' reserves are not necessarily represented by money in the bank, since in most cases the funds they represent – the accumulated profits on each year's trading – will have been reinvested in new plant or stock. The relationship between the total figure for the shareholders' contribution and that for reserves is merely an indication of the extent to which the initial capital subscribed by the shareholders has appreciated in value. The reserves may thus be thought of as undistributed dividends belonging to the shareholders, or as the capital accumulated by the company since its formation. The figures in the table show clearly that the amount of these reserves was appreciably higher in small and medium sized companies than in larger quoted companies in which the proportion of total assets represented by balancing reserves declined sharply between the early 1950s and the early 1970s.

One explanation for this trend is the increasing importance of long-term loan capital as opposed to participating share capital in these larger quoted companies. The figures in the table show that the proportion of loan capital to net assets rose from twelve per cent in 1950–2 to thirty-four per cent in 1970–2, while that of participating capital remained roughly constant. This is the cumulative result of a tendency among larger companies in recent years to rely more on banks and other financial institutions than on new issues of shares for that part of their expenditure which cannot be generated internally. It is thus a significant measure of the declining importance of the equity share market to the largest companies in the private as well as in the public sector.

The relationship or 'gearing' between share and loan capital is also of some practical importance in relation to the valuation of company shares, both for ordinary sales and in the context of takeover bids. Loan capital is normally issued with a fixed redemption value and a fixed dividend, and is valued on the market accordingly; when interest rates rise the price of fixed interest shares declines so as to produce a roughly equivalent rate of interest for all fixed interest investment. Participating or equity share capital on the other hand is valued in relation to the general profitability and asset values of the company, since the net profits and assets of the company after the repayment of all loan and preference share capital and the interest on them legally belong to the equity shareholders. The formal value of each equity share is thus the total value of the enterprise, less any prior commitments to short-term creditors and the holders of fixed value capital, divided by the number of equity shares.

The established form of balance sheet, however, regardless of the style of presentation, is often highly misleading if it is taken at its face value as a means of putting a price on a company's shares. The major difficulty is the fact that assets are generally entered in the balance sheet at their purchase cost. The formal basis of this historic cost form of account and the problems to which it gives rise will be discussed in detail in Chapter 3 (see pp. 128–37). In the present context its significance is simply that the historic cost or book value of a company's assets, and in particular of its land and buildings, is unlikely to bear any close relationship to their real current value. It is now standard practice to make provision for the depreciation of plant and machinery on a regular basis, but there is much less agreement on how to deal with the appreciation of buildings or of current stocks. Some companies now make a periodic revaluation of such assets, balancing the increase in asset values by marking up the figure for reserves or by making a special issue of fully paid shares to all existing shareholders.[21] But there is little uniformity in practice and even if there was it is notoriously difficult to fix the true current value of a factory or office block. Similar problems have arisen in relation to stock valuation in a period of rapid inflation.

The result of these uncertainties is that when an accurate valuation of company shares is required, whether for tax purposes or in the context of a take-over bid, those involved will usually wish to go beyond the balance sheet to a more realistic current valuation. The most obvious solution to this problem is to take the market price for the company's shares as the best estimate of the net worth of the enterprise as a going concern taking into account both current asset values and future prospects. Similarly for unquoted companies the

[21] Any significant change in asset values must also be disclosed in the annual Directors' Report: Companies Act 1967 (s.16).

accepted basis for valuation for tax purposes is a notional arm's length sale between a willing buyer and a willing seller.[22] The aggregate market value of the company's share capital in theory represents the true value of the company as a whole. The nature of the stock market, however, as an independent institution raises equally serious problems over the validity of current market values of quoted shares. It is this fact that has provided the opportunity for much of the take-over and merger activity among quoted companies over the past decade.

4 THE STOCK MARKET MECHANISM

The role of the stock market as the prime mechanism for the allocation of capital within the economy, and also for the exchange and withdrawal of capital by individual investors has already been described (see Chapter 1). As a means to this end the stock market must also be regarded as a mechanism for the valuation of shares. Each individual purchase and sale is carried through on the basis of an assessment of the value of that particular share in the company's assets and in its prospects of profit. To understand how this valuation is carried out and the implications of the process the workings of the stock market must now be considered in rather more detail.[23]

Values on the stock exchange as in any other market are principally regulated by the pressures of supply and demand. When the number of sellers of a particular stock or share greatly exceeds the number of buyers the price is reduced until some measure of equilibrium is reached. When buyers predominate the price rises. The way in which this system is given practical effect is as follows. A number of shares in each quoted company are held by 'jobbers' ('specialists' on the American markets) who deal in those shares. Any dealer or broker who wishes to buy or sell shares in that company for himself or on behalf of a client then approaches the jobber who quotes him a price for the transaction. The jobber, like any other trader, fixes his selling price slightly higher than his buying price and takes the difference as his personal profit. In normal conditions the jobber will fix his prices at what he considers to be the accepted level, or in the case of new issues somewhere near the amount which investors have been asked by the company to pay for the shares. But

[22] *I.R.C. v. Crossman* [1937] A.C. 26.

[23] See generally W. Baumol, *The Stock Market and Economic Efficiency* (1965).

if he finds that his holding of a particular share is being depleted by heavy buying, he will increase his price, and conversely reduce it in the event of heavy selling. He will also increase or reduce his prices in advance when he hears of any news or company statement which he knows will affect the profitability or prospects of the company concerned. His object is always to ensure that the numbers of shares bought and sold are roughly the same, so that he can maintain his holding at roughly the same level.

The function of the jobber is thus to maintain the equilibrium of the market. But in doing so he will also wish to secure for himself a reasonable personal profit. It should be clear from the account above that when the price is rising the jobber will tend to do well, since he is continually selling shares at a higher price than he anticipated, but that when the price is falling he risks having to sell them at less than he paid for them. To cover this possibility he will usually increase the margin between his buying and selling price in any shares in which there is a risk of a sudden fall. This is why the margin between buying and selling prices, as quoted on official stock exchange lists, is much greater proportionately to the price of the share in the case of small and risky enterprises than of established companies in which there is fairly consistent trading and little prospect of dramatic price fluctuations.

The jobber is also expected to help cushion the effects of overreaction on the part of investors to current information or rumour about the particular company or the state of the economy as a whole. By adjusting his prices in such a way as to discourage too much 'bull' buying or 'bear' selling he is not simply predicting or reflecting market sentiment but also helping to create that sentiment by the nature and size of the price movements which he initiates. In this he is assisted by the market authorities. The Council of the Stock Exchange and equivalent bodies elsewhere now accept the obligation of so regulating the flow of information from quoted companies as to allow the investor, assisted by comment and analysis in the financial press, to make a reasonable assessment of the prospects of the various companies in which he is interested. The grant of a quotation, i.e. permission to deal in the shares of a particular company, is closely controlled, and all quoted companies are required to comply with stringent standards as to disclosure, in addition to their obligations under the Companies Acts (see Chapter 6). The objective is to ensure that all relevant information is made available to all investors at the same time, so that no one is in a position to take improper advantage of superior knowledge. These internal controls have recently been extended to cover the conduct of take-overs and mergers in quoted and other companies (see Chapter 8).

In addition the authorities have powers to step in to prevent any form of price manipulation or fraudulent dealing. Where rumour-mongering is rife, and where the company concerned is unable to provide the necessary accurate information to clarify the situation, dealings in those shares may be suspended or the quotation revoked. Similarly if there is suspicion of concerted buying and selling with the objective of establishing a false price and profiting therefrom, the matter will be reported to the Council, and those involved in the manipulation, whether jobbers or dealers, will be subject to suspension or expulsion from the market.

The overall effect of this market regulation should be to ensure that the laws of supply and demand operate in such a way that the price of shares will at all times represent a fair valuation of the enterprise concerned. The flow of up-to-date and relevant information from the company to the market should allow investors to make rational decisions about the current performance and prospects of the company, and the oversight of the operation of the market itself should prevent any fraudulent distortion. In addition the obvious inability of the ordinary investor to peruse and digest the huge mass of information which is made available is offset by the growth of the investment analysis industry centred on the financial press, but extending to the larger institutional investors and independent investment management or advisory services. The market in this broad sense should be able to arrive at as reasonable a valuation of company shares as is possible in all the circumstances.

In practice, however, there are a number of strictly irrelevant factors which frequently distort the delicate balance of forces which the model prescribes. In the first place there is a tendency for prices of all shares to move in broad unison in accord with what is called market sentiment. In some cases these movements may reflect real economic trends which genuinely affect the prospects of all major companies. But in many instances sentiment is also affected by largely irrelevant factors such as the death of a president in the United States or what is seen as an improvement or deterioration in the international situation. This is not to say that the general question of confidence is not in itself an economic indicator of some importance, affecting in particular levels of investment and the availability of capital. But external events in themselves are unlikely to have any real impact on the performance and profitability of individual companies. In the result it is often difficult to establish any continuing close link between market prices and an objective valuation of a company's shares.

The position is further complicated by the fact that many investors are more directly concerned with buying shares at relatively low prices and selling them at higher prices than securing a continuing dividend income from the profits of the companies they invest in. Investment management is accordingly directed as much to the accurate prediction of future movements of prices as to the future performance of companies. This feature of the business of investment was commented on by Keynes :

> Professional investment may be likened to those newspaper competitions in which the competitors have to pick out the six prettiest faces from a hundred photographs, the prize being awarded to the competitor whose choice most nearly corresponds to the average preferences of the competitors as a whole; so that each competitor has to pick, not those faces which he himself finds prettiest, but those which he thinks likeliest to catch the fancy of the other competitors, all of whom are looking at the problem from the same point of view. It is not a case of choosing those which, to the best of one's judgement, are really the prettiest, nor even those which average opinion genuinely thinks the prettiest. We have reached the third degree where we devote our intelligences to anticipating what average opinion expects the average opinion to be.[24]

In simple terms the art of investment lies in predicting other investors' expectations of how companies will perform rather than how they will actually perform.

This detachment of the market pricing mechanism from the underlying value and performance of the companies concerned is borne out by statistical studies on the movement of share prices.[25] There is general agreement that the best description of the movements of individual share prices is what is termed the 'random walk path', that is, that 'the model which produces the best description of the time path of the price of any particular stock predicts that in any future period that price will be equal to the price of that same

[24] *The General Theory of Employment Interest and Money* (1936), p. 156.

[25] See generally P. Cootner (ed.), *The Random Character of Stock Market Prices* (1964).

security in the immediately preceding period plus some number randomly chosen'.[26] The implication of this model is that it is not possible or profitable to make predictions from the past price of an individual share to its future price, so that, as in the case of gaming systems, there is little point in attempting to operate any kind of mechanical investment system based on a study of prices and their movements. This does not mean of course that all investment analysis is pointless. Investigators have established some correlation between price movements and for instance dividend yield.[27] And it has been suggested that a distinction can be drawn between two classes of investors: the majority who have no time to find out the relevant facts about the companies they invest in, and thus contribute to the random walk phenomenon; and the experts who do make use of such knowledge, by buying or selling when the random walk deviates appreciably from what they consider to be the correct price, and who thus impose some control over random price movements. But the evidence on price movement as a whole does give support to the theory that the stock market as an economic institution is relatively independent of the industrial and commercial operations on which it is superimposed.

There is further evidence of this phenomenon from studies of the process of take-overs and mergers in recent years. A survey of take-over and merger activity in Britain during 1967 revealed that the final acquisition price was on average one third above the pre-bid price.[28] This in itself is some indication of the extent to which business evaluation of a company's worth differs from that of the stock market, though as we shall see below this does not mean that the take-over process can be regarded as a more objective and accurate evaluation of economic worth. An attempt in the same study to establish a relationship between the pre-bid price and various other factors such as earnings yield on the pre-bid price or the rate of return on the book value of assets, was not successful. The findings did suggest, however, that the terms of acquisition were linked not to the existing share price but to a measure of the asset value of the company and its profitability in book terms. It would appear from this that in fixing offer prices take-over and merger operators pay

[26] W. Baumol, *The Stock Market and Economic Efficiency* (1965), p. 39.

[27] A. C. Rayner and I. M. D. Little, *Higgledy Piggledy Growth Again* (1966).

[28] H. B. Rose and G. D. Newbould, *The 1967 Take Over Boom* (1967).

more attention to the company's published accounts than to the market value of the shares.

It is not surprising in the light of all this that the traditional account of the role of the stock market in resource allocation and in share valuation has frequently been questioned. Keynes, writing in 1936 of the American stock market system, concluded that 'the measure of success attained by Wall Street, regarded as an institution of which the proper social purpose is to direct new investment into the most profitable channels in terms of future yield, cannot be regarded as one of the outstanding triumphs of laissez-faire capitalism.'[29] More recently the British Monopolies Commission, in the course of a general assessment of the economics of take-overs and mergers, has concluded that 'the stock market's reaction cannot ... be relied on to reflect the efficiency aspects of a take-over':

> The connection between the shareholders' assessment of a take-over offer, and their assessment of the effects of the take-over on efficiency is not as direct or straightforward as the [traditional] argument suggests, and may indeed be tenuous, remote or even non-existent according to the particular circumstances.[30]

On the other hand, it cannot be denied that the system does play an important part both in the raising of new capital and in the evaluation of the performance and prospects of existing companies. A more balanced assessment is that of Baumol in his general account of the economics of the stock market in America:

> At best the allocative function is performed rather imperfectly as measured by the criteria of the welfare economist. The oligopolistic position of those who operate the market ... the random patterns which characterize the behaviour of stock prices, the apparent unresponsiveness of supply to price changes, and management efforts to avoid the market as a source of funds all raise some questions about the perfection of the regulatory operations of the market ... [One] can only marvel at the quality of its performance.[31]

In Britain such a relatively favourable assessment would find rather less support. The figures in Tables 2.9, 2.10 and 2.11 show that the Stock Exchange itself does not generate very much new capital.

[29] *General Theory of Employment, Interest and Money*, p. 159.

[30] The Monopolies Commission, *Report on the Rank Organisation Ltd and the De La Rue Co. Ltd.* (1969), para. 82.

[31] *The Stock Market and Economic Efficiency* (1965), p. 82.

The merchant bankers and investment institutions of the City now provide most of the funds required even by the largest companies outside the framework of the stock market. In terms of economic efficiency the Stock Exchange and the City alike have been widely criticized in recent years for channelling so much of the available capital resources into speculative office-building and commercial redevelopment projects rather than into 'more productive' investment in industry. In one sense this criticism is misguided since property development of this kind undoubtedly produced very satisfactory profits both for management and for shareholders, except in the case of a few fringe banks and property companies which over-committed themselves. It is thus arguable that the market for capital which the City provides performed reasonably well by its own criterion of profit maximization, and that if investment in manufacturing industry was lower in Britain than in other developed economies that was the fault of management in industry. On a broader level it is harder to show that the City allocated the capital which it controlled in such a way as to maximize the long-term prosperity of the British economy, as the theory of free market capitalism claims it should. It is safer to conclude that the stock market is not primarily an allocative mechanism, but a partially independent and self-sustaining system of capital exchange using the private sector of the economy as its essential base but often functioning without direct reference to that base.

5 PATTERNS OF OWNERSHIP AND CONTROL

The picture of the stock market as a self-sustaining mechanism insulated to a surprising extent from a business evaluation of the companies in whose shares it deals is mirrored by that of the companies dealt in as independent entities free from any real control on the part of shareholders and investors. In theory the company is owned and controlled by its shareholders, and directors and managers should conduct its affairs in the sole interest of those shareholders. The profit motive should prevail, in the sense that decisions on the future of the company should ultimately be determined by the search for the best possible long-term return on capital, even if that means the liquidation of a particular company and the reinvestment of the capital it employs elsewhere. The reality of course is very different. Management has an obvious vested interest in the survival of the enterprise as a source of personal livelihood and may often regard the interests of shareholders as subordinate to those of the company itself as a continuing enterprise with duties to its customers, its suppliers, its employees and even to the public at large. Management is also in a position to see that this view of the company prevails. The way in which this situation has come about may be seen from a study of the patterns of shareholding and the resulting nature of control in large public companies.

The most striking modern development in this context is the dispersal of shareholding. In their pioneering study Berle and Means found that the largest single share holding in the largest American companies was rarely more than one or two per cent of the total, and that roughly half of the largest companies studied had more than 20,000 stockholders.[32] Their figures also indicated that as the size of the company increased the tendency to dispersal increased, and the proportion of shares held by the management decreased. Furthermore, it seemed clear that this dispersal of ownership was a continuing process. Berle and Means concluded that 'parallel with the growth in the size of the industrial unit had come a dispersion in its ownership such that an important part of the wealth of individuals consists of interests in great enterprises in which no one individual owns a major part.'[33]

A similar dispersal was revealed by Sargant Florence in his comprehensive survey of share ownership in public companies in Britain.[34] The rough average number of shareholders in very large British companies was around 12,000 both in 1936 and in 1951. The degree of concentration among the largest individual shareholdings, however, decreased appreciably in the intervening period: over half the companies studied in this context had over thirty per cent of their shares in the hands of the twenty largest individual shareholders in 1936 compared with less than four in ten in 1951. But Sargant Florence also showed that though in almost every case the largest single holdings of voting shares were relatively small, there was an extreme degree of inequality in the distribution of holdings. The size of shareholdings tapered off very quickly so that though the largest twenty holdings represented only one-sixth of one

[32] A. Berle and G. C. Means, *The Modern Corporation and Private Property* (1932), Ch. IV.

[33] Ibid., revised edn. (1968), p. 64.

[34] *Ownership, Control and Success in Large Companies*, 1961.

per cent of all the holdings, they controlled about thirty per cent of the total votes.

One possible interpretation of these developments in patterns of shareholding is that most large companies are still under the potential control of a relatively small group of major shareholders. In fact Sargant Florence's choice of the twenty largest shareholdings as the basis for his analysis was linked with the idea that twenty was about the largest number of people who could be expected to get together to concert their policy over the company's affairs. In this sense it may be argued that the dispersal of shareholding has not altered the effective domination of a relatively small number of wealthy capitalists over major industrial and commercial companies.

A similar claim has been made by those who see the recent resurgence of take-overs among quoted companies as evidence that shareholders are not as subservient in relation to management as is often supposed. A number of financiers in Britain have made a practice of accumulating a substantial proportion of a company's shares, whether by open purchases on the market or more secretly through the 'warehousing' of shares under nominees, and then moving in with a controlling holding to dismiss the current management team. Such techniques have been used both in building up the industrial base of large conglomerate holding companies and also in 'asset stripping' operations. In the former case the companies acquired continue to trade within the conglomerate group; in the latter their assets are sold off by their new controllers and the proceeds distributed among the new shareholders. Pahl and Winkler, for instance, have made these practices the basis of a claim that 'shareholders are no longer weak relative to managers'; 'some capitalists recognised that shareholders were ill-organised and set about organising them, buying up scattered holdings and agglomerating them until they were able to force or agree a take-over'.[35]

Neither of these views provides an adequate account of the significance of the dispersal of shareholdings in large quoted companies.[36] There is little evidence on a general level that shareholders

[35] R. Pahl and J. Winkler, 'The Economic Elite: Theory and Practice,' in P. Stanworth and A. Giddens (eds.), *Elites and Power in British Society* (1974), p. 116.

[36] See generally C. S. Beed, 'The Separation of Ownership from Control', (1966), *Journal of Economic Studies* 29, reprinted in M. Gilbert (ed.), *The Modern Business Enterprise* (1972).

in such companies seek to exercise any real control over the directors of their companies. It is part of the basic structure of the capitalist system and of company law that directors and managers shall have exclusive control over the management of a company's affairs, both on a day-to-day basis and in terms of general policy. The only formal power of the general meeting of shareholders relates to the appointment of directors. But in practical terms the existing board of directors is in control of proceedings at annual general meetings and is almost always able to secure a majority of votes through their control over the proxy system, as described in Chapter 6. In addition, by arranging for out-going directors to retire in mid-year and for their successors to be co-opted immediately, the board is able to avoid presenting any effective choice to shareholders other than the confirmation of the existing board. In any case the mass of small shareholders are not expected to attend and could not be accommodated if they did. A few major shareholders may occasionally be consulted or exercise some influence behind the scenes, but this becomes less and less likely as the size of the company increases.

Even in the special circumstances of take-overs and mergers the formal power of shareholders is rarely exercised. Warehousing and asset stripping are best regarded as sharp practice on the fringes of the market than as evidence of a significant resurgence of shareholder power. In most cases management on either side is in effective control of the take-over or merger negotiations and of the decision whether or not to contest the bid. A study of the take-over and merger boom in Britain in 1967–8 revealed that in ninety-five per cent of cases there was no public opposition to the take-over from the directors of the 'victim' company.[37] The figures in Table 2.8 (p. 55) also indicate that the large majority of acquisitions were of unquoted companies by quoted companies. Even where the mechanism of the stock market is used to carry through a take-over, by the issue of new shares in the bidding company for those of the bid-for company, the operation is typically organized and controlled by management and its advisers. It is only in the rare case of rival bids for the same company or open warfare between two factions within a quoted company that the mass of shareholders, both large and small, are of potential importance. Even then they will rarely be in a position to make a thorough assessment of the issues or

[37] G. D. Newbould, *Management and Merger Activity* (1970).

personalities before them. The mass of the votes may be expected to divide on a fairly random basis unless one or other of the two sides has taken the trouble to foster relations with their shareholders or is able to mount a clearly superior publicity campaign.

It is important not to exaggerate the extent of this trend towards managerial independence. It is only in the largest quoted companies that the separation of ownership and control has its full effect. Both in private family companies and in smaller quoted companies a large proportion of the share capital is typically held by those who are in effective control of the company's affairs. The survey of small firms carried out for the Bolton Committee found that over eighty-five per cent of the firms in the sample covered were controlled by one or two persons, and that 'virtually all were managed by people with a stake in the firm and the majority ... by those having a controlling interest, usually the founder or members of his family'.[38] In such cases voting power in the general meeting may have a considerable impact on the general running and development of the company, especially in the appointment of directors from among the family circle. The surveys carried out by Berle and Means and by Sargant Florence revealed a similar state of affairs in many small and medium sized quoted companies.[39] There is a real danger in this as in many other aspects of company lore of assuming that developments at one end of the spectrum apply equally to all companies.

Another development which may set some limit to the extent of managerial independence in this context is the growth of large institutional holdings of shares in quoted companies, both large and small. The figures in Table 2.12 show that there has been a substantial increase in the past decade in the proportion of shares held by insurance companies, pension funds, investment companies and unit trusts. Between 1957 and 1975 the holdings of these institutional investors in quoted British companies increased from one-fifth to almost two-fifths in terms of total market value. Corresponding figures from the United States show that the proportion of total market value of shares held by institutions rose from thirteen per cent in 1949 to twenty per cent in 1964.[40] An equally significant fact, given the growing importance of loan as opposed to share

[38] Cmnd. 4811 (1971), p. 6.

[39] Berle and Means, op. cit., p. 51; Sargant Florence, op. cit., p. 75.

[40] H. Burton and D. C. Corner, *Investment and Unit Trusts in Britain and America* (1968), Chs. 10–12.

TABLE 2.12

Beneficial ownership of shares in quoted British companies as a proportion of total market value, 1957–75

Category of owner	Percentage of total market value			
	1957	1963	1969	1975
Persons, executors and trustees	66	54	47	42
Insurance companies	9	10	12	15
Pension funds	3	6	9	15
Investment companies	7	7	8	5
Unit trusts	1	1	3	2
Total institutions	*(20)*	*(27)*	*(32)*	*(37)*
Other non-personal holdings	10	14	14	10
Overseas	4	7	7	4
Unallocated				8

Source: J. Revell and J. Moyle, *The Ownership of Quoted Ordinary Shares* (1966); *Royal Commission on the Distribution of Income and Wealth,* Cmnd. 6172 (1975); figures for 1975 are for a small sample of the largest companies only.

capital, is that in 1965 ninety-two per cent of the market value of debenture or loan stock in quoted British companies was held by institutions, compared with forty-three per cent of preference shares and twelve per cent of ordinary shares.[41] These institutional investors act as intermediaries between smaller and some larger private investors and the operations of the Stock Exchange and the City, and have the skill and resources to apply themselves to a detailed analysis of the issues involved in the management of the companies they invest in and of the merits of particular take-over and merger schemes. The potential voting power of the institutions has not been exercised very frequently in Britain, except in contested take-overs and boardroom rows. Their managers appear to prefer to keep an eye on those companies in which they have substantial investment by appointing a director under the terms of a debenture or by agreement with management rather than by open use of their voting power. A survey of the interrelationship of large industrial companies and the City in Britain in 1973 revealed that thirty-one of the top forty industrial companies had a direct link by way of

[41] Ibid., Ch. 9.

interlocking directorships with one of the twenty-seven largest City companies and banks.[42] In other countries like Germany, where the fact that bearer shares are normally deposited with banks and other financial agencies with full proxy voting rights, this system of institutional oversight has been developed on a more widespread basis through the supervisory board system (see below, pp. 448 ff.).

The true effect of the potential voting power of institutional and other shareholders is thus the support which it lends to the ideology of profit and growth among top management rather than any real threat to managerial power. This aspect of corporate capitalism is of some significance in the context of proposals to provide for trade union and employee representation on company boards, as discussed in Part III. It does not alter the fact that for practical purposes the management of almost all large quoted companies may be regarded as a self-perpetuating oligarchy, free from effective intervention on the part of its shareholders.

6 THE MANAGERIAL REVOLUTION

The cumulative effect of these patterns in corporate concentration, financing and shareholding is that as the size of a company increases so the degree of managerial independence grows. The process has been aptly described as the managerial revolution, as there is a good deal more to it than the loss of direct shareholder control over large public companies.[43] Along with the changing balance in power from control by capitalists to control by managers goes a shift in emphasis from the traditional profit motive to what may be termed managerial motives. Instead of seeking exclusively to increase the net return on capital invested, those in control of company decisions will also be concerned with the preservation of the company and its business, and of their own control over it, with growth and 'empire-building' in order to increase the range and extent of their power and thus reduce the uncertainty of their operations, and even with increasing their own personal prosperity rather than that of their shareholders. And as an important part of the establishment of their independence

[42] P. Whitley, The City and Industry, in P. Stanworth and A. Giddens (eds.), *Elites and Power in British Society* (1974).

[43] J. Burnham, *The Managerial Revolution* (1942); for a general economic account see R. Marris, *The Economic Theory of Managerial Capitalism* (1964).

management will typically seek to free itself from too much reliance on the stock market as a source of new funds.

Each of these manifestations of the managerial revolution may be readily distinguished and exemplified. In the first place there can be no doubt that the large modern company has developed a separate institutional existence independent of its precise legal form. Management and senior staff increasingly conceive of themselves as company men owing loyalty to the company as such rather than to its shareholders, and visualize their own career patterns within the company or other similar companies. The mass of employees too are encouraged to look to the company as a beneficent if impersonal source not only of their livelihood, but also of all kinds of recreational activities and fringe benefits. Company paternalism of this kind is not at all new, and has been pushed further in America and Japan than in Britain, but there is perhaps more emphasis now on the company as an organization than on the individual managers or proprietors as in the nineteenth and early twentieth centuries. The growing practice of merger and take-over even among the largest companies may disturb established institutions and loyalties, but the preservation of group identities and the continuation of existing management contracts can help to bridge the gap until a new and larger institution can establish itself on the spiritual level.

The position of management within these new-style companies differs appreciably from that of their nineteenth-century forbears who typically held a substantial proportion of their company's shares. The modern company executive much less often holds a substantial block of shares in his company and has correspondingly less interest and sympathy for the shareholders' view of the company, despite the introduction of share option and share-based pension schemes for management. He is likely to be rather more concerned to maintain the business as a source of his own livelihood and prestige than as a source of dividend income, though efficiency and prosperity are, of course, the means to both these ends. And in the event of a take-over bid he will naturally think of his own future as well as of the price offered to shareholders. The legal and financial journals are full of reports of acrimonious disputes between rival groups of directors, struggling for control over their respective enterprises, and there is an appreciable number of reported cases in which the principal issue at stake has been the legitimacy of various manoeuvres adopted by company managements to protect themselves from an unwanted take-over (see Chapter 5). Conversely a recent survey of the attitudes of leading executives has shown that the principal motive of those initiating take-over and merger operations is the desire to extend market dominance or to defend an established position rather than to increase the economic return on resources.[44] This does not mean that managerial criteria of success have ceased to be financial or that ideas of social responsibility have replaced those of hard-headed capitalism.[45] But modern managers are likely to think that the power and prestige of their company, and their own position within it, is more important than earning profits for their shareholders.

There is also a temptation for managers to regard the company as essentially their own property, and for them to look primarily to their own profit in conducting its affairs. Managers are often in a position to fix their own salaries in terms of company profitability, and to arrange for themselves highly attractive pension and insurance schemes, or options for share-purchase. Finally in the event of take-over bids managers are in a strong position to secure for themselves substantial payments and benefits (the 'golden handshake') as a condition of their co-operation with the bidding company. All such practices which go beyond the confines of reasonable inducement to efficiency are condemned in such semi-official codes of conduct as the *City Code on Take-overs and Mergers*, and *Standard Boardroom Practice*, published by the Institute of Directors. They are also given their due share of publicity and criticism in the financial press when they come to light, and have often been dropped or amended as a result. The Companies Act 1967 made wider disclosure of most collateral benefits of this kind mandatory.[46] But there can be no doubt that some managers do occasionally take advantage of their controlling position in the company for their own personal profit.

Finally as a means of securing their independence of action there is a tendency for managements to seek to finance their company's expansion otherwise than through the stock market. The most important method by which this independence is secured, as has already been described, is by ploughing back the profits of the company. Where that source of funds is insufficient management may often prefer to raise a large contractual loan by way of a debenture from one of the major financial institutions rather than

[44] G. D. Newbould, *Management and Merger Activity* (1970).
[45] Pahl and Winkler, op. cit.
[46] Ss. 6–8 and 25–6.

submit themselves to the public scrutiny of the stock market and the financial press by embarking on a public share issue. The interests of shareholders as investors in the company cannot be ignored entirely. A sudden fall in dividend payments or adverse figures on profitability will naturally result in a fall in share prices, which in its turn may expose the company and its management to the threat of a take-over or an internal boardroom shake-out. The maintenance of share prices at a reasonable level is accordingly a matter of continuing managerial concern. As already suggested, this is better regarded as part of the ideological objective of profitability and growth which managers set for themselves than as evidence of their acceptance of subordination to shareholders.

Limits on managerial power

The most significant limitations on managerial powers in the largest companies are in fact imposed outside the framework of company law. The most important of these at the level of the individual company is the power of organized labour. No large company, whether in the private or the public sector, can afford to ignore the union representatives of its work force, whether on the shopfloor through its shop stewards or at a regional or national level through its full-time officials. The impact of the existing system of collective bargaining on the organization and management of companies, and the likely effect of proposals for the representation of unions or workers on company boards or works committees will be discussed in detail in Chapter 13.

The second major limitation on managerial autonomy is the increasing interference and involvement of government in the affairs of all companies but especially of those which dominate the market in any particular field of activity. Some of these governmental requirements, in particular those relating to the disclosure of accounts and other items of information, are imposed within the Companies Acts, and will be discussed in the course of the detailed analysis of company law in Part II. The powers exercised by government outside the framework of company law, however, are a good deal more significant. There is an increasing range of governmental and semi-independent agencies whose function it is to oversee and where it is thought necessary to intervene in the operations of industrial and commercial concerns. The most important of these in formal legal terms have been the Monopolies Commission, the Registrar of

Restrictive Practices (now subsumed in the Office of Fair Trading) and a number of now defunct bodies like the Prices and Incomes Board, the Commission for Industrial Relations and the Industrial Reorganization Corporation. Most of the agencies which have been abolished, however, have reappeared in different forms, whether as part of regular government departments or as new quasi-independent agencies. The work of the Prices and Incomes Board, for instance, is now carried on in part by the Price Commission and in part by that section of the Department of Employment which deals with the so-called social contract on wages. The work of the Industrial Reorganization Corporation is now shared between the Department of Industry in the exercise of its powers to give financial assistance to private companies under the Industry Acts and the newly formed National Enterprise Board. There is also an increasing degree of informal consultation between government departments and leading companies, and a power under the Industry Act 1975 (which has not often been used) to draw up formal planning agreements covering any aspect of a company's commercial and industrial policies. And at a national level the representatives of the private sector, the Confederation of British Industry, and of organized labour, the Trades Union Congress, are increasingly involved in the preparation of day-to-day government policies. The practical operation of these systems will be discussed in greater detail in Chapter 14.

One explanation for this trend towards greater governmental interference in the operations of the private sector is the acceptance of Keynesian theories of economic management. By the regulation of money supply, credit and government expenditure at the macro-economic level and of prices and wages at the level of individual firms most governments now seek to maintain a balance between levels of industrial and commercial activity, unemployment and inflation. There is a continuing dispute over the relative importance of various factors in this process, notably between the monetarists who argue that control over the money supply is the key to economic stability and those who argue that increased government spending is the correct response to a slump. But on all sides the principle of governmental economic regulation in some form or other is accepted as inevitable.

A second explanation is more directly related to the Marxist prophesy that the internal momentum of capitalist accumulation would inevitably establish monopolies and thereby require state interference (see p. 35). The various legislative attempts to prevent or to mitigate the effects of monopoly power may properly be regarded in this light. But as a general explanation of increasing state intervention it is clearly inadequate. Some forms of state intervention can be linked to the deliberate pursuit of socialist policies, as in the nationalization of certain key industries. Others are better seen as ad hoc political decisions flowing from the increasing involvement of government in the maintenance of employment, as in the support of certain declining industries such as textiles and in some instances of nationalization in which the primary motivation has been the protection of employment.

It has also been argued that government in Britain is now deliberately setting out to establish a network of informal controls over all major companies in pursuit of what has been called a 'corporatist' strategy of voluntary economic regulation through existing companies and institutions.[47] The thinking behind this strategy was simply expressed in *The Regeneration of British Industry* in 1974:

> The attitude of Government to industry ... has been too remote, too much coloured by the concept that the Government's main function ... is that of regulation to prevent the activities of industry, or the abuse of its powers, damaging the interests of other sectors of the community.... Industry and Government should also be partners in the pursuit of the objectives which spell success for industry and prosperity for this country.[48]

But there is little evidence that major companies wish to enter into the kind of relationship with government which this model prescribes, except perhaps with a view to bending government policy to suit their own objectives.

The resulting situation is perhaps better described as a three-fold division of economic power between the managerial elite, organized labour and the government, each of which is pursuing somewhat different objectives. The outcome of this struggle for dominance is not yet clear, and will obviously be influenced by the form of industrial democracy which is eventually adopted. But it is certainly not true that increasing government intervention is bound to develop into a fully planned socialist economy. Many aspects of government action in this field are designed as much to preserve as to destroy the capitalist contribution within a mixed economy.

[47] J. T. Winkler, 'Corporatism', *European Journal of Sociology* (1976), 100.
[48] Cmnd. 5710, para. 4.

7 NATIONAL AND MULTI-NATIONAL CAPITALISM

This brief account of current trends in the development of capitalism has been focused on developments within a single national economy. That is obviously a gross oversimplification. One of the most important features of capitalism, and of the Marxist critique of it, is its international character. In the early stages of capitalist development this was mainly a matter of international trade in the products of pre-industrial and industrial concerns. On the later stages the main emphasis in Marxist theory has been on the relationship between the search for markets for excess production and the development of colonialism. In market theory the main emphasis has been on the issue of free trade in manufactured goods and raw materials and the free movement of labour and capital. Each approach incorporates its own inherent value judgements: the exploitation of colonial markets, the depression of prices for raw materials from the third world and the abuse of migrant labour on the Marxist side;[49] on the other the benefits to be obtained by all peoples from the free movement of labour and capital throughout the world so that the production of every commodity can be concentrated where it can be most cheaply produced.

The merits of these two positions cannot be dealt with in this book. But there are some important aspects of the development of international capitalism and in particular of multi-national companies which cannot be avoided. The difficulty can be simply stated as an unresolved conflict between the two forces of capitalist accumulation and governmental power. The natural culmination of unfettered capitalist development in organizational terms is the multi-national company, which transcends national boundaries and thus to a large extent the power of national governments to control its activities. The natural culmination of the socialist model of development is a series of national or nationalized companies whose activities are under the direct control of the state. The difference between the two, it should be noted, is not one of size or concentration or monopoly power. Some nationalized corporations in Britain and other countries are as large and economically powerful as many multi-nationals in the private sector. There is even a degree of overlap between the two forms. Some companies, like British Leyland and

[49] Hugo Radice (ed.), *International Firms and Modern Imperialism* (1975).

the French Renault company, which are technically in the public sector in their home base operate in their overseas markets in a way which is indistinguishable from other multi-nationals in the private sector. The essential issue is the form of internal and external control over the managerial hierarchy which has developed in both systems.

The position of economic dominance which has been attained by the major multi-nationals need not be demonstrated in purely statistical terms.[50] It is well known that the annual budgets and profits of companies like General Motors, ICI and the big oil companies are much larger than those of many independent states. It is equally well known that the major multi-nationals are gaining for themselves an increasing share in the domestic economies of most developed and many developing countries. The process by which the multi-nationals have developed is fairly uniform. The typical pattern is the gradual extension into overseas markets of a company which has reached the limit of practicable growth or market dominance in its home country, at first simply by export but then by the establishment of subsidiaries in other countries for marketing and, later on, for manufacture. In many cases the foreign base is built up by taking over an already established local company in the same line of business. Initially this new subsidiary may be left to trade under its own name and with its own products, but it is likely to be progressively integrated into the larger production and marketing network of its parent company. This process can be readily observed in the motor industry in which the three American giants, General Motors, Ford and Chrysler, have gradually taken over a major part of car production in western Europe. In formal legal terms the local subsidiary like its parent company is an independent enterprise which produces its own accounts and is subject to the full range of governmental controls in the country of establishment. In practice the business of the multi-national is carried out on an international basis, with a greater or lesser concentration on the interests of the original parent company depending on the extent of its contribution to the total production of the whole group. In some cases, like those of the major oil companies whose operations are not obviously tied to any one country, the choice of a site for head office is a matter of convenience or tradition. In others American dominance, both

[50] C. Tugendhat, *The Multinationals* (1971).

economic and political, is the salient feature.[51] Ultimate control in all but a few cases of continuing family ownership is exercised by a self-perpetuating managerial elite.

The flexibility which this form of organization gives to the multinationals makes it correspondingly difficult to control them. On a purely financial level they may take maximum advantage of differential tax rates and investment incentives in different countries by so organizing their accounts that the largest profits are generated in countries with lower tax rates. 'Transfer pricing' enables them to charge high prices for those goods and services which are produced in the low-tax countries so that the profits of subsidiaries who buy these goods and services in high-tax countries are kept to a minimum. Provided prices for internal sales are kept within reasonably justifiable margins there is nothing illegal about this practice. Multinationals may take similar advantage of differentials in investment incentives in deciding where to site their new plants or which of their existing establishments to expand or run down. Many governments are under considerable political pressure to maintain employment in depressed areas, and may therefore be prepared to offer large incentives or to waive normal restrictions in exchange for favourable decisions in these matters even if the long-term cost is high. The recent negotiations between the British government and Chrysler over the future of Chrysler's British subsidiary is a good example.

The extent of the advantage which multi-nationals can obtain from transfer pricing, siting decisions and other such practices must not be exaggerated. Like other companies their freedom of action is often curtailed by the extent of their previous investment and the reluctance of local management to abandon existing plants. But the bargaining power of prosperous multi-nationals in their dealings with national governments is clearly much greater than that of national companies, however large, which cannot seriously threaten to move their operations elsewhere.

The development of national and nationalized companies may be described in a similar way, with the proviso that their operations are usually tied in one way or another to a single country. Generally speaking such companies have grown up within the private sector by the normal processes of concentration by natural growth and by take-over and merger, as for instance in the coal mining, railway

[51] See, for example, A. Sampson, *The Sovereign State* (1973).

and motor industries in Britain. Then, whether from a pragmatic need to give assistance to ailing companies, as with the railways and shipbuilding; as a natural result of increasing government finance for research and development, as with the aircraft industry; or in pursuance of a prior policy of taking over 'the commanding heights of the economy', as in the case of the steel industry, the major companies have been rationalized or nationalized into a single statutory corporation. Internally these national companies are broadly similar in structure and organization to their multi-national counterparts, with a self-generating managerial hierarchy and an ordinary commercial system of accounting. But as nationalized corporations established by specific legislation they are usually subject to direct government control on matters of policy, whether directly or through the power to appoint the controlling board. They are also dependent on government subventions as their major source of finance, both for new investment and for the writing off of accumulated deficits, though they also raise substantial sums on the open market in the form of fixed interest loan stock. The legal form through which these operational and financial controls are exercised in Britain is discussed in detail in Chapter 14. In many other respects, however, the regulation and supervision of nationalized companies raise the same issues as the regulation and supervision of multinationals, notably in the context of monopoly power and the provision of structures for the representation of employees' interests within the framework of the company. It is these issues of internal organization and external supervision and regulation with which this book is principally concerned rather than the more general political question of the relative merits of international free market capitalism and of national state capitalism.

8 CONCLUSIONS

There is no need for a detailed summary of the analysis of the current structure and operation of the capitalist system in Britain which has been presented in this chapter. In the particular context of company law, however, a number of general conclusions may be drawn.

In the first place it is clear that there is a very wide range of commercial concerns, from the small private business to the vast national or multi-national corporation, in any developed modern economy. In Britain the large majority of these, except the very smallest, are expected to operate under the same general principles of law which have been developed in the Companies Acts and in the courts. This approach is obviously unrealistic. In the detailed account of company law which is given in Part II an attempt has therefore been made to deal separately with those parts of the law which are most directly relevant to commercial concerns of three different sizes and types: the small private business in which the proprietors are all directly involved in the day-to-day management of the business; the larger family company in which there is a clear separation between the interests of internal directors and managers and external shareholders; and finally the quoted public company in which there is a much greater degree of public participation through the stock market system. This presentation has involved rather less interference with the traditional conceptual analysis of company law than might be expected. The major legal issues which typically arise in each of the three types of company are conveniently distinct: the choice of legal form and relationships with external creditors in the small private business; the relations between shareholders and directors and managers in unquoted family companies; and the problems of disclosure, public share dealing and official intervention in quoted companies. But the formal separation of the legal analysis of these various issues for different sizes of company does assist in the formulation of more satisfactory rules of law for each.

In the second place there is a fundamental imbalance in the respective rights and duties of the three main groups which contribute to commercial and industrial activity: those who supply the capital, those who organize and manage the day-to-day operations and the rank and file of employees. This imbalance is inherent in the current structure of company law which provides for the interests of only two of the three groups, shareholders and managers. The interests of employees have been dealt with in the context of the law of individual employment and industrial relations. In Part III of this book an attempt has been made to bring together these divergent strands in the law and to show how they may be related through developing structures for industrial democracy and participation in companies of various sizes and types.

The third main theme is the control of management in large modern corporations, whether in the private or the public sector.

The so-called managerial revolution and the reliance of large companies on internal as opposed to external sources of finance in the private sector clearly requires some revision of the traditional theory of control by shareholders through the mechanism of the stock market. Similarly in the public sector there is a need for a more coherent set of rules or guidelines for the supervision and control of management in nationalized companies, both by government and by their own employees. Finally there is a special problem posed by the desire of national government to exercise similar controls over the operations of multi-national companies. All this is dealt with in some detail in Part III.

PART TWO: COMPANY LAW

3 Introductory concepts: sole traders, partnerships, companies and business accounting

Whatever the actual distribution of enterprises of various types and sizes it must be remembered that there is no obligation on businessmen to adopt any particular legal form. Though the limited liability company was originally developed for large scale enterprises, it is now used by many small firms and even some one-man businesses. Conversely, though the natural application of the partnership or sole proprietorship is to small trading concerns, it is perfectly lawful for an individual or a group of individuals to carry out commercial or industrial operations on a very large scale without resorting to the raising of funds through the sale of shares in a company. Before embarking on a detailed analysis of the prevailing law and practice in respect of business operations of different sizes and types, therefore, it may be useful to set out in simple terms the basic legal rules and terminology relating to the formation, operation and dissolution of a business enterprise as a sole proprietorship, as a partnership and as a company. To complete this introductory chapter a brief description is also given of the essentials of business accounting and the way in which it has developed.

I THE SOLE TRADER

In most continental countries traders (*commerçants*) are subject to a different legal code, and often to different courts, from ordinary people. Only traders are subject to the law of bankruptcy (*faillite*) which provides for the goods and assets of an insolvent trader to be divided up among his creditors on an equitable basis, and for any outstanding liability to be nullified. And there are different rules relating to commercial contracts, making for easier proof of the oral bargains which are so prevalent and necessary in commercial dealings. There are of course difficulties in drawing the line between traders and non-traders. French law defines the *commerçant* as one who engages in 'acts of commerce' and then lists a number of activities falling under that head, for instance, 'any purchase of goods and merchandise for resale . . . or for hire. . . .' But the difficulties of definition, and the attendant dangers of slipping into circularity, are not of real importance. In almost every case it will be quite clear which law is to apply. The important point is that traders of all kinds, whether individuals or incorporated bodies, are treated as a class apart.

English law has rejected the idea of commercial law as a formally separate category. In general no distinction is made between commercial and other transactions, or between the trader and other individuals. This was not always the case. Until 1861 only the trader could benefit from the law of bankruptcy which enabled him on proof of insolvency to divide his remaining assets among his creditors, and then with the permission of the Bankruptcy Court to make a fresh start, unencumbered by his past debts. Non-commercial debtors who could not meet their obligations, on the other hand, faced indefinite imprisonment, though it was in fact normal practice for them to be released and absolved from their debts by royal decree or statute at infrequent intervals. Since 1861, however, the privilege of bankruptcy and discharge has been open to all insolvent persons with current debts of more than £50, and from 1976 of more than £200 (Insolvency Act 1976 : s. 1).

Thus there is no special legal status for traders in English law, and consequently there are no special legal rules to which a person operating a business on his own account becomes subject. Anyone may engage in business activities without for that reason alone becoming involved in legal technicalities. A trader must, of course, like anyone else pay tax on the income which he obtains out of the conduct of his business. And if he wishes to trade in a name or title other than his own he must register that name under the Registration of Business Names Act 1916. This statute has a rather limited function. It does not grant an exclusive right to any person to trade under a duly registered name. Though the Department of Trade has power to refuse to register a name as unsuitable, the power is not exercised to exclude identical or similar registrations. The main purpose of the Act is to allow other traders to check up on the real identity and addresses of persons trading under a trade name, and so to prevent notorious insolvents from concealing their identity from suppliers and customers. The register contains about a million trade names. But many of these registered businesses are defunct. Many others simply do not bother to comply with the Act. In any event most small businesses are in practice carried on in the names of their proprietors, so that registration is unnecessary. In fact, as was shown in Table 2.3 (see p. 48), most trading concerns are in law simply individuals carrying on business on their own account. It must be remembered however, that a sole trader may employ as many other workers in his business as he wishes. His status in law and for tax purposes as a sole proprietor relates only to his personal ownership of the assets and profits of the business and his personal liability for its debts. If the business fails it is the proprietor alone who is subject to the ordinary rules of bankruptcy.

2 THE PARTNERSHIP

When a number of individuals conduct a business together on an equal footing it is no longer convenient to regard them as individual traders, either for legal or practical purposes. The property of each individual participant in the business cannot easily be kept separate and for tax purposes it is natural to regard the income and expenditure of the business as a single unit. The rights and liabilities of the various partners can only be distinguished on a fractional or proportional basis. Each partner must in effect be regarded as contributing or owning a number of shares in the business. All this is achieved by the law of partnership.

The basis of a partnership is normally a formal deed drawn up to regulate the rights and liabilities of those involved. To this extent the terms of association are a matter for agreement between the parties. But in law any two or more persons who trade together are automatically regarded as constituting a partnership whether or not any formal deed has been entered into. A body of general legal principles was developed in the common law and in equity to provide for the settlement of disputes between partners which have not been expressly provided for in advance, and to regulate the relationship between the partnership and third parties. These rules are set out in codified form in the Partnership Act 1890.

A partnership for the purposes of the Act is 'the relation which subsists between persons carrying on a business in common with a view to profit' (s. 1.) This seemingly simple formulation conceals a good deal of earlier dispute on the question whether those who shared in any way in the profits from a business automatically became full partners, jointly responsible in law with other more active participants. It was finally settled that mere participation in profit was not sufficient for this purpose:

Two partners, whose business had got into financial difficulties, made a formal arrangement with their creditors to transfer the business to trustees to continue trading on behalf of the creditors who were to be paid off out of any profits realized; when the debts were discharged the business was to be transferred back to the original partners. This scheme was carried through, but the business continued to run at a loss. A number of new creditors then sought to recover from some of the original creditors on the ground that they had become partners by reason both of their share in the profits and their powers of control over the business through the trustees. It was held that no partnership had been created; the business was being carried on for the ultimate benefit of the original partners, and the interest of the creditors in the profits had been limited to the repayment of what was due to them. *Cox v. Hickman* (1860) 8 H.L.C. 268

This decision was subsequently confirmed by the Mercantile Law (Amendment) Act of 1865 (Bovill's Act) by which it was provided that the sharing of profits was not to constitute conclusive evidence of partnership. But neither that Act nor the Partnership Act which reproduced it contemplated the possibility of a partnership on the continental model in which the liability of non-active partners would be limited to the amount of their initial contribution. The basic question in English law is still whether the relationship of the parties is such as to constitute a full partnership between them in which they normally share both the profits and the losses from the business or whether the limited relationship of debtor and creditor or employer and employee persists. Even the status of so-called 'salaried partners' who do not share fully in either profit or loss must be decided on the particular facts of each individual case:

On the death of his partner a chartered accountant made an interim agreement with a younger man, under which the latter was to work with him as a salaried partner for a limited period pending agreement on a full partnership. The full partnership was never drawn up and the younger man continued to work for a salary after the initial agreement had expired. When relations between the two finally broke down the matter was taken to court to determine whether the younger man had been a true partner. Megarry J. held that though in most cases 'salaried partners' who appeared on a firm's letterhead but did not share in the firm's profit or loss were merely being held out as partners, it was impossible to say as a matter of law that a salaried partner was or was not necessarily a partner in the true sense; on the facts of the case he held that a true partnership had been created and continued. *Stekel v. Ellice* [1973] 1 W.L.R. 191

It is also settled that participation in a partnership is an essentially personal matter. This is perhaps best illustrated by the rule that the death or bankruptcy of any one partner terminates the partnership. On this the business should either be wound up, or else a new partnership agreement entered into to make provision for the alteration in membership. No partnership can in theory outlive the genuine participation of all its members.

Four partners in a whisky business contracted to employ a sales manager for a period of two years. Soon afterwards two of the partners retired, and the business was transferred to the remaining partners. When he heard of this the new manager refused to continue working for the firm on the grounds that the partnership which employed him had been terminated. He then sued the partners for wrongful dismissal and claimed immediate payment for the whole of the outstanding period of his contract by way of damages. The Court of Appeal agreed that his contract had been automatically terminated at law by the withdrawal of the two partners, but awarded only nominal damages since the remaining two partners had been quite ready to continue employing the manager on the same terms as before. *Brace v. Calder* [1895] 2 Q.B. 253

Fortunately the practical difficulties which might arise from a strict application of this rule can usually be surmounted, as in the case just cited, or ignored. Where the business is continued, the formal termination and reconstitution principally affects the rights and liabilities of the partners between themselves rather than those of the firm as such, and the necessary adjustment can be made by internal accounting. It is usual in large partnerships to provide in advance that the death of a single partner shall not operate to determine the partnership between the remaining partners.

The importance of this issue of the existence and extent of the partnership springs directly from the rule that each and every partner is jointly and severally liable for the debts of the firm as a whole. This means that any external creditor may sue any individual partner for the full amount of any debt or obligation owed to him by the firm, leaving it to the individual partner to recover any contribution which may be due from other partners. In practice, however, it is usual to institute proceedings against the partnership as a whole. The external creditor is thus not generally affected by or concerned with the internal relationships which have been agreed upon by the partners, and which would not normally be revealed to outsiders.

This rule of joint and several liability is merely an application of the ordinary law of agency to the partnership situation, in that each partner is deemed to be an agent of the firm for any transaction undertaken by him on behalf of the firm (Partnership Act 1890 : s. 5). The law of agency also governs the liability of partners as principals for the acts of their employees. Liability thus extends only to transactions which fall within the scope of the partnership. But this is widely construed to cover any transaction which falls within the ordinary course of business in the trade which the partnership has undertaken. The rights of a third party cannot be affected by any internal arrangement or limitation imposed by the partners on each other or their employees unless he has express or implied notice of it.

The rules as to participation and liability stress the essentially individual nature of the rights and liabilities of partners. In practical terms, however, the partnership or firm is generally treated as an independent unit. Its business may be carried on under any name which the partners choose, subject only to the requirements of registration and the disclosure of the names of individual partners under the Registration of Business Names Act 1916. The partnership may then sue and be sued under this name. In addition, the Partnership Act provides for partnership property to be kept separate from that of individual partners even though a partnership has no legal personality as such, so that any property employed in the business must belong in law to individual partners. In the event of an action against the firm or a dissolution of the partnership on insolvency or otherwise this partnership property will be applied to meet the firm's obligations before any question arises of individual liability on the partners (ss. 20–4). Finally, for tax purposes the accounts of the partnership will be regarded as separate from the affairs of its members. Tax will normally be levied directly on the profits of the firm, though subsequent adjustments may have to be made to the personal assessments made on individual partners.

It is also a general rule of law, applicable to all commercial associations, that any person involved in a joint enterprise must always act in the interests of the enterprise as a whole, and not allow his own personal interests to take precedence over those of the enterprise. This concept of a fiduciary duty to the firm is derived from the equitable rules on the duty of a trustee to the beneficiaries of the trust. Any personal profit made by a partner in the course of the firm's business, for example, must be handed over to the firm and apportioned in accordance with the terms of the partnership agreement (Partnership Act 1890 : ss. 29–30). Nor may one or two of the partners make arrangements to continue the business on their own to the exclusion of a third, at least while the partnership subsists.

A partnership agreement between two glass manufacturers expired after fourteen years, but was continued without any further formal agreement. Some time later the son of one of the partners was admitted as a partner with half of his father's share. The father and son then renewed the lease on the firm's premises in their own names, since the landlord would not grant an extension if the remaining partner was included. Then when the original lease expired they asked the remaining partner to remove his share of the stock from the premises. The Court of Appeal held that though the partnership could be determined immediately since there was no express agreement to the contrary, the father and son must account to the third partner for the value of the new lease. 'It was clear that one partner could not treat privately and behind the backs of his co-partners for a lease on the premises, where the joint trade was carried on, for his own benefit; if he did so treat and obtain a lease in his own name it was a trust for the partnership.' (per Grant M.R.) *Featherstonhaugh v. Fenwick* (1810) 17 Ves. Jun. 298

The Partnership Act further provides that in the absence of evidence to the contrary the property of the firm shall be deemed to belong to all the participant partners in equal shares and that any profit or loss is to be apportioned equally between them (s. 24). Similarly the management of the business is regarded as a matter for all the partners together. Each is entitled to full access to the affairs of the firm in order to enable him to participate effectively in this. But in these as in all other internal matters, the Act does not detract from the essentially contractual nature of the partnership association. The rule as to equal shares applies only in the absence of any express or implied provision to the contrary, and the partners may make what formal arrangement they wish to govern the management of the firm's affairs. They may appoint a managing committee or partner by election or otherwise. Or they may adopt a formal constitution similar to that provided for private limited companies. The only formal control on the freedom of commercial association in this context is the statutory rule that no partnership of more than twenty members is permitted (Companies Act 1948 : s. 434). Even this restriction has recently been lifted to permit larger associations of solicitors, accountants and stockbrokers and other professional partnerships (Companies Act 1967 : s. 120).

As in the case of any other association, however, the courts do have certain powers to intervene, either in the interests of the community or of the parties themselves. A partnership to carry out illegal activities would clearly be unenforceable, even if it were not a criminal conspiracy. The courts also retain a general equitable jurisdiction to dissolve a partnership on the grounds that it is just and equitable to do so (Partnership Act 1890 : s. 35). This power may be exercised if one or two of the partners attempt to exclude another from equal participation in the firm's affairs, or if circumstances have so changed that it would be unrealistic to enforce the terms of the partnership contract.

Two solicitors in joint practice agreed to take in their managing clerk as a full partner as they wished to be free from full time participation in the firm's affairs. Soon after the signature of the partnership deed, a legal action was brought against one of the former partners involving various allegations of falsification over an important account a number of years previously. The partner concerned refused to settle the action as the other two wished, and openly accused the managing clerk of attempting to squeeze him out of the business. The Court of Appeal held that the partnership should be dissolved on the principle that 'the circumstances under which the parties entered into the partnership had by matters over which they had no control materially altered, and that those altered circumstances had, combined with the conduct of the parties themselves, produced a mistrust which the court could not say was unreasonable; . . . it was impossible that the partnership could be conducted on the footing on which it was originally contemplated without injury to all those persons concerned.' (per Romilly M.R.) *Harrison v. Tennant* (1856) 21 Beav. 482

Apart from this general power of intervention, however, there is no official regulation of partnerships as such. As long as the partners trade under their own names there is no requirement for any form of registration. Nor in the event of failure is there any provision for a formal liquidation of the partnership. The individual partners, like sole traders, are subject to the ordinary law of bankruptcy if they cannot meet the firm's obligations out of their personal assets, though as will be seen there are some specific provisions regulating bankruptcy procedure in respect of partnership liabilities (see p. 193).

3 THE LIMITED COMPANY

The essential difference between a partnership and a registered company in modern law is the statutory provision of corporate personality. A registered company is a continuing legal entity entirely distinct in law from its members. It can own its own property and business, it can sue and be sued in its own name, and it is liable to tax as a company independently of the liability of its participants. The legal independence of the company also makes it relatively simple for the liability of its participants in the event of failure to be limited to the amount of their contribution to the finances of the company.

These privileges are granted subject to the terms of the Companies Acts. The company, unlike the essentially contractual partnership, is a statutory creation, and must be operated strictly within the provisions of company legislation. The more complex legal issues relating to corporate personality and the rights and duties of directors, managers and shareholders must always be considered in the light of the precise formal structure laid down by law for all companies, both for formation and subsequent operation and for eventual dissolution.

The formation of a company

The rules for the formation of a limited company are detailed and precise but essentially simple.[1] The company comes into being on the formal registration with the Registrar of Companies of the necessary formal documents, comprising principally copies of a *Memorandum of Association* and *Articles of Association* duly signed by the initial subscribers for the shares (Companies Act 1948 : s. 1). Though the memorandum is usually regarded as being the more

[1] For other forms of company without share capital or limited liability see p. 123.

fundamental, there is rarely any practical importance in the distinction between these two documents and their contents, except in so far as different procedures may have to be followed in order to make subsequent amendments. But it is convenient to describe them separately.

The memorandum of association must state the full name of the company (1948 : s. 2). The choice of name is subject to the approval of the Department of Trade and must always, in the absence of a special dispensation, include the word 'limited' (1948 : ss. 17–19). The memorandum must also set out the objects and powers of the company, for example, that it is to carry on the business of a furniture manufacturer and is to have power to do anything necessary or reasonably incidental to the carrying on of that business (1948 : ss. 2, 11 and Table B). As a statutory creation a company in English law can only do what it is expressly or impliedly authorized to do by its formal constitution. Finally the memorandum must specify the intended capital structure of the company by stating the authorized capital, and the number of units, for example, 10,000 shares of £1 each (1948 : s. 2).

The articles of association specify the way in which the affairs of the company are to be managed. The most important provisions are perhaps those concerning the voting rights of the various classes of shareholders, the procedure for the appointment and dismissal of the directors and the secretary, and the distribution of profits or assets. But detailed provision will also be made for such things as the procedure for the calling of meetings, the issue of authorized capital, the transfer of shares and the alteration of either the memorandum or articles of association. A number of these are mandatory under the terms of the Companies Acts, for example the holding of an annual general meeting, and the preparation and auditing of accounts. And the articles as a whole must follow the form of the specimen clauses set out in Table A of the Companies Act 1948 (1948 : ss. 8 and 11). Many of these will in practice be adopted, by reference or by reproduction, if only for convenience.

These detailed requirements for the formation of a company may give the impression that the whole business is exceedingly complex. In practice it is much simpler than it sounds. Specimen memoranda for businesses of all kinds, so widely drawn as to cover virtually any conceivable commercial activity, are readily available, and if the provisions of Table A are not suitable for adoption as articles there are any number of formal precedents for that too. All that needs to be done is to choose a name for the proposed company which is different from the names of the half million companies already in existence and which is not otherwise objectionable in the eyes of the Department of Trade and to arrange for the printing of the documents. The actual formation of the company will then normally take place in a solicitor's or accountant's office. The memorandum and articles will be signed by those concerned, or if they are too busy by two clerks, and copies will then be deposited at the Companies Registry for formal registration on payment of the requisite fee. It is also possible to buy 'off-the-peg' companies formed in advance by professional company registration agents for any standard type of business; if the purchasers do not like the company's name it can easily be altered (1948 : s. 18). It is only in relation to the flotation of large companies where money is to be raised by public subscription that there is any real difficulty, as for instance in the proper drafting of the necessary prospectus and in obtaining the requisite consents from all those concerned in the operation (see Chapter 6). A small company for private purposes may be formed or acquired for as little as £100 complete with all the necessary books of account and registers, and an effective company seal.

The memorandum and articles

In some cases a standard form of memorandum and articles will not meet the requirements of those forming the company. They may wish, for instance, to protect the position of certain shareholders or directors from the operation of the ordinary principle of majority rule within the company, or to limit the freedom of the company to do certain things. Provided the statutory requirements as to the content of the memorandum and articles are complied with, there is virtually unlimited scope in this context. For many purposes the memorandum and articles of a company may quite properly be regarded as an ordinary contract between the members of the company, just as a partnership deed is a contract between the partners. It is explicitly stated in the Companies Act that the memorandum and articles, when registered, shall bind the company and all its members as a legally enforceable contract (1948 : s. 20).

The most usual method of protecting the interests of individual members is the creation of a separate class of shares with special rights, whether in respect of voting or dividends or otherwise. Thus despite the statutory provision that a director may be removed from office at any time by a simple majority vote at a general meeting (1948 : s. 184), the position of any director may be safeguarded by creating multiple voting rights for his shares:

The shares in a small private company were equally divided between three shareholders, two of whom were directors. It was provided in the articles that in any motion for the removal of a director any shares held by that director should carry three votes per share, thus allowing him to outvote the rest of the shareholders. A dispute arose over the conduct of one of the directors and the others sought to remove him, arguing that the article in question was invalid in that it was an open attempt to avoid the effect of s. 184. It was eventually held in the House of Lords that there was nothing to prevent the creation of multiple voting rights for this purpose, any more than any other form of special voting rights for particular shares; the statute regulated only the majority required in any relevant resolution, not the number of votes per share. *Bushell v. Faith* [1970] A.C. 1099

The freedom of directors or managers in the conduct of a company's affairs may also be curtailed, for instance by a provision that certain things shall not be done without the prior approval of shareholders. Given the flexibility of the system in terms of multiple and variable voting rights, special majorities, and provision for casting votes there is virtually no objective in this respect which cannot be achieved by careful drafting.

Once the terms of the memorandum and articles have been finally agreed, however, it is more appropriate to regard them as a constitution than as a contract. All new shareholders are bound by their provisions and, like the constitution of any other organization or state, they are subject to interpretation and enforcement by the courts. A company is not merely a business in which the shareholders are the owners and the directors their servants or agents. It is a formal organization in which the powers and duties of shareholders and directors are balanced against each other, with the courts acting as umpire to ensure that the provisions of the company's constitution are complied with.

Two directors in a family company had been abstracting money illegitimately from the company in order to conceal their tax liability. When the matter came to light the articles of association were altered to put the control of the finances of the company into the hands of an independent board of directors who proceeded to institute actions for the recovery of the money owing. The general meeting then passed a resolution at the instigation of the two directors instructing the board not to proceed with the actions. The court held that the actions should proceed, since the articles granted full power to the new board over matters of this kind. 'A company is an entity distinct alike from its shareholders and its directors. Some of its powers may according to its articles be exercised by directors, certain other powers may be reserved for the shareholders in general meeting. If the powers of management are vested in the directors they and they alone can exercise these powers. The only way the general body of shareholders can control the exercise of the powers vested by the articles in the directors is by altering the articles, or if opportunity arises under the articles by refusing to re-elect the directors of whose action they disapprove. They cannot themselves usurp the powers which by the articles are vested in the directors any more than the directors can usurp the powers vested by the articles in the general body of shareholders.' (per Greer L.J.) *John Shaw & Sons (Salford) Ltd. v. Shaw* [1935] 2 K.B. 113

When disputes arise between the various parties interested in the affairs of a company the battle is frequently centred on the precise application of particular clauses in the memorandum and articles, or alternatively on the procedure for their amendment. For example, if the directors wish to raise new capital, necessitating an alteration in the memorandum of association, and to retain control by increasing the voting power of the shares they already hold, necessitating an alteration in the articles, the success of the operation will depend not only on control over a majority of votes in the general meeting but in addition on control over the process by which alterations in the memorandum and articles may be made. As a result the traditional distinction between the 'substantive' provisions in the memorandum and the 'administrative' provisions in the articles is likely to become blurred just when it becomes important.

The position is not made any clearer by the fact that the provisions in the Companies Act governing the alteration of both memorandum and articles have been built up in a piecemeal and confused manner. An increase in the authorized capital of the company as provided in the memorandum may be achieved by a simple majority at a company general meeting if the articles so provide (1948: s. 61). The objects of the company as stated in the memorandum, however, may only be altered by a special resolution, which requires a seventy-five per cent majority, subject to the further right of the holders of fifteen per cent of the shares to petition the court to cancel the alteration (1948 : s. 5). There is a similar provision for the alteration of any part of the memorandum which could have been contained in the articles (1948 : s. 23). In the case of a reduction of capital, which also requires a special resolution, the express sanction of the court must be obtained in all cases, and the right to petition the court is extended to creditors of the company (1948 : ss. 66–8). An alteration of the articles also requires a special resolution (1948 : s. 10). But where the alteration may affect the rights of any class of shareholders and requires the approval of a class meeting under the company's articles, the holders of fifteen per cent of the class of shares affected may again petition the court to have the alteration cancelled (1948 : s. 72).

The net effect of these various provisions is that it is theoretically possible to entrench special voting rights or any other matters normally contained in the articles by incorporating them in the memorandum since the provision which allows the alteration of anything in the memorandum which could equally have been put in the articles does not apply to class rights or to any item the alteration of which is explicitly prohibited or curtailed in the memorandum itself (1948 : s. 23). But this would require a degree of sophistication and advance planning not normally found in company constitutions. Generally speaking the entrenchment of particular provisions may be outflanked by an increase in capital. And if there is an article curtailing such an increase, all that is required to alter it is a sufficient majority to carry a special resolution. The court will rarely intervene unless there are grounds for holding that the changes have been engineered for an improper purpose or with the intention of discriminating against any members of the company, as will be seen in Chapter 5. In such cases it is necessary to consider the joint effect of both memorandum and articles as a single constitutional unit.

Share and loan capital

The formal details of the company's capital structure must also be set out in the memorandum and articles. Here too the two documents must be treated as a whole. The memorandum merely specifies the maximum authorized capital of the company. It is the articles which provide for the division of capital into ordinary or equity shares, which will normally be given full voting rights and equal rights to participate in any distribution of the company's profits or assets, and preference shares, which will typically give the holders prior rights to the payment of a fixed dividend and to the repayment of their capital in the event of a failure or dissolution but which in return may grant them only restricted voting rights. The authorized capital of a small private company, for instance, might comprise 10,000 shares of £1 each, divided into 5,000 ordinary shares and 5,000 preference shares, with a prior right to a fixed dividend of seven per cent but without voting rights unless the payment of the dividend has been suspended. But there is no limit on the number of different types and categories of shares which may be created. Provision may be made for a class of founder shares with multiple voting rights, for ordinary equity shares with no voting rights at all, or for preference shares which may be converted at some later date into equity shares.

The most important distinction in this context, however, is that between share and loan capital. Share capital is comprised of all the classes of shares into which the authorized capital of the company as provided in the memorandum is divided. Loan or debenture capital need not be so specified, though in most cases some provision will be made in the articles of association limiting the extent to which the company may raise additional funds by the issue of formal debentures.[2] The essential difference between the two is that share capital once issued may not be returned to the shareholders without following the formal procedures for the reduction of the company's capital, whereas loan capital may be repaid at any time, subject to any contractual terms specifying the maximum or minimum duration of the loan. This means that the holders of debentures rank on an equal footing with the other creditors of the company in the event of a liquidation in that they are entitled to be repaid in full before any return of capital invested is made to the holders of share capital. In practice debentures will usually be secured on the assets of the company and so rank before the ordinary unsecured creditors of the company. In addition, the interest on loan capital is deductible from the profits of the company before the assessment of tax, while any payment of a dividend on share capital of any kind must currently

[2] The term 'debenture' is defined in the Companies Act 1948 (s. 455) as including 'debenture stock, bonds and any other securities of a company whether constituting a charge on the assets of the company or not', but is generally used to refer to any loan which is secured on the assets of the company whether or not any formal bond or certificate is issued to the holder; a bank which agrees to lend money to a company in exchange for a fixed or floating charge on the company's assets will be regarded as a debenture holder.

be paid after the deduction of tax, and in addition must be paid out of profits and not capital. Of more practical importance in the future will be the EEC requirement that all public companies (see p. 121) must have a minimum capital of some £10,000, of which at least one quarter must be paid up. Under the Second Directive of December 1976 British law must be harmonized with continental practice in this respect by 1979. Most existing public companies already meet the requirement.

It should be noted in this context that there is no requirement that any more than two shares in a private company and seven shares in a public company need ever actually be subscribed and issued, nor that the amount due on a share which is issued should be fully paid (1948 : s. 1). A company with an authorized share capital of £10,000, for example, may operate on an issued share capital of two £1 shares on which only 50p has actually been paid to the company. The operations of a company may thus be financed entirely from loan capital or from accumulated profits. The fact that a share is labelled a £1 share or a £100 share accordingly means very little. Its real value can only be assessed by dividing the net assets of the company, after providing for the repayment of any outstanding loans or debts, by the number of issued shares. It has frequently been argued in the light of this that ordinary equity shares should be issued with 'no par value' to avoid any misleading implication that there is any connection between their face value and their real worth. But despite a governmental report on the subject which recommended that companies should be permitted to issue 'no par value' shares[3] nothing has yet been done to remove the provisions of the Companies Act requiring that all shares should have a nominal value (1948 : s. 2(4)).

Corporate personality and the ultra vires rule

The fact that a company, as opposed to a partnership, is an independent legal entity distinct from its shareholders or directors is not just a convenient device for the ownership of business assets, the conduct of litigation and other legal purposes. It also has a significant effect on the position of the members of the company, its directors and those who deal with it.

From the point of view of the shareholders and directors the most important aspect of corporate personality is the limitation of their

[3] Gedge Committee on Shares of No Par Value, Cmd. 9112 (1954).

own liability which the company's separate status facilitates. But the concept goes much further than this. It has been held that a company may be convicted of a criminal offence in addition to any liability on its directors or employees, on the ground that their acts and omissions may be attributed to the company itself. This applies both to regulatory offences connected with the company's business and to more serious charges:

A company and ten other individuals were charged with conspiracy to defraud. The defence accepted that a company could be vicariously guilty of regulatory offences involving no specific criminal intention, but argued that only its directors or managers could be guilty of an offence involving dishonesty. The company's conviction was upheld on the ground that the actions of the managing director were in law the actions of the company, and that his fraud was therefore the company's fraud. *R. v. I.C.R. Haulage Ltd. and others* [1944] 1 K.B. 551

The only limitation on this doctrine is a notional line drawn at offences such as perjury or bigamy which it is said a company cannot commit, or murder for which it is said it could not be punished.

In other spheres the company is regarded as entirely distinct from those who own, control or act for it. Corporate personality may operate, for instance, to deny a landlord his expected rights under business tenancies legislation:

The plaintiff owned a small butchery business which had been incorporated as a private company. She wished to expand into the adjacent shop which she had let to another business. Under the Landlord and Tenant Act 1954 she was entitled to terminate the tenancy if she required the premises for her own use but not otherwise. The tenant objected to the notice of termination and applied for an extension on the grounds that it was not the landlord personally who wished to use the premises but the company, which was in law a distinct entity. The landlord failed to gain possession. *Tunstall v. Steigman* [1962] 2 Q.B. 593

On the other hand, the courts have often been reluctant to push the separate personality of the company to its logical conclusion and have 'lifted the veil' of incorporation so as to prevent a blatant fraud or an evasion of the law. Whether or not the doctrine will be applied in a given case is thus difficult to predict. Its practical effect will be considered in Chapter 5 in relation to the particular problems which this uncertainty gives rise to (see p. 142).

In relation to company property, however, the position is a good deal clearer. The separate legal personality of the company means that its property must be regarded as distinct from that of its shareholders, despite the fact that those shareholders collectively have ultimate legal authority over its use and disposal. Thus no single shareholder is entitled to regard the company's property as his own regardless of the extent of his interest in or control over its affairs:

Gold belonging to a Dutch banking company was confiscated in 1940 by the Board of Trade as Custodian of Enemy Property, since the company fell under the terms of the definition of an enemy company. On the cessation of hostilities, the requisite sum in compensation was made over to the Administrator of Hungarian Property on the ground that all the shares were owned by Hungarians. The company itself was nonetheless ultimately held entitled to recover the money. The company's property 'was neither the property of the shareholders nor held or managed by the company on behalf of its shareholders'; it belonged to the company alone. *Bank voor Handel en Sheepvart v. Slatford* [1953] 1 Q.B. 248

Nor may the property of a company be distributed among its shareholders without following the requisite statutory procedure for the payment of dividends or the repayment of capital:

The controlling director in a small insurance broking company made surreptitious payments out of profits to himself and the only other shareholder in strict proportion to their respective holdings, probably to reduce the company's apparent tax liability. The company subsequently got into difficulties, and the director was prosecuted for fraudulent conversion of the amount of the payments. The director's defence, that the payments had been made with full knowledge of all the shareholders and without any element of dishonesty, was rejected. The operation was a fraud on the company as a separate entity. *R. v. Arthur* (1967) *The Times* 14 March

The conception of the company as a separate entity, and as such the exclusive owner of its own property is linked directly to another basic legal doctrine, that a company may not legally carry out any activity which is not expressly or impliedly authorized by statute or by the list of objects and powers in its own memorandum of association. Any such activity is *ultra vires*, literally beyond its powers, in that the legal capacity of the company is held to be exhaustively defined by the Companies Acts and its own constitution.

The explanation for this rule, which is in direct contrast to the unlimited legal capacity accorded to a partnership and to certain common law corporations, lies in the extension of the established law relating to chartered and statutory companies to the newly created registered companies in the mid-nineteenth century. Both chartered companies and those created by a private Act of Parliament were typically granted specific powers to carry out a particular undertaking, such as the building of a railway or canal, or the supply of water or gas to a stated area, and were naturally required not to exceed those powers. The extension of this doctrine to ordinary trading companies was justified on the twin grounds that the shareholders were entitled to have their capital used only for the purposes for which it was subscribed, and that any creditors were likewise entitled in exchange for the statutory grant to the company of limited liability to require that the subscribed capital be maintained and applied for the company's stated purposes and not dissipated in other ways:

One of the objects expressly authorized in a company's memorandum was to make and sell railway carriages. The directors later undertook to open a new railway in Belgium and entered into a contract with Riche to construct the railway for them. Following a dispute between the directors and the shareholders of the company Riche sought to enforce the contract. It was eventually held after protracted litigation that the contract was ultra vires and void, and could not have been ratified by the shareholders even if they had been unanimous: 'The provisions under which [the] system of limiting liability was inaugurated were provisions not merely ... for the benefit of the shareholders for the time being of the company but ... were enactments intended also to provide for the interests of ... those who might become shareholders ... and secondly the outside public and more particularly those who might be creditors.... [The memorandum] is as it were the charter and defines the limitation of the powers of a company to be established under the Act.... [The Act] does not speak of ... incorporation as the creation of a corporation with inherent common law rights, but it speaks of the company being incorporated with reference to a memorandum of association.' (per Lord Cairns, at pp. 667–8) *Ashbury Railway Carriage and Iron Co. v. Riche* (1875) L.R. 7 H.L. 653

The legal consequences of this doctrine as it was finally established are that any ultra vires contract or activity entered into by the company is technically void, so that any rights arising under it, including payment for goods or services, are unenforceable; any property which has changed hands and can be traced may thus be recovered. In some cases this may serve the intended purpose of protecting the interests of the shareholders and creditors who have invested in or traded with the company on the basis that it is carrying on a business of a certain type. But in many the result is rather more capricious. In the first place there are the usual problems in interpreting the precise extent of a company's lawful objects, and what can properly be regarded as necessary and incidental to their performance. Secondly the rule extends not only to substantial activities which fall outside its lawful objects, such as the operation of what is deemed to be a banking business by a building society, but also to the exercise of the company's general or incidental powers for an ultra vires purpose. Thus the raising of a loan for an ultra vires purpose will in itself be ultra vires, even though the company is expressly permitted to raise loans.[4] This could result in a wholly innocent party becoming involved in ultra vires activities, especially since anyone dealing with a company is deemed to have notice of its registered memorandum and thus of its lawful objects:

> A company embarked on the manufacture of veneer panels though this was clearly ultra vires. The business failed and a supplier of coke sought to recover in the liquidation for an unpaid bill. It was held that the debt could not be recovered since the coke had been used for an ultra vires purpose, and since the supplier had notice, from the company's letterhead which referred to the veneer business, that it would be used for a purpose which was not included in its lawful objects. *In re Jon Beauforte (London) Ltd.* [1953] Ch. 131

Some of the ill-effects of this rule may be mitigated by the European Communities Act 1972, which provides that a transaction decided on by the directors of a company and entered into in good faith by a third party shall not be held to be invalid on the ground that it is outside the powers of the company or its directors, unless the third party is aware of the fact (s. 9). But the provision is narrowly drawn. Transactions by agents of the company other than its directors are not covered. And the basis of the ultra vires doctrine is not affected.

The theoretical purpose of the doctrine has also been subverted by the desire of company directors and their legal advisers to avoid its effects. It soon became standard practice for company objects to be drawn as widely as possible to cover any type of business which those in control of the company might wish to turn to, and, as in many other such cases, a running battle developed between the

[4] *Introductions Ltd.* v. *National Provincial Bank Ltd.* [1970] Ch. 199 (C.A.).

courts, which in general sought to restrict the range of permissible objects, and the legal draftsmen, who sought to extend them. Thus when the courts reacted against the practice of including a long series of specific objects by holding that some items in the list must be the main objects and the rest mere powers which could be validly exercised only in the furtherance of those main objects, the draftsmen replied with a standard clause providing that each item in the list was to be construed as an independent main object. More recently it has become common practice to include a general object clause authorizing the company to carry on any business which the directors in their discretion decide to undertake:

A building and property company's memorandum included a clause which authorized it 'to carry on any other trade whatsoever which can in the opinion of the board of directors be advantageously carried on in connection with or ancillary to the general business of the company'. A director entered into a contract with another company to help it in obtaining bridging finance for a development scheme. It was held that the contract was within the powers of the company both under the terms of the discretionary clause, as long as the directors honestly believed it to be advantageous and conducive to its main objects, and also as a transaction which was in general terms incidental and conducive to the company's main objects. *Bell Houses Ltd. v. City Wall Properties Ltd.* [1966] 2 Q.B. 656

Objects of this kind, it might be thought, effectively destroy the ultra vires doctrine, but the courts have fought back by reintroducing the idea that some items in the list of objects can only be treated as 'mere' powers to be exercised in the furtherance of the company's objects:

A company was formed with the principal object of providing facilities for tourists. The usual wide range of other objects was added, including the raising of money in any way the company should think fit. Each object was to be construed as a separate and independent object. Shortly after, the company passed into the hands of new management, and was used for the operation of a pig breeding business. The directors raised a secured loan from the company's bank for the new business, but the enterprise proved disastrous and the company failed. The liquidator sued to have the bank's claim for repayment set aside on the ground that the loan had been raised for an ultra vires purpose, which the bank well knew since it had been supplied with a copy of the company's memorandum. It was held that the loan was ultra vires: the express object providing for the raising of money could not be construed as an object standing on its own but only as a power regardless of the express provision to the contrary. *Introductions Ltd. v. National Provincial Bank Ltd.* [1970] Ch. 199

The net effect of these decisions would appear to be that a general discretionary objects clause may be relied on to validate activities which are genuinely ancillary to an explicitly authorized main business or businesses which are actually being carried out. It cannot absolve a company from the statutory obligation to set out some explicit objects in its memorandum. As stated by Harman, L. J. in the *Introductions* case, a company 'cannot have an object to do every mortal thing . . . for that is to have no object at all' (ibid., p. 209).

In more general terms it seems reasonable to conclude that the *ultra vires* rule has ceased to perform any useful commercial function. It has introduced an undesirable element of uncertainty in commercial transactions, and an unnecessary prolixity in company memoranda, without affording any real protection to the company's shareholders or creditors. The Cohen Committee recommended that the rule should be abandoned and that all companies should be granted the same legal capacity to carry out any activity as a partnership or a sole trader, leaving it to the shareholders to initiate any action they may have under the terms of the company's constitution to prevent the directors from exceeding their powers.[5]

The management of companies

Once a company has been duly formed and registered the legal requirements become a good deal less demanding. Public companies as opposed to private companies (see below p. 121) must make a statutory declaration before commencing business (1948 : s. 109) and must hold an initial 'statutory meeting' within three months of the date of that declaration (1948 : s. 130). All companies must hold an annual general meeting of shareholders (1948 : s. 131), and the directors are required to convene an extraordinary general meeting on requisition by the holders of one-tenth of the voting shares in the company (1948 : s. 132). There are detailed provisions governing the calling of meetings, the circulation of resolutions, the taking of

[5] Cmd. 6659 (1946), paras. 11–12; the position taken by the Jenkins Committee was less radical and has been broadly implemented by the European Communities Act 1972, s. 9; see Cmnd. 1749 (1962), paras. 39–42.

votes and the appointment of proxies (1948: ss. 132–46). The procedure for the registration and certification of share transfers is also laid down in some detail (1948: ss. 74–83). The provisions of the company's articles in respect of all these matters must also be observed.

Apart from these procedural requirements, the main practical effect of registration as a company is in relation to accounting and disclosure. All companies must maintain registers of current shareholdings (1948: ss. 110–11), of their directors and officers and their shareholdings and sharedealings (1948: s. 195; 1967: ss. 27–9), and of any charges or mortgages on the company's property (1948: ss. 95–106). Proper books and accounts must be maintained (1976: s. 12), and annual accounts together with a directors' report containing a wide range of additional information on the company's activities must be circulated to all shareholders (1948: ss. 156–8; 1967: ss. 15–24). Copies of these registers, accounts and reports must be filed with the Registrar of Companies and are open to inspection by members of the public.

In so far as the actual management of a company's affairs is concerned the Companies Acts have very little to say. They provide for the appointment of a Board of Directors and a Company Secretary (1948: ss. 176–7). But there is no requirement that the board should actually control the day-to-day operations of the company. The internal management structure is in theory governed by a company's articles (1948: Table A, art. 80). But there is a standard form article authorizing the directors of any company which adopts it to delegate all or any part of their powers and duties as they think fit (ibid., art. 81). There is no statutory post of managing director or executive manager, and consequently no special legal duties are imposed on such persons as may be appointed (ibid., arts. 107–9). In this respect English law is a good deal less precise than that of some other countries. The Corporations Acts of many American states make provision for a company president, and the French code for a *chef d'entreprise*, each with a number of specific statutory functions. German law, as will be seen, makes detailed provision for the allocation of responsibility on various matters between a supervisory and a managing board (see Chapter 13). Whether the British approach, that it is not for Parliament or the judges to tell the business community how it should organize its affairs, can long be maintained in the context of moves towards industrial democracy remains to be seen. The arguments for and against a measure of formalization in these matters, at least for the largest companies, will be discussed in detail in Part III.

For practical purposes, therefore, the powers and duties of the directors of British companies can only be ascertained by a detailed inspection and analysis of the articles and memorandum of the company concerned. But the effect of a breach by a director of any of these internal regulations is different from that of an ultra vires act by the company itself. The result of an act in excess of his authority by a director or officer of a company is governed by the ordinary laws of agency in so far as third parties are concerned and of contract in so far as his relations with the company and its shareholders are concerned, rather than by the public law conception of ultra vires.

In law the directors of a company are its agents, as indeed are all its employees. The authority of these agents clearly cannot exceed the powers of the company itself, and any purported action on behalf of the company outside those limits thus falls under the ultra vires doctrine. But the authority of individual directors and employees, as provided in the articles, or by internal administrative direction, may fall short of the full powers of the company. The question then arises as to the legal position when directors or employees acting on the company's behalf exceed their authority, whether intentionally or otherwise. From the point of view of the company and its shareholders there is pressure to restrict the liability of the company for such actions, while third parties will obviously seek to hold the company fully responsible for the acts of any of its appointed agents.

The compromise which has been worked out on this issue is that persons dealing with a company should be expected to ensure that any transaction they are involved in is within the company's powers, of which they are deemed to have notice from its registered memorandum, and also that it falls within the permissible powers of the directors or employees, of which they are deemed to have notice from the registered articles of association. Otherwise they should be entitled to assume that directors and other agents are in fact acting within their authority, unless they have notice to the contrary. It is thus only when the third party has express or imputed notice of some lack of authority on the part of the directors or agents that he may not hold the company liable for their actions. This is the well-known rule in *Royal British Bank v. Turquand* :

The deed of settlement of a company permitted its directors to borrow money for the company if approved by general meeting. The general meeting passed a single resolution authorizing the directors to borrow as they deemed expedient, and the defendant director later borrowed £2,000 in the company's name from the plaintiff bank. When the bank sued to recover its loan the defendant objected that no specific resolution had been passed to authorize it. The courts held the bank entitled to recover; the general resolution was quite sufficient, and in any case 'dealings with ... companies were not like dealings with other partnerships ... ; the parties dealing with them were bound to read the statute and the deed of settlement; but they were not bound to do more; the party here on reading the deed of settlement would find not a prohibition from borrowing but a permission to do so on certain conditions; finding that the authority might be made complete by a resolution, he would have the right to infer the fact of a resolution authorizing that which ... appeared to be legitimately done'. (per Jarvis C.J.) *Royal British Bank v. Turquand* (1856) 6 E & B 327

In simpler terms the third party is entitled to assume that the affairs of the company are being properly conducted within the limits set by its constitution.

The application of this apparently simple rule gave rise to considerable legal difficulty and dispute, in particular on the problems which arose when a person dealing with the company relied on representations by directors or other agents of the company that they did in fact have the requisite authority. It is fortunately not necessary to delve into the complex morass of case-law on this topic since in recent years the courts have reverted to a direct application of the ordinary rules of agency, subject only to the imputed notice of the company's constitution. The third party is thus entitled to rely on what is termed the 'ostensible' authority of the agent, that is the authority which in all the circumstances he appears to possess, except where there is reason to suspect either from the peculiar nature of the transaction itself or from a knowledge of the company's constitution or otherwise that the ostensible authority assumed by the agent does not correspond with his actual authority. For this purpose the company is bound both by the ordinary usages of the trade in question and by its past or current acquiescence in the way in which its business is carried on by its directors and managers:

A property developer formed a company in association with another person, and both were appointed directors. The articles made provision for the appointment of a managing director but none was formally appointed.

The developer on behalf of the company entered into contracts with contractors, which the company subsequently argued were ultra vires in that he had no specific authority to do so. It was held that since the making of such contracts fell within the ordinary authority of a managing director and there was power in the articles to make such an appointment, the contractors were entitled to rely on the representations of authority which the company in effect made to them by permitting the director to act for it as if he were its managing director. *Freeman & Lockyer v. Buckhurst Park Properties (Mangal) Ltd.* [1964] 2 Q.B. 480

If a company permits its directors or agents to purport to act in its name, it cannot subsequently repudiate its liability for such acts on the ground of some internal irregularity or lack of authority of which third parties are not informed.

Liquidation

The provisions for the final dissolution of a company are even more complex and detailed than those for its formation (1948: ss. 211–365). Only a brief outline of the structure of the system need be given here (see further p. 194). There are three standard forms of liquidation or winding up: those initiated by members or shareholders who for some reason may wish to cease trading and to realize the company's assets; those initiated by creditors who suspect that the company is insolvent and wish to minimize their losses by securing an immediate distribution of the available assets; and those carried out by public officials in default of effective action by anyone else.

In the case of a members' winding up the whole operation is voluntary in a real sense. A creditors' liquidation is clearly less so, even though it is carried out with the co-operation of the company and its officers. Both these forms, however, are termed 'voluntary liquidations', and both involve essentially the same procedure. A meeting of members is held at which a resolution for the dissolution of the company may be approved. Then if the directors of the company feel able to make a formal declaration of solvency, the meeting may proceed to the appointment of a liquidator; if the company is not solvent, however, the creditors must also be in attendance at the meeting and it is for them to appoint a liquidator.

The actual business of winding up the company's affairs and realizing its assets, and eventually distributing them among the creditors and members, is then left entirely to the liquidator, subject only to possible supervision by a committee of inspection appointed by the creditors. The distribution must be made in accordance with strict rules as to priority : the wages of employees up to given limits and debts to the Inland Revenue and other official bodies come first, along with secured creditors; next come ordinary unsecured creditors; any balance is payable to the members, preference shareholders being entitled to priority over ordinary shareholders if the articles of association so provide. In each case the company will finally cease to exist on the passing of a further motion for dissolution when the liquidator has completed his work.

The procedures for voluntary liquidation are clearly dependent on the co-operation of all the various interested parties, and also in a more practical sense on there being sufficient assets to pay the expenses and fees of the liquidator, who is likely to be a practising accountant. In cases where the company is totally insolvent, or where the directors and shareholders are not prepared to co-operate or have simply disappeared, some other procedure must obviously be followed if the company is to be formally dissolved. Provision is therefore made in the Companies Act for a compulsory winding up at public expense in any case in which the court makes an order to that effect on the application of any creditor or other interested party. The winding up operation is then conducted by the Official Receiver under the supervision of the court, and follows roughly the same pattern as a voluntary liquidation : the establishment of the company's obligations, the realization of its assets, and their eventual distribution in accordance with the priority rules.

Not every company which ceases to trade, however, is formally wound up. Provision is therefore made for the administrative dissolution of any defunct company which for one reason or another no one has got round to winding up. Under the Companies Acts the Registrar has power subject to certain safeguards to strike such companies off the register (1948 : s. 353). Dissolutions under this provision each year far outnumber the total for both voluntary and compulsory liquidations.

Public and private companies

Brief mention should be made of the distinction between public and private companies, though it is one of decreasing practical importance. The distinction was introduced in 1907 to take account of the growing practice of incorporating what were in effect small private businesses run by one or two owner/managers. It did not seem reasonable at that time to subject such companies to the new requirement introduced in 1900 of disclosing their annual balance sheet or later their profit and loss account. A new category of private company exempt from the full disclosure requirements was thus introduced, defined as a company in which there are fewer than fifty but at least two members, in which the right to transfer shares is limited, and which may not offer any of its shares for public subscription (1948: s. 28). Share transfer is usually restricted by the standard clause in Table A to the effect that 'the directors may in their absolute discretion and without assigning any reason therefor decline to register any transfer of any share whether or not it is a fully paid share' (Part II, art. 3), or perhaps by a right of pre-emption allowing existing shareholders to buy in the shares of any other shareholder wishing to sell his interest. The effect of such powers is clearly to allow control of the company to be retained in the hands of a family or other closed group.

A 'public' company is then any company which is not a private company. It must be formed with and maintain at least seven shareholders, and may make a public offering of shares or debentures. The importance of the public/private distinction, however, has decreased appreciably since the introduction of the requirement in 1967 that *all* limited companies regardless of their status should make full disclosure of their annual accounts. Even in respect of the maintenance of control in family companies it has little practical effect. If a family company wishes to have more than fifty members or to raise money by offering shares to the public it must convert itself into a public company. But its directors need not relinquish control over the transfer of shares or the admission of new members. It is only when a company obtains a Stock Exchange quotation that it must give up any direct method of maintaining family control. Under the EEC Second Directive, however, the status of public company will gain renewed significance (see pp. 110 and 140).

Close companies

A distinction of considerably greater importance, though it does not appear in the Companies Acts, is that created for tax purposes between 'close' and 'non-close' companies. A 'closely controlled' company is defined as one in which five or fewer persons, or their immediate relatives, control the company either through a majority shareholding or by control over the appointment of directors, though any company with more than thirty-five per cent of its shares held by the public through a stock exchange quotation is excluded. This effectively covers small family companies as well as any singly or jointly owned businesses which happen to have been incorporated. The substantive provisions of the tax statutes then penalize any such company that does not distribute the 'required standard' proportion of its earnings, which is arrived at through a combination of detailed statutory provisions and discretionary powers granted to tax inspectors. The practical effects of these provisions are complex, and will be considered in later chapters where they are of special relevance.

Other types of company

Though the company limited by shares is the most common and significant, there are a number of other types of company which should be briefly mentioned. In the first place there is no obligation on a company to seek limited liability. The Companies Acts provide equally for the creation of unlimited companies (1948 : s. 1(2)(c)). Now that all limited companies must file their annual accounts there has been a slight increase in the attraction of this form. But since such a company is subject to all the other provisions of company legislation, those who wish to avoid the publicity requirements have usually prefered to operate as simple partnerships. In the second place there is no obligation to provide for any share capital. The Act provides also for the creation of companies limited by guarantee, in which the members, instead of contributing capital in the form of shares, agree in the event of a liquidation to contribute funds up to the limit of their (1948 : s. 1(2)(b)) guarantees. These companies are commonly formed for the purposes of non-commercial associations such as clubs and societies in which there is a need for continuity in the ownership of property or assets, or for some degree of formality in internal management. There is also a wide range of other forms of commercial and non-commercial organization for which there is specific statutory provision. Banks and insurance companies, for instance, are subject both to the general Companies Acts and to specialized statutory codes. Such institutions as building societies, friendly societies, industrial and provident societies, on the other hand, are constituted on an entirely different basis under separate statutes and must register themselves with the appropriate authorities (see Chapter 10). Finally there are the nationalized corporations which are established and operated by specific legislation for each particular industry or function (see Chapter 14). It is not practicable to give a detailed account of any of these statutory codes in this context. Where particular institutions are of relevance as an alternative to the ordinary limited company the broad outlines of the statutory provisions which govern them will be given in subsequent chapters.

4 BUSINESS ACCOUNTS

Some knowledge of the techniques of business accounting is essential to an understanding of certain aspects of company law and practice. This is not just a matter of the formal statutory requirements as to the preparation of an annual balance sheet and profit and loss account and their auditing. These requirements are designed more to ensure that accounts are regularly produced in accordance with accepted accounting practice than to prescribe particular accounting standards. The development of accounting practice itself has had an important and continuing impact on the way in which company lawyers and legislators have approached certain important issues, notably the difference between capital and income and the resulting rules on capital maintenance and dividend distribution. It is also arguable that the development of the 'stewardship' system of book-keeping, which permitted a simple calculation of profit and loss in any given period and provided a means of checking the honesty of those in control of business operations of all kinds, made a substantial contribution to the development of capitalism itself.[6] The continuing importance of realistic accounting is further illustrated by the difficulties which established systems have led to in dealing with the assessment of taxable and distributable profit in a period of rapid inflation. The current proposals for a new system of current cost accounting to deal with these difficulties have a number of important implications for the law.

The development of accountancy

The essential principle of almost any accounting system is that every

[6] On the development of accounting practice see generally Baxter and Davidson, *Studies in Accounting Theory* (1964); on the interpretation of modern accounts see P. A. Bird, *The Interpretation of Published Accounts*, Centre for Administrative Studies Papers, No. 14 (1971).

transaction of the business should be recorded, first as property coming into the business and then as to how it has been applied or disposed of. Thus in the earliest formal accounts each item of capital or stock would be entered as a receipt or 'charge', and eventually accounted for by an expenditure or 'discharge'. At the end of any given period the charges and discharges could then be totalled, and any difference or balance should be represented either by a surplus of cash or stock or money owed to the business (credit balance) or by debts owed by the business (loss or deficit). This simple form of account has been termed 'charge/discharge' accounting and was a simple and direct means of checking the honesty of those running a business, and also of public officials administering public funds. It appears to have been widely used in the medieval period, both by agents administering their masters' property and in trading ventures.

From this system of charge and discharge there developed from about the fifteenth century, and even earlier in Italy, what is termed 'double-entry' accounting. There is no accepted or standard meaning for this phrase, and consequently a good deal of confusion has ensued about its impact and importance. At the simplest level it amounted to no more than the physical entering of each transaction in two forms : thus goods bought on credit would be entered in the account of stock held, and also simultaneously as a debt owed to the supplier; when the goods were sold, the stock book would then be debited, and the price received or to be received entered in the cash or debtors' account; and when the original supplier was paid the debt to him would be cancelled, and the cash account debited with the payment made. By inspecting the respective accounts it would then be possible to find out the current position at any time as to how much stock was held, and how much was owing and owed. The maintenance of books of accounts in this form, classified in accordance with the needs of the business, was clearly more convenient, efficient and flexible than a single charge/discharge account.

The profit and loss account

The real significance of the developments in the sixteenth, seventeenth and eighteenth centuries, however, at least for the law of business association, was not so much the system of double-entry book-keeping as such, but the practice of dual tabulation which it facilitated. The accounts of the business as a whole would be summarized from the individual accounts by collating them on a single sheet with credits on one side and debts on the other. This process in its turn facilitated both an assessment of the current state of the business and also the calculation of profits in any given period. For example, the capital or stock at the start of the period as recorded in the stock account might be entered at the head of one side of such an account, and all expenditure incurred during the period would be listed below; on the other side all income received during the period would be listed as well as the assets and stock remaining at the end. The performance of the business during the period could then be assessed, and any balance on the credit side could reasonably be regarded as the profit earned during the period; and conversely any deficit as a loss. Summary 'profit and loss' accounts of this kind became increasingly common, and soon became the standard form from which the profits of joint stock enterprises were assessed for the purpose of dividend payments. A balance could of course be struck at any time, but at least for joint stock companies an annual assessment of profit was normal. A simple profit and loss account for a trading company might, for example, look something like this:

Stock at start of trading period	£1,000	Stock sold during period	£1,500
Stock purchased during period	£750	Stock remaining at end of period (at cost)	£1,250
Expenses during period, wages etc.	£493		
	£2,243		£2,750
Balancing item = profit	£507		
	£2,750		

The balance sheet

Summary tabulations or 'balance sheets' could likewise be produced to show the current state of the business at any time. The amounts listed in each of the separate running accounts – cash, creditors, debtors, stock and so on – would be brought together in a single account, from which the solvency or insolvency of the business could readily be seen. And if all profits made, as calculated in a profit and loss account, were added as an item on the liability side of the account, the two sides would, or should, balance perfectly, as in the following skeleton example:

Liabilities		*Assets*	
Creditors	£343	Stock (at cost)	£1,250
Loans (long term)	£1,000	Debtors	£500
Balance from profit and loss	£507	Cash	£100
	£1,850		£1,850

The practice of striking periodic balances in this way naturally led to an increasingly clear distinction being drawn between stock or capital and current income or expenditure, a distinction of obvious importance to the capitalist system of joint stock trading. The dual tabulation system was also ideal as a means of accounting for the derivation and application of a company's capital. The capital 'borrowed' from initial and subsequent subscribers could be set on one side (liabilities) and the fixed assets or circulating stock on which it was spent on the other (assets). Debts owing to or owed by the company would be likewise entered in the respective sides of the account. And finally any profit made on current trading, and not paid out by way of dividend, would be entered as a balancing item on the liability side, as in the simple example given above. In a prosperous company it is clear that fixed and circulating assets, and debts owing to the company would exceed the amount of capital paid in and debts owed by the company, so that the balancing item to be inserted, as accumulated profit, whether from trading or the appreciation of fixed assets, would become a substantial item. Accumulated and undistributed profit of this kind in time came to be regarded as the 'reserves' of the company since it represented the net excess of the value of the company's business over the amount of capital subscribed. A typical simplified capital account or balance sheet for a joint stock manufacturing or mining company might thus look something like this:

Capital subscribed 1,000 shares at £10		£10,000	Fixed assets (at cost)		£8,000
Accumulated past undistributed profit (= reserves)		£9,500	Current assets (stock, cash etc.)		£10,000
Current period's trading profit	£1,500		Debtors	£6,000	
Less dividends	£1,000	£500	*Less* creditors:	£4,000	£2,000
		£20,000			£20,000

Historical cost accounting and company law

This brief account of the origin of the profit and loss account and the balance sheet must not be taken as an accurate historical summary. The development and the final strict differentiation between the two was a gradual and complex process. There was certainly no general agreement, even among textbook writers, on the terminology to be applied. But it is clear that by the mid-nineteenth century the two forms of account had become sufficiently well established to be incorporated into the new companies legislation of 1844–5 as an essential requirement for all registered companies. Both a balance sheet and a profit and loss account had to be prepared each year by the directors and their advisers, and copies had to be circulated to all current shareholders. Since then the techniques of preparing these accounts have been progressively refined, notably in relation to provisions for depreciation, and the legal requirements have become progressively more detailed, both in relation to the form and content of accounts (1967 : sched. 2) and in relation to procedures for auditing (see p. 137). But until 1976 there has been no change in the basic principles of historical cost accounting. The principles which that system represents have in fact become progressively embedded in the law.

This may be illustrated by a number of apparently fundamental rules of company law developed by the courts in the course of the nineteenth century. The most important of these were the strict separation of capital and income, and the related notion that the capital subscribed by shareholders to the company should at all times be maintained intact. This line of thinking is clearly encouraged by the form of balance sheet which requires that a company's capital as originally subscribed shall be entered as a permanent item on every balance sheet, and has been strengthened by the statutory rule that all money raised by the sale of any new shares at more than their nominal value must be entered in a 'share premium account' and treated as an equally permanent item (1948 : s. 56). The idea of capital maintenance has likewise been strengthened by the complicated provisions governing the reduction of capital (1948 : ss. 66–8), and the rule that a company must not either purchase or assist in the purchase of its own shares (1948 : s. 54).[7]

The rationale of capital maintenance runs something like this. In an ordinary unincorporated business any loss is normally borne by the participants, who are personally responsible for the debts of the business. In a limited liability company, however, the creditors can only look to the assets of the company itself. It is therefore important, so the argument continues, that none of the capital initially subscribed should be depleted, since it represents a fund on which the company's creditors may ultimately rely, or which the shareholders may in certain circumstances seek to recover if the enterprise is wound up.

This idea that capital shall be maintained cannot be applied in any strict sense. The capital which is put up by the shareholders has to be expended on plant and materials and other running expenses of the business, and may legitimately be lost if that business proves unprofitable, as was clearly recognized in the leading case of *Trevor v. Whitworth* :

> The distinction between a company without limit on the liability of its members and a company where the liability is limited is in the latter case to assure those dealing with the company that the whole of the subscribed capital unless diminished by expenditure upon the objects defined in the memorandum shall remain available for the discharge of its liabilities. The capital might be diminished by expenditure upon and reasonably incidental to all the objects specified. A part might be lost in carrying on the business operations authorized. Of this all persons trusting the company are aware and take the risk. But they have a right to rely and were intended by the

[7] This provision is principally directed against a particular form of abuse in take-over operations and will be dealt with in detail in that context: see below, Chapter 8.

legislature to have a right to rely on the capital remaining undiminished by any expenditure outside those limits, or by the return of any part of it to the shareholders. (per Lord Herschell) (1889) 12 App. Cas. 415

The idea was none the less used in that case as justification for a rule that a company may not purchase any of its own shares:

A company was founded to carry on a flannel business with an initial capital of £150,000. Provision was made in the articles that the company might purchase its own shares from a willing seller at a price not exceeding the market value and hold them until resale. The company failed, and a number of shareholders who had sold their shares to the company but had not been fully paid claimed for the balance due to them. Their claim was rejected on the ground that no company could be permitted to buy in its own shares since it would reduce the security relied on by other creditors of the company, and in addition evade the strict controls on the reduction of capital provided in the Companies Acts: 'If the purchase of its own shares was permitted, the creditors of a company which is being wound up, who have a right to look to the paid up capital as the fund out of which their debts are to be discharged, find coming into competition with them persons who in respect only of their having been and having ceased to be shareholders in the company claim that the company shall pay to them part of that capital.' (per Lord Herschell, at p. 414) *Trevor v. Whitworth* (1887) 12 App. Cas. 409

The result of this is that specific statutory authority was subsequently required to permit companies to buy shares for their employees (1948: s. 54).

The ideal of capital maintenance has also given rise to an explicit rule of law that dividends must not be paid except out of profits. If this were permitted, it was argued, a company might run down its capital assets by continuing to make dividend distributions until there was nothing left. The payment of dividends out of capital was in fact formally prohibited in the Companies Act 1845, some time before the introduction of limited liability. Though this explicit prohibition was subsequently repealed, it was renewed in substance by an article in the model articles of association provided in the consolidating legislation of 1862 and re-enacted in each subsequent consolidation to the effect that 'no dividend shall be paid otherwise than out of profit' (1948: Table A, art. 116).

It is one thing to enact a simple rule to this effect and quite another to ensure that its objective is achieved. During the latter part of the nineteenth century directors in many companies made a point of building up secret or semi-secret reserves in order to be able to declare a regular dividend even in bad years. This practice was justified by the argument that the rule did not prevent the payment of dividends out of profits earned in a previous period. There was an even more difficult problem over wasting assets. If a company invested its capital in a mine or machinery or in a fixed term lease of property, all of which would in time lose their initial value through exhaustion or expiration, was it required to make provision for the replacement of those assets before declaring a dividend on current operating profits? Accountants had developed the technique of annual depreciation to deal with this problem, but the courts were not prepared to hold that a failure to make provision for depreciation represented a breach of the 'no dividend except out of profits' rule:

A company was formed to acquire and operate a number of mining concessions. The enterprise was sufficiently successful to pay a fairly regular dividend for five years but in the following year the proposed dividend was contested on the ground that insufficient provision for depreciation was being made. The trial judge refused to intervene, holding that 'so long as the capital remained intact and the current receipts exceeded the current expenditure ... it rested entirely with the shareholders to decide whether the excess should be divided among them or set aside as a reserve fund for replacing wasting assets'. (per Stirling J., at p. 10) This was upheld by the Court of Appeal: 'There was nothing whatever in the [Companies Acts] to prevent any excess of money obtained by working the property over the cost of working it from being divided among the shareholders; that was true although some part of the property itself was sold, and in some sense the capital thereby diminished; if it were said that such a course involved the payment of dividends out of capital the answer was that the Act nowhere forbade such a payment ... If you treated it as an abstract proposition that no dividend could properly be paid out of moneys arising from the sale of property you would find yourself landed in consequences which the common sense of mankind would shrink from accepting.' (per Lindley L.J., at p. 24) *Lee v. Neuchatel Asphalte Co.* (1889) 41 Ch. D. 1

The judges were equally reluctant to impose any binding rule on the related issue of accumulated deficits. They held that there was no legal obligation to make good capital which had been depleted by accumulated deficits in the past before paying a dividend out of profits in a new accounting period:

A mining company made a loss of some £19,000 over its first three years' operation. The directors then decided to go public, and in order to offset the deficit revalued the mining concession at some £16,000 above the original purchase price. On the basis of this unrealized profit a dividend was paid on the newly created preference shares. The company was then taken over and the legitimacy of the dividend payment questioned. The court refused to intervene: 'The Companies Acts did not impose any obligation on a limited company ... that it should not distribute as dividend the clear net profit of its trading unless its paid up capital was intact or until it had made good all losses incurred in previous years'; even if the directors had not revalued, there would have been no need to hold up payments of dividends out of current receipts. (per Swinfen Eady L.J., at p. 283) *Ammonia Soda Co. v. Chamberlain* [1918] 1 Ch. 266

More recently the courts refused to intervene to prevent a capital distribution based on an unrealized revaluation:

A company sought an opinion as to whether it was entitled to make a capitalization issue to its shareholders from reserves created by an unrealized revaluation of assets. The court could find no legal objection to such a distribution of a surplus resulting from a valuation in good faith by a competent valuer; though it might not in many cases be a wise commercial practice, there were no grounds for saying it would be illegal. *Dimbula Valley (Ceylon) Tea Co. Ltd. v. Laurie* [1961] 1 Ch. 353

The precise details of these examples are not in themselves important. But they show clearly that the practical effect of the 'no dividend except out of profits' rule in relation to the maintenance of capital is negligible. The calculation of net distributable profit for an accounting period is so much a matter of choice, depending on subjective decisions on the rate of depreciation, if any, and on levels of valuation, that there will seldom be any *legal* impediment to the declaration of a dividend out of available resources, though there will often be compelling commercial reasons for not doing so. The judges have in practice been more than content to leave all these matters to the judgement of directors and their accountants. Despite the constant reiteration of the capital maintenance rule, the actual decisions of the courts amount to little more than an application of the ultra vires rule, and, in relation to dividends, to a requirement of honesty and good faith in accounting. This was clearly stated by Lindley L. J. in the *Neuchatel* case: what is really meant by the dividend rule is 'that you must not have fictitious accounts; if your earnings are less than your current expenses you must not cook your accounts so as to make it appear that you are earning a profit . . .' (ibid., at p. 25).

Historic cost accounting has given rise to difficulties of a more practical kind. One of these is the fact that a balance sheet compiled on historic cost principles gives a highly misleading picture of the real current value of a company's assets. This defect is readily admitted by the accountancy profession :

> The primary purpose of the annual accounts of a business is to present information to the proprietors showing how their funds have been utilized and the profits derived from such use. It has long been accepted in accounting practice that a balance sheet prepared for this purpose is an historic record and not a statement of current worth. *Institute of Chartered Accountants in England and Wales: Recommendations on Accounting Principles, 1960*

Other users of company accounts have not always been so clear about the inadequacy of the system. Modern investment analysis of the return on capital employed as a guide to the relative merits of various companies has all too often relied on balance sheet figures without taking into account the fact that capital recently subscribed or assets recently purchased cannot sensibly be regarded in the same light as earlier subscriptions or purchases. Unless the measure of capital employed is standardized at a given date for all companies, any comparative analysis of the return on capital is likely to be highly misleading as a guide to the efficiency of management. For this reason most investment analysts have increasingly turned their attention to a measure of earnings in relation to the stock market valuation of a company's shares, known as the price/earnings ratio. But even this is likely to give a distorted picture of managerial performance given the fluctuating character of stock market prices (see Chapter 2).

The final blow to historic cost accounting has been the rapid increase in inflation in the 1970s. This has highlighted the irrelevance of historic costs as a guide to the current value of fixed assets. But the real problem has been the assessment of true profit. If there is a substantial increase in the cost of raw materials and other current outgoings from year to year the application of traditional cost price accounting rules may result in the profit on stock and work in progress being grossly exaggerated. Much if not all the apparent profit on the eventual sale of these goods must be used in the purchase of new raw materials at greatly increased prices if the business is to be maintained. There is a similar problem over the traditional practice of providing for depreciation by allowing a percentage of the historic cost of plant and machinery against each year's trading receipts. If the real cost of replacement is much higher than the original purchase price, it is clear that the amount of annual depreciation should be based on anticipated replacement costs rather than historic costs. The net result of these and other related problems was that in the early 1970s many companies were declaring and being taxed on profits which had not really been made at all. Some began to experience severe cash flow problems.

The first reaction to this developing liquidity crisis in British companies, as is usual in such matters, was an alteration in the rules for taxation. The Finance Act 1975 granted a special allowance in respect of stock appreciation to all but very small companies, so that tax would not have to be paid immediately on the so-called 'holding gains' on stock and work in progress caused by cost price valuation (s. 18). This was subsequently extended to all companies (Finance (No. 2) Act 1975, s. 54), and has been continued from year to year. But short-term expedients of this kind merely emphasized the need for a new system of accounting which took account of inflation. The Sandilands Committee on Inflation Accounting was appointed in 1974 to consider 'whether, and if so how, companies should allow for changes ... in costs and prices having regard to established accounting conventions based on historic costs'. In its report in 1975 the Committee recommended that historic cost accounting principles should be abandoned and replaced by a new system of current cost accounting.[8] The basis of their argument was summarized as follows:

> When costs and prices are increasing as rapidly as they have done in recent years, companies must ensure that their accounts show the effect of such increases on their financial position and their results, for the benefit of anyone using the accounts. Companies themselves also need to be aware of the effects of such increases on their position in order that management may take appropriate action. However, the realization has grown in recent years that conventional accounting practices do not lead to the effects of such increases in costs and prices being shown in a satisfactory way in companies' accounts. The apparent picture of a company's performance given by existing accounting conventions is often misleading and the ability

[8] *Report of the Inflation Accounting Committee*, Cmnd. 6225 (1975).

to compare the performance of different companies in a useful way, which is important for the investor and the investment analyst and therefore for the allocation of national resources is significantly impaired.[9]

The essence of the Committee's proposals was that any item of stock and any part of a company's fixed assets which would have to be replaced in the ordinary course of business should be valued at current replacement costs for the purpose of arriving at a figure for trading profit. In addition a clear distinction should be made in all accounts between 'operating gains' which was the best measure of real profit, 'holding gains', which might be realized or unrealized but in either case should not be regarded as profit, and 'extraordinary gains', which did not form part of the company's regular output. Finally the Committee recommended that all items in a company's balance sheet should be valued on the basis of their 'value to the business' at the date of the balance sheet, which in most cases would be its replacement cost.

These proposals have now been accepted in principle by the Accounting Standards Committee of the Institute of Chartered Accountants, and are to be implemented on a phased basis beginning with the largest companies from 1978 and smaller companies in 1979 and 1980.[10] There are a number of unresolved problems in the new system, particularly in relation to the treatment of monetary balances and deferred taxation. But the basic foundation of current cost accounting, that 'in arriving at profit the charge against income for stocks consumed and fixed assets used is based on current replacement costs and not on out-of-date and irrelevant historical costs', has been approved for immediate use in compiling all management control figures. In addition the directors of all companies using the new system are to produce for each year, in addition to a balance sheet and profit and loss account on a current cost basis, two new statements: an *appropriation account* and a *statement of shareholders' net equity interest*. The first of these is intended to show what proportion of current cost profit and holding gains the directors consider should be retained in the business having regard to their assessment of its needs; the second is intended to show the net increase or decrease in the net worth of the company from the point

[9] *Inflation Accounting: A Brief Guide to the Report of the Inflation Accounting Committee*, H.M.S.O. (1975), p. 2.

[10] *Exposure Draft 18: Current Cost Accounting*, December 1976.

of view of its shareholders, after allowing for changes in the value of money. In simple outline these might appear as follows:

Appropriation account

Current cost profit/loss for the year		£1,500
Net surplus for year on revaluation of assets	£1,000	
Less transferred to revaluation reserve for retention having regard to the directors' assessment of the needs of the business	£1,200	(£200)
Available for distribution/reinvestment		£1,300
Less dividend for year		£300
Added to general reserve		£1,000

Statement of shareholders' net equity interest

Net equity interest at start of year	£10,000
New equity capital introduced during year	£1,000
	£11,000
Amount required to compensate for the change in the value of money during year	£2,000
	£13,000
Net equity interest at end of year	£12,000
Net decrease during year	£1,000
Dividend for year	£300
Net decrease after dividend	£1,300

The figures in these examples have been chosen deliberately to illustrate how increasing inflation may affect a company's finances even when its accounts are prepared on current cost principles. In the sample appropriation account, for instance, the apparent profitability of the business has been somewhat reduced since the surplus arising from revaluation of fixed assets is somewhat less than the directors' estimate of what will eventually be necessary to maintain the business; similarly in the statement of shareholders' net equity interest the apparent increase in the overall net worth of the business has been somewhat less than the general rate of inflation. The examples also illustrate the extent to which a company's annual accounts under the new system will shift from the traditional analysis of actual transactions and become dependent on a subjective assessment of current values and future needs. This is recognized by the Accounting Standards Committee: 'It has been argued that current cost accounting will increase the degree of subjectivity in annual accounts; if this is so, then this is part of the price that has to be paid to make accounts more relevant in a period of rapidly changing costs.'[11]

There are a number of more general implications of the switch to this new form of accounting. In the first place it highlights the extent to which the concept of the maintenance of capital is a relative rather than an absolute conception, in that it is ultimately a matter for the company's directors and their shareholders whether they wish to maintain the company's business at any particular level. It also adds to the arguments in favour of the introduction of 'no par value' shares, since under the new form of accounting the historic contribution of the shareholders is as irrelevant and misleading as the historic cost of the company's assets. Finally and perhaps most important it demonstrates the extent to which all forms of accounts are a matter of choice, and in so doing opens the question whether the form which is now being proposed is the most appropriate for the various purposes for which accounts may be prepared in businesses of different types and sizes. This point will be discussed at greater length in subsequent chapters in the sections dealing with accounting for creditors in small businesses, and accounting for employees and trade unions in the context of collective bargaining and industrial democracy.

The company auditor

The development of company audit was closely linked with the development of accounting practice. In the original companies legislation provision was made for certain shareholders to be appointed as auditors to check on the accuracy of the annual accounts on behalf of their colleagues. It was also permissible, and as the complexity of accounting methods increased it became increasingly common, for professional accountants to be appointed for this

[11] Ibid., para. 9.

purpose. The status of the auditor as an external and professional agent of the shareholders was then gradually strengthened in successive Companies Acts and his legal duties progressively more tightly defined. Originally an auditor was required to do little more than see to the actual production and circulation of the annual accounts. But as the nineteenth century progressed his duty to conform to professional standards of care and skill was accepted by the courts. This did not extend, however, to a duty to guarantee the accuracy of the accounts:

> The payment of dividends by a company was contested by its liquidator on the grounds that the company's accounts had grossly overstated the value of its current stock in trade. Proceedings were initiated against the company's auditor who had signed the accounts on the ground that he had negligently failed to check the accuracy of the figures which had been given to him by the manager of the company. It was held in the circumstances that the auditor had not been negligent in failing to check the manager's honesty: 'It is the duty of an auditor to bring to bear on the work he has to perform that skill, care and caution which a reasonably competent, careful and cautious auditor would use.... An auditor is not bound to be a detective or ... to approach his work with suspicion or with a foregone conclusion that there is something wrong. He is a watchdog but not a bloodhound.' (per Lopes L.J., at p. 288) *In re Kingston Cotton Mill Co.* (No. 2) [1896] 2 Ch. 279

In practical terms the auditor continued to be largely dependent on the board of directors and the internal management of the company.[12]

Since then the independent status of the company auditor has been progressively strengthened. He now has the right to attend any general meeting of the company and to address those present on any matter within his responsibilities (1948: s. 162; replaced by 1967: s. 14). The appointment of an auditor must be considered each year at the annual general meeting (1948: s. 159), and any retiring auditor who is not proposed for reappointment has a right to make representations to the shareholders in writing (1948: s. 160). Under the Companies Act 1948 the auditor was required to make a formal report on whether proper books of account had been kept by the company, and whether the accounts gave a true and fair view

[12] On developments on the legal position of the auditor see R. Baxt, 'The Modern Company Auditor: A Nineteenth Century Watchdog' (1970) 33 *Modern Law Review* 413.

of the company's affairs (1948 : s. 162 and sched. 9). Under the Companies Act 1967 the auditor is now required to state positively if adequate books and records have not been maintained or if he has not been able to obtain from the directors all the information necessary to a proper audit (1967 : s. 14). Under the Companies Act 1976 an auditor may not resign his position without making a formal statement of any circumstances which he considers should be brought to the notice of shareholders or creditors (1976 : s. 15), and he is given the right to requisition an extraordinary general meeting and to circulate any statement to the company's shareholders (1976 : s. 16).

There has also been a progressive tightening of the professional standards expected of an auditor in carrying out his duties. A recognized professional qualification is now required except for those who were established as auditors in 1967 (1967 : s. 13), and no new individual authorizations are to be given to persons who do not belong to a recognized professional body (1976 : s. 13). And it has been established that an auditor must carry out all those checks and sample verifications which are accepted as good current professional practice :

> The managing director of a private manufacturing company consistently falsified the company's internal books of account by manipulating the amount, the value, and the dates of the receipt and disposal of stock. The company's auditors noticed some alterations on stock invoices, but as they trusted the manager implicitly they accepted his explanations without further question. On a suit by the liquidator on the eventual failure of the company it was held that the auditors had been negligent and were liable to make good the amount of the dividends which had been paid out in reliance on the inaccurate accounts which they had audited and approved. The decision in *Re Kingston Cotton Mills* in which it was stated that an auditor was entitled to rely on the stock valuations and accounts provided by the company was not followed on the ground that 'the standards of reasonable care and skill were upon the expert evidence more exacting today than those which prevailed in 1896'. (per Pennycuick J., at p. 475)
> *In re Thomas Gerrard & Son Ltd.* [1968] Ch. 455

This does not mean that the auditor as an outsider must guarantee the accuracy of all the figures produced. That is the primary duty of the company's directors and accounting staff. But the role of the auditor has clearly been extended from that of the mere watchdog on behalf of his fellow shareholders to that of an independent professional agent with duties both to the shareholders and creditors of the company, and in the case of quoted companies to the investing public at large.

EEC accounting regulations

Further developments in accounting and auditing practice will soon be required under the programme for the harmonization of company law within the EEC.[13] Under the amended Second Directive, adopted in December 1976, new controls on the maintenance of a minimum capital by public companies for the protection of creditors must be introduced in all member states by 1978–9. All public companies in Britain will be required to have a minimum capital of at least 25,000 units of account (some £10,000), of which at least one quarter must be paid up (arts. 6–9); this capital may be raised in shares either of a fixed nominal value or with merely an 'accountable par value', but no distribution or dividend to shareholders will be permitted which would reduce the assets representing the capital to less than the amount currently paid up (art. 15). Where there has been a serious loss of capital, which may not be defined as less than one half, a general meeting of shareholders will have to be called to consider the winding up of the company or other measures to remedy the situation (art. 17). There are also directives on the regulation of the purchase by a company of its own shares where that is permitted by the laws of member states (arts. 18–24). These directives will clearly require new legislation in Britain and will give new impetus to the old nineteenth-century rules on capital maintenance. But it is unclear how the problems of wasting assets, depreciation and legitimate trading losses, which minimized the practical effect of those rules, are to be dealt with or what will happen if the general meeting of shareholders decides to do nothing to remedy a serious loss of capital. Unless the draft Fourth and Seventh Directives on accounting practice for public and private companies and for groups of companies, which are currently under discussion, make current cost valuations obligatory, the search for effective capital maintenance may well prove as elusive as in the past.

[13] See generally C. Schmitthoff (ed.), *The Harmonization of European Company Law* (1973) and *European Company Law Texts* (1974); the original draft directives applied to all limited companies in Britain and Ireland, but private companies have now been excluded.

4
The small private business

The small private business, for the purposes of this chapter, may be taken to include any commercial undertaking in which all the participants are directly and personally involved as owners and managers. The formal status of the undertaking is not the primary defining characteristic. The essential legal problems which arise in such undertakings, the basis of association, the means of financing, internal organization and management, and relations with external creditors and the tax authorities, apply alike to companies and partnerships and to a lesser extent sole traders, and cannot be adequately dealt with by concentrating on any one of these. One of the main legal issues facing small businessmen in a practical sense is in fact the choice of the most convenient and appropriate formal status for their business.

The main possibilities and their respective legal consequences will be discussed under a number of general headings : first the internal structure and organization of the enterprise, covering the legal and practical effects of incorporation and limited liability, the formal basis of association and the rights of the participators among themselves, and the various methods of raising finance; and secondly the external relations of the enterprise, covering the rights and interests of creditors, the various statutory disclosure requirements, and finally taxation. Some conclusions on the relative advantages of the existing range of legal forms and on the possibility of developing a new statutory framework specifically designed to meet the needs of the small business will then be drawn.

I THE LEGAL EFFECTS OF INCORPORATION

The basic distinction in legal theory between a registered company and other forms of business is the fact of incorporation. A company is a legal entity distinct from its members, which may own its own property and sue, or be sued, to enforce its legal rights. Persons dealing with it must therefore look to the company as such for the settlement of its obligations rather than to its members or officers. A partnership on the other hand is legally no more than an aggregation of individuals trading together, and though there are important legal rules and provisions as to the rights and liabilities of partners between themselves, in so far as concerns the obligation of the business to outsiders they are for most purposes in the same position as an individual trading on his own sole account. The rights and liabilities both of partners and of sole traders are essentially personal.

The practical effects of incorporation, however, are a good deal less far-reaching than might be expected. The special rights of a company, its permanence and its technically complete separation from its members and officers can usually be simulated within the partnership form at least for everyday purposes. These special rights are not, in any case, of supreme importance to the typical small businessman. Even the limited liability currently afforded to registered companies, though as will be seen this is not a necessary incident of corporate personality, may be more apparent than real since the banks and other major creditors of a small business are likely to insist on a personal guarantee from those concerned. The fact that tax liability is assessed on a different basis for companies and other businesses is likely to be of considerably more concern to him since it directly affects his personal income from the business. The decision whether to form a company thus depends on a number of conflicting considerations.

Corporate personality

Even the strictly legal effects of corporate personality are often unclear, if only because the courts have not found it easy to maintain a consistent approach in the various situations in which the doctrine has been raised. In most cases the company will be regarded as entirely distinct from its members regardless of the consequences. But the fact of incorporation may be ignored where it impedes the due enforcement of the law.

The prime example of the strict application of the doctrine of corporate personality is the formation of a one-man company and the repudiation of personal liability. The rules for incorporation, as we have seen, stipulate that in a private company there must always be at least two members. But this does not prevent a single person from being in effective ownership and control over the whole of the company's business and assets, since the second member may be granted only a single share as a nominee merely to observe the statutory requirements. The result is a one-man company in all but the name. The question is whether the transactions of such a company can really be regarded as distinguishable from those of the sole controller, and in particular whether it is legitimate for him to use the corporate form to limit his own personal liability.

There was considerable argument and dispute over this issue in the latter part of the nineteenth century, culminating in a decision by the House of Lords that the doctrine of the separate legal identity of the company must prevail over what might otherwise appear to be the equitable solution :

Salomon ran a small business as a leather merchant on his own account. He then formed a limited company in which he himself took up 20,001 shares and his wife and children one share each, making 20,007 in all. The company then paid Salomon £39,000 for the business, settled in part by the issue of the ordinary shares and for the rest by the issue of a debenture secured on a floating charge on the business. The company failed through factors outside Salomon's control, leaving debts of some £77,000. Meantime the debenture had been transferred to a Mr Broderip in return for a loan of £5,000 to Salomon. On the liquidation of the company Broderip claimed priority as a secured creditor over the trade creditors. The liquidator's objection to this on behalf of the trade creditors was upheld in the Court of Appeal on the ground that the creation of the company was no more than 'a scheme to enable Salomon to carry on business with limited liability contrary to the true intent of the Companies Acts'. The House of Lords reversed this decision and held that in the absence of fraud the separate identity of the company must be respected: it 'was impossible to dispute that once the company was legally incorporated it must be treated like any other independent person with its rights and liabilities appropriate to itself, and that the motives of those who took part in the promotion of the company were absolutely irrelevant in discussing what those rights and liabilities were.' (per Lord Halsbury at p. 30) *Salomon v. Salomon & Co.* [1897] A.C. 22

This principle still operates to deny what ordinary people might think to be the due rights of traders:

A firm of yacht outfitters sold a new steering system to a Mr Smith. The written order for the goods, however, was made out in the name of Smith's company, Ocean Charters Ltd., in which only two shares of £1 each had been issued. When the company failed to pay, the firm sued Smith personally. The action failed: the truth of the matter was that the plaintiffs quite clearly accepted Ocean Charters as their customer . . . without making any inquiry as to its status or financial responsibility; they could not then claim payment from Smith. *Henry Brown & Sons v. Smith* [1964] 2 Lloyds List 476

The practical effects of corporate personality are not limited to the question of limited liability. Self-incorporation may also be adopted for tax purposes. An individual writer or film star may find it beneficial to create a one-man company and pay tax both as a company and as the sole effective shareholder and director. As long as the requisite formalities are complied with the law will regard the company as entirely distinct from its *alter ego*.

The legal consequences of corporate personality, however, are not always beneficial to the controlling shareholders and directors of small companies and may be entirely unpredicted. Self-incorporation, for example, may operate to deny a landlord his expected rights under the business tenancies legislation. In *Tunstall v. Steigman* (1962) (see p. 111), for instance, a landlord's decision to incorporate her business operated as a bar to her recovery under the business tenancies legislation of premises let to another trader for the expansion of her business; her personal requirements for the purposes of the statute were held not to include the requirements of her wholly owned company. And in a Northern Irish case it has been held that the owner of virtually all the shares in a company has no insurable interest in that company's property:

The plaintiff sold his timber estates to a company of which he was the sole beneficial owner, and which owed him a considerable sum of money. To protect his position the plaintiff insured the timber on the estates, and when it was destroyed by fire sued on the policy. It was held that neither as a shareholder nor as a creditor of the company could he have any insurable interest in the company's assets: as one judge put it neither his shares nor his debt were exposed to the risk of fire. *Macaura v. Northern Assurance Co.* [1925] A.C. 619

Further problems are created by the fact that the doctrine of corporate personality is not always strictly applied. The corporate veil, to use the traditional terminology, is occasionally pierced to reveal the business reality behind. In some instances there is statutory authority for this, as where those in effective control of a company's affairs may be made legally liable to its creditors under the fraudulent trading provisions of the Companies Act (see p. 204). In others the courts have developed their own exceptions to the rule. They have refused, for instance, to allow a director to be convicted of conspiring with his own one-man company, though for normal purposes a company may be convicted of criminal conspiracy:

The director of a one-man company was charged with conspiring with the company to defraud investors by representing that the company was a genuine and honest concern. There were a number of other charges against the director. The court rejected the conspiracy counts on the ground that 'where the sole responsible person in the company is the defendant himself, it would not be right to say that there were two persons or two minds', as required for a conviction of conspiracy. *Reg. v. McDonnell* [1966] 1 Q.B. 233

And in what are termed the 'quasi-partnership' cases the courts have sometimes applied the law relating to partnerships in apparent preference to that relating to companies on the ground that it is more equitable to do so. As one judge put it in the leading case on the point: 'Ought not precisely the same principles (as in a partnership) apply to a case like this where in substance it is a partnership in the form and guise of a private company?'[1] Finally there are a number of situations in which for tax purposes the courts will look behind the corporate façade: the place of incorporation of a company, for instance, will not necessarily be accepted as its place of business.[2]

It is not easy therefore to give any precise indication of the cases in which the doctrine of corporate personality will be strictly applied and those in which it may be subordinated to a more realistic approach. The most acceptable formulation of the law is perhaps that the doctrine is likely to be strictly adhered to regardless of the beneficial or detrimental effect on those concerned except where to do so would be (i) to frustrate the purpose of a particular legislative

[1] *In re Yenidje Tobacco Co. Ltd.* [1916] 2 Ch. 426, see below p. 157.

[2] *De Beers Consolidated Mines Ltd.* v. *Howe* [1906] A.C. 455.

enactment, or (ii) to permit those concerned to take fraudulent or improper advantage of the doctrine. The tax cases are probably the best examples of the application of this first head, but it may also be applied to any form of regulatory legislation. Thus it was held that a company could not evade regulations imposed on foreign companies by setting up a purely formal subsidiary in Britain:

An American film company sought to secure preferential treatment for a new film in Britain by registering it as a British production. It set up a British subsidiary company which formally contracted to make and market the film, but the company had no place of business apart from its registered office and employed no staff. The Board of Trade refused to register the film as British made on the ground that it had in effect been made by the American company. This was upheld: the intervention of the British company was 'purely colourable' in that it had been brought into existence 'for the sole purpose of being put forward as having undertaken the very elaborate arrangements necessary for the making of the film and enabling it to qualify as a British film'. *In re F G Films Ltd.* [1953] 1 W.L.R. 483

The second head, in so far as it differs from the first, may be illustrated by a case in which a company was set up with the sole object of evading a pre-existing legal obligation:

The defendant had contracted to sell freehold property to the plaintiff, but before completion decided that it would be more profitable to break the contract of sale and pay damages. In order to frustrate the courts in making any order of specific performance he registered a new private company of which he and his solicitor's clerk were the sole shareholders and directors, and conveyed the property to the company. It was held that the company was 'the creature of the defendant, a device and a sham, a mask ... to avoid recognition in the eye of equity'; specific performance of the contract of sale was granted both against the defendant and the company. *Jones v. Lipman* [1962] 1 W.L.R. 832

Any theoretical dispute about corporate criminality may also be dissolved under this general theme of legislative purpose.[3] In so far as a criminal statute is directed at the prevention of activities in which a company may engage, there is no reason at all why the company, in addition to those involved in it, should not be liable to criminal punishment. It is the company as such which benefits from any financial profit or saving which results either from a fraud

[3] See generally L. Leigh, *The Criminal Liability of Corporations in English Law* (1969).

committed through it, or from a contravention of any regulatory statute. If no financial penalty is imposed there is little reason for the company as an organization to be concerned to secure compliance, as for instance in the fencing of dangerous machinery or the submission of fully accurate tax returns. The real issue in such cases is not the proper extent of the doctrine of corporate personality but the more down-to-earth one of law enforcement.

The net effect of the doctrine of corporate personality in practical terms then is that a business will generally be expected to adhere to its choice of status and accept the conseqences of that choice, subject to the two broad exceptions in cases of fraud or the deliberate evasion of statutory regulations. In *Tunstall v. Steigman* (see p. 111), for example, since the landlord could easily have so arranged her affairs as to take advantage of the business tenancies legislation, she could not expect a special exception to be made in her favour. The actual application of these principles may be a matter of some difficulty, but the conception of legislative purpose and the distinction between positive regulation and prohibition and permissive measures will perhaps provide the best guide to the decisions of the courts. The apparent exception in the case of quasi-partnerships can readily be fitted into the picture. In these cases, as will be argued below, the courts are merely exercising their statutory discretion on what is just and equitable for the purposes of winding up or on what is oppression for the purposes of s. 210 in the light of the peculiar nature of the small one-man or two-man company (see p. 156).

The ultra vires rule in practice

There is a similar lack of precision and certainty over the practical effect of the ultra vires rule (see Chapter 3). Both incorporated companies and partnerships are legally constituted by means of a contractual settlement between the various parties concerned. The memorandum and articles of a company and the deed of a partnership are merely the formal expression of this contract, setting out the terms on which the business association is to be carried on. Any activity or transaction which is not contemplated in this contract is thus technically beyond the scope of the company or partnership, and accordingly of any person acting on its behalf.

In the case of a partnership this is of little direct concern to anyone other than the partners themselves. Since a partnership is no more than an association of individuals it may in law carry through any transaction which an individual may carry through, whether or not it is expressly or impliedly contemplated in the deed of partnership. The position of third parties in respect of acts by partners outside the scope of the partnership is thus governed by the ordinary rules of agency and notice. The firm, and thus each partner, is liable in respect of any transaction within the normal scope of the firm's business, unless the third party has notice that the transaction is not authorized (Partnership Act 1890 : s. 5). Similar rules are applied in the case of acts by employees and agents of the partnership.

In the case of a company, on the other hand, the independent legal status of the undertaking is given effect by the rule that it may only do what is specified in its memorandum of association. Any contract entered into by the company which exceeds these stated objects and powers is accordingly legally void. And any third party who suffers as a result is considered to have only himself to blame since the terms of the company's memorandum are open to public inspection.

The practical effect of this legal distinction, however, is much reduced by the fact that most modern company memoranda are drawn so widely by the proliferation of objects clauses as to permit the company to carry on virtually any honest business activity which its directors or shareholders wish to embark on. Furthermore as an additional safeguard against the ultra vires doctrine it has become common practice in recent years to insert a general discretionary clause to the effect that the company may carry on any activity which its directors consider may be profitably combined with its existing operations.[4] As long as the main business or businesses of the company are being duly carried out and the other activities are genuinely incidental to or combined with them clauses of this kind are perfectly valid.[5]

The practical effect of the ultra vires rule in so far as third parties are concerned has been further reduced by the provisions of the European Communities Act 1972 under which any person acting in good faith may rely on the capacity of the directors of the company to enter into any transaction and is not obliged to inspect the memorandum and articles for that purpose (s. 9) (see p. 114). This measure was adopted to comply with the First Directive on the

[4] *Bell Houses Ltd. v. City Wall Properties Ltd.* [1966] 2 Q.B. 656 (see p. 115).
[5] *Introductions Ltd. v. National Provincial Bank Ltd.* [1970] Ch. 199. (See p. 115).

harmonization of company law, but is broadly in line with the recommendations of the Jenkins Committee.[6] It does not abolish the ultra vires rule. It may still operate to the detriment of creditors where they have actual notice of the terms of a company's constitution, as for instance will normally be the case in a company's dealings with its bankers. In such cases the old rules will apply to prevent creditors recovering loans or payment for goods and services for an ultra vires purpose. For most purposes the resulting position will be the same for limited companies under the new Act and for partnerships under the ordinary rules of agency. But the formal invalidity of ultra vires transactions may still result in untoward and unexpected legal consequences. It would be simpler to adopt the recommendation of the Cohen Committee and abolish the rule altogether.[7] This would mean that both companies and partnerships would have the same unrestricted legal capacity, and that in each any interested party would have the same legal remedies by way of injunction or a suit in damages to prevent the breach of any internal contractual provision.[8]

Limited liability

A more important consideration than these technical issues is likely to be that of limited liability. This is not a necessary incident of incorporation. The Companies Acts make provision for the registration of unlimited companies with or without share capital which are in every other respect identical to limited companies (1948: s. 1(2)(c)). But the choice of this form was uncommon before 1967 when corporate status without limited liability was made somewhat more attractive as a means of avoiding the new requirement that all limited companies should disclose their annual accounts. In 1968 some two thousand companies took advantage of the new procedure for reregistration as unlimited companies (1967 : s. 43). But since then the number of new or existing companies registering as unlimited has dropped to little more than one hundred per year; the total number of unlimited companies in 1975 was still less than five thousand.

The availability of limited liability is usually regarded as one of the major benefits of incorporation for the small trader, who is

[6] Cmnd. 1749 (1962), paras. 39–42.
[7] Cmd. 6659 (1945), paras. 11–12.
[8] See for instance the American Model Business Corporation Act (s. 6).

thereby enabled to initiate or expand a business undertaking without jeopardizing the whole of his personal fortune and livelihood and the future of his family, and in addition to raise capital from others in exchange for a share of the profits without exposing them to the same risk.

For the smallest companies, however, the benefits are less far-reaching than might be supposed. Quite apart from the moral pressures on him to meet his obligations, if only as a means to maintain his credit in the commercial community, the small trader will find that most bank managers and some other major creditors of his business will require his personal guarantee for any overdraft or substantial loan to the company, unless the company itself has sufficient unencumbered assets of its own by way of security. He may also be required to grant a charge on his personal dwelling or place of business if that is not already in the hands of the company. The net effect is often that the limitation of liability extends only to the ordinary trade creditors of the business, and that the personal assets of the directors are as fully committed as they would be in an unincorporated business.

In this sense the institution of limited liability for the smallest participatory or partnership companies is as much a mechanism for the preferment of banks and other financial institutions to ordinary trade creditors as for the protection of the small businessman. This does not mean that a careful trader may not benefit from it in the event of the failure of a business enterprise from unforeseen circumstances, or that unscrupulous or fraudulent traders may not take advantage of it, as will be seen later. But in the typical case the principal directors of the small incorporated business will find it difficult to maintain the complete separation of their personal and business assets which the law permits. Limited liability is a complete protection for the owners and managers of trading companies only when the enterprise has established its own credit in the commercial community apart from that of its principal directors.

Administrative considerations

Though the strictly legal incidents of corporate personality and the ultra vires rule may not be of great practical significance to the small business, there are a number of important considerations on a practical administrative level which may affect the decision whether or not to incorporate. In the first place an incorporated business has a degree of permanency which cannot easily be attained through any form of unincorporated partnership association. Provision may be made in partnership deeds for the property of the firm to be held by trustees on behalf of the firm so as to avoid the need for continual reconveyances of land and premises as the members of the partnership change through time. But the corporate form does eliminate the need for continual redrafting or adjustment of partnership agreements. The transfer of company shares among members of a family for tax planning and avoidance is also a good deal more simple and less costly than the transfer of beneficial interests in property, though many practitioners now prefer to rely on discretionary trusts for this purpose. Once a company has been established the affairs of the family business or the management of family property can be managed by accountants without the need for frequent professional legal advice or assistance. It has paradoxically been the switch from the outwardly simpler legal form of partnership or direct ownership to the small family company which has removed the affairs of many small family businesses or property holdings from the hands of the family solicitor to those of the family accountant.

There is a price to be paid for permanence and for the other advantages of the corporate form. The actual formation of a small company may cost anything from a minimum of one hundred pounds to several hundred depending on the complexity of the operation and the value of the assets involved. More important than this initial cost, however, is the continuing legal obligation, as a registered company, to conduct the affairs of the business or to manage the company's property with a degree of formality and regularity which is unnecessary in the partnership form. Annual meetings must be held and directors elected and re-elected. Annual accounts must be prepared, audited and formally approved. And an annual return must be made to the Registrar of Companies giving details of any changes in the financial structure, membership or management of the company. All this is undoubtedly inconvenient, time-consuming and costly. Failure to comply renders those responsible liable to criminal prosecution, though the risk of conviction in cases of delay or negligent omission is small. Of the 2,635 prosecutions for failure to submit returns in 1975 more than one thousand were withdrawn on compliance. Some small businessmen may nevertheless prefer to remain unincorporated on these grounds alone.

The most significant consideration on this level, however, is the obligation imposed by the Companies Act 1967 on all limited companies to file copies of their annual balance sheet and profit and loss account. All companies have been required to produce accounts for their members since 1900, but small private companies were exempted from filing these accounts for possible public or commercial inspection, initially as private companies and then under the Companies Act 1948 as 'exempt private companies'. This exemption was withdrawn in 1967 on the ground that the privilege of limited liability should be granted only if certain basic information on the company's finances is regularly disclosed. The additional disclosure requirements introduced in 1967 in respect of turnover, exports, the emoluments of directors and highly paid executives, and the number and average pay of employees do not apply to companies with a turnover of less than £250,000, total directors' emoluments of less than £15,000 and fewer than one hundred employees respectively (Companies (Accounts) Regulations 1971). It was argued that the publication of such information might expose smaller companies to unfair competition from larger enterprises and that it would be an unnecessary interference in the privacy of small traders. But the obligation to publish annual accounts is in itself the principal consideration in this context. Furthermore, under the terms of the Companies Act 1976 there will be much harsher penalties on the directors of any company which fails to file accounts within ten months of the end of its accounting period (1976 : ss. 4–6).

2 THE BASIS OF ASSOCIATION IN SMALL BUSINESSES

The primary issues to be settled in any business association are the allocation of profit, of risk and of powers of control among those involved in the enterprise. There is clearly no problem in this for the sole trader. He alone is entitled to any profit realized; he alone is personally liable for the debts and obligations of the business to the limit of bankruptcy; and he alone is ultimately in control of the business, whether or not he employs assistants or a manager to operate it on his behalf.

Where more than one person is directly involved the individual rights and liabilities of the parties must be clearly settled. The simple rule is that in a partnership each partner is personally liable for the whole of the debts and obligations of the business, just as if he were a sole trader, but that his rights to share in the profit and management of the business are a matter for contractual settlement between the parties. In an incorporated company, on the other hand, the allocation of profit and control is rather more formally dealt with through the mechanism of shareholdings and directorships, and the liability of members is normally limited to the amount of share capital subscribed. In many cases, however, the practical effect of these formal distinctions is rather less than might be expected, since the terms of association in both companies and partnerships can be arranged to effect virtually any allocation of rights and liabilities, and since the impact of limited liability is frequently reduced by the personal guarantees which substantial creditors may demand from the directors of small companies. The practical position with respect to internal membership and withdrawal, management, and the allocation of profit and loss will accordingly be dealt with for both companies and partnerships together.

Membership and withdrawal

It is not strictly accurate to say that the internal relations of the parties to a partnership and to a small private company are solely a matter for contractual settlement. In a partnership each partner has an inalienable right to decide with whom he will carry on business, and therefore a right of veto against any new member regardless of the preferences of his colleagues or their formal voting power. This right to the choice of partners, or *dilectus personarum* as it is sometimes termed, is a direct consequence of the legal theory as to the personal and participatory nature of a partnership. No individual partner may be forced to maintain this close relationship with anyone against his will. In a company, on the other hand, the principle of majority rule prevails, so that a minority shareholder or director is in no position to dictate who will and who will not be permitted to join the enterprise.

There is a similar differentiation with respect to withdrawal from the enterprise. The personal participation rule for partnerships means that any partner may at any time withdraw and by so doing automatically dissolve the partnership. A partnership is no more than a contractual working association between certain named individuals, and no individual can be forced to continue to work with those he no longer wishes to work with. The only direct method of withdrawal from a company, however, is by the sale of the shares held in it, and in the case of a small private company it is not always easy to find a buyer. No shareholder has any right as such to withdraw his capital and force a formal reconstitution of the enterprise on the remaining participants as is the case in simple partnerships.

In practical terms, however, these differences are a good deal less significant than might appear. A partnership deed, as well as setting out the respective shares held by each of the partners in the joint assets and a formula for the allocation of profit, often makes provision for the partnership to last for a specific term of years thus impliedly restricting the withdrawal of any partner before the expiration of the period agreed. It may also provide for the introduction of new members with the approval of existing partners, as for instance the son of an existing partner or an articled clerk. A partner who seeks to determine the partnership before the expiration of a fixed term or who refuses to admit new partners under the terms of the partnership deed may thus be in breach of his personal contract with his fellow partners and liable for any loss which his breach may occasion. In practical terms this means that he will not normally be able to withdraw his personal assets or capital investment, unless he can show good legal cause why the partnership should be wound up prior to the expiration of the agreed term of years. Where there is no fixed term he may retire at any time on giving reasonable notice and bring about an apportionment of the partnerships assets as provided for in the Partnership Act 1890 (ss. 26–7, 40).

Conversely it is standard practice in small private companies to control the membership of the company, and thus indirectly its management, by the insertion of restrictive articles of association giving existing directors or members power to refuse to admit new members. This is normally achieved by the inclusion of a standard form clause, such as clause 3 in the second part of Table A : 'The directors may, in their absolute discretion and without assigning any reason therefor, decline to register any transfer of any share, whether or not it is a fully paid share.' The effect of this type of provision is to prevent any existing member from disposing of his shares, and thus withdrawing his capital, without the consent of the majority of his colleagues. An article of this kind will be given its full effect by the courts, in the absence of proof of bad faith on the part of the directors.

The shares in a small private company were owned equally by two directors. On the death of one director, his shares were inherited by his widow, who subsequently died, and the petitioner. They sought to force the remaining director to register them as members and to accept the petitioner as a director. He refused, but offered to buy half the shares at a price to be fixed by himself and to register the rest. The court refused to make any order: the article was drafted in the widest possible terms; the only limitation on its exercise was that it be applied bona fide in the interests of the company, and since there was no evidence of impropriety the court could not intervene. *Re Smith v. Fawcett Ltd.* [1942] Ch. 304

Where a director acts in good faith in refusing to register a transfer in such cases the only positive duty on him is presumably to secure a buyer for the shares at a reasonable price since to leave the shares permanently without voting rights or to force a sale at an undervalue would clearly constitute oppression (see p. 262).

Other more complex provisions with similar objectives may be made both in partnerships and private companies. It is fairly common, for instance, to insert a right of pre-emption under which existing members or partners may buy in the shares of any person wishing to withdraw : this permits existing participants to block the entry of new members without giving them absolute power to prevent withdrawal.

The net effect in both companies and partnerships is thus to reduce any theoretical legal differences between the two forms to negligible proportions in respect of withdrawal and the admission of new members. The contractual basis of association in each case permits provision to be made for virtually any arrangement which is desired. This is scarcely surprising since the incorporated company in historical terms is no more than a developed statutory form of the unincorporated partnership.

The management of small companies: the quasi-partnership

The law is not normally concerned with the way in which the affairs of a business enterprise are run. Business efficiency, whether in a company or a partnership, is a matter for businessmen rather than lawyers. But there are some distinctions in the formal structure of management and control between the two forms. Every partner has a right as such to be directly concerned in the management of the partnership subject only to any procedural provisions in the deed of partnership. Accordingly if any of his colleagues join together to exclude him from the day-to-day running of the business, or to refuse him access to the firm's accounts and papers, that in itself is a ground for the dissolution of the partnership. This rule applies regardless of the relative size of the partner's share. A partner is ipso facto a manager.

In an incorporated company, on the other hand, a shareholder has no right as such to concern himself in the day-to-day management of the company. That is exclusively a matter for the company's directors, at least in accordance with the usual form of articles of association (1948: Table A, art. 80). The shareholder can only influence the management of his company's affairs through the general meeting which in practical terms has control only over the appointment of directors and certain other formal statutory resolutions such as the appointment of auditors and changes in the memorandum or articles of association. It is not even possible in normal circumstances for the general meeting to issue directives that are binding on the directors, though directors who ignore the wishes of the majority of shareholders run the risk of dismissal and replacement.

The articles of a company stated that 'the management of the business and the control of the company' including the power 'to sell, leave, abandon or otherwise deal with any property rights or privileges to which the company might be entitled' were vested in the directors. A shareholder arranged independently of the directors for the sale of the undertaking to another company. He called a general meeting of the shareholders to sanction the deal and secured the passing of a resolution instructing the directors to give effect to the draft contract. The directors refused on the ground that the sale was not in the best interests of the company. Their refusal was upheld: 'If a majority of the shareholders could on a matter which was vested in the directors overrule the discretion of the directors, there might just as well be no provision at all in the articles [as was then permissible] as to the removal of the directors by a special resolution.' (per Warrington J., at p. 38) *Automatic Self-Cleansing Filter Syndicate Co. Ltd. v. Cunninghame* [1906] 2 Ch. 34 (CA)

In the case of small private companies, however, the law does take notice of the fact that the shareholders and directors are the same people, and that for many purposes the participation rule developed in partnership law is more appropriate than the more formalistic rules applied in the case of larger companies. Hence the development of the concept of the quasi-partnership, which the courts have used in certain circumstances to allow small private companies to be treated as if they were partnerships.[9] The concept appears to have originated in what may be termed the 'deadlock' cases, in which those in effective control over a company have reached such a state of enmity or disagreement that the affairs of the company cannot be carried on. This is accepted as a just and equitable ground for the grant of a winding up order (1948: s. 222(f)), just as it is an accepted ground for the dissolution of a partnership (Partnership Act 1890, s. 35(f)).

Two businessmen agreed to create a company to take over their respective businesses. Each of them had equal voting rights and each was a life director, but provision was also made for the settlement by arbitration of any disputes which could not be resolved between them. Quite soon all co-operation between the two broke down, though the operations of the company continued to be profitable. Things came to a head over the dismissal of a factory manager by one director; the other objected and eventually secured a decision by an arbitrator in his favour. In a petition for the winding up of the company on the just and equitable ground it was held that the same principles as would be applied under the Partnership Act should be applied in a case such as this, when 'in substance it was a partnership'; that 'having regard to the fact that the only two directors will not speak to each other, and that no business which deserved the name of business could be carried on . . . the company should not be allowed to continue'; and that the provision for arbitration was too slow and costly to be an effective solution in the circumstances. *In re Yenidje Tobacco Co. Ltd.* [1916] 2 Ch. 426

This line of reasoning was developed into a general rule in a subsequent case in which one joint director used his casting vote as chairman to appoint two further directors and thus effectively oust the other from all direct involvement in the company's affairs, and even from his office in the company's place of business:

The same circumstances which entitle a partner to require the dissolution of a partnership entitle a person who is equally interested with one other person in a company to have that company wound up on the ground that the circumstances render it just as equitable. *In re Davis & Collett Ltd.* [1935] 1 Ch. 693, at p. 701

The quasi-partnership concept was thus made applicable to cases of ouster as well as of deadlock, as a general extension of the partner-

[9] On this topic see generally D. Prentice, 'Winding-up on the Just and Equitable Ground', (1973) 89 *LQR* 189.

ship rule of personal participation. It was subsequently extended to three-men companies: where two directors effectively excluded a third from working in the business, though he owned half the voting shares, the third was held to be entitled to a winding up order.[10] This broad application of the concept has now been authoritatively confirmed:

The petitioner formed a company with another trader and his son. The petitioner and the father held 400 shares each and the son the remaining 200. All three earned their livelihood from the company in the form of directors' fees. Subsequently dispute arose among them, and the father and son voted the petitioner off the board in general meeting. The court was asked to intervene either to make an order under s. 210 on the ground of oppression or else to wind up the company on the just and equitable ground under s. 222(f). It was held at first instance that there was no evidence of oppression apart from the dismissal of the petitioner from his post as working director, but a winding up order was granted on the ground that 'it was an abuse of power and a breach of the good faith which partners owe to each other to exclude one of them from all participation in the business on which they had embarked on the basis that all should participate in its management'. (per Plowman J.) [1970] 1 W.L.R. 1378, at p. 1389 This decision was overruled on appeal on the ground that the removal of the petitioner had been justified, since he was perpetually complaining about the conduct of the company's affairs: a vote by a majority in general meeting to remove a director from his office in a quasi-partnership company did not form a ground for winding up 'unless it was shown that the power was not exercised bona fide in the interests of the company, or that the grounds for exercising the powers were such that no reasonable man could think that the removal was in the interests of the company'. [1971] 2 W.L.R. 618, at p. 624 In the House of Lords the original judgement was reaffirmed: the 'just and equitable' provision did not entitle a party to disregard the obligations he assumed by entering a company, nor the court to dispense him from it, but it did, as equity always did, enable the court to subject the exercise of legal rights to equitable considerations; in the circumstances of the case the right course was to dissolve the company since the petitioner as a result of losing his directorship lost his right to share in the profits as director and retained only a right to share in any dividend as a minority shareholder; he was thus at the mercy of his former colleagues who could also prevent him from disposing of his shares. Lord Wilberforce added a more general statement of some of the circumstances in which there might be grounds for equitable intervention: (i) an association formed or continued on the basis of a personal relationship; (ii) an agreement or under-

[10] *In re Lundie Bros. Ltd.* [1965] 1 W.L.R. 1051 (see p. 160).

standing that all or some of the shareholders shall participate in the conduct of the business; (iii) restriction on the transfer of shares in the company, so that if confidence is lost or one member is removed from management he cannot take out his stake and go elsewhere. *In re Westbourne Galleries Ltd.* [1973] A.C. 360

This interpretation of the quasi-partnership doctrine must not be taken too far. The judgements in the House of Lords in the *Westbourne Galleries* case continually reiterate that a company is not a partnership and that the provisions of a company's memorandum and articles must govern the relations between its shareholders and directors. If a minority participant continually disagrees with the rest of the directors on matters of business judgement, that in itself will not give him any right to seek the winding up of the company. Nor will a shareholder/director in a two-man company be permitted to secure a winding up without proof of a genuine deadlock:

A joint shareholder/director petitioned for the winding up of a company on the ground of irreconcilable differences between himself and the other director. In the absence of particulars of deadlock the action was struck out: it was not the law that in the case of a two-man company if the shareholders fall out, one of them alleging that further co-operation is impossible, then the court must at once treat them as partners and order a winding up. *In re W. R. Willcocks & Co. Ltd.* [1974] 1 Ch. 163

But where there is evidence of some prior agreement or an informal understanding on the basis of which the parties agreed to establish a company or to allocate powers and profits in an existing company the courts will not permit such an agreement or understanding to be ignored.[11] The most frequent cases will be those of deadlock or exclusion. But the courts may also intervene in other cases where the majority has acted unreasonably and in so doing has deprived a minority participant of his livelihood or of all return on the capital which he has invested. This does not mean that the constitution of the company will be ignored. The correct analysis of the quasi-partnership cases is simply that the substance of the business relationship between the parties will be taken into account by the courts in the exercise of their statutory discretion to wind up a company on the just and equitable ground.

A similar approach may be adopted in respect of the statutory power to make an order to relieve minority shareholders from

[11] See generally M. R. Chesterman, *Small Businesses* (1977), Ch. 7.

oppression within small private businesses (1948 : s. 210). The courts have generally interpreted this provision in a restrictive manner. It has been decided, for instance, that to deprive a director/shareholder in a quasi-partnership company all or a major part of his working income by dismissing him as a director does not of itself amount to oppression, since the statutory provision porvides only for the protection of shareholders :

The petitioner had been chairman of a small private company and held fifty per cent of the voting shares. The two other directors held the remainder. At a directors' meeting the two other directors voted to replace the chairman by one of themselves, thus depriving him of his casting vote. They then terminated his contract as a working director of the company at a board meeting, and confirmed this move at a general meeting immediately after. The petitioner's weekly wage was thus reduced from £22 to £2. He petitioned both for the winding up of the company on the just and equitable ground and for an order under s. 210 reinstating him as a working director. The petition under s. 210 was rejected on the ground that he had not established that the affairs of the company had been conducted in a manner oppressive to him *as a shareholder*. An order for the winding up of the company was granted on the ground that he had been excluded from what was in effect a quasi-partnership. [On this latter point the case was approved in *In re Westbourne Galleries*]. *In re Lundie Bros. Ltd.* [1965] 1 W.L.R. 1051

This is clearly a misunderstanding by the courts of the basis of this provision, as will be argued in detail in Chapter 5. The intention in providing a statutory remedy against oppression was to avoid the need to wind up a company in all cases where a fraud on the minority could be established. If the courts are prepared to adopt a broad interpretation of their power to order a winding up on the just and equitable ground in cases involving small private businesses, there is no justification for a refusal to apply similar reasoning in cases of oppression, particularly since the power to order a discretionary remedy may permit a more appropriate solution than a winding up. In a situation such as that in the *Lundie Bros.* case, for instance, an order for the controlling faction to buy out the shares of the remaining party at a fair price is likely to be more satisfactory than the dissolution of the company. The same principles as have been developed in the cases on winding up on the just and equitable ground should be applied both in cases of statutory oppression and in the exercise of the court's general equitable jurisdiction to prevent shareholders and directors from using their formal powers for an improper purpose (see p. 245). In all such cases the courts may properly look to the realities of the business relationships inside a small private company as well as to the formal provisions of the company's constitution.

The allocation of profit and loss

The allocation of the profits realized in the business of a partnership is determined by the terms of the partnership deed, which will normally provide for a certain number of notional fractions or shares in the business to be held by each partner. In a company limited by shares the same result is achieved more formally by the allotment of shares and the issue of share certificates up to the authorized limit. There is no reason in either case for the rights attaching to shares to be the same for all purposes. As has been seen it is possible in a partnership to exclude one or more partners from any direct share in profits, though most so-called 'salaried partners' are not partners in the true sense.[12] Similarly in a company shares may be created with full participation in profits but without votes, or with full voting rights and no share in the profits. There is no limit to the range and nature of preferred or deferred shares which may be created by giving special rights to payment of a fixed dividend with or without further rights to participate in any general distribution of profits. The allocation of profit, like that of control, is a contractual matter to be settled in the partnership deed or the company articles of association.

The main difference between companies and partnerships in this respect is in the formal calculation of distributable profits. The paid up capital of a company is regarded as in some sense sacrosanct, so that dividends on shares may be paid only out of profits (see p. 130). In addition, a clear distinction must be drawn between the payments made to company directors and managers by way of remuneration for services rendered and the distribution of dividends to shareholders, even if the recipients are the same people. In the case of a simple partnership, however, there is no bar on the distribution of the firm's capital, and in many cases no formal distinction will be made between payment for services to the firm and the distribution of realized profit. This distinction is of some importance for tax

[12] *Stekel v. Ellis* [1973] 1 W.L.R. 191 (see p. 99).

purposes. All profits realized in a partnership, whether retained in the business or shared out among the partners, are taxable as income in the hands of the individual partners in accordance with their share in the business, and no allowance can be made for the payment of partners before the profit figure is assessed. In a company the payment of directors and managers, whether they are also shareholders or not, is an allowable expense against profits, and profits which are retained in the business are now dealt with differently from those which are distributed as dividends, though the position is further complicated by the rules relating to the required standard of distribution in closely held companies (see p. 215).

The position with respect to the allocation of loss is rather different. As far as concerns the partners or shareholders and directors among themselves, provision may be made in the partnership deed or company articles for any form of loss allocation which the parties wish, just as in the case of profit. There is nothing to prevent a contractual arrangement within a partnership by which one partner undertakes to guarantee the full amount of any loss incurred. And the practical effect of any form of deferred share in a company is to expose the holder to the full risk of loss of capital without full participation in profit.

Any contractual settlement of this kind, however, takes effect only subject to the general legal rules relating to partnership and corporate liability. The essentials of these rules have already been stated : that all partners are jointly and severally liable for the whole of the debts of the firm to the full extent of their personal fortune, so that each is exposed to the risk of personal bankruptcy, whereas the liability of the shareholders and directors for the debts of a limited company is restricted to the amount of capital they have subscribed. In practice matters are rather more complicated.

i *Liability within a partnership.* The central conception of partnership liability is that any person dealing with the partnership is entitled to treat each individual partner as if he were a sole trader operating the whole business of the partnership on his own account. This is in part a simple deduction from the law of agency. Each partner is the agent of the firm in respect of what he himself does on the firm's behalf, and since he is also a principal he is personally liable under any contract which he makes on behalf of the firm. But each partner is in addition deemed to be a joint principal in *all* the transactions of the firm and thus liable in conjunction with his colleagues in respect of what any other partner or employee does on behalf of the firm. It is here that considerations of practical convenience intervene. A partnership lacks corporate personality and cannot therefore be directly sued by an outsider. But it would be asking too much of an outsider to require him to join all partners as defendants in the action and to execute against them severally to the extent of their individual shares. For a start he would have no way of ascertaining the relevant information. Hence as a matter of convenience and efficacy in enforcement the direct application of agency law is extended to render each partner personally and fully liable in respect of every debt or obligation of the firm. The external creditor is thus entitled in law to select any one partner and to hold him responsible for the debts of the firm, leaving that partner to enforce any internal reallocation of liability with his colleagues. This rule will apply in respect of every person who is held out as a partner, including those 'salaried partners' whose names appear on the firm's letterhead but who are not partners in the full sense of the word.

It would clearly not be right, however, to hold each partner fully liable for *whatever* business transaction his colleagues or employees entered into on behalf of the firm. In the absence of evidence to the contrary this responsibility is limited to the ordinary course of the firm's business. This too is a direct application of the ordinary rules of agency, under which the principal is only liable for the acts of the agent in so far as he has actually authorized or is deemed in law to have authorized them. The difficulty both in partnership law and in agency is to determine the extent of the authorization. In distinction to a registered company in which the objects and powers of the enterprise are formally set out in the memorandum of association, there is no requirement that the objects of a partnership should be clearly expressed, and its powers are in law identical to those of any individual trader. And even if the objects were formally agreed between the partners there would be no way in which a third party could find this out. Hence there is no way in which a third party can be sure of the extent of a partner's or an employee's authority. This difficulty is resolved in law by the presumption that the firm, and thus each partner, is liable in respect of any transaction within the normal scope of the firm's business:

Every partner is an agent for the firm and his other partners for the purposes of the business of the partnership; and the acts of every partner who does any act for carrying on in the usual way business of the kind carried on by the firm of which he is a member bind the firm and his partners, unless the partner so acting has in fact no authority to act for the firm in the particular matter and the person with whom he is dealing either knows that he has no authority, or does no know that he is a partner. *Partnership Act* 1890, s. 5

The effect of this very general formulation is to leave the decision on the precise scope of the firm's business to the court in each individual case of dispute, though the effective burden of proof is likely to be on those partners who seek to evade liability. In general terms apparent or ostensible authority is as good as actual authority from the point of view of the external creditor.

This presumption of authority within the normal scope of the business, however, does not meet every case. Partners may often wish to carry out transactions beyond the normal scope of their business. In such cases actual authority from all the other partners would be necessary to bind the firm.

In the course of the reconstruction of a partnership one partner undertook to settle the pre-existing debts of the previous firm and issued a promissory note to the major creditor. He later induced the creditor to set off credit due to the new partnership against this personal liability. The remaining partner contested this transaction in the subsequent dissolution of the new partnership, and managed to have it set aside on the ground that there could be no presumption of authority to use the firm's money to settle a personal debt: 'The one partner is agent for the other, and it is an agency to do all the matters which are within the ordinary scope of the business which the partners carry on; but when a partner does that which is beyond this prima facie authority . . . those who deal with him do so at their peril.' In such cases even an honest belief in due authority is not enough; the third party must show that the partner had actual authority to do as he did. (per Blackburn J.) *Kendal v. Wood* (1871) L.R. 6 Exch. 243

The general rule is thus that where the third party either knew or ought to have realized that the transaction was beyond the scope of the partner's ordinary authority he may only look to the individual partner concerned for satisfaction, unless he can prove that the other partners expressly approved the transaction, or gave unlimited authority to the other.

Similarly a partner, whether with a fraudulent purpose or not, may undertake a transaction which is within the normal scope of a firm's business but which has been expressly excluded from the scope of his personal authority, as in the case of a junior partner expressly forbidden to enter into large commitments without the express authority of his senior colleagues. Here again the rule is that where the third party knows of an express limitation of authority he is bound by that knowledge, regardless of the ordinary course of business rule. To render any limitation on an individual partner effective the remaining partners must ensure that the business community is expressly informed of that limitation.

ii *Liability within a company*. The major effect of incorporation is to separate the property of the company from that of the individuals concerned in it, and to render the company itself legally responsible for its own debts and obligations to the extent of that property. In strict law this does not in itself prevent unpaid creditors from looking to the assets of members or directors when the property of the company is exhausted. But the right of a registered company to limit the liability of its members is formally recognized in the Companies Act (1948: s. 1), and given practical effect by the provision that for the purposes of a liquidation 'in the case of a company limited by shares no contribution shall be required from any member exceeding the amount, if any, unpaid on (his) shares' (1948: s. 212(1)(d)). Consequently in ordinary circumstances neither the shareholders, the directors nor the employees of a company are personally liable for its debts except to the extent to which they have subscribed to its capital but have not fully paid up on their shares.

The outward simplicity of the limited liability rule is misleading. Many of the problems of partnership liability arise in relation to limited companies as well. In the first place since the company must in the nature of things act through human agents the question of the extent of the authority, and consequently of the personal liability of those agents, immediately arises. In so far as the general extent of the company's business and the powers of its directors and officers are concerned this is strictly determined by the company's memorandum and articles of association. Though under the rule in *Royal British Bank v. Turquand* (see p. 119) every person dealing with a company was deemed to have notice of these, a third party acting in good faith may now rely on the capacity of the company to enter into any transaction authorized by its directors unless he has actual notice to the contrary (European Communities Act 1972 : s. 9). But in many cases the courts must rely in practice on the more general principles of ostensible authority and notice, especially in respect of the powers of directors and managers, since it is normally on apparent or ostensible authority rather than actual authority that commercial contractors rely. In the case of a limited company the directors and officers, who are granted formal powers to act on its behalf, will normally be deemed to have delegated that authority to any servant of the company whom they allow to enter into any transaction which 'an agent authorized to do acts of the kind which he is in fact permitted to do usually enters into in the ordinary course of such business'.[13] The net result would appear to be that the company is bound by any acts of its officers or employees, whether fraudulent or not, which fall within the normal course of such an officer's or employee's duties, unless the third party has actual notice of the absence of authority, in which case he may look only to the individual concerned. This rule is virtually identical to that formulated above in respect of partnerships, and the same difficulties over the interpretation of what is the normal course of business will arise.

It should also be noted that there are certain cases where the statutory limitation of liability is suspended. The simplest case is where the number of members of the company falls below the statutory minimum (1948 : s. 31). More important is the provision that where the business of the company is conducted with the deliberate intention of defrauding creditors by sheltering behind the provision of limited liability those responsible may be held personally liable to the extent which the court in liquidation proceedings deems fit (1948 : s. 332). The precise meaning of fraudulent trading in this context is not firmly settled (see p. 204), but the provision does obviously make limited liability a rather less absolute concept than is normally assumed.

The limited partnership

The clear distinction between companies and partnerships in respect of liability has also been blurred by the creation of an intermediate

[13] *Freeman & Lockyer v. Buckhurst Park Properties (Mangal) Ltd.* [1964] 2 Q.B. 480, at p. 505 (per Diplock L.J.) (see p. 119).

statutory form of association on the model of the French *société en commandite* in which 'sleeping partners' are liable only to the extent of their capital contribution. Thus in partnerships registered under the Limited Partnership Act 1907 there are two classes of partner, the general partner who remains fully liable for the debts and obligations of the firm as in a common law partnership, and the limited partner who 'shall at the time of entry into such partnership contribute thereto a sum or sums as capital or property valued at a stated amount, and who shall not be liable for the debts and obligations of the firm beyond the amount so contributed' (s. 4(2)). The limited partner, however, loses this privilege if he takes any direct part in the management of the firm (s. 6(1)). The Act in addition requires the filing of full details of the constitution of the partnership, but for the rest the general provisions of the Partnership Act 1890 are incorporated.

The intention of this statute was to encourage small businesses to retain the simple partnership form instead of converting themselves into limited companies, a practice which at the time was felt to be undesirable. The same result could have been achieved under the common law after the decision in *Cox v. Hickman* (1860) and the Mercantile Law (Amendment) Act 1865 (see p. 98), both of which established that entitlement to a share of the profits of an enterprise did not necessarily bring with it full personal liability as a partner for the debts of the firm: all that would have been necessary was the creation of a partnership in which some of the participants were full partners with ordinary rights and liabilities and some 'external partners' who were not in strict law partners at all, but who did share in the profits of the enterprise in return for an initial capital contribution.

The precise status and novelty of the limited partnership however, is not of great practical importance since it has never been much more than an academic possibility as far as the ordinary businessman is concerned. There have never been more than a handful of such associations. The reasons for its lack of popularity are not difficult to trace. The principal participants in a limited partnership secure no advantage from their status, and with minimal extra administrative inconvenience, at least until the more stringent disclosure rules introduced in 1967, they could obtain the full benefits of limited liability for themselves and corporate personality for the business by forming a private company. The status of a limited partner is also unsatisfactory in that any action which he takes to protect his investment in the event of malpractice or inefficiency on the part of the general partners is likely to remove his privilege of limited liability. There was consequently no real reason for anyone to form a limited partnership. Nor was the continental experience with business associations of this form directly relevant since neither in France nor elsewhere on the continent was there at the time any simple form of incorporation similar to that in England. The trend in France and in Germany in recent years has in fact been away from the traditional *société en commandite* or *Kommanditgesellschaft* towards a simpler form of company with full scale limited liability on the English model.

3 FINANCING SMALL BUSINESSES

Every business enterprise, whatever its legal form, needs some form of capital to finance its operations. This is true even within a fully planned socialist economy, though the form and nature of the initial capital will not be so clearly visible as in the capitalist commercial system. Once the business is firmly established on a profitable, or socially productive, basis the principal source of funds is likely to be internal (see Chapter 2). When this happy state of equilibrium is reached there is no real problem over the precise form of financing. The enterprise simply continues its operations from year to year paying out or retaining the profit as suits those involved. In the initial stages, however, or when there is to be rapid development, or when losses are incurred, there is a need for external funds. In broad terms there are three ways in which such funds may be raised: *first* by the direct issue of shares in the business which in return for a capital contribution entitle the holder to participate in future profits; *secondly* by raising repayable loans, with or without interest, from outside sources or from those directly involved; and *thirdly* by operating on credit, that is in simple terms by avoiding the need for capital either by not paying for supplies or services until the operating profit on them has been realized, or alternatively by obtaining plant or machinery on hire or hire purchase terms.

There is little effective difference between companies and partnerships in any of these respects as far as the actual raising of funds goes. In either case a wide range of types of share capital may be issued, whether fully paid up in advance or in the form of a commitment to future contributions. Nor is there any limit in either case on the nature and extent of loans or credit which may be arranged. But there are important differences between companies and partnerships in respect of share and loan capital, the security which may be offered in return for loans and the provisions as to registration and disclosure, all of which may affect the balance of advantage between the various forms of fund raising.

Share and loan capital

The essential difference between share and loan capital in both companies and partnerships lies in the rights and liabilities attached to the shares rather than in any formal designation. In a partnership the contribution of funds in return for a right to share in profits will normally make the holder a full partner in the enterprise and thus render him personally liable for the debts and obligations of the firm. A simple loan in return for a fixed interest charge does not have this effect, and under the decision in *Cox v. Hickman* (1860) (see p. 98), the interest may be linked to the profitability of the partnership without affecting the status of the loan, as long as the lender is not also granted any rights of oversight or management. Since there is no legal requirement as to the maintenance of capital except in the case of a limited partnership, the terms on which the capital contribution or loan is repayable make no difference to its status as participatory or loan capital.

In a registered company, on the other hand, it is largely the terms as to repayment or redemption on which the distinction between shares and loan capital or debentures is based. Share capital is repayable only on the winding up of the company, or through a formal scheme for the reduction of capital (1948 : ss. 66–71), and ranks last in any list of priorities. Loan capital may be repaid at any time subject to the terms of the contractual agreement under which the loan is made, and in the absence of specific security ranks with the other debts of the company in the event of winding up on insolvency. It should be noted that the term 'debenture' has no special significance : it is used to refer both to simple loans to private companies arranged under a formal contract, whether or not secured on the assets of the company, and to the large issues of debenture stock made by quoted public companies.

There is also an important practical difference in the tax treatment of share and loan capital. The annual interest payments on loan capital are a permissible deduction from the profits of the company for the purposes of corporation tax. Dividends on ordinary or preference shares on the other hand are currently liable both to corporation tax as part of the company's profit, and to income tax as part of the income of the ultimate recipient, though tax at the standard rate is collected from the company as advance corporation tax and then credited as having been paid by the shareholder. As is often the case in tax legislation, a separate and independent definition is given of the securities which are deemed to be share capital for this purpose, namely:

> Securities convertible directly or indirectly into shares in the company . . .

and

> Securities under which the consideration given by the company for the use of the principal secured is to any extent dependent on the results of the company's business or any part of it, or under which the consideration so given represents more than a reasonable commercial return for the use of that principal. *Income and Corporation Taxes Act* 1970, s. 233 (2)(d)(ii)–(iii)

The effect of this definition is to exclude from the special treatment accorded to loan capital any loan on which the interest varies in relation to the company's profits, or on which a specially attractive interest rate is fixed, regardless of its status as debenture or share capital for other purposes. The object is to prevent the manipulation of the formal capital structure of companies for the sole purpose of securing a tax advantage.

The further rights attached to particular classes of shareholding, in terms of voting power or the right to appoint directors, or a receiver or manager to protect the interests of the particular class of shares, are less important as a means of distinguishing shares from debentures. These are a matter for contractual settlement between the parties, though in the case of a secured debenture a right to appoint a receiver is likely to be implied at common law (see p. 182).

It will be clear from this brief discussion that the exact dividing line between share and loan capital is often imprecise. In most cases the position will be quite clear, but the lack of a precise definition, except for tax purposes, and the virtually complete freedom of the parties to arrange any form of financing which suits their special circumstances, means that the borderline cases are even more a matter for the discretion of the courts than is usually the case.

Fortunately there will rarely be any need to decide the point. The distinction is mainly relevant to priorities in cases of liquidation and where there is no express provision for this purpose the courts will simply have to construe the intention of the parties from the available documents.

Security for loans

The primary concern of those who lend money in the form of debentures is not the precise legal status of their investment but the recovery of their money. The general rule is that all the liabilities of a company or partnership other than share capital, whether in the form of a capital loan or the ordinary trading debts of the business, rank equally. It is left to each individual creditor to ensure the payment or repayment of his particular debt. It is only when proceedings in bankruptcy or liquidation are instituted that the law steps in to secure some measure of equality in the treatment of the various creditors. Those who lend substantial sums, however, are naturally reluctant to take their chance with the rest. Accordingly they will often seek to secure their particular loan or credit on the assets of the business, so that in the event of insolvency or liquidation they may be assured of repayment in priority to the general run of trade creditors. This is readily achieved by creating a legal or equitable charge on the property of the business, or of those principally concerned in it.

i *Fixed charges.* The simplest and most usual form of security is a fixed charge on the premises or plant of the business, created by a formal legal contract between the lender and the borrowing concern (a legal charge) or alternatively by a simple agreement to create such a charge (an equitable charge), as for instance by the deposit of title deeds at a bank. The effect in either case is that in the event of any failure by the borrower to repay the loan or the interest on it the lender may require the property charged to be sold and the proceeds applied exclusively for the settlement of his claim, in priority to any other debts or obligations of the business including those given statutory protection.

There is no practical difference between a company and a partnership in this respect. In formal terms a charge on partnership property is a charge on the property of those individuals who are the legal owners of that property, and may thus be readily extended to cover other property of those involved in the partnership, whereas a charge on company property is restricted to the property of the company as a separate legal entity. But in the case of small private companies, banks and other large lenders may in addition require the directors to charge their own personal assets as security for the obligations of the company.

ii *Floating charges.* In the mid-nineteenth century it became common practice to create bonds and charges not only on specific items of property belonging to the business but also in more general terms on any property which might be substituted for the specific items, or more simply on all the property of the business. There were certain technical difficulties over such general charges, since lawyers understandably felt that a charge should be restricted to identifiable items. But the principle of a charge on future property was eventually approved in the case of *Holroyd v. Marshall* (1862),[14] in which machinery charged with the repayment of a substantial debt had been sold and replaced in the ordinary course of business: it was held that there was no rule of equity to prevent the court making an order for the formal charging of the substituted property which was in effect held on trust for the chargee. Any further doubts about the charging of after-acquired property were then finally removed in *In re Panama, New Zealand and Australian Royal Mail Co.* (1870)[15] in which it was held that a general charge on the undertaking of the company could be applied to all the ships of the company at the time of liquidation whether or not they were in existence at the time of the creation of the charge.

These so-called floating charges on all the existing and future property of a company or business soon became firmly established as the most comprehensive and convenient security in cases in which there was continual change in the property, plant or stock owned by the enterprise. The difficulty over the identification of the items charged was solved by the notion that as soon as action was taken to enforce the charge it descended or 'crystallized' on whatever property, in accordance with the terms of the charge, was then in the ownership of the business, though it would of course take effect subject to any prior fixed charge on specific items.

[14] 10 H.L.C. 191.
[15] (1870) L.R. 5 Ch. App. 318.

The registration of charges

The special protection for the interests of one creditor provided by a fixed or floating charge naturally affects the interests of other unsecured creditors, since the property charged will be applied to the settlement of the secured loans or debts in priority to other debts and obligations of the enterprise. This was felt to be unfair to the unsecured creditors who had no way of knowing whether property which apparently belonged to the business with which they were dealing was going to be available for execution in the event of the non-payment of their own accounts. Accordingly it was provided in the Bills of Sale Act 1854 that any contract or arrangement by which a debt or obligation was secured on moveable property should be registered and open to public inspection for the benefit of other creditors, just as any formal charge or mortgage on real property had to be registered to protect the interests of prospective purchasers of land. In the absence of registration the security could not be enforced. This legislation was subsequently extended in the Bills of Sale Acts of 1878 and 1882 which are still in force. Similar provisions for the maintenance of a register of charges, initially open to inspection only by shareholders and chargees, were included in the Companies Acts of 1845 and 1862.

The current position with respect to companies is that any legal or equitable charge on the land, undertaking or debts of the company must be registered in due form within twenty-one days of its creation, otherwise it becomes void against the liquidator or any creditor of the company (1948 : s. 95). In formal terms it is the duty of the company to ensure that the registration is made but in practice this is often left to the party in whose favour the charge is made. The definition in the section is normally given a wide interpretation :

A vending machine company made an agreement with a finance firm under which it agreed to deposit all documents and securities belonging to the company or thereafter deposited with it, which in practice meant all the hire purchase contracts which the company entered into with its customers, by way of security for its liabilities to the finance firm. Some fifty hire purchase agreements were deposited under the agreement but no attempt to register was made. It was claimed by the finance firm that the agreement was not registrable since hire purchase agreements were not book debts under the terms of s. 95 since payments under them became due only by instalments. It was held that since the hire purchase contracts created firm obligations to pay a minimum amount they did constitute book debts of the company, and the fact that they had not been so entered in the company's books was of no significance; they were accordingly registrable and the security was thus void for want of registration. *Independent Automatic Sales Ltd. v. Knowles & Foster* [1962] 1 W.L.R. 974

This means that in practice any contract or agreement entered into by a company whose effect is to give priority to any one creditor over others will be deemed to be registrable. The only major exception to this general principle is in respect of hire purchase commitments of the company, as discussed below.

No floating charges on partnership property

The development of this aspect of the law has been briefly set out to help explain an important anomaly, the fact that floating charges as a form of security are available only to incorporated companies.[16] This was not always the case. In the mid-nineteenth century no distinction was made between the various forms of business for this purpose. The abuse of general charges on future property by moneylenders and others, however, led to the introduction of a requirement in the Bills of Sale (Amendment) Act of 1882 that as a pre-condition of registration and therefore of enforceability the property covered by any bill of sale should be clearly and specificaliy listed in a schedule to the bill (s. 4); in addition after-acquired property 'of which the grantor was not true owner at the time', except in the case of substituted property, could not be validly charged (s. 5). The result of this, and of the way in which the registration requirements were formulated (s. 9), was to render it difficult to register any floating charge in the proper statutory form, and it was finally decided in *Thomas v. Kelly* (1888),[17] a case concerning a general charge on present and future property, that any bill of sale purporting to cover after-acquired property must be void for lack of compliance with the statutory form. This marked the end of the floating charge on partnership property as an effective form of business security. But the rule was not extended to registered companies: the 1882 statute specifically excluded companies and it was decided in *In re Standard Manufacturing Co.* (1891)[18] that the

[16] See generally P. G. Fitzpatrick, 'Why not a partnership floating charge?', (1971) *Journal of Business Law*, 18.

[17] 13 App. Cas. 506.

[18] [1891] 1 Ch. 627.

fact that separate provision had been made in the Companies Acts for the public registration of company charges excluded by implication the application of any other provisions of the legislation on bills of sale.

The net effect of this confused set of provisions has been to deny the advantages of the floating charge as a flexible and convenient form of security to any unincorporated business. There is no compelling reason why this should be so. The fact that in strict law the property of a partnership or sole trader must be regarded as the property of the individuals concerned does not prevent such property being described with sufficient precision to identify the extent of a floating charge in the event of crystallization. There is certainly no difficulty in this respect in relation to floating charges on corporate property. The other major consideration which is often raised as an objection to the creation of floating charges by partnerships is the reputed ownership doctrine in bankruptcy, to the effect that any property in the possession of and generally believed to belong to the bankrupt must go into the general fund for distribution among the ordinary creditors regardless of the rights of the true owner (Bankruptcy Act 1914 : s. 38). But this would appear to be no more than an ex post facto rationalization of the effect of the 1882 Act, and the decision in *Thomas v. Kelly*. The basic purpose of the requirement that bills of sale, and charges on company property, shall be formally registered is to inform creditors and prospective creditors of the fact that a prior interest has been created in property which might otherwise be thought to be available to meet the debts of the business in the event of liquidation. Thus if the charge is clearly formulated and duly registered there can be no case for the application of the reputed ownership doctrine. Reputed ownership has in any event lost much of its force in an age when many of the apparent assets of small businesses can be expected to be the subject of hire purchase or simple hiring contracts, as was stated by the Blagden Committee on Bankruptcy and Deeds of Arrangement :

> This clause has become obsolete and now serves no useful purpose whatever. . . . Any danger of a creditor being induced to give credit by an assumption that all goods in the possession of the debtor are his own property is now non-existent.[19]

[19] Cmnd. 221 (1957), para. 110.

There is no longer anything to prevent a simple rejection of the muddled policy of the 1882 Act and the decisions on it, and the restoration of a greater degree of parity between companies and unincorporated businesses in respect of the security which they may offer.

Modern financing methods: credit, hire purchase and re-financing

The unsatisfactory position in respect of floating charges is not the only shortcoming of the law in this sphere. The courts have also failed to keep pace with and adapt to other developments in business financing. Business operations need not always be financed by raising share or loan capital, with or without security. The same results may be achieved either by simple credit trading, or by means of a wide range of hiring or hire purchase transactions.

There is no special legal difficulty over credit financing. Clearly from the point of view of the debtor, delay in paying his debts is by far the cheapest means of financing his operations, since there is not normally any direct interest charge on the notional loan, though any discount for prompt payment will be lost. The only real concern of the law is to ensure that the extent of current liabilities of this kind is accurately expressed in the company's accounts, and that adequate accounting procedures are adopted for writing off bad debts.

There is a good deal more cause for legal concern over hire, hire purchase and re-financing ('sale and lease-back') transactions. The basic principle behind any transaction of this type is that the enterprise, instead of expending capital on the purchase of premises, plant, vehicles or even stock, hires or obtains them on hire purchase terms from another firm, usually a finance house, in return for a hiring charge which in effect represents the interest on the capital which would otherwise have had to be raised and laid out. The net result is that the enterprise has the full possession and use of the premises or plant or vehicles that it needs, though in legal terms the ownership remains with the finance company. Cash may be raised in a similar way on premises or plant or vehicles which already belong to the enterprise by means of a legal sale of the property in question to a finance company which then returns them to the enterprise on hire or hire purchase terms. The result in these re-financing or lease-back transactions is even more clearly a disguised loan to the enterprise on the security of its premises, plant or vehicles.

There is nothing inherently objectionable in these methods of financing business operations. They are no more than the counterpart in the business world of the modern system of consumer credit through the mechanism of hire purchase or credit sale. The difficulty is that transactions of this type are not as the law now stands subject to the same disclosure rules, nor to the same registration requirements as traditional mortgages or charges. In the first place there is no specific accounting rule which ensures that the extent to which an enterprise makes use of hire, hire purchase or re-financing is disclosed in the company's accounts, though major sale and lease-back transactions should be reflected in the accounts as a sale of fixed assets. And secondly it is settled law that an ordinary hire purchase transaction is not subject either to the Bills of Sale Acts nor to the registration requirements of the Companies Acts:

A small firm obtained a number of gas engines on standard hire purchase terms under which the property in the engines remained with the lessor until the last instalment was paid. The firm became bankrupt soon after paying the first instalment. It was argued that the lessor had no right to recover the engines since the agreement was void for want of registration as a bill of sale. This argument was firmly rejected by the court: the agreement clearly stated that the property should remain with the lessor until the final instalment was paid; hence there could be no question either of a conditional or absolute bill of sale from the firm to the lessor, nor consequently of registration. *McEntire & Maconchy v. Crossley Bros. Ltd.* [1895] A.C. 457

The position with respect to sale and lease-back transactions is a good deal less clear. Where the sale of the assets concerned to the finance company is no more than a paper transaction with no attempt to give any practical effect to the change in ownership, the courts have sometimes held that the operation is a 'mere sham' designed only to evade the registration requirements under the Companies Acts or the Bills of Sale Acts:

Polsky bought a car from a dealer which he paid for with a cheque for £895. As there was not enough in his bank account to meet this cheque he arranged to sell the car to a finance company for £400 and the finance company then let him have it back on a hire purchase agreement for a total payment of £450. Polsky later sold the car and offered full payment to the finance company, which refused to accept it. It was held that since the finance company had bought the car directly from Polsky, rather than through the dealer as is usual, the transaction was a sham sale intended only to evade the Bills of Sale Acts: it was necessary 'to look through or behind the documents and to get at the reality; and if in reality the documents are only given as a security for money then they are bills of sale.' (per Lord Goddard, at p. 188) *Polsky v. S & A Services* [1951] 1 All E.R. 185 & 1062 (CA)

This 'realist' approach is likely to be adopted where there is any element of concealment or fraud in the transaction, for instance if the value placed on the property 'sold' or 'assigned' bears no relation to its true market value or if, as in the *Polsky* case, one side is acting unreasonably. But the law on the issue is confused and uncertain. Paradoxically the more complex the transaction the less likely it is to be held to be a sham. For example where the assets are first 'sold' by the enterprise seeking finance to a dealer, who then arranges for a finance company to enter into a hire purchase agreement with the original enterprise under which it gets the goods back again, the courts seem more ready to uphold the operation as genuine. Three-party transactions of this kind are thus not normally subject to registration as company charges or bills of sale, even though there is no more physical change in the possession or control of the property involved than in the case of a two-party transaction:

A company in need of funds arranged to 'sell' a number of vehicles to a dealer who then arranged for a finance company to finance a standard hire purchase of them by the original company, despite the fact that the finance company had specifically instructed the dealer not to submit any re-financing transactions of this kind. The company went into liquidation and the question arose whether the liquidator was entitled to the proceeds of the sale of the vehicles on the ground that their sale to the dealer and thence to the finance company was no more than a sham to conceal a loan charged on the security of the vehicles which could not be enforced for want of registration. It was held that there was nothing to show that the sale of the goods to the dealer, and by the dealer to the finance company, were not genuine and effective transfers, so that there was no charge on the company's property to be registered. The vehicles were thus the property of the finance company. Sellers L.J., in dissent, argued that in reality the documents gave the finance company no more than a charge on the vehicles since no payments had actually been made as referred to in the documents and no delivery effected, and that the charge was therefore void. *Stoneleigh Finance Ltd. v. Phillips* [1965] 2 Q.B. 537 (CA)

The conflict of opinion in this and other cases shows clearly the divergent pressures on the courts, both to give effect to clearly evidenced transactions and also to prevent the evasion of the requirements as to the registration of charges by resort to complex legal forms concealing simple secured loans. Various factors are considered relevant: the price fixed for the 'sale' of the property; whether the property was newly acquired or remained all the time in the hands of the original owner; the extent to which the third parties fully realized the nature of the transaction, as they did not in the *Stoneleigh* case; and whether the transactions as documented corresponded to the actual course of events. But in the last resort it is impossible to make sound sense of the decisions. It can only be stated that the courts will probably lean against the invalidation of ordinary commercial transactions by companies, if only to avoid introducing the vagaries of the law on bills of sale into the field of company law.

A case for simplification and reform

It will be clear from this account that there is little rhyme or reason in the existing law on security for loans or in the provisions for registration. If it is accepted that the function of the law in this sphere is to provide a means by which loans to business enterprises may be secured on the property of that enterprise, it follows that there is no plausible justification for the continued denial of the benefits of the floating charge to non-incorporated businesses. It is just possible that the right of a partnership or a sole trader to create a floating charge might be established within the existing law by a tactical evasion of earlier decisions on the Bills of Sale Acts,[20] but a direct attack on the merits of the existing rules is perhaps more likely to produce a satisfactory result. In addition the concurrent objectives of a registration system, both in protecting the interests of a secured party against third parties and in making available to other existing and potential creditors details of the full extent to which a borrower's assets are already encumbered, are frustrated by the uncertainty of the law on bills of sale and re-financing transactions. They are also hindered by the fact that so many financing arrangements are concealed by the use of hire purchase or hiring contracts.

Many of these difficulties would be resolved by the adoption of the reforms suggested by the Crowther Committee on Consumer

[20] It be may argued that charges on future property fall totally outside the scope of the Acts, so that a floating charge on stock could not be attacked for want of registration: see generally P. G. Fitzpatrick, 'Why not a partnership floating charge?', (1971) *Journal of Business Law*, 18.

Credit.[21] The Committee was primarily concerned with consumer rather than business transactions and only those parts of its recommendations which affected consumers were accepted and enacted in the Consumer Credit Act 1974. But the Committee also recommended sweeping changes in the law affecting all forms of security to replace the technical distinctions between bills of sale, hire purchase, credit sale and the rest by a single simple legal form through which lenders and borrowers in all spheres may secure their loans on personal property. Under the new lending and security legislation proposed by the Committee all transactions in which in substance a loan is made on the security of a borrower's assets would be governed by the same basic rules regardless of legal form, and any non-consumer security would be enforceable in priority to third parties only if it is formally 'perfected' by registration.[22] This system, if adopted, would effectively remove any fundamental difference between unincorporated and incorporated concerns. Floating charges would be supplanted by the more general system of notice filing, under which the filing of a security notice would cover all property of the class described whether in the possession of the borrower at the time of the filing or subsequently acquired, excepting only that disposed of in the ordinary course of business.[23] And the problems over re-financing and hire purchase would simply disappear.

The scheme proposed by the Crowther Committee would not remove all distinction between companies and other concerns. The new securities registry would be separate from that maintained under the Companies Acts, and relevant transactions by companies would therefore have to be filed twice. In addition there would be some danger of continuing differences in the legal requirements under company law and the general loan and security legislation as applied to unincorporated concerns. At the simplest level, companies would still presumably be required to file details of all security agreements including those of less than the standard exemption figure of £300

[21] Cmnd. 4596 (1971).

[22] See generally Part V, and especially paras. 5.7.1–48; the system recommended is based broadly on that developed in America and codified in Article 9 of the Uniform Commercial Code.

[23] Para. 5.7.50–1; the Committee recommended that the traditional floating charge should be retained in view of its widespread popularity in the business community (para. 5.7.77); a similar view has been taken by the Cork Committee on *The EEC Preliminary Draft Convention on Bankruptcy, Winding-up, Arrangements, Compositions and Similar Proceedings*, Cmnd. 6602 (1976), paras. 364–7.

proposed by the Committee.[24] The only means of securing complete equality of treatment for all concerns would in effect be to maintain details of all charges created on business property by extending the ambit of the companies registry to include all commercial concerns. The Consumer Credit Act 1974 maintains a distinction between incorporated and unincorporated concerns, in that all credit transactions by companies are excluded from its provisions while those by partnerships and sole traders up to a current limit of £5,000 are covered (ss. 8, 189). To the extent that small traders are in need of as much protection in their transactions with large companies as consumers, as argued by the Law Commission in respect of exemption clauses (Law Commission No. 69, 1975), this distinction is hard to justify. The logic of the Committee's proposals is that regulation in this sphere should be governed by size rather than the status of those involved.

The Committee's proposals for treating hire purchase and thus many re-financing transactions as a form of secured loan would still leave the growing volume of business transacted under leasing or rental contracts outside the scope of the registration provisions, since there would be no property interest in the hands of the lessee concern. If the second objective of registration, that of informing creditors and prospective creditors of the extent to which a firm's apparent assets are in practice unencumbered, is to be fully achieved then some further provision for the express disclosure in company accounts of the extent of its commitment under hire purchase, rental and re-financing transactions alike may still be necessary. This aspect of the problem is discussed in relation to the more general question of disclosure by small business concerns (see p. 211).

4 THE RIGHTS OF CREDITORS

The creditor's view of the problems of business finance is rather different from that of the entrepreneur. The entrepreneur is primarily concerned with the range of methods by which he may raise money and the relative cost of each. The creditor or financier, in addition to his converse interest in these same aspects, is concerned about the prospects under each method of financing or trading of protecting his loan or securing payment of his debt. The rights of

[24] Para. 5.7.26.

creditors in this respect fall into two broad categories: first the right of each creditor to take action to protect his own or his co-creditors' interests *before* the enterprise has reached the stage of insolvency and liquidation; and secondly his rights in the event of a liquidation. The law in respect of these two sets of rights differs appreciably between companies and partnerships, especially in respect of bankruptcy and liquidation, though as before many of the differences are of procedure and nomenclature rather than of substance.

Creditors' rights of intervention

The prime right of any creditor is to sue for payment of his debt or repayment of his loan, and if a judgement in his favour remains unsatisfied to levy execution on the goods of the debtor. A business enterprise, whether incorporated or not, is in no special position in this respect, except of course that in the case of a limited company it is only the property of the company and not of those concerned in it which may be taken in satisfaction. Nor may those concerned in a company be subjected to the personal remedies of bankruptcy, the attachment of earnings and administration orders to which individual traders and the members of a partnership are subject.

From a practical point of view, however, the complex law and procedure of debt collection as applied to individual debts, apart from the issue of threats and writs, are less important than might appear. Businesses which fall behind in their payments are not normally indebted to a single creditor, but to a whole series of suppliers of goods and services. Accordingly, if a single creditor presses his claim to the point of execution or beyond, the fears of others will normally be aroused and formal proceedings for bankruptcy or liquidation, in which the money sought by the original creditor is likely to be swallowed up, will soon follow. The art of successful debt collection is to obtain payment without resort to the publicity which court orders and the levying of execution inevitably occasion, since a debt which has actually been paid without resort to legal compulsion, in the absence of any element of fraudulent preference, cannot be brought back into the general fund for other creditors in the event of a subsequent winding up.

Receivers and managers for secured creditors

The danger of precipitating a premature winding up applies even to secured creditors. The amount realizable on the security will not always meet the full amount of the loan or obligation, especially in the case of a floating charge on plant and goods whose value will be very much higher within a going concern than on a forced sale. In any event there is bound to be considerable delay in the realization of the money, especially where a full-scale liquidation follows. It will thus frequently be in the interests of a substantial secured creditor not to force the winding up of the business at least in the short term, quite apart from any desire he may have not to destroy the enterprise. On the other hand he may wish to impose some measure of control over its continuing operations in order to protect his security. This is normally achieved by making express provision under the terms of the contract for the loan or security for the business to be put into the hands of a receiver or manager on behalf of the secured creditor on certain eventualities. Certain powers in this respect are also implied at common law. In some cases provision may also be made for a director to be appointed to the board of a company to look after the interests of a debenture holder on a continuing basis.

Debenture deeds normally permit action of this kind to be taken by debenture holders where interest payments fall in arrears, or where execution is levied against the property of the business. Since the matter is essentially one for contractual arrangements between the parties, provision may also be made to suit the particular circumstances in which the loan or obligation was incurred. In addition to these specific provisions, however, a debenture holder is deemed at law to have the right to step in whenever his security is in jeopardy. The meaning of 'jeopardy' for this purpose is a good deal narrower than the situations usually provided for in a debenture deed. It covers only situations in which the property secured is in imminent danger of loss or dissipation. The full extent of the concept is best gauged from individual decided cases. *In re Victoria Steamboats* (1897),[25] for example, was held to be a clear case of jeopardy because interest on the debenture was in arrears, creditors were threatening and a winding up petition was pending. But the mere fact that the assets of the company are less than sufficient to meet the amount outstanding on the debenture may not be enough:

A debenture was issued by a taxi company, secured on the lease of a garage and the company's vehicles. Heavy losses were incurred in trading, and the company's insurer had failed. The company in general meeting

[25] [1897] 1 Ch. 158.

then decided not to pay the dividend due on the debentures. A debenture holder instituted proceedings to have a receiver appointed on the ground that his security was in jeopardy, but the petition was rejected: 'The assets were not in jeopardy in the sense that there was any risk of their being seized to pay claims not really prior to the claims of the debenture holders. The company was a going concern. The security was not yet enforceable ... and the fact that if it were now realised it would be wholly insufficent to pay the principal and interest was not a sufficient ground for appointing a receiver.' (per Swinfen Eady L.J., at p. 8) *In re New York Taxicab Co. Ltd.* [1913] 1 Ch. 1 (CA)

The basic duty of a receiver or manager once installed is to see to it that the property on which the debenture is secured remains intact for the settlement of the loan in due course, and he is granted full powers of control over the business for this purpose. In strict law a receiver should proceed immediately to the realization of the security, while a manager may continue to operate the business without any immediate obligation to realize the security which he is there to protect. But in practical terms there is little effective difference since a receiver is also entitled to continue the business as far as that is necessary to realize the full value of the property on which the debenture is secured. In some cases the receiver or manager will withdraw voluntarily once the crisis has passed, and before any serious attempt is made to repay the loan, leaving the business to be carried on by the original owners. But this may be conditional on some compromise arrangement for a change in management in an attempt to prevent the same difficulties arising in the future.

The rights of ordinary creditors

There is no simple mechanism comparable to the appointment of a receiver or manager by which an individual unsecured creditor may intervene in the affairs of a business debtor prior to liquidation or bankruptcy. There are, however, a number of procedures by which the full effects of a liquidation or winding up may be avoided by agreement between the debtor and the creditors. In the first place a voluntary arrangement may be made between the company or firm and the body of creditors under which each creditor agrees to forego his individual rights to force an execution or winding up in return for an undertaking that the outstanding debts or a proportion of them will be paid off by instalments over a period of time, with or without some form of continuing supervision by the creditors.

Where bankruptcy or liquidation proceedings have been started or are imminent, such an arrangement is binding on all creditors if it is approved in the case of unincorporated debtors by a majority of creditors representing more than three-quarters of the total value of all the debts proved (Bankruptcy Act 1914 : s. 16), and in the case of a registered company by three-quarters of the creditors in both number and value (1948 : s. 306). Any deed of arrangement of this kind must be registered under the Deeds of Arrangement Act 1914, which also makes provision for the filing and circulation of accounts by any trustee appointed on behalf of the creditors under the deed.[26]

In the case of small individual traders or partnerships it may also be possible for either the debtor or the creditor to persuade a court in proceedings for the enforcement of a judgement debt to make an administration order, under which the full range of the enterprise's debts will be ascertained and a scheme for the equitable payment of all creditors by instalments worked out (County Courts Act 1959, Part VII). This procedure is currently limited to cases in which the total indebtedness is not more than £1,000.

There is no equivalent procedure in Britain under which a court may impose a settlement of this kind on a registered company. In both South Africa and Australia, however, a system of judicial management has been developed under which the affairs of a company in difficulties may be placed under the control of a judicial manager, on the application to the court either by the company itself or by its creditors. It is the manager's duty to continue the business of the company in the joint interests of the owners and creditors. The institution has not proved an unqualified success in either jurisdiction. In most Australian states it has been found that the appointment of a judicial manager has frequently been arranged by the management of the company in difficulties with a view to avoiding liquidation proceedings and has simply resulted in the appointment of an associate of the existing directors with little benefit for the creditors in the long term. In South Africa there have also been allegations of irregular appointments, but the de Vries Commission (1970) reported that about twenty-five per cent of the companies to which the procedure for judicial management had been applied had not proceeded to liquidation. The procedures for the appoint-

[26] See generally the report of the Blagden Committee on Bankruptcy and Deeds of Arrangement, Cmnd. 221 (1957).

ment of provisional and final judicial managers have since been amended both in South Africa (Companies Act, No. 61 of 1973, ss. 427–440) and in Australia (e.g. New South Wales Companies (Amendment) Act 1966, ss. 199–213). A similar provision in Britain would help to strengthen the position of ordinary unsecured creditors who do not wish to force a debtor company into liquidation, but who lack confidence in the ability or bona fides of the existing directors.

As the law now stands, however, each individual creditor is ultimately left to press his own claims for payment and in default to file a petition for the winding up of the debtor business. In the case of sole traders and partnerships this will involve proceedings in bankruptcy against the individuals involved, and for registered companies a winding up petition against the company. The two systems are broadly similar in effect, but there are sufficient apparent differences to make it necessary to deal with each separately.

5 BANKRUPTCY

The law of bankruptcy provides in essence that when an individual trader or member of a partnership is unable to meet his current obligations and can no longer persuade his creditors to hold off, all his goods and assets, excepting personal necessities, may be taken and realized and the resulting fund shared out pro rata among all his creditors, at so much in the pound. In return for this the bankrupt is granted immunity from any further suits by individual creditors, though until he pays in full or secures a formal discharge from the court he will continue to be liable under the bankruptcy order to the extent of any future profits or goods which he may acquire. If he does subsequently obtain a discharge, he is formally freed from any continuing liability for his past debts, and is thus able to make a completely fresh start.

This system originated in the general jurisdiction of the King's Council and the Court of the Star Chamber to bring pressure on creditors to agree to some form of composition in order to free insolvent traders from the usual remedy of indefinite imprisonment.[27] The initial Bankruptcy Statute of 1543, which was applicable to traders only, provided both for the collection and distribution of the

[27] See generally Holdsworth, *A History of English Law*, Vol. VIII p. 229 ff., Vol. XI p. 444 ff, Vol. XII p. 387 ff, and Vol. XIII p. 376 ff, on which this account is largely based.

bankrupt's assets and also for quasi-criminal penalties to prevent collusive or fraudulent evasion of the new system. Then in 1705–6 formal provision was made for the discharge of bankrupts on proof that all available assets had in fact been distributed among creditors. Bankruptcy law was thus founded on a distinction between honest and dishonest insolvency. A similar distinction was developed for ordinary insolvents, who were able to secure their release from prison on similar terms under periodic Debtors Relief Acts from the eighteenth century onwards. A wide range of severe criminal penalties, including capital punishment for the fraudulent concealment of assets, was then superimposed on both systems.

This mixture of civil and criminal remedies has remained a feature of the law of bankruptcy and insolvency, despite the frequent consolidations and reforms of the nineteenth century. In 1861 the distinction between bankrupt traders and other non-commercial insolvents was abolished and in 1869 the general remedy of indefinite imprisonment, subject to discretionary release, was finally abandoned. But, as so often was the case, many of the complexities and inconsistencies in the law persisted, especially in the range of statutory offences. The major nineteenth-century advance was the creation in 1883 of a new system for the official oversight of all bankruptcy proceedings through the office of the Official Receiver, which meant that for the first time there was some prospect of the enforcement of the criminal provisions of bankruptcy law. The law was further consolidated and amended in the Bankruptcy Act 1914. No substantial alterations have since been made.

It is the forms and procedures through which the system of bankruptcy is operated rather than the principles on which it is based which give rise to most of the problems in practice and litigation. But the broad outlines of the system will be given since the system for company liquidation is derived from it. In addition an understanding of the differences in the two systems is important to a discussion of winding up in any new small business legislation.

Acts of bankruptcy

Bankruptcy is defined in terms of a list of situations, or acts of bankruptcy, in which a receiving order may be made against the individual involved. The most important of these, as set out in s. 1 of the Bankruptcy Act 1914, are as follows :

i failure to pay any judgement debt within seven days of a bankruptcy notice being served by the creditor concerned, provided that the total indebtedness of the potential bankrupt is in excess of £200;[28]

ii the giving of notice to creditors by the debtor that he is suspending payment of his debts;

iii the levying of execution on the debtor's goods, provided that the goods seized have either been sold or held by the sheriff for twenty-one days;

iv any fraudulent conveyance of property, or any fraudulent preference in the payment of a creditor;

v disappearance or flight of the debtor with intent to defeat or delay his creditors;

vi the making of an arrangement with the creditors;

vii the filing of a declaration by the debtor himself to the effect that he is unable to pay his debts.

In all but the last of these situations any creditor, and since 1883 the bankrupt himself, may file a petition in bankruptcy which, if granted and subsequently confirmed in a formal adjudication, has the effect of vesting the assets of the bankrupt in the official receiver as trustee in bankruptcy unless provision is made by the creditors for some other person to act as trustee on their behalf. There are considerable advantages in bankruptcy for the debtor as well as for creditors : for instance once a petition is filed all other proceedings against the debtor may be stayed, and once the adjudication of bankruptcy is formally made all such actions are automatically brought into the bankruptcy. In recent years more than half of the receiving orders made have in fact originated in a debtor's rather than a creditor's petition. But the debtor is required to assist the court by submitting a statement of affairs setting out his assets and liabilities to the best of his knowledge (s. 14). He may also be required to attend a public examination under oath at which he may be questioned both by the court and by the Official Receiver as to the circumstances of any particular transaction or more generally as to the reasons for his

[28] Substituted by the Insolvency Act 1976, sched. 1.

insolvency (s. 15).[29] The standard of disclosure imposed on a bankrupt in this respect is a strict one : he is under a positive duty to give a satisfactory account of his affairs and may be prosecuted even for a simple refusal to answer questions put to him during his public examination regardless of any proven intention to evade the provisions of the Act.[30]

The appointment of a trustee and the conduct of the winding up

On the adjudication the court must appoint as trustee in bankruptcy either the Official Receiver or the nominee of the creditors (s. 19). In practice some three-quarters of the cases are dealt with officially, that is by a fully paid official of the Official Receiver's department, and the remainder by professional accountants and other independent liquidators. In either case arrangements may also be made for the appointment of a committee of inspection elected by the creditors to oversee the process of winding up and distribution of the debtor's assets (s. 20). The trustee will then proceed to assemble all the debtor's property, both actual and potential, including any debts owing to him, and to distribute it in accordance with the rules as to priority. Thus any debt or obligation secured by a mortgage or bill of sale must be settled in priority out of the amount realized on the property charged, and statutory preference over other debts is given to rates and taxes and up to a given limit to wages and other payments due to the bankrupt's employees (s. 33).

It is only when all these prior claims have been met that the remaining assets may be distributed among the ordinary unsecured creditors who have proved their debts to the satisfaction of the trustee. And there will be many cases in which virtually nothing will be left for this purpose. Concern was expressed by the Blagden Committee[31] at the increasing proportion of assets paid out on priority debts, and in particular to the Inland Revenue, which under the decision in *I.R.C. v. Phillips* (1951)[32] may claim tax due and unpaid in respect of *any* year prior to the bankruptcy rather than for the year preceding the bankruptcy. The freedom of choice which this gives to the Inland Revenue has meant that it has been able to

[29] The obligation under s. 15 to hold a public examination in every case may now be dispensed with by order of the court: Insolvency Act 1976, s. 6.

[30] *R v. Salter* [1963] 2 Q.B. 793.

[31] Committee on Bankruptcy and Deeds of Arrangement (1957), Cmnd. 221, paras. 86 ff.

[32] [1951] 1 Ch. 225 (CA).

claim on average some ten per cent of the net assets realized. The Committee felt that any such prior claims should be limited to one of the two years preceding the bankruptcy which in the nature of things were likely to have been less profitable, and thus result in lower tax assessments. The likelihood of a sizeable dividend being available for ordinary unsecured creditors is also dependent on the costs of liquidation. In recent years roughly one-third of the total funds realized have on average been absorbed by expenses.

Fraudulent preference

A more detailed account is necessary of some of the provisions for the administration of a bankrupt's estate because of their special relevance to company liquidations. First, under the onerous property rule the trustee in bankruptcy has a discretion to disclaim any property of the bankrupt to which 'onerous' conditions are attached and which in his opinion represent a net liability rather than a net asset to the bankrupt's estate (s. 54). Secondly, under the fraudulent or voidable preference doctrine, any payment or charge made by the bankrupt in anticipation of bankruptcy with a view to preferring a particular creditor to others may be contested and set aside at the suit of the trustee, and the assets involved redistributed among all the creditors. In particular where it can be shown that within six months before the date of the adjudication of bankruptcy and while the bankrupt was insolvent he made a payment or created a charge in favour of a particular creditor with the dominant intention of preferring that creditor to others, the payment or charge is deemed to be a fraudulent preference (s. 44).[33] The objective is clearly to prevent insolvent debtors making over what property they have to a particular creditor or relation in order to avoid the full effects of a bankruptcy order. But the difficulties in deciding what is an unfair preference in distinction to a valid payment under the ordinary first come first served principle and in proving an intent to so prefer are almost insuperable.[34] It has been held, for instance, that the fact that a creditor is pressing for payment may be used as evidence to rebut an intention to prefer:

> A partner in a firm of solicitors illicitly applied for his own purposes the proceeds of a mortgage transaction undertaken by the firm for a client.

[33] See also ss. 42–3, covering fraudulent settlements or assignments.

[34] Bona fide payments are statutorily protected (s. 45).

The matter came to light in the course of a Law Society audit and on the request of his partner the solicitor repaid the money. Within six months he was adjudged bankrupt, and the repayment was contested by the trustee in bankruptcy as a fraudulent preference. It was held that the payment was voidable since the dominant intention was to prefer in that there had been no pressure from the client, who knew nothing of the affair, and in that the repayment of one defalcation among many others not so repaid could not help the solicitor: 'If a debtor deliberately selects for payment A in preference to all his other creditors, it cannot . . . matter . . . whether A is the debtor's oldest friend, closest relative or best client,' but if it is a repayment of a theft to avoid a criminal case, or if it is paid 'under pressure of some threat or to obtain . . . some immediate and material benefit or to fulfil some particular obligation the dominant intention is not to prefer, and the payment is good.' (per Lord Evershed M.R., at p. 734) *In re Cutts* [1956] 1 W.L.R. 728 (CA)

It will be clear from this example how difficult it may be to apply the voidable preference rule. It may equally be argued as it was put to the Blagden Committee that pressure from a creditor, far from enabling him to retain any payment made as a result, should have the opposite effect.[35] Where the moral arguments are so finely balanced, it is correspondingly difficult to arrive at a generally acceptable legal rule. The Blagden Committee attempted to avoid the difficulties in proof by recommending that *all* payments made while insolvent in respect of past debts and within three weeks before the date of a bankruptcy petition which *in fact* prefer one creditor to others should be set aside irrespective of the intention of the debtor.[36] This would at least have the merit of certainty, and in a situation where justice is almost impossible to attain has much to recommend it. The basic objective of the law of bankruptcy is not to secure complete equality between all the past and present creditors of the bankrupt, but to set a simple time limit beyond which all unpaid creditors shall be treated equally. It is impossible, even under the existing law, to prevent those engaged in risky ventures from alienating their personal assets to their wives or children, to protect themselves in the event of insolvency. But there is no reason why the time limit for valid payments, regardless of the intention of the debtor, should not be set somewhat before rather than on the date of the petition. Pressure on the debtor to make as full payment as is

[35] Cmnd, 221 (1957) para. 116 ff.

[36] Para. 119.

possible may more readily be operated through a discretionary discharge system, or by criminal sanctions for cases of blatant fraud or concealment, than by the uncertainties of the current fraudulent preference rule.

Bankruptcy offences and discharge

A brief account should also be given of the effect of bankruptcy proceedings on the bankrupt himself. In the first place the bankrupt is given statutory protection from the seizure of his personal necessities, including specifically his clothes and bedding and the tools of his trade (s. 38). Apart from this he must hand over all his property and give a true account of his affairs to the trustee. He is subject to severe criminal penalties for any attempt to defeat the interests of creditors by concealing assets, by making secret payments to friends and relatives or by engaging in any form of fraud or deception in the course of or in contemplation of the bankruptcy. The actual list of bankruptcy offences in the 1914 Act running to sixteen separate items in s. 154 alone is confused and often archaic, covering in addition to the concealment of assets or false accounting any indulgence in 'rash or hazardous speculations' within two years of the bankruptcy. But there is little doubt that virtually any form of direct evasion or fraud is covered somehow. In addition there is in practice an obligation on the prospective bankrupt to keep proper accounts, since he may be prosecuted for any unreasonable failure to do so within two years of the bankruptcy (s. 158). If only because of the relative simplicity of proving this form of charge, this offence has accounted for almost half the annual prosecutions in recent years.

There are also continuing penalties merely in being a bankrupt, at least until discharge. No undischarged bankrupt may obtain credit in excess of £50[37] or trade under any other name than that in which he was adjudged bankrupt (s. 155). Certain positions, such as the directorship of any company, are barred to undischarged bankrupts (Companies Act 1948 : s. 187). Any infringement of these rules may lead to criminal prosecution. In addition, and perhaps most important, until his discharge a bankrupt remains liable to all his unpaid creditors to the extent of any property or assets which he acquires or earns subsequent to his bankruptcy.

In the light of these continuing penalties it would be reasonable

[37] Substituted by the Insolvency Act 1976, sched. 1.

to expect that most bankrupts would be anxious to secure their discharge as soon as possible. In practice this did not happen. The procedure for discharge required the bankrupt to make a personal application for discharge, and to pay the fees of the hearing. Many bankrupts in consequence simply did not wish or bother to make the application, with the result that the question of discharge was considered in only one in every four or five cases. The courts were thus unable to make the intended distinction between the honest but unfortunate insolvent who would be granted a speedy discharge and those who might reasonably be penalized on a longer term basis, if only in the hope of deterring them from re-embarking on commercial activities. Following the recommendations of the Blagden Committee[38] it has now been provided that the court may order that a bankrupt shall be automatically discharged five years after his adjudication if no previous discharge is granted (Insolvency Act 1976 : s. 7).

Bankruptcy and partnership

The peculiar nature of a partnership as a business association which has no other legal status in law than that of the individuals who compose it creates special problems in the application of the ordinary rules of bankruptcy. The basic principle is that as far as possible the property and debts of the partnership are kept separate from those of the partners as individuals. But the residual liability of the partners both jointly and severally for the debts of the firm makes it impossible to maintain this strict separation. The compromise which has been reached is clearly set out in the Bankruptcy Act 1924 :

> In the case of partners the joint estate shall be applicable in the first instance in payment of their joint debts and the separate estate of each partner shall be applicable in the first instance in payment of his separate debts. If there is a surplus of the separate estates it shall be dealt with as part of the joint estate. If there is a surplus of the joint estate it shall be dealt with as part of the respective separate estates in proportion to the right and interest of each partner in the joint estate. (s. 33(6))

This means in practice that the creditors of the individual partners in respect of their personal debts may fare rather better than the creditors of the firm, where it is the business rather than the individual partners which is primarily insolvent. Some of the assets

[38] Cmnd. 221 (1957), para. 53 ff.

which in law belong to individual partners may, however, be applied to meet the debts of the firm by the operation of the reputed ownership doctrine, which provides that any property other than real property which is in the possession of a bankrupt with the consent of the true owner shall be deemed to be his property and be distributed accordingly (s. 38). In the partnership situation this means that any assets normally used in the course of the firm's business are applied as part of the joint estate.

Where the bankruptcy petition is issued against an individual partner in respect of his personal liability, on the other hand, the firm is not strictly involved at all, except to the extent that it is a rule of law that the bankruptcy of any individual partner terminates the partnership unless express provision is made to the contrary. In the last analysis, however, it is always the individual partners against whom any adjudication in bankruptcy is made. Creditors may institute proceedings in bankruptcy against any or all of the partners, subject only to the right of those concerned to consolidate any separate actions which may be initiated. Assuming that the procedural complexities are successfully surmounted, the whole of the property of the individual partners is ultimately available to meet the debts of the firm, in so far as their personal assets exceed their personal liabilities.

6 COMPANY LIQUIDATION

The system of company liquidation is derived directly from that for bankruptcy, in that the Companies (Winding Up) Act of 1890 was modelled on the Bankruptcy Act of 1883. This is especially true of the procedural aspects of the law, from the choice between official and voluntary liquidation and the provision for committees of inspection to the conduct of the winding up and distribution. The major differences are those which arise from the fact of limited liability, as will appear from the account which follows.

The types of liquidation

A company may be wound up either voluntarily or compulsorily by order of the court. The most frequent form is the members' voluntary liquidation initiated by the members themselves when for any reason they wish to dissolve their business association. Where the company is in a position to make a formal declaration of solvency

(1948 : s. 283) the oversight of the liquidation will be in the hands of the members themselves, since it is the members who will be the principal beneficiaries in the distribution of the balance of assets over liabilities (1948 : ss. 284–91). When the company is insolvent, however, the liquidation is clearly of concern primarily to creditors to whom the whole of the available assets will be distributed. In such cases the oversight of the liquidation is in the hands of a committee of creditors (1948 : ss. 292–300). But this does not in itself prevent the liquidation from being undertaken voluntarily with the consent of the company's members and officers. It is only when the members or officers refuse to take the necessary steps to wind up their company that an application to the court for an order for compulsory liquidation need be made to ensure that the matter is dealt with. In such cases the winding up will be conducted under the direct supervision of the court, usually by an official of the Official Receiver's department, though the function may be delegated to a self-employed professional liquidator. Provision is also made for a fourth type of liquidation under the supervision of the court, by which what has started as a voluntary liquidation may be converted into an official liquidation (1948 : ss. 311–15).

The grounds for liquidation

The grounds on which a petition for the compulsory liquidation of a company may be based are enumerated, like the list of acts of bankruptcy, under six heads (1948 : s. 222). Three of these relate primarily to what may be termed procedural defaults :

i the failure by a public company to hold the statutorily prescribed initial meeting, or to make the required report on it;

ii the failure to commence business within a year of incorporation, or the suspension of business for a full year;

iii the reduction of the number of members below the statutory minimum of seven for a public company and two for a private company.

Two further heads are directed primarily at the internal affairs of the company :

iv a special resolution by the company in general meeting that it shall be wound up;

v an order by the court that it is just and equitable for the company to be wound up.

The first of these is inserted only to provide for the rare case in which what should be a voluntary liquidation is blocked or impeded by those in direct control over the company's affairs. The second is more significant in that it permits the court to order the winding up of a solvent company in situations where the requisite majority of shareholders cannot be obtained, as in the case of the exclusion of a minority shareholder from a quasi-partnership company (see p. 157), or where the substratum of the company's business has disappeared.

The most important head in practical terms, however, is the one which is available to external creditors:

vi the inability of the company to meet its debts.

The precise meaning of this is spelled out in the following section, which provides that a company shall be deemed to be unable to pay its debts if a creditor for more than £200[39] has served a formal demand for payment on the company and the company has failed to give satisfaction within three weeks, or if an order for execution against the goods of the company is not satisfied in full, or more generally if the court is satisfied on all the evidence of existing and future liabilities that the company is insolvent (1948 : s. 223).

This list of grounds for liquidation, however, is not of general application. A court is not bound to grant an order for liquidation where the petitioner has nothing to gain from it. Only those with a direct and tangible interest in the winding up are entitled to demand it:

A petition was made for the winding up of a company on the just and equitable ground by a member of the company. The company was in fact insolvent. The petition was rejected on the ground that the petitioner would gain nothing from the liquidaton: where a fully paid shareholder petitioned for compulsory winding-up he must show on the face of his petition a prima facie probability that there would be assets available for distribution amongst the shareholders. (per Buckley J., at p. 72) *In re Othery Construction Ltd.* [1966] 1 W.L.R. 69

This rule clearly excludes any intervention by shareholders or others

[39] Substituted by the Insolvency Act 1976, sched. 1.

solely concerned to secure the liquidation of an insolvent company, or more generally the due enforcement of the law. Nor will an order be granted where there is any substantial dispute about the existence or validity of a particular debt:

A dispute arose among the participants in two small linked companies. One party presented a petition for the winding up of one of the companies alleging debts comprising among other items unpaid director's fees. The petition was rejected on the ground that the debts were disputed, and that the right course was to sue for the debt. *Mann v. Goldstein* [1968] 1 W.L.R. 1091

An order for the compulsory liquidation of a company, like any other legal remedy, will be granted only to those with a recognized interest in the matter, and that only where there is no other effective way in which that interest may be protected.

In practice, when an unsecured creditor begins to suspect that a debtor company is getting into difficulties and that there is little chance of his being paid in preference to other creditors, there are three courses open to him. First, he may attempt to gather together a meeting of creditors and come to a formal or informal agreement with them and the debtor company for a creditors' voluntary liquidation or perhaps for the business to be continued on condition that the outstanding debts are paid off or commuted on some equitable basis. A scheme of arrangement agreed by a majority of the creditors representing three-quarters of the relevant debts may on application to the court be made binding on all creditors (1948: s. 206). Secondly, he may petition the court on his own account for the compulsory liquidation of the company in the hope of obtaining at least some dividend to cover his costs. Finally he may decide to do nothing, leaving it to some other creditor, if any, to take action. The result, as in the case of bankruptcy, is that those cases in which there is a chance of a substantial dividend tend to be dealt with by a non-official liquidation, on which the liquidator may make a worthwhile fee, while those cases in which there is less likelihood of substantial assets tend to be channelled through the Official Receiver's department. In recent years creditors' voluntary liquidations have outnumbered compulsory liquidations by roughly two to one. But there are still a substantial number of cases in which it is not even worth the creditor's while to pay the fees for a winding up petition, in which case the insolvent company will simply cease to trade and will continue in a limbo existence until it is formally struck off the register (1948 : s. 353) (see p. 121).

The conduct of liquidations

Once the liquidator has been appointed, the procedure both in official and non-official liquidations is broadly similar to that in bankruptcy. Except where a formal declaration of solvency has been made (1948 : s. 283), a meeting of creditors will be summoned to hear an initial report on the situation, and to appoint a committee of inspection if they so desire (1948 : s. 295). There is a significant difference between bankruptcy and company liquidation, however, in the provisions for inquiring into the causes of the insolvency. While in bankruptcy a public examination of the bankrupt must be held in all cases where the requirement is not formally dispensed with, the officers of an insolvent company are only subject to public examination (1948 : s. 270) where a formal report alleging fraud or other malpractice is submitted by the Official Receiver (1948 : s. 236). There is no corresponding provision in the case of voluntary liquidations, though the liquidator has a formal duty to make a report to the Director of Public Prosecutions of any criminal offence (1948 : s. 334). Since private liquidators and their committees of inspection are typically more concerned with the speedy realization of what assets are available than with a careful examination of the conduct of those responsible for the failure, such reports are rarely made. Provisions for an independent examination and report on the circumstances of a business failure are unlikely to prove effective unless they are to be made at public expense. Creditors are more interested in recovering money than in enforcing the law.

In every type of liquidation the liquidator will then proceed to assemble and realize the assets of the company, and to distribute the proceeds. The rules as to priority are broadly similar to those in bankruptcy. Creditors with a fixed charge are afforded effective priority over all others to the extent of the realizable value of the assets on which their loans are secured. There is a statutory priority for rates and taxes, for wages and salaries up to £800[40] per claimant and for holiday pay (1948 : s. 319). These take priority over all obligations and debts except those secured on a fixed charge. Even a receiver or manager who has already taken possession of assets secured

[40] Substituted by the Insolvency Act 1976, sched. 1.

by a floating charge is bound to pay them (1948 : s. 94). They are now in addition guaranteed under the Employment Protection Act 1975 (ss. 63–4). After these items come in turn debts and obligations secured on a floating charge (1948 : s. 319(5)(b)), ordinary unsecured debts and obligations, and finally, if there is any balance available, the preference and ordinary shareholders of the company in accordance with the terms of the articles of association. It should be noted that banks and other lenders may take advantage of the statutory priorities in that a loan granted specifically for the payment of wages or holiday pay is entitled to the same priority in a liquidation as would be accorded to the wage-earners if they had not been paid (1948 : s. 319(4)) :

A company opened a separate bank account and secured special overdraft facilities for the payment of its wages and national insurance stamps. Some but not all of the money lent through the account was spent for these purposes. It was held that the bank was entitled to be treated as a preferential creditor in respect of that part of the advance which had in fact been spent on meeting preferential obligations, whether or not any formal arrangement had been made restricting the uses to which the moneys lent were put. *In re Rampgill Mill Ltd.* [1967] Ch. 1138

The major differences between bankruptcy and company liquidation practice arise from attempts to prevent the exploitation of the system of limited liability at the expense of ordinary creditors. Those in control of a company may, for instance, seek to prefer themselves in the event of insolvency by the creation of a fixed or floating charge in their own favour so that any available assets will remain in their personal possession. Alternatively they may make specially high payments to themselves as directors or managers, or repay loans or deposits made by them to the company in preference to any other of the company's obligations. The rules as to fraudulent or voidable preferences are clearly of particular importance in this context.

The main provision as to voidable preference, that *any* charge or payment created or made within six months of a liquidation shall be deemed invalid if created or made in circumstances which would in bankruptcy amount to a fraudulent preference (1948 : s. 320), is clearly directly dependent on the standard rule in bankruptcy (see p. 190), though in practice most of the leading cases on the point have arisen out of company liquidations. The same rule as to the necessity for a dominant intention to prefer is applied. But such an intention may equally be negatived by evidence that the contested payment or charge was made with a view to retaining the goodwill of a particular creditor in order to keep the business going :

A company which had borrowed money from a bank to pay for a plot of land which it was to develop agreed informally to deposit the title deeds by way of security, and an attempt to register this as an oral charge was made. The company soon got into difficulties and a formal charge was entered into with the bank to secure the company's overdraft. Three weeks later the company went into liquidation. It was held that the informal deposit of deeds had not been duly registered and was thus void, but that the subsequent formal charge, which had been registered, was valid since it had been created with the dominant intention not of preferring the bank to other creditors, but of keeping on good terms with it in the hope of maintaining the company as a going concern. *In re F.L.E. Holdings Ltd.* [1967] 1 W.L.R. 1397

On the other hand in a similar case where the benefit to the company was less apparent it was held that an intention to prefer could be inferred :

A company created a charge on its assets to a total of £5,700 in return for a cash advance of £400 and the postponement of debts which were already due. The company went into liquidation shortly after. It was held that the charge was voidable: where a creditor making an advance took from the debtor a promise to execute a charge at the request of the creditor, the court would, in the absence of any other circumstances, readily infer that the purpose of the parties was to give the creditor the right to be preferred on request. *In re Eric Holmes (Property) Ltd.* [1965] Ch. 1052

Given the obvious difficulties in deciding what is and what is not legitimate in the period before a liquidation it is impractical to attempt any precise formulation of the the way in which the court's discretion will be used.

A discretionary rule with respect to voidable preferences, which may on balance be acceptable in the case of charges or payments in favour of third parties, is less satisfactory in the case of payments made in favour of those more closely concerned with the business. The doctrine of the separate legal identity of the company permits the owner/manager of a one-man company to create a valid floating charge in his own favour.[41] To counteract this and other similar

[41] *Salomon v Salomon & Co. Ltd.* (1897), above p. 143.

abuses a special extension of the voidable preference rule has been introduced to invalidate *any* floating charge created by a company within *twelve months* of liquidation, except to the extent of any *new* money or credit provided in consideration for the charge, unless it can be shown that the company was fully solvent at the time of the creation of the charge (1948 : s. 322). This in addition to the ordinary rule in bankruptcy goes some way to prevent the worst abuses of limited liability. But like any rule which is dependent on a strict time limit, it may not always prevent the mischief against which it is directed :

The director of a small private company which had never traded profitably created a floating charge in his own favour in return for which he lent the company £400 out of the money which the company had paid him for the purchase of the business. The company went into liquidation some time later and the liquidator sought to have the charge set aside. It was held that the charge was valid despite evidence that the business of the company in the later stages had been continued merely to secure that the statutory six months (as then provided) should pass from the creation of the charge; it was not a high minded course of action, but nor was it high minded for a person forming a company to form it with a very small capital and to cause it to purchase his stock in trade by the issue of a debenture to himself, which had never been held to be fraudulent or prohibited by the Companies Acts. *In re Patrick & Lyon Ltd.* [1933] Ch. 786

The terms of this section have also been interpreted to permit banks and other lenders to protect themselves against the invalidation of charges to the extent that money is provided out of a current account on the company's cheques or bills, even if no special loan is made at the time of the creation of the charge :

A family company which owed some £67,000 to its bank was required by the bank to execute a floating charge in favour of the bank in addition to a pre-existing fixed charge. Subsequent to this payments totalling £110,000 were paid in and out of the company's account in the ordinary course of its business. Then within a year of the creation of the floating charge a winding-up order was made against the company. It was held on appeal that each time the bank honoured a cheque drawn by the company after the creation of the charge it counted as a loan of 'new' money to the company in consideration of the charge, which was thus valid to the extent of £110,000; it was admitted that the decision largely nullified the effect of s. 322 as applied to banks. *In re Yeovil Glove Co. Ltd.* [1965] Ch. 148 (CA)

In its practical effect then the voidable preference rule in respect of limited companies is scarcely more satisfactory than in the case of simple bankruptcy. It may well be that the rule has caused more trouble and expense for ordinary creditors by way of litigation than it has achieved for them in increasing the sum available for general distribution.

Liquidation frauds

There can be little doubt that the limited liability system offers considerable scope for the exploitation of the creditors of a company. Some of the methods by which the system may be manipulated, as illustrated above, are accepted as legal though undesirable. Others which involve the deliberate deception of creditors are indictable as criminal offences, whether under the Companies Acts or the general criminal law. But there is a wide range of uncertainty in between where no clear answer can be given. The resulting situation is perhaps best described in terms of typical practices rather than by a detailed analysis of individual provisions and offences.

The essence of exploitation and fraud in this context is the extraction of the assets of the company for the personal benefit of those who control it. There are a number of ways in which this may be achieved. First, as in the *Salomon* case (see p. 143), the owner/directors of a company may ensure that in the event of failure all the money that they have put into the company is returned to them in priority to other creditors through the creation of fixed or floating charges in their own favour. Alternatively the subscribed capital may be paid out to the directors in the form of fees, whether or not any profit has been realized in the business. Or more simply the company may be floated without substantial paid up capital beyond the few shares issued on its formation. The net result in each case is that the risk normally borne by the directors as promoters and shareholders is entirely eliminated, so that the company is effectively trading on other people's capital. In extreme cases the directors may simply be using the company to make money at the expense of their trade creditors. This is typically achieved by obtaining supplies or services on credit, selling the company's products before settling the bills, and in the meantime using receipts on sales to pay directors and managers for their services; the company is then eventually wound up with a large deficit.

Controlling directors may also simply appropriate the property of the company for their own purposes. The eventual need to face the consequences in such cases may for a time be postponed by false accounting, or by the submission of false tax returns, but unless the company's operations are sufficiently profitable to bear the theft of the amount taken there is bound to be an eventual insolvency. Alternatively the operators may simply abscond with the money, as for instance in a standard business credit fraud in which goods are obtained from suppliers on credit, sold off quickly at a loss and the money appropriated. There is no need for an operation of this kind to be conducted through a limited company, but in recent years at least there has been a tendency for those who specialize in this type of fraud to operate either through a newly formed company to give a veneer of respectability to their operations, or even more effectively through an established company which they have acquired for the purpose from unsuspecting former owners.

The current legal position in respect of these various forms of operation is not easy to ascertain from a study of the current range of criminal offences. Any element of direct fraud or deception in dealing with suppliers or creditors is punishable under the ordinary law of deception, and, as the decision in *R. v. Arthur* (1967) (see p. 112) shows, any illicit extraction of funds from a company, even if only for the purposes of tax evasion, is punishable as simple theft. Blatant cases of trading fraud as just described will also typically be dealt with as conspiracies under the more or less standard charge that the defendants 'conspired together to defraud the suppliers of . . . Ltd by a false pretence that . . . Ltd was an honest and genuine business.' In addition there is a long list of statutory offences in contemplation of liquidation (1948 : s. 328). The fourteen separate, complex and often overlapping offences, many of them copied directly from the equally complex list of bankruptcy offences, cover broadly the concealment of assets, the falsification of books and accounts, or any other failure to comply with the legitimate demands of the liquidator, subject always to a general defence that the accused had no intent to defraud or to defeat the law. These criminal offences, however, are generally applicable only in blatant cases, and in addition those under the Companies Acts are dependent on the initiation of liquidation proceedings. None is of great help in fixing the line between legitimate, illegitimate (voidable) and criminal conduct of the various types described.

There are only two statutory offences which are directly aimed at activities of this kind: first the offence of disposing of goods obtained on credit otherwise than in the normal course of business (1948: s. 328); and secondly the more general statutory offence of fraudulent trading introduced in 1928, which covers any case in which the business of the company is carried on with intent to defraud creditors or for any other fraudulent purpose, and which imposes both a criminal penalty and a civil remedy by way of an order of the court that those responsible shall be personally liable for some or all of the company's deficit (1948: s. 332). The essence of this 'offence' has been described in one case as 'the carrying on of business and the incurring of debts at a time when there is to the knowledge of the directors no reasonable prospect of the creditors ever receiving payment'.[42] But the provision is limited to cases in which liquidation proceedings have been instituted.[43]

The real problem over each of these offences, however, is the very generality of the charge: fraud or a fraudulent purpose under the fraudulent trading provision, for example, has been interpreted as meaning 'actual dishonesty involving according to current notions of fair trading among commercial men real moral blame'.[44] The disposal of goods 'otherwise than in the normal course of business' is an equally flexible concept. In the result it is essentially a matter of putting the facts of the case as fully as possible to a jury and leaving the decision on the criminality of the defendant's conduct to their good sense. It is relatively simple in such cases to mount a plausible defence based on a mixture of hopefulness and a desire to continue trading in order to pay off existing creditors. Proceedings are thus normally instituted only in the most blatant cases arising from police investigations of credit trading frauds. Few cases are brought as a direct result of the investigations of the Official Receiver's department or of voluntary liquidators.[45]

One possible answer to the difficulties in bringing offenders to justice would be to reduce the burden of proof imposed on the prosecution. The Jenkins Committee suggested that the offence of fraudulent trading might be extended to cover reckless trading, so that the prosecution need only convince a jury that the accused

[42] *In re Wm. C. Leitch Bros. Ltd.* [1932] 2 Ch. 71.

[43] *R v Schildkamp* [1971] A.C. 1; the requirement was to be repealed by the Companies Bill 1973.

[44] *In re Patrick & Lyon Ltd.* [1933] 1 Ch. 786, at p. 790 (per Maugham J.).

[45] T. Hadden, *The Control of Company Fraud*, P.E.P. (1968), pp. 294 ff.

closed his eyes to the obvious rather than that he deliberately set out to defraud his creditors.[46] This would also extend the court's discretion to impose personal liability on a director or manager found to have continued the company's business in reckless disregard of the creditors' interests. The difficulty with any such extension of the existing provision for fraudulent trading, however, is that the combination of a civil and criminal remedy tends to elevate the burden of proof for the civil remedy to that normally required in criminal cases. This in itself makes it difficult for the civil sanctions to be applied in ordinary liquidation proceedings, since what amounts to a specific charge must be laid and proved beyond reasonable doubt.

It would be preferable therefore to maintain a strict separation between the criminal offence of fraudulent or reckless trading and the question of civil liability and to enact an entirely new civil provision granting a wide discretionary power to the court to make an order imposing personal liability or bankruptcy on company directors or managers where it appears in the course of a liquidation that they have continued to trade when there was no reasonable prospect of meeting their obligations to creditors. In considering the reasonableness of the conduct of those concerned for this purpose the court might consider evidence of the extent to which capital had been raised to meet the risks of the business or of the relationship of the size of the deficit to the company's turnover.[47] The fact that a company has been floated with a derisory capital of a few pounds might in itself be a ground for imposing some measure of personal liability. The system of limited liability for small private companies could thus be converted into one of defeasible immunity, in which the suspension of limited liability would be dealt with in a similar way to the discharge of bankrupts as a matter for the discretion of the court in all the circumstances. This possibility will be considered further below in a more general discussion of a new statutory form for small incorporated businesses.

7 DISCLOSURE BY SMALL BUSINESSES

The question of disclosure by small companies[48] is best discussed in

[46] Cmnd. 1749 (1962), para. 503.

[47] T. Hadden, *The Control of Company Fraud* (P.E.P.), pp. 305 ff.

[48] See generally Bolton Committee on Small Firms (1971), Cmnd. 4811, Ch. 17.

relation to the rights of the various forms of creditors. From the definition of the small incorporated business which has been adopted, the owner/directors may be expected to have direct access to the accounts of the business, just as in the case of a partnership every partner has a legal right of access to all relevant information. Legal provision for the circulation of accounts and directors' reports to shareholders is thus of less importance, though it should be retained, than in the case of larger enterprises where there is a substantial external shareholding. Nor is there any pressing reason to require disclosure in the public interest from enterprises of this size. But there is every reason to consider the interests of creditors in view of the very real risk of failure and insolvency among small businesses. The provision of limited liability gives creditors a further argument to support the claim for some form of regular public disclosure of the state of the company's finances.

It is not easy to stipulate precisely the type of information which creditors might reasonably require for this purpose. Ideally a creditor who suspects that a business debtor may not be in a position to meet his obligations would like to have free access to the day-to-day accounts and bank balances of the business concerned so that he might judge for himself what action to take in his own interests. But it has never been seriously suggested that this should be permitted. Any general right of direct access for creditors and others would obviously infringe the prima facie right of individuals to conduct their businesses in reasonable privacy. The principles of free competition do not require the disclosure of trade secrets, nor of individual business methods. Total financial disclosure would in any case be impracticable since it would put a premium on dilatory and incomplete accounting, or alternatively imply a measure of uniformity in accounting methods which could not readily be expected or imposed.

In practical terms it is thus necessary to prescribe in fairly detailed terms the information which is to be disclosed, and how soon it must be made available. The onus in this context is on those who seek the disclosure of particular items of information to show that the benefit they will gain from the disclosure is not outweighed by the burden imposed on the firm which must produce it. In addition there is the difficulty that a seemingly similar formal disclosure requirement may impose a radically different level of disclosure on firms of different sizes and organization. For instance to require the disclosure of weekly turnover by a small corner shop or single product workshop will reveal relatively much more of the firm's trading position and strength than in the case of a chain of provision shops or of a multiple product firm whose accounts are aggregated. It is frequently argued, though without much supporting evidence, that detailed information on turnover and profit margins may be used by larger firms to gauge the level at which their smaller competitors may be squeezed out of business with a view to gaining a local monopoly. Too much disclosure may in this way result in less rather than more freedom of competition.

The type of information which the creditors of a small business might reasonably ask for may be listed as follows. First, they would want details of the financial structure of the business and the capital invested in it and of any prior claims on the firm's assets, for instance, a mortgage on its premises or heavy hire purchase commitments. Secondly, they would want some indication of the size and scope of the firm's undertaking so that they might judge the level of supplies and services which it could be expected to require and pay for, and of the other commitments which it has incurred or may incur in the future. Finally, they would want to be satisfied that the assets or profits of the business were not being improperly extracted from it in priority to the claims of ordinary creditors. All this might not on balance be thought to warrant a legal disclosure requirement when set against the interests of the individual firm, but it is at least worth considering how far the existing and possible future disclosure rules measure up to the list.

Current disclosure requirements

Apart from the minimal requirements of the Registration of Business Names Act 1916, providing for the disclosure both in a central registry and on all business stationery of the identity of all persons trading under a trade name or other assumed name (see p. 96) there are no statutory disclosure requirements in the case of partnerships or sole traders, though any charge or mortgage on the firm's assets must be registered as a land charge or as a bill of sale if it is to be enforceable against third parties. Nor is there any formal requirement that accounts of any kind be maintained, except to the extent that it is an offence for any bankrupt to have failed to keep adequate accounts (see p. 192).

In the case of limited companies proper books of account must be maintained; these must now be 'sufficient to disclose with reasonable accuracy at any time the financial position of the company at that time' (1976 : s. 12). Formal returns must also be made to the Registrar of Companies on a wide range of items, which will be open to public inspection by anyone prepared to pay the small fee charged by the Registrar or to commission a report from a professional credit reference agency. First, copies of the company's memorandum and articles of association must be deposited, setting out the objects and powers of the undertaking, its maximum authorized capital and the formal rules regulating the management of its internal affairs (1948 : s. 12). Secondly, returns must be made within a specified time of the appointment or resignation of any officer of the company (1948 : s. 200) and of the issue or redemption, where permissible, of any shares, and in the case of shares issued for a consideration other than cash a copy or note of the terms of the agreement on which the issue was made (1948 : s. 52). In practice this means that when an existing business is incorporated the amount of share capital issued to the previous owners for the assets and goodwill of the business must be fully disclosed. A register of shareholdings and of the directors and officers of the company must also be maintained at the company's registered office (1948 : ss. 110 and 200). Thirdly, an annual return must be made setting out the amount of authorized and issued capital, the current holders of all shares, and the names, addresses and other directorships of all officers of the company (1948 : s. 124). In addition, for any charge on the company's assets to be enforceable in priority to other creditors' claims, it must be formally registered within twenty-one days of the date of its creation (1948 : s. 95). These provisions are intended to ensure that the current capital structure, ownership and control of any company at any time may be ascertained by any interested party.

The position with respect to current accounts is rather more complex. Before 1900 the company's balance sheet and profit and loss account were circulated only to shareholders and perhaps debenture holders. From that date public companies had to disclose their balance sheet to public scrutiny, and from 1928 their profit and loss account as well, but the creation of the new status of private company in 1907 and later of the exempt private company in 1947 maintained the previous position for small private companies. The Companies Act 1967, as amended by the Companies (Accounts) Regulations 1971, now requires all limited companies to disclose by annual registration not only their balance sheets and profit and loss accounts but also the statutory directors' report. These must now include details of any major changes in the company's undertaking or in the value of its assets (1967 : s. 16); of directors' holdings in the company and its associates (1967 : s. 16); of annual turnover in each class of business and of exports (except where the turnover was less than £250,000) (1967 : ss. 17 and 20); of political and charitable donations (1967 s. 19); of the emoluments of directors (except where on aggregate these emoluments did not exceed £10,000) (1967 : ss. 6–7); of the emoluments of senior employees earning more than £10,000 (1967 : s. 8); and of the number and average wage of the company's employees (except where the number is less than a hundred) (1967 : s. 18). Details of directors' service contracts and of their share dealings must also be made available (1967 : ss. 26–9).

An immediate problem with these new requirements was that many small companies failed to file their accounts within the permissible period of up to eighteen months from the end of their accounting period, or even at all. This meant that the information on which creditors were expected to make current assessments was often hopelessly out of date. An attempt to deal with this has been made in the Companies Act 1976. The permissible delay in filing accounts has been reduced to ten months for private companies and much stiffer penalties are to be available against directors who fail to secure compliance with this limit (1976 : ss. 4 6). The practical problems of enforcing a requirement of this kind on more than half a million companies, however, must not be underestimated.

There was also some more general controversy on the merits of imposing this kind of disclosure on small private companies. The declared purpose of the Labour government was to subject all companies to the same disclosure rules in return for the universal benefit of limited liability. This was contested on the general ground that uniform disclosure rules inevitably have a differential impact on companies of different sizes and types, and that the smaller the company the greater are the claims of simple privacy. But all attempts to resolve the problem by the definition of a special class of exempt companies, along the lines of the exempt private company introduced in 1947, were rejected on the ground that any formal definition could be abused by larger companies, which are clearly not intended to fall within the test, so arranging their affairs as to take advantage of the exemption. The special position of small private companies was only recognized to the extent that specific exemption limits were agreed on for the disclosure of turnover, exports, employees, and directors' emoluments, as set out above.

This broad strategy was generally approved by the Bolton Committee on Small Firms, which discounted the most general arguments over the right to privacy and the danger of wholesale take-over of small firms by their larger competitors, but accepted that in respect of turnover there was some risk of giving an unfair advantage to larger companies over their smaller one-product or one-unit rivals.[49] The Committee's recommended extension of the exemption limit in this respect from £50,000 to £500,000, has been partially implemented by the adoption of a new figure of £250,000 (Companies (Accounts) Regulations 1971).

The Bolton Committee also recommended that serious consideration be given to the possibility of producing a new definition of the small 'proprietary' company which might be granted some more general exemption from the current accounting requirements, along the lines of the proposals of the accountancy profession.[50] There is little evidence, however, that either the accountants, or the Bolton Committee, despite its general acceptance of the value of disclosure for creditors of small companies, have seriously considered anything more than a return to some form of exemption for small companies along the lines of the 'exempt private company'. It is unlikely that any such compromise exemption scheme superimposed on the traditional disclosure rules will prove satisfactory in the long run. If the principal object of disclosure by small private companies is to permit creditors and prospective creditors to gauge the risk involved in dealing with the company, then a more fundamental assessment of the substance of the disclosure requirements is necessary.

One of the major defects in the existing law in this context, the historical cost base of traditional accounts, is already under consideration. It is clear that from the point of view of a company's creditors a valuation of the company's assets on the basis of their cost price is of little relevance. The current proposals for the introduction of current cost accounting, including the valuation of all assets at their current value to the business, however, are only to apply from 1980 onwards to companies with assets or turnover of

[49] Cmnd. 4811 (1971), paras. 17.20–17.25.

[50] Para. 17.39; the accountants' proposals were published in 1969 under the title *Companies Legislation in the 1970s*.

more than £100,000; an appropriate method of current cost accounting for smaller companies has not yet been agreed.[51] If it is accepted that accounts in small private companies are to be prepared for the benefit of creditors as well as for the assessment of tax liability, rather than for investment analysis, as with larger quoted companies, then it should not be difficult to adapt the principles of current cost accounting for that purpose. This would involve the preparation of an annual statement of the current value of the company's assets in terms of their actual market value rather than their current value to the business as is proposed for investment accounting. It would also require some statement of the full range of current and future liabilities, in particular in respect of hire and hire purchase contracts. This might be linked to the extended system for the registration of all non-consumer securities as recommended by the Crowther Committee on Consumer Credit if that is eventually adopted. For this purpose intangible assets such as goodwill which would be of little relevance to creditors in the event of a winding up would clearly be ignored.

The specific interest of creditors might also be recognized by providing that all creditors and suppliers of the company should be entitled as of right to a copy of the annual accounts of the company or to an appropriate summary. This would cover some of the objections to imposing greater disclosure requirements on small private businesses merely to satisfy the idly curious or the statistically minded. A creditor's account, for instance, might reasonably exclude details of the income derived from the company by each of its participants which will be required for tax purposes. The essential point is that accounting requirements should be directly related to the purposes of those for whom the accounts are to be disclosed.

The role of the auditor

The regular audit of accounts is an essential part of the disclosure system. It is pointless to increase the range of information to be disclosed if there is no control over its accuracy. The extent to which the auditor is genuinely independent of management and in a position to vouch for the figures produced is thus a question of some importance.

[51] Accounting Standards Committee, *Exposure Draft 18* (1976) (see generally pp. 134–7 above).

The increasing professionalization and independence of company auditors has already been described (see p. 137). In the case of small private companies, however, the detachment of the auditor from management is a more difficult matter. The fact that the auditor's appointment must be considered by the annual general meeting (1948 : s. 159) provides little protection since the controlling shareholders are typically one and the same as the directors. And it was not until 1967 that it ceased to be permissible for the partner of an accountant who held a directorship in a small private company to be appointed as auditor (1967 : s. 13). Even now the auditor may be expected to regard himself primarily as an agent of the company's management in the preparation of its accounts for taxation purposes, rather than as a guarantor of the external interests for whose benefit disclosure of the accounts is made. The auditor's duty to state on the accounts by way of 'qualification' if proper books and accounts have not been kept or if he has not been able to obtain from the directors all the information necessary to a proper audit (1967 : s. 14) could readily be evaded either by refusing to serve or by resigning. Some attempt to prevent this has been made in the Companies Act 1976 by a provision that an auditor shall not resign without making a formal statement of any circumstances connected with his resignation which he considers should be brought to the notice of shareholders or creditors (1976 : s. 15). This represents the first formal recognition that an auditor owes any duty to the creditors of a company as opposed to its shareholders or directors. If the proposal that the disclosure of accounts by small private companies should be geared primarily to the interests of creditors is to be made fully effective the duty of the auditor to inform a company's creditors of any relevant matters either in a note to the accounts or otherwise will require to be further clarified. It may even be necessary to give to any creditor the right of direct access to the auditor on certain specified issues, for instance in the context of any proposal that a scheme of arrangement should be entered into (1948 : s. 206), and to impose on the auditor a duty to report to or attend a meeting of creditors on any other matter of general concern.

8 THE TAXATION OF SMALL BUSINESSES

The principal objective of tax legislation is to raise money rather than to influence business organization and practice. There is no special reason why companies or businesses should be subject to any form of direct taxation. A general sales tax or value added tax on all commercial transactions, for instance, might be found to be a more equitable and cheaper way of raising funds from the commercial sector of the economy. But it has become accepted practice to levy tax on business enterprises in a broadly similar way to that applied to individuals, if only because incorporated businesses have increasingly become the major profit earners and also the major holders of wealth in developed capitalist societies.

There are broadly two methods of dealing with the direct taxation of business enterprises: first, to ignore the separate existence of the business and to tax those individuals who share in its profits, whether distributed or retained; secondly, to tax the business as an independent entity. Of these the first is clearly more readily applicable to unincorporated businesses, and the second to incorporated companies. Where the business is exclusively owned and controlled by relatively few persons it is natural to deal with the tax liability of each individually, if only because progressive rates of tax are normally applied to personal incomes of different sizes. But where the business has become effectively distinct from its shareholders, as in almost all sizeable companies, it is simpler to levy tax directly on the profits of the company as such, and to treat individual income derived from the business, whether in the form of dividends or salaries or capital payments, as an independent issue. This is particularly convenient when a large proportion of the profit earned is ploughed back into the business. Accordingly in Britain, as in most other western capitalist countries, companies are now subject to some form of corporation tax, while partnerships and sole traders are dealt with under the standard provisions for the taxation of personal incomes.

The development of company taxation in Britain

Within this broad structure there is a wide range of alternative schemes, each with a differential impact on patterns of business organization and practice. This is amply illustrated by the development of tax legislation in Britain in recent years.

Before 1965 both incorporated and unincorporated businesses were dealt with under the same basic tax legislation, though there were important differences in application. In the case of partnerships and sole traders tax was not levied on the business as such, but on the individuals who derived their income from it, whether as proprietors, partners, managers or employees, though for administrative convenience a provisional charge was made on the business as an independent unit. Registered companies on the other hand were subject to income tax on their profits just as if they had been individual traders, but without the benefit of any personal allowances. Any profits which were actually distributed to shareholders in the form of dividends, however, were deemed to be an allowable deduction from the company's profits for tax purposes. This was operated in practice by permitting the company to retain the money which it was required to deduct from any such dividends under the provisions for the deduction of tax at source.

The result of these arrangements was that in the case of partnerships and sole traders the whole of the assessed profit of the business fell to be taxed as part of the income of those concerned, while in the case of registered companies only that portion of the profits which was retained in the business was taxable, though any dividend paid was of course taxed in the hands of the individual recipients. In neither case was there any particular advantage to be obtained by ploughing back the profits of the business by way of reinvestment, except in the case of private companies in which wealthy owner/directors might avoid the highest rates of personal surtax by accumulating assets within the company in the form of undistributed profits, or where there was a prospect of genuinely profitable business expansion.

The generally high level of dividend distributions which this system encouraged was politically distasteful to the Labour government which came to power in 1964. A new corporation tax was thus introduced in 1965 with a view both to encouraging higher levels of reinvestment and also to simplifying the conceptual structure of company taxation. This new tax was levied at roughly the same rate as income tax for individuals on all company profits assessed before the deduction of dividends. Any dividends paid out, however, were still taxable in the hands of the recipients. The balance of advantage was thus deliberately shifted in favour of the retention of profits within a company in that any distributions were subject to double taxation.

The essentially political basis of company taxation was then further demonstrated by the proposals of the new Conservative administration for a further reform of the system aimed at 'removing the present discrimination against distributed profits'. The government was initially undecided between a new 'two-rate' system under which the corporation tax levied on distributed profits would be at an appreciably lower rate than that charged on retained profits, and an 'imputation' system, favoured within the European Economic Community, under which all company profits would be taxed at the same rate but the recipient of distributed profits would be entitled to set off part of the corporation tax already levied on the profits against his own personal tax liability.[52] It was eventually decided to adopt the imputation system under which a tax credit equivalent to the standard rate of income tax is imputed to the recipients of any dividend distributed by a company, which itself pays the amount involved to the Inland Revenue as advance corporation tax.[53] The net effect of this is to shift the balance of advantage back in favour of the distribution of profits, at least from the point of view of the shareholder, since the total tax on dividends is no higher than that on retained profits. The assumption underlying this strategy is that higher distributions result in capital being channelled into more efficient enterprises. This is almost certainly false. As has been seen, the amount reinvested in large quoted companies from external sources is less than the amount paid out in dividends (see Table 2.9, p. 60). In respect of smaller companies the government in fact accepted the argument of the Bolton Committee on Small Firms that retained profits should be taxed at a lower rate so as to encourage the reinvestment of profits. Corporation tax is now charged at a lower rate on the profits of companies with an income of less than £50,000.[54]

Tax avoidance in the small company: the 'close company' rules

This tax structure has been developed to deal with large and medium sized companies in which there is a real distinction between taxing the company and taxing its shareholders. It does not make much sense in respect of the small private companies with which this chapter is concerned. From a practical standpoint its principal shareholders and directors draw their personal income directly from the profits of the business, whether in the form of dividends or salaries, just as in the case of a partnership or sole business. Yet the company

[52] Reform of Corporation Tax, Cmnd. 4630 (1971).

[53] Reform of Corporation Tax, Cmnd. 4955 (1972); Finance Act 1972, s. 84.

[54] Finance Act 1972, s. 95; Finance Act 1976, s. 27.

will be directly subject to a corporation tax based on the assumption that the finances of the company can be clearly distinguished from those of its employees and shareholders. The essence of the problem is the fact that the dual position of directors in such companies as employees and as owners (shareholders) gives them a freedom of manoeuvre in tax planning and avoidance which is denied to other businessmen. There are several features of special importance in this respect. First, the directors are usually free of the pressures on larger public or family companies to declare a regular dividend and may therefore decide to allocate the profit among themselves either as dividends or as personal salaries depending on the relative tax advantages to be obtained. They may also retain any excess profit in the business and in theory at least subsequently distribute them in the form of a capital payment on a winding up or reconstitution of the company. By these means, until the introduction of capital gains tax in 1965 their personal tax liability as recipients of the company's past profits could be avoided altogether, and even since 1965 it may be substantially reduced by the elimination of the higher rates of income tax, since capital gains tax is levied at a flat rate.

Other tax advantages could be gained on a rather different level by the transfer of personal investment or rental income to small family investment or property management companies. Even where those concerned had no direct involvement in any business activity, some of their unearned income could be converted into earned income by the payment of a proportion of the company's income after the deduction of professional management expenses to members of the family as directors' fees or salaries. Similarly the drastic effects of death duties on family businesses and estates could be avoided by the formation of a family company and the distribution of the father's shares among his children and dependents. None of these manoeuvres were totally excluded within the framework of a partnership, and some may now be carried out more advantageously within the framework of a fixed or discretionary trust. But in practice it was very much easier to achieve the splitting of property interests and the conversion of unearned to earned income within a limited company. Hence in the 1940s and 1950s many small private companies were formed solely with a view to reducing the tax burden on self-employed and propertied persons.

An opening for tax planning and avoidance of this kind naturally led to counter measures from the tax authorities. Various legislative strategies have been adopted in different countries with a view to cutting down on the freedom of manoeuvre which the corporate form provides. In Britain special tax rules governing small private companies were enacted as early as 1922 and have been developed to a high degree of complexity in the close company provisions introduced with the corporation tax in 1965.

A close company in broad terms is any company which is:

i under the control of five or fewer persons, or of any number of shareholding directors;

ii not a subsidiary of a company which is not a close company;

iii not a company in which thirty-five per cent or more of the ordinary shares are publicly held.[55]

All such companies are required by the shortfall provisions to distribute a certain proportion of their annual income in the form of dividends. This required standard of distribution, however, is rather more flexible than the fixed statutory figure of fifty per cent implies, since there are exemptions for all income up to £5,000 and for half the income between £5,000 and £15,000; furthermore no distribution need be made if the company can show that the distribution would be prejudicial to the maintenance or development of its business.[56] In practice a figure will be agreed between the company and the Inland Revenue for this purpose. But if the agreed level of distribution is not in fact paid out those who would have received it will be taxed as if the distribution had been made. In addition until 1969 there was a statutory limit on the amount of directors' remuneration which could be set off as an expense against the company's profits.

The object of these measures is broadly to limit the amount of undistributed profit which may be accumulated in a small private company with a view to reducing the burden of higher rates of income tax on directors. Their net effect clearly depends on current tax rates and the precise level of income of the company and individuals concerned, but they have been rather more successful in reducing the tax differentials between companies and partnerships than is often supposed. The position of the very small company with a pre-tax income of less than about £5,000, whether from commercial

[55] Income and Corporation Taxes Act 1970, ss. 282–3.

[56] Ibid., s. 290; Finance Act 1972, s. 94 and sched. 16.

trading or from property or investments, is not generally affected, though there is sometimes a tax advantage to be obtained from the greater flexibility for tax planning within a company. This is particularly true in the case of self-employed persons such as authors and actors whose irregular income may be spread out in the form of a regular director's salary within the framework of a small one-man company. Even for larger concerns there has rarely been a sufficient direct tax differential between companies and unincorporated concerns to determine a choice of business status on these grounds alone.[57] Before 1961 the tax burden of small companies and partnerships was finely balanced, with the profits tax on retained company profits being roughly equivalent to the tax on personal income from an unincorporated business at least at the lower levels of surtax. The reduction in surtax rates in 1961 shifted the balance somewhat so that there was a clear tax advantage for the unincorporated form on best tax planning strategy up to about £10,000 per partner; above those levels there was an increasing advantage in incorporation. The effect of the introduction of corporation tax in 1965 was to reduce the size of the advantage in favour of unincorporated businesses at lower levels of income, and also to reduce the levels up to which that advantage might be obtained. This general trend has been confirmed by the removal of limits on directors' emoluments within close companies in 1969 and the reduction of the level of corporation tax for small companies in 1972. Since in small companies all the profit may now be paid out as fees and salaries the change in taxation on dividend distributions as a result of the adoption of the imputation system in 1972 is unlikely to affect the balance of advantage.

It would be dangerous to put too much weight on calculations such as these, since any form of tax planning must be based on the particular circumstances of the business and individuals concerned. The important point is that the balance of advantage is rarely fixed, so that unless the annual profits of a business are remarkably stable there is unlikely to be any 'correct' form of organization for tax purposes. In practice the Inland Revenue has usually achieved some measure of what may be termed 'tax neutrality' under which the choice between different forms of business organization is deter-

[57] On this topic see generally P. A. Bird, 'The Incorporation of Small Businesses: Effects of the Finance Act 1965', (1965) *British Tax Review*, 393.

mined as much by the ordinary legal incidents of incorporation and limited liability as by simple tax considerations.

Other tax considerations

This does not mean that the finances of a partnership or a company may not be successfully planned with a view to securing tax advantages. Quite apart from the issue of the legal status of the business, the amount of tax payable and the date of its payment may be affected significantly by the choice of accounting periods in relation to the likely development of the business. The precise current rules on investment allowances or grants, stock appreciation relief, and the treatment of interest on share and loan capital, all of which are frequently revised, also affect the optimum arrangement of the finances of the business. For instance, there is currently an advantage for a company in increasing the ratio or gearing of loan to share capital, since interest on loan capital is a deductible expense for tax purposes while dividends on share capital are not. It should be noted, however, that over-elaboration in tax planning may bring into operation the numerous statutory countermeasures. The most general of these is the provision, originally introduced in the Finance Act 1960, that where in consequence of any transaction in securities a person secures a tax advantage, then unless it can be shown that the transaction was undertaken for bona fide commercial reasons or in the ordinary course of making or managing investments, the tax advantage may be counteracted by an additional assessment (Income and Corporation Taxes Act 1970: s. 460). This measure was designed to counteract the classic form of 'dividend stripping' which involves the distribution of accumulated company profits in the form of capital payments to shareholders rather than as dividends so as to avoid the higher rates of tax on investment income as opposed to capital gain.

An equally significant issue in practical terms is the tax liability under capital gains and capital transfer tax which may arise when owner/directors of prosperous businesses retire or die. Since these taxes are levied on individuals in respect of the transfer or disposition of all their assets including shares in a company or business, there is no difference between companies and unincorporated businesses in this respect, except in so far as the business assets themselves may be seized to satisfy the tax liability of partners or sole traders. In addition liability under capital transfer tax and to a lesser extent capital gains tax is unlikely to pose serious problems where the assets concerned are valued at less than £30,000 or £40,000 as a result of the rapidly increasing rates of capital transfer tax above that level. The details and practical implications of these taxes will therefore be dealt with in the context of a more general discussion of problems of transition in larger unquoted companies in which the tax liability on the shares of retiring founders or directors is more likely to affect the future of the company itself (see Chapter 5).

Conclusion

There is no single criterion for assessing the impact of the tax system as a whole on small business organization. If the taxation of companies is regarded merely as a means of raising revenue the relative costs of collection under different schemes will be of major importance; if it is also intended to promote economic efficiency and expansion an element of conscious discrimination in favour of the most prosperous enterprises may be built in, as for instance in permitting capital allowances only out of realized profits; and if it is supposed to contribute to an equitable tax burden on all sectors of the community, questions of tax avoidance and the effective position of the individuals who own and control the business will be uppermost. In the narrower context of the law of business organization, and perhaps from some other points of view as well, the principal criterion should be that of neutrality between the various forms of organization as explained above, so that artificial pressures on the choice between legal forms may be minimized.

On this level the current British system scores reasonably well. At the very lowest levels of profit there is virtually no tax differential between incorporated and unincorporated businesses, and the apparent and rumoured advantages in incorporation at the middle range of income levels, from say £5,000 to £50,000, are largely wiped out by the close company rules. It is only where the business is of such a size as to earn regular profits above this level that there is a clear and consistent advantage to be obtained from incorporation. And if businesses of this size are regarded as subject to a general duty to disclose their affairs, in the interests of their employees, their suppliers and the community at large, the tax penalty on the unincorporated may perhaps be viewed as a reasonable price to impose for the privilege of privacy, in addition to that of unlimited liability. But this is achieved at the cost of considerable complexity in tax legislation, which in its turn increases the scope for complex tax planning schemes. Even if some of the most blatant avoidance operations are eventually neutralized by general or specific counter measures a considerable burden of expensive and time-consuming negotiation and litigation is borne both by the company concerned and by the Inland Revenue.[58]

It is worth considering therefore whether any other tax strategy might achieve the same level of efficacy at less cost. Most countries in which company law is modelled on the English system have also felt it necessary to introduce some form of close company legislation to counteract the anomalies which spring from treating the small owner-controlled company in a radically different way from the unincorporated business. But not all have adopted the same detailed provisions. In Australia there is a somewhat simpler but more rigid rule as to the required standard of distribution by close companies, ranging from forty to sixty per cent of the available profits, with a severe tax penalty where the required standard is not met. In the United States on the other hand a much wider discretion is granted to the 'small business corporation', which includes any corporation with fewer than ten members but excludes the subsidiaries of other companies, in that any such corporation may elect to be treated either as a corporation like any other, or else to have its income and capital gains treated as passing directly to the individual shareholder.[59] The effect of this, as with many other aspects of the American tax system, is to throw much of the burden of the choice of tax treatment and of assessment onto the corporation itself, subject always to a wide general tax evasion provision which permits the tax authorities to ignore the corporate status of a business if any person is making use of the corporation solely to secure the benefit of a deduction, credit or allowance which he would not otherwise enjoy. In addition, under the American system the rate of corporation tax is considerably less on the first slice of corporate income, so that small companies in general pay a much lower percentage of their overall profits in tax than their larger competitors. This has apparently resulted in some 'splitting' of enterprises to take advantage of the concession but it does confer a real benefit on small companies in terms of the resources available for reinvestment.

[58] Bolton Committee on Small Firms (1971), Cmnd. 4811, paras. 13.50 ff.
[59] US Tax Code, Sub Chapter S.

It is impossible in this context to argue the advantages and disadvantages of these various alternatives in detail. The Bolton Committee on Small Firms concluded that any positive discrimination in favour of small firms by tax provisions should be avoided on the ground that the complexity of administration under any discretionary scheme, and the possibility of tax avoidance by the splitting of larger firms under a fixed scheme, would outweigh any advantages which might be obtained.[60] But the Committee was equally convinced that the shortfall provisions should be abolished and that close companies should be permitted to elect to be taxed as partnerships by unanimous decision of shareholders, on the general ground that the benefits of incorporation should not be denied to small businesses by tax provisions.[61] The most important point in conclusion is perhaps that it is misleading to assume that there is any ideal neutral tax system which does not have some differential impact on large and small enterprises, in terms of the proportion of their resources which are available for distribution to shareholders and for reinvestment. In virtually every system some special provision is in fact madc for the taxation of the small closely controlled company. The general implication is again that a single uniform legal status for businesses of this kind should be created so that a rational tax strategy may be developed to give what measure of encouragement or discouragement is desired to this sector of the economy.

9 A NEW SMALL BUSINESS STATUTE

Each of the main legal and practical issues facing the small business, whether incorporated or not – those of internal organization, of external liability, of finance, of disclosure and of taxation – has now been discussed in some detail. In each case the special nature of the small incorporated business has led to the development of special rules, exemptions or informal practices to differentiate them from the larger companies for which the law was primarily developed. The main points may be summarized as follows:

i *Internal organization*. Many small enterprises are started on the basis of continuing co-operation between two or three joint owner/managers, whereas the ordinary articles of association

[60] Cmnd. 4811 (1971), Ch. 13.
[61] Ibid., paras. 13.56–13.58.

for a limited company are drawn up on the basis of strict majority rule, and the separation of the roles of shareholder and director; this has resulted in the development of special rules, adapted from partnership law, to protect minority or equal participators from exclusion or oppression in what are termed quasi-partnership cases.

ii *External liability.* The outward simplicity of the limited liability rule for incorporated companies conceals a more complex situation under which the owner/managers of small companies effectively trade with unlimited liability to banks and other major creditors who insist on personal guarantees of the company's debts, whereas the larger number of small trade creditors are strictly bound by the limitation of liability; the position of these creditors is further aggravated by the fact that banks and other financial institutions typically secure their loans and credit on fixed or floating charges so that what assets are available in the event of failure go to these creditors in priority.

iii *Disclosure.* The general disclosure provisions of the Companies Act are not wholly appropriate for the smallest businesses both in view of the claims of reasonable privacy and of the alleged commercial advantage which some of the information required may give to the firm's larger competitors; in addition, even if current cost accounting is adopted, the company accounts developed for internal accounting purposes are much less suitable for the purposes of external creditors.

iv *Taxation.* The flexibility which the corporate form affords to the owner/manager to arrange his affairs so as to minimize his personal tax liability has led to the introduction of a new category of 'close companies' subject to a whole series of complex tax assessment rules.

The natural implication which has frequently been drawn from these points is that a new statutory form of business organization should be developed specifically for the small owner-managed enterprise, combining the advantages of the partnership in terms of simplicity and equity between the participants and of the registered company in terms of administrative continuity and limited liability. Independent disclosure and tax provisions could then be designed for this class of enterprise. As was stated by the government spokesman in the debates on the Companies Bill in 1967: 'We have to see if we can find a new type of company whose structure and administration would solve some of the problems – a form of partnership or whatever it might be.'[62]

It is easier to state a conclusion in these terms than to reach agreement on the precise form of legislation called for. There are no satisfactory precedents. The Limited Partnership Act of 1907 has never made any impact, if only because there was no reason for anyone to resort to it in preference to full corporate status; the provision of limited liability for what might be termed external shareholders, on the model of the continental *société en commandite*, is no inducement for the prime movers of the enterprise, and in any case leaves the external shareholders in a difficult position since any attempt on their part to influence the conduct of the business may render them personally liable for its debts. The Incorporated Partnership Act prepared for Ghana by Professor Gower in 1961, on the other hand, was designed primarily for the particular needs of that and other developing economies. Professor Gower's prime concern was that the death or retirement of the major participants in small businesses should not result in the dispersal of the undertaking among the extended family group which is a feature of many African societies. He was also concerned to protect the businessman from his importunate friends and relatives. This he sought to achieve by providing a distinct and separate form for the business on which there would be no direct customary claim, and by requiring that there should at all times be at least two participants. But he did not recommend the introduction of limited liability on the grounds that it would inevitably require a measure of administrative and accounting complexity which could not otherwise be justified.

Within a 'developed' economy a rather different approach is called for. The primary objective is still to separate the assets and profits of the business from those of its main participators and to give the business a greater degree of continuity. But in addition some measure of limited liability for all participants, coupled with disclosure requirements which meet the practical needs of existing and prospective creditors, is desirable. The freedom to initiate a small business enterprise, or to contribute to one, without putting in jeopardy the full extent of the participators' personal assets, is

[62] *Official Report*, 12 July 1967, col. 928.

undoubtedly an encouragement to the formation of new but doubtfully viable enterprises. In addition, in a credit based commercial system, a statutory obligation to maintain accounts and to submit to a regular audit is clearly a spur to greater business efficiency as well as a protection for creditors. The problem is to achieve all this without imposing unrealistic and burdensome requirements of administration, accounting and disclosure which the small businessman cannot readily comply with, and which are expensive to administer and enforce.

The major difficulty in this context is limited liability. Much of the complexity in existing company legislation, in particular in the provisions as to the subscription and maintenance of capital, the disclosure of information and the winding up of the enterprise, stems from the attempt to protect creditors from the abuse of limited liability. But in practice many of the provisions relating to capital are unnecessary in so far as many small companies operate without substantial share capital. The owner/managers will usually prefer to finance the enterprise by the loan or deposit of funds rather than by the issue of share capital. The respective interests of the participants are more easily and equitably maintained by an initial agreement concerning their share in the business, as in a simple partnership deed, which any subsequent share issue would upset. And any provision for a minimum subscribed capital is unlikely to prove an effective guarantee of funds for distribution in the event of failure without a series of complex capital maintenance rules. What is required is a provision that the assets of the business, whether in the form of share capital, formal loans or deposits, or accumulated profits, shall be genuinely available for external creditors in the event of failure. This is most simply and directly achieved by the formal incorporation of the business, so that its assets are formally distinct from those of its owner/managers.

Some further provision may be necessary to ensure that these assets are available for the external creditors in the event of failure, and not distributed among the participants. The best means of securing this is probably to adopt and extend the conception of fraudulent or voidable preference from the bankruptcy and company liquidation legislation so that any payment, transfer or charge made within a year of winding up to any participant, directly or indirectly, may be set aside at the discretion of the court. This, in addition to a provision for personal civil liability in the event of fraudulent or reckless trading, as described above, would go a long way to discourage the deliberate abuse of limited liability. The net effect would be to subject the participators of an insolvent business to an enquiry similar to that on an individual bankrupt, except that the issue would not be that of immediate or future discharge but whether any order, and if so how large an order, for personal liability might be made against those directly involved in the running of the company. The rule of no personal liability would thus apply as a matter of course unless there was evidence of some improper business practice.

This suggestion is in line with the proposals for the harmonization of the law on bankruptcy and liquidations within the EEC. The Preliminary Draft Convention prepared for the six initial members of the EEC envisages the extension of bankruptcy to persons directing or managing incorporated companies or firms where in the opinion of the court the business has been carried on wrongfully for their personal advantage.[63] The Cork Committee has criticized the way in which the Convention seeks to implement the principle of unity and universality in bankruptcy and liquidation proceedings throughout the EEC, and has suggested a less radical approach which would recognize the different traditions in the various member countries.[64] But it has accepted the principle of the extension of liability, though not of bankruptcy except where that liability is not discharged, to any person who has conducted a business for his personal advantage and in so doing has contributed to the failure of the business.[65]

It may be objected that a provision for defeasible limited liability on this model is impractical in that any form of discretionary liability would be unworkable and unacceptable. But there is already a measure of discretion under the bankruptcy and liquidation systems, in respect of discharge and the fraudulent trading provisions, quite apart from the uncertain effect of the existing voidable preference rule. And there must be some positive inducement for businessmen to adopt the new form of organization in preference to the simple partnership with fully unlimited liability. It would in any event be politically impossible to withdraw totally the limited liability which the huge number of small incorporated companies already enjoy.

[63] *Preliminary Draft of a Convention on Bankruptcy, Winding-up, Arrangements, Compositions and Similar Proceedings*, English language version (1974).

[64] Cmnd. 6602 (1976), paras. 394 ff.

[65] Ibid., para. 330.

And there would be a good deal to be said for a system in which the activities of those in control of small insolvent companies were subjected to rather more scrutiny than at present.

A new form of statutory corporation for small businesses would also permit the development of disclosure rules more directly geared to the interests of external creditors than of shareholders and investors, but not unnecessarily infringing the privacy of small traders. The most satisfactory compromise in this context would perhaps be a provision for the annual disclosure of a current valuation of the company's realizable assets, along with a statement of the nature of its current and continuing liabilities including secured and unsecured loans, and hire purchase commitments. Details of current profitability and turnover, and of the payments made to participators, need not be included, though any major creditor could of course make the disclosure of these items a condition of his loan or credit. Provision could also be made for the immediate disclosure of any mortgage or debenture secured on the company's assets, so that creditors might gauge the extent to which the assets of the company might be available for unsecured debts. *Any* charge created within a year of liquidation could be made voidable except to the extent of any new funds supplied, on the model of the existing provision with respect to floating charges.

The remaining statutory provisions and regulations would follow from the general strategy of avoiding unnecessary complexity. Corporate status would be automatically granted on the registration of a list of those concerned in the enterprise and of the main provisions of their internal contractual arrangements. The problems of ultra vires would be avoided by dispensing with any list of authorized objects and powers and permitting the company to carry out any business transaction open to an individual trader. The company would thus be bound by the acts and undertakings of its participators and employees within the scope of its normal business as in the case of a simple partnership. A simple standard form for internal management and control should be provided, along the lines of Table A, though there would be no need for any distinction to be drawn between directors' and shareholders' meetings. Finally a general provision should be added empowering the courts to make a discretionary order for liquidation or any other form of settlement in the event of deadlock or incompatibility among the participators. This combination of the existing jurisdiction to dissolve a partnership on the 'just and equitable ground' and of the more general power to deal with cases of oppression under s. 210 would permit a rather more flexible approach to disputes than is currently possible, though the courts would undoubtedly still wish to distinguish between cases of oppression and unfair conduct and those of simple disagreement on commercial policy.

It is more difficult to prescribe a precise strategy for the taxation of this new form of small business corporation. Some form of tax incentive is probably necessary to induce acceptance of the new form in preference to the simple partnership or the more closely regulated form for larger companies, as discussed below. There may also be something to be said for a measure of discrimination in favour of the small business as such, to protect it from the monopolistic or dominating tendencies of the large modern corporation. Equally it is important not to create what is in effect simply a new mechanism for tax planning and avoidance which will lead to complex and restrictive legislation like that governing the close company for tax purposes. One possibility would be the adoption of an American style tax option system under which the company might elect to be treated either as a simple partnership, or else as a corporation entitled to some kind of tax rebate on profits actually used for the consolidation or expansion of the business.

The final major issue is that of defining the range of companies to which the new form of corporate status would be made available. It is of crucial importance to prevent larger companies from taking advantage of special privileges and exemptions intended for the small business enterprise, whether for tax planning purposes or in order to avoid the increasingly stringent disclosure regulations for larger companies. It was largely due to this difficulty in finding a satisfactory definition of the small business enterprise and so preventing other companies from arranging their affairs in such a way as to fall within that definition, as had happened with the provision for the exempt private company under the 1948 Act, that the government declined to introduce any new legal status for the small business in 1967.

The best way to proceed might be to adopt a multiple form of definition, restricting the new status to companies which are genuinely participatory, and also less than a given size on any of a number of possible criteria. A draft definition of the participatory or family company was produced in 1967 by the Conservatives, covering any company in which:

i no body corporate was the holder of any shares or debentures;

ii no person other than a director or the spouse or infant child of a director was the holder of any shares or debentures;

iii no person other than the holder had any interest in any of the shares or debentures.[66]

The inclusion of debentures in this formulation creates difficult problems in relation to bank loans and other long-term loans, which, in the Conservative proposals, were specifically exempted; so too does the provision for shares to be held by spouses and children. It might be preferable to limit the definition to participatory shares and simply to exclude the subsidiaries of larger companies or any member of a larger group of companies split into smaller units for administrative purposes from any direct involvement. The number of participator/directors could also be limited to five, or perhaps ten, as in the case of some close company definitions. The size criterion, to exclude larger closely held enterprises, which should be subjected to fuller disclosure requirements, might be based on a maximum current valuation, as disclosed on the annual return, of up to £50,000 or a payroll of up to fifty. Any company growing above these limits would then lose its small business status and be required to convert itself into a fully regulated company, as under the existing law, or at least be treated for tax and disclosure purposes as if it had so converted itself. The problem of borderline companies, sometimes above and sometimes below the line, could be solved by rendering any 'upward' change of status irreversible for a minimum period.

This brief account of how a new small business statute might be formulated is not intended to be exhaustive or precise. This is not the place to discuss questions of detail or drafting. There are a number of existing statutes and draft formulations to draw on, notably the Partnership Act, the Limited Partnership Act, the Ghana Incorporated Partnership Act, and a wide range of American precedents.[67] There are also a number of draft formulations.[68] If the need

[66] *Companies Bill 1967, Standing Committee C*, col. 4.

[67] See R. A. Kessler, 'Why not a partnership corporation?', (1967) *Fordham Law Review* 235.

[68] See, for instance, the draft bill prepared in an open competition organized by Jordans in 1975.

for such a statute is accepted there would be no real difficulty in producing a formulation along the lines discussed above providing for a form of defeasible limited liability, for the periodic disclosure of a current valuation of the company's realizable assets and of its current liabilities and continuing commitments, and for a general discretionary court jurisdiction to intervene in the event of deadlock, conflict or oppression among the participators.

Any new legislation in this sphere must now be consistent with the policy of the European Economic Community in harmonizing commercial law within its member states. But this does not rule out the proposals made in this chapter. There is as much need for a clear distinction in legislative strategy for large and small companies in Europe as in Britain. In France and Germany small limited companies, the *société à responsibilité limitée* (SARL) and the *Gesellschaft mit beschränkter Haftung* (GmbH) respectively, are already governed by separate legislation from larger public companies, the *société anonyme* (SA) and the *Aktiengesellschaft* (AG). The European Commission has been persuaded after a lengthy struggle to exclude private companies in Britain and Ireland from the requirements of the Second Directive in respect of minimum capital and related matters (see p. 140). A new British statute for small companies, parallel with the French SARL and the German GmbH, would greatly facilitate the harmonization process for small as well as for larger companies.

5
The unquoted company

This chapter is concerned with the larger unquoted company which falls between the small incorporated business and the publicly quoted company. In many cases 'family company' would be the most appropriate description, in that the concern has developed out of a small participatory business by the dispersal of shares among members of a single or perhaps several families over a number of generations. But the family nature of the shareholding is not of itself of crucial importance. The main characteristic of the unquoted company as opposed to the participatory company is the fact that there are a number of shareholders who have no direct control over, or involvement in, the operations of the company except in respect of capital appreciation and the payment of dividends. It is distinguished from the publicly quoted company, on the other hand, by the absence of a public market in its shares and thus of any control over the conduct of its affairs by the Stock Exchange authorities or market pressures. This definition is different from that of a private company in strict legal terms since the statutory limitation to fifty members and a restriction on share transfers will not always apply. The unquoted company whose shares have not been either quoted or offered to the public, regardless of its formal legal status, however, was frequently adopted by the Jenkins Committee[1] as the most natural and useful division for the purposes of legislative control.

The formal structure and many of the administrative and disclosure requirements imposed by the Companies Acts on these

[1] Cmnd. 1749 (1962), paras. 64 ff, 351 ff.

unquoted companies are no different from those for small private companies or larger public companies. Powers of control are split between the directors and the general meeting of shareholders; the distinction between share and loan capital holds good; the systems for incorporation and liquidation are identical; and all are now subject to broadly the same disclosure rules, with certain exemptions, under the 1967 Companies Act. But the practical problems which typically arise in a larger unquoted company are radically different from those within the small private business as discussed in Chapter 4. The fact that the shares are typically split between executive directors and external shareholders frequently gives rise to a conflict of interest between management and shareholders over the distribution of dividends, the level of executives' pay and the amount to be ploughed back out of profits. And since management is typically in effective control over all these matters there is an inherent danger of the oppression of minority shareholders. Similar problems and tensions may clearly arise in larger public companies, but there both the informal pressures and the formal control exercised by the stock market, institutional investors and the financial press help to redress the balance. It is in the unquoted company that there is a special need for effective legal remedies for shareholders against oppression and malpractice.

Special problems are also posed for larger unquoted companies in securing finance for expansion, in view of the unsaleability of their shares or debentures, and in dealing with the tax and other implications of the transition from one generation of owner/managers to another. The pressures caused by these problems frequently lead to a decision either to 'go public' or else to accept a take-over bid from an established quoted company.

The main issues to be covered in this chapter are accordingly:

i the powers and duties of directors and managers;

ii the remedies open to shareholders in the event of malpractice or oppression;

iii the problems of taxation, finance for expansion, and transition.

Neither the incidents of incorporation, the standard disclosure requirements nor the liquidation system which have been covered in detail in relation to smaller companies, nor the law on share dealing and the formation of groups of companies, which will be discussed in subsequent chapters, will be dealt with here.

I THE STATUS AND DUTIES OF DIRECTORS

The powers and duties of a company director are derived primarily from the company's memorandum and articles of association (see Chapter 3). But a strict application of the contractual and constitutional principles which have been developed in this respect is not sufficient to determine the position of a company director in the eyes of the law. The analogy between a director and a public official cannot be pressed very far, if only because their basic functions are so different. The official is bound to implement or administer policies within the limits of powers which are frequently expressed with some precision in the relevant legislation. The same cannot be said of directors. The Companies Acts provide very little guidance on the nature of a director's duties, beyond the formal requirements as to the holding of periodic meetings, the keeping of books of account and the like. His general function within a free enterprise system is clearly to manage his company's affairs to the best of his ability with a view to profit for the shareholders. But in doing so he is likely to face demands that he adopt a number of different roles which may not always suggest the same course of action. The two most important of these are those of 'the director as trustee' and 'the director as businessman'.

The director as trustee

It was natural for lawyers facing a situation in which corporate property is managed by directors on behalf of their shareholders to fall back on the traditional concept of a trust. Trust property in law must be managed wholly and exclusively for the benefit of the beneficiaries, and a wide range of specific rules have been developed by the courts to govern the conduct of trustees in various situations. Their prime duty is to apply or manage the trust property in accordance with the terms of the trust, both in simple family settlements in which a balance must be made between providing a reasonable income for the live beneficiaries and securing a reasonable rate of capital appreciation for the ultimate beneficiaries, and in charitable trusts in which the prime duty is to secure a regular income to enable the charity to continue its work on a long-term basis. In every case the trustees are required to exercise their powers in such a way as to conserve the trust capital and procure a reasonably consistent annual income or appreciation without exposing the fund to any unnecessary risk. Speculative ventures of any kind are strictly out of order.

In addition it is a strict rule of law that the trustee must refrain from any personal involvement in the affairs of the trust which might lead to a conflict of interest between himself and the beneficiaries. This is a natural deduction from the conception of the trustee as a disinterested custodian of other people's property. The practical consequences of the rule, however, may be far reaching in that the trustee must account to the trust fund for any personal profit which he secures from his position as a trustee:

Trustees under a will had a substantial holding in a private company, and as such were provided with information about the company's prospects. On the basis of this the solicitor for the trustees decided to buy in the remaining shares in the company in a personal capacity, wind it up and distribute the assets. This secured a substantial profit both for the solicitor personally and for the trust fund. It was held by the House of Lords that though the consent of the beneficiaries to the proposed action had been obtained, both the solicitor and one of the beneficiaries who had joined with him in the scheme in a personal capacity had obtained the opportunity for personal profit as a direct result of their special position in relation to the trust, and had not fully disclosed the extent of the possible profit to the remaining trustees and beneficiaries; they were therefore held liable to account to the trust fund for the profit made, though since they had acted in good faith and had made a handsome profit for the trust fund as well, they were entitled to a liberal payment in respect of their skill and work. *Phipps v. Boardman* [1967] 2 A.C. 46

It is arguable that this particular decision went too far both on the facts, in that there was no real conflict of interest since there was substantial benefit for the trust fund, and in law, in requiring a degree of understanding and consent from all the beneficiaries which would not in practice be obtainable. But it exemplifies the high standards of detachment which the law requires of anyone who adopts the status of trustee.

The question is how far these exacting standards can sensibly be applied to company directors. There is no doubt that directors are required to account for any personal profit which they make in their capacity as directors in the course of the company's business. This extends even to the diversion of business from the company for their personal advantage:

Three of the four controlling members of a railway construction company wished to exclude a fourth from further participation. Instead of winding up the company, as they might have done, they diverted contracts which would otherwise have been granted to the company to a firm which they set up in their own names. The remaining member was held entitled to require the others to account to the company for the profits made on the contracts. *Cook v. Deeks* [1916] 1 A.C. 554

The law in this respect is no different from that applied in the case of the partners of a firm (see p. 101).

The extent to which directors can be expected to account for personal profit resulting from the commitment of their own resources is less clear. The trusteeship concept has been applied in a case where the directors invested their own personal funds to complete a transaction which the company could not otherwise have carried through:

A company wished to dispose of a single cinema, but in order to avoid loss the directors decided to acquire two other cinemas in the area which could then be sold along with the third as a single unit. The original plan was for the company to acquire the new cinemas through a wholly-owned subsidiary, but the company was unable to raise the necessary funds for the deal. The directors instead of giving the company their personal guarantee decided to buy some of the shares in the subsidiary on their own account. There was a substantial profit on the sale of the shares in the subsidiary which was disposed of along with the original company. The new controllers of the original company then sought to have the directors account for the profit they had made on their personal shares in the subsidiary. The suit was successful: 'The rule of equity, which insists on those who by use of a fiduciary position make a profit being liable to account for that profit, in no way depends on fraud or absence of bona fides; or upon such questions or considerations as whether the profit would or should otherwise have gone to the plaintiff, or whether the profiteer was under a duty to obtain the source of the profit for the plaintiff, or whether he took a risk or acted as he did for the benefit of the plaintiff, or whether the plaintiff has in fact been damaged or benefited by his action. The liability arises from the mere fact of a profit having, in the stated circumstances, been made. The profiteer, however honest and well-intentioned, cannot escape the risk of being called upon to account.' (per Lord Russell, at p. 386) *Regal (Hastings) Ltd. v. Gulliver* [1942] 1 All E.R. 378

It has been firmly rejected in respect of the *prospective* purchasers and directors of a company, who are not expected to subordinate their own interests to those of the company:

A public company acquired all the shares in a private company as part of a wider deal in which the private company leased some of its properties to a trust on terms which suited both the trust and the public company, whose principal directors were closely involved in the trust. For fiscal reasons the leases were not executed, but when the principal directors sold their interest in the public company some years later, the trustees sought to enforce the lease. The new controllers of the private company objected on the ground that the ex-directors of the private company and the directors of the public company as 'directors-elect' of the private company had been in breach of their fiduciary duty to that company. The objections were rejected on the ground that the merits of the scheme had been properly considered by the existing directors of the private company, and that the so called 'directors-elect' owed no duty to it, either as prospective directors or as directors of its parent company: 'To hold that [the director of the parent company] was bound to protect the interests of one of its subsidiaries which had an independent board was to stretch the [trusteeship] principle altogether beyond reason.' (per Harman L.J., at p. 595) *Lindgren v. L & P Estates Ltd.* [1968] Ch. 572

The director as businessman

These cases reveal the director in his true capacity as a profit seeker for himself as well as for his shareholders. The question is whether in that capacity he should be permitted to enter into dealings on his own account with his company or associated companies, which the company could not undertake on its own, as long as full disclosure of the position is made and there is no oppression of minority holdings, or whether his position as director effectively bars him from all such personal dealing. It seems unrealistic in view of the universal acceptance of the personal involvement of directors as shareholders in their own companies, especially in small participatory and family concerns, to suggest that they may not operate in their personal capacity in other ways, as long as no unfair advantage is taken of their special position. On these grounds the *Lindgren* decision is to be preferred to the *Regal* decision. To hold otherwise is in effect to require a director either to invest his personal resources in his own company, and so to share any benefit with other shareholders, or to refrain from personal involvement altogether. On the other hand the rule in *Percival v. Wright* (1902) (see p. 421) that a director is not bound to disclose to shareholders, whose shares he is buying or selling, material information as to the state of the company's affairs which he has obtained in his capacity as director, goes too far in the other direction.

A more acceptable and workable compromise in this respect was reached in dealing with the duties of company promoters to the companies they floated. It was common practice in the mid-nineteenth century for this species of entrepreneur to acquire property or concessions with a view to making them over to newly promoted public companies at an advantageous price, which might be paid either in cash or in the form of shares in the new company which the promoter would then dispose of in the market. The most effective control over abuses in transactions of this kind is the strict disclosure requirements for prospectuses, and the vigilance of the Stock Exchange authorities, as discussed in Chapter 7. But the courts did also impose a measure of common law liability based on a conception of fiduciary duty similar to that applied to directors. Any inequitable contract arranged by the promoter with the company could thus be set aside, and the promoter required to account to the company for any illegitimate profit. But full and honest disclosure of his interest in any such contract was held to relieve the promoter of liability.

A syndicate of company promoters formed a public company to acquire their interest in a nitrate mine. They themselves were the initial directors and sole shareholders of the new company, so that in effect they sold the mine to themselves. Two years later a newly appointed independent board of directors sought to have the contract set aside on the ground that the mines had been overvalued. The action failed, the court holding that the syndicate had in fact made a sufficient disclosure of their interest as promoters to themselves as directors, and the mere fact that there had not been an independent board of directors from the start was not in itself sufficient to render them liable as promoters; though there had been some misrepresentation in the prospectus subsequently issued to the public, it was not possible after two years to rescind the contract since it was no longer possible to restore the parties to their original positions. *Lagunas Nitrate Co. v. Lagunas Syndicate* [1899] 2 Ch. 392

The actual decision in this case can scarcely be supported in view of the peculiar circumstances of the disclosure which was made. But the principle that promoters should be liable only where their profit is not disclosed to a fully independent board is perhaps more realistic in the commercial world than the inflexible duty to account applied to trustees. This is the standard which has been applied in the Companies Acts in respect of contracts in which a director has an interest, notably service contracts, of directors' share dealings and other such matters (see p. 242). The object of the law is not to prevent personal profit but to protect shareholders, and is more likely to be achieved by a discretionary power to remedy oppression.

There is a further respect in which the comparison between the director and the trustee is not appropriate. The management of a commercial enterprise may require the taking of risks of a kind which would not be legally permissible for a trustee. It is not surprising therefore that the judges have been reluctant to impose on directors the strict rules which govern the conduct of trustees, or otherwise to interfere in what are essentially matters of business judgement. The businessman in search of profit is an entirely different creature from the trustee, and cannot realistically be subjected to the same rules:

> It has sometimes been said that directors are trustees. If this means no more than that directors in the performance of their duties stand in a fiduciary relationship to the company, the statement is true enough. But if the statement is meant to be an indication by way of analogy of what those duties are ... it is wholly misleading.... It is indeed impossible to describe the duties of directors in general terms, whether by way of analogy or otherwise. The position of the director carrying on a small retail business is very different from that of a director of a railway company. (per Romer J., at p. 426) *In re City Equitable Fire Insurance Co.* [1925] 1 Ch. 407

In the face of this problem of formulating standards of conduct applicable to businesses of all kinds and sizes the courts have taken refuge in a minimal requirement of what amounts to honesty and effort. The director will not normally be required to exercise a degree of competence beyond that which can reasonably be expected of him in the particular circumstances, having regard to his actual knowledge of the matters in question: 'A director need not exhibit in the performance of his duties a greater degree of skill than may reasonably be expected from a person of his knowledge and experience.... Directors are not liable for mere errors of judgement.' (ibid. p. 428). Nor is there a legal requirement for this purpose that he should make it his business to be fully informed, or that he should apply himself full time to the affairs of the company: 'A director is not bound to give continuous attention to the affairs of his company. His duties are of an intermittent nature to be performed at periodic board meetings. . . . He is not . . . bound to attend all such meetings, though he ought to attend whenever, in all the circumstances, he is reasonably able to do.' (ibid., p. 429). In simple terms the law is that a director must do his honest best, but is not required to be competent.

2 DIRECTORS AND SHAREHOLDERS

Part of the difficulty which the courts have had in this respect can be attributed to the failure to differentiate clearly the position of directors in participatory or partnership companies, in family companies and in quoted public companies. In respect of those companies in which all the shareholders are directors the duties normally imposed by law on partners between themselves should equally be applied to directors. In respect of quoted companies it is legitimate to expect the full rigours of the trusteeship concept to be applied, though some difference in respect of standards of diligence and professional skill might be made between full-time executive directors and those acting in a supervisory capacity, as discussed in Chapter 6. It is in respect of smaller unquoted companies in which the directors are acting both as businessmen on their own account and also as trustees on behalf of external shareholders that the major problems arise. In such cases there is a conflict between the interests of shareholders and directors which does not arise in participatory or partnership companies. It becomes particularly acute where the directors are also the controlling shareholders and thus have the added duty in their capacity as shareholders of overseeing and controlling their own activities as directors.

The key to this problem is not to attempt a general formulation of the duties of directors in unquoted or family companies but to deal directly with the various situations of conflicting interest which may arise in practice in relation to the remedies which minority, and occasionally majority, shareholders may seek to enforce in the courts. There are two specially important issues in this context : first, the fact that on the existing case-law it is often almost impossible for external shareholders to find out whether they are in fact being oppressed since the directors are in total control over the flow of information about the company's affairs; and secondly, the fact that under the principle of majority rule there is every likelihood that when breaches of duty are revealed they will be ratified by the major shareholders, a doctrine which is given procedural effect in the rule in *Foss v. Harbottle* (see p. 271).

The techniques of oppression

The major types of oppression against which minority shareholders might reasonably expect to be protected, may be listed as follows:

i The directors may simply make off with the assets of the company for their private purposes: they may set about this fraudulently and subsequently conceal the depredation by false accounting; or more skilfully they may arrange apparently legitimate loans or payments to themselves for which they give no genuine consideration or which they have no intention of repaying.

ii They may take advantage of their position by diverting profitable contracts or opportunities which arise in the course of the company's business to their own personal advantage, by making use of confidential information in the buying and selling of company shares, or by arranging take-over or merger terms which are specially favourable to themselves as directors or shareholders.

iii They may take advantage of their effective control over the company's affairs to pay themselves excessive remuneration as directors, whether in cash or by way of such perks as the free use of expensive cars or foreign travel at company expense.

iv Instead of distributing realized profit among the shareholders they may insist on reinvesting all or most of it in the company's business with a view to increasing the scale of the enterprise and consequently their own power and influence, thus indirectly justifying an increase in their own remuneration.

v By entrenching themselves in control of the company by means of special voting rights or life directorships they may protect themselves from dismissal and the company from take-over regardless of their efficiency in the conduct of the company's business.

Criminal and regulatory measures

The strongest deterrent to the most blatant forms of oppression is the possibility of a criminal prosecution, whether directly for the misappropriation of assets or indirectly for false accounting or the publication of false or misleading accounts or statements. There are a large number of relevant crimes : the general offences of theft and deception, under the Theft Act 1968, the additional offences under the same statute covering consent or connivance by any director or officer of a company at false accounting, or the obtaining of property or pecuniary advantage by deception by that company (s. 18), the publication of a false or misleading statement with intent to deceive the company's members or creditors (s. 19), and the specific liquidation offences under the Companies Acts (see p. 202). Though most of the case-law on offences by directors relates to mis-statements in public issue prospectuses, all these provisions are equally applicable to frauds within unquoted companies.

There are also a number of more specific requirements and prohibitions written into the Companies Act with a view to reducing the opportunities for oppression.

Certain transactions which are likely to lead to abuse and cannot readily be justified on other grounds are absolutely prohibited. It has long been unlawful for a public company to make a loan to one of its directors or to stand guarantor for him (1948 : s. 190), and this rule has now been extended to all private companies (1967 : s. 2). There is no criminal penalty for breach of this rule, but any person authorizing the loan or guarantee is personally liable for any loss incurred by the company, except where the loan was to enable the director to carry on the business of the company and has been sanctioned in general meeting. Even if there were a stronger penalty, however, the section as it now stands does not effectively prevent directors from making use of their company's funds for their own purposes in all circumstances, since it covers only current directors and may thus be simply evaded by the resignation of the individual concerned. There is no bar on loans to managers or controlling shareholders.

A similar absolute prohibition now applies to dealings by directors and their families in share options in their own company (1967 : ss. 25 and 30). There is provision in this instance for a criminal penalty by way of a fine or imprisonment. This measure, however, deals only with a small part of the much wider problem of abuse by directors and other 'insiders' of confidential information about the company's affairs for their own private gain. Option dealings are merely an extreme example of the type of speculation in shares which is open to abuse in this way. To prove effective a preventive ban would have to be extended to all share dealing by directors, which is scarcely practicable while directors are permitted to be shareholders. A more selective attack on those dealings where there is evidence of improper use of inside information, as discussed below, would appear to be a more suitable remedy.

Disclosure provisions

There is a much wider range of transactions involving a possible conflict of interest or a risk of impropriety in which a disclosure rule has been adopted. Full particulars must be disclosed in the company's annual accounts of any loans which may legitimately be made by the company to any of its officers (1948 : s. 197). Shareholders must also be informed of, and in the case of payments by their own company approve, any payments made to a director for loss of office whether on retirement or in respect of any take-over or merger deal (1948 : ss. 191–3). Breach of these rules may render the transaction voidable : thus in one case where a director had been paid £4,000 by way of compensation for loss of office without the necessary disclosure to preference shareholders, the money was held to be refundable.[2] More generally directors must disclose to the board any interest which they may have in any contract or dealing by the company (1948 : s. 199). These rules were extended in the Companies Act 1967. All service contracts made by the company with its directors, by way of salary or otherwise, must be open to inspection by any member of the company (1967 : s. 26). A register must be kept of directors' shareholdings in the company and its associated companies and of all dealings by them in those shares, and must be open to inspection by any interested person, whether a member of the company or not, on payment of a small fee (1967 : ss. 27–9).

It is doubtful whether these various requirements provide any real protection to minority interests in unquoted private companies. Provision for disclosure to fellow directors of any personal interest in company contracts is unlikely to operate as a genuine check, particularly in the case of smaller companies where formal directors' meetings are an exceptional rather than a regular occurrence. Provision for disclosure to and even approval by shareholders is likely

[2] *In re Duomatic Ltd* [1969] 2 Ch. 365 (see p. 258).

to be equally ineffective where directors are in effective control over the general meeting. A requirement for majority approval affords little safeguard for minority interests.

Furthermore the penalty for non-compliance with the statutory requirements may not always be a real deterrent. The courts have a general power to relieve a company officer from liability for any failure to comply with the statutory provisions, where he has not been at fault (1948 : s. 448). And even where there has been a culpable failure to disclose directors' interests in contracts the result is merely to render the transaction voidable if a complaint is made:

The chairman of a public company entered into a personal guarantee to secure the company's overdraft of £50,000. Shortly after a private company bought shares in the public company from the chairman for some £100,000, and made him a director. The private company through its managing director also entered into a formal guarantee to indemnify him for any loss suffered on the guarantee and on any further loans which he might make to the public company. In reliance on this the chairman made further loans to the company of some £45,000. The chairman's interest in the indemnity as a director of the private company was not formally declared. The public company subsequently went into liquidation and the private company sought to evade liability on the indemnity. It was held that the non-disclosure merely rendered the indemnity voidable, and that since it was far too late to raise an objection, the chairman was entitled to recover on it. *Hely-Hutchinson v Brayhead Ltd.* [1968] 1 Q.B. 549

A substantial penalty or at the least a provision that any benefit accruing to the director should be held on trust for the company, as in the case of unlawful payments made to directors for compensation for loss of office (1948: ss. 192–3), would help to make disclosure requirements of this kind effective.

Civil remedies

The criminal liability of directors is limited to certain blatant and specific forms of malpractice, and it is in any event always difficult to prove a criminal intention in matters of this kind to the satisfaction of a jury. In most cases the complainant must fall back on the civil law. It is difficult to give a precise categorization of the forms of relief available, since there is a good deal of overlap between the various traditional heads of liability. Nor is it possible to relate any remedy exclusively to any particular form of oppression. But five broad heads of action may be isolated:

i an action to prevent any illegal or unconstitutional action by the company or its directors;

ii an action to have set aside any purported exercise by the directors of their powers otherwise than honestly and for a proper purpose;

iii an action for damages by any person who suffers directly as a result of fraudulent conduct or any other actionable breach of duty or trust on the part of a director;

iv an action to secure the reimbursement of any illegitimate personal profit made by a director in the course of the company's business;

v an action to prevent majority shareholders from using their powers to carry through a 'fraud on the minority';

vi an action under section 210 of the Companies Act 1948 to remedy any form of oppression of shareholders.

i *Illegal and unconstitutional acts.* The most basic right of a shareholder is to have the affairs of his company conducted in accordance with the statutory provisions of the Companies Acts, and within the limits of the company's own constitution as laid down in its memorandum and articles of association. Thus, where directors have acted or purported to act for the company in a manner which is either directly contrary to the provisions of the Acts, as for instance in failing to hold a statutory general meeting or to present accounts, or else beyond the formal powers of the company, for instance in an ultra vires extension of the company's business, any shareholder may make an application to the court for an order requiring the directors to remedy the situation. This remedy is available in any case where directors have applied company property for their own or others' advantage in circumstances in which there is no possible benefit for the company. It was held, for instance, that it was ultra vires for the directors of a company to vote a generous pension for the widow of a deceased director, since the decision was taken *after* his death when there could be no such benefit for the company as is generally assumed from the provision of pensions for employees and their widows.[3]

The main difficulty which may arise in cases of this kind is that of ratification. Acts which are ultra vires in respect of the company cannot be ratified, but where the directors have merely exceeded their powers as laid down in the company's constitution, the company in general meeting may subsequently confirm and validate their action, subject to the limitations discussed below (see p. 271).

ii *The duty to use powers for a proper purpose*. The duty imposed on a director to use his powers for a proper purpose is a simple extension of his duty to act constitutionally. It has sometimes been expressed in the context of company law as a duty to act at all times in good faith in the best interests of the company. But that formulation lays too much emphasis on the subjective intention of the director. It is better to regard the rule as an application of the general public law doctrine that office holders must exercise their powers for the purpose for which they are given. The remedy, as with illegal or unconstitutional acts, is an order of the court nullifying or restraining the improper action.

The proper purpose rule is specially relevant in cases where directors misuse their powers over the machinery of a company to their own personal advantage, for instance to entrench their position as directors in the face of a take over threat. One of the most effective weapons for directors in cases of this kind is their power to issue new shares. Like any other power vested in the directors, this power must be exercised in the best interests of the company as a whole, as opposed to those of individual directors:

The articles of a company granted power to the directors to allot new shares on such terms and conditions as they thought fit. In the face of a take-over bid the directors arranged for control of the company to be passed to a trust of which they would be the trustees and the company's employees the beneficiaries. They then proceeded to allot the remaining unissued capital of the company to the trust with special voting rights of ten votes per share. They also advanced some £28,000 of the company's funds to the trust to enable it to buy in other shares at the price offered by the take-over bidder. In an action brought by a minority shareholder to set aside the transactions it was held that the directors had no right under the articles to issue shares with multiple voting rights, and that even though

[3] *In re W. & M. Roith Ltd.* [1967] 1 W.L.R. 432.

the board may have acted in good faith and believed that the establishment of the trust would benefit the company, their primary purpose was the improper one of ensuring their own continued control; the scheme was therefore invalid, though the shareholders in general meeting could have ratified it (and in fact later did so). *Hogg v. Cramphorn* [1967] Ch. 254

The rule is not limited to cases of self-entrenchment or personal gain. It has been expressed in the most general terms by the Judicial Committee of the Privy Council in a case originating from Australia :

The directors of a company favoured one take-over bidder as against another. They used their powers of allotting new shares both to raise much needed capital for the company but also to reduce the stake held by the first bidding company to less than fifty per cent so that the second bidder might gain control. It was held that they had acted improperly: 'Where a dispute arose whether the directors of a company made a particular decision for one purpose or another, or whether one purpose or another was the substantial or primary purpose, the court was entitled to look at the situation objectively in order to estimate how critical or pressing or substantial an alleged requirement (of finance) may have been. ... It must be unconstitutional for directors to use their fiduciary powers over the shares in the company for the purpose of destroying an existing majority or creating a new majority which did not previously exist.' (per Lord Wilberforce) *Howard Smith Ltd. v. Ampol Petroleum Ltd.* [1974] A.C. 821

The practical significance of the proper purpose rule, however, must not be exaggerated. It is generally applicable only in cases in which directors have used their powers as directors for an ulterior purpose other than, or in addition to, their apparent or professed purpose. It does not prevent directors from taking advantage of their dual role as directors and controlling shareholders to establish or reconstruct companies by altering the articles, or authorizing an increase in capital and allotting shares in such a way as to secure a particular balance of power or to entrench the position of particular directors. There is no legal bar, following the decision in *Bushell v. Faith*,[4] on an article which grants overriding voting rights to a director in any motion for his removal from office. Nor is there any legal bar on the *alteration* of existing articles to achieve a similar result, if the necessary majority in the company's general meeting can be secured.

[4] [1970] A.C. 1099 (see p. 160); a clause reversing the decision was included in the Companies Bill of 1973.

The directors of a company held special management shares each of which entitled them to eight votes, thus giving them forty-seven per cent of the voting control. The company proposed to take over another company by the issue of new shares to the holders of the equity shares in the other company. In order to maintain the position of the directors a motion was proposed to double the number of votes on each management share to sixteen. This resolution, on which the holders of the management shares did not vote, was carried by a majority of nine to one of the votes cast. It was argued on behalf of the minority that the scheme should be set aside as oppressive and discriminatory, but it was held that there was nothing improper in an alteration in voting rights by the requisite majority: since the alteration in voting powers 'had been resolved upon by a great majority of those members of the company who had themselves nothing to gain by it so far as their personal interest was concerned and who . . . were actuated only by consideration of what was best for the company as a whole' there was no oppression. *Rights & Issues Investment Trust Ltd. v. Stylo Shoes Ltd.* [1965] Ch. 250

The fact that directors may generally make use of their own votes as shareholders for this purpose, despite the implication to the contrary in the *Stylo Shoes* case, reduces the impact of the proper purpose rule in small owner-controlled companies still further. It is settled law that directors may cast their own votes in a general meeting as they please, without in so doing breaching their fiduciary duty as directors.

In the course of a series of transactions prior to 'going public' a company gave an undertaking to the court to use its best endeavours to secure a quotation so as to be able to complete its contract to issue shares to the plaintiffs. The plaintiffs sought to enforce this contract, and in particular to prevent the directors of the company from voting against a motion for an increase in capital which was necessary if the scheme was to go ahead. The directors made it clear in a circular to shareholders that they thought the motion should be rejected. It was held that though the directors as directors had an obligation to carry out the company's undertaking to the court, and thus to recommend acceptance of the motion, they were not bound to use their own votes as shareholders in support of it; a director who had fulfilled his duty as a director . . . was nevertheless free, as an individual shareholder, to enjoy the same unfettered and unrestricted right of voting at general meetings as he would have had if he had not also been a director. (per Walton J.) *Northern Counties Securities Ltd. v. Jackson & Steeple Ltd.* [1974] 1 W.L.R. 1133

There is little practical point in attempting to impose a general ban on the freedom of controlling directors in unquoted companies to use their powers either of share allocation or voting to affect the ultimate control over their company. The rights of other shareholders in this context are better protected by the discretionary remedy against oppression.

It is paradoxically even more difficult to establish the impropriety of actions which are more obviously for the director's personal benefit. The terms of directors' service contracts (though not their fees as directors, which must generally be approved by the general meeting), the level of business expenses and facilities accorded to them as directors or executives, and the institution of pension and incentive schemes by way of share options or otherwise, are all typically under the sole control of the directors themselves. An individual director may not under the terms of the standard article in Table A vote on any contract in which he is personally interested (art. 84). But it appears to be established or at least accepted that the board as a whole may vote on them, and that such schemes may be taken to operate in the best interests of the company unless it is established conclusively to the contrary. In so far as company law is concerned the only control over payments and perks for directors is through the disclosure provisions discussed above. But in the case of unquoted companies where the directors are effectively in control and there are no market or institutional pressures to be faced disclosure in itself is little use to the minority shareholder who feels that too high a proportion of company profits are going to the individual directors. Nor is any limitation in tax law on the amounts which may be set off against company profits by way of directors' emoluments or expenses of direct assistance to the aggrieved shareholder, since disallowance by the Inland Revenue simply results in an increased tax liability on the company and on the directors as recipients. The tax authorities have no power to require any excess payment to be set aside or refunded. In the result the only effective legal action open to the shareholders of an unquoted company against the overpayment of directors is again the essentially discretionary remedy against oppression.

iii *Damages and the duty of honest effort.* It is well established that a director owes a duty of care to the company for which he works, and in certain circumstances to its members and prospective members, and that he will be liable to pay damages for any loss resulting directly from a breach of that duty. In principle it should make little difference whether his breach is fraudulent or unintentional, in that the duty is an objective one, the standard of care required being measured in relation to the size and nature of the company concerned, as already discussed. The formulation of a director's duty in terms of honest effort further reduces the practical difference between allegations of fraud and of negligence. This approach is given practical effect by the general provision for relief from liability on the ground that the director has acted honestly and reasonably (1948 : s. 448). Effective liability is thus usually limited to those cases in which some element of lack of probity can be established. In addition the occasions on which there is held to be a direct duty to members of the company are very restricted. The resulting minimal level of liability in practical terms is best explained in respect of the various types of breach which may arise, rather than in broad general statements.

Liability is perhaps most easily established in cases of false or misleading statements. The question of a formal prospectus does not arise in the case of a private company. But in all types of company situations arise in which statements are made by directors to shareholders or prospective shareholders as to the profitability or otherwise of the company. The law on the extent of the director's duty in such cases is well-developed but complex. He is bound in broad terms to give a true picture of the state of the company's affairs in so far as it is known to him. But his legal liability for mistakes and concealment depends entirely on the precise circumstance in which the statement was made and to whom, and on the nature of the loss suffered as a result.

The simplest situation is that in which a mis-statement is made in a formal account or report required to be circulated to shareholders or others under the Companies Act. It is well established that a company director or secretary may be civilly liable for any loss caused in such cases, in addition to any criminal penalty which he may incur for any culpable failure to comply with the statutory requirement :

A company failed to comply with the statutory requirement that details of a previous allotment of shares be included in a prospectus. It was held that though a shareholder would not be entitled to rescind his contract to buy shares merely for a minor breach of the regulations, the Act did contemplate that directors and others responsible for the prospectus would be liable in damages, since though no express provision was made to this effect, there was express provision for the exoneration of those who had not been at fault. *In re South of England Natural Gas and Petroleum Co. Ltd.* [1911] 1 Ch. 573

Thus any director of a company who fails to take all reasonable steps to secure compliance with the statutory provisions in respect of the company's annual accounts will be liable in damages to those who may suffer loss as a result, unless he can show that he had reasonable ground to believe and did believe that a competent and reliable person had been charged to secure compliance (1948 : s. 149). This liability is probably restricted to those who have a statutory right to receive the accounts, or others to whom they have been specifically made available, for instance the company's bankers, with a view to assessing the financial position of the company.

Where the mis-statement does not form part of a statutory account the likelihood of a successful action is rather more restricted, owing to the common law rule that damages cannot normally be obtained for loss suffered even as a direct result of negligent mis-statement. The traditional remedy in such cases is a suit in equity for rescission of a contract made in reliance on the mis-statement, as long as the parties can readily be restored to their respective positions before the contract was executed and there has been no undue delay (see below p. 313).

In cases of fraud, however, this rule does not apply. Damages may be obtained by anyone who suffers direct loss as a result of a fraudulent statement made to him. The standard of liability in this context is clearly established : a statement may be false both in what it includes and in what it omits, if the omission is such as to make what is stated false or misleading in itself. Any person concerned in the publication or preparation of the statement may be held liable if he knew of the falsehood or recklessly closed his eyes to it. The case-law in this respect will be discussed in more detail in relation to public issues (see Chapter 6). The main problem is proving fraud to the satisfaction of a court or jury.

This already complex position has been further confused by independent developments in the law of contract and tort.

First, under the Misrepresentation Act 1967, damages may now be awarded in respect of any mis-statement made in the course of contractual dealings subject to a general defence of an honest and reasonable belief in the truth of the facts represented. The practical effect of this measure, however, is restricted to cases in which loss results from a specific contractual dealing.

Secondly, the law of tort has been developed to permit an action for damages in respect of a negligent mis-statement made in circumstances in which one party is held to owe a duty of care to another :

A firm of advertising agents asked for a banker's reference in respect of one of their clients. The bank gave them a favourable reply, and the firm accepted orders which the clients subsequently failed to pay for. It was held that the firm would have been entitled to recover damages from the bank had it not been for the fact that the bank had explicitly disclaimed responsibility for the accuracy of their reference. Liability for negligent misstatement, it was stated, would arise in any case in which someone possessed of a special skill undertakes, quite irrespective of contract, to apply that skill for the assistance of another person who relies upon such skill. (per Lord Morris, at p. 502) *Hedley Byrne & Co. v. Heller* [1964] A.C. 465

This extension of tortious liability, however, has subsequently been expressly restricted to cases where one party is relying on the special skill or competence of the other in a professional capacity, or where the other has undertaken to advise on the strength of special skill or knowledge similar to that of a professional adviser :

A policy holder in an insurance company asked for advice from the company as to the financial stability of an associated company. The company's officers replied negligently and the plaintiff suffered loss by increasing his investment in the associated company. It was held that since it was not part of the insurance company's business to give such advice it was not bound to do more than act honestly, which it had done. *Mutual Life and Citizens' Assurance Co. Ltd. v. Evatt* [1971] A.C. 793 (PC)

In so far as statements made at large by company directors to shareholders or prospective shareholders are concerned, then, it is unlikely that the requisite professional capacity will be held to exist so as to create any general tortious liability. This does not wholly exclude the extension of liability to cases in which a direct personal communication is made to an individual shareholder or prospective investor in circumstances in which the director has, as it were, undertaken to act in the role of a professional investment adviser. But there is no reason to believe that the general rule that the director of a company owes no special duty to disclose all relevant information to a shareholder or prospective shareholder in any dealing he has with him, as established in *Percival v. Wright* (1902),[5] has been altered by this new development.

The effective duty of a director in respect of statements to shareholders and investors, and perhaps creditors as well, is thus primarily one of honesty in so far as he says anything, though where he is required to prepare a statutory account or report or where he makes a voluntary statement in the course of contractual dealing or in the capacity of an investment adviser he will be subject to the ordinary rule of liability for negligence. In order to establish liability, however, the individual complainant will have to show that he has suffered loss as a direct result of relying on the statement in question. It is unlikely in the present legal climate in such matters that this would extend to cases where a shareholder, or perhaps a creditor, has merely refrained from taking positive action to protect his interests, as he might have done had he not been reassured by the directors' statement.

The standard of conduct legally required of directors in other spheres is more easily dealt with if only because the absence of any effective liability has prevented the growth of any complexity in the law. Under the traditional formulation a director is bound to exercise that degree of care and skill which may be expected of a person in his position in respect of what he actually does in the conduct of the company's affairs; but he is not required to exercise any general oversight over the company's affairs or to perform any other duties than those prescribed by statute such as to ensure that proper books and accounts are kept and the relevant reports prepared. Any liability which does exist must then be considered in conjunction with the statutory provision for relief (1948: s. 448), and the possibility of ratification by the company in general meeting.

This formulation is not particularly helpful in dealing with the crucial practical question whether a director may ever be held liable for the mismanagement of the company's affairs. The answer to this is probably not. There is certainly no liability for what may be termed errors of commercial judgement, and this appears to be extended in practice to what can only be described as gross mismanagement of a kind which would certainly constitute actionable negligence in the conduct of an established trade or profession. A

[5] [1902] 2 Ch. 421 (see p. 255).

further difficulty is that this supposed duty of care and skill is owed exclusively to the company rather than to the shareholders, so that it is difficult to institute proceedings without the support of the majority interest in the company, which in unquoted companies is likely to lie with the directors themselves. Even if this obstacle is surmounted, it cannot be seriously argued that the office of director has yet been endowed with professional status in the sense that there is an objectively ascertainable standard of conduct to be expected of any person exercising it. The enactment of a general fiduciary duty, as proposed in the Companies Bill 1973, would not affect this position. The duty of a director in an unquoted company in default of any such professional status is merely to do his honest best.

iv *Impropriety and the duty to account.* The basis of the director's duty to account in cases of impropriety is essentially different from the duty of honesty and effort. The remedy is not the payment of damages for loss suffered, but the reimbursement of profit improperly made. In its simplest form the liability amounts to little more than the return of company assets improperly diverted by directors to their own personal use, and where any form of fraudulent intent can be established the director will also be liable to criminal sanctions. But it extends also to personal profits made by directors in the course of transactions where the opportunity for profit is deemed in law to have arisen in the course of the company's business,[6] and even to the misuse of information obtained in the capacity of director.

The defendant was made managing director of a consultancy company with a view to seeking contracts with the local gas board. When negotiations for a contract broke down, he was asked for advice in his personal capacity. In this process he acquired information not known to others in the company. He secured an early release from his directorship on the excuse of ill-health, and subsequently won the contracts from the gas board for himself. It was held that he must account to the company for any profits made, since he had started personal negotiations while he was a director; even though the company could not have won the contracts, as a director he had a duty to pass on the information he had acquired; it was an overriding rule of equity that a director must not put himself into a position in which his fiduciary duty and his own interests conflicted. *Industrial Development Consultants Ltd. v. Cooley* [1972] 1 W.L.R. 443

[6] *Cook v. Deeks* [1916] 1 A.C. 554 (PC) (see p. 235).

The trusteeship conception on which the duty to account is founded and the problem of drawing the line between the director as trustee or agent for the company and as personal profiteer have already been discussed. The basic rule is relatively easy to formulate: the duty to account arises in any case where a director makes use of company assets, facilities or information for his own personal profit within the field of business ordinarily undertaken by the company. The difficulty in any but the most blatant cases is in bringing a successful action since the directors concerned are usually in control of the company's affairs. But there are also some uncertainties as to the practical extent of the rule.

In the first place it is not entirely clear when a director will be liable to account where he undertakes a transaction in his own name which falls squarely within the powers of the company but which the company is unable to undertake without further capital or backing. The decisions in the *Regal* (*Hastings*)[7] and *I.D.C. v. Cooley* cases suggest that the practical question whether the company is genuinely willing or able to take up the opportunity is strictly irrelevant, and that the director who uses his personal resources or credit to carry the transaction through in his own name instead of assisting the company to do so will be liable to account, unless he has declared his interest and secured the approval of a majority of disinterested directors or of the company in general meeting. The difficulty is that where there are no disinterested directors, as in the *Regal* (*Hastings*) case, or where the directors are also controlling shareholders and thus in a position to ratify their own action, this approach breaks down. On the strictest trusteeship principles a director's only safe course of action would be to obtain the approval of *all* shareholders or else to resign his directorship before committing his own personal resources, and in cases where the opportunity had arisen in the course of the company's business even that might be insufficient. A self-denying obligation of this kind might be thought appropriate in quoted companies in which directors may reasonably be required to cease to do business on their own account. In owner-controlled unquoted companies a more realistic and enforceable rule would be to require directors not to divert from a company business which it is in a position to undertake, but to permit them to deal independently where the company cannot take advantage of the

[7] [1942] 1 All E. R. 378 (HL) (see p. 235).

opportunity without calling on the directors' personal resources or credit, subject only to full disclosure so that minority shareholders may seek a remedy in any case of oppression.

A somewhat different problem arises over the use or misuse of confidential information for purposes outside the scope of the company's business. The director's duty to account to the company for profit made from commercially valuable information diverted from it does not extend to profit made in dealing in the company's shares. It has been held that a director is not bound to make full disclosure to shareholders of information which would affect the price paid on the free market, even if that director is negotiating with the shareholders for the purchase of their shares:

> Shareholders wrote to the secretary of a company offering to sell their holdings to any suitable buyer at £12.25. As a result of this approach three directors of the company bought the shares on their own account at £12.50 knowing as directors that an offer was to be made for all the shares in the company by a third party at a substantially higher price. The shareholders sued to have the contracts of sale set aside on the ground that the directors were in a fiduciary position in respect of their knowledge of the prospective bid. The action failed. It was held that in such circumstances directors were under no duty to disclose, since that would place them 'in a most invidious position, as they could not buy or sell shares without disclosing negotiations, a premature disclosure of which might well be against the best interests of the company'. (per Swinfen Eady J., at p. 426) *Percival v. Wright* [1902] 2 Ch. 421

This decision has been taken to establish a general rule to the effect that a director is not bound to account either to the company or to shareholders for profit made in the course of what are termed 'insider' dealings. The case does not itself support such a widely framed rule. The judge relied to a large extent on the fact that the bid ultimately proved abortive and that there had been no unfair dealing since the original approach came from the shareholders; and since no immediate profit had in fact been realized by the directors, there was nothing for which they could be asked to account. A more satisfactory interpretation is to limit the decision to actions for rescission for non-disclosure, leaving open the possibility of liability to account for personal profits realized through the use of inside information.

This restrictive interpretation of *Percival v. Wright* is to some extent borne out by subsequent developments both in Britain and abroad. Thus in one case where a direct profit was actually realized by the directors on whose initiative the transaction in question had been undertaken, it was held that they were trustees of the profits for the shareholders:

The directors of a company arranged for the sale of the undertaking to a third party. As they held less than one-third of the shares in the company they negotiated options with the remaining shareholders to allow them to purchase their shares when the sale went through. The price fixed under the option contract amounted to some $22,000; the company was sold at some $42,000 and in addition the directors were given a substantial holding in the new company. A group of shareholders who had granted options sued for a declaration that the directors were trustees for the shareholders of the substantial profit they had made. The Privy Council upheld the decision of the Canadian courts that in the circumstances the directors were agents for the shareholders when they took the options: 'the directors must here be taken to have held themselves out to the individual shareholders as acting for them on the same footing as they were acting for the company itself, that was as agents'. *Allen v. Hyatt* (1914) 30 T.L.R. 444 (PC)

The same line of reasoning, that directors may be held liable to account for any profit made on the purchase or sale of shares in their company where they have not disclosed the existence of 'special circumstances' known to them which affect the value of the shares, has been pressed a good deal further in America. This was at first based on the ground that there was a general duty to disclose such special circumstances, so that where disclosure was not made the remedy of rescission would be granted, as in the leading case of *Strong v. Repide*:

A shareholder in a sugar plantation company offered to sell her shares through an agent. The controlling director of the company who was in negotiation with the US government for the sale of a large portion of the company's property bought the shares through his own agent without disclosing either that he was the purchaser or the state of the negotiations. It was held that in such circumstances the sale could be set aside on grounds of fraud by the director. *Strong v. Repide* (1909) 213 U.S. 419

Subsequent cases have laid more emphasis on the duty of a director in such special circumstances to account for any profit he has made, on the ground that he has in fact been making use for his own personal profit of information which he has obtained only in his capacity as director. And in *Taylor v. Wright* (1945)[8] a shareholder

[8] 69 Cal. App. 2d. 371.

who sold shares through an agent to directors in somewhat similar circumstances was held entitled to recover as damages the difference in the price paid and the true value of the shares. The 'special circumstances' doctrine is applied more or less interchangeably to refer to cases where rescission is granted and to those where the wrongdoers are required to account for their profit.

This common law liability in America has been largely superseded in respect of market dealings in quoted companies by the development of the action for breach of the Securities and Exchange Commission regulations (see p. 349). But it clearly remains applicable in the case of unquoted companies. Its effect, as in the case of the parallel liability in quoted companies, should be to place a bar on all dealings by those with inside knowledge of the company's affairs or prospects which cannot be disclosed but which affect the value of the company's shares. Directors and other insiders would thus have either to make full disclosure to any person with whom they contract to buy or sell shares, or else to restrict their dealings to occasions in which the situation is neutral between 'insiders' and 'outsiders', typically just after the publication of the company's annual report or other statements. The consensus of opinion in America would seem to be that this kind of restriction on directors' freedom to enter into dealings is reasonable in all the circumstances.[9]

The position in Britain is a good deal less satisfactory. As stated by the Jenkins Committee the result of the decision in *Percival v. Wright* is that 'a director who has by reason of his office acquired in confidence a particular piece of information materially affecting the value of the securities of his company (or any company in the same group) will incur no liability to the other party if he buys or sells such securities without disclosing that piece of information.'[10] The Committee felt that this was wrong and recommended that a director of a company who enters into any such transaction should be liable to compensate a person who suffers from his action in so doing unless the relevant information was known to that person. In the case of unquoted companies a statutory remedy of this kind, or the active development of the 'special circumstances' doctrine at common law, is likely to prove more effective than the general ban on insider dealings proposed in the Companies Bill of 1973 (cl. 12)

[9] R. H. Mundheim, 'The Texas Gulf Sulphur Complaint', (1966) *Journal of Business Law* 284.

[10] Cmnd. 1749 (1962), para. 89.

(see p. 349). For the moment the only effective restriction on the freedom of directors to deal as they please is the statutory ban on option dealings and the obligation to maintain a register, open to inspection by any interested person, of their dealings (1967 : ss. 25, 27 and 29). This obligation to disclose dealings is of little help to shareholders in unquoted companies in the absence of an effective remedy in cases of impropriety.

Statutory relief for directors

The effective extent of the four heads of liability discussed so far must all be considered in the light of the statutory provision for relief. The court has a discretionary power to relieve any officer of a company in any proceedings 'for negligence, default, breach of duty or breach of trust' of all or part of his liability if it is satisfied that he acted honestly and reasonably and that in all the circumstances he ought fairly to be relieved' (1948 : s. 448). Relief is most likely to be granted in cases where there has been a minor breach of the statutory regulations over the conduct of the company's affairs, though it extends to any breach of a director's duties at common law as well. In practical terms, therefore, the final decision on the extent of a director's duties over the whole range of his activities is left to the discretion of the court, which is thus able to make a clear distinction between the conduct to be expected of full-time and of part-time directors, and to lay down more general standards of business practice and morality. In one recent case, for instance, it was decided that in respect of the settlement of a possible legal claim against the company a reasonable director would normally take professional legal advice :

> The directors of a company consistently failed to secure a resolution of the general meeting authorizing their emoluments, and in addition agreed to make a special payment to another director to induce him to leave the board without taking action against the company for wrongful dismissal. It was held that the failure to secure a vote of the general meeting did not invalidate the payments drawn by the directors from time to time by way of salary, since all those eligible to vote had in fact tacitly approved the payments; that further drawings on a similar basis in the following year which had not been so approved were prima facie unlawful, but that in view of the practice in the previous year the director concerned ought to be excused under s. 448 from his liability to repay the money; but that the payment to the retiring director by way of compensation for loss of office

was ultra vires since the approval of the preference shareholders had not been sought under s. 191, and since legal advice had not been sought as to the validity of any possible claim against the company, those concerned would not be relieved of their liability to refund the money. *In re Duomatic Ltd.* [1969] 2 Ch. 365

v *Fraud on the minority.* Different considerations arise in respect of the remaining heads of liability, in which neither relief nor ratification will normally be possible. The controlling faction in a company is not permitted to exercise its power in such a way as to constitute what is termed a fraud on the minority. This concept was developed in the common law with primary reference to the duties of majority shareholders. But in practical terms it is often pointless to distinguish the precise duties of directors and shareholders in owner-controlled companies.

The essence of the rule is best expressed in modern terms by the notion of discrimination. The controlling faction must not exercise its powers in such a way that one group of shareholders, typically but not necessarily the majority group, is treated preferentially in relation to the rest. The majority will not be permitted to expropriate the property of the company by selling it to themselves at less than its real value. Nor may it in its own interest seek to exonerate any person from liability to the company for fraud or other illegitimate activities if that would have the effect of depriving the minority of its right to recover a share in what the company has lost. In *Cook v. Deeks* (see p. 235), for instance, an attempt by the directors to use their powers as controlling shareholders to exonerate themselves from liability to account to the company was rejected on this ground :

> Directors holding a majority of the votes would not be permitted to make a present to themselves; that would be to allow a majority to oppress the minority... if directors have acquired for themselves property or rights which they must be regarded as holding on behalf of the company, a resolution that the rights of the company should be disregarded in the matter would amount to forfeiting the interest and property of the minority of the shareholders in favour of the majority, and that by the votes of those who are interested in securing the property for themselves. (per Lord Buckmaster) [1916] A.C. 554, at 564

The rule against the expropriation of the property of the company at the expense of the minority, however, does not extend to cases in which the minority is effectively excluded from participation in future profits, for example by a scheme involving the winding up of one company and the creation of another from which the minority is excluded, as long as all the shareholders in the original company are paid a fair price for their interest in the company as a going concern. This follows from the fact that the ultimate remedy in cases of fraud on the minority is an order for the winding up of the company and the distribution of the assets among the shareholders. The same principle should be applied where the majority simply seeks to buy out the shares of a minority in an existing company. But the case-law has been taken to establish that minority shareholders have a right not to be bought out against their will. It has been held that a company may provide in its articles for the compulsory purchase at a fair price of the shares of any shareholder whose continued involvement is detrimental to the company, for instance if he or his associates are engaged in direct competition with the company.[11] This was justified on the ground that competitors should not be allowed to obtain information about a company merely by buying a few shares. Now that all companies must file for public inspection all information required to be disclosed to shareholders this argument is no longer valid. It has also been held that a majority may not alter the articles of a company to permit compulsory purchase of some shares and not others:

A group of tinplate companies set up an independent company to supply them with steel. One of the group later made other arrangements for its steel supply, and the remaining members sought to buy out its holding in the supply company by passing a resolution by the requisite special majority altering the articles of the company to permit the general meeting to require any shareholder, with one specific exception, to dispose of his shares in the company. In an action brought by the minority shareholding company it was held that the new article was so widely drawn as not to be justifiable in the interests of the company as a whole, and therefore invalid: 'The majority could not alter the articles in such a way as to place one or more of the minority in a position of inferiority, as for instance by attributing to his or their shares a smaller proportional share of the available profits than that which the others received, nor could it ... confer on one or more of its number benefits or privileges in which other shareholders of the same class did not participate.' (per Peterson J., at p. 143) *Dafen Tinplate Co. v. Llanelly Steel Co.* [1907] 2 Ch. 124

But it is arguable that these cases do not and should not rule out

[11] *Sidebottom v. Kershaw, Leese & Co.* [1920] 1 Ch. 154.

compulsory purchase at a fair price and within the terms of a company's constitution, even if an alteration of that constitution is required for the purpose. The best approach in cases of this kind is to draw a distinction between alterations in the articles which merely affect the internal management of the company and those which result in a clear depreciation in the value of the shares affected in relation to the rest. Even this test is difficult to apply. Any increase in share capital may be said to diminish the voting power and value of existing shares. But it has been held that a bonus issue of new shares to ordinary shareholders does not affect the rights of preference shareholders:

A preference shareholder objected to a bonus issue of shares to ordinary shareholders on the ground that it had not been approved by a class meeting of the preference shareholders who were entitled by the company's articles to block any scheme which affected their rights unless it had been approved by a special resolution in a class meeting. It was held that since the rights of ordinary shareholders could not be said to be affected by the issue of further ordinary shares, nor could the rights of preference shareholders. *White v. Bristol Aeroplane Co.* [1953] Ch. 65

It has also been held that a majority may legitimately extinguish a right of pre-emption:

A small minority shareholder instituted a long series of actions against the directors and controlling shareholders of his company. The directors eventually decided to dispose of their controlling interest. They secured the passing of a resolution in general meeting to alter the existing articles which provided a right of pre-emption for existing shareholders in the event of the sale of any shares in the company. The minority shareholder objected that this effectively prevented him from exercising his right to buy some of the shares. The court dismissed the complaint on the grounds that there had been no deliberate dishonesty or fraud on the part of the majority. *Greenhalgh v. Arderne Cinemas* [1951] 1 Ch. 286

The difficulty of applying the general concept of fraud on the minority to cases such as these eventually led to the creation of more flexible and discretionary statutory remedies. In respect of the alteration of a company's objects or of the rights of specific classes of shareholders, provision has been made for an application by the holders of fifteen per cent of the shares in question for an order of the court refusing to sanction the alteration (1948: ss. 10 and 72). And in the case of schemes for the reduction of capital or for the reconstruction of a company the company itself must obtain express court sanction in all cases, and the right to petition is extended to creditors of the company (1948 : ss. 66–8 and 206–8). The discretion of the court under these various provisions is not bound by the old common law rules, so that each case may be treated on its merits:

An investment company proposed a scheme for a reduction of capital under which the preference shareholders were to receive an equivalent amount to their existing holding in unsecured loan stock. A separate meeting of the preference shareholders approved the scheme but a minority among them later opposed the company's application for court confirmation of the scheme under ss. 67–8. The court refused to confirm the scheme on the grounds that the majority preference shareholders, who also held substantial amounts of equity capital, had not genuinely considered the merits of the scheme for preference shareholders as a class, and that in substance the scheme was unfair in that the slight increase in interest payable on the new loan stock did not compensate the preference shareholders adequately for the postponement of the date of repayment. *In re Holders Investment Trust Ltd.* [1971] 1 W.L.R. 583

vi *The statutory remedy against oppression* (*section 210*). The old rules developed in the cases on fraud on the minority continue to affect the most general statutory remedy for the protection of minorities. This was introduced in 1947 with the deliberate intention of removing the difficulties in proving and in granting a suitable remedy in cases of fraud on the minority, and permits the court to make any remedial order which it thinks fit where it is established that the affairs of the company are being conducted 'in a manner oppressive to some part of the members' (1948 : s. 210). The section specifically authorizes the court to order the offending majority shareholders to buy out the minority at a price to be fixed by the court. But there is an explicit requirement that an order under the section shall be made only where an order for the winding up of the company 'would unfairly prejudice [the oppressed members] but otherwise the facts would justify the making of a winding up order on the ground that it was just and equitable' (s. 210(2)). This cross-reference to the power to wind up a company on the just and equitable ground (1948 : s. 222(f)), which is itself subject to the restriction that the court must be satisfied that no other suitable remedy is available (1948 : s. 225(2)), has made it difficult for the courts to develop the new remedy against oppressive conduct in a liberal manner.

The usefulness of the new remedy has been further curtailed, quite apart from these formal restrictions, by the highly cautious approach adopted by the courts. General judicial statements to the effect that oppression is conduct which would normally be regarded as 'burdensome, harsh and wrong', or 'a visible departure from the standards of fair dealing and a violation of the conditions of fair play on which every shareholder who entrusts his money to a company is entitled to rely' are not lacking.[12] But the remedy has in fact been granted in only three cases which have been reported, and in one of those the decision was subsequently reversed on appeal. It is nonetheless more revealing to concentrate on the types of conduct which may justify a remedy as indicated in these and other cases than to take refuge in generalities. On this approach three broad categories of oppression may be isolated: *first*, the deliberate running down of the assets or worth of a company in such a way as to deprive shareholders of the legitimate return on their investment; *secondly*, the allocation of the profits of the company, whether by way of excessive directorial remuneration or otherwise, in such a way as to discriminate against minority shareholders; and *finally*, the misuse of the procedures for the formal control of the company's affairs in such a way as to exclude the minority from participation in its affairs.

The first of these is clearly exemplified in a case where the directors of a subsidiary company deliberately ran down its operations with a view to increasing the profits of the parent company, thus rendering the minority holding in the subsidiary valueless:

A group of rayon dealers formed a company jointly with a firm of weavers for the exploitation of the market in rayon fabric which was then new and difficult to obtain. The company was controlled by the weaving company by a small margin both on the board of directors and in general meeting. When rayon became more readily available the weaving firm found it more economic to obtain supplies otherwise than through the dealers and diverted its orders away from the joint company which was thus left in a state of decline from lack of business. The dealers, as minority shareholders, alleged that this constituted oppression and petitioned for an order under s. 210 that the weaving firm should buy out their interest at a reasonable price before liquidating the company. The court granted the order: 'The truth is that whenever a subsidiary is formed . . . with an inde-

[12] See *Elder v. Elder & Watson Ltd*, [1952] S.C. 49 at p. 60; (per Lord Keith) *Scottish Co-operative Wholesale Society v. Meyer Ltd*, [1959] A.C. 324 (HL), at p. 342 (per Lord Simmonds).

pendent minority of shareholders the parent company must, if it is engaged in the same class of business, accept as a result of having formed such a subsidiary an obligation so to conduct what are in a sense its own affairs as to deal fairly with the subsidiary.' (per Lord Cooper [1954] S.C. 381 at p. 391) The House of Lords upheld the order on the ground that the policy of the weaving firm in running down the subsidiary was clearly oppressive in the sense of being 'burdensome, harsh and wrong'. *Scottish Co-operative Wholesale Society v. Meyer* [1959] A.C. 324

The similarity between this decision under section 210 and the earlier application of the concept of a fraud on the minority in *Cook v. Deeks* (1916) (see p. 235) where the directors of the company also sought for their own personal profit to divert business which might have been channelled through the company will be obvious. Grossly negligent conduct or misconduct of the company's affairs, however, will not be sufficient to justify an order under section 210, even if it leads directly to a lower level of profitability or to a trading loss and thus to a general reduction in the value of shares in the company:

A small minority shareholder in a car washing company complained that the controlling director was acting oppressively, for instance by issuing car wash vouchers at a discount in order to secure a rapid cash inflow, though the price of the vouchers was less than the cost of washing, and more generally by not attending to the payment of the company's creditors so as to make the continuance of its business difficult. It was held that such allegations of mismanagement or inefficiency were not sufficient to establish oppression for the purposes of s. 210 since there was no suggestion that the director had acted unscrupulously, unfairly, or with any lack of probity . . . or that he had disregarded the wishes of the board of directors'. *In re Five Minute Car Wash Service Ltd.* [1966] 1 W.L.R. 745

It would appear from this that there must be some element of personal profit or advantage, however indirect, for the controlling directors or shareholders so that the decrease in the value of the minority's shareholding amounts to discrimination against them. Where there is no such discrimination the minority must fall back on an ordinary action in the name of the company against the directors or managers for a breach of their duty to the company, or a motion for their removal by the general meeting. But since both of these require majority support, they are not genuine alternatives.

It is more difficult to give a compelling example of the second head. In one case at first instance it was held that the continued payment of large directors' fees after the main burden of managing the company's business had been entrusted to a management company for a substantial annual fee could amount to or at least form part of a course of conduct which was oppressive to the minority shareholders:

The sole founder members and directors of a small private company each took up 50 £1 shares, and supplied additional capital by way of direct loans and guarantees for the company. The business did not prosper and one of the two sold his interest to a Mrs Peskoff. The other died shortly after. Mrs Peskoff then arranged for a further hundred shares to be issued to her, to secure her control over the company, and supplied an additional £1,000 of her own money and her own personal guarantee to tide the company over its current difficulties. Under her management the business soon prospered, and for a time the company paid her a flat fee of £1,550 per annum plus five per cent commission on turnover. Then the management of the major part of the business was transferred to a new company under the sole control of Mrs Peskoff and her family at an annual fee of between £3,000 and £5,000. Notwithstanding this new arrangement director's fees of between £6,000 and £12,000 continued to be paid to Mrs Peskoff. In addition a loan due to the deceased director was repudiated. It was held on a petition by the representatives of the deceased director that the issue of the new shares for the principal purpose of increasing Mrs Peskoff's interest could be set aside; that the repudiation of the loan, though time barred, was invalid, and that though Mrs Peskoff's skill in making the company profitable must be recognized and paid for, the continued payment of the very large director's fees after the introduction of the management company in itself amounted to oppression; the court accordingly ordered Mrs Peskoff *either* to buy in the petitioner's interest in the company on the basis that (i) he still owned a full half share, (ii) the excessive director's fees over and above a net amount for management and direction of £6,000 per annum would be refunded, and (iii) the loan was reacknowledged, *or* to permit the petitioner to buy her out on a similar basis; the remedy was held to be available to a shareholder's personal representatives, though the section mentioned only the shareholder himself. *In re Jermyn Street Turkish Baths Ltd.* [1970] 1 W.L.R. 1194

This decision was subsequently reversed on appeal on the ground that the issue of the shares was perfectly valid as an integral part of the rescue operation which was wholly financed by Mrs Peskoff, that the loan was statute barred, and that Mrs Peskoff had not in any way used her position as controlling shareholder to procure or retain the excessive remuneration in accordance with the initial arrangement and that accordingly there had been no continuing course of oppressive conduct.[13] Here too the reluctance of the courts to intervene in the assessment of what is reasonable remuneration and the refuge taken in the formal distinction between action as a director and as a controlling shareholder may be compared to their attitude under the common law remedy.

It is only in respect of the deliberate disregard of the formal procedures for the control of a company that the statutory remedy against oppression has been applied more liberally than the prior conception of fraud on the minority. In the single reported case on this the court held that a section 210 order could be made to enforce the right of minority shareholders to have the affairs of their company conducted in a proper fashion :

The founder of a stamp dealing business caused it to be incorporated, largely for tax purposes, and though he retained voting control over the company through his own and his wife's shareholdings, his two sons were elected as directors. Despite this, the founder, who had secured for himself the position of chairman for life, continued to act as if the business was still under his sole control, and as he became older acted increasingly in disregard of the decisions of the board of directors, notably in dismissing company employees and in his dealings with the company's American subsidiary. In an application by the two sons for relief under s. 210 the trial judge and the Court of appeal held that there had been oppression of the sons as minority shareholders: the founder's belief that he was entitled to ignore the decisions of the board as long as he retained voting control over the company could not be accepted, since the shareholders as a whole were entitled to have the affairs of the company conducted in the way laid down in the company's constitution. An order was accordingly made restraining the founder from interfering with the affairs of the company except in accordance with the decisions of the board, and appointing him as Life President, though without specific powers or duties as such. *In re H.R. Harmer Ltd.* [1959] 1 W.L.R. 62

Even in this sphere, however, the extent of the remedy as interpreted by the courts is strictly limited. It has been held, for instance, that it is not oppression for a majority shareholder to use his voting control to oust a fellow shareholder and director from his directorship and thus from the management of the company, even if that means that he loses all effective income from the company.[14] Here

[13] [1971] 1 W.L.R. 1071 (CA).
[14] *In re Lundie Bros. Ltd* [1965] 1 W.L.R. 1051 (see p. 160).

too the courts have been reluctant to interfere with the power of the majority to order the affairs of the company they control, unless there has been some impropriety not just in the motive of the controllers but in the means which they use to secure their ends.

A precise formulation of the extent of the remedy against oppression is further complicated by a number of more technical considerations arising from the form of words used in the statute. In the first place the remedy is provided against conduct 'oppressive to some part of the members' of the company, a phrase which has been interpreted to deny a remedy to a member in his capacity as a director. This has been applied even to the ouster of a director in a small private company in which all profits are paid out in the form of directors' fees and salaries so that the ex-director's financial interest in the company is effectively terminated, as in the *Lundie Bros.* case.[15] Similar reasoning has been applied where a shareholder/director who had been excluded from the business by his colleagues sought to obtain an order under section 210 to secure the repayment of a substantial loan from the failing company to his own company: relief was refused on the ground that his exclusion from the affairs of the company in his capacity as director had no bearing on his rights as shareholder, and that even as a shareholder he had no remediable interest since if the company had been wound up there would have been no assets left to distribute among the shareholders after the repayments of the company's various prior loans and debts.[16]

The phrase 'course of conduct' has also caused some trouble. In *In re Westbourne Galleries* where the major claim under s. 210 against the ouster of a director failed on similar grounds to those in the *Lundie Bros.* case a further complaint about the reversal of a decision to dispose of a lease was rejected on the grounds that as an isolated incident it would not be sufficient ground for an order under the section, 'which requires a course of oppressive conduct up to the date of the petition'.[17]

Some of these problems might be eased by the replacement of section 210 by a new provision along the lines of that included in the Companies Bill of 1973: this was explicitly drafted to cover past, present and future acts of oppression, to exclude all reference to a winding up order as a condition of relief and to extend to

[15] Ibid.

[16] *In re Bellador Silk Ltd* [1965] 1 All E.R. 667.

[17] [1970] 1 W.L.R. 1378 (see p. 158).

personal representatives of a deceased shareholder (cl. 70). An extended formulation of this kind has already been adopted in other jurisdictions, as for instance in Northern Ireland.[18] The real problem, however, is the reluctance of British judges to intervene in the internal affairs of companies. The inefficacy of section 210 as a genuine protection for minority interests is better attributed to this general approach than to the precise wording of the existing provision. The view is borne out by the fact that the judge at first instance in the *Jermyn Street Turkish Baths* case felt able to extend relief to the successors of a deceased shareholder on the simple ground that to deny it merely because it was not expressly covered would be to frustrate the objective of the remedy. Certainly the decisions of the higher courts in that case and *In re Westbourne Galleries* have destroyed section 210 as a remedy against some of the most frequent and effective techniques of oppression, notably the payment of excessive directors' fees, and the ousting of major shareholders from their position as working directors, linked in both cases to the failure to make any regular distribution of profits by way of dividend. It is significant that the Jenkins Committee drew special attention to cases of this kind:

> We may perhaps usefully mention as illustrative of the situations in which action under s. 210 might be appropriate those in which directors appoint themselves to paid posts with the company at excessive rates of remuneration, thus depriving the complaining members of any dividend, or any adequate dividend, on their shares; or in which directors . . . refuse to register personal representatives in respect of shares devolving upon them in that capacity, and by this expedient (coupled with the absorption of profits in payment of the directors' remuneration) force the personal representatives to sell their shares to the directors at an inadequate price.[19]

The Committee was careful to refer to the special circumstances of every case, but there can be little doubt that in the light of these remarks the decisions referred to above can at best be regarded as unfortunate exercises of the court's discretion and at worst as a plain misinterpretation of the proper meaning of oppression. In particular the attempt to distinguish between the rights of a minority shareholder as a shareholder and as a director in a small joint venture is a complete misreading of the practicalities of the situation in

[18] Companies Act (N.I.) 1960, s. 201.
[19] Cmnd. 1749 (1962), para. 205.

such cases. It may be difficult to decide on a fair allocation of trading profits in situations of this kind. But that in itself is not a reason for refusing to intervene when minorities are in effect being denied any income from their investment at all. The order at first instance in the *Jermyn Street Turkish Baths* case is a good example of the way in which the problem can be resolved.

It is ironic in this context that the courts have found it necessary to fall back on the older remedy of a winding up on the just and equitable ground to provide a relief against oppression in small participatory companies (see p. 156), since it was precisely the drawbacks to winding up as a remedy that prompted the introduction of section 210. There has been similar resort to equitable intervention in other cases which might have been dealt with more satisfactorily by a discretionary order under section 210:

The voting shares in a prosperous building company were divided between an ageing aunt who held 1,000 shares, and her niece, who held 800. The directors, other than the aunt, proposed to increase the share capital by issuing 200 shares each to themselves and 850 to a trust for the company's employees. The niece objected to the scheme on the ground that it would reduce her holding to less than twenty-five per cent, and sought an injunction to prevent the aunt from using her votes to carry the necessary resolutions. It was held that the aunt's right to use her votes must be subject to equitable considerations, and that since she had misled her niece as to her intentions it would be unjust for her to use her votes to deprive her niece of the right to block any special resolution. *Clemens v. Clemens Bros. Ltd.* [1976] 2 All E.R. 179

The merits of this decision, in so far as it goes beyond the particular facts of the case, are questionable, since it implies that the shareholders in a small private company are locked into the existing distribution of ownership and control, and that those who are effectively running the company may not issue new shares merely to alter the balance of power or give themselves a stake in it. The power to order the purchase of minority shareholdings provided in section 210 is perhaps the only satisfactory solution in such cases. It is all the more difficult to explain why the courts are prepared to use their powers to wind up on the just and equitable ground or to control the use of voting power in a liberal manner, and yet remain so reluctant to develop the much more flexible statutory remedy. Once the principle of discretionary intervention is accepted there are strong arguments for using the wide powers under section

210, or any replacement, to deal with oppression in a way which takes account of the realities of the interlocking roles of directors and shareholders both in unquoted companies and in quasi-partnerships.

It is significant in this context that though there is no equivalent in most American states to the British remedy against oppression, American courts have developed a general equitable jurisdiction to require a company to declare a dividend out of accumulated profits on the application of minority shareholders.

The controlling shareholders and directors of a corporation withheld payment of all dividends with a view to reducing the personal tax liability of the controlling shareholder. Minority shareholders petitioned the court to require the declaration of a dividend out of the company's substantial profits. It was held that shareholders had a fundamental right to share in the net profits of the corporation, and that this right was personal to each individual shareholder and thus enforceable by a minority action: 'It was an elementary principle of corporation law that the declaration of dividends out of net profits rested on the discretion of the board of directors; however there were circumstances under which shareholders could compel the declaration of dividends; if directors had acted fraudulently or arbitrarily in refusing to declare a dividend when the corporation had a surplus which it could divide among shareholders without detriment to the business, a shareholder might invoke the equitable powers of a court for relief.' *Knapp v. Bankers Securities Corporation* (1956) 230 F. 2d. 717

If the reluctance of the British courts to make active use of their powers under s. 210 is due to any feeling that it is inappropriate for a court to intervene in commercial matters of this kind, the American precedents on the shareholder's right to a dividend may perhaps be cited to assist in dispelling that feeling. The techniques of oppression are themselves so flexible that the rights of minorities in many cases can only be upheld by superimposing the will of the court on the controlling shareholders and directors on matters of commercial policy and judgement. The object of providing a general discretionary remedy is after all to allow the courts to do justice in all the circumstances.

Practical problems of enforcement

The value to the shareholder of a precise formulation of his legal rights is directly related to the prospects for enforcement. Even if the conduct of directors does fall within the restricted conceptions of a breach of duty or oppression, there are very real difficulties in the path of the shareholder who seeks to bring an action against them. In the first place unless he can secure a majority in general meeting he must face the possibility that the directors' misconduct will be ratified, a possibility which under the rule in *Foss v. Harbottle* may even prevent him from getting his action off the ground at all. Secondly he may have considerable difficulty in obtaining the necessary information and evidence on which to base his action. And finally there is the very practical matter of the costs of the action.

i *Ratification and the rule in Foss v. Harbottle.* The weakness of the minority shareholder's position in seeking to protect his interests against those of a controlling faction is formally reflected in the established rule in *Foss v. Harbottle* that when a director or other employee of the company has acted in breach of his duty to the company the company and only the company is the proper plaintiff in any action against him. The basic question was whether an individual complainant shareholder was entitled to initiate action on the company's behalf. This was answered in the negative, on the grounds that it would be pointless for a minority to be permitted to establish a legal case against the directors or others in default, at considerable cost to all concerned, only to find the company in general meeting ratifying the breach or default:

An action was brought by two shareholders against the directors of a chartered company for fraudulently acquiring for the company at inflated prices property in which the directors had a personal interest, for raising illegitimate loans and for making false statements at company meetings. The directors refused to permit the action to be instituted in the company's name, a power which was entrusted to them in the company's constitution. The court refused to order them to do so: 'The statutes clearly showed that while the proprietors could control the company through the general meeting, they could not sue individually. . . . If the court declared the directors' acts void at the suit of the plaintiffs, who might be the only objectors, the governing body of the proprietors might lawfully defeat the decree by confirming the directors' acts.' (per Wigram V.C., at pp. 493–4) *Foss v. Harbottle* (1843) 2 Hare 461

The same considerations are applied to actions to enforce the company's rights against third parties as well as directors.

There is a large body of case-law on the precise application of the rule in *Foss v. Harbottle* and the numerous exceptions to it. But the rule is now so attenuated as to make a detailed exposition unnecessary. It is more helpful to deal separately with the two main issues involved, those of ratification and the right to initiate proceedings.

The position in simple terms in relation to ratification is that any breach of duty by a director may be ratified by a simple majority in general meeting, except where to do so would (i) commit the company to an ultra vires or illegal activity, (ii) deny the personal rights of individual shareholders, or (iii) constitute an act of oppression.

The fact that ratification is barred in such cases may readily be explained. In the first place each shareholder has a right to insist that the activities of the company be strictly limited to its expressed objects, which are usually taken to exclude any illegal or criminal acts, and which may be altered only by the procedure laid down in the Companies Act. Equally he is entitled to insist that the company's articles and the various statutory provisions in respect of procedure and voting, the circulation of accounts, the alteration of articles and the like, are strictly adhered to. In either case this amounts simply to requiring the majority to comply with the company's constitution. There is a direct relationship in this respect between the rights of a company shareholder against his company and those of a trade union member against his union :

> Some members of the National Union of Vehicle Builders objected to paying increased dues, and claimed that the resolution approving the increase was invalid in that it had been passed only by a show of hands rather than a secret ballot as provided for in the union rules. It was argued for the union that since this was merely a procedural defect the rule in *Foss v. Harbottle* would operate to bar any action otherwise than on behalf of the union as a whole, and that the defect had in fact been ratified by the acquiescence of the mass of the members. It was held that the individual members had a right to require a secret ballot and a vote by the requisite special majority before they could be required to pay the increase: 'It was implicit in the rule [in *Foss v. Harbottle*] that the matter relied on as constituting the cause of action should be a cause of action properly belonging to the general body of corporators or members of the company or association as opposed to a cause of action which some individual member could assert in his own right.' (per Jenkins L.J., at pp. 1066–7) *Edwards v. Halliwell* [1950] 2 All E.R. 1064 (CA)

In such cases the question of ratification cannot arise. Likewise the very nature of the remedy against oppression as a protection of minority interests makes it clear that ratification by the general meeting of an oppressive action is a contradiction in terms.

Ratification is permissible, on the other hand, in other cases of breach of duty, such as negligence by directors, the use of the power to issue shares for an improper purpose, and some cases of more serious misconduct falling short of oppression, on the ground that the general meeting has the power to relieve directors of any personal liability to the company where that can reasonably be argued to be in the best interests of the company as a whole. This was confirmed in a case in which it was claimed that directors had misused their power to issue shares by issuing a block of shares to an associated company with a view to fending off a take-over bid:

> Impropriety by directors in the exercise of their powers is a matter for waiver or disapproval by ordinary resolution.... The allotment of shares by directors not bona fide in the interests of the company is not an act outside the articles but in breach of the general duty laid on them ... to act in all matters committed to them bona fide in the interests of the company. (per Russell L.J., at p. 242) *Bamford v. Bamford* [1970] Ch. 212 (CA)

The power to issue shares may be compared to writing off a bad debt or deciding not to pursue an action against a third party in the name of the company. It is only where such a decision can be shown to have been taken with the deliberate purpose of benefiting some members of the company at the expense of others or their associates that it is not permissible. And that, as will be obvious, would simply be another instance of oppression. It is significant that the last type of oppression discussed above, covering the deliberate disregard of the formal procedures for the control and management of the company, is broadly similar to the first two types of non-ratifiable breach, and that the same argument on the right of individual shareholders to have the affairs of their company conducted in a proper constitutional manner is raised in support of each. In this sense the two concepts of oppression and non-ratifiable breaches of duty may be seen as two sides of the same coin.

The remaining issue in this area concerns the extent to which the votes of those at fault may be used to support the ratification of their own breach of duty. The position is not wholly clear. It is established that where the breach of duty consists in the issue of new shares for an improper purpose, the votes of the newly created shares may not be used to ratify the impropriety. Thus in *Hogg v. Cramphorn*,[20] another case concerning the issue of shares for an improper purpose, the trial judge held over an action for a declaration that the issue in question was a nullity to allow a motion for ratification by the general meeting on the express condition that the newly issued shares would not be used; he did not, however, place any bar on the exercise of voting rights by any of the existing shareholders including the directors themselves. This suggests that there is nothing to prevent directors who are themselves in control of the general meeting from voting to ratify their own misconduct. Thus in the last case in which the rule in *Foss v. Harbottle* was strictly applied, it was assumed without argument that the directors of a holding company may use the company's controlling holding in a subsidiary to ratify their own misconduct as directors of the subsidiary:

> The directors of a subsidiary company sold a substantial mining asset which had been acquired for £142,000 in 1936 for £182,000 in 1947, a transaction which was beneficial to the holding company, of which they were also directors. A minority shareholder in the subsidiary objected on the ground that the sale price was a gross undervaluation of the assets. It was held that even if this were so, the directors' action could be confirmed by the general meeting: 'It was open to the company on the resolution of a majority of the shareholders to sell the mine at a price decided by the company . . . and to decide that if the directors by their negligence or error of judgement had sold it at an undervalue proceedings should not be taken.' (per Danckwerts J., at p. 576) *Pavlides v. Jensen* [1956] Ch. 565

This issue has not been conclusively settled in the courts, but the balance of argument, as already suggested in relation to the proper purpose rule, is probably that shareholding directors may validly exercise their voting rights in general meetings even if that involves a direct or indirect ratification of their own misconduct as directors. There is certainly no general rule that voting rights must be exercised solely in the interests of the company as a whole. There is nothing, for instance, to prevent a controlling director from using his majority voting power to force the liquidation of a company in order to realize his personal investment in it, even if his decision to do so is taken for wholly selfish reasons, as long as the assets are fairly realized and distributed. Nor is it established that it is necessarily improper for a director to use his own voting power to maintain himself in

[20] [1967] Ch. 254, see above p. 245.

office or even to ratify his own negligence or misconduct. It is only where some element of discrimination or oppression of minority interests can be established that the principle of majority rule is suspended. It is more appropriate to assess this by an objective test of loss or injury actually suffered than by the subjective notion of self-justification by wrongdoers. This does not imply that the present interpretation of the concept of oppression is adequate. But it does suggest that the true application of the 'wrongdoers in control' slogan is to the separate issue of the institution of proceedings.

ii *The initiation of proceedings: actions by the company.* The conceptual basis of the rule in *Foss v. Harbottle* is the idea that any wrong suffered by a company is suffered by the company itself as an independent entity, rather than by its members as individuals. It follows that the natural plaintiff in any action arising out of the wrong suffered is the company itself, and that no individual shareholder has the right to institute proceedings without first assuring himself of the support of the company as a whole. In particular he has no right to institute proceedings where there is any chance that the cause of action may disappear through ratification of the misconduct by the company or more simply by a decision not to sue.

This simple exposition of the rule in *Foss v. Harbottle*, however, ignores the equally simple fact that the company as a whole is an abstraction, and that somebody must always act on its behalf. There is considerable academic dispute as to who may institute, or waive, an action in the name of the company.[21] There is a clear implication in most of the *Foss v. Harbottle* line of cases that the ultimate authority in such matters lies in the general meeting. On the other hand, the directors' normally exclusive control over the day-to-day administration of the company's affairs undoubtedly includes the power to institute proceedings in the company's name and on its behalf. It has been held that where the board of directors has such power, the general meeting cannot direct them to discontinue an action.[22]

There is no simple answer to this conflict of authority. The idea that the powers of the board and the general meeting in this respect are concurrent does not help to resolve instances of direct confronta-

[21] See generally K. W. Wedderburn, 'Shareholders' Rights and the Rule in *Foss v. Harbottle*', *Cambridge Law Journal* (1957), 194; (1958) 93.

[22] *John Shaw & Sons (Salford) Ltd. v. Shaw* [1935] 2 K.B. 113 (see p. 106).

tion, and a decision in principle in favour of either the board or the general meeting is equally unsatisfactory. It is perhaps better to conclude that the power is shared and that a final decision can only be made in relation to the particular circumstances. In ordinary cases involving the day-to-day administration of the business, it is up to the board of directors to decide whether or not it is in the interests of the company to institute proceedings on behalf of the company whether against an employee or a third party. Where there is an allegation of misconduct by individual directors or by the board as a whole, on the other hand, it is natural to look to the general meeting to determine whether or not proceedings should be instituted. It is in this context that the 'wrongdoers in control' conception is specially relevant. The power to institute proceedings, or to waive a possible action, cannot be left to those against whom the action would lie. Thus the question of an action against directors will normally be a matter for the general meeting, but where, as in the *Shaw* case, a wholly new and independent board has been appointed with the express purpose of rectifying the company's affairs, the general meeting will not be permitted to interfere, especially where, as in that case, it is under the control of the allegedly delinquent ex-directors. The frequent overlap in the roles of director and shareholder makes it impossible to lay down precise rules. The matter must be left to the discretion of the courts in cases of dispute to determine in all the circumstances which line of authority is to prevail. In doing so they will obviously apply the general principles that potential defendants must not be allowed to judge their own cause, but that a genuinely independent body may legitimately resolve to waive a possible action.

iii *The initiation of proceedings: shareholders' direct and derivative actions.* The precise allocation of the right to institute proceedings between the board and the general meeting is not of great concern to individual minority shareholders who find their efforts to initiate proceedings blocked by the rule in *Foss v. Harbottle.* The crucial question for them is how far they are entitled to institute proceedings, whether in their own right or on behalf of the company, against directors or managers or third parties who have been involved in transactions or conduct which in the shareholders' view is detrimental to the company. They may also in certain circumstances wish to institute proceedings to ensure that their company complies with the law in respect of monopolies, restrictive practices and industrial relations, or even to prevent activities which they consider to be morally or politically wrong. Here too, as in the case of the powers of the board and general meeting, no hard and fast rules can usefully be laid down. The main objection to the rule in *Foss v. Harbottle* is precisely that in purporting to solve the problem it obscures the essential flexibility of the law in relation to the particular circumstances of each case.

The resulting position can best be explained by adopting the categorization of shareholder actions which has been developed in America. The two most important forms are the shareholder's direct or non-derivative action, and the shareholder's derivative action; in addition there is what is termed the shareholders' class action, which is an extension of the former.

There are no major problems in respect of the non-derivative action. In any case where his individual rights have been infringed or threatened any shareholder has an independent right of action in his own name against the company, or in certain circumstances against its directors or managers. This form of action is directly related to the concept of oppression or non-ratifiable breaches of duty as discussed above. In such cases there is no need for the shareholder to concern himself with the rights of other shareholders, though for reasons of convenience and expense he may wish to join with others in a class action, in which the costs and benefits are shared between all those affected by a particular breach of duty.

Where a breach of duty or misconduct by directors is ratifiable the reasoning behind the rule in *Foss v. Harbottle* is directly applicable, in that an action by an individual shareholder may be outflanked by a subsequent decision to ratify by the general meeting. Hence the requirement that any such action should be initiated in the name of the company, and the ensuing difficulty facing a minority shareholder. The idea of the shareholder's derivative action is an attempt to get round the dilemma by permitting individual shareholders in certain circumstances to institute proceedings on behalf of the company. Thus, where an individual shareholder considers that the company should be taking proceedings against the directors or some third party, but neither the board of directors nor the general meeting is prepared to do so, the right to take action in the company's name passes to the individual shareholder. Though the company may for technical procedural reasons be joined as a defendant, the action is genuinely derivative in the sense that it is an attempt to assert the rights of the company as such. If it succeeds, any damages or compensation will be payable to the company and not the shareholder.

The shareholder's derivative action has been developed to a high degree of precision and technicality in the United States in an attempt to balance the legitimate rights of minority shareholders with the somewhat less desirable activities of 'professional' activists who may seek to hold a company to ransom for their own personal profit. As so often in American company law the position differs from jurisdiction to jurisdiction, but in general the conditions under which a derivative action is permitted are strictly drawn. First, the complainant must have been a shareholder at the time of the misconduct complained of, and must retain his shares until the completion of the action. A derivative action by a director, on the other hand, is not affected by the subsequent removal of the director from office. Secondly, the shareholder must show that he has taken all practicable steps to induce the board of directors and the general meeting to institute proceedings before initiating his own derivative action, though these requirements may be waived where the directors themselves are the defendants, or where the cost of contacting all shareholders through the proxy mechanism or otherwise would be prohibitive. In most jurisdictions the shareholders must also make a substantial deposit by way of security for costs in the event of the proceedings proving unsuccessful. And finally, to prevent the circumvention of the rule that all damages or compensation recovered shall be paid to the company, any settlement between the initiating shareholder and the defendant company is normally subject to court approval, and there is an explicit bar on payments to the initiator of the action :

> Generally where a stockholder's action is successful and it is established that a pecuniary benefit to the corporation results, a stockholder is compensated for the money paid to his attorney but in no instance is the stockholder himself entitled to any separate compensation. *Eisenberg v. Central Zone Property Corp.* (1957) 335 U.S. 884

This is due in part to the fact that derivative actions in America are frequently initiated primarily with a view to direct personal profit for the initiator through the negotiation of a settlement with the defendant company or directors. The courts' restrictive attitude to the full payment of expenses in 'strike' actions of this kind is wholly understandable. The restriction extends also to the reimbursement of directors' expenses, but as a result a clause has been written into many company constitutions authorizing such payments.

The development of a derivative action in Britain has been long delayed by the commitment to the rule in *Foss v. Harbottle*. But in recent years there has been some progress. It is established that an individual shareholder may sue in a representative capacity on behalf of his company: in *Hogg v. Cramphorn* it was held that a shareholder's action in respect of improper dispositions by the directors of money belonging to the company would not be barred, even though the company itself was the proper plaintiff.[23] The conditions under which such an action may be instituted have now been clearly formulated:

A minority shareholder undertook a lengthy series of actions against the controlling director of a group of companies for the misapplication of some £230,000. He eventually obtained judgement for that sum, but had exhausted his own and other shareholders' contributions to the cost of the litigation which had dragged on for more than ten years, mainly as a result of the director's dilatory tactics. It was held that when the wrongdoers were in control of a company the court had power to order that the costs incurred by a shareholder in a representative action be indemnified by the company whether the action succeeded or not; in such cases the shareholder might sue in his own name on behalf of the company; if he wished to seek an indemnity he should make an application to the court and on proof that there was a reasonable cause of action the master might make an order for all costs incurred up to the close of proceedings to be borne by the company; the shareholder would not be entitled to legal aid or to take action on a contingent fee basis. *Wallersteiner v. Moir (No. 2)* [1975] Q.B. 373

The net result is that a shareholder who is prepared to initiate proceedings may do so at the ultimate expense of the company, which itself will receive any damages or reimbursement which results from the action. Provided the company is solvent and the authority of the court is obtained in advance, the initiating shareholder is reasonably safe from having to pay the costs of the action himself. But he will have to take the risk of paying for counsel's opinion, which the court may require before sanctioning further proceedings at the company's expense, and he may also have to persuade other share-

[23] [1967] Ch. 254.

holders at any minority shareholders' meeting which the court may require to be summoned. If further proceedings are not sanctioned any costs incurred will have to be paid by the individual or group concerned. In this the situation in Britain is somewhat different from that in America where most shareholders' actions are launched on a contingent fee basis : this means that if the action fails only the costs of the other side must be raised; only if it is successful do the lawyers on the shareholders' side claim for their services, the bulk of which will presumably be paid by the defendants. It is sometimes argued that a system of this kind is necessary to the successful pursuit of derivative actions. The idea of making an exception to the general ban on contingent fees in British courts was raised in *Wallersteiner v. Moir* and was favoured by Lord Denning, in dissent on this issue. It remains to be seen whether the provision for an indemnity will prove sufficient incentive to make legal action by shareholders a more practical proposition than it has hitherto been, without running the risks of abuse and personal profiteering which company litigation has sometimes led to in America.

A second issue on which further clarification will be required is on the circumstances in which a derivative action and thus a possible indemnity will be permitted. The suggestion that such an action will be possible only where the wrongdoers are in control is similar to the original American rule for derivative actions, under which the initiating shareholder had to show that the board of directors and the general meeting had explicitly refused to take action. This rule, obviously derived from *Foss v. Harbottle*, has since been extended first to permit an action where the directors or controlling shareholders simply fail to act, regardless of whether they themselves have been at fault, and then to cases in which it would be unduly burdensome to the complaining shareholder to obtain a decision on the matter. It is to be hoped that the British courts in developing their own rules on derivative actions will finally dispense with the legacy of *Foss v. Harbottle* and focus on the merits of the particular action.

iv *Problems of access and information: the common law.* In order to mount a successful derivative action, a shareholder who suspects that the directors of his company are acting improperly must gain access to detailed information on the company's affairs. He is entitled to copies of the company's annual accounts, and to inspect the various statutory minute books and registers which should be maintained at the company's registered office. But this formal disclosure will not usually be sufficient to enable him to formulate any precise allegation against the directors or the company. In so far as the financial accounts are concerned he will be largely dependent upon co-operation from the company's auditor, which may not always be forthcoming. And in respect of the day-to-day management of the company's affairs he may not be able to get beyond the stage of vague suspicions and general allegations, unless he secures the co-operation of an insider.

What the shareholder needs in order to test his suspicions is direct access to the internal accounts and records of the company. But this he is generally denied. Once he gets a legal action under way the courts will insist on the discovery of documents and correspondence reasonably necessary to the conduct of the proceedings. But it appears to be generally accepted that shareholders as such have no right of access to the books and records of their company for the purpose of discovering what precise claims might properly be made, except in so far as special provision is made for this purpose in the articles of association. The standard article on access to accounts and records states explicitly that a shareholder must gain the authorization of the directors or the general meeting before inspecting anything other than statutory registers (1948: Table A, art. 125). But the cases which are usually cited in support of this restrictive view on access in fact suggest that the courts may order access to be given in appropriate circumstances:

> A number of shareholders petitioned for access to a banking company's books in order to ascertain whether the terms offered to them for their shares in a reconstruction of the company were fair and reasonable. It was held that no such order was necessary in view of the pending arbitration which had been agreed, though it was added that 'if fraud or inaccuracy were suggested the court would exercise its discretion to see that justice was done'. (per Bacon V.C., at p. 625) *In re Glamorganshire Banking Company* (1884) 28 Ch. D. 620

Despite this explicit reservation of a discretionary power to make an order for access, however, conventional legal wisdom denies the shareholder any right of access, and there is accordingly little to induce a shareholder to apply to the courts for special permission to inspect his company's books and records.

The position in the United States in this respect is rather different. The American courts have generally regarded a right of access to be a natural accompaniment of the right of the individual shareholders to institute proceedings as discussed above, and are sympathetic to requests from shareholders to inspect their company's books and records where that is reasonably necessary to the enforcement of their rights :

A minority shareholder in a banking company suspected that the directors were not conducting the affairs of the bank in accordance with its charter, and applied for a court order to require the directors to give him access to the company's books. The Supreme Court upheld the order, stating that 'decisive weight of authority allowed the common law right of a shareholder for proper purposes and under reasonable regulations as to place and time to inspect the books of the corporation of which he is a member', though the writ would not be granted 'for speculative purposes or to gratify idle curiosity'. *Guthrie v. Harkness* (1905) 199 U.S. 1149

As in the case of the derivative action, this difference in approach is probably due more to the greater propensity to resort to legal action and the natural consequences of that in terms of a developed case-law than to any basic differences in legal theory.

v *Problems of access and information: statutory inspection.* The absence of an accepted common law right of access in Britain is implicitly recognized and to some extent remedied in the Companies Acts. First, there is provision for a court order against a company requiring the production of books and records on application by the government, by the Director of Public Prosecutions or by a chief officer of police where there are reasonable grounds to suspect that an offence has been committed (1948 : s. 441). The limitation of this power to criminal matters, however, and the fact that it is normally exercised only for the collection of evidence in support of charges which have already been preferred effectively destroy its potential for the prior investigation of complaints of civil misconduct or oppression.

The suspicious shareholder is thus thrown back on the much wider powers of investigation conferred on the Department of Trade, in succession to the Board of Trade (1948 : ss. 164–75). These powers will be considered in detail in Chapter 7, since it is in respect of quoted public companies that most of the major issues arise. In so far as unquoted and private companies are concerned it is sufficient to state the position briefly. First, though this is rarely a genuine alternative for a minority shareholder, if a formal resolution of the general meeting or a court order can be obtained the Department is required to proceed to the appointment of inspectors (1948: s. 165(a)). More important, for obvious reasons, is the procedure whereby an application may be made by *any* individual shareholder for an inspection of the affairs of his company on the ground that it is being conducted fraudulently or oppressively, that those in control have been guilty of fraud, misfeasance or other misconduct, or that the shareholders have not been given all the information which they might reasonably expect (1948: s. 165(b)). Provision is also made for an application by at least 200 shareholders, or the holders of one-tenth of the issued share capital, for an inspection on the less precise condition of showing to the satisfaction of the Department, if it so requires, that they have good reason for requesting the inspection (1948: s. 164). There is little need to distinguish precisely between this and the more general provision since in both cases the effective decisions are made by the Department, which appears to exercise its discretion under both sections on similar principles. The number of complaining shareholders may in itself have some influence on the outcome, but it should also be noted that where an application is made under section 164, the Department may levy the full costs of the inspection from the applicants (1967: s. 40). Finally, the Department has general power to call for the production of books and papers from any company at any time if it thinks there is good reason to do so (1967: s. 109), a power which will normally be used in connection with applications for inspections, though it is not restricted to that.

The procedure adopted by the Department with respect to unquoted companies is as follows.[24] First, the complainants will be required to submit a 'statement of facts' setting out the grounds on which they seek an inspection, and sufficient facts to support their application. This statement will then be forwarded by the Department to the directors of the company against which the complaints are made for their observations. On the basis of this exchange the Department then attempts to secure some compromise settlement between the parties. Only where this is not possible will the Department seriously consider the institution of a formal inspection or the

[24] See generally Jenkins Committee, Cmnd. 1749 (1962) para. 213 ff.

use of their powers of preliminary investigation under the 1967 Act. It may be that an order requiring the production of accounts or records under this latter will in itself be sufficient to establish the true position, and form the basis for a settlement or for legal proceedings. Where a full-scale inspection is decided on it will normally be conducted by a single full-time official of the Companies Division of the Department, or less frequently by an independent lawyer or accountant. In either case the inspector is required to submit a formal report to the Department in due course. In respect of unquoted companies this will be published only in exceptional circumstances, but copies will be made available both to the complainants and to the company, leaving the question of further proceedings to the parties, except where serious criminal offences requiring official action by the Department or the Director of Public Prosecutions are disclosed. The Department may now also institute civil proceedings in the name of the company to recover assets which may have been wrongfully applied or appropriated, where such action appears to be in the public interest (1967 : s. 37). This power is unlikely to be exercised in respect of unquoted companies.

There is a good deal of dispute over the efficacy of this procedure. Critics of the system allege that the Department requires complainants to go too far in establishing a prima facie case against the company or its directors before making use of its formal powers of investigation, and in particular that more frequent and early use should be made of the power to investigate either by the appointment of an inspector or by the use of powers to call for the production of documents with the sole purpose of providing shareholders with the information which the common law, as it is generally interpreted, denies them. The Department, on the other hand, has claimed considerable success in meeting the legitimate requests of shareholders by their conciliation policy, and argues that the formal appointment of an inspector may often do more harm than good. As will be seen in Chapter 7 (see p. 355), however, it was still claiming in 1973 that it could only act if there was prima facie evidence of wrongdoing, despite the explicit statutory provision for the appointment of an inspector on the sole ground that shareholders have not been given all the information they might reasonably expect.

The major question, however, is whether this system of administrative investigation is wholly appropriate to the needs of minority shareholders in unquoted companies. There are inevitable drawbacks in any system which is dependent on the decisions of a government department, with its inherent problems of manpower and official caution and delay. A simplified court procedure for the supply of information or access to records as of right for individual shareholders or their representatives, along the lines of the existing American jurisdiction, might fulfil the needs of the parties more adequately and more quickly, whether for the preparation and formulation of a petition for relief against oppression or misconduct or with a view to an agreed settlement. The Department's powers are not for that reason unnecessary, and may in certain cases fill a useful function. But this does not reduce the need for a right of direct access to information for individual shareholders on proof of reasonable cause.

Conclusion: the strengthening of shareholder rights

The conclusion of this survey of the balance of power in unquoted companies can only be of the relative impotence of shareholders, and especially minority shareholders, in relation to directors or others in de facto control. To a large extent this is due to the basic principle of majority rule and to the related fact that in many unquoted companies there is a substantial overlap between controlling shareholders and directors and managers. The crucial decisions from the point of view of the external investor on the balance between managerial salaries, dividends and reinvestment of profit are thus concentrated in the hands of individuals who are unlikely to have the interests of shareholders as such uppermost in their minds. And since there is no market in the company's shares they are not subject to the pressures in this respect which apply to quoted companies.

Even if this structural imbalance is allowed for, however, there is little doubt that the minority shareholder's effective powers of intervention are insufficient to allow him to protect his legitimate interests. As already explained this is not so much attributable to the inadequacy of the remedies which are theoretically available to him, as to the restrictive attitude of the courts, and indeed lawyers in general, to the application of those remedies. The main difficulty is the reluctance of the courts to use to the full their discretionary powers of intervention in cases of oppression. The statutory power is widely drawn, but has been interpreted with wholly unnecessary restriction. As a result there has been a lack of procedural inventiveness in the development of the minority shareholder's action and of the attendant right of access to the books and records of the company in the event of suspicion of actionable impropriety or inefficiency.

The principal requirement if there is to be any effective strengthening of the relative power of shareholders is thus a change in the attitude of the courts in the application of existing remedies and procedures. In particular there is a need for the rejuvenation of the concept of oppression to cover all the various forms of discriminatory conduct discussed above. This could be facilitated by a measure of statutory reformulation, not to alter the nature of the remedy but to specify the types of conduct which might in appropriate circumstances be deemed oppressive, as for instance the unreasonable conversion of profits into managerial remuneration or the cessation of direct dividend payments. Minor alterations in wording might also be made to avoid the technical restrictions discussed above, as for instance the supposed requirement of a 'course of conduct' rather than a single act, and the restriction of a remedy to cases in which a winding up order would otherwise have been available. The practical and procedural problems facing the external minority shareholder could also be considerably eased by statutory recognition of his right of access on reasonable grounds to the books and records of the company prior to any formal allegation of oppression or request for an official inspection.

Greater protection for shareholders' rights, however, may well run counter to other more practical and perhaps more important considerations, notably those of business efficacy. This is of particular relevance in relation to schemes for ensuring the smooth transition of management in family companies from one generation to another. If lawyers and the courts are to intervene more directly and positively in the affairs of unquoted companies some balance must be struck between protecting the proprietary rights of minorities and fostering the effective future management of the company. This suggests, as will be seen, that other more far-reaching remedies, perhaps by way of rights to initiate management audits or to appoint representative supervisory directors, may be required in addition to the formal discretionary relief against oppression discussed in this section.

3 PROBLEMS OF TRANSITION

The substance of the law in relation to financing, liquidation, disclosure and taxation is the same for larger unquoted companies as for smaller participatory companies and will not be covered again in this chapter. There are a number of issues, however, in these spheres of sufficient practical importance to larger companies to merit special consideration. These are the difficulties in finding finance for expansion, the legal technicalities involved in handing over control of family companies from one generation to another, and the implications for the company of the tax liabilities on the death or retirement of founders. In each case the issue facing those in charge of the company's affairs is whether to try to maintain the business as a family concern, or to accept a radical change by bringing in outsiders, by 'going public' or by accepting a take-over bid. The answer will clearly depend on the particular circumstances of each case, but the three issues may conveniently be dealt with under the general heading of problems of transition.[25]

Finance for expansion

The principal sources for raising finance for larger unquoted companies are essentially the same as for smaller businesses : the reinvestment of profits, bank loans, hire purchase or hiring contracts, and the issue of new equity capital or long-term debenture stock. The difficulty is that as a company expands the sources which can readily meet the needs of smaller concerns, notably personal loans or new capital from directors and short-term bank overdrafts, are likely to become increasingly inadequate in relation to the cost of major schemes for expansion, which may involve the purchase or building of a new factory or substantial investment in the development and launching of a new product. Even if the money could be found, there are drawbacks inherent in financing in these forms. Direct investment in the form of equity capital is not always an attractive proposition either to the private or to the institutional investor, in view of the unsatisfactory position of a minority shareholder in a private company. Yet the existing directors will not always wish to share their control over the enterprise by the issue of new voting capital equal to their own. In addition the raising of very large sums in the form of short-term loan capital may result in serious imbalance in the capital structure or gearing of the enterprise, notably in the liability to make substantial and regular interest payments unrelated to the performance of the company.

[25] On this subject generally see the more detailed analysis in M. R. Chesterman, *Small Businasses* (1977), Ch. 7.

The problems in raising finance for expansion for the larger unquoted company, the so-called Macmillan Gap, have long been recognized. Some remedial measures have been taken. The government and the larger private sector banks joined in setting up the Industrial and Commercial Finance Corporation, with a view to providing substantial funds by way of equity investment or long-term loan capital for unquoted companies. The Bolton Committee on Small Firms, however, pointed to a continuing problem of lack of knowledge of these and other sources of funds.[26] This resulted in the establishment of a series of regional Small Firms Advisory Bureaux. Even where contact is made with one or other of these institutional lenders, the drawbacks to substantial and continuing investment in unquoted companies from the point of view of the investor remain. A successful and expanding business must eventually face the decision of whether or not to 'go public'. The advantage of such a move is that in the very process of doing so the company will be able in almost every case to raise an amount of new capital which might otherwise be quite beyond its reach. Once a company secures a Stock Exchange quotation many of the disadvantages inherent in the situation of minority equity shareholders disappear. The company will be subjected to the pressures for increased disclosure and for the maintenance of a regular dividend payment which public quotation entails, and in addition any investor, whether institutional or individual, may at any time withdraw his capital by disposing of his shares. The various institutional investors will thus be all the more ready to put up substantial sums for expansion. In addition, from the point of view of the existing shareholders, there are important advantages in the move. For perhaps the first time the major shareholders will be able to realize some of the capital which they have committed to the development of the company. This is of special importance in the context of tax liability on the death or retirement of controlling directors, as will be seen below.

On the other hand there are aspects of going public which may not be so attractive to the controlling shareholders and directors of the company. The Stock Exchange rules for admission to quotation require at least a third of the equity capital of the company to be made available where the issue is to be made by the placing of

[26] Cmnd. 4811 (1971); see generally Chapter 12.

existing shares in the company, and in any event a newly issued security must have a market value of £200,000. This means that a substantial holding in the company must pass out of the control of the directors, who will also by the very fact of the conversion into a quoted company lose any power of veto over the subsequent transfer of any of the shares in the company. The company will thus be open to direct take-over bids for the equity capital of the company without any agreement with the existing directors being necessary, though the directors may still retain control over the company by virtue of their own personal holdings of the voting capital. In addition the directors will be subject to the much more stringent standards of disclosure and managerial conduct which are required of the directors of publicly quoted companies both through the General Undertaking which each quoted company is required to sign and more generally through the powers of the Stock Exchange Council (see Chapter 7).

Handing over control

Whether a company decides to opt for expansion and the ensuing pressures to go public or to maintain itself as a family concern, it must eventually face the issue of providing for a smooth transition of management on the death or retirement of the controlling directors who have built up or expanded the firm's business. In many companies the natural successors are the next generation of the family or families concerned, who will expect to inherit their fathers' or uncles' holdings. The difficulty is that the natural processes of inheritance do not usually coincide with business efficiency. The members of the second generation of the founder's family may not be either willing or able to take over and run the company as effectively and successfully as their fathers and uncles. There is a good deal of hard evidence that second and third generation directors and managers in family companies typically display less drive and business sense than their founders.[27] Many such firms go into a slow but continuing decline in the second and third generations, and are eventually taken over by larger public companies or else liquidated.

One solution to this problem is to accept the inevitability of an eventual take-over, and to make arrangement for disposing of the

[27] J. Boswell, *The Rise and Decline of Small Businesses* (1973).

family interest while the company is still prosperous, either before or on the death of the founders. This option, as will be seen, helps to solve the taxation problem. But it not only leaves the future choice of managers and directors to the new parent company, which will typically phase out the remaining family directors and managers in a relatively short period, but also leaves the future of employment in the factory at the mercy of the longer term plans for rationalization which the parent company may have. Many controlling directors in family concerns prefer to remain independent and thus protect the jobs both of their relatives and of their employees.

If this second option is followed, whether deliberately or by default, the retiring directors should clearly make advance provision for a smooth succession, whether within the family or otherwise. This can readily be achieved by the direct transfer of a controlling shareholding to the chosen successor or by the issue of new shares. The difficulty is that neither company law nor tax law facilitates this kind of advance planning.

The law on the relations between directors and shareholders as set out in the preceding section takes little account of matters of this kind. If a controlling director dies without making advance provision for his succession, there is no mechanism other than the ordinary rules of property inheritance to determine what shall happen within the company. The various factions within the family are left to fight it out among themselves in accordance with the provisions of the company's constitution. Where this includes the standard article giving directors an absolute discretion as to the registration of new shareholders, the remaining directors are in an unassailable position, except in so far as they may have to pay a fair price for any shares which they refuse to register.[28] There are also some formal legal difficulties in advance planning. The concentration of the law on the proprietary rights of minority shareholders may curtail the freedom of a retiring director to structure the future of his company. The suggestion in some cases that shares may not be issued or votes used with the sole object of affecting the future control over the company,[29] could, if further developed, have the effect of invalidating any scheme for reallocating control which involves the issue of new shares. In some cases the difficulty might be resolved by adopting

[28] *In re Smith & Fawcett Ltd.* [1942] Ch. 304 (see p. 154).

[29] As for instance in *Howard Smith Ltd. v. Ampol Petroleum Ltd.* [1974] A.C. 821 (above p. 246), and *Clemens v. Clemens Bros. Ltd.* [1976] 2 All E.R. 179 (see p. 269).

a rule that the courts will not interfere with any scheme which has been explicitly or tacitly agreed by the interested parties in advance.[30] But this will not help where the scheme has been drawn up by the controlling faction without the consent of the minority. Once the issue of planned succession is admitted in reply to a claim of oppression of minority interests there is no easy method by which the courts can avoid making a decision openly or covertly on the relative merits of the existing property rights of individual shareholders and the prospective future management of the company as a whole. The essence of a planned succession will frequently be a deliberate dilution of the interest of an existing or potential shareholder who is deemed to be ineffective as a businessman or prospective director. The courts in Britain have always rejected any suggestion that they might involve themselves in the merits of business decisions. If they are to do justice to shareholders without at the same time preventing retiring directors from looking to the future in a constructive manner, they cannot entirely avoid the role of management consultancy as well as that of property protection.

Taxation and business succession

Tax law is equally unhelpful to the planning of succession with a view to business efficacy. The relevant taxes in this context, capital gains tax and capital transfer tax, are not levied on the company itself but on those who own it. The objective in each case is the raising of revenue and the pursuit of a greater redistribution of wealth. But since one or other of the two taxes, and sometimes both, are payable on any transfer of the shares in a company, whether by sale or gift, they play a major part in the planning of any business succession.

Taxation in this form dates back to the introduction of estate duty in the nineteenth century. This was originally levied on the total value of all assets on the death of the owner. But since property could be distributed in anticipation of death the tax could be readily avoided. Though all gifts made within seven years of death were eventually brought into account, estate duty was generally regarded as a voluntary payment by those who did not wish to make the necessary arrangements to avoid its impact. The net result was that until 1965 there was strong pressure on the controlling directors of

[30] Chesterman, op. cit., p. 221.

family firms to disperse their shareholdings well in advance of retirement or possible death. To this extent estate duty acted as a powerful incentive for advance planning in family companies, though the desire to make arrangements for the equitable distribution of the father's wealth among members of his family by way of trusts or otherwise did not necessarily coincide with the desire to pass control over the family business to the member of the family with most business sense and ability.

This position did not satisfy those in Labour governments who wished to secure a greater degree of redistribution of wealth through taxes on capital. In 1965 capital gains tax at a basic rate of thirty per cent, similar to that on earned or unearned income, was introduced : this is now levied on the net real or notional gain to the owner on any sale or disposition of property, including gifts to members of his or her family, though transfers on the death of the holder are exempted.[31] Then in 1975 estate duty was replaced by a new capital transfer tax designed to cover all transfers of wealth, whether before or on death : this is levied on a cumulative basis on all transfers made by an individual throughout his life and on death, though the rates of tax on transfers up to £300,000 during life are somewhat lower than those on or within three years of death and there is a special relief on transfers between spouses; the effective rates of tax range from nil on the first £15,000 transferred and a further £2,000 exemption per year to a maximum rate of seventy five per cent on transfers in excess of £2m.[32] Both capital transfer and capital gains tax are levied on the transferor, though there are also provisions for recovering any capital transfer tax due from the transferee. Both capital gains and capital transfer tax may have to be paid on lifetime transfers, and since each is assessed separately on the gross value of the transfer account cannot be taken of capital gains tax when assessing the amount of capital transfer tax.

The combined impact of these new taxes on the future of family companies is likely to be substantial. It has already been estimated that the previously avoidable estate duty was the primary cause of the rapid increase in the number of take-overs of privately owned companies by quoted companies since the 1950s (see Table 2.8, p. 55). The effect of the much less readily avoidable capital transfer

[31] Finance Act 1965, Part III; Finance Act 1971, sched. 12.
[32] Finance Act 1975, Part III.

tax can only be to accelerate the trend. Though the tax is payable by individuals rather than the companies in which they own shares, the need to raise hard cash to pay any tax due on the transfer of those shares is bound to involve the companies themselves, whether through pressure to increase the level of dividend distribution or pressure to sell shares to outsiders or a larger company. The greater the prosperity of the company, the greater will this impact be, in terms both of the capital gain to a controlling director and of the value of any eventual transfer, since both are assessable on the market value of the shares at the time of the disposition or transfer.

The importance of these factors has been recognized by the government. In response to pressure from various sources[33] a number of concessions have been introduced with the express objective of lessening the burden on businessmen on the transfer of their shares in companies or their assets in unincorporated concerns. In the first place, capital gains tax is payable at a substantially reduced level on the disposition of business assets on retirement between the ages of sixty and sixty-five up to a current level of £40,000.[34] Secondly, there is a thirty per cent reduction on the valuation of business assets held for at least two years by a controlling shareholder or sole proprietor for the purposes of capital transfer tax.[35] Thirdly, there is provision for extended payment over a period of eight years of capital transfer tax on business assets.[36] And, finally, there is provision for complete exemption from capital transfer tax where the whole of a controlling holding is transferred to a trust for the benefit of a firm's employees with no possible reversionary benefit for the transferor.[37]

It will be clear from this brief account that the policies of taxing wealthy businessmen in the interests of the redistribution of wealth and of promoting the interests of the small business sector as against their larger competitors are difficult to combine. Any system designed to tax the wealth which is accumulated in family companies and businesses through the reinvestment of profits over a period of years is bound to cause problems since what is being taxed is a slice of the

[33] See for instance the Bolton Committee on Small Firms, Cmnd. 4811 (1971) Ch. 13.

[34] Finance Act 1965, s. 34; Finance Act 1974, s. 34.

[35] Finance Act 1976, s. 73 and sched. 10.

[36] Finance Act 1975, sched. 4, para. 13.

[37] Finance Act 1976, s. 90.

business itself rather than the money which has been paid out to the members of the family. It is arguable in view of the typically poor performance of second generation family directors and managers that it is economically desirable for pressure to be put on the family to sell out their interests on the retirement or death of the founder or principal developer of the business. But there are also strong economic and social arguments for maintaining a strong small business sector to offset the dominating position of the major companies in any sector of trade or industry. It has even been suggested that the system of capital taxation should be openly used as a means of discriminating between efficient and ailing family companies: this could be done by establishing a formal tribunal with powers to relieve the tax pressure on family companies or at least to assist in meeting it through state loans, on proof that a viable scheme for the continued effective management of the business on the retirement of the current controllers had been drawn up.[88] It seems unlikely that the government would be prepared to institute a formal structure of this kind, though the Estate Duty Investment Trust (EDITH), a subsidiary of Finance for Industry, established to make loans to family companies to assist in the settlement of capital taxation, already operates as a filtering device of a similar kind. The concession which encourages family companies to establish a trust for the employees of the company as a means of avoiding capital transfer tax represents a more coherent strategy, since it is designed to secure both the redistribution of wealth and the continued independence of the company itself by removing all pressure to raise cash for tax payments.

In more general terms the only possible conclusion to this review of the problems of transition in unquoted family companies is that in the absence of any clearly defined governmental or legal policy the fate of individual companies will continue to be determined by a large number of interacting and often conflicting considerations. If it is desired to shift the balance of advantage in favour of smaller unquoted and family companies it will be necessary to establish more clearly the respective interests of controlling directors, other members of the family and employees. One possibility suggested by the more detailed analysis of similar problems in quoted companies

[88] Boswell, op. cit., Ch. 11.

in Part III is that control over management in such companies should be exercised through some form of supervisory body representing the interests of all those involved. But any moves of this kind are likely to follow developments in larger companies.

6

The quoted company: legal controls and the disclosure system

The fact that shares in a company are quoted on a recognized stock exchange or are otherwise available for public investment does not alter the essential nature of the enterprise. Shareholders and directors in quoted companies[1] are governed by the same formal rules as in unquoted companies, as set out in the preceding chapters. But the existence of a public market in a company's shares raises new issues. The independence of stock exchange dealings from the affairs of the companies whose shares are bought and sold, and the notorious herd instinct of investors coupled with their relative lack of sophistication in assessing the performance and prospects of commercial companies, creates a need for a further set of controls for the protection of shareholders in their capacity as investors. The huge increase in the number of shareholders also creates an entirely different situation in relation to general meetings of shareholders. In practice, as described in Chapter 2, the directors and managers of large quoted companies and their subsidiaries are an independent and self-perpetuating elite, whose activities are controlled otherwise than through their legal subordination to shareholders.

These factors have given rise to a system of administrative regulation over quoted companies which is largely separate from that developed under the Companies Acts and in the courts. This second set of controls is operated by the semi-official authorities in the City of London and to a lesser extent by the Department of Trade. In

[1] Though official Stock Exchange terminology now refers to 'listed' rather than quoted companies, the established usage has been retained except for technical references.

many respects the two systems are complementary, as for instance on the question of disclosure, though the unofficial requirements of the Stock Exchange are typically more demanding than those of the Companies Acts. But there are certain inherent differences which make it difficult to give a single coherent account on any particular issue. In the first place, many of the statutory controls are imposed on public companies in the strict legal sense rather than on quoted companies, though there are some additional statutory requirements for companies whose shares are actually offered to the public. In the second place, there is a crucial difference in the processes of administration and enforcement. The various legal requirements and prohibitions must be strictly interpreted by the courts when the issue is raised, but their enforcement is essentially a matter for the parties involved. The administrative control system, on the other hand, is applied in an essentially flexible manner by a body of permanent officials whose job it is to see to it that the regulations are in fact complied with, and the sanction for non-compliance is not so much the possibility of civil or criminal penalties in the courts, but the equally effective sanction of the refusal or withdrawal of permission to operate through the normal market channels.

For these reasons it is convenient to deal separately with the application of traditional legal and statutory rules to quoted companies and with the operation of the alternative regulatory system by the Stock Exchange, the City and the Department of Trade.[2] In this chapter attention will be focused primarily on the *legal* rules on the following issues:

i public issues of shares and the disclosure system;

ii criminal sanctions and civil remedies in respect of misrepresentation or fraud;

iii the non-commercial activities of quoted companies and the special duties of their directors;

iv the formal rights of shareholders in general meetings to control or influence the activities of their companies.

The operation of the system of *administrative* controls will be dealt

[2] For a detailed and comprehensive account from a legal standpoint with useful comparisons with foreign law and practice see R. R. Pennington, *The Investor and the Law* (1968).

with in Chapter 7. The particular problems raised both in law and in practice by take-overs and mergers, market dealings and investment institutions will then be dealt with independently in Chapters 8 and 10.

1 PUBLIC ISSUES AND THE DISCLOSURE SYSTEM

The basis of formal legal control over public issues is the familiar one of disclosure backed by civil and criminal sanctions. The key item in the system is the prospectus which must accompany any invitation to the public to subscribe for or purchase shares or debentures in a company. The rules governing the prospectus, however, were developed in the nineteenth century to deal primarily with the flotation of entirely new companies when it was standard practice for capital to be raised by a direct offer of new shares for subscription on the open market. This is no longer the case. Most public issues are now of shares in companies which have existed for some time and which for one reason or another have decided or been forced to go public, or in established quoted companies seeking additional capital. This has led to increasing complexity in the statutory requirements for prospectuses, which can only be unravelled in the light of current practice in the new issue market.

Types of public issue

The most direct form of public issue is a *prospectus issue* by the company to the public of newly authorized share or loan capital, either by a company which is coming to the market for the first time or by an established quoted company. In most cases this will differ little from the pattern of issues for which the statutory rules were first developed. The fact that the company is already in existence will affect the contents rather than the form of the various documents. Similar to this is the *offer for sale* in which a block of shares which has already been issued is offered for sale on behalf of the company, usually by an issuing house or other agent to which the shares have been allotted. In either case the offer may be made either at a fixed price which will be settled in advance by the company and its advisers in the light of the general state of the market for new capital, or else by the recently developed and more flexible tender system under which the shares will be allotted or transferred to those who offer the highest price. This helps to ensure that the company itself benefits from any measure of oversubscription if the issue is favourably received or alternatively if it is not generally recommended that some of the shares may still be taken up at a lower price. A prospectus issue or offer for sale, however, is likely to be expensive in view of the wide publicity which must be given to the prospectus in the financial press, and is likely to be uneconomic except for the largest issues. A simple prospectus issue is also risky because the full amount may not be subscribed. From the point of view of the company the risk may usually be avoided by arranging for the issue to be underwritten for a suitable premium. In the case of an offer for sale any premium will be included in the price at which the shares are issued to the issuing house.

A somewhat cheaper method of raising capital is to address the offer to a more restricted range of potential investors, by way of what is termed a *placing*. Under this system a large block of new or existing shares is issued to an issuing house or broker which then endeavours to place the shares with the requisite number of new investors through its own contacts and mailing lists. The issuing house or broker makes a charge for this service by way of a percentage discount on the capital involved. From the point of view of the company any such payment may be considered justifiable, since in normal circumstances the issuing house underwrites the issue through its obligation to retain any shares which are not disposed of.

The simplest and cheapest form of issue, however, is a *rights* issue, by which new shares in the company are offered exclusively to existing shareholders in proportion to their existing holdings. This is administratively simple since the company will already have a mechanism for circularizing its members. It is relatively cheap since there will be no need to publicize the documents. To ensure acceptance these issues are usually made on favourable terms, the price for the new shares being fixed at less than the market value so that shareholders may accept the offer and then if they wish, immediately dispose of their new shares to a third party at a slight profit. This is facilitated by making the offer to the shareholders on what is termed a renounceable letter of acceptance, which the shareholder may accept and then renounce in favour of a third party. The new capital is thus effectively supplied by the market without the need for a formal new issue. Rights or *bonus* issues may also be made free of charge to shareholders as a means of 'distributing' the accumulated profits or reserves of the company, though in such cases there is no question of actually raising any new capital.

These are not the only methods of arranging public issues. There are special rules for foreign securities, and for the introduction of securities in which there is already a public market without any specific offer of new shares. There is a wide range of possibilities, particularly in the context of take-overs and mergers, for the conversion or exchange of one class of security for another. But direct offers, placings and rights issues form the basis of current practice, in respect of which the various formal provisions of the Companies Acts must be viewed.

The prospectus

The original object of the statutory obligation to file a formal prospectus with the Registrar of Companies was to inform those subscribing for shares in new companies of the identity of those behind the flotation and of the precise nature of the enterprise. The range of information required was then cumulatively extended, in the face of continuing malpractices by promoters, to include details of pre-incorporation contracts and arrangements, reports from experts and accountants, and, where appropriate, the actual performance of the enterprise in the years before flotation. To counter the avoidance of these requirements by the offer for sale to the public of shares which had already been subscribed and allotted, a requirement was introduced in 1908 that a similar statement in lieu of a prospectus should be filed by all companies, except private companies, before the allotment of any of its shares. Since then additional provisions have been introduced under which both offers for sale and placings are deemed to fall under the general prospectus requirements.

The resulting position under the Companies Acts is thus somewhat complex. A prospectus in accord with the statutory definition must be prepared and filed in respect of any offer to the public to subscribe for or purchase shares or debentures in any company (1948 : s. 455). Offers for sale are included in this by the provision that an offer to the public of shares already allotted with a view to subsequent public offer is deemed to be a prospectus issue (1948 : s. 45); placings are covered by the provision that an offer is deemed to be made to the public where it is made either to existing shareholders or to the clients of the person issuing the offer (1948 : s. 55(1)). Exceptions are made in three cases :

i where the offer is restricted to existing shareholders of the company, without permitting them to renounce in favour of a third party (1948 : s. 38(5) (a));

ii where the shares are simply a further issue of a class of shares already quoted on a recognized stock exchange (1948 : s. 38(5) (b));

iii where a certificate of exemption has been issued by a recognized stock exchange on the ground that in all the circumstances the preparation of a formal prospectus would be unduly burdensome (1948 : s. 39).

It has also been decided that the provisions do not apply to offers to exchange the shares of one company for another, since such an exchange could not be held to be either a subscription or a purchase under the terms of the statutory definition.[3] This exempts many take-over bids from the prospectus requirements.

These formal requirements and exemptions are closely tied to the ordinary operations of the various recognized stock exchanges. But the concept of a public issue in strict law is a good deal wider than this. There is no legal rule restricting public offers and dealing in shares to the stock exchanges. The main protection for the public from exploitation in such extra-market offers and transactions lies in the various administrative controls over circulars and solicitation, and over dealers themselves.[4] But the prospectus requirements also extend to non-market offers. A public offer is defined to cover not only an offer to all the world, but offers restricted to a particular section of the public, whether as members of a company or clients of a firm or otherwise (1948 : s. 55(1)). On the other hand, it is provided that an offer shall not be deemed to be a public offer if it is 'not calculated to result directly or indirectly in the shares or debentures becoming available for subscription or purchase by persons other than those receiving the offers or invitation, or otherwise as being a domestic concern of the persons making and receiving it' (1948 : s. 55(2)). The interpretation of the net effect of these partially

[3] *Governments Stock and Other Securities Investment Co. Ltd. v. Christopher* [1956] 1 All E.R. 490.

[4] Prevention of Fraud (Investments) Act 1958 (see p. 338).

conflicting provisions is not assisted by the cases which have been reported and it can only be left to the court to decide in cases of doubt. This is less than satisfactory in a sphere where the legal consequences of a dispute may be far-reaching. There would be a good deal to be said for a definite ad hoc cutting off point, as in America where the Securities and Exchange Commission has adopted a rule to the effect that any invitation to take shares which is addressed to fewer than twenty-five persons is deemed not to be a public offer.

In addition, any public company which does not make a public offer of shares on its formation must file a statement in lieu of a prospectus at least three days before the allotment of any of its shares or debentures (1948 : s. 48). This requirement, as pointed out by the Jenkins Committee,[5] no longer serves its original function, in view of the inclusion of offers for sale and placings under the standard prospectus provisions. The statement in lieu is thus not in any way connected with public issues as such. It simply operates as a further disclosure requirement in respect of the registration of any company which is not a private company. This does not mean that it serves no useful purpose, as the Jenkins Committee implied, since the information included may be of importance to investors and others, for instance in respect of the flotation of a new subsidiary by a quoted company.

The actual contents of a statutory prospectus as prescribed in the Companies Act can be described briefly under three main heads (1948 : Schedule 4). First, full details must be given of the actual offer, including the number of shares offered, the rights attaching to them, any minimum subscription before allotment is to be made, and the precise administrative arrangements for the making of applications and allotments.[6] Second, details must be given of all material contracts in respect of property or other rights which the company is to acquire and which have been entered into within two years of the issue. This rule was prescribed in order to curb various malpractices common in the nineteenth century. For instance, details are required in respect of the purchase of real property or existing businesses, of the expenses of the flotation including any commissions or discounts arranged by the promoters, in so far as these are per-

[5] Cmnd. 1749 (1962), paras. 247–8.

[6] These matters are further regulated in ss. 47 and 49–53.

mitted by the company's articles or otherwise (1948 : s. 53), and of any interest held by any director or prospective director in any of these matters. Finally, there must be a report from the company's accountants on the results of the company or group, or of any business to be acquired, over the five previous years, setting out the profits and dividends over that period.

These are the minimum prescribed contents. Other details and reports will normally be included : for instance, from the company's technological advisers and experts, subject to the inclusion of a statement that they have given and not withdrawn written consent to its inclusion in the prospectus (1948 : s. 40). The express responsibility of directors is also secured by the provision that before it is issued a copy of the prospectus signed by all directors and prospective directors must be lodged with the Registrar of Companies (1948 : s. 41).

These rules follow the normal pattern of statutory control in matters of this kind. The list of items for disclosure has been built up over the years in response to particular forms of malpractice, rather than in an attempt to specify the full range of information which a prospective investor would ideally like. A prospectus which contained only the statutory details would not give a complete view of the nature of the enterprise or of the prospects and risk for investors. Nor is there any general requirement that all relevant or material information should be included even in respect of those items which are prescribed. The law on this, as will be seen, is simply that an omission may be held to affect the truth of what is actually stated. The net result is that a formally perfect statutory prospectus may do no more than confuse the people it is intended to protect by a list of disparate and complex items of information unrelated to each other or to any overall pattern of disclosure.

In practice, however, as far as quoted companies are concerned, these various defects are largely remedied by the independent rules of the Stock Exchange, which now controls all stock exchanges in the British Isles. The list of prescribed items for disclosure is considerably more comprehensive.[7] It requires a statement of the general nature of the business, the location and size of its operations, its turnover over five years, its profits and losses over five years and a general statement as to its financial and trading prospects; in addition the

[7] *Admission of Securities to Listing* (1976 version), sched. 2.

directors are required to accept responsibility 'for the accuracy of the information given and to confirm, having made all reasonable enquiries, that to the best of their knowledge and belief there are no other facts the omission of which make any statement in the prospectus misleading' (para. 2). The auditors are similarly required to report on the company's financial results and on 'any other matters which appear . . . to be relevant having regard to the purpose of the report' (para. 20).

These additional requirements increase the length and complexity of a typical prospectus as it appears in a circular or in the financial press. But there can be no doubt that the supervision of the Quotations Department produces a considerably more comprehensive and useful picture for the prospective investor than is required by law. The less sophisticated will in any event rely more on the comments in the financial press or on advice from their brokers and financial advisers than on the prospectus itself. The main function of the very demanding disclosure requirements for public issues is to provide the material on which professional investment analysts may work, rather than to make things immediately clear to the ordinary investor.

Continuing disclosure requirements

The position in respect of continuing disclosure requirements is similar to that for prospectuses. In strict legal terms there are few special rules for quoted companies as such, though they will rarely be able to take advantage of the exemptions for smaller companies from the general disclosure rules in respect of turnover, directors' and executives' pay and other such matters imposed on all companies in 1967.[8] The rules in respect of the immediate disclosure of directors' dealings and share-ownership, however, are restricted to quoted companies. A director must now disclose any interest or dealings in the shares of his company or its subsidiaries within five days, and the company must pass the information on to the stock exchange concerned (1967 : ss. 27–31; 1976 : ss. 24–5). In addition any person who owns or acquires more than five per cent of the voting shares in a quoted company must inform the company within five days (1967 : ss. 33–4; 1976 : s. 26), and the company may require any person to disclose any beneficial interest in its voting shares (1976 :

[8] The basic rules are set out above in Chapters 4 and 5.

s. 27). These provisions are designed to ensure that voting control over quoted companies is not concealed by nominee holdings or anonymous market purchases.

The requirements of the Stock Exchange are a good deal more demanding. Every company admitted to listing in the British Isles is now required to sign a general undertaking to provide information both for shareholders and for the Quotations Department of the Stock Exchange in London on a regular basis in accordance with the current regulations.[9] These provide for the disclosure of substantial holdings in the company and of directors' dealings, for a statement in the annual directors' report of the general nature and geographical location of the company's activities, and of its subsidiaries, and for a half-yearly statement of interim results covering the company's profit (mentioning specifically the provision for taxation and any special credits, transfers from reserves or debits), the proposed rate of dividend, comparative figures for the previous year and 'any other information necessary to enable the shareholders and the public to appraise the position of the company' (para. 4). Advance notice must be given to the Stock Exchange on a wide range of other matters in relation to the company's formal structure and administration.

The extension of these disclosure rules beyond those of the Companies Acts can be attributed primarily to the much greater flexibility in amendment and updating open to the Stock Exchange authorities. The additional requirements suggested by the Jenkins Committee were imposed on quoted companies soon after the publication of the report, and by the time these had been given statutory backing in the 1967 Act, the Stock Exchange had imposed extra requirements, for instance in respect of half-yearly statements. The fact that the Stock Exchange is dealing with a clearly defined range of companies allows more stringent rules to be imposed without fear of inflicting unnecessary harm or undue administrative burdens on smaller unquoted companies. Until a similar cutting off point is adopted in the Companies Acts there is likely to be a continuing divergence between the statutory standards for disclosure and those of the Stock Exchange.

The absence of statutory backing for the Stock Exchange rules is not of great practical importance. The scrutiny of the Stock Exchange

[9] *Admission of Securities to Listing* (1976 version), Ch. 2.

authorities, backed by the threat of the suspension or withdrawal of quotation, is a highly effective sanction for securing compliance with the rules. This is in direct contrast to the absence of any simple means of enforcing the statutory rules. The major civil and criminal remedies against false or misleading disclosure apply irrespective of the statutory or non-statutory nature of the obligation both in relation to prospectuses and continuing disclosure.

2 LEGAL SANCTIONS AND REMEDIES

Cases of false or misleading statements, unlike those of insufficient disclosure, are not always immediately apparent even to the most searching scrutiny. When they eventually come to light the discretionary powers of suspending or withdrawing a quotation may no longer be an effective sanction. The authorities and those most closely affected in such cases, if they wish to pursue the matter, are usually forced to fall back on legal rather than administrative remedies.

The civil and criminal law in this respect gives the appearance of considerable complexity, owing to the piecemeal introduction of special statutory provisions in the aftermath of major frauds. Behind the various overlapping and sometimes apparently conflicting statutory rules and the mass of case-law, however, there is a relatively simple basic structure. This can best be explained by dealing first with the criminal law and the meaning of falsehood, and then with civil remedies.

Criminal sanctions

Though the Companies Acts contain a specific offence, punishable with up to two years' imprisonment, of authorizing the issue of a prospectus which includes any untrue statement (1948 : s. 44), the basic offences in this context are contained in other statutes. The most general is the offence under the Theft Act 1968, covering the publication by an officer of a company with intent to deceive members or creditors of any written statement or account which to his knowledge is or may be misleading, false or deceptive in a material particular (s. 19).[10] There is also the more specific though more widely drawn offence under the Prevention of Fraud (Investments) Act 1958, covering any fraudulent or reckless inducement of invest-

[10] This replaces the offence originally introduced in 1857 and re-enacted in the Larceny Act 1861 : s. 84.

ment or deposit in any enterprise by means of any statement, promise or forecast which is misleading or deceptive (s. 13);[11] this was introduced in 1939 to extend the law to newer forms of investment such as unit trusts, deposit companies and any other form of property management for which subscriptions were sought, excepting only certain forms of betting and gambling, and also to avoid the restrictive effect of the then 'no future false pretence' rule. Charges have been laid under either of these two statutes in most of the cases in which criminal proceedings have been instituted following major company failures, though in some instances the even more general common law charge of conspiracy to defraud by the publication of false accounts or statements has been preferred.[12]

The precise definition of each of these offences, and the case-law upon them, cannot be dealt with in detail here. But there are certain general principles regarding the meaning of falsehood and the standards of culpability which are applicable to all of them and to the attendant civil remedies.

It is not necessary in order to establish that a statement is false, misleading or deceptive to be able to point to a particular claim or sentence that is false in itself. It is quite sufficient if the general impression given by the document as a whole, both in what is included and what is left out, is false or misleading or deceptive. A good example of this is the *Royal Mail* case in which a leading City figure was imprisoned for the tacit concealment in a prospectus of the fact that the company had been maintaining its dividend payments out of secret reserves rather than current profits:

The Royal Mail Steam Packet Company issued a prospectus in 1929 in which it was stated that over the previous five years there had been an annual balance available for distribution, after depreciation and interest charges, sufficient to pay the dividend on the new issue five times over. It was later revealed that this balance was not current profit, since the company was losing heavily on its current operations, but an accumulated secret reserve built up in the prosperous years immediately following the 1914–18 war. In defence to a charge under the Larceny Act 1861 of publishing a false prospectus the directors and auditors argued that there was nothing improper in using a secret reserve for the purpose of equalizing dividends in less profitable years, and that none of the figures in the pros-

[11] As amended in the Protection of Depositors Act 1963: s. 21.

[12] See generally T. Hadden, 'Conspiracy to Defraud', (1966) *Cambridge Law Journal* 248.

pectus had been in any way false or inaccurate. The jury was directed that they might convict if there had been such an economy of the truth as to deceive; the document as a whole might be false not because of what it stated but because of what it did not state, because of what it implied. (per Wright J., at p. 445) The Chairman, Lord Kylsant was found guilty and imprisoned, though the auditors were acquitted; his appeal was dismissed. *R v. Lord Kylsant* [1932] 1 K.B. 442

The high standards of accuracy imposed in this and other civil and criminal cases in respect of anything expressly or impliedly contained in company reports, statements or accounts are offset as far as criminal proceedings are concerned by the strict rules relating to the proof of criminal intent. Convictions are rarely obtained in the absence of clear evidence of prior deliberation on the part of the accused. In one of the leading cases, arising out of the failure of an established and respectable banking company, the judge ruled that 'it is not because the defendants have taken too sanguine a view of their affairs ... that ... they are to be visited with a criminal prosecution.'[13] An allegation of any form of criminal or fraudulent intent is notoriously difficult to establish in the face of the standard defence that the accused misled himself as well as others as to the true state of affairs.

Recognition of the extreme difficulty in discharging this burden of proof eventually led to the introduction in 1939 of a new statutory formula permitting conviction under what is now the Prevention of Fraud (Investments) Act 1958 on proof of recklessness as well as fraud. In strict law this measure should not have been necessary in that recklessness has always been regarded as equivalent to deliberation in criminal cases. The explicit inclusion of recklessness has eased the task of the prosecution. Even so, further amendment of the Act[14] to insert 'dishonest or otherwise' after 'recklessly' was found to be necessary in view of a decision that absence of an honest belief in the truth of the statement, promise or forecast recklessly made was essential to a conviction.[15] The best formulation of the resulting position is perhaps that used in the *State Building Society* case, in which the defendants had made a series of take-over bids which their company was not in a position to pay for, despite an express commitment in the offer documents: it was held that a statement,

[13] *R v. Gurney* (1868) 11 Cox, C. C. 414, at p. 453.
[14] Protection of Depositors Act 1963: s. 21.
[15] *R v. Mackinnon* [1959] 1 Q.B. 150.

promise or forecast might be deemed to have been recklessly made if it was rash in fact, and there was no real basis of facts upon which the person making it could support it.[16] To this extent the extension of criminal liability to include recklessness has introduced an element of objectivity in that the onus of establishing that there was some credible basis upon which the statement, promise or forecast could be made is effectively shifted on to the defence. The task of the prosecution in cases where a charge is laid under the Prevention of Fraud (Investments) Act as opposed to the Theft Act is thus to establish that the document in question did in fact give a misleading impression and that the true position could have been readily established by those responsible at the time when the document was issued. Accordingly where there has been a direct attempt to induce investors to enter into a contract or arrangement to buy shares, to make deposits or to enter into other forms of property management with a view to profit the broader offence under the Prevention of Fraud (Investments) Act is likely to be preferred; where there has merely been an attempted deception of existing shareholders or creditors, the more restrictive rules on the proof of an intent to deceive or guilty knowledge under the Theft Act must be met. The maximum penalty in each case is imprisonment for seven years.

In practical terms, however, the difficulties of proving a case in a criminal court remain considerable. The complexity of the documents and accounts which are involved even in the simplest cases are likely to prove too much for most ordinary jurors before whom such cases must still come. The need to explain the whole story in terms which a jury can understand in itself adds considerably to the length of the trial, and thus to the cost of the proceedings. A decision to prosecute is therefore likely to be taken only in the clearest cases. As a result it is often argued that complex financial frauds should be dealt with before a panel of jurors or assessors skilled in the interpretation of financial documents and transactions, or even by a judge sitting alone. Furthermore where there has been any deliberate intent to defraud the culprits have usually taken the precaution of removing themselves from the jurisdiction before the crash.

There have consequently been relatively few successful prosecutions in cases of large scale financial fraud, though public pressure

[16] *R v. Grunwald* [1963] 1 Q.B. 935, (per Paull J., at p. 940).

for action typically increases in proportion to the size of the crash. Those cases which have been brought have often involved matters in which the culpability of the defendants in so far as it can be proved has not been such as to merit a heavy penalty. The overall efficacy of the control of large scale financial malpractice by means of criminal prosecution is thus a good deal less satisfactory than might appear from an analysis of the range and extent of the offences which have been developed. It is for this reason that the emphasis in recent reforms has increasingly been on prevention by administrative controls rather than on tightening the criminal sanctions.

Civil remedies

The two basic remedies available to those who purchase shares on the strength of a false or misleading prospectus, as developed during the nineteenth century, are damages and rescission. Damages were formerly available in a common law action for deceit in any case where the subscriber for shares could establish, first, that he had been induced by the misrepresentation to subscribe, secondly, that those responsible for the prospectus had acted fraudulently, and thirdly, that he had suffered financial loss as a direct result. In addition, the courts of equity were prepared to intervene in certain cases of non-fraudulent misrepresentation to rescind a contract under which shares had been subscribed for or allotted. Though the formal separation of these two remedies is now a matter of legal history, and a number of statutory remedies have been superimposed, many of the old distinctions persist.

As far as the legal interpretation of falsehood and fraud is concerned there is little difficulty. The rule that a prospectus may be rendered false by omission as well as by direct mis-statement was in fact developed in the civil rather than the criminal courts:

A prospectus for a mining company stated that the money raised was to be used to exploit mining concessions in Venezuela. No mention was made of the fact that two previous companies which had attempted to work the concessions had gone into liquidation. In a suit by the company against a subscriber to require him to pay a further call on the shares he had taken up, the subscriber argued that he was not bound to pay in view of the fraudulent nature of the prospectus. The trial court found in his favour, on the grounds that the previous history of the mines was relevant material which should have been disclosed, and that it had been concealed with fraudulent intent. The decision was upheld in the House of Lords, despite the fact that there was no statutory requirement for the disclosure of this information: 'In an honest prospectus many facts and circumstances may be lawfully omitted although some subscribers might be of opinion that these would have been of materiality as influencing the exercise of their judgement. But the statement of a part of the truth accompanied by suggestions and inferences which would be possible and credible if it contained the whole truth but become neither possible nor credible whenever the whole truth is divulged is ... neither more or less than a false statement.' (per Lord Watson, at p. 287) *Aaron's Reefs Ltd. v. Twiss* [1896] A.C. 273

The same stringent rules as to the proof of fraud were applied in actions both for damages in deceit and for the setting aside of a contract on grounds of fraud:

A prospectus was issued to raise capital for a tramway company, stating that the special attraction of the company was its right under a special Act of Parliament to use steam power in place of horse power. No mention was made of the requirement that official permission be obtained for this purpose. When this permission was later refused and the company wound up, a subscriber sued for damages. The action was dismissed at first instance on the finding that the directors had honestly believed in the truth of their claim. This was reversed in the Court of Appeal on the ground that there could be liability in damages if there was no reasonable ground on which the directors could base their belief, but the original decision was restored by the House of Lords: 'In order to sustain an action for deceit there must be proof of fraud and nothing short of that will suffice. ... Fraud is proved when it is shown that a false representation has been made (1) knowingly, or (2) without belief in its truth, or (3) recklessly, careless whether it be true or false. ... Making a false statement through want of care falls far short of and is a very different thing from fraud, and the same may be said of a false representation honestly believed but on insufficient grounds.' (per Lord Herschell, at pp. 374–5) *Derry v. Peek* (1889) 14 App. Cas. 337

Damages were thus available at common law only on proof of fraud, or at the least a reckless disregard of truth. And there were further restrictions on the action for deceit. In the first place, only direct subscribers could sue. In addition, it had been established that no action in deceit for damages arising out of a false prospectus would lie against the company, as opposed to its directors, unless rescission could also be granted.[17] The ground for this decision is not at all clear. But the practical result was that the only effective remedy

[17] *Houldsworth v. City of Glasgow Bank* (1880) 5 App. Cas. 317.

available to a shareholder who had subscribed on the basis of a false prospectus but who could not prove fraud was a suit for the equitable remedy of rescission, which as will be seen was not always easy to obtain.

The ruling in *Derry v. Peek* was regarded as highly unsatisfactory at a time when suits for damages arising out of misleading prospectuses were relatively common. Amending legislation was immediately introduced in the form of the Directors' Liability Act of 1890. Under this measure, now incorporated in the Companies Acts (1948 : s. 43), any person who authorizes the issue of a misleading prospectus, whether as a director, a promoter or an expert whose report or opinion is included, is liable to pay damages to any person who subscribes for shares on the faith of the prospectus for any loss sustained as a result of the misrepresentation. The standard of liability imposed is effectively that of negligence, in that the statute provides a defence for any person who has withdrawn his consent to the publication and given reasonable public notice of the fact, or who can show that he had reasonable ground for believing and did so believe the statements in question to be true. The statutory remedy is none the less expressly limited by two of the most restrictive of the old common law rules. In the first place only those who have actually subscribed for the shares in question may sue, thus excluding those who may subsequently purchase shares on the market even if they do in effect rely on the prospectus. And the action must be brought against the directors personally rather than the company.

It is sometimes suggested that the extent of this liability has been altered by recent developments in ordinary tortious liability for negligent mis-statements (see p. 251). This seems unlikely in that the relationship between directors or promoters and shareholders would certainly fall outside the ambit of the type of special professional relationship envisaged in *Hedley Byrne & Co. v. Heller* (see p. 241). Further development along these lines is not excluded, but for the moment the only extension in potential liability in damages stems from the Misrepresentation Act 1967. Though this too is restricted to negligent mis-statements, and to cases in which there is a direct contractual relationship between the parties, it may have the effect of extending liability to the company itself and in addition to statements made outside the confines of the formal prospectus as well as those contained in it. But this is offset by the express limitation of the new statutory remedy to cases in which the existing remedy of rescission would have been available.

If liability is established the measure of damages both at common law and under the statutory remedies will be settled on the ordinary principles of compensating the plaintiff for any loss directly resulting from the defendant's action. In prospectus cases this will amount to the difference between the amount paid on the shares and their real value at the time of the issue. No account is taken of the loss of any future profit which the plaintiff could have expected if the statements in the prospectus had been true. Difficulties under these rules are likely to arise only where the company has continued in business. Where it has gone into liquidation the simple solution of regarding the shares as valueless even at the date of the prospectus is usually adopted.

The question as to whether the contract under which a subscriber has agreed to take up shares from a company should be set aside on grounds of misrepresentation is distinct from that of damages. The basic issue is whether the subscriber is to be forced to remain a shareholder. In many cases there will be little practical difficulty. Where the company has gone into liquidation and the shares have been fully paid up, rescission will often be of theoretical importance only. And where fraud can be established the contract may always be set aside either at common law or in equity. But where the misrepresentation was merely negligent or entirely innocent the availability of rescission may be crucial. For instance, where the initial subscription on the shares was only a small proportion of the full nominal value, and the shareholders would thus be liable to pay further calls, or where the assessment of any damages which might be payable would come to less than the total depreciation in the value of the shares, it would clearly be to the advantage of the subscriber if he could give up his shares in return for the amount he has paid on them.

Rescission is theoretically available in any case where a subscription has been induced by a misleading prospectus, whether or not there has been any fraud or negligence on the part of the company or its officers. But like other discretionary equitable remedies it will be granted only on stringent conditions. Any form of affirmation of the contract, or any undue delay on the part of the subscriber may result in the court's discretion being exercised against him. The most important rule in the context of company law, however, is that which bars rescission in any case where the parties cannot be restored to their original position, or where third parties have acted on the strength of the validity of the contract. This means in effect that unless the misrepresentation comes to light immediately on the issue of the shares or soon after, rescission is unlikely to be granted. Thus if the subscribers' capital has been expended on the company's business, or if others have dealt with the company on the basis of the capital which has been subscribed, as in the *Lagunas Nitrate Co.* case,[18] rescission cannot be granted. This applies with particular force to prospectus cases, since to grant rescission to a single subscriber in what must be regarded as a test case would be tantamount to ordering a return of the whole or much of the capital subscribed in response to the prospectus. The further restriction suggested in *Seddon v. North East Salt Co.* (1905),[19] on the other hand, that rescission cannot be granted in any case where the contract has been executed, can safely be dismissed in so far as prospectus cases are concerned. But it is clearly settled that only the allottee can rescind, so that any subsequent sale or transfer of the shares alloted will bar any possibility of rescission in respect of those shares, just as it will bar any suit for damages.

The range of cases in which either rescission or damages in respect of a misleading prospectus can be obtained is thus severely restricted. In either case only those who actually take up shares on the strength of the prospectus and who can show that the misrepresentation was a material factor in their decision to subscribe have any cause of action. Then to obtain damages proof of negligence or fraud against individual directors or promoters must be produced. And to obtain rescission proceedings must be started not only as soon as is reasonably practicable after the misrepresentation comes to light but before the money subscribed has been expended on the purposes for which it was raised.

The position in respect of the continuing disclosure requirements, unrelated to any particular issue of shares, is scarcely more encouraging. There will clearly be no question of rescission in cases of misleading statements in a company's annual accounts or otherwise, in that no specific contract will have been made with the company in reliance on the statement which may be set aside. Nor is rescission

[18] [1899] 2 Ch. 392 (see p. 314).
[19] [1905] 1 Ch. 326.

likely to be extended to cover cases in which shares are purchased on the market, since there is again no direct contract between the company and the new shareholder. It is equally doubtful whether any successful action in damages could be mounted. Even if a fraudulent intention could be established for the purposes of an action in deceit, the duty of those making the statement or account is likely to be limited to existing shareholders, thus excluding liability to any investor who purchases shares on the market in reliance on the fraudulent statement or account. Existing shareholders could only recover by establishing some direct loss resulting from the statement or account, for instance if they have increased their holdings in direct reliance on it, or perhaps if they have reversed a prior decision to sell on receiving the accounts. Similar difficulties will arise in respect of the cause of action for any deliberate or negligent breach of the statutory duty to make accurate annual returns or accounts (see p. 249).

It is scarcely surprising, therefore, that there have been relatively few successful actions in matters of this kind. Quite apart from the danger of running foul of one of the many procedural and substantive rules on who is and who is not entitled to take action, and what loss may be recovered, there is always the possibility that in a case where the default on the part of the directors is not blatant the court will exercise its discretion to relieve them of any liability (1948: s. 448). Furthermore the uncertainty of the law and the complexity of the proceedings combine to raise costs to a level where the necessary financial guarantees in the event of failure will be difficult to raise. There is little inclination on the part of investors to commit further resources to an unsuccessful venture in the faint hope of recovering some of what they have already lost. And even if all these obstacles can be surmounted, the culprits will frequently not be worth suing, or if they are may well have taken the precaution of removing themselves from the jurisdiction of the court.

Deficiencies in the disclosure system

It will be clear by now that there are serious deficiencies in the disclosure system in respect of public issues and other statements and accounts made by quoted companies. These may be summarized as follows: first, the absence of a legal obligation to disclose all material information in a prospectus or on a continuing basis, as opposed to those items prescribed in the various statutory provisions; secondly, the legal complexity of the various remedies that are available by way of damages, rescission or criminal sanctions; thirdly, the serious practical difficulties of organization and expense which face any shareholder who wishes to initiate proceedings against the company or its directors; and finally, the absence of any effective remedy for those who buy shares on the market on the strength of prospectuses or public statements and accounts issued by a company. Most of these deficiencies could be remedied by legislation. The formal obligation imposed by the Stock Exchange on all quoted companies to make full disclosure of all information relevant to the value of their shares both in formal prospectuses and accounts and also on a continuing basis could readily be incorporated in the Companies Acts. Likewise there would be little difficulty in extending the right of action in respect of false or misleading statements to all who have dealt in the shares, provided some direct tangible loss could be established. And on a procedural level the problems of expense and organization could be eased by permitting representative actions through which active shareholders could in effect undertake proceeding on behalf of the general body of those who may have suffered without incurring huge personal expense. American experience suggests, however, that some form of contingent fee arrangement over costs, whereby the legal advisers of the shareholders are paid only where the action is successful, is necessary to the development of this type of action. The main emphasis in Britain has not been on the development of legal remedies, but on the creation of alternative methods of enforcement and control through administrative channels.

3 QUOTED COMPANIES AND THEIR DIRECTORS

There are similar problems for shareholders who seek to control the activities of large quoted companies and their directors, either through court actions or the exercise of their rights in general meeting. Quoted companies are subject to the same legal rules on ultra vires activities as any other company, and their directors are if anything bound by stricter standards of conduct than those in unquoted companies. Their shareholders have the same rights over the appointment and dismissal of directors and other matters requiring the sanction of the general meeting. But in practice it is difficult for shareholders to enforce these rights and duties in the manner envisaged in the Companies Acts. What controls there are are typically exercised in other less formal ways.

Non-commercial activities

The first question which arises is how far the directors of a quoted company may use its funds for other than strictly business purposes. How far may they go in spending money on the welfare of their employees, in making contributions to charities or to political parties, or in joining in political campaigns on issues of current concern? And how far may ordinary shareholders control them in relation to such matters by relying on the ultra vires doctrine?

The simple answer to this question is that the company may incur any expenditure which is expressly authorized in its constitution, which is reasonably incidental to carrying out its authorized objects or which otherwise contributes to the profitable exercise of its business. The law takes a broad view of these matters, as is clear from the following leading statement of principle:

> [A company's directors] are not to keep their pockets buttoned up and defy the world unless they are liable in a way which could be enforced at law or in equity. Most business requires liberal dealing. The test is not whether it is bona fide, but whether as well as being bona fide it is done within the ordinary scope of the company's business, and whether it is reasonably incidental to the carrying on of the company's business for the company's benefit. . . . A railway company . . . might send down all the porters at a railway station to have tea in the country at the expense of the company. Why should they not? . . . A company which always treated its employees with Draconian severity . . . would soon find itself deserted. . . . The law does not say that there are to be no cakes and ale, but that there are to be no cakes and ale except such as are required for the benefit of the company. (per Bowen L.J.) *Hutton v. West Cork Railway* (1883) 23 Ch.D. 654

Most expenditure of a strictly non-commercial kind can clearly be justified on these grounds. Swimming pools for employees, prestige advertising, refreshments for shareholders before a general meeting, grants to outside bodies for research or for charity may all be of long-term benefit to the company in creating attractive working conditions for employees, in promoting a better understanding of the company's activities by shareholders and the public at large, or in increasing the supply of well-trained recruits. As long as the company remains prosperous there will be few objections to such expenditure except perhaps on political grounds.

Different considerations arise when the company ceases to have a long-term future in relation to which the expenditure can be justified. If a company is about to be wound up or even absorbed by another it is no longer possible in a strict legal sense for expenditure on its employees or other external purposes to be for the long-term benefit of the company, and any shareholder who will participate in the eventual distribution of the company's assets may legitimately object to such largesse. In *Hutton v. West Cork Railway*, for instance, it was held that large terminal payments to certain of the company's chief officials on the transfer of the whole of the company's undertaking to another company could not be held to be reasonably incidental to the company's business, since the business was about to cease. This rule is applicable no matter how exemplary the motives of the directors may be in making the payments, as for instance in arranging redundancy grants for long-term employees of a company going into liquidation:

> On the winding up of the *News Chronicle* in 1960 the controlling directors of the company proposed to apply the balance of the sum to be paid by the *Daily Mail* for the company's goodwill, after meeting outstanding liabilities, by way of compensation to those of the *News Chronicle* staff who would lose their jobs in the merger. One of the shareholders objected to the proposal on the grounds that all the remaining assets should be distributed to the shareholders. The objection was upheld: the directors' motives, 'however laudable and however enlightened from the point of view of industrial relations, were such as the law does not recognize as a sufficient justification'; the application of funds in payments to former employees in order to benefit those employees rather than the company was ultra vires, though the individual directors were of course entitled to use their own share of the distributable balance as shareholders in that way if they wished. (per Plowman J.) *Parke v. Daily News* [1962] Ch. 927

The most satisfactory solution to this dilemma would perhaps be a provision that employees should for this and other purposes be deemed to be members of the company they work for.

The more difficult issues of principle in respect of political and charitable contributions have not yet come before the courts in a direct form in this country. It has been decided that for tax purposes a company may deduct political contributions from its assessable profits:

The directors of Tate and Lyle in 1949 felt that their business was threatened by the Labour Party's plans for nationalization, which made specific reference to public ownership of sugar manufacture and refinement. They accordingly contributed some £15,000 of the company's funds to an advertising campaign sponsored by a pro-Tory organization against nationalization. To strengthen their position a general meeting of shareholders was called at which a resolution was passed empowering the directors 'to do everything in their power to meet the threats of the nationalizers'. The Inland Revenue argued that the company was not entitled to tax relief since the expenditure was not money 'wholly and exclusively laid out for the purpose of the company's trade', but the House of Lords eventually held that relief was allowable, since the payment had been made in the honest belief that it was necessary to preserve the company's assets and business from appropriation, and so to enable the company to carry on its business and earn profits. *Morgan v. Tate & Lyle* [1955] A.C. 21

This decision is generally taken as having settled the legality of political donations for all practical purposes, though many companies take the additional precaution of including an express power to make both political and charitable donations in their memoranda of association. The Jenkins Committee certainly thought that the practice of making contributions to charities which were of no direct interest to the company's business would be acceptable to the courts as a means of creating or preserving public goodwill for the company.[20] In America payments for research purposes have also been sanctioned on the general ground of the duty of large corporations as public benefactors:

A company donation to Princeton University was challenged by a shareholder. The New Jersey Supreme Court eventually held that the making of such corporate contributions 'if held within reasonable limitations was a matter of direct benefit to the giving corporation', and might well be regarded as a 'major though unwritten corporate power' and even, in the Court's opinion, 'a solemn duty'. *A. P. Smith Mfg. Co. v. Barlow* (1953) 346 U.S. 861

In Britain company donations have typically been relatively low, and appear to have been declining rather than increasing as a proportion of total company income. An independent study found that in 1967 they represented less than half of one per cent of net company income compared with a figure of one per cent for American companies, and concluded that 'the smallness of dona-

[20] Cmnd. 1749, para. 52 (1962).

tions as a proportion of company funds, the absence of objection from shareholders, and the uncertain character of shareholders' rights over company assets favoured the view that company donations are an acceptable business practice.'[21] Any remaining doubt over the general legality of political and charitable contributions has now been removed by the statutory requirement that details of all such payments should be disclosed (1967 : s. 19). It appears to be generally accepted that the position of large companies as the major holders of wealth in the private sector in itself helps to legitimate a liberal approach to company largesse, and that any objection to their political contributions, most of which go to the Conservative Party, can scarcely be sustained while trade unions continue to contribute large sums to the Labour Party.

The legitimacy of other forms of political involvement by major companies and multi-nationals, from the support of favourable regimes to outright political or commercial bribery, is more widely questioned. There is little doubt that under-cover political operations of this kind are fairly widespread, both in developed countries and in the third world, as shown by recent disclosures concerning the overseas activities of the American ITT and Lockheed corporations and the involvement of some major oil companies in Italian politics. Apart from the intrinsic illegality of bribery, the issue is not generally discussed in the context of company law. But it is reasonably clear that all unlawful activities are ultra vires. It follows that a shareholder could obtain an injunction to prevent a company from embarking on or continuing any unlawful activities, whether at home or abroad, if sufficient evidence could be produced of the reality of the allegations. Apart from this the ordinary rule that a company may carry on any activity within the scope of its objects which can reasonably be held to contribute to long-term profitability would be applicable, however distasteful that activity may be to individual shareholders. In such cases the only remedy for the shareholder is to raise the issue at the company's general meeting, though for reasons which will be discussed below that is unlikely to prove very effective.

Directors' duties

The principal issues of company law in respect of the directors of

[21] B. Shenfield, *Company Giving* (1969).

quoted companies in their individual capacity concern the respective duties and responsibilities of executive and non-executive directors and the control of excessive payments and perks to directors and senior managers.

It is accepted practice in many large British companies for the board of directors to operate in a largely supervisory capacity. This is achieved by making a clear distinction between executive management, which controls the day-to-day operation of the company, and non-executive directors who may be recruited from any source outside the company, but will typically include prominent industrialists and City personalities and perhaps politicians. The board of directors itself will then be constituted of senior executive directors and non-executive directors, perhaps in the ratio of two to one respectively, and a chairman who may fall into either category.[22] It will meet perhaps once a month to receive reports from management and generally to review the progress and prospects of the company. The function of the board in such cases is to act as a more or less independent check on the activities of full-time management. The role of the chairman is to act as a link between the internal and external members of the board.

This allocation of functions is quite lawful, given the standard article of association permitting the board of directors of any company to delegate any or all of its statutory duties in running the affairs of the company (1948: Table A, art. 81), or to appoint a managing director with full executive powers (ibid., arts. 107–9). It is also likely to become increasingly institutionalized with the appointment of employee or union representatives on company boards, as discussed in Chapter 13. But it raises difficult issues in relation to the respective formal responsibilities of full-time executive directors and their part-time colleagues.

It is now generally accepted that executive directors of quoted companies may properly be regarded as professional managers who may be expected to carry out their duties with standards of care and skill analogous to those imposed on accountants or doctors. Any failure to maintain such a standard, for instance by failing to seek proper advice where the need for it is generally accepted or as a result of excessive drinking or illness, would thus in theory leave the

[22] R. E. Pahl and J. T. Winkler, 'The Economic Elite: Theory and Practice', in P. Stanworth and A. Giddens (eds.), *Elites and Power in British Society* (1974).

director open to an action in damages for negligence. This liability is unlikely to be enforced given the power of the company to ratify any such breach of duty. If it were the delinquent director would be liable to reimburse the company for any loss sustained as a result of his negligence.

It seems clear that a non-executive director is not expected to exhibit this standard of professional care and skill. The question then arises as to what are his legal duties and responsibilities. Given the large numbers of bankers, City representatives and politicians who sit on the boards of quoted companies in a non-executive capacity the question is not wholly academic. The old rule that company directors are not bound to do more than act honestly and to the best of their ability in whatever they actually do (see p. 238) is clearly inadequate. But there is no relevant modern case-law on the issue. Current commercial attitudes, as exemplified in some recent Department of Trade inspectors' reports and in the financial press, is certainly more demanding. Non-executive directors are now expected to be alert to any danger signals of impropriety or impending failure and to inform their shareholders and the investing public at the earliest possible opportunity if their suspicions are not adequately answered by management. The precise extent of a non-executive director's liability, if this formulation of his duty is accepted, is more difficult to state. In theory he will be liable to the company for any breach to the extent of the loss which flows from his failure to act in time, which in the case of a failing company could be very substantial. A more effective and readily enforceable remedy would be a discretionary court power to order the delinquent director to contribute a specified sum to the assets of the company in relation both to his means and to the amount of payment he has received from the company.

The second major issue is the control of self-interested conduct by directors and senior managers. The standards expected of the directors and senior executives of quoted companies, as reflected in the financial press, are fully equivalent to those of legal trustees. Evidence of private profit-making within the sphere of the company's business or even by dealings in the shares of the company or its subsidiaries usually results in substantial public criticism and strong informal pressures for reimbursement. This suggests that the directors and senior executives of quoted companies, unlike those in family or proprietory companies, should abandon all operations as businessmen on their own account while they remain directors. The difficulty is that the law does not draw any sharp distinction between the duties of directors in these various types of company, though different standards are likely to be applied in practice. This raises special problems in respect of the very substantial payments and perquisities which directors and senior executives are in a position to award themselves. Directors and executives may be rewarded in a number of different ways, from simple directors' fees and executives' salaries to incentive schemes by way of share-options and valuable payments in kind. In addition to the standard provision in company constitutions that directors' fees must be formally approved in general meeting (1948 : Table A, art. 76), all companies are now required to disclose the aggregate amount of directors' and senior executives' emoluments in stated bands (1967 : ss. 6–8) and also to permit directors' service contracts to be inspected by shareholders (1967 : s. 26). In addition details must be disclosed of any subsisting contracts in which directors are interested and of any schemes for the purchase or transfer of shares or share-options to directors (1967 : s. 16). Directors must further disclose to the board any interest which they may have in any contract or dealing by the company (1948 : s. 199). Quoted companies must also undertake under Stock Exchange regulations to secure the approval of their general meeting for all service contracts for more than ten years, and to make available for inspection at the annual general meeting all service contracts not determinable within one year.[23]

These disclosure requirements are more effective in respect of quoted companies than of unquoted companies, given the power of the financial press to bring the pressure of publicity on any directors who are felt to be taking improper advantage of their position. The usual result in such cases is a voluntary refund or abandonment of the payment or perks in issue. But the authorities have yet to reach the obvious solution which is that the actual amount paid or payable to each director and senior executive in quoted companies should be disclosed, including the value of any perquisites which are now to be taxable under the Finance Act 1976 (ss. 60 ff.). Further protection might be afforded if all arrangements for such payments, as opposed to long-term contracts, had to be formally laid before the

[23] Stock Exchange, *Admission of Securities to Listing* (1976 version), Listing Agreement, para. 10.

annual general meeting subject to annulment by a specified proportion of shareholders. A more far-reaching and equitable solution would be to require all schemes in which payments or share-options are linked to the performance of the company, which may give rise to huge personal profits, to be extended to cover all employees of the company, as discussed in Chapter 13.

4 SHAREHOLDERS AND INVESTORS

The final resort for a shareholder or group of shareholders dissatisfied with the policies or performance of their company is the annual general meeting at which the broad lines of policy are supposed to be open to discussion. Shareholders may wish, for example, to raise the desirability or morality of certain company activities or to question directors on any public statements which they may have made on such matters. The basis of this is the notion of the company as a kind of democracy in which the directors, like the government of a country, are elected on a periodic basis and must account to their electors for their performance. The theory of disclosure which now forms such a large part of modern company law is likewise based on the idea that shareholders armed with the relevant information may exert more effective control over the activities of their company and its directors.

Shareholder democracy in theory and practice

This conception is built into the Companies Acts by the provision for annual general meetings (1948 : s. 131), and for the election or dismissal of directors by a straight majority vote of the shareholders (1948 : s. 184). It is specifically provided that the holders of ten per cent of the shares in a company may requisition the summoning of a general meeting at any time (1948 : s. 132); that the holders of five per cent of the shares may require the distribution of resolutions and explanatory memoranda to all shareholders at the expense of the company preparatory to any general meeting (1948 : s. 140); and that any shareholder who is unable to attend the meeting and register his vote may appoint a proxy to exercise that right on his behalf (1948 : s. 136).

In small companies, as discussed in Chapters 4 and 5, these provisions are of little use to external shareholders, given the fact that the general meeting is usually dominated by the voting power of the directors themselves. In quoted companies it might be thought that the wide dispersal of shareholding and the fact that the directors themselves typically hold only a handful of the total voting shares might make for greater shareholder democracy. In practice things work out somewhat differently. The board of directors in large quoted companies are usually in a position to dominate the general meeting just as effectively as their counterparts in smaller companies, and thus to secure their own unfettered control over the conduct of the company's affairs on an equally permanent basis.

In the first place, the wide distribution of share-ownership in quoted companies means that a relatively small concerted block of voting shares will generally be sufficient to control the general meeting. In normal circumstances the large majority of small and medium shareholders are unlikely to exercise their voting rights at all, or if they do to act in a concerted way. A block of votes amounting to as little as one in ten or twenty may thus be sufficient to ensure control. Recent surveys of shareholding in large British companies, as set out in Chapter 2, have shown that the twenty or so largest holdings do typically account for a much larger proportion of the total voting power than any other manageable group.[24] As long as this controlling group acts in a concerted way its position is virtually impregnable.

Secondly, the management of the company is in a position to utilize the provisions for proxy voting to consolidate its position. It used to be standard practice for management to send to all shareholders open proxy cards offering themselves as proxies. The Stock Exchange now requires all quoted companies to send out proxy cards in a two-way form which permits the recipient to vote for or against any resolution to be proposed.[25] But management can usually count on a sufficient number of general proxies authorizing them to act on their discretion to counteract any attempt by an opposing group of shareholders to dispute any important resolution. Thus even if an opposing group does exercise its right to propose critical resolutions the well-established inertia of ordinary shareholders when faced with a request for actual involvement in the affairs of their companies by exercising their votes in a specific way removes any serious threat to the position of management.

[24] Sargant Florence, *Ownership, Control and Success of Large Companies* (1961).
[25] Listing Agreement (1976 version), para. 5.

Thirdly, there is no way in which a dissatisfied shareholder may insist on a satisfactory answer, or indeed an answer at all, to a question which he wishes to raise and discuss. There is no legal obligation on directors to answer questions, though they will normally seek to give at least the appearance of doing so. Where a shareholder wishes to pursue an issue in any depth, however, they will usually take refuge in the general principle that the day-to-day administration of the company's affairs is a matter for the directors and not the shareholders. Alternatively, the chairman may rule that any discussion of an issue which is not directly relevant to a resolution which has been duly circulated is out of order. In one recent case in which a shareholder wished to discuss a company's investment in South Africa, the chairman, having heard the shareholder's initial question and given an unsympathetic answer, simply proceeded with the rest of the formal business of the meeting allowing the shareholder in question to continue his harangue at the back of the hall. It is only where a majority of shareholders present wish to pursue an issue that there is any effective pressure on directors to deal with it in detail. Even then the directors may refuse to reveal the facts on grounds of confidentiality or the absence of any legal obligation to do so.

Finally and perhaps most important of all, the directors are usually able to secure that there is no serious question of a contest over the election of new directors or the re-election of existing directors. The Companies Acts require that votes on the election of directors be taken individually (1948 : s. 183) and that any director may be removed by an ordinary majority vote notwithstanding any provision in the articles to the contrary (1948 : s. 184). And it is usual for the articles of a company to provide for the retirement of directors by rotation (Table A : articles 89–92), so that in theory the general meeting is required to give its attention to the matter. In practice the board will normally arrange for any retiring director to resign in mid-term, and then make use of its power to co-opt new directors (Table A : art. 95) to make any new appointments. In this way the general meeting is rarely given an opportunity to do other than confirm those members of the existing board who retire by rotation. And if any opposing candidates are actually put up the existing board will usually be able to muster sufficient votes in the manner just described to defeat the attempt. The only serious contests likely to arise over the election of directors in publicly quoted companies are those arising out of contested take-over bids in which large blocks of shares are accumulated by opposing groups.

The shareholder militant

The virtual elimination of the general meeting as an effective controlling agency, and the resulting domination of the affairs of large companies by a self-perpetuating body of managers has not been universally accepted as either necessary or desirable.[26] The first line of attack has usually been to seek to control the more blatant examples of abuse of managerial power, for instance by the diversion of profits or the misuse of confidential information, through the development of a more effective system by which complaining shareholders may take legal action against those responsible (see Chapter 5). But there has also been pressure for the adoption of measures which will allow ordinary shareholders to exercise general control over their companies in situations where it cannot seriously be argued that the management has been in breach of any formal legal duty, but has none the less acted irresponsibly or inefficiently or simply contrary to the wishes of a substantial body of shareholders or public opinion.

The idea of active involvement by shareholders in matters of this kind, like that of shareholder actions in the courts, has been developed a good deal further in the United States than in Britain. The activities of a few well-known 'professional shareholders' like the Gilbert brothers, who have made a practice of attending company meetings and questioning management on matters which appear from a detailed study of the company's accounts to require further explanation, have resuscitated the general meetings of large corporations both as a forum for probing the conduct of corporate affairs and also as a spectacle or even an entertainment worth attending in its own right. As a result the numbers of shareholders actually attending meetings has tended to grow to a sufficient level to force management to pay a good deal more attention to them. And it has become relatively common for associations of shareholders to be formed with a view to monitoring the activities of management in the interests of shareholders on a more or less permanent basis.

Shareholder militancy of this kind has perhaps had some beneficial effect in increasing management's awareness of their duties to

[26] Alex Rubner, *The Ensnared Shareholder* (1965).

shareholders as distinct from the company, despite the slighting references to trouble-makers and time-wasters which are sometimes made. Some large American corporations have even sought to encourage greater attendance at annual meetings by offering food and drink or other attractions, though this kind of public relations expenditure is not usually welcomed by the militants. But even if five or ten thousand shareholders attend and can be accommodated at a meeting, they are still likely to represent only a small minority of the total voting power. Furthermore, as small voters tend to be divided on major issues, there is rarely any danger of defeat for management on important resolutions. It is the forms of shareholder democracy which do not require physical attendance, notably the procedures for cumulative voting for the election of directors and the regulation by the Securities Exchange Commission of the proxy system, which constitute the most serious potential threat to managerial voting control.

The basic objective of cumulative voting is to permit individual shareholders to cast all their votes for a single director instead of one for each vacancy, thus allowing a concerted minority of shareholders to ensure the election of at least one director to represent them. This system was first introduced in the State of Illinois in 1870 and has since been adopted, usually on a permissive basis, in many other American jurisdictions. The pro forma provision in the Model Business Corporation Act prepared by the American Law Institute is as follows:

> At each election for directors every shareholder ... shall have the right ... to cumulate his votes by giving one candidate as many votes as the number of directors to be elected multiplied by the number of his shares shall equal, or by distributing such votes on the same principle among any number of candidates. *Article 31*

The system does not appear, however, to have made any real impact. It has been adopted by only one in five of listed American corporations. And even where it does apply, its effect has often been minimized by managerial action to secure that there are never enough vacancies at any one election for the cumulation of sufficient votes to threaten the status quo. In any event the system no longer attracts the enthusiastic support which it once did.[27]

[27] See H. F. Sturdy, 'Mandatory cumulative voting: an anachronism', (1961) *The Business Lawyer*, 550.

The official regulation of the proxy system under the Securities Exchange Act, 1934 (s. 14), is of rather more practical significance. Under the Securities and Exchange Commission rules any public company which issues proxy solicitations must conform to the regulations governing the form and content of the solicitation and the proxy card itself, which are designed to ensure that the shareholder is given the full details and background of the various proposals to be voted on and a clear opportunity to vote either for or against each individual proposal. The company must also deposit copies of all documents with the SEC for scrutiny. The regulations apply equally to solicitations and proxies issued by other shareholders, but these are relatively infrequent: in 1963, for instance, all but twenty-three of the 2,396 proxy statements filed originated from management, most of them in respect of routine matters such as the election of retiring directors or the appointment of auditors. These figures in themselves demonstrate the limited extent to which the proposals of management are seriously contested. The major impact of the SEC regulations appears to lie in the potential sanctions against management for any false or misleading proxy statements issued rather than in any real increase in the powers of shareholders to influence the outcome of resolutions or elections. Despite the efforts to turn it into an effective weapon for shareholders, the proxy system remains firmly in the hands of management.

It is doubtful therefore whether these various practices and procedures have resulted in any substantial increase in shareholder democracy in America, or any corresponding diminution in the extent to which large corporations are effectively under the sole control of top management. This is all the more true in Britain where there is no developed tradition of co-operative action by shareholders. Here too the proxy system is almost exclusively a tool in the hands of management, despite the provisions of the Companies Acts and the Stock Exchange Listing Agreement to facilitate its use by individual shareholders. Though there is currently some evidence of increasing interest and involvement in company annual general meetings following the American practice, a substantial turn-out of shareholders is only likely where there has been some crisis in the company's affairs such as the appointment of a receiver or a contested take-over bid.

The shareholder as investor

It would be a mistake to deplore this apparent failure of the movement for shareholder democracy to make any genuine impact on management without first considering some of the wider implications. There are serious deficiencies both in theory and in practice in the conception of the company which the movement represents. On a simple practical level there is no reason to suppose that the general meeting of shareholders, or even a formal postal vote of all shareholders, is a suitable body to make final decisions on the complex economic and social issues involved in major company policies, any more than a direct poll of all voters on major political issues is likely to produce satisfactory results within a democratic state. Even if it is conceded that some form of ultimate 'democratic' control over management is beneficial and necessary, there is a serious objection to entrusting this to shareholders alone. It is now widely recognized that a large company cannot limit its obligations to the maximization of its long-term profitability in the interests of its shareholders. The company has equally important obligations to its employees and to the community at large, and it cannot be assumed that these will always be met by entrusting ultimate control to its shareholders.

This wider view of the company as an independent institution with a wide range of obligations to a number of conflicting internal and external interests clearly raises issues which cannot be resolved within the traditional capitalist framework. Some of the possible alternatives, such as the creation of a supervisory board, representative of all interested parties, to exercise general control over management, will be discussed in Part III. But this does not exclude the development of new procedures or rules through which the legitimate interests of shareholders in their limited capacity as detached investors may be better protected. These may perhaps be formulated in simple terms as the right to a reasonable return on capital invested in terms of an annual payment by way of interest or dividend, the right to share in any capital appreciation which their investment may help to make possible, and finally the right to ensure that the capital invested is profitably employed and not put in jeopardy through inefficient or fraudulent management. There may be some disagreement about the adequacy of this formulation. But there can certainly be little dispute that even these minimal rights of investors are inadequately protected under the existing system.

The most radical suggestion in respect of the first of these rights of investors is that all companies should be required to pay out in the form of dividends the total amount of net profit made each year.[28] This would have the theoretical advantage of permitting the shareholder to decide whether the profits on his capital should be ploughed back into the company or invested in other enterprises, and thus of restoring the balance of power between management and investors by forcing management to compete on the market for new capital. Despite its theoretical attractions in terms of capitalist economic theory, however, the suggestion is unlikely to win much favour. The actual result would almost certainly be to cause a sharp decline in the proportion of profit actually reinvested as shown by the analysis of company financing in Chapter 2. There would also be serious problems in calculating what constituted profit for the purposes of distribution and what was reasonable by way of an allowance for depreciation in order to maintain the capital of the company. A more practical proposal might be to require the distribution out of profit of a basic minimum percentage return on the net value of capital invested, perhaps related to current market interest rates, at least in the case of quoted companies. This type of provision has been adopted on a notional basis in connection with certain schemes for profit-sharing among employees as a means of calculating the legitimate interest of investors as a prior charge on profits (see Chapter 13). The net effect is to emphasize the limited contribution of shareholders in established companies and to equate the status of share and loan capital, though further entitlement to a share of profits over and above the required minimum charge would not be excluded. But any such suggestion assumes the acceptance of a fundamental revision of the conventional conception of capitalism which is best discussed in relation to the rights of employees. Until a fundamental change in this respect is accepted, the only pressures to maintain a regular minimum dividend are likely to be those applied on an informal basis through the market and the financial press.

Formal provisions to assist investors in monitoring the performance of management within the existing framework are more likely to be acceptable. The shortcoming in existing procedures for the disclosure of accounts and directors' reports on a periodic basis

[28] See, for example, A. Rubner, *The Ensnared Shareholder* (1966).

is that both are effectively under the control of management, subject only to the requirements of the company's auditor in respect of accuracy and completeness. Management may thus present to shareholders its own explanations of the company's performance which shareholders are not always in a position to verify. To counteract this the idea has been launched that shareholders as such should be given the right to initiate what is termed a management audit to provide a wholly independent report on the performance of the company's management. A Bill to this effect was presented in Parliament in 1969 under which the shareholders of a quoted company would have been permitted to establish a shareholders' committee with power to require management to co-operate in a management audit to be carried out at the expense of the company; the report would then be distributed to all shareholders, subject only to a power of veto by management on the publication of any confidential commercial information.[29] The latest version of the Bill follows American practice in proposing that quoted companies should be required to appoint a minimum of three non-executive directors and an audit committee to review internal reports and accounts and make independent reports to shareholders.[30] These proposals have attracted some interest as a means of increasing the power of investors to exercise genuine control over the efficiency of management and so over the policies of the company. In practice any such system would be likely to be operated largely by institutional investors who would be able to supply active and skilled manpower for shareholders' committees. But that would not in any way reduce the general benefit to ordinary shareholders. It does not seem unduly rash to predict that some provision along these lines will eventually be adopted, whether in conjunction with an acceptance of the principle of a supervisory board, or merely through a formal shareholders' committee. The concept of management audit is in effect a logical extension of the principle of disclosure, in giving investors a fuller and more searching picture of the state of their company's affairs than is possible on the current system of reports and accounts.

Institutions as investors

The most important practical development in this sphere may not lie in the creation of new rights and remedies based on the ideal of

[29] Companies Bill 1969.

[30] Companies (Non-executive Directors and Audit Committee) Bill 1976.

investor democracy, but in the formal recognition of the growing importance of investment institutions as a means by which the interests of investors may be protected from managerial self-interest. The figures on the ownership of quoted shares show very clearly the importance of the investment institutions on the market. Their holdings of quoted ordinary shares as set out in Table 2.11 (see p. 66) amounted to more than one-third of the total value of such shares in 1963, and if holdings of fixed interest preference shares and debenture stock were included, the proportion would be higher still. There is no reason to believe that this trend will not continue.

The importance of this trend in the pattern of share-ownership in quoted commercial and industrial companies is the fact that the institutions are increasingly in a position to dominate the general meeting of shareholders. In contrast to the position of most individual shareholders there is little practical difficulty for institutions in actually exercising this power. Each maintains a staff of skilled investment analysts who are fully competent to take on the management of any company on their own terms, and who are in a position to attend company meetings as part of their paid employment. The gradual withdrawal of the small individual investor from direct participation in large companies and the corresponding increase in the practice of leaving investment management to the professionals in investment companies and unit trusts has in this way increased the power of investors to influence the conduct of company management.

In practical terms, however, the influence of the investment institutions is rarely observable at company meetings. It is more usual for substantial institutional investors in a company to maintain a direct line of contact with management through personal visits and discussions. Where a number of institutional investors are involved, a meeting of their representatives may be arranged in the City at which a common policy will be worked out.[31] Attempts to formalize institutional action of this kind, however, have met with little success. Any concerted policy is usually restricted to a single type of institution through its City association and to situations in which a boardroom or take-over battle has already developed. Direct pressure on management is more likely to be applied in an informal manner by a single institution. If there is doubt about the

[31] R. Spiegelberg (ed.), *The City* (1973), Ch. 2.

competence of an individual director or board, an institution with a substantial shareholding may put pressure on the company to bring in management consultants or to undertake a boardroom shake-out. The conduct of specific development projects may also be affected by the conditions which investment institutions may impose in exchange for the funding of new issues of loan or preference capital. In some cases the institution may insist on the appointment of a representative to the board of directors with a view to maintaining a more effective continuing oversight of the conduct of the company's affairs.

These developments create new problems, in particular the risk of the misuse of confidential information obtained by investment institutions in the course of their informal contacts with a company (see Chapter 7). They also create an opportunity for the development of a more effective formal structure for the control of management in quoted companies. Any new legislation in the field of management audit or watching committees of shareholders must take account of the fact that it is the investment institutions who will in practice dominate the proceedings. The natural result will be that any control exercised on management is likely to remain firmly within the framework of the capitalist system as it is understood in the City.

Social audit

Those who wish to subject management in large companies to other than purely financial criteria must therefore look to other methods than the development of shareholder democracy. One suggestion which has attracted some attention is the proposal that all large companies should be required to produce or submit to a social audit in which their performance on matters of public concern, such as safety and anti-pollution measures, should also be subject to independent scrutiny. The possibility of bringing such matters into the framework of existing disclosure requirements has been raised by the accountancy profession and in an official discussion paper.[32] The drawback to this approach is that if such reports are prepared by the company itself they are unlikely to provide the kind of information which is intended. Many large companies already include such

[32] Institute of Chartered Accountants, *The Corporate Report* (1975); Department of Trade, *Aims and Scope of Company Reports* (consultative document) (1976).

anodyne statements as the following in their annual directors' reports: 'Attention continued to be given throughout the year to improving the effectiveness and safety of industrial explosives at all stages from manufacture to final use.'[33] If a social report is to achieve any real improvement in the content of company reports on matters of general public interest, it would have to be compiled on the basis of an independent enquiry either by a social audit committee within the framework of the general meeting or else by a professional social auditor. One model for such reports has been provided by some independently financed pressure groups which have published 'alternative' company reports for selected companies. But there is as yet no clear and workable proposal as to the coverage and criteria for independent social audit of a kind which could be made obligatory for all large companies.

[33] *I.C.I. Annual Report*, 1975.

7 The quoted company and public dealing: administrative controls

The power to order official inspections of registered companies as a necessary addition to formal disclosure requirements was built into the Companies Acts as early as 1862. This was a natural development from the existing practice under which the power to appoint an ad hoc parliamentary or governmental inquiry to look into allegations about the conduct of a company's affairs was assumed to follow from the fact that it was Parliament or the government which had granted the right of incorporation. But the powers of official inspection under the initial Companies Acts do not appear to have been used. The main focus of attention throughout the nineteenth century was on the extent of the disclosure requirements and on the pursuit of legal remedies through the courts in the event of any breach of duty.

The first practical move towards administrative control was in 1890 when an official system was established under which the circumstances of any failure by a registered company were to be investigated by the Official Receiver. This was backed up by an express provision for a report to be made in suitable cases to the newly created office of the Director of Public Prosecutions, so that for the first time there would be a real prospect that criminal proceedings would actually be brought against fraudulent promoters and directors who sought to take advantage of the repeated cycle of booms and slumps. This was a substantial improvement on the pre-existing situation under which legal proceedings, both civil and criminal, were wholly dependent on action by individual shareholders who were unlikely to want to commit further resources in addition to the money they had already lost merely for the satisfaction of seeing offenders brought to justice. A series of major trials and convictions followed at the turn of the century. But it was not until the crash of 1928–9 that it became generally accepted that something more than the deterrent effect of civil and criminal liability was necessary if the investing public was to be effectively protected. It was only at that late stage that the Stock Exchange authorities finally accepted the responsibility not merely to see to it that the relevant requirements in respect of prospectuses and other issue documents were formally observed, but to prevent the flotation of unsound ventures and to curtail the activities of promoters whose past record was suspect.

The vetting of new issues and quotations on the stock market was not in itself sufficient. During the 1920s the practice of share pushing by circular and even by house-to-house salesmanship spread to Britain from America. At the same time investment through unit trusts and other similar organizations operating separately from the ordinary stock market took on a new lease of life (see Chapter 10). Control over these new outlets for speculation and the malpractice which went with them could not be exercised by the Stock Exchange authorities. A second line of administrative control over non-market dealings in securities and the operations of unit trusts was accordingly developed. This was entrusted to the Board of Trade, which had already been given similar supervisory powers over savings banks, insurance companies and other institutions catering for small investors. As an indirect result of these developments, the existing 'police' powers of the Board to appoint inspectors and to initiate both civil and criminal proceedings were resurrected and extended. Specialist units of the ordinary police forces were created to investigate suspected criminal offences under the new legislation. In London these units were reorganized in 1946 as the City of London and Metropolitan Police Fraud Squad, which now undertakes all major investigations of company frauds, whether in connection with quoted companies and share pushing or with small business credit frauds. Similar specialist police units have also been developed in other major commercial centres in the provinces.

The development of this network of administrative controls and powers of intervention has been a piecemeal and continuing process. Substantial new powers of intervention have been introduced in the last decade, and a start was made on the policing of the take-over and merger market by the creation of the City Code and Panel on

Take-overs and Mergers in 1968 (see Chapter 8). But it is convenient for the purposes of analysis to regard the various developments as part of an overall strategy with three main objectives: first, to channel as many dealings in securities as possible through the authorized stock exchanges and to impose rigorous controls on any remaining extra-market operations; secondly, to exercise stringent discretionary controls through the stock market authorities over the admission of securities to quotation and over all dealings on the market; and finally, to create sufficient powers of official investigation and intervention to deal quickly with any cases in which there is reason to suspect impropriety in the conduct of a company's affairs or a serious risk of failure. These three aspects of the system will be dealt with in turn.

I THE CONTROL OF NON-MARKET DEALINGS

The first attempt to control non-market dealings by a specific prohibition against the house-to-house touting of shares was not a success.[1] In its place the Bodkin Committee on Share Pushing recommended a system based on the absolute prohibition of any form of public dealing and of the distribution of circulars by any person not authorized to do so. Those who worked through the normal market channels were to be granted automatic authorization, while other applicants would be considered individually.[2] The net result was to grant to the authorities wide discretionary powers to exclude any person from operating in this sphere.

The formal details of this system were introduced in 1939 and are now controlled under the Prevention of Fraud (Investments) Act 1958. There are two entirely separate schemes of authorization. In so far as share dealing is concerned it is a criminal offence to carry on or purport to carry on the business of dealing in securities except under licence (s. 1). Formal exemption is then granted to the members of any recognized stock exchange or association of dealers, and to building societies, unit trusts and other similar institutions (s. 2). In addition any individual or firm may apply for an individual licence on deposit of a guarantee of £500 (s. 3). But this may be refused or revoked by the authorities if it appears that the applicant or holder is not a fit and proper person through having been con-

[1] Companies Act 1929, s. 356.

[2] Cmd. 5539 (1937).

victed of any offence involving fraud or dishonesty or a breach of the law relating to sharedealings, or more generally 'by reason of any other circumstances whatsoever which either are likely to lead to the improper conduct of business by or reflect discredit upon the method of conducting business of the applicant or holder' (s. 5). Though provision is made for formal representations in the event of the refusal or revocation of a licence, it is clear that the final decision is entirely a matter for the judgement of the authorities. Provision is also made for the making of regulations to govern the activities of licensed dealers.

The scheme of the legislation in respect of investment circulars is virtually identical, but the exemption provisions are somewhat wider. It is a criminal offence to distribute or to have for distribution any circulars or other documents which contain a direct or indirect invitation to buy securities or any other form of share giving the holder a right to participate in the profits from the management of property (s. 14). This broad definition, which is the same as that for the purposes of the offence of issuing false or misleading prospectuses (see above p. 306), is designed to catch not only the touting of shares in ordinary companies but also such forms of 'investment' as the buying of shares in land or livestock or vending machines or any other enterprise from which attractive profits may be promised to the investor. The object is to help protect the ever gullible small investor from his incurable desire to participate in schemes which in many cases are no more than a front under which the promoters are enabled to collect cash from the public. The only schemes which are not covered by the definition are those in which the 'investor' is induced to deposit money with the operators to gamble with on his behalf.[3] This somewhat surprising exemption was intentional. When the wording of the relevant provisions was altered in 1962 to cover the latest fashion in property management schemes,[4] gambling schemes were excluded on the ground that they fell outside the range of investment proper. It is hard to justify this somewhat technical distinction.

The express exemptions from this general prohibition cover the distribution of any prospectus fulfilling the requirements of the

[3] See *Hughes v. Trapnell* [1963] 1 Q.B. 737, in which it was held that 'the management of property other than securities' could not cover the application of the investor's own property in the betting schemes.

[4] Protection of Depositors Act 1963, s. 21.

Companies Acts, and any other documents or invitations to invest issued by members of a recognized stock exchange, by a company to its existing shareholders or creditors, or by unit trusts and other similar investment institutions (ss. 14–15). In addition there is a general category of exempted dealers who may be exempted both from this prohibition and from that on dealing on the condition that dealing in securities is not the major part of their business, that the major part of their dealing is with members of a recognized stock exchange or dealers association, licensed dealers, unit trusts or other exempted dealers, and that any circulars issued by them relate only to quoted shares (s. 16). The object of this additional exemption, which is available as of right, is to protect issuing houses and other financial institutions whose ordinary business involves such operations and which do not embark on soliciting subscriptions for unquoted companies or other enterprises.

Despite the formal complexity of these provisions, the system as a whole appears to have worked well in restricting if not entirely eliminating the evils of share pushing. It has been sporadically attacked on the ground that an effectively unlimited administrative discretion to exclude individuals from operating in this sphere is unacceptable in a free market economy. But the argument that continuing discretionary control of this kind, in contrast to the faint chance of bringing civil or criminal proceedings after a fraud has been completed, is the only means of affording some protection to the investing public has always prevailed.

2 CONTROL OVER QUOTATIONS

The necessary counterpart to the policy of channelling all possible dealings through the recognized stock exchanges is stringent control over the admission of companies to quotation. The requirements of the Stock Exchange in relation to disclosure both in prospectuses and on a continuing basis have regularly been more demanding than those in the Companies Acts (see Chapter 6). Companies applying for a quotation must also comply with the standard requirements as to the type and number of shares which will be available to the investing public: at least thirty-five per cent of the voting shares in any quoted company must be in the hands of the public, and the company's quoted shares must have a minimum expected market value of £500,000, though these limits appear to be liberally applied.[5]

Outward compliance with requirements of this kind is not in itself a sufficient protection for investors, as was obvious from the relatively frequent failures of newly quoted companies floated during the speculative booms of the later nineteenth and early twentieth centuries. In the 1920s the London Stock Exchange authorities began to undertake a much more thorough scrutiny of applications for quotations with a view to excluding all companies over which there is any substantial doubt as to the bona fides of the promoters or the soundness of the enterprise. The separate right of provincial exchanges to grant their own quotations, sometimes after less searching investigations, was controlled by the federation of all existing stock exchanges in the British Isles in 1966, and finally phased out on their amalgamation in 1971 in the Stock Exchange, which controls all British and Irish quotations.

There is no statutory basis for this scrutiny. The Stock Exchange is a voluntary association of brokers and jobbers who may deal together on whatever basis they choose. Admissions to quotation are thus a matter for the discretion of the Quotations Committee of the Council of the Stock Exchange, subject only to the power of the Bank of England to control the timing of new capital issues involving more than a million pounds so that a fairly regular flow of new issues is maintained in the interests of stability.[6] In practice the routine work of scrutinizing the application documents for all new quotations is carried out by the Quotations Department of the Stock Exchange in London. The Department attempts to establish the general validity of the claims made in the various documents through independent sources, though without in any way seeking to guarantee the accuracy of the prospectus or the soundness of the company. In addition a check will be made to ensure that there is no connection between the new applicant company and any of those individuals or companies which appear on the Department's files to have been involved in impropriety or malpractice in the past. Clearance of any application or conversely any recommended rejection by the Department will then be accepted in almost every case by the Quotations Committee.

The Stock Exchange also undertakes a similar scrutiny of the formal disclosure documents and accounts of all listed companies,

[5] *Admission of Securities to Listing* (1976 version).

[6] Control of Borrowing Order 1958.

a copy of each of which must be deposited with the Quotations Department. Compliance with the various current requirements both in form and in substance is secured through the unfettered power of the Council, or of the officers or any two members of the Quotations Committee, to suspend or cancel the grant of a quotation (Rule 159(7)). Any dealing in the shares of the company concerned is then formally prohibited (Rule 165). The power to suspend or cancel a quotation may also be exercised in any situation where it is impossible for any reason for the market to place a realistic value on the shares of a company. Thus a company's quotation will normally be suspended if it declares that it is unable to meet its obligations, as in the case of Rolls Royce in 1971, or where doubts have been cast on the accuracy of a company's accounts, as in the case of Pergamon Press whose quotation was suspended following on a dispute about the validity of published accounts arising out of the Pergamon/Leasco merger negotiations in 1969–70. Where possible, dealings will be resumed as soon as sufficient information is available on the true financial state of the company to allow a reasonable estimate of the value of its shares to be made. The authorities also have power to suspend a quotation on the ground that a false market has been engineered, as will be seen below.

There can be little doubt that this system of discretionary control has proved more successful than the simple disclosure system which preceded it. The number of patently reckless or unsound flotations which have escaped the net since the 1930s is relatively small. This does not mean that there have not been cases in which investors have suffered as a result of impropriety by company promoters and directors. But the losses which have occurred have usually resulted from incompetent or fraudulent management of the company's trading operations rather than from the unloading on to the market of inherently unsound enterprises, as was so often the case in earlier decades. The most frequent abuses in recent years have stemmed more from the failure to withdraw quotations from dormant or semi-dormant companies which have passed into the control of unscrupulous operators, or from take-over and merger schemes, than from any deficiency in the control of new issues.

3 THE CONTROL OF MARKET DEALINGS

The sale and transfer of shares does not of itself cause many problems.[7] The basic rules are a mixture of ordinary contractual principles and of the established customs and practices of the Stock Exchange:

The plaintiff gave instructions to his broker to acquire put options in a certain company. The company was taken over before the options expired and the Council of the Stock Exchange made a ruling as to the value of the shares for option purposes. The plaintiff sought to exercise his option on an ex-bid basis but his broker refused to do so except in accordance with the Council's ruling. It was held that the option contracts were made subject to the rules and customs of the Stock Exchange which the ruling of the Council accurately reflected. *Cunliffe-Owen v. Teather & Greenwood* [1967] 1 W.L.R. 1421

This applies also to the more sophisticated transactions which the market provides for, such as option dealings in which the parties contract for a future transfer of shares at the option of the 'buyer' at a price which takes into account the parties' expectations as to future price movements, and the equally speculative technique of 'selling short' in which the 'seller' sells shares which he does not possess with a view to buying in a sufficient number to meet his obligations before the end of the account. In practice any disputes which arise will usually be settled through the internal agency of the Stock Exchange Council and its committees. The reliance of stockbrokers and jobbers on their own informal rules and sanctions as opposed to those of the law goes far to nullify the effect of legislative intervention. The provisions of Leeman's Act 1867, for instance, which was introduced to curb speculative dealings in banking shares by requiring that all transactions should be in respect of specific numbered shares, are simply ignored. Legislation is only called for when established market practices require some measure of legal backing to bind third parties, as for instance in the case of the Stock Exchange (Completion of Bargains) Act 1976, which exempts certain stock exchange transactions from the requirements of the Companies Acts in respect of share certificates and authorizes the maintenance of records of dealings on computers.

There are two aspects of market dealing of special importance to the protection of investors which merit some further discussion. First, there is the risk of the creation of what is termed a false market, whether by the manipulation of shares in a new issue or take-over

[7] For an account of the mechanism of the market, see Chapter 2.

situation, or more generally by the use of large scale buying or selling to influence the price of a share. Secondly, there is the related risk that those with 'inside information' on the affairs of a company may seek to use this information for their own personal profit in advance of its public release. In either case the question arises whether those who suffer loss as a result of such operations should be granted a legal remedy in the courts, or whether the practices should be controlled by administrative means.

Market rigging

An attempt to influence the price of a share by means of market transactions is not always reprehensible. The directors of a company may in certain circumstances wish to support the market in the shares of their company to prevent a substantial decline in price which in their honest opinion would be wholly unjustified. But others with less respectable motives may seek to manipulate the movement of prices for their own personal profit by selective dealings or rumour mongering. The incidence of the more blatant forms of this practice has declined considerably since the nineteenth century, when the rigging of the market in newly issued shares was relatively common. The difficulty lies in gauging the extent to which the remedies developed at that time for the most blatant forms of malpractice may be extended to the less serious forms of manipulation which are still used.

It is generally accepted that it is a criminal offence to conspire to affect the price of the shares in any company by false rumours, though there is continuing dispute over the precise basis of the criminality:

A number of people arranged for false reports of the death of Napoleon to reach London. The price of Government securities, of which they had recently made large purchases, rose sharply. Those involved sold out and made a handsome profit. The ring leaders were subsequently indicted and convicted of conspiring to cause a rise in the price of the public funds by false rumours. The conviction was upheld on appeal as a fraud on the public: it was a conspiracy to effect a public mischief by giving a false price to a vendible commodity on the market by means of false rumours. *R. v. de Berenger* (1814) 3 M. & S. 67

This line of reasoning was later extended to cases where the false market was to be created by fictitious purchases, though no actual prosecutions have been recorded:

The promoters of a company and their associates gave instructions to their brokers to purchase shares in the company at a premium in order to induce the public to believe that the shares were sought after. Instead of doing so the brokers transferred some of their own holdings in the company to the promoters and associates. Their suit against the brokers for failing to carry out their instructions was dismissed on the ground that the whole transaction was illegal; the judge added that 'if persons for their own purposes of speculation create an artificial price in the market by transactions which are not real, but are made at a nominal premium merely for the purpose of inducing the public to take shares they are guilty of gross fraud ... which can be brought home to them in a criminal court'. (per Wright J., at p. 727) *Scott v. Brown Doering & McNab* [1892] 2 Q.B. 724

It should follow that any person who suffered loss as a direct result of the criminal conspiracy to rig the market could sue those responsible. But the case-law is confused on the point. It was held that a dealer who sold short on a false expectation that shares had been issued to the public could not recover any loss he made in buying in the shares at a premium.[8] It is unclear whether this decision was based on the narrow ground that the complainant had not established that he had in fact relied on any false statement or implication on the part of the defendants, or on the more general ground that those who deal on the market have no right of action arising out of false statements issued to the market.

Whatever the position in strict law, however, it remains a fact that no successful civil or criminal case has been brought in cases of market rigging since the nineteenth century, despite a number of notorious instances of manipulation and malpractice. In practical terms the only effective control over practices of this kind, as in the case of most other promotion frauds, is that exercised by the Stock Exchange authorities through their overall control over the operations of the market. The Stock Exchange Regulations expressly forbid any member knowingly or without due care to deal in such a manner as to promote or assist in the promotion of a false market, which is defined as follows:

... a market in which a movement of the price of a share is brought about or sought to be brought about by contrived factors, such as the operation of buyers and sellers acting in collaboration with each other, calculated to create a movement of price which is not justified by assets, earnings or prospects. *Rule 73b*

[8] *Salaman v. Warner* (1891) 65 L.T. 132.

The formal sanction against any contravention of this rule lies in the power of the Council to discipline or expel any member in default, as was done in one case in 1964. But the power is more often used on an informal basis as a threat to curb undesirable or suspicious dealings as they become known. The provision in the City Code requiring all parties to a take-over or merger transaction 'to use every endeavour to prevent the creation of a false market' is used in a similar way.[9]

These administrative controls appear to work reasonably well despite the general reluctance of the market authorities to resort to formal disciplinary measures. But they are of no assistance to those who suffer as a result. There might be some advantage in adopting a formal statutory provision, like that in the Canadian Criminal Code prohibiting the use of the facilities of a stock market 'with intent to create a false or misleading appearance of active public trading ... with respect to the market price of a security,'[10] or the regulation of the United States Securities and Exchange Commission against 'any act, practice or course of business which operates as a fraud or deceit upon any person' (Rule 10(b) (5)). The Canadian and SEC codes also contain specific prohibitions against what are termed 'wash sales', that is the prior fixing of share sales and purchases with a view to influencing the market. The adoption of specific measures of this kind in Britain in place of the existing vague common law rules would help to provide a clear standard of conduct for all those dealing on the market, as well as for Stock Exchange members, and to lay the foundation for the development of civil remedies for those who suffer loss from any malpractices. The question of civil liability, however, is best discussed in relation to the more specific problem of insider trading.

Insider trading

Allegations of the misuse of inside information by directors and their associates, in contrast to those of market rigging, are of relatively frequent occurrence, particularly in the context of take-over bids. A survey of price movements in 1967, for instance, showed clearly that there was a general tendency for the price of shares in bid-for companies to rise sharply before the announcement of take-

[9] General Principle 5 (see Chapter 8).

[10] See generally J. P. Williamson, *Securities Regulation in Canada* (1960).

over bids, which is in itself prima facie evidence of 'inside' buying.[11] And there has been a continuing series of cases in which specific allegations of improper conduct by insiders have been made. The question of control over insider trading has consequently been a matter of general concern in recent years.

The law in this respect, however, is even less satisfactory than on market rigging. The decision in *Percival v. Wright* (1902)[12] is taken to exclude the possibility of any civil action by an aggrieved shareholder who has sold shares to a director who knows that their value is likely to increase sharply on the announcement of a take-over bid of which he has prior notice. And there is certainly no general rule at common law that an insider who has prior knowledge of information which is likely to affect the price of shares must compensate an external investor who buys or sells his shares without the benefit of that knowledge. The Jenkins Committee recommended an immediate reform of the law in this respect.[13] The provisions of the Companies Act 1967, however, were restricted to the tightening of the rules for the disclosure of all dealings by directors and their close relatives (1967 : s. 27), and the prohibition of a limited class of option dealings by directors (1967 : s. 25). In the absence of some special relationship between the insider and the aggrieved buyer or seller of the shares in question which is sufficient to create a legal duty to disclose all material facts, the insider is thus legally entitled to retain any profit which he may be able to make from dealing on the basis of his special knowledge.

For all practical purposes then the only current sanctions against insider dealing are those wielded by the Stock Exchange authorities and the Panel under the City Code on Take-overs and Mergers (see Chapter 8). The Code lays down stringent requirements as to the disclosure of any personal interest by directors of both bidding and bid-for companies in offer documents and circulars (Rule 17), and as to the vital importance of absolute secrecy as to any negotiations between the boards of companies before an announcement is made (Rule 7); in addition it imposes a specific ban on insider dealing while negotiations continue :

No dealings of any kind (including option business) in the securities of

[11] *The Economist*, 13 May 1967.
[12] [1902] 2 Ch. 421 (see p. 255).
[13] Cmnd. 1749 (1962), para. 89.

the offeree company by any person, not being the offeror, who is privy to the preliminary take-over or merger discussions or to an intention to make an offer may take place between the time when there is reason to suppose that an approach or an offer is contemplated and the announcement of the approach or offer or the termination of the discussions. No such dealings shall take place in the securities of the offeror except where the proposed offer is not deemed price sensitive in relation to such securities. *Rule 30 (1976 version)*

Where a breach of this rule is alleged or suspected, the Panel will either direct an investigation by the Stock Exchange authorities or undertake an enquiry of its own. Where irregularities are discovered it will take what action it may to enforce the rule :

A director in Norbury Insulation Ltd. instructed his broker to buy shares in Hayeshaw Ltd., for which Norbury was about to make a take-over bid, on behalf of a family trust in which the director was interested. After an investigation by both the Stock Exchange and the Panel, the Panel made a public ruling that both the director and the broker had been in breach of their obligations under the Code and that they had attempted to conceal this fact in the course of the investigations; the case of the broker was referred to the Stock Exchange Council for their consideration; the director, in the light of the Panel's statement doubting his fitness to remain managing director of the company, agreed to submit his resignation to the shareholders; the profits made by the trust were paid over to Norbury Insulation. *Financial Times*, 3 April 1971

In addition the Panel has intervened in a general preventive capacity in an attempt to minimize the danger of leaks of take-over information from the advisers of interested parties. Following allegations of the improper use of confidential information by certain parties for the benefit of independent investment clients during the course of the Pergamon/Leasco battle, the Panel instituted a wide-ranging enquiry into the problems facing merchant banks involved both in advising parties to take-over operations and in maintaining their regular investment advisory service for their clients. The resulting report of the Panel on *The Use of Confidential Price-Sensitive Information* (1970) rejected the idea of legal regulation in matters of this kind, but emphasized strongly that 'inside or confidential information obtained in the corporate advisory capacity was not to be used in the capacity of investment advising, still less in the personal investment of the firm or individuals concerned.' Accordingly the Panel recommended that 'in order to avoid the risks of mistake or abuse the two functions should as far as practicable be physically segregated in different departments and be the concern of separate executives', and drew up a list of specific principles to guide the activities of merchant banks in this field.

Notwithstanding the successful outcome of the Panel's intervention in the *Norbury* case, however, and its general approval of the practice of merchant banks, there have been continuing doubts on the adequacy of the existing controls. The Panel itself has admitted that its enquiries into specific cases have occasionally proved inconclusive. Even where it does succeed in tracing those responsible for an abuse, in the absence of any legal backing for the rules it seeks to uphold, it may not always be in a position to enforce a ruling on those who are not directly dependent on the favour of any of the City institutions. This could be of special importance in respect of the reimbursement of profits improperly made by independent directors or associates. The Panel has recently retracted the view it expressed in 1970 that the disciplines of professional discredit, expulsion and public reprobation were more effective than formal legal regulation, and has called for a criminal sanction to be imposed on insider dealings.[14] A provision to prohibit dealings by any person associated with a company who is in possession of information which is likely to affect share prices but is not generally available was included in the Companies Bill 1973 (cls. 12–15), but has not yet been reintroduced.

Pending final resolution of this issue it may be helpful to consider the experience in the United States of civil liability for insider trading. There are two broad heads under which the liability of insiders to those who deal with them has been developed: first, the 'special circumstances' doctrine by which the rule in *Percival v. Wright* has been outflanked (see p. 256); and, secondly, the action for breach of statutory duty founded on the SEC regulations governing market dealings.[15] In respect of quoted companies the second of these, until recently at least, has been the more significant.

The Securities Exchange Act 1934 created a new cause of action by which a corporation, or a security holder suing in the corporate name, might recover any profit realized by a director or substantial

[14] Panel on Take-overs and Mergers, Reports for 1969–70 and 1975–6.

[15] This aspect of American law is fully discussed by Professor Loss in 'The Fiduciary Concept as applied to Trading by Corporate "Insiders" in the United States', (1970) 33 *MLR* 34.

shareholder on short-term dealings in his corporation's securities, regardless of any question of the misuse of confidential information (s. 16(b)). This statutory action, in conjunction with the general duty imposed on directors at the same time to disclose their dealings in the corporation's shares (s. 16(a)), has proved generally successful in curtailing speculation of this kind. But liability under this provision extends only to officers and major shareholders, and to purchases or sales undertaken within six months of each other. Liability for the misuse of confidential information in itself is based on the breach of regulations issued by the SEC under s. 10(b) of the same statute, which in broad terms prohibit the use of any fraudulent device or course of business which would operate as a fraud or deceit on any person, or the issue of any false statement, or the concealment of any material fact in connection with the sale or purchase of any security. Any person who deals directly with an insider who fails to reveal all relevant information in his possession may thus recover any loss which he suffers as a result. But liability under this head has been progressively developed and seems now to extend not only to insiders and their associates, who have themselves engaged in improper dealings, but to those who have merely misstated material facts without themselves buying or selling any shares :

The Texas Gulf Sulphur Company struck rich mineral deposits in preliminary drilling operations. A number of officials and employees of the company and their associates bought shares and rumours of a major strike became rife. The company then issued a press release discounting the rumours and stating that to issue details of the prospects would be premature and possibly misleading. The SEC took proceedings against the company and its officers and employees seeking an injunction against further violations of Rule 10(b)(5), rescission of all share contracts entered into by insiders, and compensation for those who had sold the shares affected. It was held that the company had been in breach of the Rule in issuing the press release, as had those who had purchased shares or given tips to others. The issue of compensation was deferred, but it was implied that those responsible for making the public statement to investors might be liable to market buyers 'if such assertions are false or misleading or are so incomplete as to mislead irrespective of whether the issuance of the release was motivated by corporate officials for ulterior purposes'. *SEC v. Texas Gulf Sulphur Co.* (1968) 401 F. 2d. 833

The full extent of this doctrine is still a matter of dispute. The Supreme Court in the United States has held that some form of wilful intent is required to establish a cause of action in damages, and also that any plaintiff must actually have bought or sold shares before asserting any claim.[16] But there is little doubt that the possibility of personal liability, whether to compensate external investors who suffer direct loss or to reimburse any improper profit, is a real deterrent both to insider trading and to any attempt to influence the market by misleading public statements.

The older head of liability at common law under the special circumstances doctrine has also been extended to cover market transactions:

> The directors of a management consultancy firm sold a large number of shares in their company in the knowledge that the profits of the firm had slumped drastically. When the results were finally released the price of the shares fell from around $28 at which the directors had sold their holdings to around $11. A number of those who had purchased shares instituted a derivative action against the directors in the name of the company to compel them to account for their profits. The suit was dismissed at first instance, but upheld on appeal: 'corporate officers and directors who trade on undisclosed inside information violate their fiduciary duty to the corporation . . . and may be held accountable to the corporation for their personal gain'. *Diamond v. Oreamuno* (1969) 24 N.Y. 2d. 494

Here too the full extent of the potential liability is still unclear, and the primary liability is to the company rather than to individual investors. But the development is a further deterrent to any form of insider trading.[17]

The net effect of these developments is to discourage any person with inside information of any kind from speculating or intervening in the market in any way, at least until full disclosure has been made. Dealings by company directors would thus be increasingly restricted to periods immediately after the release of company statements, a restriction which is becoming generally accepted in America.[18] It amounts in effect to little more than a generalization of the rules already written into the City Code in respect of dealings in take-over

[16] See *Ernst & Ernst v. Hochfelder* (1976) 96 S. Ct. 1375 and *Blue Chip Stamps v. Manor Drug Stores* (1975) 421 U.S. 723, noted in (1976) 41 *Missouri Law Review*, 296.

[17] The case is noted and discussed in 83 *Harvard Law Review*, 1421. The supreme court of Florida refused to follow the New York precedent in *Schein v. Chasen* 313 So. 2d 739 (1975); see the note in (1975) *University of Florida Law Review*, 223.

[18] R. H. Mundheim, 'The Texas Gulf Sulphur Complaint', (1966) *Journal of Business Law*, 284; see also above p. 257.

situations. But some form of legal liability along American lines would seem to be a necessary condition if any similar rule is to become accepted in Britain. A committee of Justice has recommended that all insider dealing on stock exchanges should be a criminal offence, but that in view of the difficulty of establishing and identifying loss in such cases civil liability for non-disclosure should be restricted to non-market dealings.[19] If the active enforcement of the prohibition can be guaranteed, this is probably the most satisfactory solution.

4 OFFICIAL INTERVENTION

There is a good deal of overlap in the functions of the various agencies of official intervention in the affairs of quoted companies. Inspections by the Department of Trade often duplicate investigations by the Official Receiver and the police. This explains many of the problems of delay and seeming bureaucratic inertia which have frequently been experienced and criticized in individual cases. But for the purposes of explanation the provisions for inspection, investigation and liquidation are best seen as integral parts of a unified system for official supervision and control extending from the power of intervention in going concerns by the appointment of inspectors, to the procedures for dealing with companies which have already gone into liquidation, and for securing that offenders are duly brought before the courts on the relevant civil or criminal charges.

Company inspections

The powers of the Department of Trade to appoint inspectors to look into the affairs of registered companies were created long before the development of active supervision over quoted companies by the Stock Exchange authorities. But they were very rarely exercised in the period before 1945, whether from a commitment to the ideals of laissez faire capitalism or from an absence of any clearly defined responsibility within the Board of Trade, as it then was, for the oversight of the market. The first reported case of an inspection was in 1896,[20] and the published figures for the early twentieth century show that there were only three inspections in the period

[19] Report on Insider Trading (1972).

[20] *Re The Grosvenor and West-end Railway Terminus Hotel Co.* (1897) 76 L.T. 337.

from 1909 to 1925, and nine between 1930 and 1944. The criticisms of the Cohen and Jenkins Committees,[21] however, induced the Board to adopt a somewhat more positive approach to the exercise of its powers. The number of inspections made increased from three or four per year in the 1950s to around twenty per year. And after 1967 a corps of inspecting officers was established on a full time basis to undertake the more routine inspections which would not merit the appointment of eminent professional lawyers and accountants, as had previously been the accepted practice. Much of the increase, however, as the figures in the accompanying table show, was attributable to appointments in respect of private and unquoted

TABLE 7.1

The use of powers of preliminary inquiry and of inspection, 1958–75

	Applications	Initial inquiry (s.109)	Appointment of inspectors s.164	s.165 (a)	s.165 (b)	s.172	Public cos.	Private cos.
1958	64	–	2	–	1	–	1	2
1959	67	–	2	–	1	–	1	2
1960	72	–	–	–	14	–	13	1
1961	81	–	–	–	5	–	3	2
1962	88	–	1	–	10	–	3	8
1963	90	–	–	5	2	–	2	5
1964	121	–	–	2	12	–	7	7
1965	146	–	–	2	2	–	3	1
1966	150	–	1	–	13	–	3	11
1967	240	27	–	–	18	–	12	6
1968	338	47	1	1	14	–	–	16
1969	390	62	–	–	26	–	3	23
1970	400	61	–	–	15	–	3	12
1971	432	103	–	24		–	n.a.	n.a.
1972	403	110	–	6		–	n.a.	n.a.
1973	408	81	1	9		1	n.a.	n.a.
1974	438	130	1	25		2	7	20
1975	456	150	3	16		2	9	10

Source: *Parliamentary Answer, 26 July 1971; Department of Trade Reports on Companies*

[21] Cmnd. 6659 (1945) paras. 154 ff; Cmnd. 1749 (1962), paras. 213 ff.

companies. More recently there has been an equally rapid growth in the use of the power to call for documents and a levelling off in the use of full inspections.

The formal provisions governing the appointment of inspectors are the same for quoted companies as for private and unquoted companies. The Department of Trade may be required to make an appointment by order of the court or on the vote of the company in general meeting (1948 : s. 165(a)). For practical purposes, as shown in Table 7.1, the important procedures are those under which the Department may make a discretionary appointment, either of its own motion or on the application of a shareholder. The two broad grounds upon which the Department may act are, first, that the affairs of the company appear to have been conducted fraudulently or oppressively or that the directors appear to have been guilty of any misfeasance, and, secondly, that the shareholders have not been given all the information which they might reasonably expect (1948 : s. 165(b)). No such grounds are specified under the alternative procedure which provides for an appointment at the discretion of the Department on the application of 200 shareholders or the holders of one-tenth of the shares (1948 : s. 164), but the Department appears to regard this as governed by the same general principles. In addition there is provision for the appointment of an inspector with the sole object of reporting on the effective ownership and control of the company where that has been masked by means of nominee holdings or otherwise (1948 : s. 172), or on sharedealings by directors and others (1967 : s. 32).

The Department has in general adopted a cautious approach to the exercise of its powers under these sections. In its evidence to the Jenkins Committee it took the view that the basic function of an inspector was to ascertain and report on the facts rather than to act as an agent of law enforcement.[22] But the neutral position of arbiter between the parties which the Board has adopted as described in respect of unquoted companies (see p. 283), has largely nullified the utility of the inspection procedure as a means of securing further information for shareholders and others who suspect but cannot establish that something important is being concealed from them. The position was aptly stated by Professor Gower in the course of oral evidence taken by the Jenkins Committee from the Department:

[22] Minutes of Evidence, p. 1572.

> The attitude seems to be that if one makes out a prima facie case of oppression then you say. 'We are not going to appoint an inspector because you already know the facts'. On the other hand if you do not make out a prima facie case you say, 'You have made out no prima facie case and therefore we cannot appoint an inspector'. *Minutes of Evidence*, 1534

Part of the problem used to be the official view that to make an appointment before it was absolutely necessary, especially in the case of a quoted company, might cause irreparable damage to the company and destroy whatever chance there might have been of its weathering the storm of public suspicion if the allegations made against it turned out to be without foundation. This difficulty has been removed by the grant to the Department of new powers of preliminary enquiry, under which it may demand the production of documents and accounts from any company without necessarily proceeding to the appointment of a full inspection (1967 : s. 109). This new power has been widely used, as is shown by the figures in Table 7.1. On a number of occasions the information obtained has led directly to the prosecution of company officers or the presentation of a winding up petition. But the Department maintained its view that a prima facie case of wrong-doing had to be made out, as was made clear in its official report for 1972 :

> As regards the use of investigation powers, the correct legal interpretation ... is that the Department can exercise these powers *only* where there is prima facie evidence of fraud, misfeasance or other wrong-doing. *Companies in 1972*, 3

Though this statement was legally inaccurate in view of the explicit provision for the appointment of inspectors in cases where shareholders have not been given all the information which they might reasonably expect (1948 : s. 165(b)(iii)), and has been withdrawn, the Department remains reluctant to act on the sole ground that shareholders have been denied specific items of information.

The conduct of an inspection

Once appointed, an inspector or pair of inspectors have full powers to require the production of documents and accounts and to summon witnesses, who are then bound to give answers to their questions on pain of committal for contempt of court (1948 : s. 167). On the basis of the evidence thus obtained the inspectors must then prepare a formal report, or interim and final reports, for the Department. In the case of quoted companies these reports will normally be published. Any further action is then a matter for the Department or other authorities. To this extent the inspectors are limited to what has been termed a 'statutory fact-finding capacity'. But it is generally recognized that the report of an inspector cannot in practice be so limited. Where fraud or misconduct are in issue, it is difficult for an inspector to refrain from drawing conclusions on the legality or propriety of the conduct of those responsible for the company's affairs, or on the proceedings which might lie against them. In many cases the report in effect amounts to a preliminary prosecution report. In others there have been general comments and criticisms on individuals. In their report on Pergamon Press, for instance, the inspectors stated of the principal director that 'despite his acknowledged abilities and energy, he was not in the inspectors' opinion a person who could be relied on to exercise a proper stewardship of a publicly quoted company.'[23]

Public allegations and condemnations of this kind, which have been made with increasing frequency in recent reports, have led to complaints of unfairness and 'Star Chamber' procedures on the ground that those criticized have not been properly informed of the 'charges' against them or given a proper opportunity to answer them. The courts have ruled that inspectors must act fairly to all such persons, notwithstanding the administrative rather than judicial nature of their function:

Following the breakdown of take-over negotiations on the grounds that the bid-for company had not fully disclosed the true state of its finances, the Department appointed inspectors to inquire into the affairs of the company and certain of its subsidiaries. The principal director and his colleagues, with a view to protecting their interests in foreign proceedings instituted by the bidding company, sought assurances from the inspectors that their inquiries would be conducted in accordance with the rules of natural justice and in particular that the directors would be given access to a full transcript of any evidence and documents hostile to them and the right to cross examine the witnesses concerned. The Inspectors refused to give these assurances and took proceedings to require the directors to attend and answer questions put to them. The Court of Appeal held that the inspectors as a fact finding body were not acting in a quasi-judicial capacity and so were not subject to the rules applicable to a judicial inquiry; they

[23] Department of Trade and Industry, *Interim Report on Pergamon Press Ltd.* (1971), para. 343.

were masters of their own procedure, but since their report might well contain findings damaging to those named in it, they were bound to act fairly by giving any person a chance to correct or contradict what had been said against him before condemning or criticising him. As this was what the inspectors proposed there was no ground for complaint against them. *In re Pergamon Press Ltd.* [1971] Ch. 388 (CA)

In further proceedings on essentially the same issue after the publication of a series of reports critical of the directors of Pergamon Press the Court of Appeal reaffirmed that an inspection should not be regarded as a trial in which accused persons had a right to be informed of and to answer specific charges, but as a private inquiry as a result of which the inspectors must report their findings on the evidence and their opinions on matters referred to them; provided they acted fairly in putting to any person concerned the points at issue and gave him an opportunity of answering them, they need not put their tentative conclusions to each witness before publishing them. *Maxwell v. Department of Trade and Industry* [1974] Q.B. 523

In addition leading City representatives have argued that the terms of reference for inspectors should be much more precisely defined in order to tie inspectors down to findings on specific issues rather than general assessments on companies and their directors.[24]

The Department has rejected the need for any major change in inspection procedures in the light of these criticisms. But the uncertainty as to the precise role of inspectors remains. In some cases the main objective of an appointment appears to be to restore public confidence after a major crash or scandal, and the inspection is conducted in conjunction with an Official Receiver's or Fraud Squad investigations. In other cases the inspector is expected to give what amounts to a legal opinion on the propriety of a particular course of conduct, as in the *Savoy Hotel* case in which the inspector concluded that a scheme to dispose of an hotel in order to put it and its employees beyond the control of a take-over bidder who was thought to want to demolish it and redevelop had been devised for reasons which 'however meritorious would not seem ... to form part of a true legal definition of the interests of the companies'.[25] More recently inspections have been ordered at the instigation of the Panel on Take-overs and Mergers to look into allegations arising out

[24] See, for instance, the representations made by the Chairman of the Stock Exchange and the Chairman of the Panel on Take-overs and Mergers in July 1976.

[25] Board of Trade, *Inspector's Report on Savoy Hotel Co.* (1954).

of breaches of the City Code and at the instigation of the Stock Exchange to look into allegations arising out of a breach of a Stock Exchange listing requirement.[26] It is impossible in many such cases for an inspector to report on the facts without at the same time turning his attention to possible breaches of the law. And yet an inspector as such has no formal role in the processes of law enforcement.

Civil and criminal proceedings

The primary duty of instituting any further proceedings which may seem desirable on the basis of an inspection report is now cast on the Department of Trade. The Department may petition for the winding up of the company (1967 : s. 35), for which purpose the inspector's report may be used as prima facie evidence that sufficient grounds for the petition exist, subject to any objections on behalf of the company concerned.[27] It may institute civil proceedings in the name of any company against directors or others to recover any property of the company or damages in respect of any fraud or misfeasance (1967 : s. 37). And where inspectors indicate in a formal report or otherwise that a criminal offence has been committed, the Department may refer the matter to the Director of Public Prosecutions, or institute proceedings on its own account. For the purpose of both civil and criminal proceedings it is expressly provided that answers given by any person to an inspector shall be admissible in evidence in subsequent proceedings (1967 : s. 50).

There are similar provisions in respect of investigations made by an Official Receiver in the course of a compulsory liquidation. His initial duty is to make a report to the court where there is any indication that an offence has been committed (1948 : s. 236), on which the court may order a public examination of any director or other person concerned (1948 : s. 270). The court may then direct that any matter be referred to the Director of Public Prosecutions (1948 : s. 334(1)). It is also the duty of the liquidator in a voluntary winding up to make a report to the Director where it appears that a criminal offence has been committed in relation to the company (1948 : s. 334(2)).

[26] See, for instance, the inspections ordered in the case of *Pergamon Press* (1969) and *Scotia Investments* (1976).

[27] See, for instance, *In re Allied Produce Co. Ltd* [1967] 1 W.L.R. 1469.

These various provisions give something of a false impression both of order and of formality in the official enforcement system. In practice things are a good deal more haphazard. In any case where criminal proceedings are contemplated, the matter will usually be referred immediately to the police Fraud Squad or its provincial equivalents for an independent investigation. This will often take place simultaneously with an inspection or liquidation enquiry. In due course a report will be made by each to the Director of Public Prosecutions or the Department on the basis of which proceedings may be authorized. The shortcoming in enforcement is thus less a matter of unnecessary formality and complexity than of duplication by a multiplicity of agencies whose functions overlap with each other to such an extent that constant contact is necessary between them. This causes special difficulties when a detailed scrutiny of the company's books of account is necessary. Provision has been made to permit inspectors to draw the attention of the authorities to offences which appear to have been committed without making a formal report (1967: s. 41), to avoid the kind of delay which resulted in the *Rolls Razor* case, in which three and a half years passed between the appointment of inspectors and the initiation of criminal proceedings. But the time scale of inspections is still reckoned in years rather than months. This is due in part to the complexity of the issues. It is also due to the fact that eminent non-official inspectors work only part-time, though their fees in 1974 absorbed more than £600,000 of the total of £900,000 spent on inspections. But there is little doubt that the major cause is the overlapping yet separate responsibilities of the various agencies involved.

The Securities and Exchange Commission

It is often suggested that the only satisfactory answer to the problems caused by this fragmentation and duplication is the creation of a single unified enforcement agency along the lines of the United States Securities and Exchange Commission. The SEC, as it is called, was set up in 1934 in the immediate aftermath of the Wall Street crash and ensuing depression as an important part of the 'New Deal' to regulate trade in securities as far as that was possible on a federal basis, given that the registration and control of companies is a matter for state legislatures.

The basis of the SEC's operations is the virtually unlimited rule-making power granted to it under the Securities Act of 1933 and the Securities Exchange Act of 1934. By the progressive formulation of detailed regulations under these and subsequent statutes the SEC has developed a comprehensive system of control over the securities market in respect of any security which is dealt with in more than a single state and thus subject to federal jurisdiction. The level of public disclosure by the companies affected is governed by stringent regulations backed by a comprehensive system for the filing and scrutiny of all documents issued to the public. The operations of brokers and dealers are similarly controlled by licensing and by the scrutiny of all investment circulars. And in 1940 the net was thrown still wider to cover the operations of investment institutions, or mutual funds, through which the funds of ordinary investors are channelled onto the market. More recently the SEC has begun to impinge on the dominating position of the New York Stock Exchange by requiring it to lift its embargo on dealing by members otherwise than through the floor of the exchange.

In all these spheres the SEC, like other regulatory agencies in the United States, has developed wide powers of intervention, whether by the issue of a stop order on any particular transaction which appears to be in breach of an SEC regulation or by the withdrawal of a licence from any broker or dealer. In the case of a new issue, for instance, all the relevant documents must be cleared by the SEC before the issue may proceed. More generally the SEC has powers to conduct any investigation, and to call for any witnesses and documents which appear necessary to the discharge of its functions, either in respect of an individual company or transaction where there is suspicion of impropriety or illegality, or in respect of any wider issue which may arise over the operation of the market, as for instance, insider trading or corporate bribery. Disputes over the exercise of any power by the SEC are dealt with initially by informal negotiation between the parties, for example, over the disclosure requirements affecting documents for issue to the public. Where the matter cannot be settled in this way there is provision for formal semi-judicial hearings at which the parties are entitled to put their case before an independent arbiter, and ultimately for an appeal to the federal courts.[28]

[28] The simplest account of the origin and work of the SEC is that given by its then chief executive, Manuel Cohen in (1960) *Journal of Business Law*, 104. The standard American work on the SEC is Louis Loss, *Securities Regulation*, 3rd edn., 1969.

To perform all these functions the SEC has not unnaturally grown into a vast bureaucracy with a permanent staff of more than 1,000. And there have been increasing complaints over the slowness of its operations, not least from certain laissez-faire economists of the Chicago school who have objected to the SEC's unproductive and time-consuming interference in the self-regulating mechanisms of the market.[29] But the SEC has generally been accepted as a necessary and highly effective organ for investor protection. In particular its power to formulate and enforce its own rules and regulations has allowed it to keep somewhat ahead of British practice in matters of disclosure, and it has played a large part in the development of civil remedies for mis-statement in publicily issued documents, and for insider trading. It has also initiated action on corporate corruption.

An SEC for Britain?

There is a good deal of force in the argument that a flexible and independent agency of this kind with wide powers to create new rules and regulations without the need for formal legislation is essential if the balance of advantage is not to remain with those who seek to avoid the strict regulation of investment activities. A centralized enforcement agency could certainly improve on the existing fragmented British system which relies on the concerted efforts of the Stock Exchange, the City Panel, the Department of Trade and other official agencies.

It does not follow that the SEC should be taken as a model for the reform of the British system. The British securities market, unlike the American, is very highly centralized. It is dominated by the Stock Exchange in London, not only in terms of size and volume of business, but also through the unified procedures for the admission of companies to the market. The cumulative effect of recent legislation in Britain has been to make a Stock Exchange quotation more or less essential to any form of public dealing, whereas in America the SEC has been building up a structure of licensed broker/dealers which is largely independent of the major American stock exchanges. Many of the functions of the SEC in America can thus be effectively carried out in Britain by the Stock Exchange authorities and the City Panel without formal statutory authority. The major drawbacks to this voluntary system, especially in respect of take-over and merger

[29] George Stigler, 'Public Regulation of the Securities Market', (1964) *Journal of Business* 117.

operations and the newer forms of investment bond, are, first, the lack of any effective sanction against those who do not depend for their livelihood on the approved City channels, and, secondly, the inability to create effective legal remedies for those who suffer from fraud, negligence or impropriety. In this context there would be a clear advantage in giving formal legal backing to the internal rules and regulations of the City authorities. This would not in itself necessitate the creation of an SEC. What is required is a much wider power for the government to give statutory support to the existing organs of the City where there is an obvious need for formal as well as informal sanctions, as in the case of insider trading.

There is a stronger case for a more fundamental restructuring of the existing enforcement and investigatory agencies. The functions of the Department of Trade and its inspectors, the Official Receiver, the Director of Public Prosecutions and the Police Fraud Squad in this sphere could all usefully be brought together in a single company law enforcement unit with a degree of independence of action which is currently denied to any single part of the system. Such a unit would be able to maintain a body of skilled and experienced investigators and its own complement of legal and accounting advisers, who under the existing arrangements are not always available at short notice. It could thus move a good deal more quickly in investigating and reporting on individual cases when called upon to do so by individual complainants or by the City authorities. Close co-operation between the investigating and legal departments could also lead to considerable saving in time and manpower where formal proceedings were necessary. The most appropriate model for this is not the SEC but rather the much smaller investigatory and enforcement organization which has been developed around the office of Attorney-General in most Canadian jurisdictions.

The precise form of the structure which is created is a good deal less important than the spirit in which its powers are implemented. The principle of flexibility in regulatory power was clearly accepted by the Cohen Committee as necessary to the effective control of impropriety in the new issue market, though a clear distinction was drawn between the essentially voluntary nature of this power and the necessarily inflexible nature of formal legal controls.[30] The key to the effective reform of the British system is the acceptance of the

[30] Cmnd. 6659 (1945), para. 24.

principle of flexibility linked with formal statutory backing. Legislation in this sphere, however, is as likely to be determined by the wider political issue of state control as opposed to free market capitalism than the practical efficacy of the resulting structure. Further developments must await the conclusions of the Wilson Committee established in 1977 to report on the role and functions of financial institutions in the UK and their value to the economy; the Committee is explicitly required to consider what changes are required in the existing arrangements for the supervision of these institutions, including the possible extension of the public sector.

8

Take-overs and mergers

Criticism and concern over the working of the stock market system has been transferred in recent years from the question of new issues and quotations to that of take-overs and mergers.[1] The main focus of discontent has been the fact that in many take-over bids and battles the interests of the ordinary investor appear to have been subordinated to those of controlling shareholders and directors, either through the inadequacy of the disclosure system as applied to take-over bids, or because of the inequality of the terms offered to various classes of shareholders. The only law which prevailed was that of the jungle. In 1968 the first City Code on Take-overs and Mergers restored some semblance of order and equity to the take-over market. Since then the terms of the Code and the ability of the City Panel to enforce it have been progressively strengthened. But there has also been continuing criticism of the voluntary and informal nature of the Code and the absence of legal sanctions.

I THE CAUSES AND TYPES OF TAKE-OVERS

Before discussing the details of the legal and administrative controls which have been developed it is important to correct some of the misapprehensions which this type of approach to the question of take-overs may encourage. In the first place there is nothing inherently undesirable in the absorption of one company by another. In economic terms the advantages of size and the economies of scale

[1] On this topic generally see M. A. Weinberg, *Take-overs and Mergers*, 3rd edn. (1971), and Paul Davies, *The Regulation of Take-overs and Mergers* (1976).

must be set off against the disadvantages which growth for the sake of growth, or empire building by individual company executives may bring in their train (see Chapter 2). But within a capitalist framework the transfer of productive assets from the ownership of shareholders in one company to those of another can readily be justified on the grounds that a greater return on the capital employed may be obtained by improved management. The fact that a company is deemed to be ripe for take-over is thus simply an indication that there is some deficiency in the existing management policies so that the market price of the controlling shares in the company has sunk below the potential value of the assets it owns. Two basic causes for this 'disparity between market price and true value, which is the take-over bidder's opportunity', have been isolated in *Standard Boardroom Practice*:

> The first is that the directors have failed to utilize the assets of the business, whether in cash, securities or property, to the best advantage. It may be that the directors have failed to realize that in a period of rapid inflation properties have reached an intrinsic value greater than their value merely as working assets in the business and have failed, whether by way of sale and lease back or some other method, to take advantage of the situation for the benefit of the company. It may be that the directors have failed to make adequate dividend distributions with the result that reserve funds are built up in excess of the requirements of the business and have not been put to full use. The other main cause of a disparity between the market price and true value is the absence of proper and full information, whether as to profits and reserves or as to asset values. If these are properly made known the market is quick to adjust values accordingly. There have been cases where directors have tried to ward off a take-over bid by increasing dividends, by hiving off properties or by capitalizing reserves. These steps are usually indications that in the past one or other of the above mentioned defects in the directors' policy have taken place.[2]

These are not the only circumstances in which a take-over may materialize. A prosperous and well-managed small company may be sufficiently attractive to a larger group for the group to offer more than the true value of its shares in order to secure control of its business or even to tap the skill of its managers. Other small companies are forced into take-overs by the pressure of tax liability (see Chapter 5). Some of the larger mergers and amalgamations of leading companies have been initiated or pressed through by govern-

[2] Institute of Directors, 3rd edn. (1968) p. 43.

mental pressure, in order to secure a more integrated and ideally more competitive unit of production in the face of foreign competition, or allow a more rational policy of government development aid in the more advanced technological industries. In a typical take-over situation, however, there is likely to be some genuine weakness in management or financing in the bid-for company.

Non-market bids

It is also important to remember that the vast majority of take-overs are amicably negotiated with the full consent of all the parties. The most frequent form of take-over is that in which a quoted company absorbs an unquoted company (see Table 2.8). In such cases the agreement of the controllers of the bid-for company must be obtained, since there is no other way of forcing a sale. But there is still a danger of discriminatory treatment of minority holdings in these circumstances, whether by the offer of specially favourable terms to controlling directors, leaving minority shareholders to make the best terms they can, or more simply by the negotiation of a partial take-over of a controlling block of shares. Conversely there may be an element of oppression or impropriety in the action which the directors of a bid-for company may take to entrench themselves against a bidding company. The rules of the City Code are now expressly stated to cover the conduct of non-market bids for all but private companies in the strict legal sense:

> The City Code is drafted with listed public companies particularly in mind. Nevertheless, the spirit of the City Code and, where appropriate, the letter will apply also to take-overs of unlisted public companies. The City Code will not apply, however, to cases where the offeree company is a private company, nor will it normally apply to take-overs of companies which are not resident for exchange control purposes in the United Kingdom. *Introduction, para. 6*[3]

The most important provision in this context is that which requires all the shareholders of the same class to be treated similarly (General Principles 8–9). This means that where a bid is made for an unquoted company it would be a clear breach of the Code for the directors to accept in respect of their own controlling shares without securing

[3] See also *Practice Note No. 1*, as amended in 1976, which excludes offers for companies not resident for exchange control purposes in the United Kingdom other than listed Irish companies. All quotations from the City Code are taken from the revised version of April 1976.

an identical offer for the remainder of the shares. It would also be a breach of the Code for the directors to take any action, for instance by the issue of new shares or the hiving off of property and assets, with a view to frustrating the bid without the approval of a general meeting of shareholders (General Principle 4; Rule 38). The Panel requires the deposit of documents in respect of all bids for unquoted public companies and for any private company where as a result of the bid any person, together with persons acting in concert, will control more than thirty per cent of the voting shares in the bidding company.[4] Earlier editions of the Code stated that the general principles of the Code might also be relevant to transactions in the shares of private companies, as for instance where a private company is taken over by a quoted company, though the Panel did not claim any jurisdiction in such cases. This ruling has now been withdrawn. It is hard to see why the same rules should not be applied to all take-overs by quoted companies given the tenuous distinction in real terms between public and private companies in the strict legal sense. Minority shareholders in private companies may seek to enforce their formal legal remedies against oppression or the misuse of directors' powers, as set out in Chapter 5. But there is no legal principle which forbids the payment of a special premium for a controlling block of shares or the making of a partial bid for control which leaves the minority in possession of its shares in the bid-for company. The Code in this context represents a clear attempt to extend the range of existing legal remedies.

Market bids and offers

There are broadly three ways in which a bid may be made for a quoted company. First, the bidder or bidding company may set out to buy sufficient shares in the bid-for company through the ordinary market channels, or by private arrangement with the principal shareholders. Secondly, a formal public offer may be made to existing shareholders to purchase for cash all or perhaps a controlling block of shares in the bid-for company. And thirdly, a similar offer may be made which in place of cash offers an exchange of shares in the bidding company for those in the bid-for company. These may be termed respectively *direct purchase bids, cash bids* and *paper bids.* There is of course nothing to prevent a combination of the three

[4] *Practice Note No. 1*, as amended in 1976, para. 3.

forms. Bidding companies frequently make a public offer which links an exchange of shares with a cash payment of any balance in the assessed values of the respective shares. Nor does a public offer exclude a simultaneous attempt to acquire shares in the bid-for company on the market.

There is no special practice or procedure to be adopted in respect of the initial purchases on the market which may still be made without triggering a formal bid. The bidding company and its advisers simply purchase the maximum permitted number of shares in the bid-for company at minimum cost, whether over a period of time or in a quick market 'raid'. In some cases an attempt is made to conceal what is happening by 'warehousing' the shares purchased under the names of nominees. One attraction of this method of operation used to be the possibility of gaining control without the expense and formality of a formal public offer. Now, as will be seen below, a direct purchase bid will usually give rise to an obligation under the City Code to make a formal offer for the whole of the company's share capital at a later stage (Rule 34). But there may still be an advantage in launching a bid in this way, in that the initial shares may be acquired more cheaply, though buying on a substantial scale is in itself likely to cause a rapid increase in the market price.

The procedure in respect of cash and paper offers, on the other hand, has been progressively standardized by the market authorities. The basic principle, adopted long before the formalization of the City Code, was succinctly stated in the original notes of guidance prepared by the City Working Party in 1959 : that 'so far as possible all shareholders of the company for whose shares an offer is being made shall have full, timely and equal information on all relevant matters and adequate time in which to consider the offer.' Accordingly rules similar to those governing formal prospectuses were developed by the Stock Exchange and later by the City Panel for all offer documents prescribing the information which must be given, including the precise terms of the offer, the time limit for acceptance and the commercial justification for the bid.

The range of possible developments in take-over situations, however, is much wider than in simple prospectus issues or offers. An offer which has been previously negotiated with the board of the bid-for company is normally accompanied by a statement from that board recommending acceptance. Where the offer is contested, the board of the bid-for company may instead issue an independent circular recommending their shareholders to reject it, or perhaps to hold out for a better price. The situation may then be further complicated by the intervention of a second or third external bidder offering a better price either in cash or paper, leading to a full scale take-over battle in which the shareholder will be bombarded with a series of offers, counter offers, statements and advice from all sides. The course of events is also influenced by the growth of market opinion, as conveyed to the ordinary investor by the various financial columnists or by his broker, in favour of one or other of the contestants, in the face of which others may concede or withdraw. The outcome is then finally determined by the number of acceptances actually received by a bidding company from directors or controlling shareholders and other institutional or individual investors.

2 LEGAL CONTROLS

Prior to the introduction of the City Code in 1968 the main controls over take-over operations, other than the general Stock Exchange and licensed dealer guidelines, were the statutory restrictions on take-overs or mergers which would result in a monopoly situation as defined in the monopolies and mergers legislation (see Chapter 14), and the standard civil and criminal remedies in respect of false or misleading statements and the misuse of directors' powers. These were sometimes effective. The courts intervened in some cases to control the misuse of directors' powers to issue shares to ward off a take-over (see Chapter 5), or to secure that the terms of a company's constitution were strictly applied.

The holders of a large block of shares in a private company were persuaded to sell their holdings to an external bidder. The company's articles provided for a right of pre-emption for existing shareholders from any other shareholder who wished to transfer his holding. It was held on a petition by an existing shareholder that despite the fact that the bidder had secured contracts for a controlling interest, paid the price and obtained proxies in respect of the shares concerned, the articles of the company could not be overridden and that existing shareholders had the right to block the bid by buying in the shares. *Lyle & Scott Ltd. v. Scotts Trustees* [1959] A.C. 763

In a few blatant cases criminal liability was enforced, as in the *State Building Society* case in which the directors were convicted for making a reckless undertaking that the necessary finance would be forthcoming to pay for a large property deal.[5] But in general terms these formal legal remedies were even less relevant in take-over situations than in respect of new issues. The speed of developments and the difficulty of proving the inaccuracy of the forecasts and undertakings made by the various parties, especially where the bid-for company was to be merged into a larger unit, often left minority shareholders at the mercy of a *fait accompli*.

A property company agreed terms with the directors of a canal company which owned valuable derelict sites for the purchase of their shares. The directors recommended acceptance of a similar offer to their shareholders, even though they had received independent advice that the price was too low. This information was belatedly conveyed to the other shareholders some time after the formal offer from the property company. A number of shareholders sought an injunction to prevent the take-over from proceeding. The judge held that it would not be right to intervene, given that the directors honestly believed the offer to be advantageous; aggrieved shareholders could bring any action they wished at a later stage. *Gething v. Kilner* [1972] 1 W.L.R. 337

Apart from the application of these standard rules to take-over situations, formal provision for the control of take-overs and mergers under the Companies Acts is limited to three relatively minor issues: the approval of schemes of reconstruction and amalgamation (1948: ss. 206–8); the compulsory purchase of small minority interests which stand in the way of a hundred per cent take-over (1948: s. 209); and the prohibition of the use of a company's own funds to assist in the purchase of its own shares (1948: s. 54).

The power of the court to sanction schemes of arrangement and reconstruction is provided to facilitate the process of amalgamating two enterprises where a direct cash offer by one for the shares of the other is not practicable. Thus where shares in the bidding company are to be issued to the shareholders in the bid-for company in part or full settlement, it may be expedient, in order to avoid unnecessary complexity in the resulting capital structure of the bidding company, to transfer the assets in the bid-for company to the bidding company and to cancel the shares of the bid-for company. Alternatively it may be convenient to create a new company to acquire the assets of both the bidding and the bid-for companies, and to issue shares in the new company to the shareholders of the old ones, whose shares

[5] *R. v. Grunwald* [1963] 1 Q.B. 935.

will then be cancelled. In cases such as this the court is enabled by the statutory provisions to dispense with the requirement for a formal winding up of the companies which are to disappear, provided that the consent of three-quarters of the shareholders in the companies concerned is obtained, a requirement which will readily be fulfilled in the case of a successful bid for total control (1948: ss. 206 and 208). The detailed procedure laid down for such transactions does not appear to cause any undue difficulty.

There has been rather more conflict and litigation over the provision for the compulsory purchase of the holdings of dissenting minorities following a successful take-over bid (1948: s. 209). The purpose of the section is two-fold: first, to permit a bidding company which obtains acceptances in respect of ninety per cent of the shares in the bid-for company (excluding those which it already holds) to require the remaining shareholders to sell out so that the bid-for company may become a wholly owned subsidiary; and, secondly, to allow any shareholder who has not accepted the offer to require the bidding company to buy him out in similar circumstances, and so to avoid the possibility of any future oppression of his interests as a small minority shareholder in a subsidiary of the bidding company. The conditions on which either of these powers may be exercised, as might be expected, are strictly drawn. First, they are applicable only in the immediate aftermath of a genuine take-over or merger operation: a bidding company must exercise its right by serving notice on a dissenting shareholder within two months of the requisite acceptances being received; and in the case of an application by a shareholder to be bought out action must be taken within one month of the statutory notice which the bidding company must serve on the dissenting shareholders. Secondly, the shares already held by the bidding company, or by its subsidiaries or nominees, are ignored in the calculation of the requisite proportion of acceptances, and, somewhat illogically where those holdings exceed ten per cent, there is an additional requirement that three-quarters of the remaining shareholders (as opposed to shares) must have accepted. Thirdly, the compulsory purchase must be made on similar terms to those for shares already purchased. And finally, any dissenting shareholder may apply to the court to relieve him of the obligation to sell out or to make any other order which the court thinks fit as to the terms of the purchase.

The decisions in the decided cases reinforce this cautious approach to what amounts to a power of expropriation. The courts will not readily interfere to block the operation of the section on the ground that the price offered to the dissenting shareholders is unfair, as long as it is based on the current market price, which is taken to be cogent evidence of the true value of the shares.[6] Accordingly a dissenting minority will not be permitted to hold out for a higher price on the ground that the acquisition of their shares will give the bidding company the additional advantage of total control. Nor conversely will the holders of a controlling block of shares be permitted to obtain a higher price for their shares than a dissenting minority on the ground that control in itself is a valuable asset. But the courts will require that dissenting, or non-assenting, shareholders be given the same terms as those who accept the original offer for any shares which are compulsorily acquired:

An offer was made on behalf of a bidding company for shares in another company on terms which gave the shareholders a choice of an exchange of shares or a cash alternative in the form of an option to sell the new shares to the bidding company's merchant bank. The petitioner did not receive the offer in time to act on it. The bidding company having obtained more than ninety per cent acceptances sought to buy in his shares on the direct exchange basis. It was held that the petitioner as a non-assenting shareholder was entitled to the benefit of the cash alternative; the policy of the Act was that he should receive no less favourable treatment than an approving shareholder. *In re Carlton Holdings* [1971] 1 W.L.R. 918

Nor will the courts allow the section to be used as a means of expropriation where there is no bona fide take-over or merger.

The two major shareholders in a small publishing company sought to exclude the remaining shareholder who held only ten per cent of the shares. To achieve this they set up a new company in which each held half of the shares and made a formal offer for the shares of the original company at a price which was a reasonable assessment of its value. When the minority shareholder rejected the offer they sought to buy him out compulsorily under s. 209. The court exercised its discretion under the section to 'order otherwise' and refused to sanction the purchase on the ground that there was no genuine scheme or contract as intended by the section: if the manoeuvre were approved it would allow any ninety per cent majority to get rid of a minority whom they did not happen to like, which would be contrary to the fundamental principle that prima facie if a man has a legal

[6] *Re Grierson Oldham & Adams Ltd.* [1967] 1 W.L.R. 385.

right which is an absolute right, then he can do with it or not do with it what he will. *In re Bugle Press* [1961] 1 Ch. 270

In general terms, however, the section represents a sensible approach to the protection of small minority interests in take-over situations. The same principle, that those taking over control of a company should be required to purchase all the shares offered to them, has been further extended in the City Code.

The rationale of the provision prohibiting the giving of assistance by a company towards the purchase of its own shares is a good deal less clear (1948 : s. 54). The rule is usually regarded as an extension of the common law rules on the reduction of capital through the purchase by a company of its own shares (see p. 130). But contravention of the statutory ban does not in itself necessarily result in any such reduction. It was originally introduced in 1928 in an attempt to curb a particularly prevalent form of 'asset stripping'. The essence of this practice consists in obtaining control of a company whose shares are undervalued by making an attractive offer to existing shareholders and then selling off the company's assets; the balance between the price paid for the shares and the money realized from the assets is pure profit for the asset stripper. If operations of this kind can be financed by using the company's own resources, there is obviously no need for the organizer to raise any money at all on his own account. It is arguable that there is no harm in the end result, in so far as the company's assets may not have been profitably employed by the company. But the Greene Committee considered that there was a risk to minority shareholders where asset strippers gained control without buying up all the shares, and that allowing the company's own assets to be used to pay for the purchase increased the opportunities for abuse.[7]

The results of the prohibition have not been satisfactory. The maximum penalty of £100 has certainly not served to deter those who engage in self-financing stripping operations with an improper motive. Though the section is broadly drawn to include any form of indirect assistance by the company by way of guarantee as well as direct subvention, it may be avoided by means of a simple independent bridging loan, or evaded by introducing a series of intermediary transactions and a number of finance houses or banks. None of these is in a position to unravel the full complexity of the transaction and

[7] Cmd. 2657 (1926).

so to recognize a breach of the section, even if they wished to do so. The usual effect of the prohibition has accordingly not been to prevent such transactions but simply to create new problems over the enforceability of contracts involving a deliberate or accidental breach of the section. The resulting legal uncertainty creates an additional risk for innocent parties. The Jenkins Committee was satisfied that the section was no more than 'an occasional embarrassment to the honest, without being a serious inconvenience to the unscrupulous'.[8] This assessment has been fully borne out by the continuing series of cases in which it has been flagrantly ignored, leaving only a hopeless tangle for the courts to deal with after the event. The position appears to be that any breach of the section renders the whole transaction void, and any money or security given by the company under it irrecoverable, though this does not bar an action in misfeasance against those responsible.[9]

It is clear from this that the section has failed to achieve whatever objective was expected of it. The Jenkins Committee accordingly recommended its repeal and replacement by a new provision specifically designed to deal with the abuses which can arise in self-financing take-overs. This new provision would require prior authorization by a special resolution of any scheme involving the use of company resources in the purchase of its own shares, subject to the right of any ten per cent minority holding to petition the court for relief. In addition it would require a declaration of solvency on behalf of the company guaranteeing the due payment of all obligations arising out of the scheme.[10] The Committee hoped in this way to permit legitimate schemes and at the same time to provide some guarantee to dissenting minorities and to creditors of the company. No action has yet been taken on this matter.

3 THE CITY CODE

The lack of any more far-reaching controls over the conduct of take-over and merger operations does not appear to have occasioned any serious concern until the take-over boom of the 1960s was well

[8] Cmnd. 1749 (1962), para. 176.

[9] *Selangor United Rubber Estates Ltd. v. Cradock* (No. 3) [1968] 1 W.L.R. 1555; the complex case-law is summarized in a series of articles by J. H. Farrar, *New Law Journal*, January 1970, pp. 52, 85 & 97.

[10] Cmnd. 1749 (1962), paras. 178–9.

under way. The Jenkins Committee in 1962 limited itself to a recommendation that the Board of Trade should be authorized to strengthen the City's informal guidelines of 1959 by issuing general regulations along the lines of the rules which it had introduced in 1960 for licensed dealers. These would lay down the procedure to be followed in public bids in respect of the period for acceptance, the conditions under which the bid might be withdrawn and the heads of information to be contained in any take-over circular.[11] But there is no indication that the matter was regarded as more than the regularization of what was already accepted practice.

The take-over boom and ensuing abuses

As the number and size of bids and mergers continued to increase, however, a variety of malpractices and inequities began to attract more and more attention in the financial press. The most frequent complaint was the inequality of terms offered to investors. There were allegations of excessive payments to the retiring directors of bid-for companies, either for their shares or by way of compensation for loss of office. Less seriously there were instances in which shares were bought on the market while a general take-over offer remained open so that those who sold on the market obtained a better price than those who accepted the formal offer, as for example in the Courtaulds bid for Wilkinson & Riddell in 1967. Similar objections were raised against any form of partial bid, in which inequality of treatment is inherent unless a strict pro rata offer is made to and accepted by all shareholders.

Complaints were also raised at some of the manoeuvres adopted by companies involved in major take-over battles, whether by way of attack or defence. Thus in the course of the GEC/AEI battle in 1967 AEI disposed of its electric lighting interests to Thorn Electrical in order to place them beyond the reach of GEC; and in the course of a bid by Aberdare Holdings for Metal Industries, also in 1967, Aberdare's apparent victory was thwarted by the issue of a new batch of shares by Metal Industries to Thorn Electrical. This move was sanctioned by the grant of a quotation for the new shares by the Stock Exchange authorities, despite an earlier undertaking by Metal Industries not to issue the shares without first obtaining the approval of existing shareholders. Manoeuvres of this kind might fall within

[11] Cmnd. 1749, paras. 265 ff.

the rules governing the misuse of powers by directors, but in the context of a large market bid legal proceedings are not always easy to initiate.

The most general complaint, however, was the quality of the disclosure made to the market in respect of take-over deals. In a number of cases profit forecasts made in the course of take-over battles turned out to be wholly unjustified, as for instance in the GEC/AEI battle in 1967:

> In 1967 GEC made a take-over bid for AEI. In the course of the battle which developed as a result of the opposition to the bid on the part of the AEI directors, AEI made a forecast in October 1967 that profits of £10m were expected for the year ending in December 1967; this was later supplemented in November by forecasts of profits of £16m for 1968 and £20m for 1969. The battle was eventually won by GEC, which announced in July 1968 that the actual results for 1968 for the old AEI group, calculated in accordance with GEC's standard accounting techniques, showed a loss of £½m instead of the forecast profit of £10m. The report of the accountants for both companies which was commissioned as a result stated that while accounts of this kind involved the exercise of judgement and were not matters of precision, 'of the total shortfall of £14½m we would attribute roughly £5m to adverse differences which are matters substantially of fact rather than of judgement, and the balance of £9½m to adjustments which remain substantially matters of judgement'.

Frequent complaints were also raised over the secrecy surrounding the purchase of shares in bid-for companies during the course of bids, either by the bidding company itself, as in the Phillips bid for Pye of Cambridge in 1967, or by its associates. The failure to make full and accurate disclosure on these and other relevant matters during the course of a take-over battle clearly destroyed the argument that the market was the best arbiter of the dispute, since the ultimate decision had to be made by investors on the basis of inadequate information. There was also frequent complaint over the misuse for their own personal profit by insiders of information which had not been released to the market (see Chapter 7).

The introduction of the City Code

These malpractices were not as serious, as far as the ordinary investor was concerned, as the activities of fraudulent promoters in earlier decades. But the fact that established companies and their advisers were ignoring the spirit of the general notes of guidance on take-over practice, which had been drawn up in 1959 by the City Working Party and adopted in 1966 by the Federation of Stock Exchanges, led to pressure for the introduction of more precise and stringent rules of conduct backed by effective sanctions. The various City authorities finally set up a working party which produced the first City Code on Take-overs and Mergers in April 1968. The immediate impact of these new rules and principles was disappointing. The voluntary Panel set up to administer the Code seemed powerless to do anything when the rules were broken. In the face of continuing adverse comment, a greatly strengthened Panel was eventually set up in April 1969 with a permanent secretariat and full powers to sanction offending parties through the discretionary powers of the Stock Exchange and other City institutions to discipline their members. Further general revisions of the Code were made in September 1970, February 1972 and April 1976.

The resulting structure is firmly based on the concept of self-regulation. 'The choice before the City', as it was stated in the Introduction to the 1969 Code, 'was either a system of voluntary self-discipline, based on the Code and administered by the City's own representatives, or regulation by law enforced by officials appointed by Government.' The City chose self-regulation. The advantage claimed for this is that it permits a much greater measure of flexibility in implementation than could be achieved by formal legislation. The Code itself reflects this difference in approach by its clear separation of General Principles, which provide in broad terms for full disclosure and equity between one shareholder and another, and more formal Rules, which set out in detail the procedures to be followed in their implementation, and by the explicit declaration that 'the spirit as well as the precise wording of these General Principles and of the ensuing Rules must be observed' (General Principle 1). This is achieved in practice by the scrutiny of all relevant documents by the Secretariat of the Panel, and by the rule that the Panel shall be consulted in advance in any case of doubt and where necessary asked for a ruling. Alternatively the Panel may intervene in any take-over situation where it appears that the parties have not been acting in accordance with the spirit or letter of the Code, and make what order or ruling may seem necessary. The implementation of a ruling is then left either to the parties themselves, as for instance in the temporary suspension of voting rights in respect of any newly issued or newly purchased shares. Or it may be left to the other City authorities, as for instance in the case of the suspension of a quotation by the Stock Exchange or the disciplining of a member by the Issuing Houses Association.[12] The Panel will normally make its ruling known by public statement, and there is provision for an appeal to an independent committee of the Panel chaired by an appeal judge. The Panel may also from time to time issue general statements or practice notes on the interpretation of points of general application arising out of rulings in individual cases. Amendments in the Code may also be made in consultation with the full City Working Party which has final jurisdiction in such matters.

The principles of the Code

The fundamental principles on which the Code is based can be simply summarized. First and foremost is the commitment to the ideal that the ultimate decision in take-overs or mergers shall be left to the shareholders of the companies concerned, who must therefore be given all the information necessary to an informed and rational decision:

> Shareholders shall have in their possession sufficient evidence, facts and opinions upon which an adequate judgement and decision can be reached, and shall have sufficient time to make an assessment and decision. No relevant information shall be withheld from them. *General Principle 3*

> At no time after a *bona fide* offer has been communicated . . . or . . . might be imminent, shall any action be taken by the board of an offeree company in relation to the affairs of the company, without the approval in general meeting of the shareholders . . . , which could effectively result in any *bona fide* offer being frustrated or in the shareholders . . . being denied an opportunity to decide on its merits. *General Principle 4*

Closely linked with this are the principles and rules which impose on the directors of the companies concerned a duty to subordinate their own interests at all times to those of their shareholders, and where appropriate to seek competent outside advice to that end:

> Directors . . . shall always, in advising their shareholders, act only in their capacity as directors and not have regard to their personal or family shareholdings or their personal relationships with the companies. It is the shareholders' interests taken as whole, together with those of employees and creditors, which should be considered. *General Principle 11*

[12] See Policy Statement of 28 April 1969 and the Introduction to the 1976 Code, para. 2.

A board which receives an offer or is approached with a view to an offer being made should in the interests of its shareholders seek competent independent advice. *General Principle 6*

The second cardinal principle is that all shareholders shall be treated equally, both in the terms which they are offered and in the information which is supplied to them :

All shareholders of the same class of an offeree company shall be treated similarly by an offeror. *General Principle 8*

If . . . an offer has been made to one or more shareholders . . . any subsequent general offer made by or on behalf of the same offeror to the shareholders of the same class shall not be on less favourable terms. *General Principle 9*

. . . neither the offeror, the offeree company nor any of their respective advisers shall furnish information to some shareholders which is not made available to all shareholders . . . *General Prinicple 10*

Finally there is the unexpressed but equally fundamental principle that it is undesirable to fetter the market by imposing any bar on market dealings by any of the parties to a bid, subject only to the rules as to the misuse of confidential information and the duty to make full disclosure of any relevant purchases or sales (Rule 31).

The implementation of these principles in the formal Rules of the Code is a matter of some complexity. The standards of conduct to be followed by the directors of both bidding and bid-for companies, from the time when the first confidential approach is made to the completion or rejection of the bid, are laid down; the heads of information to be included in all relevant offer documents and circulars are listed; and detailed procedural rules are formulated in respect of the mechanics of any formal offer which may be made. For instance, a minimum time limit of twenty-one days for the acceptance of an offer is prescribed, and the precise timing of the various formal announcements on the market is laid down. These rules need not be set out in detail here, since they have been drafted in a rather more intelligible and self-explanatory form than is usual in statutory regulations. But there are several issues which merit some further discussion, both in their own right and as a means of illustrating the system of self-regulation in action : these are the inherent uncertainty of profit forecasts, the conflict between the principle of equal treatment for all shareholders and the desire not to fetter the market, and the problem of bids which are withdrawn or cannot be completed. The part of the Code relating to the misuse of confidential information and the creation of false markets has already been discussed in Chapter 7.

The Code in operation: disclosure

The problems of disclosure in take-over documents and circulars are not essentially different from those which arise in relation to new issues. In both cases the major difficulty lies in the fact that what the investor really wants to know about is the future rather than the past. But the matter has been given rather more prominence in relation to take-overs than new issues. In deciding on the merits of rival take-over offers or defence circulars, the shareholder has to adjudicate on rival claims as to likely future profits under new or existing management or within the framework of a large organization. The strength with which these forecasts are pressed in the heat of the battle has focused attention on the results which are actually achieved in the event, as in the AEI/GEC take-over battle. The Panel's concern over this issue is amply demonstrated by the fact that its first public intervention in the course of a public bid took the form of a lengthy published analysis by the Panel of the bases on which certain profit forecasts had been made in the battle which arose out of Dufay Bitumastic's bid for International Paints in the summer of 1968. The Panel was careful, however, to refrain from giving any opinion of its own on the dispute, or indeed from examining the detailed figures. This approach is followed consistently both in the Code itself and the two practice notes which have subsequently been issued. The Code expresses the matter in the very broadest terms:

> ... Notwithstanding the obvious hazard attached to the forecasting of profits, any profit forecasts must be compiled with the greatest possible care by the directors whose sole responsibility they are. ... the assumptions, including the commercial assumptions, upon which the directors have based their profit forecasts must be stated. ... The accounting bases and calculations for the forecasts must be examined and reported on by the auditors or consultant accountants. Any financial adviser mentioned in the document must also report on the forecasts. *Rule 16*

The interpretation of what amounts to a forecast has subsequently been clarified, to include statements such as that profits are likely to be similar to last year. It also includes estimates of past profits which have not yet been publicized in annual accounts or half yearly statements. In each case the required auditor's and adviser's report must be obtained.[13] The essential objective is thus to ensure that any forecast is subjected to some external scrutiny. The Panel's intention in respect of the assumptions on which the forecasts are based has also been clarified, after consultation with the accountancy profession.[14] These assumptions, like the forecast itself, are the sole responsibility of the directors, but it is for the auditors or consultants 'to satisfy themselves that the forecasts so far as the accounting bases and calculations are concerned have been properly compiled on the footing of the assumptions made.... Neither should allow an assumption to be published which appears to them to be unrealistic (or one to be omitted which appears to them to be important) without commenting on it in their reports.'[15] As to the assumptions themselves, the Panel directs that they should wherever possible be 'specific rather than general, definite rather than vague', and that 'all-embracing assumptions and those relating to the general accuracy of the estimates', such as that 'there will be no significant unforeseen circumstances' or that 'provisions for outstanding legal claims will prove adequate', should be avoided.[16] The form of these practice notes in themselves is perhaps the best indication of the approach adopted by the Panel in this as in other matters. The Code itself expresses a general standard, and the Panel then vets each document submitted to it in the light of that general statement. Where there is substantial difficulty, the Panel issues practice notes explaining in the light of experience the way in which it is likely to treat future submissions. The difference between this method of discretionary control and that which would follow from a more legalistic prescription, with the sanction of court proceedings in the event of disagreement, is clear cut and important.

The commitment of the Panel to securing full disclosure in all take-over and merger operations goes very much further than the provisions of the Code as to the offer documents and other circulars. There is also specific provision, adopted as a result of widespread complaints over secret market buying by participants in a contested bid, for full disclosure on the following day of the full amount of

[13] *Practice Note No. 3* (originally introduced June 1970).
[14] *Practice Note No. 4* (originally introduced June 1971).
[15] Ibid., para. 5.
[16] Ibid., paras. 10 and 13.

any relevant dealings by the principals or their associates, whether for themselves or on behalf of investment clients; in the latter case disclosure to the press as well as to the Stock Exchange and the Panel is not required (Rule 31).[17] The intent of this rule is to keep the market fully informed of any dealings over which the parties or their advisers might have direct or indirect control or influence, and so to ensure both that uncommitted shareholders may make their decision in full knowledge of the extent to which the outcome has already been determined on the market, and that no illegitimate advantage is obtained by those with inside knowledge. More generally the Panel will intervene in any case where it appears that the proper progress of a bid is impeded by any lack of material information or distorted by misleading statements. In a serious case the Panel may require the postponement or withdrawal of the bid and the suspension of quotations until the situation is clarified, as in the Pergamon/Leasco affair in 1969:

> In the course of a bid in August 1969 by the American controlled Leasco World Trade Co. (UK) Ltd. for Pergamon Press Ltd. doubts were raised as to the adequacy of the information made available by Pergamon in relation to the profitability of its subsidiaries; in addition certain undisclosed dealings entered into by family trusts closely connected with Mr Robert Maxwell, the Chairman and Managing Director of Pergamon, came to light. As a result Leasco sought to withdraw its offer, upon which Maxwell made public allegations to the effect that Leasco had insufficient resources to complete the deal. The Panel intervened to request the suspension of dealings and made a lengthy report questioning whether the directors of Pergamon 'had properly discharged their obligation to inform their shareholders sufficiently in regard to the affairs of their company'; in view of the fact that 'the withdrawal of a public offer once announced was a matter of serious concern' in its effect on market values and on the interests of shareholders, the Panel arranged a compromise with Pergamon and Leasco under which the offer would be continued at a price to be determined in relation to the actual earnings of Pergamon for the years in question. The Panel also recommended the appointment of a Board of Trade inspection into the affairs of Pergamon. *The Times* 29 August 1969

The Pergamon affair was not settled by this intervention. As a result of an independent accountants' report published in August 1970,[18] which confirmed the uncertainty as to Pergamon's financial position,

[17] *Practice Note No. 7* (originally issued June 1970).

[18] *Financial Times*, 27 August 1970.

Leasco finally withdrew its amended offer in November 1970, leaving the Pergamon shareholders without either an offer or a market quotation for their shares. Neither the Panel nor any other authority can be expected to guarantee the completion of all bids. But the affair established the determination of the Panel to pursue a policy of active intervention in any situation where the required standard of full and frank disclosure has not been adhered to.

The Code in operation: equality and market dealings

It is a basic principle of the Code that all shareholders of the same class shall be treated equally in so far as that is possible. Where a bidding company receives sufficient acceptances to give it control of the bid-for company, and may accordingly declare the bid unconditional, the offer must remain open for a further fourteen days to allow hitherto dissenting shareholders to accept it on the same terms (Rule 23). Partial bids used to be discouraged as 'undesirable' and were permitted only with the prior consent of the Panel; this consent is still required but a more liberal attitude is now adopted to most partial bids, subject to a requirement that any shareholder who accepts may do so in respect of the same proportion of his shares as every other accepting shareholder (Rule 27).

Complete equality, however, is often difficult to attain. Problems have arisen in cases where the capital of the bid-for company has been divided into voting and non-voting shares, and the offer for the voting shares has been at a higher price than for the rest. The Panel has adopted the position that voting and non-voting shares are of different classes and that voting control is itself a valuable asset:

> The directors who controlled a majority of the voting shares in Swears and Wells accepted an offer for their shares, and in accordance with the Code insisted that a comparable offer be made to the rest of the ordinary shareholders. The price offered for the voting shares was about fifty per cent more than that for the non-voting shares. The holders of the non-voting shares appealed to the Panel. It refused to intervene on the ground that voting shares were normally worth more than non-voting shares; since the difference depended on the relative sizes of the two classes and the concentration of the holding, no formal rules for valuation could be imposed.
> *Financial Times* 18 February 1970

The holders of non-voting shares, however, must be made a 'comparable offer' (Rule 21). This is usually taken to permit a discount of some ten or twenty per cent.

The fact that market dealings in the shares of the bid-for company by the bidding company and its associates are generally permitted (Rule 31) also creates considerable difficulties in this context, in that the price which the bidding company pays on the market will not always be the same as the offer price. The Code requires the bidding company to increase the price paid to accepting shareholders to not less than the highest price paid for the shares which it buys on the market during the period of the offer (Rule 32). The same principle applies in the case of paper bids or mixed cash and paper bids. Accordingly in the American Tobacco/Galaher battle in 1968 in the course of which American Tobacco bought a substantial block of shares on the market, the Panel ruled that all the shareholders should then be offered cash in place of the fifty per cent cash/paper terms in the formal offer. Though the Panel was not at the time able to enforce this ruling, the principle has subsequently been applied and reinforced. When the dual battle for Cementation in 1970 between Trafalgar House Investments and Bovis Holdings ended with Trafalgar buying the twenty-six per cent holding which had been amassed by Bovis on cash terms under a special contract, the Panel insisted that the remaining Cementation shareholders should also be paid fully in cash. But the Panel Executive also ruled in a number of cases that where the purchases on the market were not of significance to the outcome of the bid, the offer terms need only be adjusted upwards under Rule 32 in paper terms. As a result it became relatively common for bidding companies to make a formal paper offer, to secure working control through selective cash purchases on the market or through individual contracts with institutional investors and then to adjust the offer terms upwards in paper in a way which would not have been acceptable to the institutional investors. In this way they would obtain their objective without having to pay cash to all the shareholders. The Panel is only prepared to intervene in cases of this kind where there are special circumstances rendering the procedure under Rule 32 inadequate, as for instance in the *Adepton/Williams Hudson* case in 1971 in which a smaller company with uncertain future profits was acquiring a much larger one. This special circumstances doctrine was then formalized in a new rule to the effect that unless prior approval of the Panel is obtained a cash alternative will be required in any case in which fifteen per cent of the shares in the bid-for company have been purchased for cash within a year of the offer being made, or otherwise where the Panel considers it necessary to secure equal treatment for shareholders (Rule 33). The matter is thus essentially one for the discretion of the Panel in the light of the nature and size of the market purchases.[19] As long as market dealings are permitted during the course of a bid, there can be no absolute equality of treatment for all accepting shareholders short of a requirement that all bids should include a cash alternative.

Similar problems arise in respect of defensive action by the bid-for company and its associates. It is a general principle that the directors of the bid-for company shall not take any action which will prevent their shareholders from deciding on the merits of the bid (General Principle 4; Rule 38). This is not taken to prevent the directors of a bid-for company buying shares on the market, provided the purchases are disclosed (Rule 31). The Code provides in addition that any person with a commercial interest in the outcome of an offer should consult the Panel before making any purchases on the market which might affect the outcome, and should be prepared to justify the purchases after the event (Rule 37). Where such purchases are made the Panel may rule that the shares shall be held in abeyance:

During the course of a bid for the *News of the World* by Pergamon Press in 1968 the advisers of an Australian company, also interested in acquiring control of the paper, bought sufficient shares on the market to give voting control in *News of the World* to the Australian bidder and the *News of the World* directors who favoured the Australian offer. Though the purchases had been formally declared in accordance with the Code, the Panel intervened to obtain an undertaking from the advisers that the votes would not be used at the crucial shareholders' meeting to consider the Australian offer, 'so that the voting at this meeting may be seen to be influenced by the shareholders' judgement and not by any change in the shareholding of the parties or their associates since the original announcement of the intended offer by Pergamon.' *Financial Times* 2 November 1968

But the balance of power may be altered in such a case by the very fact that a certain number of votes are rendered inoperative.

These various examples illustrate the virtual impossibility of ensuring full equality of treatment for all shareholders in take-overs and mergers without imposing some fetter on free market dealings.

[19] *Practice Note No. 9* (first issued April 1976).

The commitment of the City authorities to the principle of equality and the attempt by some bidding companies to avoid the terms of the Code by resort to direct purchase bids thus led inexorably to the introduction in 1972 of a new rule under which any person or company which attempts to gain control of another company by market purchases must if successful make an unconditional offer to buy out the remaining shareholders at the highest price paid for shares on the market. This obligation now extends to any person or company that together with persons acting in concert acquires a holding of thirty per cent of voting shares in a company, or increases an existing holding of between thirty and fifty per cent by more than two per cent in any period of twelve months (Rule 34). Any attempt to buy control of a company through the market or otherwise is thus deemed to constitute a take-over bid, and is subject to the same general principle of equality of treatment as other more formal bids. It is impossible to guarantee that a purchaser who brings this obligation into operation will have the resources to carry it through. But the Panel has demonstrated its intention to secure that the objective of the rule is fulfilled, by putting pressure on merchant bankers associated with the bid or by facilitating an alternative take-over.

In 1973 a consortium which included a South African financier acquired a forty-seven per cent holding in Ashbourne Investments. One of the British companies involved in the consortium went into liquidation and the other was not in a position to raise the finance to buy in the remaining shares as required by the Code. The Panel initially sought to persuade the South African financier, who denied all knowledge of the Code, and the consortium's merchant bankers to carry out the obligation. It eventually abandoned this strategy and ruled that the remaining members of the consortium must not use their shares to block an alternative bid which had materialised or otherwise dispose of them without the Panel's consent; it also ruled that 'any person who seeks to gain control of a public company in the U.K. must be familiar with the rules, regulations and practices' of the U.K. *Financial Times* 16 April 1976

Even where the obligation is successfully enforced, however, the shareholders may complain that they have not at any time been given the information necessary to enable them to reach a reasoned decision on the merits of the take-over, as required by the Code (General Principle 3). The logic of the principles on which the Code is based suggests that the Panel should impose the same general disclosure requirements on those who embark on a take-over by market purchase as already apply to formal offers, or at least require a successful bidder to pay the final bid price to those whose shares have been acquired on the market. The maintenance of an unfettered market as currently understood in the Code is in practice incompatible with the primary objective of the Code, that all major transfers of shareholdings in quoted companies should be rigidly controlled in the interests of an orderly market and equality between shareholders.

Conclusion: self-regulation or official control

Despite some initial shortcomings, the City Code and Panel have succeeded in imposing a degree of control over take-overs in which quoted companies are involved which critics of the City in the late 1960s predicted would be impossible. To that extent they have demonstrated the advantages of a voluntary and flexible system of self-regulation.[20] The system has been built up gradually. In many instances the Panel has only been able to impose controls to prevent the repetition of practices which it has been unable to prevent when they first appeared. Much of the driving force has been provided by the continual threat of government intervention. The question remains whether a governmental agency with statutory powers would have achieved better results.

It is important in this context to distinguish between legislation of the kind found in the Companies Acts and regulation by a governmental agency. It is virtually impossible to legislate in advance for all the malpractices which may emerge in matters of this kind, as the history of official regulation of insurance companies and other investment institutions has shown (see Chapter 10). A more useful comparison is with those governmental agencies which already operate with the same freedom of action and flexibility within stated guidelines as the City authorities have set for themselves. The work of the Monopolies Commission and the new Office of Fair Trading in dealing with take-overs and mergers within the framework of the criteria established in the Monopolies and Mergers Act 1965 and the Fair Trading Act 1973 is perhaps the best example (see Chapter 14). It seems unlikely on that basis that a statutory agency would

[20] See generally the Panel's response to a Department of Trade questionnaire on the supervision of the securities market, 1975.

have acted in a very different way from the Panel, except perhaps in the control of insider dealing. In the absence of a clear political policy of replacing the objective of securing equal treatment for shareholders in the context of stock market take-overs by an entirely different set of criteria, for instance to discourage or prohibit such operations altogether, there seems little point in replacing a relatively effective and inexpensive agency like the City Panel by an official body.[21]

[21] The expenses of the Panel were originally met wholly by the Bank of England, but they are now shared equally by the Bank and the sponsoring City bodies; the total annual cost in 1976–7 was of the order of £250,000.

9
Groups

The natural result of a take-over is the complete absorption of one company in another. In practice those in control of the successful bidding company often find it convenient to leave the company they have purchased in existence as a formally independent unit. Where the bidding company has not secured control over all the voting shares, or of sufficient to enable it to force a sale by the recalcitrant minority (1948 : s. 209) or to secure approval for a scheme of arrangement (1948 : ss. 206–8), there is no alternative to maintaining it as a partially owned subsidiary. Wholly and partially owned subsidiaries are also frequently created by established companies quite apart from the ordinary processes of take-over or merger. In either case it may be simpler for the parent company to maintain a number of formally separate subsidiary companies than to organize a series of informal managerial or accounting units or divisions within a single company. As the number of subsidiary companies becomes larger and the network of shareholdings becomes more complex, the original parent company may eventually hive off its original business, in the form of a further wholly owned subsidiary, and operate exclusively as a holding company through which the original shareholders participate at one remove in the operations of a series of wholly or partially owned trading companies.

The development of complex groups of companies raises important issues in all areas of company law and practice. In its simplest form, where one company merely owns a block of shares in another and takes no other interest in its operations than the collection of dividends and the exercise of its ordinary rights as a shareholder, there are few problems other than the need for special tax provisions to deal with the dividends passing from one company to another. Where one company effectively controls the operations of another, whether it owns all its shares or not, more difficult problems of responsibility and accounting arise. There is an obvious risk in such circumstances that the controlling company will dictate the affairs of its subsidiaries in such a way as to prejudice minority shareholders or creditors of the subsidiaries. In addition the precise financial position of any one company in the group cannot be ascertained from its separate accounts, given the facility with which assets and liabilities can be transferred from one member company to another. The various aspects of accounting, taxation and the control of impropriety within groups of company will be dealt with in turn. But first the essentials of the relationship between a holding company and a subsidiary company must be set out.

Holding companies and subsidiaries

The legal relationship of 'holding' and 'subsidiary' companies is defined in the Companies Act in terms of the control of one company by another (1948 : s. 154). This control may be exercisable either directly through ownership by the holding company of more than half the equity share capital of the subsidiary, or through its control by any other means of the composition of the subsidiary's board of directors. For this purpose it is beneficial rather than legal control which counts. Accordingly shares or voting powers held on trust for another are ignored, while the holdings of nominees are deemed to be those of the principal for whom they are held. Similarly it is effective control over the appointment of the majority of directors on the subsidiary's board which counts, whatever the legal form through which that control is exercisable. In addition, a holding company is deemed to be a holding company in respect of any company which is a subsidiary of a subsidiary. The relationship of holding and subsidiary, however, is strictly one way; there is a formal bar on the holding of shares by a subsidiary in its own holding company (1948 : s. 27). Accordingly any allotment or transfer of shares in the holding company to a subsidiary is void, and voting rights on any shares already held by a subsidiary in its holding company are suspended.

Group accounting

The primary purpose of these statutory definitions is to make special provision for group accounting. Where two technically independent commercial enterprises are under the same control it is obviously possible to arrange transactions between the two on terms which would not otherwise be commercially acceptable, and thus to create profit or loss in respect of each individual company more or less at will. This is especially easy in respect of the transfer from one company to another of real property and other assets without a readily ascertainable market value since the price may be fixed either at an exaggerated or a nominal level. Even in the ordinary course of commercial operations it is often difficult to gauge a proper level of pricing for transactions with wholly owned subsidiaries which are the sole suppliers of components or materials within an integrated production chain. There is a similar problem in respect of the transfer of loans with or without security between members of the same group. This flexibility in the channelling of liquid assets is one of the advantages of group organization. It may also be used for or result in confusion as to the precise financial position or even the solvency of individual companies or indeed the group as a whole. A debt from what is in effect an insolvent subsidiary may lend a spurious air of solvency to the holding company. Similar problems may arise in giving a realistic value to the holding company's shareholdings in its subsidiaries. Many of the most notorious commercial frauds have been based on the inherent obscurity of group accounts.

The centrepiece of the statutory provisions in this sphere is the requirement that consolidated group accounts should be produced each year to show the profitability and solvency of the holding company and its various subsidiaries as a single unit (1948 : s. 150; 1976 : s. 8). These group accounts must follow the general form of the standard balance sheet and profit and loss account, except where some variation is deemed necessary in the interests of presentation and accuracy by the holding company's directors. A company is exempted from the inclusion of a particular subsidiary in the consolidated accounts where in the opinion of the directors it is impracticable or unnecessarily expensive, where it would be misleading or harmful to any company in the group or where the business of the subsidiary is so different as to make it unreasonable to include it, though in the last two cases governmental permission to exclude a subsidiary is required (1948 : s. 150 (2)).

The production of group accounts does not affect the obligation of each individual company to produce its own statutory accounts. But there are additional requirements in respect of these individual accounts. First, in the interests of clarity and to prevent the juggling of temporary balances, the holding company's directors must secure that the financial year of all companies in the group shall coincide, except where there are good reasons against it (1948 : s. 153). Secondly, each company in the group must state separately in its own accounts the amounts of any assets or liabilities consisting either in shares held in other companies in the group or in loans or other forms of indebtedness (1967 : sched. 2, paras. 15 and 16). Special provision is also made for the disclosure of group turnover, employment and exports (1967 : ss. 17, 18 and 20), and the requirement as to the disclosure of the emoluments of employees earning more than £10,000 per annum covers emoluments from any company within a group (1967 : s. 8). Explicit disclosure must be made of the holding company's shareholdings in all subsidiaries and other companies in which it holds more than one-tenth of the equity shares, and every subsidiary must disclose the identity of its ultimate holding company (1967) : ss. 4–5).

Despite some minor loopholes, such as that the emoluments of directors from all companies in the group need not be aggregated for the purposes of disclosure, these measures are generally adequate to secure that a reasonably clear picture is presented of the affairs of groups of companies where there is nothing to hide and no attempt to hide it. They are less than adequate where that is not the case. There is a wide measure of discretion for directors of holding companies to exempt themselves from the requirements that accounting periods shall coincide or that the accounts of all subsidiaries shall be consolidated. Nor is there any specific control over intra-group transactions, to prevent the evasion of the disclosure provision in relation to intra-group loans by arranging suitable absolute transfers of assets which will appear only in so far as overall asset valuations are affected. The only safeguard against such practices for external shareholders, whether of the ultimate holding company or for minorities within individual subsidiaries, is the general duty of the auditors to report on any matter which appears to them to affect the validity of the accounts as a true and fair description of the state of the group's affairs. Some additional protection in this respect is provided by the new rule that auditors of a subsidiary must supply to the auditors of its holding company any information reasonably required by them for the compilation of group accounts (1976 : s. 18). But as long as different auditors are permitted to deal with the accounts of different companies in a group, there will be scope for the manipulation of group accounts through the use of different accounting and valuation bases and complex intra-group transactions. Further regulation of these and other matters may be required when the EEC Draft Seventh Directive on group accounts is adopted (see p. 140).

Groups and taxation

For the purposes of taxation, unlike those of accounting, the law does not take general note of the special position of subsidiaries. Each company is assessed for corporation tax as an independent unit on the basis of its own annual accounts. The ordinary tax rules in respect of dividends and distribution and franked investment income will thus be applied to all such payments between companies in the same group. But the Inland Revenue does in certain circumstances require its own rules of valuation and assessment to be applied rather than those applied in the company's statutory accounts. These exceptions as might be expected apply to those transactions where the freedom of manoeuvre within a group could be used to minimize its tax liability. Thus, in respect of the transfer of assets from company to company within the group, the Inland Revenue is entitled to disregard any purported capital gain or loss arising from the transaction, and so in effect to ignore any changes of ownership within the group, though for this purpose a company is deemed to be the subsidiary of another only where the principal company holds over three-quarters of its shares (Income and Corporation Taxes Act 1970, ss. 485, 486 and 488). It is significant that as in the case of the special tax rules for depreciation and directors' emoluments, the tax authorities have felt the need to impose their own accounting rules in the very areas where the need for additional protection for shareholders has been raised.

The group as a legal entity

These rules on accounting and taxation do not affect the formal independence of each company as a separate legal entity within the group. As in the case of individual companies, however, the courts are prepared in certain circumstances to look to the reality of the group situation rather than the strict legal position. In one case the parent company of a group has been held to be entitled to compensation for disturbance to the business of the group as a whole:

In order to assist in the financing of the purchase of premises for a grocery business a subsidiary company was set up to hold the legal title. Initially the shares were held by the bank, but they were later transferred to the main trading company. The subsidiary carried out no trading and did not have a bank account. When the premises were compulsorily purchased it was argued that the only compensation payable was to the subsidiary for the value of the premises. It was held on appeal that compensation for the extinguishment of its business must also be paid to the trading company since it controlled the subsidiary in every respect; the group must be treated as a single economic entity. *D.H.N. Food Distributors Ltd. v. Tower Hamlets L.B.C.* [1976] 1 W.L.R. 852

It has also been held that for the purposes of the approval of a scheme of arrangement the votes of a wholly owned subsidiary of a purchasing company must be treated as being in a different class from those of other ordinary shareholders of the company which is being purchased:

A merchant banking company sought to purchase the shares of an investment company. Slightly more than half the shares in the investment company were already held by a subsidiary of the banking company. In a petition by the banking company for court sanction for the proposed scheme of arrangement it was held that the shares held by the subsidiary must be treated as different from those of other shareholders since the interests of the parent and its wholly owned subsidiary were for practical purposes identical; therefore since the requisite approvals of the scheme of arrangement by separate classes of shareholders had not been obtained, the petition must be rejected. *In re Hellenic & General Trust Ltd.* [1976] 1 W.L.R. 123

The increasing readiness of the courts to treat a group of companies as a single unit cannot be relied on for all purposes. The most important exception for practical purposes is the fact that the status of each company as a separate entity with limited liability means that any member company of a group may be wound up without affecting the group as a whole. Where such a company is solvent there is no difficulty in this. But where it is insolvent, the external creditors and any minority shareholders may well find themselves bearing a loss which could readily be met by the assets of other members of the group. It is often argued that the group as a whole should be required to guarantee the liabilities of any member company, especially since the flexibility of inter-group transactions may be used to accumulate substantial losses in a single insolvent subsidiary. The current legal position on this issue, though there is no direct authority, would appear to be that there is no obligation on a holding company to meet the liabilities of its subsidiaries. It has been held that the directors of each individual company within a group must act in the interests of that company and not sacrifice it to the interests of other companies in the group or to the group as a whole:

The controlling director of a group of companies arranged for one of the subsidiaries to guarantee the debts of an associated company in the group. Subsequently the company's property was charged to support the guarantee, and then later sold to a third company. The third company sought to have the prior charge set aside on the ground that it was ultra vires the company. It was held that the charge was valid in that the subjective intentions of the controlling director were irrelevant to the decision whether or not the charge was objectively within the powers of the company, and that even if his motives had been relevant he had in all the circumstances validly considered the interests of the individual company in relation to the group as a whole; but this did not mean that it was sufficient for the directors of a subsidiary to look only to the interests of the group in conducting the affairs of a subsidiary: 'Each company in the group was a separate legal entity and the directors of a particular company were not entitled to sacrifice the interest of that company; that became apparent when one considered the case where the particular company had separate creditors'. (per Pennycuick J., at p. 74) *Charterbridge Corporation Ltd. v. Lloyds Bank Ltd.* [1970] Ch. 62

Nor, conversely, is there any duty on the directors of a parent holding company to protect the interests of a subsidiary which has an independent board of directors.[1] It is only where there is evidence of a deliberate scheme to defraud creditors that the courts are likely to intervene to hold the holding company or its directors liable on the ground of fraudulent trading. But this will be difficult to establish except in the most blatant cases. It would seem more reasonable that the concept of the group as an integrated entity for accounting purposes should be extended to this substantive level. In normal cases, of course, a group would not wish for commercial reasons to allov

[1] *Lindgren v. L. & P. Estates Ltd.* [1968] Ch. 572 (see p. 236).

external creditors of a subsidiary to go unpaid in the event of a winding up, but a legal guarantee at least for wholly owned subsidiaries should be added.

There are similar risks of abuse in respect of minority holdings where the subsidiary is not wholly owned, for example by the shuttling of assets within the group to the detriment of the partly owned subsidiary, or more simply by so organizing prices and profit-margins within the group as to deny it any substantial profit or dividend. There is no theoretical difference in the rules applicable to cases of oppression within a group as opposed to a single company. But it will be clear that minorities within a larger group are in a specially vulnerable position. Major policy decisions will often be taken in the interests of the group as a whole rather than of each individual company within it. There may be good reasons, in a group context, for running down the business of a partly owned subsidiary in favour of another enterprise within the group, or there may be important tax considerations for minimizing profit or distributions within a particular unit.

There is clear authority that such conduct may amount to oppression. It has been held that it is the duty of the directors of a holding company to conduct the affairs of any subsidiary so as to deal fairly with the interests of minority holdings and that this might extend to the buying out of those interests at a fair price where the business of the subsidiary was to be run down.[2] The net effect is that policies which will put the interests of the group as a whole before those of an individual subsidiary may be pursued only where the subsidiary is wholly owned. But the obstacles which face a minority in asserting its rights in matters of this kind detract considerably from the usefulness of this line of authority.

Rather more progress has been made in the German company legislation of 1965 towards the protection of both shareholders and creditors of subsidiaries. Every holding company in Germany must now either enter into a formal control agreement with its subsidiaries guaranteeing the position of minority shareholders and creditors, or else make specific compensation to the subsidiaries for any transaction which it is required to enter into to its own detriment. The adoption of a provision of this kind would clearly go some way to prevent the oppression of creditors and minorities. But the concept

[2] *Scottish Co-operative Wholesale Society v. Meyer* [1959] A.C. 324 (see p. 263).

of a wholly controlled subsidiary as an independent legal entity within an integrated group is in itself unsatisfactory. Serious consideration should be given to the creation of a prima facie right for minorities to require the holding company to buy them out at a fair price at any time, and for creditors to look to the holding company in the event of liquidation. The only permissible holding/subsidiary relationship, unless otherwise agreed by the interested parties, would thus be in substance one of total ownership.

The entrenchment of control

The final problem in this context is the use of interlocking shareholdings to entrench control.[3] The current definition of a subsidiary linked with the bar on crossholdings by a subsidiary in its holding company (1948 : s. 27) prevents the establishment of the simplest form of unbreakable chain in which each of two companies holds majority control over the other. It also prevents the holders of a relatively small proportion of the shares in one company from protecting themselves against any form of adverse vote or take-over by means of crossholdings short of control, as for instance in Figure 9.1 :

Figure 9.1

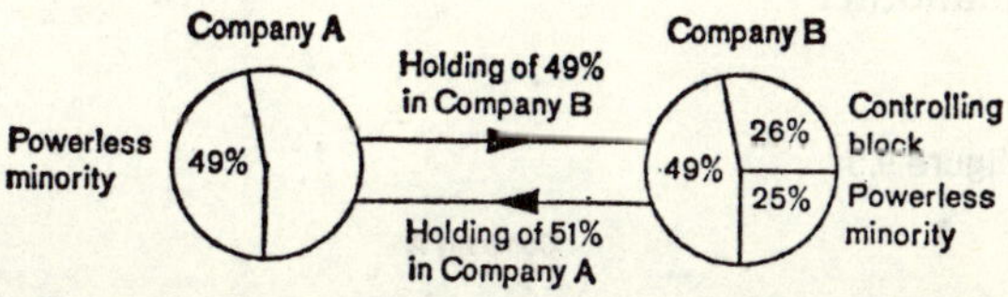

The rationale of the statutory prohibition in this context is to ensure that in any group there is one single holding company in which a majority in the general meeting of shareholders can exercise ultimate control, and conversely that control is exercised by the holders of the largest beneficial interest in the group's operations.

The flexibility of group organization, however, allows this simple principle to be outflanked without a great deal of difficulty. In the first place the creation of a chain of companies each with a bare majority holding in its subsidiary allows the controllers of the holding company to maintain control over each company in the chain,

[3] See generally M. Pickering, 'Shareholders' Voting Rights and Company Control', (1965) 81 *LQR* 248.

or 'pyramid' as it is often called, even though the net value of the minority holdings in the various companies exceeds that of the controllers. An extreme case where a holding of £51,000 controls nets tangible assets of £198,000 in all is illustrated in Figure 9.2.

Similar results may be achieved by circular holdings or crossholdings short of control. Thus, as shown in Figure 9.3, the ban on

Figure 9.2

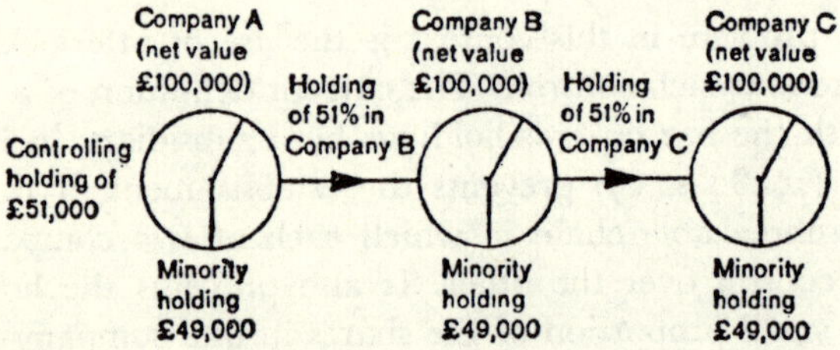

controlling crossholdings may be circumvented by means of a circular relationship between three or more companies, none of which is a subsidiary of another, but each of which has a substantial minority holding in another:

Figure 9.3

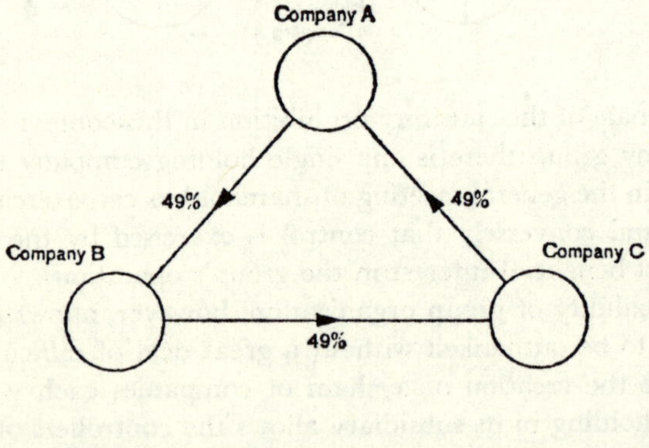

Nor is there anything to prevent the extension of this type of circular grouping to include crossholdings between the various companies, as for instance in Figure 9.4:

Figure 9.4

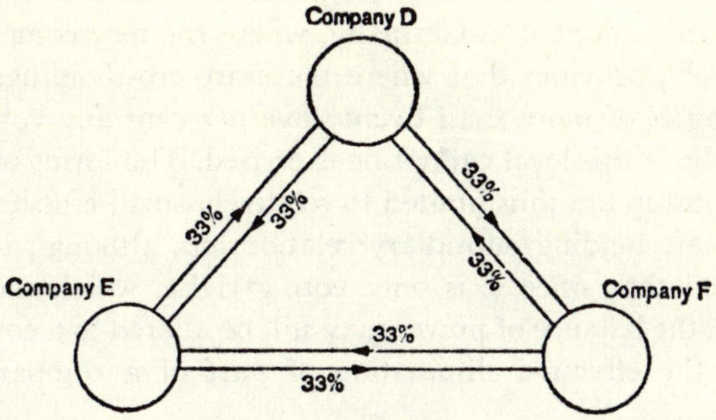

In either case a relatively small holding in two of the companies will give overall control over the whole 'group': in the examples illustrated holdings of twenty-six per cent in companies A and B, and of seventeen per cent in Companies D and E respectively would give total control over net assets of the 'group' leaving the remaining holdings in all three companies as powerless minorities.

Crossholdings of any kind have the additional effect, as will be clear from the above examples, of raising the apparent capital of the group as a whole, since a proportion of the assets are effectively counted twice. This point was raised by the Jenkins Committee as a further argument for imposing some form of control in this sphere.[4]

Company interrelationships of this complexity are not met with in ordinary commercial practice, since they will clearly give rise to equal complexities in day-to-day accounting and management. But the fact that they may legally be created demonstrates the absence of effective control over manipulations of this kind. The Jenkins Committee, while recognizing the possibility of abuse within groups and near-groups, both through the indirect depletion of capital by crossholdings, and through the various forms of entrenchment, considered that any remedial legislation would be too complex for adoption: it would be difficult, it was argued, to determine which of two companies holding shares in the other short of control should lose its voting rights.[5] The Committee concluded, somewhat optimistically, that sufficient protection would normally be granted by the statutory

[4] Cmnd. 1749 (1962), paras. 148 ff.
[5] Paras. 151–2.

disclosure of any holding larger than ten per cent and by the existing remedy against oppression in section 210.

More extensive controls over the permissible extent of crossholdings have been adopted in Germany, where the new company legislation of 1965 provides that where there are crossholdings between two companies of more than twenty-five per cent any voting rights over and above this level cannot be exercised. The forms of effective interrelationship are thus limited to relatively small crossholdings, or to a full scale holding/subsidiary relationship, although it must be remembered that since it is only voting rights which must be relinquished, the balance of power may still be altered to a considerable extent by the effective elimination of part of a company's share capital.

To place a more effective bar on the abuse of interlocking shareholdings it will be necessary to place an absolute ban on the holding of shares in a company by any other company which directly, or indirectly through the intermediary of another company, holds shares in it. It would thus be the duty of the directors of any company interested in buying a holding in another company to ensure that there was no prior inverse shareholding. This would cause some difficulties in respect of market dealings, especially in certain forms of take-over battle where each company is attempting to acquire control over the other, and in some investment company operations. But measures of this kind are necessary if the problems of entrenchment and the consequent concealed depletion of capital are to be avoided. As in the case of the oppression of minorities and creditors the only effective solution to the problems of complex group organization is to prevent the development of unnecessarily complex forms of interrelationship.

10

Investment institutions

Despite the widely publicized increase in the range and extent of investment in the stock market by all sections of the community it would be unrealistic to claim that direct investment in the shares of publicly quoted companies is not largely restricted to the propertied classes. A recent official survey has shown that in 1972–3 just over two million taxpayers in the United Kingdom received dividends or other forms of investment income taxable at source, but that the top ten per cent of these taxpayers received about seventy per cent of the total income.[1] Allowing for the fact that younger members of a family and some wives are excluded this means that about one-tenth of the population may be regarded as investors, but that most of these are very small investors. There is no formal bar on the number of shares which may be purchased or the amount of money which may be invested through a stock broker, but small investors dealing in sums of less than £100 or so are certainly not encouraged except with a view to business on a larger scale in the future. The small investor from the point of view of the Stock Exchange is one who deals in hundreds or thousands of pounds rather than tens or hundreds of thousands.

The genuinely small investor is not thereby excluded from the operations of the capitalist system. Since the eighteenth century a wide range of financial institutions has developed through which the savings of the lower middle and working classes, however small in

[1] *Royal Commission on the Distribution of Income and Wealth*, Report No. 2, Income from Companies and its distribution, Cmnd. 6172 (1975), Tables 12 and 17.

individual terms, may be aggregated and channelled into commercial and industrial investment. These second order investment institutions may be categorized into two broad groups : those in which savings are invested or deposited with an institution on a fixed interest basis, as for instance in savings banks and deposit companies, and then invested by that institution on the market with a view to profit over and above the agreed interest; and those in which the small investor is enabled to participate more directly in the profit or loss from the investment of his money, as for instance through investment companies and unit trusts. There are in addition a number of institutions such as insurance companies and building societies whose principal objective is rather different but which also invest subscriptions or deposits from small investors and savers on the stock market.

The main focus of the law in this sphere, as will be seen, has been on the protection of small investors. In recent years, however, increasing attention has been focused on the importance of institutional investors within the general framework of the stock market and industrial investment. As shown by the analysis in Chapter 2, second order investment institutions now hold more than one-third of equity shares in quoted companies (see Table 2.12), and have an increasing influence on the allocation of investment throughout the economy. This has raised the question whether these investment institutions should be subjected to some more effective control in respect of their investment policies than is practicable within the existing law.

The protection of savings

The first formal institutions for the collection and investment of small savings were the insurance and annuity societies of the eighteenth century. In view of the great increase in 'the pernicious practice of raising money by the sale of life annuities' these were subjected to registration and enrolment as early as 1777. Similar provisions for the regulation by local magistrates of all friendly societies engaged in the collection and administration of the savings of the working classes were introduced in 1793. The precise terms of these measures are of historical importance only. But they set a pattern of regulation by continuing official oversight which has been followed in respect of every other form of institution whose business involves the direct solicitation and collection of money subscriptions from the general public.

The basic objective in all such cases is to permit the benefits from the operation of such institutions to be as freely and widely available as possible without exposing those who entrust their money to them to unnecessary risk. This is normally pursued first, by exercising control over the internal rules under which such institutions operate, and where practicable over the establishment of new ventures, and secondly, by maintaining a system of regular scrutiny over the form and content of their periodic accounts. Within this framework there is wide variation in the form and intensity of regulation over the various types of institution. Each is governed by its own legislation, often as complex and detailed as the Companies Acts themselves, so that only the broad outlines can be described here.

The most extreme form of intervention and protection is that provided for the Post Office Savings Bank, now the National Savings Bank, which was set up in 1861 on the failure of a number of private savings banks and has official backing both for deposits and for interest. In every other case the legislature has stopped short of any kind of official guarantee. Other trustee savings banks are subject to the more usual controls of registration, the scrutiny of annual accounts and a statutory limitation on the types of investment into which the depositors' money may be put. In many cases this type of oversight is maintained through an independent registrar, as for instance for industrial, provident and friendly societies, and building societies. The registrar is granted wide powers both to refuse to sanction any rule under which the society proposes to operate its affairs and also to intervene by way of ad hoc investigation where any suspicion is raised from the scrutiny of the periodic accounts or otherwise. In all these cases the basis of official intervention is the conception of the institution as a trust fund governed by the specific purposes of the society, whether that be to provide money for sickness or other distress for members, as in industrial, provident and friendly societies, or to provide money for house-purchase as in building societies. The basic task of the registrar is to see to it that the terms of the trust are observed, and that any protective rules as to the investment or application of members' funds are strictly observed.

The trust conception is not in any way a prerequisite of official intervention. Building societies have in practice developed in a very different direction from friendly and provident societies, and have grown more and more like ordinary commercial institutions. In form a building society is an association of members whose savings as members are pooled and used as capital for house-building and house-purchase. But the idea of co-operative membership is fast disappearing, and the societies are increasingly regarded merely as a source of loan capital for the general public financed by the return on money deposited with them and invested by them in the ordinary course of business. The fact that the original legal form has survived this fundamental though gradual change in function, however, does not appear to have created any serious problems. The substance of modern building society business itself justifies the kind of supervision to which it is subjected.

Nor does the trust form of itself make official supervision necessary. One of the largest and most significant groups of institutional investors are the independent pension funds set up by larger enterprises. These funds are accumulated from employers' and employees' contributions and invested by the fund managers with a view to financing pensions and other benefits for employees who are members of the scheme. The similarity of these funds to other industrial and provident societies is obvious. Yet they are not subject to any statutory supervision as such, except that in order to gain tax exemption for the employers' contributions the rules of the fund must be approved by the Inland Revenue. The introduction of governmental controls has always been dependent on positive proof by way of actual cases of failure and fraud that intervention is necessary, and there has not yet been any sufficiently serious case of the manipulation or misuse of pension funds to bring that about.

Deposit-taking companies

One of the major difficulties in legislating for the protection of small savers is the flexibility of legal forms. It is almost impossible to formulate a satisfactory range of definitions of savings institutions of the various types already discussed which excludes the possibility of carrying out similar functions under a different form and thus escaping official regulation. Savings banks and building societies and other such bodies are in practice largely self-classified by the fact that they have opted to register under a particular statute, and to subject themselves to the relevant statutory provisions. But as controls are tightened over older established institutions, there is a tendency for new forms to be adopted. The development during the 1950s of public advertising by ordinary companies for deposits from small savers at attractive rates of interest is a good example of this process.

There was nothing in any existing legislation to prevent the raising of finance in this way, since it did not fall within the terms of the legislation on public issues of share and loan capital. As so often happens, the loophole was exploited by a number of unsound and unscrupulous enterprises, culminating in the failure of the Mias group of deposit-taking companies in 1958.

Legislative control was eventually introduced in the Protection of Depositors Act of 1963. Under this statute any company, whether public or private, which advertises for deposits is subject to special accounting requirements similar to those imposed on other savings institutions. Copies of accounts in the prescribed form must be deposited with the Department of Trade before any advertisements are issued. The Department is also given wide powers to control the form in which advertisements may be issued, and the information which must be included in them. In addition every depositor must be supplied with copies of the most recent accounts, and may withdraw any deposit, regardless of any contrary contractual terms, if the company embarks on any business operations not expressly covered in the circulars soliciting the deposit. The net effect of this is to extend to deposits the type of controls long established in the sphere of share issues, and to subject the accounts of deposit-taking companies to similar official scrutiny as those of other savings institutions. The Department of Trade is also given extensive powers of intervention, to require the production of documents or accounts, or enter and search premises. Finally, it has power, where necessary, to halt the operations of any company which appears to be insolvent or only able to repay existing depositors by obtaining additional deposits, or which has failed to comply with the accounting requirements of the Act, by petitioning for a winding up order.

Insurance companies

The initial provisions for the supervision of insurance companies were based on the same principles as those for other institutions soliciting funds from the public. But these have gradually been extended to include a large element of control designed specifically to counteract the risks of loss or failure inherent in insurance business. In addition to the requirements for the scrutiny of annual accounts by the Department of Trade, linked to powers to demand additional information with a view to establishing the solvency of the company and if necessary to petition for a winding up order, provision was made in 1946 for a statutory margin in excess of solvency to be maintained by all insurance companies as a condition of continuing in business. This was intended to permit the authorities to intervene before a state of actual insolvency is reached. Following a renewed outbreak of frauds and failures in the cut-price motor insurance business in the 1960s these provisions were further strengthened in the Companies Act 1967 by requiring positive official authorization for any new company starting in business. The Act also extended the Department's powers of intervention to permit temporary orders forbidding a company to write any new business, and more general restrictions on the type or amount of business undertaken. These powers and that of prescribing the form of annual accounts are now consolidated in the Insurance Companies Act 1974. They should ensure that a genuine assessment of a company's financial position, including its future contingent liabilities, is possible, so that official action may be taken to prevent the continuance of any unsound insurance activity which threatens the solvency of the company. Certain rights are also protected by the Policy Holders Protection Act 1975.

The problems of intervention

It is not possible in the space available to discuss individually the details of these various schemes for official supervision and intervention. But the broad strategy in each case is sufficiently similar to permit some general assessment.

There can be no absolute guarantee that savings will not be lost in whole or in part without a government guarantee. Short of that, there is always the possibility that those in control of a savings institution will make off with funds deposited with them, and perhaps for a time conceal the depredations by skilful false accounting. The objective of official supervision is simply to minimize this possibility. The real difficulty is that the regular scrutiny of accounts, as provided in most of the statutes, cannot of itself provide much genuine protection for depositors. It is almost impossible to relate accounts prepared on the traditional basis to the practical question of the realizability of assets and the actual repayment of deposits. Some progress has been made in most cases by the formulation of more functional accounting requirements under the power usually provided to prescribe in detail the form of accounts to be submitted to the supervising authority. Under the Insurance Companies Acts, for instance, there are now detailed provisions requiring the provision of precise details of the company's provision for contingent liabilities and its reinsurance arrangements, so that an assessment of their adequacy may be made. But in the end all that the scrutiny of accounts can provide is evidence of or grounds for suspecting unsoundness in the company's finances.

The crucial question is what is to be done when suspicions are aroused. From the point of view of the depositor the best move would be to insist on the replacement of the current management and the initiation of more satisfactory policies. But this has never been accepted as a real option within a free enterprise system. The authorities are accordingly forced back on a number of second-best alternatives. Under most of the statutes there is provision for the supervising authority to call for additional information and accounts, or to appoint an inspector, so that the true position may be ascertained. There is usually also a provision permitting the authority to petition for the winding up of the suspect institution on the grounds of insolvency. Pending a decision on the petition or the report of inspectors the authority may also be granted power to impose a stop order on any further business by the institution. In the case of insurance companies, for instance, this extends to the imposition of an upper limit on the amount of business of a particular kind which may be undertaken. More direct and positive powers of intervention are occasionally granted, as, for instance, the power to require an insurance company to realize certain investments which appear to the supervising authority to be unsatisfactory. But these are the exceptions. The problem which usually faces the authority is whether to step in formally by initiating an inspection with a view to making a winding up petition, or simply to use the threat of such action as a means of securing some voluntary remedial action on the part of the suspect institution's managers.

The policy of the Department of Trade and other regulatory agencies in this respect has typically been to adopt a strategy of persuasion and veiled threats. It has not been wholly successful. The Pinnock Finance Company, for instance, failed disastrously in March 1967 with a total deficit of more than £8m. The report of the inspectors appointed to enquire into the group revealed that the deficits in the various subsidiary companies into which the depositors' money had been poured over a period of years were of long standing. Yet despite its brand new powers of intervention to clarify any doubtful accounts under the Protection of Depositors Act 1963 the Department took no formal action until some months after the crash.[2] Similarly in the case of the rash of cut-price insurance companies in the mid-1960s little positive action appears to have been taken by the Department under the Insurance Companies Acts until it was too late to do anything but clear up the mess. It was argued at the time that the powers of the Department were inadequate. But the Tribunal of Inquiry into the failure of the Vehicle and General Insurance Company revealed that the Department consistently took the narrowest possible interpretation of its powers.[3] The opinion of one of the Department's principal witnesses before the Tribunal is revealing:

> This is what freedom with publicity is all about. This was the basic principle of the 1958 Act, which has only been modified in some degree in the 1967 Act. The insurer is free to conduct his business as he thinks fit. The only power the Department had under the 1958 Act was to to pick up the pieces.[4]

This approach was an effective denial of the policy of the legislation, which, as stated by Sir Stafford Cripps in 1946, was 'to make as certain as possible that there were no failures of British insurance companies'. The Tribunal concluded that while the Department's approach prior to 1967 had been strictly justifiable, it had been unnecessarily restrictive, but that in any event there had at all times after that date been grounds for intervention and that action should have been taken long before it was.[5]

The justification which has frequently been produced for this restrictive attitude is that precipitate formal action by the initiation of an inspection or otherwise could cause irreparable harm to a company from which it might never recover, since the appointment of an inspector is generally thought to be conclusive evidence of insolvency. But this argument is self-defeating. It is only the fact that the Department has consistently used its formal powers only at the last possible moment which has encouraged the deduction that any company sub-

[2] Department of Trade and Industry, *Report on Pinnock Finance Company (Great Britain) Ltd. and Associated Companies* (1971).

[3] *Report of the Tribunal appointed to inquire into certain issues in relation to the circumstances leading up to the cessation of trading by the Vehicle and General Insurance Company Limited* (1972), para. 147.

[4] *Minutes of Evidence*, Day 18, p. 20 (Mr Homewood).

[5] *Report*, para. 147; Summary of Findings, para. 5.

jected to an inspection must be near to insolvency. A more active policy of intervention as soon as there is any reasonable doubt as to a company's financial state might well have bred a rather different public expectation.

The implication of this is clear. If the powers of supervising authorities are to have a genuine preventive force, and so operate as a real protection for small savers, the restrictive policies of the past must be replaced by a strategy of more active intervention to establish the true position whenever there is any suspicion that a company's financial position is unsound. And since to establish that this is indeed the case is not in itself enough, the powers of the authorities might also be extended to permit the installation of a temporary receiver or manager on behalf of the depositors or members along the lines of the standard provisions for debenture holders. The logic of a policy of providing genuine protection to small savers must go further than the idea of freedom with publicity as it is currently interpreted.

Investment companies and unit trusts

Investment companies and unit trusts are based on an entirely different principle from other savings institutions, in that their shareholders or unit-holders participate directly as investors in the success or failure of the company or trust.[6] The only difference between them and shareholders in ordinary quoted companies is that instead of making their own investment decisions they place their capital in the hands of the management of the company or trust to invest on their behalf. The profit or loss on the operations of the enterprise, after the deduction of the salaries of the directors or managers and other expenses, is then allocated among the share or unit holders either as dividends or as capital appreciation. The company or trust is simply a channel through which the investors' money is directed onto the ordinary market for investment.

The simplest form of organization for second order investment of this kind is the investment company, which is for all practical purposes an ordinary limited company whose business happens to be

[6] There is a good account of the historical development of investment (trust) companies and unit trusts in R. R. Pennington, *The Investor and the Law* (1968), Ch. 8; see also H. A. Ford, 'Unit Trusts' (1960) 23 *MLR* 129, and for an economic appraisal H. Burton and D. C. Corner, *Investment and Unit Trusts in Britain and America* (1968).

investing the funds of its shareholders in other companies or enterprises. It is accordingly subject to the standard rules of company law in respect of the division of power between the board of directors and the general meeting of shareholders. The fact that such companies are frequently referred to as investment trust companies or even simply as investment trusts is a confusion of terminology which should be avoided wherever possible. The only reason for the formal recognition of the investment company as a distinct category is the need for special rules for the assessment of trading and capital profit for tax purposes.

A unit trust on the other hand is not a company but a trust. Those who invest their savings in the units offered by the management of the trust fund are in law the beneficiaries in whose sole interest the trust fund constituted by their contributions must be administered. In practice the management of the trust sets up the formal legal organization of the fund in advance, providing a set of rules for the investment of the funds (perhaps specifying a particular type or area of investment), for the payment of dividends and for the valuation of units for the purposes of purchase or sale. The units are then offered to the public, initially at a fixed price and subsequently at the average current valuation of the existing units. A unit holder is entitled to withdraw at any time by selling his units back to the management at current valuation. To give a simple example : if 1,000 units had been created at an initial price of £1 per unit and the purchase money profitably invested in stocks and shares which, after allowing for the expenses of management, had risen in value to £2,000, the price payable to a unit holder who wished to withdraw would be £2 per unit; any new investor would then have to pay £2 plus a small commission to the managers for each new unit issued. In this way the small investor is enabled to spread his investment over a wider range of equities than would be possible if he simply went to a stockbroker with £50 or £100. In addition he is spared the problem of deciding what to buy and what to sell and what to hold on a continuing basis. All this is done for him by the managers of the unit trust, who make a charge on the fund for their services and expenses; they are not usually permitted to hold units themselves. The growth of the fund in terms both of the number and the value of units is thus directly dependent on the investment skill or luck of the managers and on their ability in bringing in new investors on the strength of their past performance. Though in the early stages of their development unit trusts were limited in size to a fixed number of units, it is now almost universal practice for them to be operated on a flexible or open-ended basis which permits the managers to sell as many units as they can find buyers for.

The distinction between investment companies and unit trusts, which clearly serve a similar function, is largely a historical accident. Both forms were developed in the later nineteenth century. But following a decision in 1879 that a unit trust was illegal in that it contravened the restriction in the Companies Acts on non-corporate business associations of more than twenty members,[7] most of the existing unit trusts transformed themselves into investment companies. It was decided a year later that unit trusts were perfectly legal since the members had no intention of carrying on business together, but simply deposited their funds with the trustees for investment.[8] But the trust form did not become popular again until the 1930s when it was taken up on the American model as a means of evading the increasing controls which were being imposed on the flotation of new issues on the stock market. Many of the new unit trusts, however, were little more than a means of extracting money from unsuspecting small investors, and in the face of growing public concern the Anderson Committee of 1936 recommended the introduction of stringent statutory controls over all unit trusts.[9] Action was finally taken in the Prevention of Fraud (Investments) Act of 1939, which gave wider powers of control to the authorities than were available for any other investment institution. No unit trust was to be operated without official sanction and the Board of Trade, as it then was, was granted absolute discretionary power to refuse to grant a licence to any person. In addition, the rules for the internal management of any fund, including those which governed the commission and expenses which might be deducted by the managers, had to be officially approved, and there were the usual stringent provisions as to the form of the accounts to be deposited with the Board.

These provisions, re-enacted in the Prevention of Fraud (Investments) Act 1958, appear to have been singularly effective in preventing any return to the malpractices of the pre-war years. Investment companies are not subject to any special form of regulation. But the general schemes for the supervision of quoted companies and for the

[7] *Sykes v. Beadon* (1879) 11 Ch. D. 170.

[8] *Smith v. Anderson* (1880) 15 Ch. D. 247.

[9] Committee on Fixed Trusts, Cmd. 5259 (1936).

control of extra-market dealings have also proved sufficient to prevent any major abuses in that sphere. The major criticism of the current situation is that enterprises as similar in function as unit trusts and investment companies are dealt with under two entirely separate codes. This is in direct contrast to the position in the United States where all forms of investment company, or mutual funds, as they are termed, are subject to the same general provisions for disclosure and supervision under the Investment Companies Acts of 1940 and 1967. In some respects the American legislation is less stringent than that for unit trusts in Britain, for instance in the lack of control over the commission which may be charged by fund managers which is consequently many times higher in America than in Britain. But the disclosure requirements imposed on all mutual funds, whatever their formal status, are a good deal more demanding. There is a strong theoretical case for the standardization of the law for the various types of investment institution, perhaps on the basis of the investment company rather than the unit trust in view of the greater control exercisable over the managers by the investors.[10]

The adoption of a general functional provision designed to regulate the substance rather than the form of investment institutions would also have the advantage of providing in advance for new forms of organization in this sphere. The latest development in Britain has been the property bond, which in essence is a simple insurance policy, the premiums for which are invested directly in specified equities or in property development. The attraction of this is to allow relatively small investors to tie their investments to rising equity or property values and at the same time to take advantage of the tax reliefs granted on insurance premiums. The companies through which these bond schemes are operated are usually subject to the general regulations affecting insurance companies. But, as has frequently been pointed out, these regulations do not extend to the control of standards of disclosure in respect of the valuation of investments or properties or of commission charges which are generally thought to be desirable in operations of this kind. Some measure of self-regulation on these matters was initiated in 1970 by some of the larger and better established operators in the field, and has resulted in some measure of standardization of the information to be included in advertisements and circulars, as for instance an express statement that

[10] R. R. Pennington, *The Investor and the Law*, pp. 241 ff.

no given rate of capital appreciation can ever be guaranteed. But in the absence of any statutory or institutional sanction against fringe operators who do not choose to accept this voluntary code the position can scarcely be said to be satisfactory. Even if the revelation of some particularly scandalous malpractice in the coming years does lead to specific legislation, the prospect of yet another separate code to add to those already governing deposit companies, unit trusts and the rest is not attractive.

Some consolidation of the existing structure of prudential supervision in this field has been promised in the aftermath of the secondary banking crisis of the early 1970s. The government proposes to require all deposit-taking institutions other than those formally recognized as banks to operate under licence from the Bank of England and to meet required standards of liquidity and solvency.[11] But trustee savings banks, building societies and friendly societies, all of which take deposits, are to be excluded from the new system as will be other investment institutions like the insurance companies, pension funds, investment companies and unit trusts which raise their money in different forms. There is a strong case for a more thorough review of the system of legislative and administrative supervision of all investment institutions both from the point of view of protecting investors' money and of giving them greater control over the way in which their investment is applied.

[11] *The Licensing and Supervision of Deposit-Taking Institutions*, Cmnd. 6584 (1976).

11

Co-operatives and communes

There are forms of business organization which lie outside the framework of capitalism. There is no clear cutting off point in this context between capitalist and non-capitalist structures, as will be clear from the discussion in Chapter 13 of schemes for profit sharing and participation in larger companies. But for the purpose of analysis two additional forms of organization, the co-operative and the commune, may usefully be isolated.

A co-operative is a business enterprise in which membership and participation in profit is linked to the provision of labour or produce, or the use of facilities, rather than the contribution of capital. It may still be necessary to raise capital for the establishment and operation of such an enterprise, whether in the form of contributions from members and supporters or loans from ordinary commercial sources on a fixed interest basis. But this does not affect the formal basis of the association in which capital as such plays no part. Participation in a co-operative, as in a simple partnership, is essentially personal. Any profit resulting from trading operations, after the usual provision for re-investment, is shared among the members as members on some equitable basis. In a consumer or service co-operative dividend payments are based on the use made by each of the members of the facilities provided. In a producer co-operative they will be assessed on the basis of the amount of labour contributed. Thus in a typical retail co-operative members will receive a dividend on the total amount of their purchases. Similarly in an agricultural marketing co-operative members will receive payment at the market rate for their produce and a dividend based on the proportion of the total value of goods processed or sold which they have supplied. And in an agricultural service co-operative members will pay at an agreed rate for materials or services and receive a dividend out of profits in proportion to the amount they have spent. The net result is not in any sense a rejection of the basic economic principle of evaluating and paying for goods and labour at a rate which is determined primarily by market forces. But the suppliers of capital are denied any share in profit over and above an agreed rate of interest on their contribution or loan. Any profit or surplus value created in the enterprise is divided exclusively among the members. In this way the rights of capital as such are subordinated to those of production or consumption.

In a commune, as the term is used here, the basic principle of market economics is rejected. The members of a commune need not in theory receive any direct payment for work done or goods supplied. There is no sharing out of profit in proportion to any assessment of each member's contribution. Instead the benefits of joint enterprise are distributed among members and their dependants on the basis of whatever political or religious conception the members may share about the nature of a just society. Thus in accordance with traditional communist ideals, all payments or distributions to individuals would be made on the basis of need rather than of merit or work done or goods supplied. Furthermore, since there are no calculable costs of production, there can be nothing which can reasonably be thought of as profit. The benefits of communal enterprise are simply absorbed by the community as a whole. If there is a good harvest or a high level of manufacture, the community is simply better off, and must decide whether to celebrate in consumption or alternatively to seek still further increases for the future by the 'reinvestment' of energy or resources.

This formal account of communism bears no observable relationship to any established party or state. A determined application of communist principles in this strict sense would involve a radical departure from the practice of buying and selling goods, services and labour which has not been achieved in any large scale economy either in developed western countries or elsewhere. For this reason the main focus in the account which follows will be on the development and formal organization of co-operative enterprises within a wider capitalist or market economy.

Co-operatives in Britain

The development of the co-operative movement in Britain, despite the wide claims of its more committed adherents, has been curiously limited and fragmented.[1] The ideals of the movement may readily be traced to the schemes of Robert Owen and others for factory communities in the early nineteenth century, and later to the more limited proposals of the Christian Socialists for facilitating the establishment of producer co-operatives. The only forms of co-operatives to establish themselves on a widespread and lasting basis, however, have been retail consumer co-operatives, and agricultural marketing and service co-operatives. The former were a more or less direct development out of the friendly and provident societies which had been formed in many working class communities from the middle of the eighteenth century onwards to provide some protection for members against sickness and unemployment in the new industrial conditions. The Rochdale Pioneers who established the first lasting retail co-operative in 1844 merely extended the established principles of co-operation from communal thrift and mutual assurance to the supply of ordinary daily requisites at fair prices from a society shop. Others before them had tried similar operations, but it was in Rochdale that the right mixture of hard-headed financial management, notably in the refusal to grant any form of credit, and of local communal organization was found. The recipe was copied in other towns and areas, and later extended to wholesaling and manufacturing on a co-operative basis for the established retail societies. The form of organization usually adopted was quite simple. Individual members would appoint a managing committee from among themselves to supervise the operation of the business on ordinary commercial lines, and to arrange for the periodic distribution of any surplus in the form of a percentage dividend on the amount purchased by each member. This structure then became standardized in the model rules for co-operatives which were developed and promoted by the central Co-operative Union established in 1869. Agricultural co-operatives in which individual farmers pooled their marketing and purchasing of supplies followed a similar pattern of development with the founding

[1] See generally A. M. Carr-Saunders, P. Sargant Florence & R. Peers, *Consumers' Co-operation in Great Britain* (1938); M. Digby, *Agricultural Co-operation in Great Britain* (1949); P. Backstrom, *Christian Socialism and Co-operation in Victorian England* (1974).

of the Irish Agricultural Organization Society in 1894 and the Agricultural Co-operatives Association in Britain soon after. In neither case has there been any radical break with established principles of business organization within the various retail shops and processing plants, in which the same division in status and authority between management and employees is to be found as in traditional capitalist companies. The members who support, and benefit from, the co-operative movement in Britain are individual consumers and farmers rather than the employees of the co-operatives.

This fragmentation in organizational terms is clearly reflected in the legislation under which most co-operatives in Britain now operate. The form of statutory control, like the co-operative movement itself, may be traced to the friendly societies of the later eighteenth century. Defalcations by officers and treasurers in these societies were relatively common. Accordingly in the first friendly societies legislation in 1793 provision was made for the registration of the rules of all such societies with local magistrates. This pattern was followed in subsequent statutes which gradually extended the principle of official supervision to cover the scrutiny by a full time official registrar of the rules and annual accounts of all organizations and associations in which there was an element of co-operative saving or investment (see Chapter 10). The first statute directed principally at co-operatives as such was the Industrial and Provident Societies Act of 1852 which was sponsored by the Christian Socialist movement in the hope of giving encouragement to the establishment of producer co-operatives. This measure, though frequently amended, still forms the basis of legislative control over co-operatives, as set out in the major consolidation of 1893 and in the current Industrial and Provident Societies Act 1965.

The registration of a co-operative under this statute is strictly voluntary, though any association of more than twenty persons would be technically unlawful under the Companies Acts (see Chapter 3). But registration does afford the benefits of corporate status and limited liability (s. 3). The conditions for registration are set out in very general terms, namely that the association shall be of a bona fide co-operative nature (s. 1). This is generally taken to mean that its affairs are controlled by its members equally, that there shall be no artificial restriction on membership with a view to increasing the proprietary interests of existing members in the assets of the society, and that the amount of interest on shares and the amount of any capital contribution from any member in the form of either shares or loans are limited to prescribed figures. A society whose objects include carrying on business mainly with a view to paying interest or dividends on its share or loan capital is expressly excluded (s. 7). There are also certain formal requirements in respect of the rules governing the internal affairs of the society. In practical terms, however, the rules will be based on one of the sets of model rules which have been prepared by the various central promotional bodies referred to above. Provision is also made for the investigation of the affairs of any society by the Registrar (s. 47), for determination of disputes by the Registrar (s. 60), and for a petition by the Registrar for dissolution by court order (s. 56). In so far as members or creditors are concerned the winding up provisions of the Companies Act 1948 apply. Where dissolution is finally agreed or ordered, any surplus assets of the society will be distributed among existing members in accordance with its rules; the standard rule for agricultural co-operatives, for instance, provides for the division of the surplus in proportion to the use made by current members of the facilities of the society in the seven years preceding dissolution.

Some societies of a broadly co-operative nature are also registered under the Friendly Societies Act 1974. This statute, which replaces the earlier consolidating statute of 1896, is primarily intended for organizations which provide mutual benefits for their members, notably in cases of sickness or loss of employment. This particular form of voluntary mutual assistance, however, has been largely superseded by the welfare state. Most friendly societies are now working men's clubs or benevolent associations of a charitable nature which provide benefits for persons other than members. Friendly societies are controlled by the Registrar of Friendly Societies under broadly similar provisions to those governing industrial and provident societies. The accounts of all societies registered under the Industrial and Provident Societies Act and the Friendly Societies Act must be audited annually by a qualified accountant under similar rules to those which govern companies (Friendly and Industrial and Provident Societies Act 1968). The Registrar of Friendly Societies also deals with the registration and supervision of building societies (see Chapter 10).

At the end of 1975 more than 9,500 societies were registered under these two statutes.[2] This figure conceals a wide range of different enterprises. More than 4,000 of the societies were housing associations, and more than 3,500 were social and recreational clubs; of the remainder some 1,500 were agricultural, fishing and general service societies. There were 313 retail co-operative societies and only 73 wholesale and productive societies. These figures indicate that the co-operative movement has made little or no headway in manufacturing and business activity other than the traditional retail and agricultural spheres. The tiny number of producer co-operatives registered under these statutes, however, may be misleading, in that many of the best known 'co-operatives' are registered as companies under the Companies Acts. Co-operative principles may readily be incorporated into the memorandum and articles of ordinary limited liability companies, for instance by eliminating all equity capital and entrusting the ultimate control of the company to trustees for the benefit of existing employees or to the general meeting of employee members. Employees as members would also share in any distributed profit after the payment of interest on loan capital and any provision for reinvestment. The John Lewis Partnership and the so called Meriden Co-operative are examples of large enterprises organized in this way (see Chapter 13).

Some additional government support for co-operative enterprises may now be provided under the Industrial Common Ownership Act 1976. This provides that grants or loans may be made to organizations which themselves advise or make loans to common ownership and co-operative enterprises. Common ownership enterprises are defined as companies or industrial or provident societies whose constitutions ensure that only employees may be members, that no assets of the enterprise other than profits shall be distributed to the members, that on dissolution all surplus assets shall be made over to a fund for the benefit of other common ownership enterprises, and that the enterprise is controlled by the majority of those who work for it (s. 2(1)). Co-operative enterprises are defined as those which the Secretary of State has certified as being in substance a co-operative association and being controlled by a majority of those who work for it (s. 2(2)). The intention of this statute is to encourage the formation of new enterprises in which all direct proprietary rights for members have been eliminated and in which all employees share both in any dis-

[2] *Report of the Chief Registrar of Friendly Societies for the year 1975* (1976).

tributed profit and in the ultimate control of the enterprise. It is doubtful whether this strategy of leaving each individual enterprise to draw up its own constitution in consultation with some appropriate advisory body and to register as a company or an industrial or provident society is the most appropriate. A new statute providing a simple and intelligible structure for the incorporation of co-operative enterprises, with a draft constitution along the lines of Table A in the Companies Act 1948, would help to dispel the confusion which many people still feel over the mechanics of registration and incorporation in this context.

Communes

There has been no widespread development in Britain of any form of enterprise which could reasonably be described as a commune, and for the reasons already discussed it is unlikely that such enterprises could flourish in the prevailing political and economic framework. But there is no reason why pure communist principles should not be applied and promoted in other countries. The best known and most successful example in the western world has been the development of the Israeli Kibbutz. In so far as any valid assessment can be made of these without becoming involved in matters of religion rather than economics, it would appear that their success has been closely linked to the crusading spirit in the reclamation of virgin land and to a tightly controlled social and communal framework. A similar difficulty in assessment arises in relation to the widely publicized development of rural and industrial communes in the People's Republic of China. Objective information on the true nature of these communes is almost impossible to obtain,[8] but it would appear that what success may be claimed in the establishment of pure communism in Chinese villages has been the result of careful policies of gradualism. Since the revolutionary victory of 1948 the authorities in China have been pursuing a deliberate strategy to wean the peasants away from the established conceptions of private ownership and profit towards those of communal service. Thus in the early period collective production was organized in what were termed 'lower socialist co-operatives' in which rental payments continued to be paid to ex-landlords for any land taken for communal production, and in which payment to members was on a simple piecework basis. In the period of the

[8] For some interesting details see C. S. Chen, *Rural People's Communes in Lien-Chiang* (1969).

'higher socialist co-operatives' these rental payments were phased out, though wages and rents continued to be paid on a market basis to members for contributions in the form of labour or materials. The move from this stage to pure communes in which payment to members is on the basis of need rather than of work done has been widely heralded, but it is impossible to say how far a genuine structural change has actually been made. The established conceptions of individual property and of payment for work done would appear to be as firmly embedded in Chinese as in western culture. The results of the Chinese policy of socialist education must be awaited before it is possible to say whether such ideas are in any way necessary or natural, or merely the result of a particular ideological framework.

No satisfactory conclusion on these issues is possible in this context. The justification for such a brief reference to the Israeli and Chinese systems is simply to emphasize that other than capitalist structures can be implemented if the conditions are suitable, and that the laws of market economics are no more fixed than any other aspect of political and social organization. In those countries where the conception of communal rights in land still prevails over that of individual ownership there is clearly no reason why the commune and the co-operative should not remain the primary form of economic organization as long as adequate measures are implemented to prevent the intrusion of alien structures of capitalist organization, and to ensure that as in capitalist companies the opportunities for impropriety and fraud are reduced to a minimum by the establishment of adequate structures for accounting and control.

PART THREE: THE MIXED ECONOMY

12

Perspectives for the future

British company law is based on a precise and limited conception of the company as a means through which capital may be invested in commercial enterprises. The basic essentials of the structure may be stated quite simply, and are highlighted in the accompanying model (Figure 12.1): first, the shareholders are regarded as owning

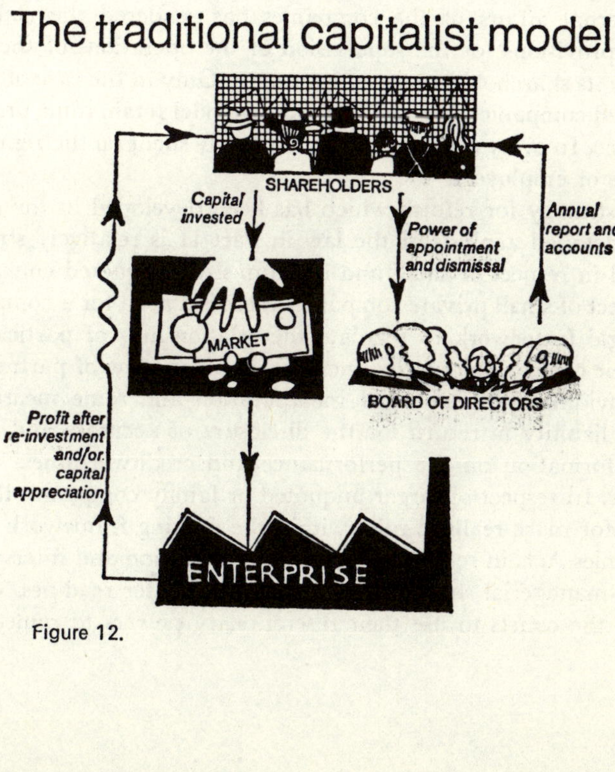

Figure 12.

the enterprise and in return for their initial capital contribution are entitled to the whole of the profit from the business, whether it is distributed to them in the form of dividends or accumulated in the company by reinvestment; secondly, the control of the enterprise is shared between the shareholders, who appoint the directors and must approve certain basic transactions, and the directors, who manage the enterprise but must account to the shareholders for their performance; thirdly, in the case of quoted companies the flow of capital is ideally channelled through the stock market in such a way as to secure the optimum allocation of resources in the private sector of the economy. Most of the complex rules in the Companies Acts and the case-law discussed in Part II can be traced back to these relatively simple ideas.

This model, as the analysis in previous chapters has shown, does not reflect the realities of the commercial world. In the smallest companies the fact that shareholders and directors are the same people upsets the basis upon which the various legal controls and protections are based. In large quoted companies the growth of an independent and largely self-perpetuating managerial elite and the increasing detachment of shareholders and the stock market from the internal affairs of the companies has rendered the elaborate formal provisions for the supervision of the operations of the company by its shareholders largely irrelevant. Only in the case of larger unquoted companies does the traditional model retain some practical relevance. In every case the law is completely silent on the rights and interests of employees.

The strategy for reform which has been developed in the course of the detailed analysis of the law in Part II is relatively straightforward in respect of small and medium-sized unquoted companies. In respect of small private companies there is a need for a completely new legal framework to regulate the relationships of participators and their creditors along the lines of the existing law of partnership, but providing the benefits of incorporation and some measure of limited liability in return for the disclosure of accurate and up-to-date information on the performance and creditworthiness of the business. In respect of larger unquoted or family companies there is a need for more realistic rules within the existing framework of the Companies Acts in respect of access to information and intervention by non-managerial shareholders, and for a greater readiness on the part of the courts to use their discretionary powers to remedy the oppression of minorities by the failure to pay dividends or otherwise. Whatever provision is made for the recognition of employees in these smaller companies is likely to follow the pattern set in larger companies.

The basis for legal reform in larger quoted and unquoted companies is less settled. Though there is some agreement that employees should be afforded greater recognition within the company, the extent to which they should participate in the control or supervision of the management of the company or in its profits is a matter of political controversy. So too is the extent to which formal provision should be made for greater governmental involvement in the affairs of major companies, though it is generally accepted that some degree of governmental interference in the interests of economic regulation is inevitable if not desirable. The purpose of this chapter is to introduce some of the basic conceptions underlying the existing structures for employee participation and governmental regulation and the various possibilities for the extension of industrial democracy and state intervention.

The conflict model

The response in most countries to the exclusion of employees from any formal involvement in the affairs of the companies for which they work has not been the proletarian revolution envisaged in Marxist theory but the spontaneous growth of trade unions and a system of collective bargaining through which the interests of workers have been pursued with considerable effect. Wage bargaining at national and shop-floor level has won for most industrial workers a progressive improvement in pay and conditions of work and some degree of influence for shop stewards over the day-to-day organization of most large companies.

The system of collective bargaining has been legally institutionalized in some countries. In Britain, mainly as a result of the prolonged struggle of the trade unions throughout the nineteenth and early twentieth centuries for the legalization of their activities, there is a deeply felt suspicion of legal processes among most active trade unionists. This was forcefully demonstrated in the highly successful opposition by the trade-union movement to the attempt of successive Labour and Conservative governments to introduce a much greater degree of legal control over union activities. In 1969 the Labour government was forced to drop its plans for legal regulation of

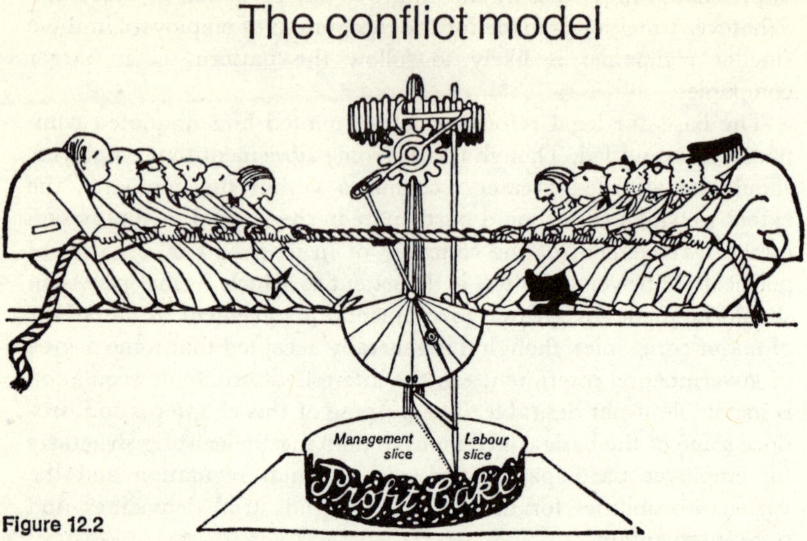

Figure 12.2

collective bargaining outlined in *In Place of Strife.*[1] And in 1974 the Trades Union Congress finally won its campaign to secure the repeal of the Industrial Relations Act 1971, which had been introduced by the succeeding Conservative government and which contributed in large measure to its ultimate fall.

The commitment to free collective bargaining has led to the development of a powerful conceptual thesis which is based on a supposedly natural and fundamental antagonism between capitalists and workers as representatives of the 'two sides' of industry. The 'conflict theory' of industrial relations, as illustrated in Figure 12.2, portrays the operation of a company's business as a perpetual struggle between workers and management for a larger share in the profits from their joint enterprise.[2] The side with the greatest bargaining strength in terms of its resources and political backing in relation to the state of the economy as a whole will be in a position to increase its share of the profit cake at the expense of the other side. If agree-

[1] Cmnd. 3888 (1969).

[2] A good account of the difference between a conflict model and the more traditional conception of the enterprise is given by A. Fox, *Industrial Sociology and Industrial Relations*, Royal Commission on Trade Unions and Employers' Associations, Research Paper No. 3 (1968); the author has subsequently revised his approach in *Beyond Contract: Work, Power and Trust Relations* (1974).

ment cannot be reached through the processes of peaceful collective bargaining the conflict will eventually be decided by industrial warfare in which the side with the greater capacity to withstand a strike or a lockout will triumph. There is a direct relationship between this theory and the Marxist account of the appropriation of surplus value by the owners of capital and the resulting exploitation of the workers.

The result of this pattern of development on a more formal legal level has been a strict separation of labour law and company law. Labour law has focussed attention on the contract of employment between employer and employee, on the protection of the system of collective bargaining and the right to strike from legal interference, and to a lesser extent on trade-union organization. Company law has been exclusively concerned with the means of raising capital for the enterprise, the treatment of profit arising from it and the relations between shareholders and directors. The possibility of any constructive interrelationship between the two has been further thwarted by the commitment of most British labour lawyers to what may be termed the 'abstention' theory of labour law, under which any form of legal intervention in the mechanism of collective bargaining is regarded as likely to cause more problems than it solves.[3] The only area of genuine contact between the two fields has been that of disclosure, in that the release of full details of the state of a company's affairs is thought by some to be an essential precondition of realistic and effective collective bargaining. Even in this sphere, however, the statutory provisions for disclosure, as will be seen, have been developed in two entirely separate codes.

This approach to industrial relations is an accurate reflection of the real historical struggle in which the trade-union movement has been involved since the early nineteenth century. But there are certain drawbacks to a continued reliance on the conflict model in current industrial and commercial conditions.

In the first place the emphasis on conflict between management and labour has tended to obscure the extent to which there is a shared interest in the generation and reinvestment of profits on the part of employers and employees alike. In many instances the

[3] This theory may be traced to the influence of Professor Kahn-Freund on a generation of British labour lawyers: see his lecture 'Labour Law', in M. Ginsberg (ed.), *Law and Opinion in England in the Twentieth Century* (1959), and also K. W. Wedderburn, *The Worker and the Law* (1st edn., 1965), p. 13.

primary conflict of interest is between different groups of workers within the enterprise in respect of pay differentials and restrictive practices, rather than between employees as a whole and shareholders. It may be argued that it is even less appropriate and mutually beneficial for this internal conflict to be carried out by a strategy of industrial confrontation between workers and management. There is certainly no evidence that the performance of British industry in the post-war period under the prevailing conflict approach to industrial relations has been more effective than that of other countries, though there is continued dispute on the practical impact of strikes and other forms of industrial action on levels of production.[4]

A second drawback is that the emphasis on the inherent conflict between the two sides of industry makes more difficult the kind of direct involvement by workers or their representatives in managerial decision-making which critics of the capitalist system have wished to promote. Instead it promotes a form of arms-length bargaining between management and unions in which each side prepares its plans and strategies in conditions of secrecy in order to strengthen its bargaining position. To that extent it reinforces the existing position of management as the ultimate authority within the company. This problem has been recognized by some trade-union leaders in recent years, as in the following TUC report:

> There are a number of specific questions of close concern to workpeople which are not being effectively subjected to joint regulation through the present processes of collective bargaining . . . , particularly as capital becomes more concentrated and the central decisions of boards of directors seem increasingly remote from any impact by workpeople through their own organizations.[5]

Hence the demands, culminating in the majority report of the Bullock Committee on Industrial Democracy,[6] for equal representation of trade unions on the boards of major companies so that collective bargaining may be effectively extended to matters of longer-term planning and investment, as opposed to immediate issues of pay and conditions and methods of work.

The prospects for this form of industrial democracy will be

[4] H. A. Turner, *Is Britain really strike-prone?* (1969).

[5] Trades Union Congress, *Interim Report on Industrial Democracy* (1973), p. 7.

[6] Cmnd. 6706 (1977).

discussed in greater detail in Chapter 13 in the light of experience in other countries of employee representation at board level. But it is important to recognize that the extension of collective bargaining represents only one of a number of possible alternatives to existing capitalist structures. Though it proposes an important alteration in the balance of formal authority within the company it does nothing to change the basic legal rules of company law on the ultimate ownership of the company by its shareholders and the resulting rules as to the distribution of profit or allocation of capital appreciation. The implications of the Marxist analysis of the capitalist mode of production is more accurately reflected by the two strands of socialist thinking represented by the state capitalist and workers' co-operative models of the enterprise.

State Capitalism

Marx's remedy for the evils of the capitalist system was usually expressed as a form of social or collective ownership of the means of production, under which individual workers would have greater control over, and involvement in, their daily work. But this formulation conceals two widely differing approaches. One strand of socialist thinking, associated with Proudhonist and anarchical theories, found its expression in Russia in 1917 in the widespread workers' control movement and in Britain in the guild socialist movement of the 1920s. The other, which was closer in its inception to Marx's own views, is a policy of state centralization under which the 'commanding heights' of the economy are taken over by the state and subjected to direct political control in the interests of the community as a whole. This latter view, illustrated in Figure 12.3, eventually triumphed both in Russia and in the British Labour Party.

The reasons for the abandonment of the notion of workers' control in both Britain and Russia, which may be taken as representative in this respect of the pursuit of socialism by revolutionary and parliamentary means respectively, are instructive. In post-revolutionary Russia the primary concern of the new Bolshevik government was to restore some kind of economic stability in the exceptionally chaotic conditions which resulted from the war with Germany and the revolution itself.[7] This involved stringent central controls on wages, prices, hours of work and the distribution of raw materials,

[7] See generally M. Dewar, *Labour Policy in the USSR, 1917–28* (1956).

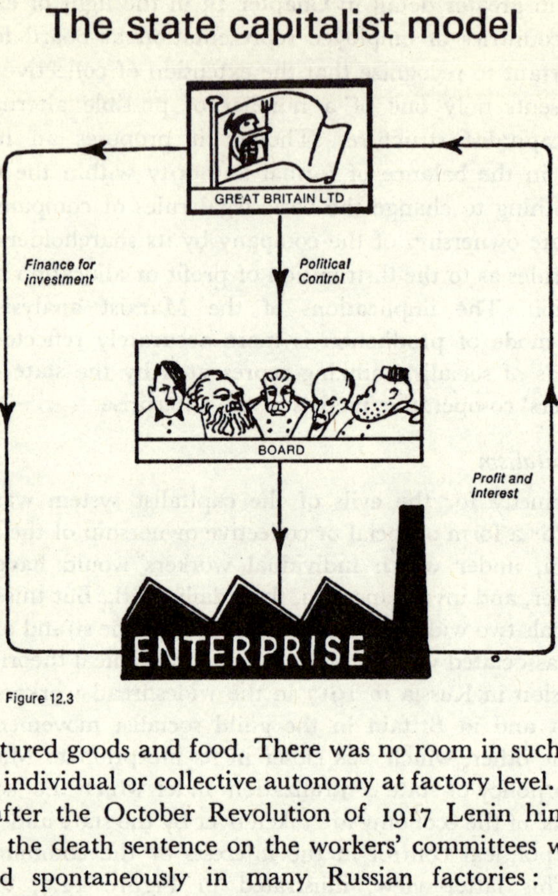

Figure 12.3

manufactured goods and food. There was no room in such a framework for individual or collective autonomy at factory level. Less than a year after the October Revolution of 1917 Lenin himself pronounced the death sentence on the workers' committees which had developed spontaneously in many Russian factories: 'Workers' control, which in all the important branches of industry was bound to remain chaotic, scattered, primitive and incomplete, was to give way to workers' management of industry on a national level.'[8] In practice that meant party control, which in time developed into the bureaucratic socialism of present-day Soviet Russia. In post-war Britain, where nationalization was adopted as a deliberate policy both for industries like coalmining and the railways in which there was an urgent need for state finance to maintain services, and for others like air transport and steel on more ideological grounds, there were similar pressures to exert strong central control in the interests

[8] Ibid., p. 35.

both of general economic management and of short-term political advantage.

Centralized state capitalism of this kind eliminates any profit for individual capitalists, except in so far as they are compensated for the compulsory purchase of their shares. It makes less difference to the status of ordinary workers within the enterprise. The state simply takes over the role of the individual or corporate capitalist, both in supervising or controlling the internal management of the enterprise and in extracting from it whatever profit or surplus value is generated by the wages, pricing and investment policies adopted. In theory the workers benefit from the change in that the state ideally controls wages and prices and directs resources in the best interests of all the people. In practice their position is little different from that in capitalist enterprises in a free market economy. Provision may be made in either system for consultative committees through which management may communicate with their employees. Collective bargaining may likewise be permitted or prohibited in either. But the ultimate ownership and control, and the right to extract profit or surplus value, is vested in the state or the shareholders as external capitalists rather than in those who work in the enterprise. There is no greater need for formal provision for employees within the framework of company law under state capitalism than under traditional capitalism.

The co-operative

An outright assertion of the prior right of employees to the fruits of their labour leads to a conception of the enterprise radically different from both traditional and state capitalism. The basis of workers' ownership and control, as shown in Figure 12.4, is the denial of the right of capital to anything but a reasonable return by way of a fixed interest charge. Any profit remaining after the payment of this charge on borrowed capital is then attributable to the employees of the enterprise and may be distributed among them equally or in proportion to their notional contribution or, alternatively, reinvested in the enterprise with a view to future profit. Control over the enterprise is also exercised by the main body of employees both in the appointment and discharge of managers and in major issues of policy. The net result, as the figure makes clear, is simply to reverse the position of capital and labour in the traditional model, so that it is capital which is paid for at the going market rate,

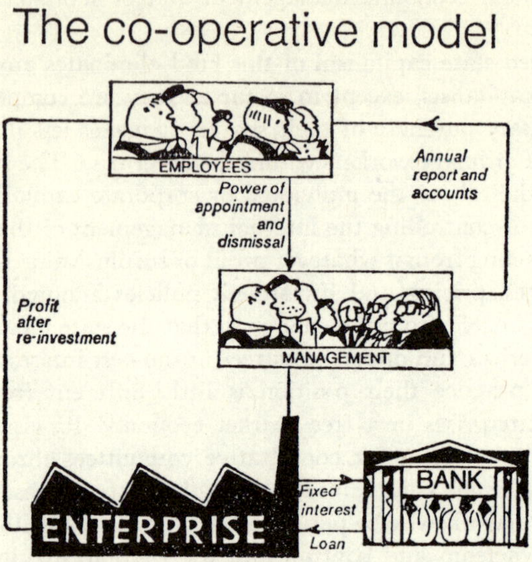

Figure 12.4

leaving any surplus value or profit to be appropriated by the employees.

An enterprise organized on these lines is usually described as a producers' co-operative, on the analogy of the retail co-operative movement which developed in Britain in the nineteenth century (see Chapter 11). But there is no reason why the ordinary rules of company or partnership law should not be adapted to produce the same result. The similarity of a producers' co-operative to a simple partnership in which all who work for the enterprise are full partners will be obvious. Alternatively the standard framework of company law may be used simply by allocating the shares in an ordinary limited company to its employees or to trustees to hold on the employees' behalf. As will be seen in Chapter 13, this approach has been adopted in most of the larger co-operative enterprises in Britain. It is also possible to develop an entirely new structure for the allocation of control and profit within large modern enterprises, as for instance under the structures for workers' control in Yugoslavia.

The managerial corporation

The most powerful alternative to these various forms of socialism is not the traditional capitalist model but the conception of the corporation as a continuing institution run by management in the joint interests of both investors and employees, and indeed of the consumer and the community at large. This conception is a direct development from the traditional model in that lip service is usually paid to the ultimate ownership and control of the shareholders. But there is, typically, a significant shift in the largest national and multi-national companies away from the objective of profit maximization for shareholders towards a more general notion of corporate self-interest and occasionally of communal service. The task of senior management in this model is to strike a fair balance between reasonable dividends to shareholders, good wages for employees and fair prices to consumers after the primary requirements of the company itself by way of reinvestment and expansion have been met. The duty of the company to make provision for the welfare and recreation of its employees and their families, and to make reasonable contributions to local and national charities is also accepted.

These objectives of responsible management are not always achieved.[9] Those in control of large corporations are often tempted to pursue their own financial or political interests at the expense of employees or the community at large. Employees may not always accept their obligation to co-operate with management in seeking higher levels of productivity from which all will benefit. Multinational corporations in particular have the power to shape or to evade national governmental policies which threaten the stability or expansion of the corporation. But the ideal of the corporate universe, illustrated in Figure 12.5, and of the prerogative of management which goes with it, is no more invalidated by these shortcomings than are the ideals of traditional or state capitalism by the abuse of power by capitalists or politicians.

The company in a mixed economy

The drawback with all these models is their assertion of a single overriding ideal or interest group and the implicit denial of other competing claims and interests. The traditional capitalist and cooperative models make formal provision for representation within the enterprise only for shareholders and employees respectively. State and managerial capitalism alike assert the priority of political

[9] For a critical account of this approach to the company see J. Burnham, *The Managerial Revolution* (1942) and P. F. Drucker, *The Concept of the Corporation* (1964).

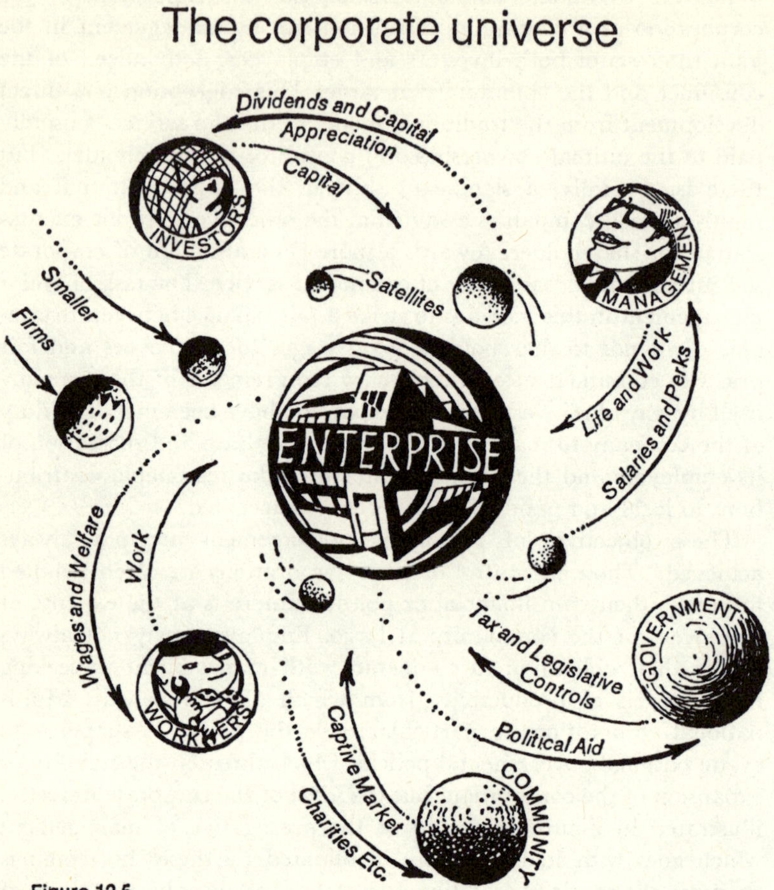

Figure 12.5

or managerial authority in the allocation of resources and rewards to the exclusion of local or individual autonomy. The pursuit of these ideal forms of authority and resource allocation is not for that reason invalid or illegitimate. But in the context of the western democratic tradition, in which the free assertion of competing interests is regarded as beneficial, an attempt to build a workable structure for the regulation of large modern corporations on the basis of any of these exclusive models is inherently unrealistic.

The standpoint of the chapters which follow is that proposals for industrial democracy and the various forms of governmental inter-

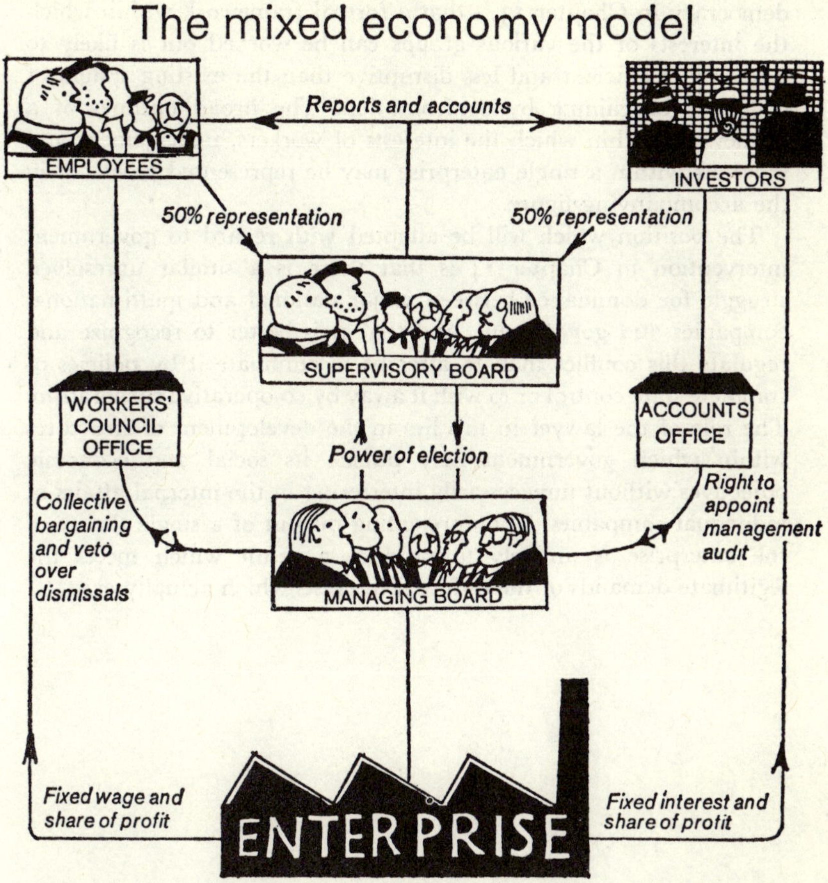

Figure 12.6

vention in major companies must be based on the recognition of the legitimate interests of all the various groups which contribute to the operations of the enterprise. There are bound to be conflicts in objectives between the providers of capital, labour and managerial skill for any large scale enterprise. There are also bound to be differences between the objectives of government in the regulation of economic activity and those of individual companies whether in the private or the public sector. But this does not mean that an attempt to accommodate these conflicting interests within the formal framework of company law is futile.

The argument which will be developed in respect of industrial democracy in Chapter 13 is that a formal framework within which the interests of the various groups can be worked out is likely to prove more efficient and less disruptive than the existing system of collective bargaining by confrontation. The broad outlines of a framework within which the interests of workers, management and investors within a single enterprise may be represented is set out in the accompanying figure.

The position which will be adopted with regard to government intervention in Chapter 14 is that there is a similar unresolved struggle for dominance between major national and multi-national companies and government, and that it is better to recognize and regulate this conflict than to attempt to eliminate it by policies of complete state control or to wish it away by co-operative corporatism. The role of the lawyer in this lies in the development of structures within which government may pursue its social and economic objectives without unnecessarily interfering in the internal affairs of individual companies. The unrelenting pursuit of a single theory of the enterprise is unlikely to produce a result which meets the legitimate demands of the different interests which actually exist.

13
Industrial Democracy

It is no longer necessary to argue the case for some form of industrial democracy in large companies. The 'democratic imperative' that those substantially affected by decisions must be involved in the making of those decisions has been accepted in respect of large companies both by the European Commission and by the majority and minority reports of the Bullock Committee on Industrial Democracy.[1] The main issue is the form in which this involvement should be promoted. One view is that it is no longer acceptable or realistic for the employees of large companies to be excluded from all recognition in the body of law which governs the constitution of such companies and the control of their activities. This is based on the argument that the employees of an enterprise, who are typically as numerous as its shareholders,[2] make a much greater practical and continuing contribution to the profitability of its operations than external shareholders and investors who may have contributed some initial or new capital but who play no active or continuing part in running it. If this is accepted it follows that employees should be granted rights at least as great as those of shareholders both in controlling the activities of management and in participating in profits, and that the foundations of company law must be altered accordingly. The other main view is that the interests of workers are

[1] *Employee participation and company structure*, Bulletin of the European Communities 8/75, p. 9; *Committee of Inquiry on Industrial Democracy*, Cmnd. 6706 (1977), p. 25.

[2] See the analysis by Sargant Florence, *The Logic of British and American Industry* (2nd edn., 1961).

best represented by the development of existing structures for consultation or collective bargaining, and that workers as such should not become in any way involved in the operations of the capitalist system.

The objective of this chapter is to analyse the implications of these two approaches for company law and practice both in respect of the proposals for board-level representation made by the Bullock Committee, and in respect of possible longer-term developments. The main focus will be on companies in the private sector, though some of the additional problems which arise in nationalized industries will also be discussed. Before dealing with the specific recommendations of the Bullock Committee, however, it is important to recognize that industrial democracy covers a much wider range than board-level representation, and that the success of any scheme for board-level participation may well depend on parallel developments in shop-floor and financial participation. The interrelationship of these three aspects of industrial democracy will therefore be outlined in general terms before the potential for legal regulation in respect of each is dealt with in any detail.

I LEVELS OF INDUSTRIAL DEMOCRACY

There is a basic paradox in proposals for industrial democracy. This is that rank and file workers rarely express much enthusiasm for it, at least in so far as schemes for participation in decision-making at board level are concerned. For the most part workers prefer to trust in established procedures for collective bargaining at shop-floor level. This pattern has been reported in numerous surveys both of employee attitudes to the idea of participation in a wide range of industries, and of the reaction to participation schemes already in operation. A survey of the attitudes of more than two thousand workers in companies employing more than twenty persons carried out in 1974 reported that participation in management was low in the general scale of priorities for most workers compared with better information from management, better incentives to productivity and better pay (see Table 13.1). Similar results have been obtained from surveys in Yugoslavia, where there has been a form of representative democracy in all large enterprises for many years, and in the John Lewis Partnership in Britain: in each case rank and file workers expressed much less interest in the structures for participation (and

TABLE 13.1

Attitudes of a sample of workers in private sector companies on aspects of industrial democracy, in terms of the two aspirations they considered most and least important, 1974

	Most important aspirations % of responses	Least important aspirations % of responses
More information from the top on what is happening and why	26	3
Better incentive to improve productivity and efficiency	23	2
Bigger say in day-to-day running of company	19	7
Bigger say in how own work is planned and organized	15	4
Better working conditions	12	3
Part-ownership or shares in the company they work for	12	14
More interesting/less boring work	11	6
Better pension arrangements	10	3
Bigger say in management decisions on finance and investment	6	31
Workers having seats on the board	3	26
Better canteen and welfare arrangements	3	21
Other answers (all less than 10% in most important scale)	31	49
None of these/Don't know	4	14

Source: Opinion Research Centre, *The Times*, 14 January 1975; the percentages in each column add up to 200% since each is based on the two items mentioned.

were much less frequently involved in them) than lower and middle managers.[8]

Intrinsic and instrumental job-satisfaction

A partial explanation of this paradox may be found in the distinction

[8] See generally P. Blumberg, *Industrial Democracy: The Sociology of Participation* (1968) and A. Flanders, R. Pomeranz and J. Woodward, *An Experiment in Industrial Democracy* (1969).

drawn by industrial psychologists between intrinsic and instrumental job-satisfaction.[4] There is a good deal of evidence that workers appreciate and value jobs which give them a greater degree of freedom in organizing and controlling their own methods of operation. To this extent the Marxist concept that alienation stems from the loss of individual control over the processes of production is valid. But it is equally true that many workers are primarily concerned about the amount of money which they earn and the security of their jobs. This is amply demonstrated by the fact that it is these issues which lie at the root of most industrial disputes. This concern is related mainly to the external standard of living which earnings make possible, but also to the comparisons which are made between the earnings of different groups of workers. It is a strange fact that more dissatisfaction is often caused by the knowledge that a fellow worker is earning a little more than by the knowledge that senior managers are earning four or five times as much.[5] It is perfectly possible to find a great deal of personal satisfaction and fulfilment in doing a particular job and yet to be highly dissatisfied with the payment received for doing it.

This distinction between the intrinsic element in job satisfaction, based on the quality of the work itself and the scope for individual self-regulation and initiative, and the instrumental factor, based on the rewards which are obtained from it, may be illustrated by a study of relatively affluent workers in the motor and engineering industries in Britain in the 1960s. It was reported that the majority of assembly-line workers would have preferred some other job in their factory and that what satisfaction they got from their work was directly related to the financial rewards; craftsmen and setters who had much greater control over the pace of their work and the organization of their working day reported a much greater degree of intrinsic satisfaction, though they also gave the level of their pay as an important reason for staying in the job (see Table 13.2).

These particular findings are not important in themselves. But the distinction which they illustrate is crucial to an understanding of the criteria on which schemes for industrial democracy will be judged at the shop-floor level. Participating in decision-making may

[4] On this section see generally Guest & Fatchett, *Worker Participation: individual control and performance* (1974) and N. Wilson, *On the Quality of Working Life*, Manpower Papers No. 7 (1973).

[5] See generally W. R. Runciman, *Relative Deprivation and Social Justice* (1966).

TABLE 13.2

Levels of job-satisfaction reported by a sample of workers in the motor and engineering industries, 1962–4

	Craftsmen	Setters	Process workers	Machinists	Assembly workers
Find job monotonous	14%	13%	22%	46%	67%
Would prefer some other job on shop floor	16%	9%	9%	29%	62%
Prefer present job	84%	87%	74%	64%	36%
Level of pay as a reason for staying in job	68%	57%	48%	66%	76%
Level of pay as only reason for staying in job	7%	9%	9%	17%	31%
Number in sample	(56)	(23)	(23)	(41)	(86)

Source: Goldthorpe, Lockwood, Bechofer & Platt, *The Affluent Worker: Industrial Attitudes and Behaviour* (1968); adapted from various tables in Chapter 2.

afford some intrinsic satisfaction to those who feel that they have played some part in it. If it is not seen to produce some tangible benefit it is unlikely to be regarded as worthwhile by those who are not directly involved, or to make much difference to the relations between management and the general body of workers. And if it is seen to bring a decrease rather than an increase in instrumental rewards it is likely to be regarded with a great deal of suspicion and resentment. The mechanics of schemes for the improvement of intrinsic job-satisfaction at shop-floor level, by job-enrichment or the introduction of autonomous work groups as for instance in the new Volvo works in Sweden, have little bearing on the formal organization of the enterprise as a whole and cannot be discussed here. But the same principles may be applied to schemes for participation at every level in the enterprise. Unless rank and file workers can see some tangible benefit arising from the participation of their representatives at board level they are unlikely to take much interest in it. This has important implications for the relationship between any system for board-level representation and the existing structures of collective bargaining through which most of the instrumental benefits for workers have hitherto been obtained.

Levels of decision-making

The nature of decision-making itself at various levels of the enterprise is also likely to have an important impact on the type of industrial democracy which develops. It is only in the very smallest units that everyone can be directly involved in every significant decision. In large enterprises there is an accepted hierarchy within which decisions of different types are made. Major issues of policy and investment are supposed to be resolved, or at least confirmed, at board level, though the preparatory work is usually left to senior executives. The appointment or promotion of top management is dealt with in a similar way. The planning and maintenance of regular production, on the other hand, is regarded as a matter for middle management. The organization of the work force and plant is left to shop-floor managers and foremen. This hierarchy is not absolute. Any accepted practice or proposed change may be called in question at any level of the enterprise. But in normal circumstances the accepted allocation of decision-making functions is not called in question; deliberate decisions are thus made only within a small range of variability on a few issues at a particular level in the hierarchy. Collective bargaining, for example, has traditionally been restricted to levels and systems of payment and conditions of work.

One of the reasons for this is the fact that decisions at board level and by extension in senior management are likely to be on a large scale and to be correspondingly divorced from the immediate concerns of rank and file workers and their shop stewards. The issues involved – plans for investment or diversification, the development of new products and the organization of the overall finances of the enterprise – are inherently complex and require detailed prior analysis and preparation if they are to be properly considered. This does not mean that the decisions themselves are determined by the preparatory briefs. The most important issues often have to be decided under conditions of great uncertainty. No amount of preparation or analysis can ensure that forecasts on future interest rates or the cost of raw materials or the demand for a product will prove to be accurate. Decision-making at board level does not require any special qualifications other than a clear perception of objectives and an ability to absorb the relevant briefs and ask the right questions. But the basis of the discussion is typically pre-determined by the kind of information which has been prepared by middle and senior management. This inevitably puts non-specialist board members, whether they are representatives of employees or of other external interests, at a disadvantage. Simplified versions of production plans and of past, current and projected accounts can be prepared as an aid to decision-making by non-specialists. But these simplifications themselves involve crucial choices in the method of presentation and the choice of assumptions which are bound to influence the direction of the eventual decision. This control over the information supplied to decision-makers is one of the most powerful weapons in the hands of senior executives in their dealings both at board level and in collective bargaining with union officials or shop stewards.

Decisions at a lower level within the enterprise, on the other hand, are usually less complex and their impact is correspondingly more immediate and obvious to rank-and-file employees, as for example those on levels of pay, conditions of work or redundancies. The issues involved from the point of view of employees are relatively simple, and it is natural for them to have strong views on the rights and wrongs of managerial decisions. The difficulty is that the broad parameters within which these lower-level decisions can be made are effectively determined by decisions made, often on entirely different criteria, at higher levels in the enterprise months or years before. Participation at a lower level, whether through collective bargaining or works committees, is thus restricted in practical terms to the methods by which decisions made elsewhere are to be implemented. Where a company or plant is part of a large group of companies, in which major decisions are made at head office or even by a foreign parent company, the difficulty in making plant-level participation appear more than an exercise in gaining consent for decisions which have already been made is even greater. Management is required to negotiate with recognized trade unions on procedures for dealing with collective redundancies under the Employment Protection Act 1975 (ss. 99–107), and may be prepared to bargain on the time-scale over which a particular production line is to be phased out or reorganized. But it is often not in a position, even if it wished, to have meaningful discussions on the merits of the policies which have been adopted.

This distinction between high- and low-level decisions is not absolute. All major decisions, and many apparently routine ones as well, have ramifications up and down the hierarchy. This is especially true of those issues on which there is an established right of collective bargaining or which involves rates of pay or conditions of work. An apparently straightforward decision on production schedules or methods initiated by management in the interests of greater productivity, or a more even flow of work on the shop floor, may in turn interfere with established patterns of overtime and take-home pay and spark off an industrial dispute which in its turn may escalate into an issue of principle for the board. But the details of payment systems and methods of work are often regarded by senior executives as a matter for plant or personnel managers, who are expected to negotiate the best deal they can at a lower level, rather than as an integral part of long-term planning or policy-making at board level.[6]

These features of industrial decision-making do not facilitate the position of employee representatives at board level. If they press for the recognition of employee interests by way of higher wages or better conditions of work there is a danger that board meetings may turn into another form of collective bargaining in which each side will seek to maintain a strong bargaining position by concealing as much as possible of their real intentions. The natural result would be that the open discussion of long-term policies and investment plans would be carried on elsewhere by management in the absence of employee representatives. If, on the other hand, employee directors accept that wage bargaining is best left to lower levels in the enterprise, they risk losing touch with the rank and file of employees whom they are supposed to be representing and may be thought to have 'sold out' to management, or at best to have been unable to make any real impact on board decisions. This dilemma, which lies at the root of the opposition by some trade unionists to the idea of worker directors in any form, poses a serious threat to the successful operation of any scheme for employee representation on the board. Its resolution, as will be argued below, is almost certainly

[6] J. T. Winkler, 'Directors: The ghost in the boardroom', *BJIL*, XII, 191.

dependent on parallel developments in the conduct of collective bargaining and in financial participation at plant or company level. Industrial democracy cannot be introduced in any meaningful form at one level of the enterprise without affecting established mechanisms for decision-making and profit allocation within the enterprise as a whole.

2 BOARD LEVEL PARTICIPATION

There are a number of reasons why the main focus of attention in relation to industrial democracy in Britain has been on board-level representation for employees. It is natural to think that the best way of securing a larger say for employees within the framework of the enterprise is to provide for their representation at the ultimate seat of authority in the company. The Trades Union Congress adopted this position in 1974 when it argued that collective bargaining could only effectively be extended to major issues of policy and planning by the representation of trade unions on company boards.[7] The Bullock Committee has similarly argued that while a statutory right of representation at board level is not in itself sufficient to secure a real extension of industrial democracy, it is an essential prerequisite to the joint regulation of major policy decisions and is more likely than any other legislative strategy to strengthen existing forms of industrial democracy below board level.[8] The principal reason for government action in this field, however, has been the pressure from the European Economic Community for the introduction of employee representation at board level in all large companies: the Commission initially recommended the universal adoption of the two-tier structure developed in West Germany, though it has subsequently adopted a more flexible approach.[9]

The principal argument in favour of the German model for co-determination at board level is that it has operated successfully for some twenty-five years. It cannot be proved that co-determination as such has made any direct contribution to the success of the German economy. But it is hard to avoid the implication that it has played some part and that it is a more effective method of dealing

[7] Trades Union Congress, *Industrial Democracy* (1974).

[8] Cmnd. 6706 (1977), p. 46.

[9] *Draft Fifth Directive on Company Law* (1972); *Employee Participation and Company Structure* (1975).

with the inherent conflicts within an enterprise than the British model of arms-length collective bargaining. The difficulty is that there are sufficient differences in the patterns of industrial and trade-union organization in Germany to make any direct transfer of the German system to other countries impractical. Co-determination in Germany is based on a long-established and precise division of power between a supervisory and an executive board which cannot easily be introduced in other countries. There is also an important difference in practice between the parity system of representation which has been in operation in the limited coal and steel sector and the minority (one-third) system applied in other industries. The Bullock Committee has recommended that employee representation on the boards of large British companies should be based on a rather different model, with parity between shareholder and employee representatives on all boards, a more flexible allocation of supervisory and executive functions, and a monopoly for trade-union members in the selection of employee directors. However, a detailed account of the structure and practical operation of the German system is necessary to a full understanding of these proposals and their likely impact.

Co-determination in Germany: formal structures

The German system of co-determination grew out of the post-war reconstruction. Direct representation of employees on company boards, first in the coal and steel industry and later in other companies, was intended to give an effective voice to worker representatives in the absence of an established and independent trade-union movement. But it was grafted onto a peculiarly German system of company management which dates back to the nineteenth century. A large privately owned company in Germany (*Aktiengesellschaft* or *AG*) is not formally controlled by a single board of directors, as in Britain, but by two boards. The day-to-day affairs of the company are under the sole control of an executive board (*Vorstand*). This is not directly elected by the general meeting of shareholders, as in Britain, but by a supervisory board (*Aufsichtsrat*) of shareholders' representatives. The executive board must report regularly to the supervisory board on a wide range of specified matters, including future policy, and must submit further reports on specific items raised by the supervisory board. The formal consent of the supervisory board must be obtained for certain major transactions such as plant closures or take-overs and mergers. This structure was developed to permit the more effective supervision of companies on behalf of shareholders than was likely to be achieved by an annual general meeting. It was and is particularly suited to Germany since many small shareholders there deposit their shares with banks and other financial institutions which may then secure the election of a representative on the supervisory board. One in four of the total number of seats on supervisory boards within the co-determination system are held by banks.[10]

When the new Federal German government formalized the system of joint and equal management and union control over the coal and steel industry which the allies had set up in 1947, it was natural to make use of this familiar framework. Under the Co-determination Law of 1951 (*Mitbestimmungsgesetz*) each company in the coal and steel sector employing more than one thousand workers was required to establish a supervisory board on which there was an equal number of shareholder and employee representatives and one independent member nominated by agreement. All these representatives are formally elected by the shareholders, but the employee representatives must be selected from names put forward by the works council and trade unions recognized within the company. There is a formal procedure for resolving deadlock over the appointment of the independent member, through a joint conciliation panel and ultimately by reference to the labour court. In 1956 this structure was extended to cover holding companies of industrial groups more than half of whose business is in coal and steel; in these the employee representatives are elected by an electoral panel covering the employees of each company in the group.

Similar but less far-reaching structures for co-determination have been developed for companies employing more than five hundred workers outside the coal and steel sector. Under the Works Constitution Law of 1952 (*Betriebsverfassungsgesetz*) only one-third of the members of the supervisory board in such companies have been elected by employees. The shareholder representatives have thus always been able to outvote the employee representatives. Another formal difference from the coal and steel sector has been that there is no provision for the nomination of employee representatives by

[10] *Biedenkopf Report on Co-determination* (1970; English translation, 1977), Schedule 3, Table 1.

trade unions, though in practice most of those elected appear on informal trade-union canvassing lists.

These structures are to be amended under the Co-determination Law of 1976. The supervisory boards of all companies employing more than two thousand workers are to be formed of twenty members, ten to represent the shareholders and the employees respectively. In order to meet the requirements of their coalition partners, the Free Democrats, however, the governing Social Democrats had to agree that only three of the ten employee representatives should be directly linked to trade unions, and that of the remaining seven one should be a representative of staff and middle managers (*leitende Angestellte*). And to meet the objection that full parity would infringe the property rights of shareholders, which are indirectly guaranteed in the German constitution, it has been provided that the chairman of the supervisory board, who will have a casting vote, cannot be chosen against the wishes of the shareholders' representatives.

Two further institutions must be described before the operation of these structures can be fully understood. Companies in the coal and steel sector are required to appoint to their executive boards a labour or personnel director (*Arbeitsdirektor*) who is acceptable to the employee representatives on the supervisory board. The labour director has specific statutory responsibility for industrial relations and for other 'social' matters, which in Germany cover all aspects of safety and welfare for employees, including leisure and pension provisions made by the company. It is sometimes argued that the dual role of the labour director as a working member of the executive board and at the same time as an indirect representative of employees must create such divided loyalties as to make his position untenable. In practice it appears that while labour directors have usually been selected with full co-operation from trade unions, they have not been expected to and have not in fact sided with unions or employees against the collective view of the executive board.[11] But their presence on the board as of right and their direct personal links with company unions, and the right of employee representatives to veto their dismissal, has helped to ensure that important issues of industrial relations are not left out of account in the preparation and discussion of company policies.

[11] *Biedenkopf Report*, Part III, paras. 60–1.

In addition, under the Works Constitution Law of 1972, which extends a similar measure of 1952, all companies employing more than five people are required to establish a works council (*Betriebsrat*). In small companies the works council is elected by a direct ballot of all employees. In larger enterprises the employees are usually divided into separate electoral constituencies to ensure a reasonable spread of representation. All those who are elected to the works council are given statutory protection from dismissal during their term of office. They are also entitled to exemption from work without loss of pay so far as is necessary for the conduct of works council business. In larger companies with more than three hundred employees some of the leading works council members are entitled to devote all their time to works council business, though they continue to draw full pay from their employers. In this respect full-time works council members are in a similar position to full-time shop stewards or convenors in large British plants. German employers are also required to provide the requisite office facilities and staff for the proper conduct of works council business.

The principal functions of works councils lie in the field of 'social' matters at plant level and will be discussed in the context of shop-floor participation. But they are also tied into the structure for co-determination at board level. In the coal and steel sector they have the right to nominate two of the five members of the supervisory board on the employee side. And in all plants with more than one hundred employees there is provision for the establishment of an economic committee under the auspices of the works council; this is intended to provide a forum for the discussion of all major plans for investment, expansion or closures at plant level, though the power of decision-making on such matters rests with the executive and supervisory boards.

The overall structure of the co-determination system in the two main sectors as it was before the reforms of 1976 is illustrated diagrammatically in Figure 13.1.

Co-determination in Germany: the system in operation

The reason for describing in detail a system which has been partially superseded by new measures is that the pre-1976 German system is the only one on which there is satisfactory evidence on the actual operation of employee representation at board level over a period of years. The most thorough study was carried out by an official

Figure 13.1 The formal structure for co-determination in Germany in the coal and steel sector and in other companies prior to 1976

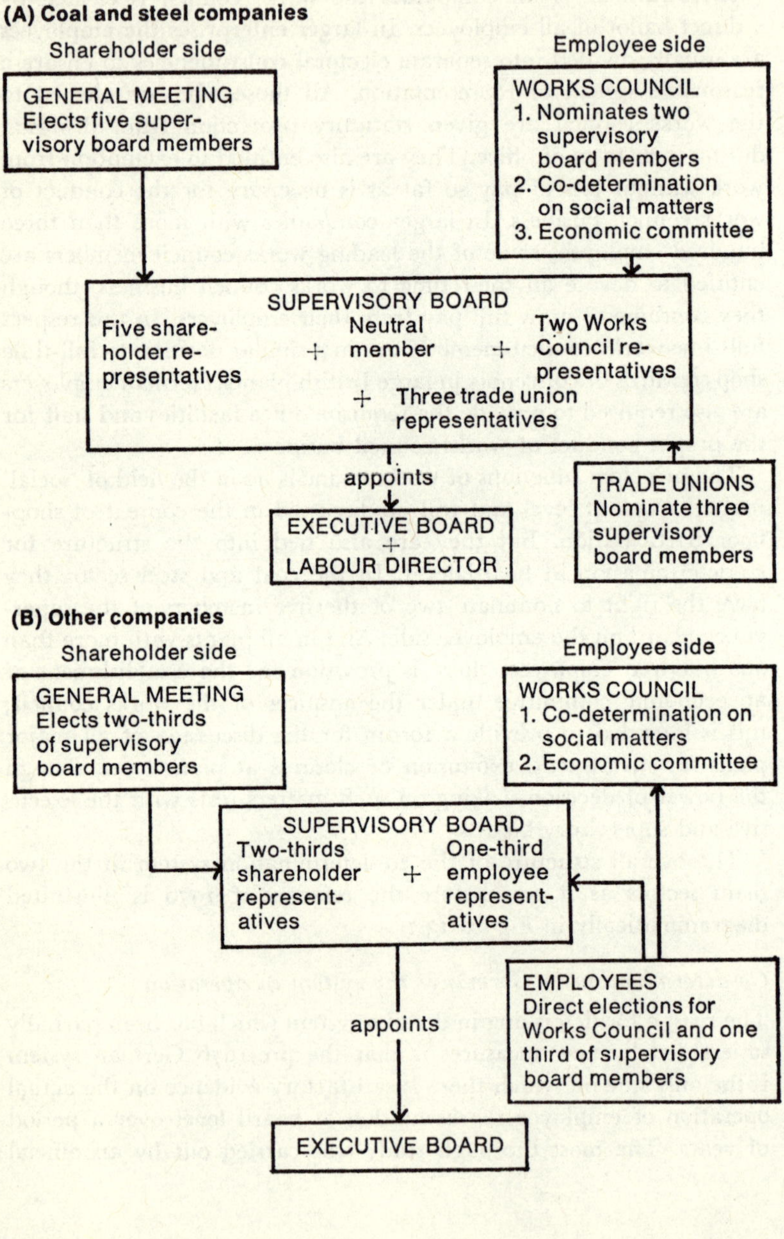

commission appointed in 1968 to report on how the system should be reformed or developed. Much of the resulting report, known as the Biedenkopf Report from its chairman Professor Kurt Biedenkopf, is now of historical interest only.[12] But it contains the results of a survey of the experience of co-determination in some fifty companies in the coal and steel sector and almost three hundred other companies likely to be affected by any extension of the parity principle. The replies by these companies to the commission's questionnaires, on which the tables which follow are based, were supplemented by lengthy hearings with representatives from both sides of the supervisory board in selected companies.

The most significant general finding by the Biedenkopf Commission was that the formal structures for co-determination had resulted in the development of a much more extensive informal network of communication between management and the representatives of employees at all levels of the enterprise. It was reported that almost

TABLE 13.3

Decision-making on supervisory boards in German companies in 1968

	Coal & Steel			*Other companies*		
	All unanimous	Mainly unanimous	Other/NK	All unanimous	Mainly unanimous	Other/NK
Managing directors	65%	27%	8%	80%	14%	6%
Supervisory board chairmen	62%	26%	12%	84%	14%	2%
Works council chairmen	52%	44%	4%	58%	28%	14%
Labour directors	67%	33%	—	(not applicable)		

Source: Biedenkopf Report, Schedule 3, Table 4; the figures are based on separate estimates by managing directors, supervisory board chairmen, works council chairmen and labour directors.

[12] *Mitbestimmung im Unternehmen* (1970); quotations are from the English translation published by the Legal Research Committee, Queen's University, Belfast (1977).

TABLE 13.4

Prior consultation between management and employee representatives on supervisory board business in German companies in 1968

	Coal & Steel			Other companies		
	Prior discussion	No prior discussion	Not known	Prior discussion	No prior discussion	Not known
Managing directors	92%	2%	6%	60%	30%	10%
Supervisory board chairmen	66%	4%	30%	57%	31%	12%
Works council chairmen	81%	—	19%	56%	28%	16%
Labour directors	94%	6%	—	(not applicable)		

Source: Biedenkopf Report, Schedule 3, Table 5; for basis see note to Table 13.3.

TABLE 13.5

The use of casting votes by the neutral chairman on supervisory boards in German coal and steel companies, 1964–8

	Managing directors	Supervisory board chairmen	Works council chairmen	Labour directors
No casting votes	72%	64%	60%	71%
Once for employees	2%	6%	6%	10%
More than once for employees	2%	2%	—	—
Once for shareholders	10%	11%	15%	11%
More than once for shareholders	4%	2%	4%	4%
Other/Not known	10%	13%	13%	4%

Source: Biedenkopf Report, Schedule 3, Table 12; for basis see note to Table 13.3.

all decisions at supervisory board level were unanimous, largely as a result of prior negotiation between the parties. This pattern was found both in the coal and steel sector and in other companies, as shown in Tables 13.3 and 13.4. The fear that parity in representation on supervisory boards would lead to frequent deadlock was also shown to be unfounded. It was reported, as shown in Table 13.5, that between 1964 and 1968 the neutral member on the supervisory board in coal and steel companies had never been called on to give a casting vote in two-thirds of the companies in the survey; in the remaining third the replies indicated that the casting vote went in favour of the shareholder side a good deal more frequently than in favour of the employee side. The Biedenkopf Commission concluded from these findings that the appointment of a neutral chairman was not essential to the smooth running of co-determination with equal representation, though it did recommend a formal system of conciliation for the few cases of deadlock which might be expected to occur.

This system of informal consultation was not restricted to supervisory board business, but extended down through the enterprise to dealings between management and leading works council members. The Biedenkopf Commission described the process as follows:

> There is an inseparable connection between co-determination of workers at supervisory board level and co-operation between management and workers' representatives at plant level under the Works Constitution Law. ... This co-operation between management and the works council became institutionalized first in the sphere of co-determination in coal and steel companies but has become increasingly prevalent in other companies. This has led to a move from co-operation between management and workers' representatives on the supervisory board and economic committees to co-operation between management and the works council. ... The importance of this co-operation was seen as lying mainly in the comprehensive information received by the plant representatives and in the opportunity to discuss with management at the earliest possible stage all problems of the plant and the company.[13]

The requirement of joint discussion on formally constituted bodies appears to have given way, both at the supervisory board and the works council level, to an informal search for consensus or compromise between the leaders on each side, with the result that proceedings at the meetings themselves have become less significant.

[13] *Biedenkopf Report*, Part III, para. 62.

It was reported that in more than two-thirds of the coal and steel companies a small presidium of leading supervisory board members on both sides had been formed to assist in this kind of negotiation. A further indication of the way in which compulsory institutions for co-operation have been superseded by informal arrangements is the fact that in some companies it was no longer considered necessary to maintain a formal economic committee: this position had been reached in more than a quarter of the companies in the coal and steel sector and in some fifteen per cent of other companies.[14]

These findings must not be taken out of context. The supervisory board in German companies has no direct executive power. Most of its 'decisions' in practice amount to little more than the confirmation of management policies or the approval of management reports and accounts. All that the supervisory board can do in most cases is to refer back particular items for further consideration by management. The dominant position of management was often stressed in the hearings of the Biedenkopf Commission: 'It was constantly stated that only in exceptional circumstances did controversy arise in supervisory board meetings over management's investment proposals; . . . as a rule the individual member of the supervisory board has neither the technical ability nor the time to examine the calculations which are attached to the substance of investment proposals.'[15] Co-determination had resulted, however, in management plans being subjected to rather more scrutiny, particularly as to their impact on the workforce. In some cases this had led to delays in decision-making while the stipulations of employee representatives were dealt with. Some directors also reported greater problems in preparing major investment plans, since a balance had to be struck between technical and economic considerations and the social demands of employee representatives. The Commission concluded nonetheless on the basis of its hearings that there was no fundamental difference in approach by shareholder and employee representatives over basic company policy or over the criteria to be applied in making decisions on investment, lay-offs or even closures. But the importance of real bargaining power may be deduced from the finding that the extent of prior consultation was appreciably greater in coal and steel companies where there is parity of representation than in companies in which management can rely on the built-in majority of shareholder

[14] Ibid., Part III, para. 65.

[15] Ibid., Part III, para. 62.

representatives. It is equally significant that where presidia of leading supervisory board members were formed outside the coal and steel sector, it was extremely rare for an employee representative to be included : this was reported in fewer than one in seven of the companies in which presidia had been formed.[16]

A second significant finding by the Biedenkopf Commission was that co-determination, both at supervisory board and at works council levels, had operated without interfering in established patterns of collective bargaining with trade unions on a national or regional level. It was reported that in the coal and steel sector management and unions tacitly agreed to keep the two spheres separate by ensuring that the same individuals were not involved in both systems.[17] Some doubt was expressed, however, on whether this position could be maintained, given the tendency of trade unions to seek to extend the collective bargaining process from simple wage bargaining into spheres covered by co-determination. German trade union leaders have in general accepted and co-operated in structures for co-determination, though they have consistently pressed for the extension of the parity principle to all sectors of the economy. But the reports of the Biedenkopf Commission and other studies suggest that many unions regard representation on the supervisory board as a means of obtaining more information on company performance and planning with a view to increasing their relative bargaining power in collective bargaining. There is little evidence that trade-union officials or internal employee representatives have sought to use the co-determination structures as a means of involving themselves directly in the processes of management, or that management would welcome such a trend.

Whatever view is taken on the proper relationship of co-determination and traditional collective bargaining, however, it is clear that co-determination both at board level and in works councils is firmly established in Germany. No major political party or pressure group seeks to dismantle the structures which have been developed, though there is still considerable disagreement on the merits of the extensions provided for in 1976. Numerous opinion polls and surveys have reported that most German workers are happy with the system, even though they are apparently less convinced that it had brought

[16] Ibid., Sched. 3, Table 9.

[17] Ibid., Part IV, para. 95.

about any real change in their position within their own companies and plants.

The purpose of this detailed account of the German structure for co-determination at board level is not to suggest that it provides an ideal model for industrial democracy in other countries. It has frequently been pointed out that workable structures for co-operation between management, as representative of shareholders, and employees or unions cannot be imposed without taking into account established practices in management and trade union organization and in collective bargaining. The European Commission has dropped its initial proposal for the introduction of the German two-tier model in all EEC countries,[18] and is now recommending 'a framework which provides for the objectives to be reached in a way which leaves discretion to the member states as to the precise models which they may adopt.'[19] Experience in Germany, and in those countries which have followed the German lead in this sphere, however, does bear out the general points made in the preceding section, that management through its control of the development and explanation of company policy has been able to maintain effective control of decision-making both on parity and less than parity boards, and that rank and file workers typically express little interest in board-level decision-making.

Board-level representation in Britain

The recommendations of the Bullock Committee on Industrial Democracy[20] for the introduction of employee representatives on the boards of large British companies are broadly based on the German approach, which has likewise formed the basis of board-level representation in Holland, Denmark, Belgium and Sweden. In each case, however, there have been substantial modifications to the formal two-tier German structure to reflect the existing organization and practice of management and unions. In Britain the strong industrial and political position of the trade unions was recognized both in the membership and the terms of reference of the Bullock Committee, and the majority report put corresponding emphasis on the representation of employees through the 'single channel' of their unions. The essence of the majority proposals was that companies

[18] *Draft Fifth Directive to harmonise company law in Member States* (1972).
[19] EEC Commission, *Employee participation and company structure* (1975).
[20] Cmnd. 6706 (1977).

employing more than two thousand workers, amounting to some eighteen hundred companies in seven hundred and fifty groups, be required to proceed within a year of legislation to the appointment of a new board of directors on which there would be an equal number of shareholder and union or employee directors and a third group chosen jointly by both sides, the so-called $2X + Y$ formula.

This new board would have specific non-delegable and exclusive authority for submitting proposals to the general meeting of shareholders on five issues: the winding-up of the company; changes in its memorandum or articles; dividends; increases or reduction in capital, including the issue of shares on a take-over or merger; and the disposal of substantial parts of the enterprise. It would also have responsibility, which it might delegate, for the appointment of management and the allocation of resources within the enterprise.[21] The method of selecting the directors representing employees would be the responsibility of a joint committee of the unions established in the enterprise. But the system would not come into operation unless a proposal to introduce it were carried in a referendum of all employees in which the majority in favour represented at least one-third of those entitled to vote.

The precise details of these proposals and the method recommended for their implementation will not be discussed here, given the political uncertainty at the time of writing on the form of the legislation which will eventually emerge. The minority report on the Bullock Committee, effectively representing the Confederation of British Industry, recommended a much more flexible and gradual implementation of any requirement for the representation of employees on company boards; it suggested legislation to facilitate the adoption of the German two-tier model with one-third representation on a supervisory board for shareholders, employees and neutral interests, and a statutory obligation to negotiate structures for industrial democracy at plant level on the model of the German works council. It seems unlikely that any government will seek to press through the package recommended by the majority in the face of concerted opposition from employers. There are certain practical and legal issues, however, which are raised in the Bullock Report and which will be of continuing relevance under any scheme which is eventually implemented. These are the choice between a two-tier

[21] Ibid., pp. 77–8.

and a unitary board, the powers of the board in relation to shareholders, the duties of directors, access to and confidentiality of information, and the special problems raised by groups of companies. All these matters, as will be seen, ultimately revolve around the basic issue, which will be dealt with in conclusion, of who is to control the majority of seats on the board.

i *Unitary and two-tier boards.* The principal reason for the rejection of the German two-tier model by the Bullock Committee was the fact that the boards of large British companies have traditionally combined both executive and supervisory functions. A survey of the board membership of the one thousand largest British companies carried out by the Committee showed that four out of five of the companies employing more than two thousand workers and therefore likely to be affected by the Committee's proposals had some non-executive directors on their board, and that two out of five had at least three such directors (see Table 13.6). It is generally accepted that these non-executive directors act in a supervisory capacity, often on behalf of external financial institutions. Provided the principle of employee representation is accepted, there can therefore be no formal objection to bringing in additional non-executive directors to act in a similar capacity on behalf of employees. The Committee accepted, however, that the precise allocation of responsibility for executive and supervisory functions was best left to each individual company, given the wide range of different managerial structures in companies and groups in various sectors of the economy. Its main concern in prescribing precise functions for the reconstituted boards which it recommended was to avoid the risk that senior executives and directors might seek to starve the new boards of any effective decision-making power by delegating all important issues to executive managers, either on a formal or informal basis. A survey of existing practice in two hundred large British companies carried out by the British Institute of Management in 1972 reported that seven out of ten of the companies had some kind of management committee composed of executive directors and senior managers to which the board delegated the business of running the company and the preparation of policy.[22] This form of delegation is perfectly

[22] Ibid., p. 67; see also E. Batstone and P. L. Davies, *Industrial Democracy: European Experience* (1976), p. 62, and P. L. Davies, 'Employee Representation on Company Boards and Participation in Corporate Planning', (1975) 38 *MLR*, 254.

TABLE 13.6

The total number of directors and the number of non-executive directors on the boards of large British companies, 1975–6

No. of UK employees	Number of companies	Number of directors				Number of non-executive directors			
		2–5	6–10	11–15	16+	None	1–2	3–5	5+
Under 2,000	357	95	232	23	7	92	151	89	25
2,000–5,000	325	54	232	36	3	78	130	90	27
5,000–10,000	145	4	80	50	11	36	44	42	23
Over 10,000	155	7	51	72	25	37	57	40	21
Total	982	160	595	181	46	243	382	261	96

Source: *Bullock Committee on Industrial Democracy*, Table 11; 18 companies from *The Times 1,000, 1975–76* on which the table is based did not disclose the number of their employees.

lawful, as has been seen in Chapter 6, and is usually provided for in the company's constitution (1948: Table A, arts. 81, 107–9).

A second reason given by the Bullock Committee for retaining a unitary board rather than introducing even an optional two-tier system was its view that supervisory and executive functions could not be satisfactorily distinguished unless all effective power was removed from the supervisory board. The Committee contrasted in this respect the German two-tier system with its rigid allocation of supervisory and management functions, and the Danish system introduced in 1973 which provides that management shall run the affairs of the company but that transactions of special importance cannot be undertaken, except in cases of urgency, without the authorization of the board of directors.[23] In practice, however, the list of specific functions which would be reserved for the board of directors as such if the proposals of the Bullock Committee were adopted are remarkably similar to those which require the authorization of the supervisory board under German law. The difference

[23] Cmnd. 6706, pp. 71–7.

between the German two-tier model and the existing unitary board in Britain is likely to be a good deal less than might be thought at first sight. The German system achieves a clearer allocation of powers. The British system is more flexible. But the real issue in either system is whether, and to what extent, employee representatives are to be given a veto over managerial decisions of a given type.

ii *The board and the general meeting.* Similar issues arise over the allocation of powers between the board and the general meeting of shareholders. The proposals of the Bullock Committee envisage a substantial derogation from the existing powers of the general meeting to initiate a winding-up or a reconstruction of the company, for example in the context of a take-over or merger. Some such provision is theoretically necessary if employee representatives on the board are to be given effective influence on such matters. But the change would in practice be little more than a formal recognition of the existing situation. The proposal of dividends in most companies is already reserved for the board of directors. And it is extremely rare for shareholders of large quoted companies actually to exercise their right to propose resolutions in general meeting without the approval of the board. In real terms the only occasion on which such a right might be of value to shareholders would be in the course of a take-over bid which the board opposed. But the provisions of the City Code on Take-overs and Mergers already provide that any such proposal shall be put to the shareholders for their decision (see Chapter 8).

iii *The duties of directors.* Two issues in respect of directors' duties are raised by proposals for employee representation at board level. The first, which should cause little difficulty, is the reformulation of the traditional statement of the duty of a director to look to the long-term interests of the company to include the interests of its employees. A provision entitling directors to have regard to the interests of their employees as well as their shareholders was included in the Companies Bill of 1973 (cl. 53). The Bullock Committee recommended that any such provision should require rather than entitle the interests of employees to be taken into account.[24] In practice the difference is unlikely to be significant except in the case

[24] Ibid., p. 84.

of a winding-up, since it is already established that looking to the long-term interests of a company must involve looking to the interests of its employees (see Chapter 6). But neither formulation would in itself be sufficient to meet the problem raised in *Parke v. Daily News*[25] over payments to employees in anticipation of liquidation. The simplest way of including employees within the permissible range of distributions on liquidation would be to enact that existing employees should be regarded as full members of the company entitled to share in the distribution of any surplus assets in accordance with the company's constitution. If employees are to play a part along with shareholders in the appointment of the board of directors, it is hard to see why they should not be accorded the status of members for other purposes as well. This would also facilitate, as will be seen, provision for financial participation.

A potentially more difficult issue is the conflict of interest which may be experienced by the representatives of employees on company boards. The matter has been raised in a number of court cases in Germany: in one instance two union members of the supervisory board of a metal company were ordered by the court to refrain from active support of a strike on the ground that they were bound to act in the interests of the company as a whole rather than the sectional interests of employees.[26] The Bullock Committee took a similar view: while there was bound to be conflict between the representatives of shareholders and employees on the reconstituted boards which it proposed, and while it was right and proper for the issues to be openly discussed on the board, the existing rule that no director may bind his personal discretion by agreeing to vote in accordance with the instructions of any other person or group should be applied to prevent the mandating of employee representatives by their trade unions or otherwise.[27] All directors would thus continue to be bound by the same duty to balance the various conflicting interests within the company in the best interests of its long-term future.

iv *Provision and confidentiality of information.* The directors of a company, unlike its shareholders, are entitled to require the production of any information from within the company which is necessary

[25] [1962] Ch. 927 (see p. 318).

[26] See the cases cited in D. T. Vagts, 'Reforming the Modern Corporation: Perspectives from the German', (1966) 80 *Harvard Law Review*, 23, at pp. 74 and 82.

[27] Ibid., p. 85.

to the proper fulfilment of their supervisory or executive roles.[28] This raises the issue of confidentiality in respect of employee representation at board level. In respect of unauthorized disclosure to competitors of the company or for personal profit, the Bullock Committee took the view that there was no more risk of impropriety by employee representatives than by existing directors, and concluded that all directors should be subject to the same legal duty not to use company information for personal profit or advantage. There is a more serious problem in respect of the disclosure of confidential facts and plans for the purposes of collective bargaining, given the fact that many trade unionists are prepared to support board-level participation only as a means of extending the scope and effectiveness of trade-union bargaining power. In Germany, as has been seen, this problem is avoided partly by the separation of supervisory and executive responsibility, so that supervisory board members do not have a right of direct access to all managerial information, and partly by an informal practice of entrusting collective bargaining and co-determination to different people. The proposals of the Bullock Committee for representation on a unitary board with formal responsibility for resource allocation and its insistence that employee or trade-union directors on company boards must be expected to report back to their constituencies, might give rise to greater difficulties over the classification of information which would be disclosed to board members as of right.

Several attempts have already been made to resolve this problem within the framework of labour law. The Industrial Relations Act 1971 made provision for the disclosure of information without which trade unions would be to a material extent impeded in carrying on collective bargaining or which it would otherwise be in accord with good industrial relations practice, as defined in the proposed Code of Practice, to disclose for collective bargaining purposes (s. 56); there was also provision for direct disclosure to employees of specified items of information in companies employing more than 350 persons (s. 57). This statute was repealed before this could be brought into force, and the Draft Code of Practice issued in 1972 merely stated that management should aim to meet all reasonable requests from trade unions for information relevant to negotiations in hand (para. 97). A subsequent report by the Commission on

[28] *Conway v. Petronics Clothing Co. Ltd*, *The Times*, 28 April 1977.

Industrial Relations proposed more detailed guidelines, in which it was suggested that trade unions should be entitled to the financial information supplied to shareholders and information on immediate or longer term prospects and plans which might affect employees; where this was refused unions would have had a right to complain to the Industrial Court of an unfair industrial practice.[29] Similar provisions have now been incorporated in the Employment Protection Act 1975: this re-enacts the basic duty to disclose information for collective bargaining purposes in similar terms to those in the earlier statute (s. 17), with a similar list of formal exceptions covering in particular any items the disclosure of which would cause substantial injury to the employer's undertaking for reasons other than its effect on collective bargaining, and exempting the employer from being required to produce specific documents or to compile information which would be unreasonably expensive to produce (s. 18). Complaints over any failure to comply with these obligations are to be dealt with by a Central Arbitration Committee under the auspices of the Advisory Conciliation and Arbitration Service (ss. 19–21), which has also produced a formal Code of Practice governing disclosure procedures.[30]

It is clear that these measures envisage a somewhat lesser degree of compulsory disclosure than would be available to a director under the ordinary rule of company law. It may be that some trade-union officials and shop stewards will prefer to retain an arms-length relationship with management for collective bargaining purposes, and even to avoid becoming too directly involved in assessing the state of the company's financial affairs in the context of wage bargaining, since that would inevitably involve them in some responsibility for decisions on the allocation of resources within the company. If joint management/union decisions are to be made at board level on the resources to be allocated to reinvestment, wage increases and dividends, the nature of collective bargaining at lower levels would be very different from what it is now, in that individual unions would be bargaining over the allocation of a given sum to various sections of the workforce, rather than seeking the best settlement obtainable from management for their particular constituency. Considerations of this kind render it likely that board-level participation will be rather less far-reaching than is anticipated

[29] Report No. 31, *Disclosure of Information* (1972).

[30] ACAS, *Code of Practice 2: Disclosure of information to trade unions* (1977).

by the Bullock Committee, unless some further provision is made for the development of financial participation as discussed below.

v *Groups and multi-nationals.* The organization of companies into groups, whether on a national or multi-national basis, creates special problems for any form of board-level representation for employees.[31] If the employee representatives on the board of a subsidiary were entitled to thwart decisions made at a higher level within the group, any rationalization of group activities which involved closing or running down a particular subsidiary might be difficult to carry through. To remove this threat to the power of holding companies to control the activities of their subsidiaries, the Bullock Committee recommended that the controlling company of a British-based group should be entitled to appoint the 'neutral' members of the board in any subsidiary within which there had been a vote for board-level representation. To prevent an established management/union partnership on the board of an independent company from being outflanked by a sale of a majority of its shares on the stock market to a new holding company, the Committee also recommended that such a company should not formally become a subsidiary of the company taking it over until its reconstituted board had signed a 'control' agreement, and that the legal relationship of all holding and subsidiary companies should be amended accordingly (1948: s. 154) (see Chapter 9). The similar danger that employee representation on British subsidiaries of foreign-based multi-nationals might be outflanked by the foreign holding company taking advantage of a right to appoint the 'neutral' board members would be dealt with by suspending that right and providing that the proposed Industrial Democracy Commission should not proceed to the nomination of 'neutral' members in the event of deadlock without consulting the government.

These particular recommendations were designed to secure the effective implementation of the principle of parity representation at the top level within Britain of any national or multi-national group covered by the measures proposed by the Bullock Committee. Other provisions have had to be made to secure the effective implementation of the different forms of board-level representation adopted in Germany, Denmark and Sweden. In this sense the imposition of

[31] See the detailed discussion of this issue by the Bullock Committee, Ch. 11.

schemes for industrial democracy on groups and multi-nationals is a technical issue, which follows from a decision in principle on a particular structure for simple companies. But national and multi-national groups are dominant in many sectors of the economy. It is therefore essential to develop a system of industrial democracy which can in practice be effectively applied to such companies. The reluctant admission by the Bullock Committee that it may not always be possible to impose effective parity in decision-making on British subsidiaries of multi-national groups is a useful illustration of the drawbacks to its exclusive concentration on board-level representation as opposed to structures for participation at plant level.

Selection, parity and control

The crucial issue in any scheme for employee representation at board level is that of control over decision-making, and thus indirectly the proportion and method of selection of the employee representatives. The Bullock Committee concluded that parity of representation between employees and shareholders, together with a jointly appointed 'neutral' element to help resolve any deadlock, was the only method of transferring real power and responsibility to employee representatives. It also took the view that the method of selection of employee representatives at board level must be left to the trade unions established within the enterprise. These conclusions, which have been at the centre of the continuing controversy over the Bullock Report, were based largely on the Committee's assessment of the experience of board-level representation in Germany and Sweden and, to a lesser extent, on the initial results of an experiment in the appointment of worker directors to the divisional boards of the British Steel Corporation.

The appointment in 1968 of a small number of shop-floor employees to the internal divisional boards of the newly nationalized British Steel Corporation was the result of a personal non-statutory initiative by the Corporation's first chairman, Lord Melchett.[32] The trade unions eventually agreed to produce a list of names with the proviso that no employee directors were to retain any direct link with their sponsoring unions, so that there could be no interference with established collective bargaining systems. The experiment did

[32] This account is based upon the description of the initial years of the experiment in P. Brannen, *et al.*, *The Worker Directors* (1976), supplemented by information on subsequent developments supplied by the Corporation.

not start well. After an initial period of enthusiasm, the new employee directors found themselves being cut off from all contact with their unions and their shop-floor colleagues. They were also squeezed out from any real involvement in decision-making by their full-time managerial colleagues, partly as a result of the failure of management as a whole to work out precisely what it was that the new employee directors were meant to be doing other than bring an element of grass-roots thinking into the boardroom. Following the reconstruction of the Corporation into a number of product divisions in 1970, and a highly critical report by a research team which had been monitoring the experiment, however, these initial problems were largely resolved. In January 1972 a new job description for the employee directors was produced, and they were able to play a more constructive role within the structure of managerial committees and working parties. They were also permitted to resume direct contact with their unions: by mid-1974 twelve of the fifteen current employee directors held continuing union office and all were active union members. Though no one claims that the employee directors have made a substantial impact on managerial decision-making, it is generally accepted by both management and unions that the system provides a useful channel of communication to supplement the structures for collective bargaining.

Similar complaints about the exclusion of employee representatives from real involvement in managerial decision-making have been made in Germany and Sweden. In Germany this is due more to the separation of supervisory and executive functions than the issue of parity in representation. But the Biedenkopf Commission reported that the parity system of co-determination in the coal and steel sector had led to a more thoroughgoing structure for informal co-operation than in other companies where there was less than parity in representation. In Sweden a report on the first three years of a system of minority representation for employees indicated that managerial decisions were being delegated to committees and working parties from which employee directors were excluded in two-thirds of the cases studied.[33] In both systems there have been complaints that employee representatives have been denied access to the preparatory reports and working papers necessary to a full

[33] National Swedish Industrial Board, *Board Representation of Employees in Sweden* (1976); see also E. Batstone and P. Davies, *Industrial Democracy: European Experience* (1976).

understanding of the issues involved, or alternatively that they have been unable to digest and master what is provided in the time available.

It is difficult to gauge the extent to which these problems are due to lack of parity in representation, as opposed to the fact that employee representatives cannot be as fully engaged in the preparation and development of managerial plans and decisions as full-time managers without becoming full-time managers themselves. The considerations introduced at the start of this chapter suggest that even in a parity system the representatives of employees are unlikely to be able to operate effectively in other than a supervisory capacity. To that extent many of the benefits of employee representation in terms of better communications and mutual understanding may be gained without proceeding immediately to parity. On the other hand it is clear that the power of a supervisory board to remove individual managers from their positions, as in Yugoslavia, or to veto certain key decisions on take-overs, mergers or closures, as in Germany, cannot be exercised on behalf of employees without some form of potential voting control. If the political and economic objections to granting full equality to employee and shareholder directors are too great, as is suggested by the retention of a casting vote for shareholders in the appointment of supervisory board chairmen in Germany under the 1976 legislation and by the introduction of a neutral element in most other systems, then there are strong arguments for a more formal division of powers through which employee representatives may be given a veto on certain matters without threatening the effective control of management on other matters. A limited formal power of supervision and veto may give more effective power to employee representatives than an apparently more equal allocation of authority on a flexible unitary board where ultimate control is, in one way or another, retained by the management side.

The main alternative to limited supervision and veto on the German model is the development and extension of collective bargaining to board-level issues. This concept has been most fully explored in Sweden. Legislation was introduced in 1976 with a view to extending established trade-union negotiating rights to a wider range of issues, and providing unions with information and documents relatings to important developments within the enterprise.[34] Swedish laws on the appointment of employee directors are best regarded in this general context as a means of complementing a plant bargaining system which has been developed over a number of years. As has already been indicated in relation to the disclosure of information, the difference between this approach and that of formal co-determination is that each side is likely to minimize the extent of its disclosure except in so far as the information will support its bargaining position. If this is the case then parity representation will not necessarily make a great deal of difference, since effective managerial decision-making is likely to be shifted from open discussion on boards and joint working parties to other less formal channels.

The approach of the Bullock Committee to the selection of employee representatives indicates that it favoured the extension of collective bargaining on the Swedish model rather than a more formal German system of co-determination on specific issues. The recommendation that employee representatives on company boards in Britain should not be directly elected by all employees but selected in accordance with a scheme drawn up by existing trade unions in the enterprise, subject to a conciliation procedure in the event of deadlock, follows from the Committee's prior commitment to the maintenance of a single channel of employee representation through trade-union machinery. Even in Sweden, however, the procedure for union selection is subject to a statutory provision that representation must be related to the level of membership in the company. Given the fragmented structure of union organization in many large British enterprises and the substantial number of non-union employees, estimated by the Bullock Committee at some twenty to thirty per cent in larger manufacturing and non-manufacturing companies,[35] it is difficult to justify the denial of the ordinary principles of elective democracy. In Germany the vast majority of directly elected board members have always been active trade unionists. A statutory code of practice governing the drawing up of constituencies in complex enterprises and other relevant matters would afford a greater degree of legitimacy to employee representatives. As with the issue of parity

[34] Act on the Joint Regulation of Working Life 1976, noted in (1976) 5 *Industrial Law Journal*, 237; see also, for a more general discussion of these issues, H. Gospel, 'Disclosure of Information to Trade Unions', ibid., p. 223.

[35] Ibid., pp. 11–15.

in control, however, the method of selection of board-level representatives is less important than the relationship of the system to collective bargaining on financial rewards and other matters at lower levels in the enterprise.

3 SHOP-FLOOR DEMOCRACY

The creation of structures for industrial democracy at plant and shop-floor levels is not directly related to the traditional concerns of company law and did not form part of the terms of reference of the Bullock Committee. But it is widely recognized that if legislation for employee representation at board level does not produce some observable results at shop-floor level it is unlikely to gain much general support. The majority on the Bullock Committee argued that progress in the development of democratic structures at lower levels was likely to be dependent on direction from the board; the minority, that the development of consultation at lower levels should be pursued in priority to board-level representation. Neither gave any serious consideration to the relationship of the two.

In practical terms a similar contrast to that already noticed at board level may be drawn between the development of collective bargaining and of more formal structures for joint decision-making at plant and shop-floor levels. In Britain there is a highly developed system of low-level bargaining through shop stewards. In Germany there is a highly developed and formalized system of works councils. A description of the main features of these two systems may help to explain the relationship of the immediate issues of pay, working conditions and security of employment to board-level participation.

Shop stewards and plant bargaining in Britain

The basis of industrial democracy at shop-floor and plant level in Britain is the local bargaining carried out by shop stewards. In most plants and workshops in large companies there is some formal or informal procedure for the selection or election of stewards from those union members who are prepared to serve as such. Their function is to take up with management any issue of immediate concern to their fellow workers, from levels of pay and conditions of work to threatened dismissals or lay-offs, and to seek a favourable settlement by the usual processes of compromise and confrontation. A general picture of how the system operates may be gathered from the following extracts from the summary of an official survey of workplace industrial relations carried out for the Donovan Commission on Trade Unions and Employers Organizations in 1966:

> 80 per cent of all union members claimed to have a shop steward or someone who did the work of a steward.... More than two-thirds [of the stewards] either went through no form of election or were the only candidates for the job. Workplace elections outnumbered union branch elections by nearly five to one, and a show of hands was more than twice as frequent as a ballot. 65 per cent [of stewards] said that in practice they had to stand for re-election and another 15 per cent had to do so only technically.... The average size of constituency was 60 members for ordinary stewards and 350 for senior stewards.
>
> Only 1 per cent of informants were full-time stewards.... There were some kinds of meeting between stewards in two-thirds of the workplaces.... More than half the stewards could leave the job to contact members whenever they wanted to or with only courtesy permission, and only 13 per cent could not leave the job at all. 71 per cent of stewards said there existed at their place of work 'a joint committee where stewards meet jointly with management to discuss and settle problems'.... 72 per cent of stewards said they had 'unofficial' ways of approaching management, and almost all thought these were very important. Three out of five stewards said they were sometimes able to increase members earnings as a result of their personal efforts.... The most common arguments used by stewards were comparisons with other workers in the same or different places of work, abnormal conditions of work, and changes in the nature of the job.[36]

It is important to distinguish this network of local workplace representation and bargaining from the collective bargaining carried out at national level on basic rates of pay by full-time union officials and employers' organizations. In many cases agreements are reached and claims pursued by shop stewards which are contrary to official union policy. So-called 'unofficial' disputes and strikes are a good deal more frequent than 'official' union-backed disputes and strikes. Shop stewards have often continued to press the sectional interests of their fellow workers in terms of special payments and fringe benefits without much regard for the national rules or guidelines laid down by their unions or by government. In the largest plants where shop stewards are traditionally exempt from the whole or a large part of ordinary working duties, there is often fierce competition for the posts and a corresponding anxiety on the part of those

[36] Government Social Survey, *Workplace Industrial Relations* (1968), pp. 2–3; see also S. Parker, *Workplace Industrial Relations 1973* (1975).

elected to represent the interests of their constituencies as forcefully as they can.

The strength of this system is the fact that shop stewards are able to reflect the feelings and aspirations of their fellow workers in a more democratic manner than national or regional trade-union officials. They are more directly, if less formally, elected and their authority can usually be revoked as soon as they lose the confidence of their constituencies. Its weakness lies in its fragmented and decentralized character and the fact that it frequently results in disruptive sectional claims by one group of workers in terms of parity or differentials with other groups. As a result, there has gradually developed the idea that an orderly and equitable structure of payment and differentials within a company or plant can only be worked if all the stewards representing all the various groups of workers can be brought together to agree a scheme which covers all employees and to which all unions and shop stewards are in some sense committed. Plant bargaining of this kind is usually limited to a specific period of one or two years, after which a new set of payments and differentials may have to be worked out; it will frequently involve a general all-round increase in pay or other benefits, as a means of securing general agreement from all sections of the workforce.[37]

The natural impetus of employee representation through shop stewards is thus towards a system of plant or company bargaining in contrast to the system of national bargaining by the independent trade unions representing each group of workers. In most large companies and plants there is already a joint shop stewards committee on which the stewards and convenors representing each trade or workshop meet together to co-ordinate their policies and sometimes to engage in unified collective bargaining with management. The recommendations of the Bullock Committee clearly envisaged that most of the employee representatives on the board would be selected by such a shop stewards committee, which would then act as a focus for the transmission of issues and information from the shop floor to the board and from the board to the shop floor. Similar patterns have been developed for extended collective bargaining in those nationalized companies like British Leyland and Harland & Wolff in Belfast in which negotiations on industrial democracy

[37] On plant and productivity bargaining generally, see A. Flanders, *The Fawley Productivity Agreements* (1964); Prices and Incomes Board, *No. 36* (1967) and *No. 123* (1969).

have been pursued with government support independently of the work of the Bullock Committee.[38] The main legal issues in this context are whether informal committees of this kind should be left to operate on an extra-legal basis, whether they should be granted some form of legal recognition and given specific powers or functions, or whether they should be replaced by a more orderly and uniform structure of works councils on the German model.

Works councils and formal democracy in Germany

Statutory schemes for plant-level democracy have been introduced in most European countries. In Germany the *Betriebsrat* dates back to the 1930s; in France the *comité d'entreprise* to the post-war reconstruction under de Gaulle; similar provisions have been made in Belgium (1948) and Holland (1950). Non-statutory schemes have been developed under national collective agreements in the Scandinavian countries and Italy. In most cases the obligation to form a works council is geared to the size of the enterprise or plant, in terms of the number of people employed. But in many countries the obligation has been widely ignored and, even where the law has been formally complied with, the councils have had little influence or impact. This appears to be directly related to the fact that works councils have had few powers and have been isolated from the structures for collective bargaining. In Germany, where works councils have a number of significant functions and are closely integrated with the structures for collective bargaining and co-determination, they are generally regarded as useful and effective.

In Germany, as already outlined (see p. 451), the obligation to form a works council was extended in 1972 to all establishments with more than five employees. Though compliance is low in the smallest of these, it has been reported that councils have been established in some eighty to ninety per cent of establishments with from fifty to five hundred employees, and in all establishments with more than five hundred employees.[39] The main functions of the works council lie in the field of 'social' issues such as working hours, washing and eating facilities, holiday arrangements, pensions, housing and other company-based provisions for the benefit of employees.

[38] See for instance *Industrial Democracy: a discussion paper on worker participation at Harland & Wolff* (1975).

[39] Commission on Industrial Relations, Report No. 4: *Worker Participation and Collective Bargaining in Europe* (1974).

All major economic plans such as a merger or shut-down or the introduction of new production methods must also be submitted to it, and in establishments with more than one thousand employees it has statutory authority to draw up and administer guidelines on suspensions and dismissals. On all these matters the management of the company must work in conjunction with the works council, and where agreement cannot be reached the issue must be referred to an arbitration board and ultimately to the labour court. This is known in Germany as the right to co-determination as opposed to mere consultation or collective bargaining. The works council is also directly involved in plant-level bargaining through a joint plant committee (*Lohn und Akkord Kommission*) composed of equal numbers of works council members and of management. This deals both with any improvements on basic regional or national wage rates and with methods of job evaluation and piece-rate measurement. Any agreement reached must then be submitted to the full works council for formal approval. Though in theory the works council is not permitted to involve itself in any form of industrial action, individual councillors, the vast majority of whom are active trade unionists, may lend their support to unofficial industrial action in their union capacity.

The sheer volume of work carried out in German works councils, particularly in larger plants, has created its own problems. Leading works councillors frequently lose contact with their fellow workers as they become involved on a full-time basis in processing the mass of paper-work and consultation at the works council office. It has also been reported that works council members tend to adopt an increasingly managerial approach to the issues which come before them, and that the particular grievances of individual employees may become submerged in the pursuit of wider objectives. Poor attendance at the statutory plant meetings which are supposed to be held every three months is a further indication of the formality and lack of relevance to ordinary workers of work of the routine works councils. All these factors have led to the development of a separate system of trustmen (*Vertrauensmann*) whose function it is to take up individual and group grievances with management as soon as they arise. Nonetheless there is clear evidence that both workers and management are generally satisfied with the works council system. A survey of employee attitudes in 330 companies with more than one hundred employees reported that two-thirds of those interviewed regarded the works councils as effective and that more than nine in ten thought them an indispensable part of the company structure. A more recent study by the British Commission on Industrial Relations reported that 'management generally considers that the works council is essential and conducive to effective management'.[40]

Bargaining and authority

This brief comparison of the operation of shop-floor bargaining in Britain and of works councils in Germany highlights the important distinction between the extension of collective bargaining and the reallocation of authority. In Germany the system of co-determination alters the basis of legal authority for certain specified decisions both at board level and on works councils. The development of collective bargaining may achieve similar results on particular issues but it leaves intact the principle of managerial authority. There is also a difference in the extent to which employee representatives themselves become involved in making and taking responsibility for decisions of a managerial kind. Experience in Germany shows that there are drawbacks to involvement of this kind, in terms of a loss of direct contact between rank and file employees and their 'managerial' representatives. Where there is no shift in authority, however, there is an equal risk that decisions will continue to be taken by management behind the backs of employee representatives and that full details of managerial planning and calculation will not be revealed for collective bargaining purposes.

This suggests that there are advantages in the creation of formal structures for joint decision-making on specific issues of special importance to employees, such as industrial safety and dismissals, or for a power of veto in relation to take-overs and mergers,[41] which may not be so readily achieved by informal collective bargaining. In Britain there have been very few developments of this kind. Formal legal controls over managerial authority have been introduced in relation to unfair dismissal under the Industrial Relations Act 1971 and the Trade Union and Labour Relations Act 1974. But these do not involve any direct control of employers by employees. Nor do the provisions of the Health and Safety Act 1974

[40] Ibid., p. 31.

[41] As, for instance, in the revised *Draft Statute for European Companies* (1974) (see p. 309).

which require management to consult with trade unions or employee representatives on safety matters (s. 2). Though the regulations and code of practice prepared by the Health and Safety Commission under this statute will give formal authority to safety representatives and members of safety committees to make inspections and to investigate accidents with a view to improving standards of safety, any disagreements which arise are to be dealt with through normal industrial relations procedures.[42] The pursuit of the collective bargaining model to the exclusion of any element of co-determination may in practice serve to prolong rather than diminish the principle of managerial authority.

4 FINANCIAL PARTICIPATION AND WORKERS' CONTROL

There is a basic problem in any scheme for the transfer of authority to employees or their representatives on the German model as an alternative to collective bargaining. This is the fact that financial benefits for employees continue to be dealt with exclusively by collective bargaining. If employee and union representatives must continue to bargain for their share in any increase in productivity or profitability by a direct increase in wages, while shareholders take their benefit either as dividends or as capital appreciation, there is likely to be a continuing imbalance in board-level decisions on investment, and continuing confrontation in wage bargaining at plant level. Employee representatives will naturally wish to ensure that employees secure an immediate benefit from any concessions, while management, on behalf of shareholders, may wish to take a longer view. Co-determination at board level or on the shop floor cannot sensibly be divorced from the issue of financial participation for employees.

Profit sharing and share distribution

In its simplest form profit sharing for employees may amount to little more than an incentive scheme. The idea that the performance of employees, and hence the general level of productivity, could be improved by linking the wages paid to each individual to his personal output, as in the piece rate system, became widely accepted as a

[42] *Health and Safety at Work: Safety representatives and safety committees* (1976); at the time of writing these regulations were expected to come into force in 1978.

basis for the payment of wages during the nineteenth century.[43] It is a short step from this to the payment of a periodic cash bonus linked to the performance of the enterprise as a whole. Profit sharing of this kind, however, is usually regarded merely as a managerial technique through which the profitability of the enterprise may be increased in the interests of shareholders, rather than as a recognition of the independent rights of employees. Those who have been concerned to give employees a real interest in the company for which they work have usually preferred to concentrate on schemes through which a share in profits is distributed in the form of shares, with a view to building up a substantial body of employee shareholders who will participate in both dividends and capital appreciation on a par with other shareholders. In some cases this is pursued by the direct issue of fully paid shares to all employees in proportion to their wages or length of service; in others by the issue of shares to trustees to hold on their behalf. In the case of directors and executives it is also common practice to promote share-option schemes under which substantial blocks of shares are issued to independent trustees and eventually offered to the beneficiaries at attractive discounts related to the interim appreciation in the market price of the company's shares. Any formal difficulties which may arise over the purchase by a company of its own shares or the issue of shares at a discount in this connection have been removed by statute (1948 : s. 54).

Share distribution schemes on these general lines have been adopted by some large public companies both in Britain and America, and have from time to time been given official support and encouragement.[44] But schemes of this kind, however generous and enlightened, make no essential alteration to the traditional framework of company law. The terms of each individual scheme are wholly dependent on the approval of the board of directors and ultimately of the general meeting of shareholders, and even if share issues are maintained on a regular basis from year to year they constitute no more than a continuing voluntary payment by the company to its employees which differs only in degree from a simple wage increase or other incentives related to performance. The linked

[43] See for instance the work of J. W. Taylor and the 'scientific management' school.

[44] See generally W. Wallace, *Prescription for Partnership* (1959) and Acton Society Trust and G. Naylor, *Sharing the Profits: an inquiry into the habits, attitudes and problems of employees' shareholding schemes* (1968).

objective of creating a block of employee shareholders to counterbalance external investors in the general meeting has usually been frustrated by the fact that most employees prefer to realize whatever shares are issued to them by disposing of them as soon as they are permitted to do so.

The idea of granting employees a legal right to a share of company profits after the deduction of a fixed prior return on capital invested has been given a statutory base in France. Under a law pressed through in 1967 by de Gaulle all companies with more than a hundred employees must set aside a proportion of their annual profit, after the deduction of tax and of a fixed rate of interest of five per cent on capital employed, for distribution to employees in the form of shares or other investment units. The actual proportion of profit to be applied in this way is calculated from the relationship between the company's total wage bill and the net value of its output, so that employees in a capital intensive industry do not enjoy an unfair advantage over those in a labour intensive industry. The apportionment among employees is also regulated on the basis of each individual employee's wage with a ceiling on the amount attributable to any one person of approximately £500. And as in many voluntary British and American schemes there is a formal bar on realization by employees of their shares for a period of five years, so that the company may have the benefit of the capital set aside for that period. Finally there is a provision which permits the management and employees of any firm to replace the statutory scheme by any other arrangement which is at least as beneficial to employees as the statutory scheme, subject to the approval of an official supervisory agency (*Service de l'interessement et de la participation*). By the end of 1974 agreements had been reached in more than ten thousand companies covering some five million employees. Many of these were negotiated by works councils or trade unions. The total sum involved for all schemes in 1974 represented three per cent of the wages and salaries paid and two per cent of the capital value of the companies concerned, though these figures varied widely between individual companies. Unofficial surveys have indicated that roughly half of the shares actually distributed in 1974, at the end of the prescribed five-year waiting period in respect of the 1968 allocation, were immediately sold on the market. The Sudreau Report has recommended the extension of the scheme, and the replacement of the five-year ban on realization by a new system of individual tax incentives to encourage reinvestment.[45]

It is difficult to give a valid assessment of the success of profit-sharing schemes. There is little doubt that they are popular with employees in so far as they result in appreciable extra payment. It is less clear whether they make any lasting contribution to the efficiency of an enterprise or the commitment of employees to it. None of the studies on companies which have adopted profit sharing on a voluntary or guaranteed basis have established that they are any more successful or that they survive longer than other companies. Official surveys in Britain in 1912, 1920 and 1956 reported with remarkable consistency that somewhat more than half of the schemes started had been abandoned due to lack of profit or to apathy or dissatisfaction among employees; the average life of abandoned schemes was eight years and of continuing schemes from twelve to fourteen years.[46] The tendency of employees to dispose of any shares issued to them as soon as they are entitled to do so is further evidence that they are primarily interested in immediate financial benefit as opposed to continuing participation as shareholders. To counter this tendency and promote a progressive take-over of companies on behalf of their employees some writers and politicians have proposed that any shares or profit attributable to employees under a compulsory profit-sharing scheme should be invested in a national fund, so that a substantial and permanent holding in all large companies could be built up and exercised on behalf of current employees by a central or local agency.[47] But such proposals have met with little support. It is difficulty to resist the conclusion that profit sharing which is divorced from immediate and effective involvement in the control of the companies concerned is of little interest to most employees other than as a source of additional income.

Constitutional participation

Some companies have sought to overcome these difficulties by altering the fundamental basis of their constitution in such a way as to

[45] *La reforme de l'entreprise* (1975), Ch. 5; the report also deals with proposed structures for participation in the control of French companies.

[46] Ministry of Labour, Reports on Co-partnership: C. 6267 (1891); C. 7458 (1894); Cd. 6496 (1912); Cd. 7283 (1914); Cmd. 544 (1920); and 1956.

[47] See for example the proposals of the British Labour Party, *The Community and the Company* (1974) and the scheme proposed in Denmark in 1973.

place the rights of employees and shareholders on a more equal footing. One example of the complex structure which has to be created within the existing legal framework to achieve this is that of the John Lewis Partnership, which runs a chain of large department stores. The rationale of the Partnership in terms of the respective rights of capital, management and labour is simply expressed in the company's own literature:

> The fundamental economic ideas upon which the partnership is based are simple.... Capital should receive a reasonable fixed cumulative dividend, and the rewards for taking a financial risk should never be unlimited. Management should receive an ample remuneration properly related to the earnings of able hard-working professional men in general. No worker should receive less than a decent living, and between this bottom limit and the top limit every pay rate should be governed by the Partnership's aim of first rate efficiency in its service to the general community. After meeting these prior claims and providing proper reserves, all profits should be distributed among all the workers, managers and managed alike, in proportion to their pay, which should be taken as the best measure of their contribution to the total result.

This conception has been put into operation in formal terms by transferring the sole voting control over the group as a whole to a trust company which is bound to exercise its powers in accordance with the above principles, and by converting all the ordinary equity capital into fixed interest preference shares with voting rights only when the dividend is in arrears. Any surplus profit after paying this dividend and providing for reserves must then be distributed direct to employees either in cash or in the form of new preference shares issued to ensure that a proper level of capitalization is maintained. The employees may if they wish dispose of these shares without delay, thus in effect raising the additional capital for the enterprise on the external market, though the shares may sometimes have to be sold at a discount. The rights of employees under this scheme are created by the effective abolition of the ordinary equity shareholder.

The structure for control in the John Lewis Partnership is as highly formalized as that for profit sharing. Provision is made in the constitution of the trust company for the election of a central council from all employees, which in its turn nominates a majority of the trustees who control the voting power over the group as a whole. This council may at any time initiate a resolution for the removal of the chairman of the group, the chief executive, on the ground of any infringement of the constitution. There is also a directly elected branch council in each establishment. These bodies can exercise a real influence on the decisions of management without actually using their powers. A recent study of the operation of the John Lewis system showed clearly that top management did regard themselves as restricted by the principles of the partnership, even though in formal terms the chairman has absolute authority over matters of day-to-day management.[48] Important commercial decisions have been carried through by individual branch councils against the wishes of management, as for instance over the question of Saturday opening hours.

Workers' control

Control by employees rather than shareholders may be pressed considerably further than this. But there has been an understandable absence of extreme examples of industrial democracy in the western world. A model for a system in which the power of capital and management has really been subordinated to that of workers must be sought elsewhere. The best example is that of Yugoslavia which has managed to avoid the high degree of centralization and party control that effectively nullifies any real element of industrial democracy in most other communist countries.[49]

The formal structure of the enterprise in Yugoslavia is broadly similar to the abstract co-operative model (Figure 12.4). The basic organ of control, on a par with the general meeting of shareholders in the west, is the *workers council* elected directly by all employees. This council, which may have as few as fifteen members and as many as a hundred, depending on the size of the enterprise, is in general control over the policy and production plan of the enterprise, and over the distribution or reinvestment of profits. The executive organ of the council is the *managing board,* composed of from three to fifteen members elected by the council, which draws up the details of these policies, plans their implementation and is in general control

[48] A Flanders *et al.*, *An Experiment in Industrial Democracy* (1969).

[49] A good up-to-date account of the Yugoslav system is contained in P. Blumberg, *Industrial Democracy*: *The Sociology of Participation* (1968); there are also useful details from the socialist and capitalist viewpoints respectively in F. Singleton and A. Topham, *Workers' Control in Yugoslavia,* Fabian Society (1963), and in C. de Hoghton, *The Company*: *Law, Structure and Reform in Eleven Countries* (1970), pp. 320–9; for an economic assessment see J. Vanek, *The Economics of Workers' Management*: *A Yugoslav Case-Study* (1972).

over the accounts of the enterprise. The actual day-to-day management of the enterprise is undertaken by a *director* who is now appointed by the workers council from a recommendation prepared by a selection committee on which half the members are workers' representatives and the rest local and governmental officials. The director may be dismissed by the council either for illegality or inefficiency. The director is an ex officio member of the managing board, but is also subject to considerable though apparently waning pressures from the local party organization.

It is clear from reports of the actual operation of this system that the tensions between management and workers are by no means wholly eliminated. The director and his immediate subordinates, and to some extent the managing board, face many of the same problems as their western counterparts in balancing the costs of production and revenue from sales, and are inevitably forced into confrontations with the workers' council and the main body of employees over the extent of managerial authority. But real control is exercised by the council. Directors have been removed from office with surprising frequency, and there have been numerous instances in which the workers' councils have insisted on the distribution of profits to the detriment of the firm's requirements for reinvestment, and even cases in which monopolistic and restrictive pricing and production policies have been pursued with the full approval of the councils. These are perhaps no more than the counterparts of the self-interested policies frequently adopted by management and controlling shareholders within the capitalist system. There is no doubt in general terms that the Yugoslav system of corporate organization is as fully workable as the traditional capitalist model.

5 CONCLUSION

This account of the formal structure and practical operation of schemes for employee participation at various levels in the enterprise suggests three general conclusions of relevance to the essentially political issues involved in the development of industrial democracy.

The first is that it is impractical to attempt to give effective managerial power to employees in general. It is no more convincing to recommend that the management of a large and complex enterprise should be entrusted to several thousand employees than that it should be entrusted to several thousand shareholders. It is equally unrealistic to expect part-time or even full-time employee representatives at board level to be a match for full-time professional managers. The relatively short life-span of most enterprises which have sought to continue their operations under direct workers' control following a successful 'work-in' suggests that commitment and enthusiasm cannot make up for the lack of effective managerial planning for a viable market.[50] It does not follow that management cannot be made accountable to employees, as experience in Yugoslavia demonstrates. But this is more likely to be achieved by giving employee representatives effective powers of supervision and veto on specific and limited issues rather than by pursuing the initially more attractive goal of joint employee/management control on all issues at board level. To this extent a modified form of co-determination which shifts authority on certain matters may prove more effective than the proposals of the Bullock Report.

The second is that it may be difficult to secure greater managerial accountability without making a greater change in the basis of managerial duties than merely authorizing or requiring directors to take the interests of employees into account. There are dangers in this context in concentrating on the extension of collective bargaining at all levels in the enterprise, since that assumes that managers are naturally committed to the 'other side' and will seek to promote shareholders' interests in preference to those of employees. More progress might be made in dismantling the current ideological base of the capitalist system by developing the conception that management is employed jointly by both employees and investors and that any profit generated in an enterprise after paying the current rates for capital and labour should be shared among employees and investors, or invested on their joint behalf, as indicated in Figure 12.6.

The third is that the natural tendency of industrial democracy is towards a degree of decentralization which runs counter to current trends in economic organization. To grant effective power to employees or their representatives at company, plant or shop-floor level necessarily curtails the power of management at higher levels to operate their enterprises as appears to them to be most economic. This poses special problems in national and multi-national groups of

[50] See the review of experience in three government assisted worker-controlled companies, Scottish Daily News, Kirkby Manufacturing and Engineering and Meriden Motorcycle Co-operative: Committee of Public Accounts, *Sixth Report 1975–76* (1976), paras. 18 ff.

companies, particularly in respect of mergers, closures and redundancies. Some protection for employees in this respect may be sought by providing for their representation at company and group level, as proposed by the Bullock Committee. But it is questionable whether this is an adequate substitute for the reallocation of authority at company, plant and shop-floor levels on those issues, notably redundancies and dismissals, which most affect those working there and which can be granted without unduly fettering the rationalization of production in the face of market forces.

All these issues create additional problems in state-controlled companies and industries, since government may wish to impose policies which are unpalatable to employees and management alike and since there is greater difficulty in developing structures for financial participation. The inherent conflict between workers' control and state capitalism and socialism has already been discussed in Chapter 12. This suggests that realistic proposals for industrial democracy in the public sector must be focused on structures for implementing externally imposed policies. The framework within which such structures must be developed is discussed in Chapter 14.

14
The modern corporation and government

A major feature of both the capitalist and the conflict models of the company is their concentration on the interests of shareholders, management, employees and unions to the exclusion of any consideration of the public or community interest. This limitation is acceptable in the case of smaller companies whose employment and pricing policies are subject to the ordinary pressures of market competition. But competition has much less apparent impact on the larger corporations which dominate industrial and commercial activity in particular spheres. In addition, many companies at this level expect to receive government aid and support on a continuing basis, whether by way of assistance towards the huge development costs of new products in the advanced technological industries, as in the field of aircraft and computers, or support for declining staple industries, as in the case of cotton or shipbuilding, or more simply by way of substantial government contracts. In the discussion of cases of this kind attention is naturally directed away from the conception of the company as a means for the production of profit to that of the provision of a service to the community in the production of essential goods and services or the maintenance of exports or employment. The question for the lawyer in such cases is whether the interests of the consumer and the community may safely be left to the management, or indeed the employees, of the companies concerned or whether some additional formal control or supervision is necessary.

Further problems are created by the development of multi-national companies whose operations are so extensive as to make any attempt at control by a single national government largely ineffective, since the company will often be in a position to switch its production and investment, and the employment and wealth which it creates, to other areas.

All these matters have a high political content, and the various strategies for legislative control and nationalization are constantly changing. But a satisfactory legal framework for the large modern corporation can not realistically be developed without taking this governmental and community interest into account. The various possibilities may be considered under four general heads: first, the modes of governmental intervention which do not involve any direct government participation in the affairs of the company; secondly, the various forms of direct intervention by way of aid to private sector companies or of rationalization; thirdly, nationalization; and finally, the question of control on an international level, in particular the prospects for control within the context of the European Economic Community.

I MONOPOLIES, RESTRICTIVE PRACTICES AND PRICE AND INCOMES POLICIES

The control of monopolies and restrictive practices has been the most generally accepted and stable form of governmental intervention in the affairs of individual companies under free enterprise capitalism. The need for some intervention of this kind, if the forces of economic competition were not to become wholly ineffective, was apparent by the end of the nineteenth century. In most industrialized countries a number of very large enterprises had developed and were in a position either individually or in combination to dominate the market in particular spheres. This development was most pronounced in the transport, chemical and oil industries in the United States, but the control of markets and prices by large cartels became firmly established in Europe in the 1920s and 1930s. If the traditional economic model of the role of the free market in protecting the consumer and the public interest against overcharging and in securing the optimum allocation of resources was to have any meaning at all it was clear that some intervention was necessary, both to control the growth of monopoly power by single companies, and to prohibit restrictive agreements and arrangements between those firms which should in theory be competing with each other.

These twin objectives are now pursued with varying degrees of enthusiasm and effectiveness in most capitalist countries.

Legislation on these lines was first introduced in the United States under the Sherman Act of 1890. This declared any restrictive agreement or monopoly to be illegal and subjected those involved to penal sanctions. These broad formulations, however, proved largely ineffective, and it was not until the Clayton Act of 1914 that any real progress was made. This Act introduced a more precise prohibition against any form of unfair competition including price discrimination and established the Federal Trade Commission to enforce its provisions.[1] The Commission typically seeks to achieve its objectives by a process of negotiation with the companies concerned, but in the last resort it has power to make orders requiring large companies to divest themselves of assets or holdings in other companies where these can be shown to operate against the interests of free competition, as in the famous cases of Standard Oil of New Jersey in the 1920s and the Du Pont holding in General Motors in the 1950s, or to cease and desist from restrictive agreements with other companies.

Monopolies and mergers

Legislation on monopolies in Britain was introduced much later and is less well developed.[2] The Monopolies Commission was established in 1948 to inquire into and report on cases in which competition in the production or supply of goods appeared to be prevented or restricted. This might arise where a monopoly situation defined as the concentration of at least one third of the market in particular goods or services in the hands of a single company or group of companies, existed, or where restrictive agreements were found to exist and to operate against the public interest. The Board of Trade, as it then was, was given wide powers to order the break up of the monopoly or the cessation of the restrictive agreements.[3] The operations of the Commission, however, tended to be excessively long

[1] Further provision along the same lines was added in the Robinson/Patman Act of 1936, the Wheeler/Lea Act of 1938 and the Celler/Kefauver Act of 1950; for a simple account see G. C. Allen, *Monopoly and Restrictive Practices* (1968), Ch. 10, and a more detailed analysis A. D. Neale, *The Anti Trust Laws of the United States of America* (1960); for a critical view see J. K. Galbraith, *Economics and the Public Purpose* (1974).

[2] For a simple account see either G. C. Allen, *Monopoly and Restrictive Practices* (1968) or V. Korah, *Competition Law in Britain and the Common Market* (1975).

[3] Monopolies and Restrictive Practices (Inquiry and Control) Act 1948.

drawn out and were particularly ineffective against take-overs and mergers between large concerns which were often effectively completed before the Commission could take preventive action.

The powers of the Commission and the government in respect of monopolies and mergers were increased under the Monopolies and Mergers Act 1965 to enable the authorities to intervene in any proposed take-over or merger which involved assets of more than £5m or which might result in the creation of a monopoly situation, initially by ordering a stay for a period of six months pending investigation by the Commission and ultimately by prohibiting the proposed transaction in whole or in part. Further amendments have been introduced under the Fair Trading Act 1973, which also consolidates the existing law. The power of initial investigation and reference now rests with the Director-General of Fair Trading, who is formally independent of the government (s. 2). The definition of a monopoly situation has been extended to cover the control of one quarter (previously one third) of the supply of any goods or services by any one person, company or group (ss. 6–7), either in the United Kingdom as a whole or in any part of it (s. 9). The exemption from investigation previously enjoyed by nationalized industries and other statutory trading bodies has been removed. The power to stay a proposed take-over or merger to permit a reference to the Commission, however, remains with the Department of Trade (s. 64), as does the exercise of the various powers of governmental intervention where the Commission reports that a proposed merger or take-over or an existing monopoly situation may be expected to operate against the public interest (ss. 56, 73). In such cases the appropriate Minister may prohibit any transaction, order the division of any business or the sale of any assets, or declare specific practices in the supply or sale of goods or services, including any discrimination in pricing or supply, to be unlawful (Sched. 8). In practice the use of these powers is usually avoided by inducing the companies concerned to enter into voluntary undertakings designed to protect other traders or the public from any future abuse, as for instance by maintaining supplies to independent producers at fair prices, or by the continued publication of separate accounts for the constituent parts of a merged enterprise.

These provisions have been rather less stringently applied in respect of monopoly than the equivalent powers of the Federal Trade Commission in the United States. It has been clearly estab-

TABLE 14.1

The use of governmental powers of intervention in take-overs and mergers, 1965–75

	Cases considered	Referred to Commission	Cases found to be against public interest	Cases not so found	Proposed merger abandoned
1965	50	1	–	1	–
1966	60	5	1	4	–
1967	90	2	1	1	–
1968	130	2	1	1	–
1969	110	4	1	2	1
1970	90	2	1	–	–
1971	110	1	–	–	1
1972	120	3	1	1	1
1973	150	9	2	2	5
1974	128	6	–	3	1
1975	157	5	–	3	1

Source: Adapted from Paul Davies, *The Regulation of Take-overs and Mergers* (1976), Table 2 and Office of Fair Trading, *Second Report 1975* (1976); in 1974 and 1975 some references were outstanding at the end of the year.

lished in America that the promotion or maintenance of competition is an end in itself and that monopoly power cannot be justified as being on balance to the advantage of the consumer.[4] In Britain it is rare for cases to be sent to the Monopolies and Mergers Commission until there is some evidence of abuse, and it is standard practice for the government to accept undertakings from enterprises in a monopoly situation rather than to require them to re-establish competition. When the Office of Fair Trading was established in 1973 twelve such undertakings were already in existence, and this policy has been continued.[5] Even when the Commission finds in its reports that a monopoly exists and is likely to operate against the public interest there is no obligation on the government to take any action. Monopolies of size are not in themselves regarded as undesirable.

[4] See *Otter Tail Power Co. v. U.S.* (1973) 410 U.S. 366, discussed in S. M. James, 'The Concept of Abuse in EEC Competition Law: an American Perspective', (1974) 92 *LQR*, 242.

[5] See Office of Fair Trading, *First Report 1973–74* (1975), p. 30.

In respect of take-overs and mergers the government has habitually taken a similarly permissive view.[6] The figures for the use of governmental powers, set out in Table 14.1, show clearly that only a small percentage of the proposed take-overs covered by the legislation have been referred to the Commission, and of those that have been referred only one in five have been found to be against the public interest, though almost as many have in practice been abandoned on reference to the Commission.[7] In a few cases, such as the bid by the Rank Organisation in 1969 for De La Rue, the Commission has reported that there is no economic justification for the proposed merger. But the approach of the authorities is that specific disadvantages as opposed to a mere decrease in potential competition must be established to justify any intervention.

Restrictive Trade Practices

The strategy for government intervention in the field of restrictive agreements between companies has had a more direct and observable impact than that for monopolies and mergers.[8] Initially most of the references to the Monopolies and Restrictive Practices Commission under the 1948 Act fell under this general heading. Little notice, however, was taken of its reports on the manufacture and supply of individual commodities, such as those on *electric lamps* (1951) and *matches* (1953). General dissatisfaction with this system, as expressed in the Commission's general report on collective discrimination in 1955,[9] eventually led to the introduction of an entirely new system of control under the Restrictive Trade Practices Act 1956. This provided for the registration of all agreements between manufacturers or suppliers restricting the freedom of any party to make independent decisions on such matters as the pricing, range, quality and supply of goods or services. Under the Restrictive Trade Practices Act 1968 control was extended to agreements for the exchange of information and other less formal arrangements. Under the Restrictive Trade Practices Act 1976, which consolidates the law, all such agreements which, on reference to the Restrictive Practices Court by the Director-General of Fair Trading, who has taken over

[6] *Mergers: a guide to Board of Trade Practice* (1968).

[7] See generally P. Davies, *The Regulation of Take-overs and Mergers* (1976).

[8] For a detailed analysis see R. B. Stevens & B. S. Yamey, *The Restrictive Practices Court* (1965).

[9] Cmd. 9504.

the functions of the Registrar of Restrictive Trading Agreements, are not shown to be justifiable in the public interest, under one or more of a list of eight 'gateways' (ss. 10, 19), may be declared illegal and unenforceable (ss. 1–2). Any company which fails to register an agreement or which gives effect to an unlawful agreement may be subjected to a substantial fine. In the case of the *Galvanised Tank Manufacturers' Association's Agreement*,[10] for instance, fines totalling £102,000 were imposed on eight companies which had continued to charge identical prices for their goods through a 'notification agreement' despite a previous order of the Court that an earlier registered agreement was contrary to the public interest.

The case-law on the justification of individual agreements under the eight heads is detailed and complex. The law permits the validation of an agreement where it does not discourage competition or where a specific benefit to the community may be expected from the preservation of employment or exports, from protection against discriminatory pricing or supply policies by other companies, from reduced risk of physical injury, or more generally from any specific and substantial benefits to the public. There has been considerable dispute on the interpretation of this final general benefit 'gateway' and the courts have taken seemingly inconsistent approaches.[11] But relatively few cases have in fact come before the courts, and in those which have the majority of agreements have been struck down or curtailed. As a result many agreements which were originally registered by the parties with a view to justification have been voluntarily abandoned. The Registrar in his review of the first ten years of the Act was able to report that the mass of price fixing agreements which had been evolved by trade associations over the preceding quarter of a century had been dismantled.[12] Those agreements which have been justified have been concerned with the standardization of products or the regulation of supply, rather than with pricing. By the end of 1974 there were 2,996 agreements on the register, while 2,684 had been voluntarily or compulsorily terminated.[13]

[10] (1965) L.R. 5 R.P. 315.

[11] See for instance *Re Black Bolt and Nut Association's Agreement* (1960) L.R. 2 R.P. 50, (1961) L.R. 3 R.P. 43 (CA).

[12] *Report of the Registrar of Restrictive Trading Agreements*, 1963–6 (1967) Cmnd. 3188, p. 1.

[13] Office of Fair Trading, *First Report 1973–74* (1975), p. 33.

Under the statute of 1956 collective agreements by suppliers to require their retailers to maintain a fixed price on their goods were treated in the same way as other restrictive agreements. Under the Resale Prices Act 1964, now consolidated in the Resale Prices Act 1976, control was extended to transactions between a single supplier and its retailers, whether enforced through a contractual agreement or by the withholding of supplies. The structure of the legislation is similar to that of the Restrictive Trade Practices Acts in that suppliers who wish to validate a scheme for resale price maintenance may register an agreement covering specified goods, which must then be justified before the Restrictive Practices Court under one or more of five 'gateways' (s. 14). As under the earlier statutes, the courts have been reluctant to permit exemptions. In the case of the *Net Book Agreement* publishers persuaded the court that resale price maintenance was essential to the maintenance of a network of well-stocked bookshops.[14] But the statute has generally been strictly applied with the result that resale price maintenance has been effectively abandoned in almost all trades.

These controls on restrictive trading and pricing agreements have operated rather more successfully than those on monopolies and mergers. There is a clear presumption in law that restrictive agreements are contrary to the public interest. To rebut this it must be established to the satisfaction of the Office of Fair Trading or the Restrictive Practices Court that there is some positive benefit to the public from the restriction which could not otherwise be achieved. The fact that all agreements must be disclosed and registered in itself contributes to the creation of a climate of business opinion contrary to secret cartels. The system is not wholly effective. Leading firms in some sectors undoubtedly maintain channels of communication on pricing policy, as evidenced by the fact that prices of competing products often move together. But the relative efficacy of the controls on cartels is offset by the weakness of those on mergers between previously competing enterprises. The degree of concentration in many sectors of the British economy is higher than in most other western countries.

Competition policy in the EEC

There is a similar distinction between the control of restrictive

[14] (1962) L.R. 3 R.P. 246.

agreements and of monopoly power within the European Economic Community.[15] The Treaty of Rome contains a detailed and explicit formulation of the ideals of free-market economic theory, which were reasserted in more general terms in the first report on competition policy by the Commission in 1972:

> Competition is the best stimulant of economic activity since it guarantees the widest possible freedom of action to all. . . . (It) enables enterprises to continuously improve their efficiency, which is the sine qua non for a steady improvement in living standards and employment prospects within the countries of the Community.[16]

But there is no formal prohibition in the Treaty of Rome on the creation of a monopoly as long as other enterprises are in practice free to set up in competition with it. The main focus of the competition policy enshrined in the Treaty is against restrictive agreements which may interfere with free competition (Art. 85), and against the exercise of unfair or discriminatory practices by a dominant enterprise in any given sector (Art. 86).

The Commission has established an administrative structure similar to that in Britain for the notification of all restrictive agreements (Reg. 17/62), except those which have been formally exempted, notably two-party exclusive-dealer agreements (Reg. 67/67), agreements between small enterprises designed to promote co-operation and economic efficiency, and agreements of minor importance affecting less than five per cent of a relevant market. The Commission must then consider all non-exempt agreements and decide whether to declare them unlawful under Article 85, on the ground that their object or effect is the prevention, restriction or distortion of competition. These provisions have been stringently applied. It has been held that instructions from an American parent company to a number of its EEC subsidiaries not to sell their products in other EEC countries could amount to an unlawful agreement or concerted practice between the subsidiaries, and that a German manufacturer could not appoint a sole agent with exclusive territorial

[15] See generally J. P. Cunningham, *The Competition Law of the EEC* (1973), and W. van Gerven, 'Twelve Years of EEC Competition Law', (1974) 11 *Common Market Law Review*, 38.

[16] EEC Commission, *First Report on Competition Policy*, in Fifth General Report (1972), p. 11.

rights in France, since to allow that would be to limit competition by other potential distributors of the company's products.[17]

The system of control over the abuse of a dominant position within the common market or a substantial part of it is less well developed. Monopolies and mergers as such are not prohibited under Article 86 unless they may affect competition. Each individual case must therefore be considered on its merits. Substantial fines have been imposed on an American chemical company and its Italian subsidiary for attempting to deprive an independent competitor of essential raw materials.[18] And it has been decided that it may be unlawful for any company to maintain such a domination over a specifically defined market within a substantial part of the Community as to exclude effective competition, and that take-overs or mergers which strengthen an existing dominant position so as to substantially fetter competition may also be unlawful.[19] But there is no EEC procedure for the prior vetting of mergers. The Commission has proposed that all large companies within the common market should be required to give three months notice of any proposed merger, and that the laws of individual member states should be harmonized to provide greater protection for shareholders and employees.[20] These proposals have not yet been adopted (see p. 508).

Price and incomes policies

The development of prices and incomes policies in recent years has resulted in further increases in the powers of government to control the affairs of all companies. In Britain this was initially limited to a power to refer any proposed increase in prices or wages to the quasi-independent Prices and Incomes Board under the Prices and Incomes Acts 1966 to 1968. Though the government had certain reserve powers to order companies to carry out the Board's recommendations, these were rarely used. In its final report the Board concluded that 'the effectiveness of its reports rested ultimately not on statutory backing but on the soundness of the facts, analysis and

[17] *Re Kodak* [1970] C.M.L.R. D19; *Consten and Grundig v. EEC Commission* [1966] C.M.L.R. 418.

[18] *I.C.I. and Commercial Solvents Corp. v. EEC Commission* [1974] C.M.L.R. 309, noted in (1974) 11 *Common Market Law Review* 248.

[19] *Europemballage Corp. and Continental Can Co. v. EEC Commission* [1973] C.M.L.R. 199.

[20] *Proposed Third Directive on Mergers* (1970); *Proposed Directive on the Retention of Employees' Rights in Mergers, Take-overs and Amalgamations* (1974).

conclusions which they embodied', and that despite its abolition in 1970 some form of continuing governmental control on the freedom of large companies to set their own price and wage levels was likely to be found necessary.[21] When the second round of statutory wage and price controls was introduced in 1972 under the Counter-Inflation (Temporary Provisions) Act 1972 and the Counter-Inflation Act 1973 the formal structures were broadly similar, until the abolition of the Pay Board in 1974. But much greater emphasis has been placed on the enforcement of the strict terms of the successive Price Codes which have been enacted by statutory instrument under the Counter-Inflation Act 1973 (s. 2). All proposed price increases by large concerns must be notified to the Price Commission, which may then order any person or concern to restrict its prices or charges (ss. 5–6). Though the terms of the Price Code have been progressively eased to permit greater freedom to raise prices to fund investment as well as to meet increased costs, a statutory framework under which individual price rises may be controlled if on investigation by the Price Commission they do not appear to be justified in the public interest is to be continued.[22]

2 GOVERNMENTAL INTERVENTION: AID AND RATIONALIZATION

Statutory controls on monopolies and mergers, restrictive practices and prices may be justified within a free-market economy as a mechanism for increasing workable competition and controlling the abuse of economic power by major national and multi-national enterprises. But governments in developed economies have other reasons for intervening in the affairs of large enterprises in the private sector, notably in the context of the management of supply and demand, the maintenance of employment, the pursuit of regional development and the promotion of exports. These objectives may be pursued by general administrative or legislative action on money supply, taxation, investment incentives and prices and incomes policies. In some cases, however, the government may wish to intervene in the affairs of particular industries or companies on a more selective basis, to maintain regional employment, to prevent the collapse of a strategically significant enterprise or to promote rationalization or investment

[21] Prices and Incomes Board, *Final Report*, Cmnd. 4649 (1970), paras. 78 & 96

[22] *Consultative Document on Prices Policy* (1977); Prices Bill 1977.

in major national companies with a view to meeting foreign competition. In certain high technology industries in which the cost of research and development is especially high, it is now accepted that government finance is essential and that a monopoly national enterprise is the only realistic method of countering the power of major foreign or multi-national companies. The natural tendency of such policies, if they were pursued to a logical conclusion, would be towards a fully directed economy on a state capitalist or socialist model. But there is a large intermediate area between a totally free-market economy and a fully directed economy. Most western countries are now committed to the maintenance of a mixed economy of this kind.

Financial assistance

Government aid for ailing firms or industries can readily be arranged without any direct or formal interference in the operations of the companies concerned by making direct grants or guarantees, with or without attending conditions, as for instance under the Cotton Industry Act 1959 and the Shipbuilding Industry Acts 1967 and 1971. But it is natural for the authorities to wish to retain some continuing control over the use of the funds which they supply, particularly in the case of very large subventions to individual companies. In Britain this has usually been achieved by state acquisition of substantial blocks of shares in the recipient companies and the appointment of government representatives to their boards of directors. Until recently action of this kind required specific legislation in each case, as for instance in the partial take-over and removal to Belfast of the Short Brothers aircraft firm in the 1930s and the rescue and division of Rolls Royce in 1971. The only general powers of the government were those granted to the National Research Development Corporation under the Development of Inventions Acts 1948 and 1954 to make grants, to enter into guarantees or to purchase shares for the limited purpose of promoting new inventions and developments.

The powers of the government in this sphere have been substantially extended in recent years. Under the Industrial Expansion Act 1968 the government took permanent powers, subject to Parliamentary approval, to make grants or guarantees and to purchase shares or assets in any enterprise as part of an industrial investment scheme designed to develop the efficiency or productivity of an industry or section of an industry. These powers were further extended and generalized under the Industry Act 1972, which authorizes the Department of Industry to give selective financial assistance to undertakings, both in development areas with a view to maintaining employment (s. 7), and elsewhere, with Treasury consent, with a view to benefiting the economy of part or the whole of the United Kingdom (s. 8); the further requirements that the Department should not acquire more than fifty per cent of the equity shares in any company assisted and that it should be satisfied that the assistance could not be provided in any other way were removed by the Industry Act 1975 (s. 22). Responsibility for the administration of assistance may be delegated to the National Enterprise Board (s. 2), or to the Scottish and Welsh Development Agencies.

These powers have been widely used. In the period from 1972 to 1975 a total of some £170m was paid out to more than two thousand applicants.[23] The large majority of these were in development areas, though some large individual payments and guarantees were also made to major firms in the motor industry. The Department of Industry produced detailed guidelines in 1975 setting out the criteria which are applied in assessing applications : companies which receive assistance are expected to establish the viability of their proposals over a period of three to five years and to show that an appropriate return on capital invested can be realized, though special consideration may be given to short-term rescue operations for companies facing liquidation; for a time specially favourable consideration was also given to applications from worker-controlled enterprises on an experimental basis.[24]

Rationalization

Direct aid to individual companies, whether by loans, guarantees or share purchase, is not always sufficient to secure the objectives of government. The long-term safeguarding of employment or the development of a national undertaking of sufficient size and economic strength to meet international competition may be thought to require a greater degree of rationalization within a particular sector of the economy. The government may consider it necessary in this context to take positive action to encourage the formation of a single national

[23] Committee of Public Accounts, *Sixth Report 1975–76* (1976), p. 542.

[24] Ibid., p. 537; for the Committee's criticisms of this policy see its report, paras. 18–29.

company in a given sector rather than to permit foreign-controlled enterprises to establish themselves or take over existing companies by the ordinary processes of market competition.

The first formal move in this direction was the establishment of the Industrial Reorganisation Corporation in 1966. The Corporation was given power to enter into financial arrangements with individual companies, to promote and if necessary to give financial support to schemes for take-overs and mergers, and to purchase shares on the open market, whether in support of one or other side in a take-over battle or more generally, with the broad objective of encouraging the rationalization of important sectors of the economy within the ordinary machinery of the market. In its last full year of operation before it was wound up in 1970 by the incoming Tory government, the Corporation spent a total of some £30m in thirty-two separate projects with three explicit objectives: the reorganization of specific sectors of industry through mergers, the stimulation by advice and persuasion of the 'sleeping giants and industrial coffins of the British industrial scene', and selective investment in areas of high growth and export potential.[25]

In 1975 a new body, the National Enterprise Board, was established with similar entrepreneurial functions to those of the Industrial Reorganisation Corporation, but with the additional tasks of making large-scale and sustained investment in British industry to offset the short-term pull of market forces and of acting as a holding company for major government holdings in industrial and commercial companies.[26] Under the terms of the Industry Act 1975 the Board is an independent statutory corporation with power to spend up to £1,000m (s. 8) in any way which is calculated to assist new or existing enterprises, to promote their reorganization or development, to extend public ownership into profitable areas of manufacturing or to promote industrial democracy in its subsidiaries (s. 2). The financial duties of the Board, however, are to be determined by the Department of Industry and the Treasury (s. 6) and it must give effect to any direction given to it by the Secretary of State for Industry (s. 7). In this respect, as will be seen, the Board is subject to controls similar to those of nationalized industries. It has no powers of compulsory acquisition.

[25] See generally Industrial Reorganisation Corporation, *Report and Accounts for 1970*.

[26] See generally *The Regeneration of British Industry*, Cmnd. 5710 (1974).

The role which the National Enterprise Board is to play in the overall strategy of government intervention is not yet clear. By the end of 1976 it had invested some £575m in thirteen companies. Its investment in British Leyland and Rolls Royce, however, which it inherited from the government, represented more than £500m of the total, and in eight of the remaining eleven companies the Board was a minority shareholder.[27] The very diverse nature of these holdings and the continuing problems of its relationship with British Leyland have made it difficult for the Board to develop any effective industrial strategy separate from that of the Department of Industry itself in the exercise of its powers to give direct assistance to private-sector companies under the Industry Acts. In theory the Board is in a position to exercise continuing control over its subsidiaries in the public interest and to eliminate any untoward effects of free-market capitalism. State capitalist holding companies have long been established in other countries, notably in Italy where the *Instituto per la Reconstruzioni Industriale* (IRI) was set up in 1933 to help counter the effects of a collapse in private banking and now operates as a permanent state holding company with wide powers to involve itself in any area of industry in which public intervention appears necessary.[28] A similar body, the *Statsföretag* group, was established in Sweden in 1970 to co-ordinate the operations and policies of some thirty companies in which previous governments had already acquired an interest. As with nationalized industries, however, there has been continuing tension between the short-term political objectives of governments and the development of longer-term industrial development plans.

The potential role of the National Enterprise Board as a key agent of state capitalism in Britain has been further undermined by the attempt of government to exercise more direct but less formal influence over the operations of major companies in the private sector. Specific provision was made in the Industry Act 1975 for government departments to enter into voluntary planning agreements with private-sector companies or groups (s. 21), with a view to promoting greater certainty in the relationship between government and major and strategic firms in key sectors of manufacturing industry. In addition the government took powers to require

[27] National Enterprise Board, *Annual Report and Accounts 1976* (1977).

[28] See generally M. V. Posner & S. J. Woolf, *Italian Public Enterprise* (1967), and S. Holland (ed.), *The State as Entrepreneur* (1972).

such companies to disclose any information which in the opinion of the government is necessary to form or further national economic policies or to assist in consultations between government, employers and trade unions on the outlook for a particular sector of manufacturing industry (s. 28). Before the company can be compelled to disclose any such information, however, a preliminary notice must be served on it; three months must elapse before a formal order can be made; and any such order may be annulled by a resolution in either House of Parliament. There are also tightly drawn provisions governing the release of information to trade unions (ss. 31–2). By mid-1977 none of these powers had been exercised and only one planning agreement had been drawn up. Closer continuing relations between government departments and major companies have been more effectively pursued by the appointment of high-level liaison officials in departments directly concerned with industry and commerce. The existence of reserve powers may assist these officials in the pursuit of voluntary planning and co-ordination. But there is no evidence that management in major companies and groups regard this as more than a useful means of keeping in touch with government intentions and where possible influencing them in their own interests. The objectives and thinking of government departments and leading industrialists are not sufficiently convergent for the policies enshrined in the Industry Act 1975 to achieve any major change in the relationship between the state and private sector companies.[29]

3 NATIONALIZATION

The ultimate step in governmental intervention is nationalization. The traditional justification for nationalization is that state control of the means of production and distribution will eliminate the evils of the capitalist system and permit a generally more equitable and beneficial distribution of resources throughout the community. The close relationship between this conception and socialist and communist political parties has then resulted in a stereotyped response to nationalization on the part of both its supporters and its opponents. The reality is a good deal more complex. The justification for the nationalization of a particular industry or service may be as much

[29] For an extended discussion of this issue see (1976) 39 *MLR*, 318.

economic or social as political. The fact that the supply of electricity and the railways and airlines are nationalized in most countries, for instance, is better attributed to the nature of the industries than to the politics of the ruling parties. In the first place, direct internal competition over the same areas or routes in the provision of these services will rarely be economically beneficial; in addition, there are substantial economies of scale to be gained in the concentration of research, development and investment; and, finally, there is a clear social and economic benefit in the maintenance of a regular and efficient supply or service throughout the country. Further arguments in respect of uniformity and quality of service may be produced for the nationalization of certain social and administrative services, whether on a total or partial basis, as, for instance, the prison system, medical treatment, legal aid and advice, housing or broadcasting. This list of examples of existing or potential areas of nationalization indicates that the issue is a good deal wider than is usually assumed, and also that there is a huge range of different forms which nationalization may take.

The simplest means of securing state control of a firm or industry short of total nationalization is for the government to acquire the equity share capital of the existing companies, which may then be operated on a continuing basis within the formal framework of the traditional law by the appointment of directors by the government. This technique is most often used for the nationalization of individual companies, as for instance Rolls Royce in 1971.

Where nationalization is extended to a whole industry a different strategy will usually be adopted to secure unified control and direction over the various enterprises. In the initial burst of nationalization following the victory of the Labour government in 1945 it was the usual practice to create a single national board in which the assets of the existing companies in the industry concerned would be vested. This board would have general control over the conduct of the industry as a whole, subject only to the right of the controlling minister or government department to issue directives of a general character as to the exercise of its duties. Thus, under the Coal Industry Nationalization Act 1946, a National Coal Board consisting of a chairman and eight other members was established as a body corporate (s. 2). The assets of all existing coal mining companies were then transferred to the Board in return for what later turned out to be rather generous compensation based on an individual valuation of each enterprise on a local basis (s. 10). The Board is charged with the duty of carrying on the business of coalmining and any ancillary activities with a view to securing the safety, health and welfare of its employees (s. 1(4) (a)) and ensuring that the revenues of the Board shall not be less than sufficient for meeting all their outgoings properly chargeable to revenue account ... on an average of good and bad years' (s. 1(4) (c)). The Board is also expressly directed to give effect to any directions issued by the Minister as to the performance of its functions in the national interest (s. 3), and to enter into consultation and negotiation with the employees' unions (s. 46). Finally there is a system of consumer councils which may make representations to the Minister as to the performance by the Board of its duties (s. 4).

This general pattern has been followed in subsequent nationalization statutes in the industrial sphere, though in some instances there has been considerably more statutory regulation of the internal organization of the nationalized industry on a regional or sectional basis, as in the case of the electricity and gas supply industries. The internal administrative structure of nationalized corporations has worked tolerably well. But there has been continuing criticism of the fact that sponsoring government departments have so rarely resorted to formal ministerial directions, as opposed to continuing informal involvement in the running of the nationalized concern. The result has been that the precise allocation of responsibility for key decisions has not always been clear. And the chronic unprofitability of certain nationalized industries, such as the railways, has made the statutory duty to balance revenue and expenditure accounts a somewhat academic issue. It is now becoming more generally accepted that the proper relationship between the government and the relevant board is for the government to set a general financial objective in terms of the percentage return on individual investment decisions. Where a particular service or policy which the Board is required to provide or pursue cannot be maintained within this limit, or within the more general obligation to balance current revenue and expenditure, the board should then ask the government to make a specific grant to cover the expected loss. In this way an essentially commercial framework for the nationalized industries can be preserved without jeopardizing their wider social obligations to the community, for instance in the maintenance of unprofitable railway lines, the provision of employment or the holding down of price rises in the interests of national economic policy.[30]

Whether such a relationship can be effectively established and enforced under existing statutory provisions is more doubtful. The National Economic Development Office has recently proposed that each nationalized industry should be protected from continuing short-term interference by government departments by the creation of a policy council, composed of representatives of government, consumers, trade unions and others, which would set performance criteria for the board of the corporation and maintain continuing supervision over its operations.[31] The similarity of this proposed structure to that which has been developed in Germany for the supervision of large companies in the private sector is clear. Its effect might be to create a more workable distinction between the setting of policy objectives and the control of the efficiency of management in carrying them out.[32]

The creation of a supervisory board or policy council in nationalized corporations might also help to resolve the paradox that nationalization as a policy has failed to make any progress in breaking down the barrier between capital and labour. On the introduction of nationalization in the 1940s it was intended that the interests of labour should be represented by the appointment of leading trade unionists on the boards of the new national corporations. But any direct relationship between these representatives and the employees within the corporations was effectively ruled out, and it soon became obvious that the position of employees in nationalized industries was not effectively different from what it had been before nationalization. The appointment of employee representatives on policy councils or supervisory boards, with the power to monitor the performance of management in carrying out externally imposed policies, might help to increase the accountability of management in the public sector to their employees. Nor is the development of schemes for participation in the profits from greater productivity impossible, if financial

[30] For a general discussion of these issues see the report of the Select Committee on Nationalized Industries, 1966–7; see also A. H. Hanson (ed.), *Nationalization: a book of readings* (1963).

[31] NEDO, *A Study of UK Nationalised Industries* (1976).

[32] The possibility of creating a similar structure for large corporations in both public and private sectors was raised in M. Fogarty, *Company and Corporation—One Law* (1965).

performance criteria are established and achieved. Provision for collective bargaining on the traditional conflict model, however, was built into the framework of the early British nationalization statutes, and there have been few developments in any other form of industrial democracy either at board or lower levels. A scheme for the appointment of employee representatives on divisional boards has been successfully developed in the British Steel Corporation (see p. 467), and the National Enterprise Board has encouraged plant-level productivity councils within British Leyland. But until the Aircraft and Shipbuildings Industries Act 1977 (s. 2(8)) there has been no formal provision for industrial democracy in any nationalized industry.

Nationalized industries may equally be taken right out of the traditional commercial sphere and operated simply as a public service without specific regard to the balancing of revenue and expenditure. This may be achieved either by the operation of the service in question as an integral part of a government department or local authority, as in the case of the British National Health Service or the system of state schools, or by the creation of an independent corporation which is given a block grant to finance its operations or permitted to raise what amounts to a tax on consumers, as for instance in the case of the British Broadcasting Corporation. In this way the preoccupation with commercial viability that seems so natural and even inevitable within a generally free market economy may be effectively sidestepped and replaced by an entirely different set of criteria related to administrative efficiency and quality of service. It is somewhat strange that this general approach to nationalized industries has not been more forcefully argued, in view of the desire of many socialists to break free of the straitjacket of traditional capitalist thinking. But where so-called 'trading' enterprises in which the public have become accustomed to paying an economic price for goods or services are concerned the pressures to retain a traditional framework are not easily surmounted.

4 MULTI-NATIONAL COMPANIES

The growth of multi-national companies with interlocking operations in many different countries has made the discussion of the interrelationship of companies and government within a single state an increasingly unrealistic frame of reference. The establishment of a company in a particular country obviously subjects its operations within that country to domestic laws on taxation, monopolies and restrictive practices, as well as other forms of government intervention including the risk of nationalization. But the largest multinational companies are free to concentrate their operations in the most favourable economic and political climate. The balance of power is thus appreciably shifted away from governments to the companies themselves as powerful, independent and international organizations. This freedom should not be overestimated. Most multinationals are effectively forced to locate their main operations in one of the advanced industrial countries, and once established they will be reluctant to incur the huge expense of a major re-allocation of their resources. But decisions on future development and expansion are clearly a powerful bargaining counter in their dealings both with national governments and with trade unions, especially in those areas where unemployment is a major problem. To this extent the multinationals constitute a genuine threat to the controls which have been built up against the power of capital in relation to that of organized labour and the state.

Effective controls for some purposes may be developed by individual states through legislation specifically directed against the abuse of power by multi-nationals. In Britain the Inland Revenue has been given power to counteract the practice of 'transfer pricing' through which multi-nationals may seek to produce minimum profits in high-tax countries. Under the Income and Corporation Taxes Act 1970 the tax authorities may themselves reallocate reported profits to different parts of a multi-national enterprise where it appears that the true amount of taxable profit realized in Britain has been understated (s. 485). This power, together with those permitting the tax authorities to require the production of papers under the Finance Act 1976 (sched. 6), have been used with increasing stringency in recent years, particularly in the case of American-controlled groups in which the proportion of intra-group transactions is typically more than fifty per cent compared with an average figure of some twenty-five per cent for British-based groups.

In addition under the Industry Act 1975 the Secretary of State for Industry has power to prohibit any change of control over any important manufacturing undertaking which would result in effective control passing to a foreign company or person and which would be contrary to the national interest (ss. 11–13); where control has already passed and the Secretary of State is satisfied that it is necessary in the national interest, he may make an order for the compulsory purchase of the undertaking (s. 13(2)). The recommendations of the Bullock Committee on Industrial Democracy also envisage specific controls to ensure that any scheme for the introduction of industrial democracy in Britain is implemented in British subsidiaries of foreign-controlled groups (see p. 466).

An alternative to the threat of nationalization is to accept the technological dominance of the multi-nationals as inevitable and to impose specific discretionary controls on their operations in both physical and financial terms. Many developing countries have imposed stringent conditions and heavy taxes and royalties on foreign companies in return for licences to operate. A similar approach has been adopted in Britain for the exploitation of North Sea oil and gas. The British National Oil Corporation, established under the Petroleum and Submarine Pipe-lines Act 1975, has been given powers to enter into participation agreements with the major oil companies with a view to subjecting their operations to current governmental policies. It was originally envisaged that the Corporation would take a controlling equity interest in all oilfields in return for a contribution to exploration and development costs. It has since been decided to restrict direct equity participation to new fields. Control over existing fields is to be restricted to general taxes and royalties, leaving the oil companies to bear the full development costs. The Corporation has entered into participation agreements with most of the major companies under which a proportion of the oil and gas extracted must be sold to the Corporation at market prices. As stated in its first Report and Accounts for 1976, the Corporation is neither a regulatory body nor a nationalized industry, but a hybrid which 'combines functions of an instrument of national policy, of a commercial enterprise and of an adviser to the government.'

International controls

Internal legislation of any kind is inherently limited in its impact on multi-national companies which are in a position to shift their operations or otherwise to play one government off against another in such a way as to obtain more favourable treatment than would otherwise be granted. Effective action in such cases requires some form of international supervision. The best example is that which is being developed within the European Economic Community. The provisions of EEC competition policy, which have already been described (see p. 493), clearly apply to any multi-national enterprise which wishes to establish itself in any member country. As the membership of the EEC is extended, these will be increasingly difficult to evade by setting up factories in adjacent low-cost countries such as Spain and Portugal. More far-reaching measures have also been proposed within the context of the EEC Commission's programme for the harmonization or approximation of economic legislation in all member states. The initial directives and draft directives in the programme for the harmonization of company law were mainly concerned with technical issues of company formation, accounting and structure.[33] Apart from the First Directive, which has already been implemented in Britain under the European Communities Act 1972, little progress has been made with this policy. The proposed Fifth Directive, requiring all member companies to adopt the German two-tier structure for company boards, has been effectively abandoned. Rather more progress has been made in inducing member countries to adopt their own structures for the development of industrial democracy (see Chapter 13). The Commission is now concentrating its efforts on specific proposals for the protection of employees where their companies are taken over, on the control of stock market operations, on international co-operation on the recovery of tax and control of transfer pricing, and on the development of a body of law on groups of companies.[34] A directive requiring all member states to adopt measures under which the established rights of employees in respect of protection from dismissal and of compensation for redundancy must be guaranteed by any undertaking which takes over control of another undertaking is likely to be adopted in 1977; similar protection would be granted to established structures for industrial democracy.[35] This may result in the closing of some loopholes in the existing British law on redundancy and unfair dismissal for individual employees. But the commitment of the EEC Commission to the principle of freedom

[33] See generally C. Schmithoff (ed.), *The Harmonisation of European Company Law* (1973) and *European Company Law Texts* (1974).

[34] *Multinational Undertakings and the Community*, Bulletin of the European Communities, Supplement 15/73 (1973).

[35] See generally B. Hepple, 'Workers' Rights in Mergers and Take-overs: the EEC Proposals', (1976)5 *Industrial Law Journal*, 197.

of establishment for all enterprises, whether controlled within a member country or by a foreign undertaking, rules out the most effective sanction against multi-nationals, namely the refusal of permission to establish subsidiaries or to take over existing enterprises. The effective control of multi-nationals requires the adoption of more flexible and discretionary powers by international authorities than have yet been considered by the Commission.

The European company

The most far-reaching proposal within the framework of freedom of establishment and of competition is for the creation of a single legal framework within the Community for large enterprises whose operations extend to several member states. If the proposal were adopted, all such companies would be permitted, and might be required, to register themselves as corporations on a European level and thus submit themselves to a single framework of legal regulation. They would also avoid the complexities currently experienced by multinationals in establishing separate subsidiaries in each country of operations or in entering into inter-state take-overs or mergers.[36]

The proposed legal framework for the European Company has been progressively amended since the idea was propounded by Professor Sanders in 1960. Under the latest draft[37] a European company could be formed only by two or more existing companies respectively registered in more than one member state. The traditional basis of corporate personality, share capital and limited liability has been adopted, and there is also provision for a substantial minimum capital measured in terms of the accounting units of the Community. Most of the basic rules and concepts of company law, which are broadly similar on the continent to those in Britain, will thus be directly applicable to European companies.

The proposed draft, however, also incorporates detailed provisions for supervisory and managing boards, and for the statutory representation of employees on the supervisory board and on works

[36] On these problems and the various solutions which have been adopted in the Unilever and Dunlop/Pirelli mergers see M. A. Weinberg, *Take-overs and Mergers*, 3rd edn. (1971), Appendix K.

[37] *Amended Proposal for a Statute for European Companies*, Bulletin of the European Communities, Supplement 4/75 (1975); for a general assessment of the original proposals see D. Thompson, *The Proposal for a European Company*, Chatham House/PEP (1969) and G. Hornsey, (1970) 20 *Northern Ireland Legal Quarterly*, 1.

councils as developed in France and Germany. Thus day-to-day control over the company's affairs is to be exercised by a board of management appointed by and subject to the general supervision of a supervisory board (Art. 62). In particular the board of management is subject to the express prior authorization of the supervisory board for the closure or transfer of the company's undertaking, or any substantial extension or curtailment of its activities (Art. 66). The board of management must also submit quarterly reports of progress to the supervisory board, and inform it immediately of any matter of importance (Art. 73a), in addition to the provisions for annual reports and accounts. One third of the supervisory board is to be constituted of shareholders' representatives, one third of employees' representatives and one third of persons co-opted by those representatives (Art. 74a). This third group is to be chosen by shareholders, the employees' representative body and management (Art. 75a). In addition, there is to be provision for the election by employees of a European Works Council within any company which has establishments in more than one member state (Art. 100). This council will have powers to represent the interests of employees in consultation with the board of management, which must submit a quarterly report on progress to the council and inform it of any event of importance, as in the case of the supervisory board (Arts. 119–20). The council is also entitled to receive the same communications and documents as shareholders (Art. 121). Any decision relating to the recruitment, promotion and dismissal of employees, the terms and computation of provisions for social facilities and holidays, may only be taken by the board of management with the agreement of the European works council, subject to a provision for arbitration in the event of deadlock (Art. 123).

The underlying aim of the proposed European Company was to provide a formal means of controlling American and multi-national investment.[38] This could be achieved by restricting the right of establishment as a European Company in such a way as to exclude or discourage American firms, or by requiring all companies above a given size to register their subsidiaries under the statute. But it has proved impossible to secure the agreement of member states to any such policies, and discussion of the proposal has focussed on more technical legal issues. Nor has there been sufficient political

[38] See generally J. Servan-Schreiber, The American Challenge (1968).

agreement within the EEC to make it possible to impose effective controls on the eurodollar money market through which many multi-nationals have been able to organize their finances beyond the direct control of any member government.

Attempts have also been made on a broader international front to secure greater governmental cohesion in dealing with multi-national investment. In 1976 a set of guidelines for multi-national enterprises was drawn up by the members of OECD to govern the terms on which such investment should be permitted : in return for 'treatment under their laws, regulations and administrative practices . . . no less favourable than that accorded in like situations to domestic enterprises', multi-national companies would be expected to adhere to general guidelines on the disclosure of information on their local operations in their overall context, to compete fairly with local enterprises, to follow local practice in recruitment and industrial relations, to refrain from anything like transfer pricing which might lessen the tax properly payable on their activities, and to abstain from any improper involvement in local politics and from all other forms of bribery and corruption.[39] Though provision was made for a review of progress on the implementation of these guidelines by 1979 there are no formal powers of enforcement, and complaints were already being made in 1977 that the guidelines were being ignored.

[39] Organization for Economic Co-operation and Development, *Declaration on International Investment and Multinational Enterprises* (1976), Cmnd. 6525.

INDEX

Accounting:
  Accounting Standards Committee, 210–11
  audit, development of, 137–9
  balance sheet, 65–9, 126–8
  capital and income, 128–9
  charge/discharge accounts, 125
  for creditors, 210–11, 223, 227
  current cost, 134–7, 210–11
  depreciation, 68, 131, 134
  development of, 124–8
  double entry, 125
  EEC regulation, 140
  effect on law, 128–33
  group accounts, 391–3
  historical cost, 128–9, 133
  judicial attitudes to, 129–32
  profit and loss account, 125–6
  reform of, 134–7
  reserves, significance of, 67, 127
  Sandilands Committee, 134–5
  for shareholders/investors, 331–2
  true and fair view, 138–9
Agency:
  directors as agents, 118–20, 165–6
  excess of authority, 119–20, 163–5
  ostensible authority, 119, 164
  partners as agents, 100, 162–5
Anderson Committee on Fixed Trusts (1936): 411
Annual returns: 117, 152
Articles of association:
  alteration of, 108, 261
  contents, 104
  contractual basis of, 106
  model in Table A, 104
Asset stripping, 77–8, 373
Auditor:
  as agent of shareholders, 138
  development of audit, 137–9
  duty of care, 138–9
  duty to creditors, 139, 212
  group audit, 393
  professional status, 139, 212
  report to shareholders, 138
  resignation of, 139, 212
  as servant of management, 212
  in small companies, 211–12
  social audit, 334–5
Authority:
  ostensible and actual, 119, 164
Balance sheet:
  economic analysis, 65–8
  modern presentation, 65
  orgin of, 126–8
Banki of England: 15, 413
Banks:
  avoidance of limited liability, 150
  avoidance of voidable preference rule, 201
  early legislative control, 15
  savings, 403
  sharedealings in controlled, 343
  source of finance, 60–2
  supervision of, 413
Bankruptcy:
  acts of bankruptcy, 187–8
  bankrupt's statement of affairs, 188
  Blagden Committee: *see* main entry
  committee of inspection, 189
  Convention on, 180, 226
  Cork Committee, 180, 226
  discharge, 192–3
  duty to keep accounts, 192
  early limitation to traders, 95–6
  fraudulent (voidable) preference, 190–2
  offences in, 192
  onerous property, 190
  origin of, 186–7
  and partnership, 103, 193–4
  priorities for distribution, 189–90
  public examination, 188–9
  reputed ownership, 175, 194
  trustee in, 189
Berle and Means: 53, 76, 79
Biedenkopf Report: 449, 450, 453–7, 468
Blagden Committee on Bankruptcy and Deeds of Arrangement Law (1957):
  on deeds of arrangement, 185
  on discharge, 193
  on fraudulent preference, 191
  on priority for tax, 189
  on reputed ownership, 175
Board of Trade: *see* Department of Trade
Bodkin Committee on Sharepushing (1937): 338

Bolton Committee on Small Firms (1972):
on concentration, 54–6
on decline of, 54–5
on disclosure, 205, 210
on duration of firms, 43–4
on legal status, 57
on Macmillan gap, 63
on ownership/control, 44, 79
on role of small firm, 57
on taxation, 215, 221–2
British Leyland: 500, 505
British National Oil Corporation: 507
British Steel Corporation: 433–4, 451
Bubble Act: 12–13
Building societies: 403-4
Bullock Committee on Industrial Democracy:
on confidentiality, 464
on directors' duties, 462–3
on groups, 466–7
minority report, 459
on powers of board, 459, 462
on selection of employee directors; 459, 467, 470
on unitary boards, 460–2
Business names, registration of: 96–7, 100, 207

Capital:
authorized, 104, 109–10
maintenance of, 129–32, 140
Marxist analysis of, 32–3
minimum, 110, 140
reduction of, 108, 129, 169, 262
share and loan distinguished, 108–10, 169–71
share premium account, 129
significance in accounts, 65–9
sources and uses of, 58–65
Capitalism:
defined, 3–4
development of, 4–9
state capitalism, 431–3
theory of, 3–4, 25–35
traditional model of, 425–6
Capital gains tax: 291–4
Capital transfer tax: 291–4
Charges:
fixed, 171–2, 198–9
floating, 172, 174–6, 179–80, 199–201
reform of law on, 179–81
registration of, 173–4
Charitable donations: 60, 318–20
City Code on Take-overs and Mergers: 83, 337, 347–9, 364–8, 374–88
(*see* main entry on Take-overs)
Close company: 122–3, 215–17
Co-determination: 448–58, 475–6
Cohen Committee on Company Law (1945):
on discretionary regulation, 362
on ultra vires, 116, 149
Collective bargaining: 427–31, 457, 464–5, 471–4, 476
Commission on Industrial Relations: 464–5, 474, 476
Commune: 415, 420–1
Companies Bill 1973: 204, 253, 257, 267–8, 349, 462
Company:
accounts, 124–40, 152, 208–9, 227, 391–3
articles of association: *see* main entry
audit/auditor: *see* main entry
board of directors, 117, 460–2
books, 117
capital: *see* main entry
classification: *see* main entry
close company: *see* main entry
constitution, 106–8
contractual basis of, 105–6, 153–5
corporate personality, 110–12, 142 7, 393 4
corporate property, 112
criminal liability of, 111, 145, 146–7
development of, 43–4
director: *see* main entry
disclosure: *see* main entry
distributions, 132, 214–17
dividends, legality of, 130–3
dividend stripping, 219
donations, 60, 318–20
extended partnership, 45
family: *see* Unquoted company
financing: *see* main entry
formation, 103–5
fraud on minority, 259–62
fraudulent trading, 145, 166, 204–5
general meeting: *see* main entry
group organization: *see* main entry
holding company: *see* main entry
inspection: *see* main entry
limited by guarantee, 123
limited liability, 20–1, 110–11,

149–50, 165, 395–6
liquidation: *see* main entry
majority rule, 247–8, 271–5
management of, 116–18, 155–61
memorandum of association: *see* main entry
merger: *see* Take-overs
multi-national, 87–90, 505–11
name, choice of, 104, 105
number of companies, 38–46
number of members, 122
objects, 104, 112–14, 148–9
offences by, 111, 145, 146–7
one-man, 44, 143–4
oppression (s. 210), 159–61, 228, 262–70, 400
participatory, 44–5
powers and objects, 112–16, 148–9
private: *see* main entry
proceedings by, 275–6
public: *see* main entry
quasi-partnership: *see* main entry
quoted: *see* main entry
reconstruction, 262, 370–1
reduction of capital, 108, 129, 169, 262
secretary, 117
share and loan capital, 108–10, 169–71
shares: *see* main entry
shareholders: *see* main entry
small private: *see* main entry
subsidiary: *see* main entry
take-over: *see* main entry
ultra vires, 113–16, 147–9
unlimited, 123
unquoted: *see* main entry
Conflict theory: 427–30
Co-operative: 414–20, 433–5
Cork Committee: 180, 226
Corporate personality: 110–12, 142–7
Corporate property: 112
Corporatism: 86, 438
Corruption: 320, 360–1
Creditors:
accounting for, 210–11, 223, 227
committee of, 189, 198
deeds of arrangement, 184–5
disclosure for, 177, 179, 205–6, 211
judicial management for, 185–6
rights of intervention, 181–6
secured, 171–2, 182–4
Crowther Committee on Consumer Credit (1971): 179–81, 211
Cumulative voting: 328
Current cost accounting: 134–7, 210–11

Davey Committee on Company Law (1895): 30
Debentures:
defined, 109
in jeopardy, 183–4
right of intervention, 183–4
Debtor:
bankruptcy: *see* main entry
imprisonment of, 96
relief of, 187
Department of Trade:
deposit-taking companies, control of, 404–5, 407–8
inspections, 282–5, 337, 352–8
insurance company supervision, 405–6, 408–9
monopolies, powers on, 489–91
problems of intervention, 406–9
sharedealing, control of, 338–40
unit trusts, control of, 411
Deposit-taking companies: 404–5, 413
Depreciation:
accounting practice, 131–2
effect on financing, 60–1, 64
effect on valuation, 68
Derivative action:
shareholders' right to, 276–80
in United States, 278–9
Director:
bar on undischarged bankrupt, 192
as businessman, 236–9
civil liability of, 243–58, 310–13
compensation for loss of office, 242–3
cumulative voting for, 328
delegation by, 117, 321
disclosure of contracts and fees, 242, 304, 323
disclosure of interests, 242–3, 323
disclosure of shareholdings and dealings, 242, 304–5
dismissal of, 106, 324, 326
dividends, control of, 462
duty to account, 234–5, 253–5
duty of care, 238–9, 248–53, 320–2
duty to company, 271
duty of disclosure, 242–3
duty to employees, 462–3
election of, 324, 326
excess of authority, 118–20, 165–6
executive, 321–2
fraud by, 241, 306–7, 250

fraudulent misstatement by, 311–12
insider trading by, 255–8
liability for misstatement, 249–50
liability for negligence, 238–9
loans to, prohibited, 241
managing, 117
mismanagement by, 252–3
misstatement by, 249–50
non-executive, 320–1, 332
offences by, 241–2
oppression by, 240, 262–70
option dealings prohibited, 241
perks, 322–3
powers, 118
power to issue shares, 245–6, 273–4
proper purpose rule, 245–8
prospective directors, duty of, 236
relief for, 243, 249, 252, 258–9
register of, 117
register of shareholding and dealing, 117, 242
report, 117, 209, 335
retirement by rotation, 326
share-options for, 323
status of, 233–9
as trustee, 233–6
voting in general meeting by, 247
wrongdoers in control, 274–5, 280
Director of Public Prosecutions: 282, 284, 336, 358–9, 362
Disclosure:
of accounts, 152, 208–9
Bolton Committee on, 205, 210
for creditors, 177, 179, 205–6, 211
Davey Committee on, 30
delay in, 152, 209
of directors' fees and contracts, 152, 209, 242, 304, 323
early provisions on, 19–21
of number of employees, 152, 209
exemption for unlimited companies, 149
of exports, 152, 209
proposals for new small business corporation, 227
by quoted companies, 300–6
register of charges, 208
register of directors, 117
register of directors' holdings and dealings, 242, 304–5
by small companies, 205–11, 223
to trade unions, 464–5, 470
of turnover, 152, 209
Distributions:
required standard, 217, 221
Dividends:
level of, 64–5
no dividends except out of profit, 130–2
shareholders' right to, 270
stripping, 219
tax on, 170, 218
Donations:
disclosure of, 209, 320
legality of, 318–20
statistics on, 60, 319–20
Donovan Commission on Trade Unions and Employers' Associations (1968): 428, 472

Economic analysis:
of companies, 47–58
patterns of finance, 59–69
role of small firms, 57–8
of stock market, 29–30, 69–75
theory of capitalism, 25–9
Employees:
collective redundancy, 445
control by, 482–3
councils, 474–6
as directors, 447–71
disclosure to, 464–5
job-satisfaction, 441–4
as members, 463
profit sharing, 477–81
rights on mergers, 495, 508
safety committees, 477
shop stewards, 471–3
unfair dismissal, 476
Entrenchment: 106, 240, 246, 326–7, 397–400
Equity capital: 108–9
Estate Duty Investment Trust: 294
European Economic Community:
competition policy, 493–5
First Directive, 148
Second Directive, 140
Fourth Directive, 140
Fifth Directive, 447, 458
Seventh Directive, 140, 393
harmonization of law, 140, 230, 507
monopolies, control of, 495
multi-national companies in, 507–8
proposals for European company, 508–10
European company:
proposals for, 508–10

Financing:
credit financing, 60–2, 176
economic analysis, 58–69
flow of funds, 59–63
hire and hire-purchase, 176–81
for industry, 63, 74–5, 297, 497–8
Macmillan gap, 63, 288
public issues, 74–5, 298–300
refinancing, 176–81
sale and lease-back, 176–81
share and loan capital, 108–10, 169–71
in unquoted companies, 287–9, 294
Fixed charges:
legal and equitable, 171–2
priority in liquidation, 198–9
registration, 173–4
void for preference, 190, 199–202
Floating charges:
origin, 172
priority in liquidation, 198–9
prohibited for partnerships, 174–6
registration, 173–4
void for preference, 199–202
Foss v. Harbottle, rule in: 240, 271–80
France:
chef d'entreprise, 117
commerçants, 95–6
employee councils, 474, 479
profit sharing, 479–80
société en commandite, 20, 167–8, 224
société á responsabilité limitée, 203
Fraud on minority: 259–62
(*see also* Oppression)
Fraudulent preference:
see Voidable preference
Fraud squad: *see* Police
Fraudulent trading: 145, 166, 204–5
Friendly societies: 402–3, 417–9

Gearing: 67–8, 219
Gedge Committee on Shares of No Par Value (1954): 110
General Meeting:
alteration of articles and memorandum, 107–8, 261
Bullock Committee on, 462
control over dividends, 462
control over directors, 77, 106–7, 324–8
control by management, 324–9
distribution of holdings, 75–81
proxy voting, 324–5, 329
questions at, 326–7
requisition of meeting, 324
resolution for inspection, 283, 354
resolution for winding up, 120, 194–5
special resolution, 107
Germany:
AG, 448
Biedenkopf report, 449–50, 453–7, 468
co-determination, 448–58, 475–6
GmbH, 230
groups, control over, 396, 400
supervisory board, 448–9, 453–7
works councils, 451, 474–6
Ghana:
incorporated partnership, 224, 229
Gladstone Committee on Joint Stock Companies (1843): 19
Government intervention:
mergers, 488–91
monopolies, 488–90
multi-nationals, 506–7
nationalization, 501–5
rationalization, 498–501
restrictive practices, 491–3
theory of, 86
(*see also* Inspection)
Greene Committee on Company Law (1926): 373
Groups:
abuse in, 390
accounting, 391–3
cross-holdings, 398–400
EEC regulation, 140
entrenchment, 397–400
as legal entity, 393–7
taxation, 393

Historical cost accounting: 128–9, 133
History:
accounting, 137–9
bankruptcy, 186–7
capitalism, 3–9
joint stock company, 9–22
stock market, 13–16
Holding company:
avoidance of liability for subsidiary, 395
definition, 390
duty to subsidiary, 396

Individual trader:
bankruptcy, 96, 186–93
status, 95–6
taxation, 213, 218–19

Industrial and Commercial Finance Corporation: 63, 288
Industrial democracy:
  board level, 447–71
  Bullock Committee, 430, 439, 447–8, 458–71, 473–4
  financial participation, 477–81
  in France, 474, 479
  in Germany, 448–58, 474–6
  shop-floor level, 471–7
  in Sweden, 468, 469–70
  in Yugoslavia, 482–3
Industrial Relations Act: 428, 464, 476
Industrial Relations Code of Practice: 464–5
Industrial Reorganization Corporation: 85, 499
Inflation accounting: 133–7
Insider trading:
  City Code on, 347–9
  incidence of, 346–7
  Jenkins Committee on, 257, 347
  Justice Report on, 352
  merchant banks and, 348–9
  United States law on, 256–7, 349–51
  in unquoted companies, 255–8
Inspection:
  of books, 282, 283–4, 355
  charge on applicants, 283
  civil proceedings after, 284, 358
  conduct of, 355–6
  by court order, 283, 354
  criminal proceedings after, 284, 358–9
  criticism of Department of Trade, 284–5, 354–6
  delay, 359
  development of system, 336, 352–3
  grounds for, 283, 354–5
  Jenkins Committee on, 354–5
  natural justice, 356–7
  Pergamon Press, 356
  powers of inspectors, 355–6
  practice of Department, 283–4, 354–6
  quoted companies, 352–8
  report on Savoy Hotel, 357
  resolution of general meeting for, 283, 354
  shareholders' right to apply, 283, 354
  statistics on appointments, 353
  unquoted companies, 282–5
Investment analysis: 133, 135
Investment circulars: 339, 360
Investment company: 360, 409–11
Investment institutions:
  building societies, 403–4
  deposit companies, 404–5, 413
  insurance companies, 405–6
  investment companies, 409–11
  pension funds, 404
  savings institutions, 402–3
  as shareholders, 80–1, 332–4
  share ownership of, 79–80
  unit trusts, 409–11
  United States law on, 360
Investors:
  protection of, 337–40
  rights of, 330–2
Italy:
  IRI, 500

Jenkins Committee on Company Law (1962):
  on disclosure, 305
  on fraudulent trading, 204–5
  on groups, 399
  on insider dealing, 257, 347
  on inspection, 354–5
  on oppression, 268, 400
  on political and charitable donations, 319
  on purchase by company of own shares, 374
  on statement in lieu of prospectus, 302
  on take-overs, 375
  on ultra vires, 116, 149
  on unquoted companies, 231
Jobber: 69–70
Joint stock company:
  origin and meaning, 11–12
  (*see also* Company)
Judicial management: 185–6

Keynes, J. M.:
  on stock market, 72, 74
  economic management, 85

Labour law:
  and company law, 429
John Lewis Partnership: 419, 440–1, 481–2
Limited liability:
  corporate personality and, 110–11
  formal basis, 165
  in small private business, 149–50

introduction of, 20–1
proposals for reform, 223, 225–6
Limited partnership: 166–8, 224, 229
Liquidation:
committee of inspection, 121, 198
compulsory, 120, 195
creditors' voluntary, 120, 195
declaration of solvency, 120, 194–5, 198
early systems, 21
frauds in, 202–6
fraudulent trading, 204–5
grounds for petition, 195–6
just and equitable ground, 156–60
members' voluntary, 120, 194–5
offences in, 202–5
priority in, 121, 198–9
public examination, 198
reckless trading, 204–5
report by liquidator, 198
subject to court, 195
voidable preference, 199–202
Loan capital: 108–10, 169–71

Macmillan gap: 63, 288
Majority and minority:
buying out the minority, 260–1, 371–3
fraud on the minority, 259–62
majority rule, 247–8, 271–5
minority action, 276–80
oppression by majority, 159–61, 262–70
ratification by majority, 271–3
wrongdoers in control, 274–5, 280
Management audit: 332
Managerial revolution:
control of voting, 324–9
independence of stock market, 83–4
limits on managerial power, 84–5
managerial attitudes, 82–4
managerial model, 434–5
Marshall, Alfred, 28
Marxist analysis of capitalism: 32–5
Meeting: *see* General meeting
Memorandum of association:
alteration of, 107–8
contents of, 104
discretionary objects, 115, 148
objects, 104, 114–15, 148
powers, 104, 115, 148
signature of, 105
Minority:
fraud on, 259–62
oppression of, 159–61, 262–70
right of action, 276–80
Misstatements:
criminal sanctions, 306–10
damages for, 310–13, 314–15
reckless, 308
rescission, 313–14
Monopolies and Mergers Commission: 74, 387, 488–91
Monopolies:
control of, 488–91, 495
United States law on, 487–8, 490
Multi-national company: 87–90, 505–11

National Coal Board: 502–3
National Economic Development Office: 504
National Enterprise Board: 85, 499–501
National Research Development Corporation: 497
Nationalization:
by holding company, 499–500
public service or trading, 505
by share purchase, 502
Nationalized industries:
duty to break even, 503
industrial democracy in, 504–5
relationship with government, 503–4
News Chronicle case: 318, 463
Non-commercial companies: 46, 123
No par value shares: 110

OECD, guidelines for multinationals: 510
Offer for sale: 298–9
Official Receiver:
establishment of, 187
as liquidator, 197
power to investigate failures, 336, 357–8
report to court, 198, 358
as trustee in bankruptcy, 189
Oppression:
deprivation of dividends, 268–9
ground for remedy, 262
within groups, 396, 400
Jenkins Committee on, 268, 400
judicial definition, 263
origin of remedy, 262
reform of, 267–8
in small companies, 159–61
techniques of, 240

Option dealings: 241
Ostensible authority: 119, 164
Ownership and control:
  patterns of, 175–81
  share ownership in Britain, 80, 401

Participatory company: 44–5, 141
  (*see also* Small private business)
Participation: *see* Industrial democracy
Partnership:
  agency in, 100, 162–4
  authority of partners, 148, 162–5
  bankruptcy in, 193–4
  capacity of, 148
  choice of partners, 153
  contractual nature of, 97, 101
  definition of, 98
  duty of partner to account, 101
  floating charge, bar on, 174–6
  internal management of, 101
  Ker Report on, 19
  liability of partners, 100, 162–4
  limited partnership, 166–8
  limit on number of partners, 102
  participation in profit, 98
  partnership property, 100, 193–4
  personal participation, 99
  presumption of authority, 164
  profit, apportionment of, 101, 161
  quasi-partnerships, 155–61
  registration of name, 100
  salaried partners, 98–9, 161
  scope of, 163–4
  taxation, 100–1, 213, 217–18, 220
  termination, 99
  winding up, 102, 157
  withdrawal, 153–4
Pension funds: 404
Percival v. Wright, rule in: 236, 252, 255–7, 347
Placing: 299
Police fraud squads: 337, 359, 362
Political donations: 209, 318–20
Pre-emption: 155, 369
Price Commission: 85, 496
Prices and Incomes Board: 85, 495
Private company: 122
  (*see also* Small private business)
Profit:
  assessment of, 125–6, 130–2
  economic analysis, 27
Profit and loss account: 125–6
Profit sharing:
  in France, 479–80
  in John Lewis Partnership, 481
  official surveys, 480
  share distribution schemes, 478–9
  share options, 323
Promoter:
  duty to company, 237
Proper purpose rule: 245–8
Property bonds: 412
Prospectus:
  contents, 302–4
  falsehood in, 307–8, 310–12
  issues, 298–9
  legal control of, 300–1
  liability for, 303, 312–13
  statement in lieu of, 302
  Stock Exchange control, 303–4
Proxy voting:
  statutory control, 324–5
  Stock Exchange regulations, 325
  United States practice, 329
Public company: 116, 122
  (*see also* Quoted company)
Public issue:
  control of circulars, 338–40
  disclosure rules, 302–4
  definition, 301
  economics of, 62–3
  governmental control, 341
  offer for sale, 298–9
  placing, 299
  prospectus issue, 298–9
  rights issue, 299–300
  Stock Exchange requirements, 303–4, 340–2
  types of, 298–9

Quasi-partnership: 145, 147, 155–61
Quotations:
  control of, 340–2
Quoted company:
  administrative control of, 336–8
  directors' duties, 321–3
  disclosure rules, continuing, 304–6
  disclosure rules, new issues, 302–4
  disclosure system, deficiencies in, 315–16
  discretionary controls, 340–42
  inspections of, 352–8
  number of, 38–9
  prospectus: *see* main entry
  public issue: *see* main entry
  Stock Exchange requirements, 288–9, 340–1
  Stock Exchange scrutiny of documents, 341–2

Ratification:
- bar on, 274–5
- of impropriety, 273
- rule in *Foss v. Harbottle*, 271–3
- voting by wrongdoers, 280
- when permissible, 273–4

Receiver:
- for debenture holders, 182–4
- duty of, 184

Reckless trading: 204–5
Reduction of capital: 108, 129, 169, 262
Registrar of Companies:
- annual returns, 117, 208
- initial registration, 103
- power to strike off, 41, 121

Registrar of Restrictive Trading Agreements: 491–2
Registration of charges: 173–4
Regulated companies: 11
Rescission: 313–14
Reserves:
- significance of, 67, 127

Restrictive trade practices:
- control of, 491–3
- EEC regulation, 494–5
- registration of agreements, 491–2

Revaluation of assets: 68, 132, 211
Rights issue: 299–300
Royal British Bank v. Turquand, rule in: 118–19
Rule in: *see* case name

Samuelson, P.: 26–7
Sandilands Committee: 134–5
Savoy Hotel: 357
Scheme of arrangement: 197
Schumpeter, J. A.:
- on economics of capitalism, 28–9

Secured loans: 171–4
Securities and Exchange Commission:
- control of market, 359–61
- on corporate corruption, 360–1
- definition of public issue, 302
- establishment of, 359
- insider trading, 256–7, 349–51
- practice of, 360–1
- proxy rules, 329
- an SEC for Britain, 361–3

Shares:
- compulsory purchase, 260–1, 371–3
- equity, 108–9
- multiple voting rights, 106
- no par value, 110
- no purchase by company, 130, 370, 373–4
- non-market dealings, 338–9
- patterns of ownership, 75–81
- origin of, 11–12
- preference, 109
- random price movement, 71–3
- share premium account, 129
- valuation, 68–9, 293

Sharedealing:
- control of, 338–9
- insider trading, 255–8, 346–52
- licensed dealers, 338–9
- market dealing, 342–4
- market rigging, 344–6
- Stock Exchange regulations, 343, 345
- in take-overs, 376, 379, 383–7
- wash sales, 346

Shareholders:
- class action, 277
- class rights, 108, 261–2
- costs of action, 279–80
- cumulative voting, 328
- decline of, 325–6
- democracy, 324–6
- direct and derivative action, 276–80
- disclosure: *see* main entry
- distribution of, 75–81
- expropriation of, 260–1
- institutional, 332–4, 402–11
- as investors, 330–2
- militancy, 327–9
- right of access to accounts, 280–2
- right of action, bar on, 271, 275–6
- right to dividend, 270, 331
- right to management audit, 332
- right to requisition meeting, 324
- right to statutory inspection, 283, 354
- rights in take-overs, 378, 383–6
- strengthening of rights, 285–6

Sharepushing: 338–40
Small private business:
- advantages of corporate form, 150–1
- annual returns, 151–2
- bankruptcy, 186–94
- basis of association, 152–68
- cost of incorporation, 151
- credit financing, 176
- creditors' rights, 181–6
- deadlock, 157

definition of, 141, 228–9
disclosure, 151–2, 205–11
effects of incorporation, 142–7
exclusion of member, 157–60
financing, 168–81
fixed charges, 171–2
floating charges, 172
hire purchase financing, 176–81
incorporated partnership, 224, 229
judicial management, 185–6
lease-back financing, 176–81
limited liability, 149–50
limited partnership, 166–8
liquidation, 194–205
loss, allocation of, 162–6
management, 155–6
membership, 153–5
oppression, control of, 156–61
pre-emption, right of, 155
profit, allocation of, 161–2
proposals for statutory reform, 222–30
quasi-partnership, 156–61
registration of charges, 173–4
secured creditors, 182–4
security for loans, 171–2
share and loan capital, 169–71
size criteria, 228–9
taxation, 212–22
transfer of shares, 154–5
ultra vires, 147–9
withdrawal, 153–5

Adam Smith:
on joint stock companies, 27

Social audit: 334–5

Société en commandite: 20, 167–8, 224

South Sea Bubble: 16

Special resolution: 107

Standard Boardroom Practice:
on directors' duties, 83
on take-overs, 365

Stock Exchange:
brokers, control of, 343
Council of, 341, 343, 346
disclosure requirements, 303–4, 305–6
Federation of Stock Exchanges, 341
general undertaking, 305
insider trading, 346–52
market mechanism, 69–75
origin of public dealing, 13–16
quotation, admission to, 288–9, 340–2
Quotations Department, 341–2
rigging, 344–6
suspension of dealings, 342, 382
take-overs: *see* main entry

Stripping: 77–8, 373

Subsidiary:
bar on shareholding in holding company, 390, 397
definition, 390
estimated number of, 46
oppression of, 394–6

Supervisory board: 448–9, 453–7, 450

Take-overs:
abuses in, 375–6
Aberdare/Metal Industries (1967), 375
Adepton/Williams Hudson (1971), 384
American Tobacco/Galaher (1968), 384
Ashbourne Investments (1973), 386
Bovis/Cementation/Trafalgar House (1970), 384
causes of, 364–6
City Code, 83, 337, 347–9, 364–8, 374–88
City Panel, 367, 380–8
City Working Party, 368, 377–8
Courtaulds/Wilkinson & Riddell (1967), 375
compulsory purchase, 371–3
disclosure rules, 380–3
Dufay Bitumastic/International Paints (1968), 380
equality for shareholders, 379, 383–7
GEC/AEI (1967), 376, 380
General Principles of Code, 378–9
government control over, 488–91
incidence of, 55
insider trading: *see* main entry
introduction of Code, 376–7
Jenkins Committee on, 375
Leasco/Pergamon (1969), 382
legal controls, 369–74
management and, 78–9
market dealings in, 376, 379, 383–7
Monopolies Commission assessment, 74
News of the World bid (1968), 385
non-market bids, 366–7

Norbury bid (1971), 348
Notes of Guidance (1959), 375
partial offers, 383
Phillips/Pye (1967), 376
procedural rules, 379
profit forecasts, 380–1
reconstructions, 370–1
share prices in, 73–4
suspension of dealings, 382
Swears & Wells bid (1970), 383
types of market bid, 367–8
warehousing, 368
Taxation:
avoidance, 215–17
balance between company and partnership, 218
Bolton Committee on, 215, 221–2
capital gains, 219, 291–4
capital transfer, 219, 291–4
close company, 122–3, 217
corporation tax, 214–5
development of British system, 213–5
on distributions, 170, 214–5, 218
dividend stripping, 286
group taxation, 393
impact on company formation, 40
imputation, 215
neutrality, 220–2
optional assessment basis, 221
proposals for new small business corporation, 228
on share and loan capital, 109–10, 169–70
on small businesses, 212–22
tax advantage, 219
in United States, 221
Trade unions:
collective bargaining, 427–31, 472–3
conflict model, 427–31
disclosure to, 464–5, 470
industrial democracy, role, in 439–40, 467–71
plant bargaining, 473
shop stewards, 471–3
single channel of communication, 458
theory of legal abstention, 429
workplace bargaining, 472–3
Trustee:
director as, 233–6
partner as, 101
Ultra vires:
avoidance of, 114–15
consequences of, 113–14, 147–9
origin of, 112–13
in partnership, 147–8
reform of, 116, 148–9
in United States, 149
Unincorporated companies: 16–19
Unit trust:
definition, 410
origin, 411
regulation, 411–12
United States:
insider trading, 256–7, 349–51
investment institutions, 360
monopolies (trusts), 487–8, 490
Securities and Exchange Commission: *see* main entry
shareholders' actions, 278–9, 327–8
taxation, 22 1
Unlimited company: 123
Unquoted company:
capital taxes, 291–4
definition, 231
disclosure in, 242–3
finance for expansion, 287–9
going public, 288–9
inspection, 282–5
Jenkins Committee on, 231
Macmillan gap in financing, 63, 288
oppression in, 240, 268
shareholders' actions, 275–80
transition in, 289–91

Valuation:
of assets, 67–8, 133–4
of shares, 68–9, 293
Vehicle and General Insurance Company Inquiry: 408
Voidable preference:
in bankruptcy, 190–2
in liquidation, 200–2
reform of, 191–2
de Vries Committee (1970): 185–6

Warehousing: 368
Winding up: *see* Liquidation
Workers: *see* Employees
Wrongdoers in control: 274–5, 280

Yugoslavia:
employees' control in, 482–3